Resisting The Empire: The Plan to Destroy Syria and How the Future of the World Depends on the Outcome

Brandon Turbeville

Resisting The Empire

The Plan To Destroy Syria And How The Future Of The World Depends On The Outcome

Brandon Turbeville

Copyright ©2016

False Flag Publications

Damascus has seen all that has ever occurred on earth, and still she lives. She has looked upon the dry bones of a thousand empires, and will see the tombs of a thousand more before she dies. – Mark Twain

Table of Contents

Preface

Syria, where to start?

I love every part of my homeland.

But now, when Syrians utter this word, it is with a heavy heart. It is a visceral pain. But it is not the pain that is cured by modern medicine. It is the pain caused by love, nostalgia, and longing to be with a loved one who is struggling to stay alive. It is the pain of being in love but being forced to watch as your lover is stabbed to death.

Syria is not a typical country. It is a history. It is the mother of civilization. Syria taught the hand of the world to write and to store knowledge on paper, to share it with subsequent generations.

It was Syria, not Greece, that brought the world the first alphabet.

Syria was created when this world was created. Our ancestors told us that this land was the land of Adam, the first prophet and that every prophet has this land as his motherland.

Al-Sham. Jasmine. Damashq. Damascus. All names for the oldest city in the world.

Today, despite the war, destruction, and death brought upon her by the West, Damascus remains full of life, still teeming with inhabitants as it has since the 6th Century BC.

For Syrians, we know our land was born when life itself was born. Ask the residents of the ancient city of Maloula, the land of Jesus Christ, about the age of mother Syria?

Syria, we miss you.

We miss walking in your beautiful old streets, with flowers along the way. We miss that cup of tea with our families, our sons, brothers, fathers, kids. We miss the songs of birds every morning. We miss the simple life. We miss Syria.

And why do we miss our country? Why do we miss the good times? Who set fire to our land?

Who sends monsters from every cave in the world to kill humans in the name of humanity?

No more birds' songs. Instead, we have suicide bombs.

No love. No Freedom. All of it is banned in the name of religion, the Saudi Wahhabi cult.

Where are our families, if only to suffer with us? They have been killed by those barbaric mercenaries sent by the West. They say they demand freedom. They are backed by the country of freedom. But they are backed by savage grandson of the Ottoman Sultan. The USA has the statue of liberty but the real liberty is in Syria.

Today there is no peace in our streets. There are bombs, mortars, rockets. There is no money for food. Most of our men have gone to the army to defend their families and their country.

But Syria will be the Phoenix who will rise from the ashes.

You can no longer smell the jasmine in Syria now. You can only smell fire and blood.

But we will smell jasmine again.

Syria has seen many empires in its time and always the jasmine returns.

Afraa Dagher

June 2016

INTRODUCTION

Much has been made over the difference between ISIS, al- Nusra, and the allegedly "moderate rebels" in Syria as a result of a shaky ceasefire agreement between the Syrian government and the jihadist "moderate" terrorists. That ceasefire has seen the United States act as the public protector of known terrorist organizations like Ahrar al-Sham and refuse to allow that group to be listed as terrorist organization. In so doing, the United States has only driven more nails into the coffin of its credibility and has publicly revealed its actual support for terrorist organizations yet again.

Yet the U.S. will admit that it supports terrorists in Syria although the White House will never actually call them terrorists. Instead, the preferred name is "moderate rebels," despite the fact that, beyond the name, one cannot distinguish any of these groups from ISIS. The United States will never admit, however, that it is actually funding ISIS since that would reveal not only the existence of the proxy war itself but the fact that the world's most feared terrorist organization is actually a product wholly created and directed by the Western and NATO intelligence community. It would also expose the fact that the global boogeyman is actually a proxy army for the NATO agenda.

When analyzing the nature of ISIS and who exactly funds, directs, arms, and controls it, there are a number of points that must be addressed.

The differences between ISIS and the "moderate opposition."

The difference between ISIS, al-Qaeda, and al-Nusra.

Who is funding and facilitating ISIS?

ISIS' Strategic Supply Lines

Whose agenda lines up with the agenda of ISIS? Who benefits from ISIS?

The following pages of this book aim to answer all of these questions as well as to explain the relevance of the crisis and the world's response to it. In addition, it is necessary to understand who created the situation on the ground in Syria and the direction in which the creators of this agenda desire to the take Syria, the Middle East, and, ultimately, the rest of the world. It is the intention of this book to do just that.

Chapter I: The Moderate Opposition
There Are No Moderates

The so-called "opposition" in Syria is anything but moderate. As Tony Cartalucci wrote in his article, "In Syria, There Are No Moderates,"

> . . . . . there were never, nor are there any "moderates" operating in Syria. The West has intentionally armed and funded Al Qaeda and other sectarian extremists since as early as 2007 in preparation for an engineered sectarian bloodbath serving US-Saudi-Israeli interests. This latest bid to portray the terrorists operating along and within Syria's borders as "divided" along extremists/moderate lines is a ploy to justify the continued flow of Western cash and arms into Syria to perpetuate the conflict, as well as create conditions along Syria's borders with which Western partners, Israel, Jordan, and Turkey, can justify direct military intervention.[1]

Indeed, even the New York Times has been forced to admit that there are, as Cartalucci expertly argues in his article, no moderates in the ranks of the Syrian death squads. As Ben Hubbard wrote in April, 2013,

> In Syria's largest city, Aleppo, rebels aligned with Al Qaeda control the power plant, run the bakeries and head a court that applies Islamic law. Elsewhere, they have seized government oil fields, put employees back to work and now profit from the crude they produce.

> Across Syria, rebel-held areas are dotted with Islamic courts staffed by lawyers and clerics, and by fighting brigades led by extremists. Even the Supreme Military Council, the umbrella rebel organization whose formation the West had hoped would sideline radical groups, is stocked with commanders who want to infuse Islamic law into a future Syrian government.

> Nowhere in rebel-controlled Syria is there a secular fighting force to speak of.[2]

Even one of the FSA commanders, Bassel Idriss, recently admitted to openly collaborating with ISIS and al-Nusra, revealing yet another example of the fact that the "moderate rebels" are not moderate at all. In an interview with the Daily Star of Lebanon, Idriss stated "We are collaborating with the Islamic State and the Nusra Front by attacking the Syrian Army's gatherings in . . . Qalamoun . . . . Let's face it: The Nusra Front is the biggest power present right now in Qalamoun and we as FSA would collaborate on any mission they launch as long as it coincides with our values."[3]

---

[1] Cartalucci, Tony. "In Syria, There Are No Moderates." Land Destroyer Report. September 20, 2013. http://landdestroyer.blogspot.com/2013/09/in-syria-there-are-no-moderates.html#more

[2] Hubbard, Ben. "Islamist Rebels Create Dilemma On Syria Policy." New York Times. April 27, 2013. http://www.nytimes.com/2013/04/28/world/middleeast/islamist-rebels-gains-in-syria-create-dilemma-for-us.html?pagewanted=all&_r=1

[3] Knutsen, Elise. "Frustration Drives Arsal's FSA Into ISIS Ranks." The Daily Star. September 8, 2014. http://www.dailystar.com.lb/News/Lebanon-News/2014/Sep-08/269883-frustration-drives-arsals-fsa-into-isis-ranks.ashx

Idriss also admitted that many FSA fighters had pledged allegiance to ISIS. He said, "[ISIS] wanted to enhance its presence in the Western Qalamoun area. After the fall of Yabroud and the FSA's retreat into the hills [around Arsal], many units pledged allegiance [to ISIS]".

Abu Fidaa, a retired Syrian Army Colonel who is now a part of the Revolutionary Council in the Qalamoun, corroborated Idriss' statements by saying that "A very large number of FSA members [in Arsal] have joined ISIS and Nusra. In the end, people want to eat, they want to live, and the Islamic State has everything."

Not only the FSA, but also the Syrian Revolutionary Front has also openly admitted to working with Nusra and al-Qaeda. The leader of the SRF, Jamaal Maarouf admitted that his brigades coordinate with Nusra and al-Qaeda regularly.[4]

Demonstrating yet again the jihadist nature of the so-called Syrian "rebellion" as well as the fracturing command structure the top "rebel" commander, General Selim Idriss, was forced to flee Syria as a result of attacks by the more extreme jihadists of the Islamic Front.

According to the Wall Street Journal, TIME, UPI, and a host of other mainstream sources, Idriss fled Syria into Turkey after Islamic Front jihadists overran his weapons warehouses full of US-donated military gear as well as his own headquarters located near the border of Syria and Turkey. From Turkey, Idriss flew to Doha, Qatar. The warehouses were controlled mainly by the Supreme Military Council, the loose umbrella group which contains the FSA.[5] [6] Reports of Idriss' flight were corroborated by both an anonymous senior U.S. Official and a spokesman for the Islamic Front.

A spokesman for the FSA, however, attempted to claim that Idriss was merely in Turkey for talks between the Islamic Front and the FSA. Doha plays an important role for the FSA forces as the Syrian National Coalition, the governmental wing of the "moderate extremist" version of the Syrian "rebels," is based the country.

As a result of the Idriss abandonment of his position, the United States and Britain announced that they would be freezing the delivery of "non-lethal military aid to rebels in northern Syria," though they also stated that "humanitarian aid" will continue to be distributed through organizations like the United Nations. In further response, Turkey closed its side of the border. Yet the threats to halt shipments of "lethal" military aid lasted as long as the attention span of the general public since aid to terrorists fighting against the government of Bashar al-Assad has continued apace.

The Islamic Front is a powerful alliance of seven openly Jihadist fighter groups that publicly broke away from the more moderate (only in comparison) Free Syrian Army on

---

[4] "'I am not fighting against al-Qaeda . . . it's not our problem,' says West's last hope in Syria." The Independent. http://www.handsoffsyriasydney.com/articles/i-am-not-fighting-against-al-qaida-its-not-our-problem-says-wests-last-hope-in-syria/?print=pdf

[5] Rayman, Noah. "Top U.S. Backed Rebel Commander Flees Syria." TIME. December 12, 2013. http://world.time.com/2013/12/12/top-u-s-backed-rebel-commander-flees-syria/

[6] "U.S.-backed Syrian Rebel Commander Flees Country." UPI. December 12, 2013. http://www.upi.com/Top_News/US/2013/12/12/US-backed-Syrian-rebel-commander-flees-country/UPI-96541386829631/

November 22. While the IF claims to have no ties to either the SNC or al-Qaeda, the ideology and methods of the organizations are indeed quite similar. Although there may be no clear paper trail and cache of membership cards linking the groups, the truth is that they are indelibly linked to one another by virtue of their extremist ideology and their goal of a fundamentalist caliphate under Sharia law.

 While the official Western narrative is that the Anglo-American governments are concerned that the "moderate" rebels are being outmatched and overtaken by "extremist" elements, the fact is that these governments know and have known full well that the entire "rebellion" in Syria is made up of fanatics, mercenaries, dupes, and fundamentalists. Indeed, even the New York Times, admitted that, in Syria, a secular "activist" or fighter was almost impossible to find

 The myth of moderate fighters in Syria is collapsing almost as fast as the claims that Assad gassed his own people in Ghouta, a claim that was later disproven and shown to be the work of the death squads.[7] As Tony Cartalucci writes in his article, "Syria's War: The Next Phase,"

> The alleged fleeing of General Selim Idriss of the so-called "Free Syrian Army" (FSA), was more symbolic than anything else. Whether or not he really fled, and whether he is in Turkey or Qatar is of little consequence. The so-called "moderates" he commanded were nothing more than a smokescreen, a cheap veneer applied to the hardcore Wahabist extremists of Al Qaeda's Al Nusra franchise and similar fronts that have formed the core of foreign-backed militancy turned against the Syrian people from the very beginning of the conflict.

> [...]

> And while the West has attempted to portray these extremist groups as entities entirely separate from the "moderates" they have claimed to be openly training, funding, arming, and equipping to the tune of billions of dollars, there is no other logical explanation for Al Nusra's ability to rise above these Western-backed "moderates," unless of course they never existed and the West was, as was planned in 2007, simply arming Al Qaeda all along.[89]

Indeed, even as far back as 2005, the plan to arm religious fundamentalists to destabilize and destroy the Assad government was being reported in the mainstream Western press. The only true development which exists as a result of Idriss' flight is that one group of fighters that once appeared more politically palatable has been publicly castrated by the more extreme elements of an already extreme movement.[10] The

---

[7] Turbeville, Brandon. "5 Ways 'Incontrovertible Evidence' On Syria Is Controvertible." Activist Post. September 12, 2013. http://www.activistpost.com/2013/09/5-ways-incontrovertible-evidence-on.html

[8] Cartalucci, Tony. "West Attempts Syria Cover Up – Claims 'Twitter Donations' Behind Rise Of Al Qaeda." Land Destroyer Report. September 22, 2013. http://landdestroyer.blogspot.com/2013/09/west-attempts-syria-cover-up-claims.html

[9] Cartalucci, Tony. "Syria's War: The Next Phase." Land Destroyer Report. December 13, 2013. http://landdestroyer.blogspot.com/2013/12/syrias-war-next-phase.html

[10] Hirsch, Michael; Barry, John. "The Salvador Option." Newsweek. January 9, 2005. http://web.archive.org/web/20050110030928/http://www.msnbc.msn.com/id/6802629/site/ne

fanaticism and savagery of the death squads operating in Syria will continue, as will their funding by the United States and the rest of the Anglo-American powers via Saudi Arabia and other Gulf state feudal monarchies. While the geo-political posturing may shift; make no mistake, the goal of Syria's destruction will remain the same.

Official Classifications

So what's the big difference between the "moderate" terrorists and the extremist terrorists running rampant in Syria today? At one time, we were told there were no terrorists at all. Then, we were told terrorists were indeed present but that there were also moderate, secular, democracy-loving freedom fighters in the country. Now, after the nature of the so-called "rebels" has been revealed ad infinitum by the alternative and independent press, it is admitted that the "fighters" in Syria are terrorists but, apparently, some are moderate and some are extreme.

Of course, they all have the same goal of Sharia. They all hate minorities, Christians, Alawites, Shiites, etc. They all torture. They all rape. We could go on and on. In the world of the West's "rebels," there is not one shred of difference between any of the armed groups fighting against the secular Syrian government besides the names they call themselves.[11] [12]

Still, we are told there are clear differences and that the U.S. State Department knows just what they are. Only, they aren't telling the American people. Or the Russians. Or the Syrians. Or anybody. The "moderate" terrorists are thus a very mysterious force, a group of which we may speak but also one that never shows itself.

Of course, there are groups that the United States admits are brutal killers but somehow rationalizes to the public that they are "our" brutal killers. The U.S. can, at times, be forced to admit that the groups it supports as "freedom fighters" have committed atrocities, rapes, murders, torture, and establishment of Islamic theocracy upon unwilling inhabitants. Essentially, the U.S. can admit (when pressed) that these groups have the same ideology as ISIS, although the State Department will never say these exact words.

Thus, it is clear that any designation of terrorists groups as "extremist" or "moderate" is obviously based on political motivation and geopolitical designs, not the nature or action of the terrorist group in question. If that were the case, then Ahrar al-Sham, Jaish al-Islam, and other groups would easily be listed as terrorist organizations that would subsequently not be covered under the "ceasefire" agreement. After all, there is no distinguishing characteristic that sets these groups apart from ISIS or Nusra other than a name.

---

wsweek/

[11] Hubbard, Ben. "Islamist Rebels Create Dilemma On Syria Policy." New York Times. April 27, 2013. http://www.nytimes.com/2013/04/28/world/middleeast/islamist-rebels-gains-in-syria-create-dilemma-for-us.html?_r=2

[12] Turbeville, Brandon. "The Roots Of ISIS." Activist Post. September 11, 2014. http://www.activistpost.com/2014/09/the-roots-of-isis.html

But when the Russians attempted to remove these groups from the list of non-protected terrorists in Syria (terrorists protected at the insistence of the West), the United States, Britain, France, and Ukraine rushed to their rescue and blocked the Russian proposal. This is, of course, despite the fact that both of these groups, which make up around half of the "Syrian opposition forces" thanks to Western name changes, have repeatedly worked together with Nusra and ISIS forces. Jaish al-Islam and Ahrar al-Sham have both worked so closely with ISIS and Nusra that the groups themselves are virtually interchangeable. Nevertheless, the U.S. is only digging its own international public relations grave with its refusal to designate known and obvious terrorists as precisely that, particularly when it has launched campaigns of destruction and death across the world on the basis of allegedly "fighting terror."[13]

The results of this policy was that the Russians forced the Western nations to admit that, despite their rhetoric, terrorist organizations are doing their bidding and have never truly been the targets of NATO forces. While the Western public remains entirely befuddled as to the nature of the crisis in Syria (many do not even know there is a Syrian crisis) Western propaganda has created such a complex and distorted view of the situation that any newcomer or casual observer would find it incredibly difficult to navigate through the lies and deceit.

For the rest of the world, however, much of that propaganda is ridiculous and transparent and, for that reason as well as many others, the United States and NATO are losing more and more credibility by the day.

The United States' narrative of "moderate" rebels was dealt a series of serious blows in late 2012 and early 2013 as the alternative media began reporting on the atrocities of the so-called "rebels."[14] Since the beginning of the crisis, Syrians had been reporting that the West's democracy-loving freedom fighters were, in reality, brutal theocratic psychopaths who were raping and pillaging their way across the country committing unspeakable horrors. For instance, in August, 2012, it was reported by Iranian FARS News Agency that "armed rebel groups attacked the house of a Shiite Iraqi family in the Seyede Zainab neighborhood in the capital city of Damascus, killed all members of the family and hanged the last one, a little child."[15] The original report had come by way of Iraq's Qanon news website and Iraqi human rights activists. FARS News Agency accompanied their own article with an alleged picture of the child.

Only a few days prior, a graphic video below was produced by RT showing the Free Syrian Army rounding up prisoners in Aleppo and summarily executing them. After the

---

[13] Tomson, Chris. "Western U.N. Bloc Rejects Russian Bid To Blacklist Islamist Groups In Syria." Al Masdar. May 12, 2016. https://www.almasdarnews.com/article/western-u-n-bloc-rejects-russian-bid-blacklist-islamist-groups-syria/

[14] Turbeville, Brandon. "Iranian News Reports Child Hanged By Syrian 'Rebels.'" Activist Post. August 7, 2012. http://www.activistpost.com/2012/08/iranian-news-reports-child-hanged-by.html

[15] "Terrorists Hand Shia Child After Killing Family Members." Fars News. August 7, 2012. Reposted at this link: http://navideshahed.com/en/news/361390/terrorists-hang-shia-child-after-killing-family-members

executions, chants of "Allahu Akbar" were clearly audible thus demonstrating the fanatical nature of the "rebels."

Even the Soros-funded Human Rights Watch was forced to admit the executions constituted "war crimes."

The fact that al-Qaeda terrorists were now fully part of the Syrian "revolution" was no longer debatable. Much like the situation in Libya, the "rebels" were clearly not rebels at all. They were, and still are, merely NATO-backed death squads used for the purpose of destabilization and regime change.[16] [17] [18]

Perhaps the most notorious and shocking incident elucidating the nature of the alleged "rebels" was the infamous "heart eating" video that even made its way across the mainstream channels. The video showed Syrian "rebel" leader Abu Sakkar cutting out the heart of a Syrian soldier and then biting it for the camera to see. Shortly before biting the man's heart, Sakkar states to the camera "I swear to God we will eat your hearts and your livers."[19] [20]

The video came fresh on the heels of a pledge by U.S. Secretary of State John Kerry to provide $123 million in aid to the Syrian death squads and £40 million by the UK, all in the midst of a worldwide economic depression and the imposition of brutal austerity measures in both countries.

However, while the footage was clearly shocking, it should only have been shocking in its savagery as an act in and of itself, not in the fact that Syrian "rebels" (aka death squads) were engaging in such brutal acts. After all, it was well known in the alternative media by the time of the video's release that the death squads were responsible for unspeakable atrocities against innocent people ever since the destabilization effort began.[21]

In October, 2012, the death squads, in typical terrorist fashion, conducted at least four suicide bombings in Aleppo that killed around 40 innocent civilians.

---

[16] Abdul-Ahad, Ghaith. "Al-Qaida Turns Tide For Rebels In Battle For Eastern Syria." The Guardian. July 30, 2012. https://www.theguardian.com/world/2012/jul/30/al-qaida-rebels-battle-syria

[17] Rosenthal, John. "Al Qaeda In Rebel Syria." National Review. March 8, 2012. http://www.nationalreview.com/article/292904/al-qaeda-rebel-syria-john-rosenthal

[18] Husain, Ed. "Al-Qaeda's Specter In Syria." Foreign Policy. Council On Foreign Relations. August 6, 2012. http://www.cfr.org/syria/al-qaedas-specter-syria/p28782

[19] Nelson, Sara C. "Syrian Rebel Leader Abu Sakkar Filmed Cutting Out And 'Eating' Soldier's Heart." Huffington Post. May 15, 2013. http://www.huffingtonpost.co.uk/2013/05/14/syrian-rebel-leader-abu-sakkar-cutting-eating-soldiers-heart-video_n_3271067.html?utm_hp_ref=uk

[20] Abdulaziz, Salma; Yan, Holly. "Video: Syrian Rebel Cuts Out Soldier's Heart, Eats It." CNN. May 14, 2013. http://edition.cnn.com/2013/05/14/world/meast/syria-eaten-heart/?hpt=hp_t1

[21] Clabough, Raven. "Evidence Shows Rebels Behind Chemical Weapons Attacks." The New American. March 27, 2013. http://www.thenewamerican.com/world-news/asia/item/14929-evidence-shows-syrian-rebels-behind-chemical-attack

Receiving more attention in the media, however, at least until the death squads were found to be responsible, was the infamous Houla Massacre of 2011 where approximately 90 people were killed.

Another high profile event was the public execution of a teenager for a flippant comment regarding the prophet Muhammed.

Fifteen year old coffee vender Mohammed al-Qatta was captured and killed for stating that he would not extend credit to an unspecified individual "Even if Muhammad comes down," a common phrase used by many Syrians. This statement was construed as blasphemy by the death squads who are portrayed as "freedom fighters" by the Western media and government agencies supporting them.[22]

Upon making the statement, al-Qatta was abducted by the death squads and tortured before being publicly executed. UPI reports "When they brought him back, the teen's head was covered with his shirt and his body bore marks of whipping."[23]

The death squads then paraded the young man in front of a crowd that included his parents and siblings, announcing that "cursing the prophet" is a horrible act and others committing such crimes will be punished. The death squads then shot the boy once in the mouth and once in the neck.

The Huffington Post wrote that the murderers were believed to be "members of a rebel group known as the Islamic State of Iraq and Syria, formerly known as the al-Nusra Front. "[24]

Even the pseudo-organizations like the Syrian Observatory for Human Rights found it impossible to obfuscate the animalistic brutality of the death squads in this latest act. Indeed, death squad supporter Rami Abdul Rahman was forced to admit the savagery of groups he had supported for the previous two years.[25]

What is more interesting is that Rahman was forced to admit that the killers were likely foreign fighters – not native Syrians fighting for freedom against their oppressive government, as Western audiences have been propagandized to believe.

"They spoke classical Arabic, not Syrian dialect," he said.[26]

---

[22] "Syrian Rebels 'Execute Teenager' In Aleppo." Al-Jazeera. June 9, 2013.
http://www.aljazeera.com/news/middleeast/2013/06/201369175918244221.html

[23] "Syrian teen killed after rebels accuse him of blasphemy." UPI.com. June 10, 2013.
http://www.upi.com/Top_News/World-News/2013/06/10/Syrian-teen-killed-after-rebels-accuse-him-of-blasphemy/UPI-25501370881538/

[24] Stuart, Hunter. "Muhammad al-Qatta, 15-Year Old Boy, Reportedly Executed By Syrian Rebel Group For Blasphemy." Huffington Post. June 10, 2013.
http://www.huffingtonpost.com/2013/06/10/muhammad-al-qatta-15-year-old-syria-rebels_n_3415901.html

[25] Turbeville, Brandon. "New U.N. Chemical Weapons Report On Syria Blames Assad." Activist Post. June 5, 2013. http://www.activistpost.com/2013/06/new-un-chemical-weapons-report-on-syria.html

[26] "Syrian Rebels 'Execute Teenager' In Aleppo." Al-Jazeera. June 9, 2013.
http://www.aljazeera.com/news/middleeast/2013/06/201369175918244221.html

"They shot the boy twice, once in the mouth, another in his neck, in front of his mother, his father and his siblings," he added.[27]

Ironically, it was reported that the 15-year old victim had taken part in protests against the government prior to his "blasphemous" remark, thus proving that the death squads which are now being mopped up by Assad's forces, are incapable of even the slightest cognitive functions that allow for coexistence.

The Syrian Observatory for Human Rights has criticized the killing as "criminal" and as a "gift to the regime of Syrian President Bashar al-Assad."[28]

"This kind of criminality is exactly what makes people in Syria fear the fall of the regime," Abdel Rahman said.[29]

Yet this kind of criminality and "gifts" to Assad were taking place ever since the invasion of foreign-backed death squads into Syria in 2011 when those efforts began in earnest. Indeed, Rahman and his Observatory supported the death squads throughout the entire ordeal in full knowledge of the atrocities being committed against the Syrian people.

Rahman and his organization were clearly aware of videos showing the death squads machine gunning captives, beheading prisoners, and forcing young children to behead them. I, myself, had written an article dealing with reports regarding the death squad's hanging of a young child after murdering his family in front of him. One can also view the videos of the death squad members beating and humiliating the famous elderly "Yellow Man" in Aleppo.[30] [31] [32] [33] [34] [35]

---

[27] "Syrian Rebels 'Execute Teenager' In Aleppo." Al-Jazeera. June 9, 2013. http://www.aljazeera.com/news/middleeast/2013/06/201369175918244221.html

[28] "Syrian Rebels 'Execute Teenager' In Aleppo." Al-Jazeera. June 9, 2013. http://www.aljazeera.com/news/middleeast/2013/06/201369175918244221.html

[29] "Syrian Rebels 'Execute Teenager' In Aleppo." Al-Jazeera. June 9, 2013. http://www.aljazeera.com/news/middleeast/2013/06/201369175918244221.html

[30] Turbeville, Brandon. "Syrian Rebel Eats Soldier's Heart: Paid For By The U.S. Taxpayer." Activist Post. May 14, 2013. http://www.activistpost.com/2013/05/syrian-rebel-eats-soldiers-heart-paid.html

[31] "Rebels Massacre 11 Prisoners in Saraqib, Syria." Youtube. Posted by SyrianRebelWatch on November 2, 2012. https://www.youtube.com/watch?v=t5OLmnYpIXs Footage shows 11 wounded prisoners being beaten, forced to lie down, and shot to death.
Video description by SyrianRebelWatch is as follows: At least 11 wounded prisoners are forced to lie down before being beaten and then shot to death by insurgents in the central town of Saraqib. The victims are taunted, insulted and stamped on before a hail of gunfire is directed at their prone bodies.
The men were said to have been captured after Syrian rebels overran a checkpoint.
This is one of hundreds of such mass executions carried out by rebel forces since the conflict in Syria began, the methods varying from shooting to beheading. While such atrocities are arguably far more common than those often falsely attributed to Syria government forces they are often completely ignored by Western journalists and politicians keen to portray the insurgents in a positive light despite all the evidence to the contrary. Numerous other examples of such executions are available on my channel and facebook page.

Indeed, the videos of the torture of prisoners in the hands of the death squads are legion and were viewed with ease at the time of this atrocity. One need only type the relevant keywords into a YouTube search engine to be greeted with generous results. It should also be mentioned that a number of chemical attacks directed against innocent civilians on the part of the Syrian death squads took place over the months leading up to the killing of Muhammed.[36]

Although the mainstream media and Western governments attempted to blame these attacks (and every other atrocity) on the Assad government, each and every one turned out to be the work of the Syrian death squads, who are themselves funded by Western governments, intelligence agencies, and NATO command structures.[37]

Neither Rahman or any other individual or organization supporting the "rebels" could have overlooked the video of Syrian "rebel" leader Abu Sakkar cutting out the heart of a Syrian soldier and then biting it for the camera."[38] [39]

---

[32] "Syrian Rebels Behead A Man In Aleppo, Syria. 11/08/12." Youtube. Posted by 3TimeToFightBack on August 13, 2012. https://www.youtube.com/watch?v=FL0uGSBhORc&bpctr=1471049673 Footage shows a man being beaten and berated before being beheaded by a man with a small knife.
The description of the video from the user account is as follows:
This footage, first posted by a member of the opposition purports to show the beheading of an Assad supporter in Aleppo. The man is beaten and insulted before being executed by a man wielding a small knife who proceeds to cut his throat. His captors suggest that he was a 'Shabiha' a term now frequently used to describe all those deemed loyal to the Syrian [government]

[33] Watson, Paul Joseph. "Gruesome Video Shows Syrian Rebel Beheading Civilian" Infowars.com. March 21, 2013. http://www.infowars.com/gruesome-video-shows-syrian-rebel-beheading-civilian/

[34] "Syrian Rebels Use Child In Beheading Unarmed Prisoners In Homs." Youtube. Posted by Human Rights Investigations on December 11, 2012. https://www.youtube.com/watch?v=yjmH5kU8msc The footage shows "rebels" marching a man to the street where he is forced to lie down. A young boy is then handed a machete and forced to behead the man.
Video description from the Youtube account user is as follows:
This is the footage of the incident where a child is made to behead a prisoner. This version has been edited by Sama TV to make it more acceptable to a general audience. For the background to this appalling war crime see https://humanrightsinvestigations.org/2012/12/10/syrian-rebels-use-a-child-to-behead-a-prisoner/ "Syrian Rebels Use A Child To Behead Prisoner." Human Rights Investigations. December 10, 2012.

[35] "Salafist Jihadis Beat 'Yellow Man' In Aleppo Syria." Youtube. Video shows "rebels" insulting and beating the elderly "Yellow Man," a beloved fixture of Aleppo. The Yellow Man is humiliated and the "rebels" pluck his beard. The man is shoved into a car and driven away.

[36] Turbeville, Brandon. "False Flag Attacks In Syria Pin Atrocities On Assad And Justify 'Red Line' Engagement." Activist Post. May 14, 2013. http://www.activistpost.com/2013/03/false-flag-attacks-in-syria-pin.html

[37] Turbeville, Brandon. "Globalist Hidden Hand Revealed In Destabilization Of Syria." Activist Post. April 9, 2013. http://www.activistpost.com/2013/03/false-flag-attacks-in-syria-pin.html

[38] Turbeville, Brandon. "Syrian Rebel Eats Soldier's Heart: Paid For By The American Taxpayer."

Always known for their brutality and inhumanity to innocent men, women, and children, America's "rebels" sunk to a new low with the beheading of a child (under the age of 12) they had accused of fighting alongside the Liwaa al-Quds (Quds Brigade), a Palestinian militia fighting alongside the Syrian government in 2016, another act that was videotaped and shared via the terrorists' online social media accounts.

The video, which was recorded by the terrorists of Nour al-Din al-Zinki, an American-backed "rebel" group, shows the child in ragged clothes sitting in the back of a pickup truck surrounded by five bearded terrorists. The child is then laid on his stomach and his hands tied behind his back. After a short intro speech by the executioner, the child's head is then lifted up and the executioner begins sawing with a small and, apparently, dull knife through the child's neck. After a few muffled attempts at screaming, the knife having severed the vocal chords early enough to prevent most of that, the executioner holds the child's head above his own and utters the familiar cry of "Allahu Akbar!" At this point, his chanting friends, more akin to a pack of crazed apes more than anything resembling human, begin repeating the chant and holding their hands in the air, celebrating their kill.

In the video, it should be noted that the terrorist says "We will leave no one in Handarat," an open admission of the intent and purpose of committing an act of genocide.

The Jerusalem Brigade (al-Quds Brigade) released a statement saying that the boy was not a fighter with the brigade and identified him as Abdullah Issa.

"He lived in al-Mashhad [Aleppo] with his family, among multiple poor families that live in the area under the control of terrorists," said al-Quds, adding that the boy was ill. "By taking one glance at the child - the argument that he was a fighter is immediately disapproved."[40]

Meanwhile, the United States continued its funding to the so-called "rebels" amid yet another horrific atrocity while claiming moral high ground over Assad despite the fact that the U.S. has yet to produce a shred of evidence to show that he or his forces have ever committed attacks, much less atrocities, on civilians.

State Department Spokesman Mark Toner responded to the reports saying, "If we can prove that this was indeed what happened and this group was involved in it, I think it would certainly give us pause." Of course, there was video evidence of the crime if Toner was interested. In addition, for most people, although admittedly not for the U.S. government, the beheading of a child is reason enough to do more than simply pause. Nevertheless, the United States continued supporting their terrorist proxies to the fullest

---

Activist Post. May 14, 2013. http://www.activistpost.com/2013/05/syrian-rebel-eats-soldiers-heart-paid.html

[39] Abdulaziz, Salma; Yan, Holly. "Video: Syrian Rebel Cuts Out Soldier's Heart, Eats It." CNN. May 14, 2013. http://edition.cnn.com/2013/05/14/world/meast/syria-eaten-heart/?hpt=hp_t1

[40] "Syria War: Rebels 'Behead 12-year-old boy' On Video." Al Jazeera. July 20, 2016. http://www.aljazeera.com/news/2016/07/syria-war-rebels-behead-10-year-boy-video-160720065358507.html

extent possible until their goal of destroying the secular government of Bashar al-Assad is accomplished or until the plan is stopped by other actors.

Interestingly enough, reports from Business Insider in 2015 reveal that the United States had indeed supported and armed Nour al-Din al-Zinki in the lead up to the heinous act. What's even more damning, however, is the fact that the group was considered one of the U.S. "vetted" organizations, a designation that was touted as a sure way to avoid arming "extremist" terrorists like ISIS or al-Qaeda.

The lie of vetting and "moderation" is now thoroughly debunked if, for no other reason, than the public beheading of a child.

But there is more! Not only has the United States "vetted," endorsed, and armed Nour al-Din al-Zinki, it has armed them with TOW missiles, a type of guided missile that is capable of piercing and damaging tanks, armored personnel carriers, and other forms of vehicles found on the battlefield. These missiles are especially dangerous for a number of reasons including the fact that they can be used from a considerable distance.

As Jeremy Bender wrote for Business Insider in his article, "These CIA-Vetted Syrian Rebel Groups Fighting Assad Are Russia's Primary Targets,"

> Since 2013, the CIA has been training and equipping various moderate rebel elements in the Syrian civil war in an effort to undermine the regime of Syrian President Bashar al-Assad and force him to the negotiating table.

> Among the range of munitions and supplies that the CIA has funneled to the various brigades of the Free Syrian Army and other moderate groups through Saudi Arabia, Jordan, and Turkey are TOW anti-tank missiles.

> . . . . . .

> These weapons have helped decimate Syrian armour and pushed a recent regime offensive against rebel-held territory to a standstill in reported "tank massacres."[41]

> For instance, on October 8, a Syrian armoured offensive suffered massive casualties as, rebels armed "with US-made TOW missiles … [and] other guided rockets … caused the destruction … of over 15 armoured cars, vehicles, and tanks," according to the Syrian Observatory of Human Rights.

> What is striking is just how many CIA-vetted groups now exist throughout Syria receiving TOWs.

> According to Syrian observer Hasan Mustafas, no fewer than 42 vetted groups now receive TOWs from a Saudi supply originally provided by the US. These weapons are funneled into Syria through Military Operations Command (MOC) posts in Turkey and Jordan that are co-operated by Western and local intelligence agencies.[42]

---

[41] "'Tank Massacre:' Rebels Hit Syrian Forces Hard After Initial Offensive." Business Insider. October 8, 2015. http://www.businessinsider.com/tank-massacre-rebels-hit-syrian-forces-hard-after-initial-offensive-2015-10?IR=T

[42] "The Moderate Rebels: A Growing List Of Vetted Groups Of Vetting Groups Fielding BGM-71 TOW Anti-Tank Guided Missiles." Hasan Mustafa.com. May 8, 2015. https://hasanmustafas.wordpress.com/2015/05/08/the-moderate-rebels-a-complete-and-growing-list-of-vetted-groups-fielding-tow-missiles/

The various groups are well documented due to the nature of TOW provisions. Saudi Arabia can not deliver the US-supplied TOWs without prior CIA approval. Additionally, Mustafas notes, the various vetted groups must apply to receive the TOWs. They are then provided with small batches of arms.[43] [44]

Bender provides a list of the groups who received the TOW missiles but, among them, is the name of Nour al-Din al-Zinki, the child beheading and carcass boiling "moderate" rebels that allegedly representing freedom and democracy.

Still, State Department Spokesman Mark Toner was only able to state that the beheading of the boy might only cause the United States to "pause" and reflect upon its relationship with the group, meaning arming and supporting it.

At the end of the day, the horrific atrocity that was committed by Nour al-Din al-Zinki was really nothing more than several more pints in a massive ocean of blood created by the United States, Israel, the GCC, and NATO. Still, it stands as yet another example of why this treacherous and immoral war against Syria must be ended immediately.

The "Syrian Rebels" Are Not Syrian
Foreign Elements

The fact that the Syrian people were essentially immune to propaganda efforts designed to instill the fear of the inevitable collapse of the government or to insight rebellion, demonstrates at least two things. First, that the propaganda directed back home regarding the nature of the Syrian government and its citizens is largely false. Second, it shows that the information present on the ground inside Syria is readily visible to anyone open to seeing it. As a result, the fundamentalist nature of the death squads sweeping throughout the country is apparent to any Syrian citizen.

Of course, one of the reasons the death squads are so transparent (in addition to their fundamentalist rantings and brutal violence) to native Syrians is the fact that the overwhelming majority of the members of such groups are not Syrian at all. After all, when Webster Tarpley toured Syria for a week as a part of a fact finding mission, the reports he received from Syrian citizens and, indeed, his own firsthand accounts revealed that many of the "rebels" were not native to the country. This raises an interesting question as to how one can rebel against the laws of a nation in which he does not reside. How one can be considered an insurgent while he is fighting in a foreign nation? Obviously, the situation is Syria is not a rebellion, insurgency, or insurrection. It is an invasion.

---

[43] Bender, Jeremy. "These CIA-Vetted Rebel Groups Fighting Assad Are Russia's Primary Targets." Business Insider. October 21, 2015. http://www.businessinsider.com.au/cia-vetted-syrian-rebels-fighting-assad-2015-10

[44] "The Moderate Rebels: A Growing List Of Vetted Groups Of Vetting Groups Fielding BGM-71 TOW Anti-Tank Guided Missiles." Hasan Mustafa.com. May 8, 2015. https://hasanmustafas.wordpress.com/2015/05/08/the-moderate-rebels-a-complete-and-growing-list-of-vetted-groups-fielding-tow-missiles/

Foreign Death Squad Network In Syria Much Larger Than Stated By West

Although evidence supporting the claims that the overwhelming majority of the Syrian "rebels" are made up of foreign fighters is not surprising to anyone who has investigated the unfolding crisis in Syria at any length, it might indeed come as a shock to those whose only source of information are mainstream Western media organizations like CNN, FOX, MSNBC, and other similar corporate outlets.[45]

Yet the extent to which foreign mercenaries and religious fanatics make up the majority of the "rebel" (more aptly named "death squad") ranks might surprise even those who would otherwise be considered well-informed regarding the Syrian situation.

Western governments and media outlets have attempted to downplay both the role and the number of foreign fighters in Syria. This is, of course, understandable, considering the agenda of the NATO forces in regards to the country. [46]

However, it should be noted that although mainstream corporate media outlets were eventually forced to admit that there was, at least, a contingent of foreign fighters making up the ranks of the death squads they choose to call "rebels," these same media outlets attempted to silence, ignore, and even deny this fact for a significant amount of time. Unfortunately, the atrocities of the death squads became so great that they can scarcely be kept secret any longer.

Nevertheless, while such outlets were forced to admit the presence of foreign fighters, these same outlets attempt to keep the reported numbers artificially low. For instance, consider the article by Mike Brunker, Investigations Editor of NBC News, entitled "Study uses 'martyr' posts to analyze 'foreign fighters' aiding Syrian rebels."[47]

Brunker's article deals with a "study" released in 2013 by the security firm Flashpoint Partners and the Neo-Con think tank Washington Institute for Near East Policy (WINEP) entitled, "Convoy of Martyrs in the Levant: A Joint Study Charting the Evolving Role of Sunni Foreign Fighters in the Armed Uprising Against the Assad Regime in Syria."[48]

---

[45] Sarich, Christina. "Censorship Abounds: The Handful of Companies That Control Your Perceptions." Activist Post. June 13, 2013. http://www.activistpost.com/2013/06/censorship-abounds-handful-of-companies.html Accessed on July 17, 2013.

[46] Turbeville, Brandon. "Globalist Hidden Hand Revealed in Destabilization in Syria." Activist Post. April 8, 2013. http://www.activistpost.com/2013/04/globalist-hidden-hand-revealed-in.html Accessed on July 17, 2013.

[47] Brunker, Mike. "Study uses 'martyr' posts to analyze 'foreign fighters' aiding Syrian rebels." NBC News. June 3, 2013. http://openchannel.nbcnews.com/_news/2013/06/03/18728823-study-uses-martyr-posts-to-analyze-foreign-fighters-aiding-syrian-rebels?lite Accessed on July 17, 2013.

[48] Zelin, Aaron Y.; Kohlmann, Evan F.; al-Khouri, Laith. "Convoy of Martyrs in the Levant: A Joint Study Charting the Evolving Role of Sunni Foreign Fighters in the Armed Uprising Against the Assad Regime in Syria." Flashpoint Partners. June 2013. https://flashpoint-intel.com/upload/syria_martyrs/2013-06-02_Convoy_of_Martyrs_Report.pdf Accessed on July

This report, "broke down 280 'martyr' postings on jihadist websites, Facebook and Twittter marking the deaths of the foreign recruits" in order to estimate the amount of foreign fighters operating inside Syria.[49]

Brunker writes, "The report notes that social media have 'provided a critical online bedrock for foreign fighters in Syria . . . Each day on Facebook, new names of deceased foreign fighters are posted by rebel supporters who hope that their willingness to sacrifice will inspire others to follow in their footsteps."[50]

The Flashpoint/WINEP study incredibly attempts to claim that the majority of "rebels" were, in fact, Syrian and that the foreign contingent of the death squads made up, at most, 10% of the ranks of the "rebellion."[51]

Going beyond the realm of absurdity, the study even goes so far as to suggest that foreign fighters engaging in atrocities all over Syria were mostly those fighting in the service of Assad. While Assad has cooperated, to his own intellectual credit, with Hezbollah and PFLP (Popular Front for the Liberation of Palestine), the suggestion that Assad is taking advantage of the use of mercenaries as a substitute army is ludicrous.[52]

Brunker's article states the following regarding the findings of the Flashpoint/WINEP study:

> The numbers from the admittedly small sample of foreign fighters show that even within the radical elements, there is a broad range of participants.

> "A wide variety of international terrorist organizations have become deeply involved in Syria," Kohlmann said. "In fact, based on our data, Sunni foreign fighters in Syria include former Hamas militants from Gaza, relatives of Abu Musab al-Zarqawi (the late leader of al Qaeda in Iraq) and leaders of Fatah al-Islam (a Lebanon-based radical Sunni group).

17, 2013.

[49] Brunker, Mike. "Study uses 'martyr' posts to analyze 'foreign fighters' aiding Syrian rebels." NBC News. June 3, 2013. http://openchannel.nbcnews.com/_news/2013/06/03/18728823-study-uses-martyr-posts-to-analyze-foreign-fighters-aiding-syrian-rebels?lite Accessed on July 17, 2013.

[50] Brunker, Mike. "Study uses 'martyr' posts to analyze 'foreign fighters' aiding Syrian rebels." NBC News. June 3, 2013. http://openchannel.nbcnews.com/_news/2013/06/03/18728823-study-uses-martyr-posts-to-analyze-foreign-fighters-aiding-syrian-rebels?lite Accessed on July 17, 2013.

[51] Zelin, Aaron Y.; Kohlmann, Evan F.; al-Khouri, Laith. "Convoy of Martyrs in the Levant: A Joint Study Charting the Evolving Role of Sunni Foreign Fighters in the Armed Uprising Against the Assad Regime in Syria." Flashpoint Partners. June 2013. https://flashpoint-intel.com/upload/syria_martyrs/2013-06-02_Convoy_of_Martyrs_Report.pdf Accessed on July 17, 2013.

[52] Zelin, Aaron Y.; Kohlmann, Evan F.; al-Khouri, Laith. "Convoy of Martyrs in the Levant: A Joint Study Charting the Evolving Role of Sunni Foreign Fighters in the Armed Uprising Against the Assad Regime in Syria." Flashpoint Partners. June 2013. https://flashpoint-intel.com/upload/syria_martyrs/2013-06-02_Convoy_of_Martyrs_Report.pdf Accessed on July 17, 2013.

"What should be particularly worrying for Western governments is the fact that at least a third of the fighters in our sample were affiliated with the most extreme rebel faction, al Qaeda's Jabhat al-Nusra -- and that at least seven of the 280 dead fighters we analyzed were from Western countries, including France, Denmark, Australia, the U.K., and the United States."[53]

The Flashpoint/WINEP study thus puts the number of foreign fighters dead inside Syria as follows (totaling 280):[54]

Libya 59	France 1
Kuwait 3	Palestine 8
Algeria 1	Azerbaijan 1
Tunisia 44	United Kingdom 1
United Arab Emirates 3	Russia 7
Ireland 1	Bulgaria 1
Saudi Arabia 44	United States 1
Australia 2	Chechnya 5
Kabardino-Balkaria 1	Denmark 1
Jordan 32	Other 12
Morocco 2	Dagestan 4
Uzbekistan 1	Turkey 1
Egypt 27	Iraq 3
Bahrain 2	Kosovo 1[55]

However, it should be noted that, while few involved in the Syrian conflict will be able to provide a perfect picture of just how many foreign fighters there are, their identity, or whether or not these fanatics are still alive, a study which attempts to do so by using Facebook posts as the source of its data must not be taken as an authoritative account.

Much more authoritative reports would, obviously, come from individuals and organizations that are on the ground in Syria. In addition, it would stand to reason that organizations who are dedicated to the weakening and/or destruction of a nation should not be considered an unbiased or reliable source of information, particularly when that

---

[53] Brunker, Mike. "Study uses 'martyr' posts to analyze 'foreign fighters' aiding Syrian rebels." NBC News. June 3, 2013. http://openchannel.nbcnews.com/_news/2013/06/03/18728823-study-uses-martyr-posts-to-analyze-foreign-fighters-aiding-syrian-rebels?lite Accessed on July 17, 2013.

[54] Zelin, Aaron Y.; Kohlmann, Evan F.; al-Khouri, Laith. "Convoy of Martyrs in the Levant: A Joint Study Charting the Evolving Role of Sunni Foreign Fighters in the Armed Uprising Against the Assad Regime in Syria." Flashpoint Partners. June 2013. https://flashpoint-intel.com/upload/syria_martyrs/2013-06-02_Convoy_of_Martyrs_Report.pdf Accessed on July 17, 2013.

[55] Zelin, Aaron Y.; Kohlmann, Evan F.; al-Khouri, Laith. "Convoy of Martyrs in the Levant: A Joint Study Charting the Evolving Role of Sunni Foreign Fighters in the Armed Uprising Against the Assad Regime in Syria." Flashpoint Partners. June 2013. https://flashpoint-intel.com/upload/syria_martyrs/2013-06-02_Convoy_of_Martyrs_Report.pdf Accessed on July 17, 2013.

organization's information would go some distance in shaping the opinion of the American and Western public with regard to the target nation.

Thus, it is important to understand that WINEP is nothing more than a Neo-Con/Israeli/Zionist think-tank which has long held Syria as one of its main targets. Indeed, WINEP is attached at the hip to AIPAC (American Israel Public Affairs Committee) and is largely considered to be merely another wing of the Israeli lobbying organization.

As the Institute for Policy Studies describes WINEP,[56]

> The Washington Institute for Near East Policy (WINEP), a spin-off the American Israel Public Affairs Committee,[57] is an influential beltway think tank whose members have advocated a host of hawkish, "pro-Israel" policies over the years. It is considered a core member of the "Israel lobby," a constellation of policy shops and advocacy groups devoted to pushing an Israel-centric U.S. agenda in the Middle East. Many of WINEP's current and former scholars have been closely associated with neoconservatism, and the organization has generally been supportive of the "war on terror" policies pushed by representatives of groups like the American Enterprise Institute (AEI)[58] and the Foundation for Defense of Democracies.[59]

> Iran and Syria have long been at the center of WINEP's work, with the group's scholars promoting a host of aggressive U.S. policies towards these countries, which often dovetail with the goals of other hawkish "pro-Israel" campaigns.[60]

Although one could successfully argue that think tanks such as WINEP are "close to the ground" in Syria by virtue of their connections (direct and indirect) to those individuals and organizations who have organized, trained, and set loose upon secular Syria, it is also true that Middle Eastern news organizations such as Al-Manar of Lebanon are not only literally "close to the ground," but that they are largely free of a blinding anti-Syria pro-death squad psychosis.

That being said, Al-Manar, banned in the United States (because free speech is respected in the U.S.A.), is not to be construed as an unbiased observer either. The network is owned by Hezbollah and is an avowed supporter of the Assad regime.

---

[56] "Washington Institute For Near East Policy." Institute For Policy Studies. October 15, 2012. http://www.rightweb.irc-online.org/profile/washington_institute_for_near_east_policy Accessed on July 18, 2013.

[57] "American Israel Public Affairs Committee." Institute For Policy Studies. November 9, 2012. http://www.rightweb.irc-online.org/profile/american_israel_public_affairs_committee Accessed on July 18, 2013.

[58] "American Enterprise Institute." Institute For Policy Studies. http://www.rightweb.irc-online.org/profile/american_enterprise_institute Accessed on July 18, 2013.

[59] "Foundation for Defense of Democracies." Institute for Policy Studies. November 16, 2012. http://www.rightweb.irc-online.org/profile/foundation_for_defense_of_democracies Accessed on July 18, 2013.

[60] "Washington Institute For Near East Policy." Institute For Policy Studies. October 15, 2012. http://www.rightweb.irc-online.org/profile/washington_institute_for_near_east_policy Accessed on July 18, 2013.

Nevertheless, Al-Manar has reported that 6,113 foreign fighters have been killed in Syria so far. The numbers and ethnic breakdown according to Al-Manar are as follows:[61]

[61] "First Post – June 11, 2013 – Qatar's Prince Porky To Call It Quits; Syrian Army Bashes Rat Mercenaries; News From Around The World." Syrian Perspective. June 12, 2013. http://www.syrianperspective.blogspot.com/2013/06/first-post-june-11-2013-qatars-prince.html Accessed on July 18, 2013.

729 Saudi Arabians
640 Kurds from the Mujaahedeen Khalq (recently declassified as a terrorist organization by the U.S.)
489 Egyptians
439 Libyans
439 Chechens
301 Afghans
263 Libyans
261 Pakistanis
208 Iraqis
188 Russians
167 Turks
129 Jordanians
117 Somalis
129 Jordanians
109 Kuwaitis

90 French
67 Germans
66 British
50 Tunisians
55 Indonesians
53 Algerians
52 Yemenis
19 Qataris
45 Belgians
40 Uzbekis
35 Americans
31 Kosovars
21 Azerbaijanis
31 Maltese (Of Lebanese descent)
7 Mauritanians
6 Sierra Leone
6 Surinam[62]

It should be noted that individuals at the Syrian Perspective website,[63] have stated qualms with the breakdown provided by Al-Manar. Syrian Perspective suggests that Libyans have made up the majority of foreign fighters.[64]

While the evidence does point toward Libyan fighters making up a larger contingent of foreigners as a whole in the death squad network, it should also be noted that the number produced by Al-Manar and Flashpoint/WINEP only represented the death squad members that have been found or reported dead, not necessarily the number of members currently in action.

Also note that many other nationalities have been included by a variety of other sources, almost all with different numbers. For instance, other sources have also reported the following nationalities:

Belgium;[65] Afghanistan;[66] Albania;[67] Algeria;[68] Bosnia;[69] Sweden;[70] Tajikistan;[71] China;[72] Kyrgystan; Sudan; Chad; Spain;[73]

---

[62] "First Post – June 11, 2013 – Qatar's Prince Porky To Call It Quits; Syrian Army Bashes Rat Mercenaries; News From Around The World." Syrian Perspective. June 12, 2013. http://www.syrianperspective.blogspot.com/2013/06/first-post-june-11-2013-qatars-prince.html Accessed on July 18, 2013.

[63] Syrian Perspective Website Homepage. http://syrianperspective.blogspot.com/ Accessed on July 18, 2013.

[64] "First Post – June 11, 2013 – Qatar's Prince Porky To Call It Quits; Syrian Army Bashes Rat Mercenaries; News From Around The World." Syrian Perspective. June 12, 2013. http://www.syrianperspective.blogspot.com/2013/06/first-post-june-11-2013-qatars-prince.html Accessed on July 18, 2013.

[65] Fontaine, Daniel. "La Belgique, pépinière de djihadistes pour la Syrie." RTBF.BE. May 24, 2013. http://www.rtbf.be/info/belgique/detail_la-belgique-pepiniere-de-djihadistes-pour-la-syrie?id=7994552 Accessed on July 18, 2013. English translation of title: "Belgium, nursery of

It is extraordinarily difficult to obtain accurate numbers regarding simply the number and nationality of dead foreign fighters. Even then, the number of dead foreign fighters does not provide us with an accurate number of living foreign fighters. Thus, we are unable to compile a list of the total number of foreign fighters as a whole.

Bill Van Auken of the World Socialist Website, however, wrote an article in which he stated that the Syrian Observatory for Human Rights reported that 2,219 foreign fighters have been killed as of 2013, thus suggesting that the number of foreign fighters still active inside the country at the time "must be in the tens of thousands."[74]

Interestingly enough, this is the same figure which Hezbollah Secretary General Hassan Nasrallah cited when he stated "Tens of thousands of (rebel foreign) fighters did not bother the so-called Friends of Syria countries whose representatives met in Amman a couple of days ago. . . . . . But the interference of a small group from Lebanese Hezbollah was considered a foreign intervention."[75]

---

jihadists to Syria."

[66] "Syria names 142 slain foreign fighters from 18 countries." Ahram. November 27, 2012. http://english.ahram.org.eg/NewsContent/2/8/59294/World/Region/Syria-names--slain-foreign-fighters-from--countrie.aspx Accessed on July 18, 2013.

[67] "Ten Albanians Were Killed In Syria." PTC. April 13, 2013. http://www.rts.rs/page/stories/ci/story/2/%D0%A1%D0%B2%D0%B5%D1%82/1304802/%D0%94%D0%B5%D1%81%D0%B5%D1%82+%D0%90%D0%BB%D0%B1%D0%B0%D0%BD%D0%B0%D1%86%D0%B0+%D0%BF%D0%BE%D0%B3%D0%B8%D0%BD%D1%83%D0%BB%D0%BE+%D1%83+%D0%A1%D0%B8%D1%80%D0%B8%D1%98%D0%B8.html Accessed on July 18, 2013. Original language title: "Десет Албанаца погинуло у Сирији

[68] Roggio, Bill. "African jihadists killed in fighting in Syria." Long War Journal. September 10, 2012. http://www.longwarjournal.org/threat-matrix/archives/2012/09/african_jihadists_killed_in_fi.php Accessed on July 13, 2013.

[69] "Another Bosnian Salafi dies in Syria conflict." B92. May 21, 2013. http://www.b92.net/eng/news/region-article.php?yyyy=2013&mm=05&dd=21&nav_id=86284 Accessed on July 18, 2013.

[70] "HS: Man with Finnish roots killed in Syria fighting." YLE. May 3, 2013. http://yle.fi/uutiset/hs_man_with_finnish_roots_killed_in_syrian_fighting/6523548 Accessed on July 18, 2013.

[71] "Tajiks, Kyrgyz confirmed fighting in Syria." Central Asia Online. May 24, 2013. http://centralasiaonline.com/en_GB/articles/caii/newsbriefs/2013/05/24/newsbrief-01 Accessed on July 18, 2013.

[72] Barkan, L. "Facebook Page Documents Foreigners Who Come To Syria From Western Countries To Fight The Regime." Right Side News.

[73] Zelin, Aaron Y. "Deciphering the Jihadist Presence in Syria: An Analysis of Martyrdom Notices." Combating Terrorism Center at West Point. February 20, 2013. http://www.ctc.usma.edu/posts/deciphering-the-jihadist-presence-in-syria-an-analysis-of-martyrdom-notices Accessed on July 18, 2013.

[74] Van Auken, Bill. "White House convenes meeting on Syria escalation." World Socialist Web Site. June 11, 2013. http://www.wsws.org/en/articles/2013/06/11/syri-j11.html Accessed on July 18, 2013.

[75] Ahmed, Amir; Watkins, Tom. "Hezbollah leader acknowledges fighters' presence in Syria town." CNN. March 27, 2013. http://www.cnn.com/2013/05/25/world/meast/syria-violence

Yet one of the most obvious examples of foreign involvement in the Syrian death squad movement is the fact that the Libyan Islamic Fighting Group (LIFG) made up a large portion of the allegedly "Syrian" death squad fighters. Indeed, the LIFG, a contingent of terrorists, mercenaries, madmen, and religious fanatics that led the destabilization effort against Colonel Ghaddaffi in Libya and the subsequent genocide of black Africans after the murder of the aging leader, were thus been exported to Syria to wreak the same level of havoc and brutality upon the Syrian people as they did to their own country.[76]

The LIFG, however, did not simply ship a few fighters here and there for tactical support. The organization has actually commanded entire brigades of death squads, themselves made up of a diverse number of nationalities as evidenced by the above body counts.[77]

In fact, it was known as far back as November 2011 that around 600 LIFG terrorists had traveled to Syria in order to engage in combat against the secular government and the civilian population.[78] This provision of actual military support and "boots on the ground" on the part of the new terrorist Libyan regime (itself made up of nothing but Western-backed death squads) was only thinly veiled if at all.

Remember, Abdul Hakim Belhaj, the LIFG death squad leader in his own country actually traveled to the Turkey-Syria border and promised weapons, funding, and manpower to "Free Syrian Army" (FSA) killers only days before the promised material arrived.[79]

Although claims that Syrian death squads were made up mainly of foreigners were denied then and continue to be denied now by Western governments and their media mouthpieces, these same media outlets have been forced to admit that, at the very least, these death squads contained foreigners. As Ivan Watson and Raja Razek of CNN reported,

> Meanwhile, residents of the village where the Syrian Falcons were headquartered said there were fighters of several North African nationalities also serving with the brigade's ranks.
>
> A volunteer Libyan fighter has also told CNN he intends to travel from Turkey to Syria within days to add a "platoon" of Libyan fighters to armed movement.

Accessed on July 18, 2013.

[76] Tarpley, Webster G. "The CIA's Libya Rebels: The Same Terrorists Who Killed US, NATO Troops in Iraq." Tarpley.net. March 24, 2011. http://tarpley.net/2011/03/24/the-cia%E2%80%99s-libya-rebels-the-same-terrorists-who-killed-us-nato-troops-in-iraq/ Accessed on July 18, 2013.

[77] Cartalucci, Tony. "UN Designates 'Free Syrian Army' Affiliates as Al Qaeda." Land Destroyer Report. August 12, 2012. http://landdestroyer.blogspot.com/2012/08/un-designates-free-syrian-army.html Accessed on July 18, 2013.

[78] "Libyan fighters join 'free Syrian army' forces." Albawaba. November 29, 2011. http://www.albawaba.com/news/libyan-fighters-join-free-syrian-army-forces-403268 Accessed on July 18, 2013.

[79] Sherlock, Ruth. "Leading Libyan Islamist met Free Syrian Army opposition group." The Telegraph. November 27, 2011. http://www.telegraph.co.uk/news/worldnews/africaandindianocean/libya/8919057/Leading-Libyan-Islamist-met-Free-Syrian-Army-opposition-group.html Accessed on July 18, 2013.

. . . . .

On Wednesday, CNN's crew met a Libyan fighter who had crossed into Syria from Turkey with four other Libyans. The fighter wore full camouflage and was carrying a Kalashnikov rifle. He said more Libyan fighters were on the way.

The foreign fighters, some of them are clearly drawn because they see this as … a jihad. So this is a magnet for jihadists who see this as a fight for Sunni Muslims.[80]

The admission of the presence of al-Qaeda among the death squads has been yet another aspect of the so-called "civil war" that the Western mainstream media attempted to avoid until avoidance was no longer possible. Unfortunately for the propagandists, the fact that the death squads are indeed al-Qaeda either officially or in ideological sympathy is no longer hidden nor debatable and has not been a lie that has been able to keep up for years now.

Consider the fact that the Council on Foreign Relations itself has not only admitted the presence of al-Qaeda amongst the death squads but also their necessity to the tactical success. The CFR report, entitled, "Al-Qaeda's Specter In Syria," states,

The Syrian rebels would be immeasurably weaker today without al-Qaeda in their ranks. By and large, Free Syrian Army (FSA) battalions are tired, divided, chaotic, and ineffective. Feeling abandoned by the West, rebel forces are increasingly demoralized as they square off with the Assad regime's superior weaponry and professional army. Al-Qaeda fighters, however, may help improve morale. The influx of jihadis brings discipline, religious fervor, battle experience from Iraq, funding from Sunni sympathizers in the Gulf, and most importantly, deadly results. In short, the FSA needs al-Qaeda now.[81]

Tony Cartalucci of Land Destroyer expounds the subject even further by writing,[82]

Also, to be clear, the Libyan Islamic Fighting Group (LIFG) is in fact an affiliate of Al Qaeda with its commanders having occupied the highest echelons of Al Qaeda's command structure and having participated in every combat engagement Al Qaeda has conducted since its inception via US-Saudi cash and arms in the mountains of Afghanistan in the 1980's. This was documented meticulously in the US Army's West Point Combating Terrorism Center report, "Al-Qa'ida's Foreign Fighters in Iraq."[83]

---

[80] Watson, Ivan; Razek, Raja. "Faces of the Free Syrian Army." CNN. July 27, 2012. http://edition.cnn.com/2012/07/24/world/meast/northern-syria-violence/index.html Accessed on July 18, 2013.

[81] Husain, Ed. "Al-Qaeda's Specter in Syria." Council on Foreign Relations. August 6, 2012. http://www.cfr.org/syria/al-qaedas-specter-syria/p28782 Accessed on July 18, 2013.

[82] Cartalucci, Tony. "UN Designates 'Free Syrian Army' Affiliates as Al Qaeda." Land Destroyer Report. August 12, 2012. http://landdestroyer.blogspot.com/2012/08/un-designates-free-syrian-army.html Accessed on July 18, 2013.

[83] Felter, Joseph; Fishman, Brian. "Al-Qaeda's Foreign Fighters in Iraq: A First Look At The Sinjar Records." Harmony Project. Combating Terrorism Center at West Point. 2007. http://tarpley.net/docs/CTCForeignFighter.19.Dec07.pdf Accessed on July 18, 2013.

LIFG is also listed by both the US State Department[84] and the UK Home Office (page 5, .pdf)[85] as a foreign terrorist organization and a proscribed terrorist organization respectively.

Foreign Policy's admission of al-Harati's role in organizing and leading the FSA in Syria, and the inclusion of Libyan terrorists in his brigade are by no means the only role LIFG is playing in the Syrian violence. LIFG commander Abdul Hakim Belhaj had visited the Turkish-Syrian border[86] in late 2011 pledging Libyan arms, cash, and fighters to the FSA - with the nation of Libya itself having already become a NATO-created terrorist safe-haven.

It is clear that LIFG, and by implication Al Qaeda, played a significant role in the violence in Syria, not only undermining the narrative of the unrest being an "indigenous" "pro-democracy uprising," but also implicating foreign nations who are funding and arming militants as state sponsors of terrorism.

Included amongst these state sponsors of international terrorism are Turkey, Saudi Arabia, Qatar, and the Hariri faction in northern Lebanon, as well as the NATO-installed government of Libya. This also includes both the United States, who is admittedly providing cash and equipment for the FSA[87] as well as coordinating efforts to arm militants, and now the UK once again with their latest announcement.

A similar scenario unfolded in Libya,[88] where LIFG terrorists were likewise carrying out a campaign of nationwide genocide with NATO providing air support. Similarly, by funding, arming, and coordinating acts of violence with LIFG fighters, NATO, and in particular, France, England, and the United States, were guilty of violating both their own respective anti-terrorism legislation, as well as international provisions against terrorism.[89]

---

[84] "Foreign Terrorist Organizations." U.S. Department of State. Bureau of Counterterrorism. September 28, 2012. http://www.state.gov/j/ct/rls/other/des/123085.htm Accessed on July 18, 2013.

[85] "Proscribed Terror Groups." UK Home Office. http://www.homeoffice.gov.uk/publications/counter-terrorism/proscribed-terror-groups/proscribed-groups?view=Binary Accessed on July 18, 2013.

[86] Sherlock, Ruth. "Leading Libyan Islamist met Free Syrian Army opposition group." The Telegraph. November 27, 2011. http://www.telegraph.co.uk/news/worldnews/africaandindianocean/libya/8919057/Leading-Libyan-Islamist-met-Free-Syrian-Army-opposition-group.html Accessed on July 18, 2013.

[87] Schmitt, Eric. "C.I.A. Said to Aid in Steering Arms to Syrian Opposition." New York Times. June 21, 2012. http://www.nytimes.com/2012/06/21/world/middleeast/cia-said-to-aid-in-steering-arms-to-syrian-rebels.html?_r=1&pagewanted=all Accessed on July 18, 2013.

[88] Cartalucci, Tony. "Libyan Rebels Listed by US State Department as Terrorists." Land Destroyer Report. http://landdestroyer.blogspot.com/2011/09/libyan-rebels-listed-by-us-state.html Accessed on July 18, 2013.

[89] Cartalucci, Tony. "UN Designates 'Free Syrian Army' Affiliates as Al Qaeda." Land Destroyer Report. August 12, 2012. http://landdestroyer.blogspot.com/2012/08/un-designates-free-syrian-army.html Accessed on July 18, 2013.

In continuing to address the foreign nature of the death squads, it is also worthwhile to consider the claims made by Abou Zayd Attounssi, a former fighter with the death squads who became disillusioned with the movement.[90]

As reported by Salma Bouzid of Tunisia Live, the Tunisian television show, Attasiaa Massaa, featured a clip of a young Tunisian man named Abou Zayd Attounssi who claimed that he had recently returned to Tunisia after fighting for eight months alongside the inappropriately named "Syrian rebels."[91]

Further supporting the fundamentalist nature of the majority of the members of the NATO death squads (aka rebels) operating in Syria, Attounssi stated that his initial reason for traveling to Syria to engage in murder, plunder, and torture against innocent people was because "he felt his religion required him to engage in jihad against 'the enemy.'"[92]

Although it was apparently not the killing that turned Attounssi off from the death squad movement, he nevertheless became disillusioned with it because, "most of the fighters within the Free Syrian army are fighting for the spoils of war and the foreign aid they supposedly get."[93]

Also featured on the show was the father of Hamza Rjeb, another former death squad member who is now disabled. Rjeb's father claimed that "the Tunisian government should take full responsibility for his son's situation and for allowing groups in the country to 'brainwash' his son."[94]

In an interview with Tunisia Live, Ahmed Youssef, a journalist described by Bouzid as "pro-Assad," stated, "For every Tunisian fighter brought to Syria, Qatar pays 3,000 dollars to the Syrian rebels." He also claimed that, "most of the Tunisians come from disadvantaged regions in Tunisia with low unemployment," and stated that the Tunisians fighting in Syria are "considered mercenaries." Youssef estimated that the number of Tunisian fighters wreaking havoc in Syria is more than 3,500.[95]

---

[90] Turbeville, Brandon. "Tunisian Terrorists Are Now Confirmed Members of Syrian Death Squads." Activist Post. March 26, 2013. http://www.activistpost.com/2013/03/tunisian-terrorists-are-now-confirmed.html Accessed on July 18, 2013.

[91] Bouzid, Salma. "TV Show Renews Controversy Over Tunisian Fighters In Syria." Tunisia Live. March 22, 2013. http://www.tunisia-live.net/2013/03/22/tv-show-renews-controversy-over-tunisian-fighters-in-syria/ Accessed on July 18, 2013.

[92] Bouzid, Salma. "TV Show Renews Controversy Over Tunisian Fighters In Syria." Tunisia Live. March 22, 2013. http://www.tunisia-live.net/2013/03/22/tv-show-renews-controversy-over-tunisian-fighters-in-syria/ Accessed on July 18, 2013.

[93] Bouzid, Salma. "TV Show Renews Controversy Over Tunisian Fighters In Syria." Tunisia Live. March 22, 2013. http://www.tunisia-live.net/2013/03/22/tv-show-renews-controversy-over-tunisian-fighters-in-syria/ Accessed on July 18, 2013.

[94] Bouzid, Salma. "TV Show Renews Controversy Over Tunisian Fighters In Syria." Tunisia Live. March 22, 2013. http://www.tunisia-live.net/2013/03/22/tv-show-renews-controversy-over-tunisian-fighters-in-syria/ Accessed on July 18, 2013.

[95] Bouzid, Salma. "TV Show Renews Controversy Over Tunisian Fighters In Syria." Tunisia Live. March 22, 2013. http://www.tunisia-live.net/2013/03/22/tv-show-renews-controversy-over-tunisian-fighters-in-syria/ Accessed on July 18, 2013.

Although the exact number of foreign fighters making up the ranks of the death squads is unknown and will likely never be made public, the fact that the majority of the militants were drawn from outside of Syria's borders. Even while the mainstream Western media did its best to obfuscate and pretend that the "rebellion" was organic in nature, only tainted with a few bad apples, the reality on the ground was and still is quite the opposite.

Chapter II: Fake Humanitarian Organizations

White Helmets

Despite the failure to award the White Helmets with the Nobel Peace Prize and the pathetic propaganda film that accompanied the run-up to the decision, there remains a continued effort to not only promote the White Helmets as being a humanitarian organization and hide their actual terroristic nature, but also to conceal the real humanitarian heroes in Syria, the Syria Civil Defense.

Indeed, if one searches the web for Syria Civil Defense, he will be met with links to a White Helmets website operating under the domain of SyriaCivilDefense.org. Wikipedia also lists the Syria Civil Defense as "aka" the White Helmets.[96]

It is, of course, a necessity for the NATO powers to erase the real Syria Civil Defense and replace them with the White Helmets so that the corporate outlets' information sourcing can come from a "respected" humanitarian organization whenever false claims leveled against the Syrian government. Propaganda sounds so much better when it comes from selfless, humanitarian, rescue operations.

Vanessa Beeley,[97] the researcher who has ripped the mask of the White Helmets numerous times before and who may be the person most responsible for preventing the terrorist support group from receiving the Nobel Peace Prize, describes the real Syria Civil Defense in the following way:

> The REAL Syria Civil Defence was established as an organisation, in 1953, some 63 years before the White Helmets were a glimmer in the eyes of CIA and MI6 operatives.

> The REAL Syria Civil Defence is a founding member of the ICDO (International Civil Defence Organisation). Other ICDO partners include the UN Department of Humanitarian Affairs (OCHA), Secretarian of the International Strategy for Disaster Reduction (UNISDR), International Search and Rescue Advisory Group (INSARAG), World Health Organisation (WHO), United Nations of Geneva (UNOG), Red Cross and the Red Crescent.

> To our knowledge and according to the Head Quarters of the REAL Syria Civil Defence in Damascus, the White Helmets are NOT a member of the ICDO. The REAL Syria White Helmets have received awards for their participation in the training of other member states in USAR (Urban Search and Rescue) and for their contributions to the Civil Defence community, prior to the NATO dirty war on Syria that began in earnest, in 2011.

> Later in Part II, we will go into further detail regarding this affiliation with the ICDO and the role the REAL Syria Civil Defence has played in global civil defence

---

[96] "Syria Civil Defense." Wikipedia. https://en.wikipedia.org/wiki/Syrian_Civil_Defense November 18, 2016.

[97] Vanessa Beeley's work can be read at her website, TheWallWillFall.org.

developments for the last 63 years – which is tremendous, and something the White Helmets could never lay claim to in reality, despite all the superficial accolades being rained down upon them by the US and NATO fueled organisations, foundations and cosmetic award bodies.

This is an introduction to the unsung heroes who, unlike the counterfeit White Helmets, do truly risk their lives every day, working not only in government controlled areas, but forging deep into terrorist strongholds to rescue civilians living under the brutal US-NATO-backed terrorist siege and occupation that engulfs all of Syria.

When Syrian civilians are at risk, injured, or buried under the rubble of homes, schools and hospitals destroyed by terrorist mortar showers, it's not Le Mesurier's White Helmets who rush to their aid – it's the REAL Syria Civil Defence, a real civic organization who, up until the publication of this article, have never been mentioned by any western media outlets.[98]

Beeley traveled to Syria in 2016 in order to get a firsthand feel for the situation on the ground and to investigate the Syria Civil Defense/White Helmet issue. She traveled all over the country, most notably in Aleppo and Damascus, the latter city being the headquarters of the real Syria Civil Defense. She, along with journalist Eva Bartlett,[99] was able to interview members of the SCD and inspect the organization's equipment and facilities.

Beeley writes,

On the 15th of August, I entered the work yard of Aleppo's REAL Syria Civil Defence and was greeted by an exhausted team of about fifteen crew-members. That morning from 11am until around 3 pm, just before our visit, they had been fighting a fire in a cement and plastics factory which had been ignited by Al Nusra Front mortar fire.

They were understandably wary, but they still gathered around us (my colleague and independent journalist, Eva Bartlett and our translator) in the searing arid summer heat. Over the course of this 5 years and 6 months of this dirty war against Syria, not one western media journalist had ever asked to speak to them.

This extraordinary omission and failure to follow the most rudimentary journalist text book rules by the western media is staggering, but hardly surprising considering the level of spin and propaganda employed daily by the likes of the BBC, CNN, FOX News, The Guardian, New York Times, and Washington Post.[100] Sadly, western media lap dogs end up simply wagging their tails to their masters voice and turning somersaults with the truth to merit reward.

---

[98] Beeley, Vanessa. "The REAL Syria Civil Defence Exposes Fake 'White Helmets' As Terrorist-Linked Impostors." 21stCenturyWire. September 23, 2016. http://21stcenturywire.com/2016/09/23/exclusive-the-real-syria-civil-defence-expose-natos-white-helmets-as-terrorist-linked-imposters/

[99] Eva Bartlett's work can be read at InGaza.Wordpress.com.

[100] Beeley, Vanessa. "'Aleppo Media Centre' Funded By French Foreign Office, EU And US." 21st Century Wire. September 20, 2016. http://21stcenturywire.com/2016/09/20/exclusive-aleppo-media-centre-funded-by-french-foreign-office-eu-and-us/

Unfortunately for the Syrian people, western pundits have only reported on crucial and pivotal events in the war on Syria based largely on 'evidence' supplied by the US-UK-NATO construct, the White Helmets, who are ensconsed only in Al Nusra Front aka Al Qaeda and ISIS held areas.

As a result of western media outlets not bothering to make contact with the volunteer Syrians in the REAL Syria Civil Defence, western audiences never received a balanced view of the situation. Instead, western media only disseminates what amounts to a biased, one-sided view which mirrors anti-Syrian state and Syrian Arab Army rhetoric issued by the US State Dept and British Foreign Office.

I explained in detail, why I had come to talk with them, that my objective was to find out who were the real heroes inside Syria, the multi- million NATO funded White Helmets created in 2013 or the Syrian Syria Civil Defence established in 1953.

Aleppo's REAL Syria Civil Defence informed us there are 150 volunteers working across all units in Aleppo, the headquarters are in the Hamadaniya area which is one of the most severely targeted civilian areas, by Al Nusra Front Hell Cannon mortar fire and explosive bullets. The volunteers ages range between 25-45 years old, and the minimum age for training is 18.[101]

All members of the crew were genuine volunteers. They spoke proudly of the intensive training process they undergo before they can be accepted into the unit. They are fully trained in urban search and rescue techniques (USAR). They are also fully qualified paramedics.

A glance around their yard revealed that their equipment is tired and worn. The fire trucks were gleaming in the sun but showed signs of heavy use. Tattered jackets hung from the fenders and wing mirrors of the trucks and a Syrian flag had been draped across the radiator of one truck, perhaps in honour of our visit.[102]

She adds,

The West Aleppo crew is forced to attend missions without the standard issue equipment and to deal with situations like chemical weapons attacks with only the ineffectual paper breathing masks. This is another result of the EU-US sanctions being enforced against Syria, and effectively against the Syrian people. The REAL Syria Civil Defence is unable to replace equipment or replenish supplies, unlike the NATO White Helmets who enjoy an endless stream of kit and replacement materials via the Turkey supply chain that has remained unbroken for much of the four years that Aleppo has been under terrorist siege.[103]

---

[101] "Huge explosion as Hell Cannon hits "weapons cache" in Syria – Truthloader." Youtube. Posted by Truthloader. April 24, 2014. https://www.youtube.com/watch?v=mqd2InhOj90 Video shows a rudimentary "Hell Cannon" being launched. Video cuts to "weapons cache" which is possibly a factory or some other facility being hit by the explosive launched from the cannon.
[102] Beeley, Vanessa. "The REAL Syria Civil Defence Exposes Fake 'White Helmets' As Terrorist-Linked Impostors." 21stCenturyWire. September 23, 2016.
http://21stcenturywire.com/2016/09/23/exclusive-the-real-syria-civil-defence-expose-natos-white-helmets-as-terrorist-linked-imposters/
[103] Beeley, Vanessa. "The REAL Syria Civil Defence Exposes Fake 'White Helmets' As Terrorist-Linked Impostors." 21stCenturyWire. September 23, 2016.

Beeley's article, "The REAL Syria Civil Defence Exposes Fake 'White Helmets' As Terrorist-Linked Imposters," details firsthand accounts of SCD volunteers risking (and sometimes losing) their lives in order to save the lives of civilians. The article also details stories from volunteers regarding the horrific aftermath of terrorist hell cannons, missiles, and other indiscriminate strikes against civilian areas. This author highly recommends reading the entirety of Beeley's article.

When Beeley asked the volunteers their opinions on the White Helmets, an image was painted that appears much different from the fantasy portrayed by Western media and Hollywood film sets as well as the Nobel Prize committee. She writes,

> When we got on to the subject of NATO's White Helmets, the West Aleppo REAL Syrian Civil Defence crew became animated. One of them, stepped forward and began to talk excitedly to our translator. He had been stationed in East Aleppo at a REAL Syrian Civil Defence unit based in an area that has since been overrun by Al Nusra Front and their associate terrorist gangs.

> Again, we are unable, as we have said, to provide names of the men we spoke with. They are prime targets for the Al Nusra Front and company in East Aleppo. This crew member, lets call him 'Khaled,' described what happened when the terrorists (western media still call them "opposition" or "moderate rebels") started to invade East Aleppo in 2012.

> "They came in and they drove us out of our homes and they came to the Syria Civil Defence yard and they killed some of my comrades, they kidnapped others. They wanted to force me to work with them. I escaped at night. I was forced to leave my teenage sons behind. They burned my house to the ground and they put my name on all the terrorist checkpoints so if I go back, they will kill me."

> Khaled went on to explain how those men who later became the White Helmets were among this first wave of terrorists:

> "They are terrorists, not rescuers. They stole our ambulances and three of our fire engines. They don't do any rescue work. They drive round with guns in the back of their car like any other terrorist. Some are from East Aleppo, some are from Syria but not from Aleppo and some are even coming in from abroad."

> Granted, this might come as a shock to anyone who has already bought into the public relations image of the group that's already been developed over three years by various agencies in New York, Washington DC and London, but these are the real accounts regarding what one might say is the true unmasked nature of the west's White Helmets.[104]

---

http://21stcenturywire.com/2016/09/23/exclusive-the-real-syria-civil-defence-expose-natos-white-helmets-as-terrorist-linked-imposters/

[104] Beeley, Vanessa. "The REAL Syria Civil Defence Exposes Fake 'White Helmets' As Terrorist-Linked Impostors." 21stCenturyWire. September 23, 2016. http://21stcenturywire.com/2016/09/23/exclusive-the-real-syria-civil-defence-expose-natos-white-helmets-as-terrorist-linked-imposters/

Beeley also writes that the volunteers of the SCD had a chance to view some of the White Helmets' "rescue videos" and found a number of oddities if the White Helmets were truly rescuing trapped civilians or even simply retrieving bodies.

Beeley continues,

> At this point other crew members interjected and told me that they had watched the White Helmet "rescue" videos.

> "They are fake. They don't carry out any correct procedures, either as paramedics or as search and rescue experts."

> They described how the White Helmets use a heavy-duty power drill to dig down for civilians buried under the rubble of homes allegedly targeted by "Syrian or Russian airstrikes."

> "It's the wrong equipment to use. It is not sensitive enough and because it vibrates powerfully, it can displace the rubble which is dangerous if anyone is genuinely buried beneath it."

> They went on to describe other aspects of the White Helmet videos that they believe contravene all standard procedures that are followed by genuine search and rescue experts, paramedics and first responders.

> In the following very recent video made by a White Helmet camera crew, men pretending to be genuine rescuers attack an area of rubble where they seem to know where a body buried. They start with a mint condition JCB digger, which attacks the heap of rubble with gusto. Then, alarmingly, they begin to pound the rubble with a heavy duty mallet without employing any devices to actually determine where the body is located, under the impenetrable concrete blocks. Finally, the JCB digger returns to the mound of rubble and enters the teeth of its bucket into the rubble without any hesitation, surely not standard procedure if there is a chance of a body being under the debris.

> Miraculously, as with all White Helmet videos, they seem to find exactly where the bodies are, despite having displaced the majority of the rubble in the process. They also, miraculously, avoided staving in the first body's head with the mallet. There is no intention to downplay or belittle the deaths that have obviously occurred but we do ask the questions:

> 1. How did the White Helmets know the bodies would be exactly where they found them?

> 2. Where is this rescue being filmed?

> 3. "Activists", "citizen journalists", the White Helmets and western media would have us believe that East Aleppo is under almost constant Russian or Syrian aerial attack yet the White Helmets make, on average, 4 or 5 films per day and we never see or hear any sign of an attack, only the "aftermath".

---

[105] Beeley, Vanessa. "The REAL Syria Civil Defence Exposes Fake 'White Helmets' As Terrorist-Linked Impostors." 21stCenturyWire. September 23, 2016. http://21stcenturywire.com/2016/09/23/exclusive-the-real-syria-civil-defence-expose-natos-white-helmets-as-terrorist-linked-imposters/

4. Where do these bodies come from? Are they victims of air strikes as we are told by these NATO funded "activists" and "first responders" or are they taken from among the thousands of "disappeared" that have been kidnapped by Nusra Front and other terrorist gangs in East Aleppo? Are they gruesome props being used inhumanely, to polish the image of this faux NGO embedded in East Aleppo, HQ for Al Nusra Front.[105]

Indeed, upon my own travels to the Middle East, I spoke with Syrians (not volunteers with the SCD) who had similar questions about White Helmets rescues. How do they always know right where to find the bodies? How do they not kill living victims or damage dead bodies with the equipment they are using in the videos? Why are they always videotaped? These were all questions the individuals that I spoke with were asking about the White Helmets. Another issue was the extraordinary budget this group receives from the U.K. and the U.S., a budget that is more akin to a military coffer than a humanitarian one.

Beeley went further, however, and met with the real Aleppo Medical Association. She asked them about the White Helmets and the alleged work they do in East Aleppo (they only operate in terrorist-held territory). Interestingly enough, according to Dr. Bassem Hayak, the man in charge of the medical teams that assess civilians fleeing East Aleppo to West Aleppo, stated that the White Helmets are unknown to civilians in East Aleppo.

Beeley writes,

One of the other meetings we had during our time in Aleppo, was with the Aleppo Medical Association. We met with the Director, Dr Zahar Buttal and Dr Bassem Hayak, who is in charge of the medical teams assessing refugees from East Aleppo who fled to West Aleppo via the Russian and Syrian state humanitarian corridors, created on the 29th July, which have allowed over 2000 people to escape the terrorist strongholds to safety, food and medical care in government-protected West Aleppo. These figures were given to us by the Aleppo Medical Association on the 15th August 2016.

One of the questions I asked Dr Hayak, who spoke good English, was what he knew of the White Helmets. His response was concise and without preamble. His family is still in East Aleppo and although he has not been able to get back into East Aleppo for the last year, his family have told him that the White Helmets are not known in East Aleppo. I asked again to be sure, and was told again, people, civilians do not know of the White Helmets in East Aleppo. Any actual first response work is carried out by foreign workers from various countries, Pakistan and the Gulf region among them. These foreigners work with Syrian people who are not properly trained in first response. They might only receive 2 or 3 months training before being allowed to work.

Dr Hayak says, "Even with our relationship with WHO (World Health Organisation) and the UN, we still didn't hear about the White Helmets."

Are the White Helmets, NATO ghosts?

Dr Hayak also states quite clearly, he has a cousin, working as a surgeon in East Aleppo. ISIS and other terrorist factions have forced her to stay in East Aleppo by threatening to kill her family, should she leave for West Aleppo.

Dr Hayak also said that the majority of civilians in East Aleppo are "hostages" of the NATO/US allied terrorists.

In East Aleppo, civilians living under Al Nusra Front occupation, do not know the White Helmets.

It is possible to view a portion of her interview with Dr. Hayak on YouTube.[106]

The History And Formation Of White Helmets – The Founders And Directors

White Helmets was founded by James Le Mesurier, an admitted former British army officer and mercenary with the Olive Group, a private contracting organization that is now merged with Blackwater-Academi into Constellis Holdings.[107] [108] Although White Helmets half-heartedly attempts to hide its source of funding, the organization is linked to George Soros through a PR firm named Purpose Inc., a pro-war firm that argues for Western intervention against Assad.[109] [110] The co-founder of Purpose is Jeremy Heimans, who also helped found Avaaz, a "pro-democracy" group connected to Soros' Open Society Foundation, SEIU, and MoveOn.org.[111]

In her expose of White Helmets, "White Helmets: War By Way Of Deception," Vanessa Beeley summarizes the history and funding of the organization when she wrote:

The White Helmets were established in March 2013, in Istanbul, Turkey, and is headed by James Le Mesurier, a British "security" specialist and 'ex' British military

---

[106] "Dr. Bassem Hayak Aleppo Medical Centre." Youtube. Posted by Vanessa Beeley on September 22, 2016. https://www.youtube.com/watch?v=G66GSSwpc_w

[107] LeMesurier, James. "MayDay Rescue. http://www.maydayrescue.org/content/james-le-mesurier-0 Accessed on November 18, 2016. The bio reads:
"James has spent 20 years working in fragile states as a United Nations staff member, a consultant for private companies and the UK Foreign and Commonwealth Office, and as a British Army Officer. Much of his experience has involved delivering stabilisation activities through security sector and democratisation programmes. Since 2012, James has been working on the Syria crisis where he started the Syrian White Helmets programme in March 2013. In 2014, he founded Mayday Rescue, and is dedicated to strengthening local communities in countries that are entering, enduring or emerging from conflict."

[108] Anderson, Tim. The Dirty War On Syria. Pg. 75.

[109] "Homs Airstrike: White Helmets Caught Faking Syria Casualties Report." Sputnik. September, 30, 2015. https://sputniknews.com/middleeast/201509301027807644-ngo-caught-faking-syria-casualties-report/
See also,
Nimmo, Kurt. "Soros NGO Fakes Casualties After Russia Strikes CIA Terrorists In Syria." PrisonPlanet.com. October 2, 2015. http://www.prisonplanet.com/soros-ngo-fakes-casualties-after-russia-strikes-cia-terrorists-in-syria.html

[110] "Avaaz, Soros, Israel and the Palestinians." NGO Monitor. March 6, 2013. http://www.ngo-monitor.org/reports/19/

[111] Turbeville, Brandon. "Avaaz: The Online Pro-War Propagandist And Color Revolution NGO." Activist Post. January 12, 2016. http://www.activistpost.com/2016/01/avaaz-the-online-pro-war-propagandist-and-color-revolution-ngo.html

intelligence officer with an impressive track record in some of the most dubious NATO intervention theatres including Bosnia and Kosovo, as well as Iraq, Lebanon, and Palestine. Le Mesurier is a product of Britain's elite Royal Military Academy at Sandhurst, and has also been placed in a series of high-profile pasts at the United Nations, European Union, and U.K. Foreign and Commonwealth Office.

The origins of The White Helmet's initial $300k seed funding is a little hazy, reports are contradictory but subsequent information leads us to conclude that the UK, US and Syrian opposition [Syrian National Council] are connected. Logistical support has been provided by given by Turkish elite natural disaster response team, AKUT.

A further $13 million was poured into the White Helmet coffers during 2013 and this is where it gets interesting. Early reports suggest that these "donations" came from the US, UK and SNC with the previously explored connections to George Soros in the US.

However, subsequent investigations reveal that USAID has been a major shareholder in the White Helmet organisation.

The website for the United States Agency for International Development (USAID) claims that "our work supports long-term and equitable economic growth and advances U.S. foreign policy objectives by supporting: economic growth, agriculture and trade; global health; and, democracy, conflict prevention and humanitarian assistance."[112]

In a USAID report update in July 2015 it is clearly stated that they have supplied over $ 16m in assistance to the White Helmets.[113]

In addition to Soros and the $16 million, White Helmets is known to receive approximately $23 million dollars from the U.S. State Department via USAID, a figure that was confirmed more recently by Deputy State Department Spokesman Mark Toner when questioned by reporters at a State Department briefing on April 27, 2016.[114]

It is thus no surprise that White Helmets have been publicly calling for Western intervention in Syria, particularly a No-Fly Zone since their creation. The organization is, after all, a fully funded arm of U.S./Western imperialism. It is, therefore, reasonable to expect the group to publicly call for the same desires as their bosses in the United States and Europe.

Raed Saleh, head of White Helmets (aka Syrian Civil Defense) has publicly called for the implementation of a "No-Fly Zone" over Syria by the United Nations Security Council, an act that is tantamount to direct military warfare, an example of which can be seen in the rubble of Libya. Indeed, such a decision would simply be a repeat of the Libyan tragedy.

Saleh has stated on the White Helmets website:

---

[112] Beeley, Vanessa. "White Helmets: War By Way Of Deception." The Wall Will Fall. October 23, 2015. https://thewallwillfall.org/2015/10/23/white-helmets-war-by-way-of-deception/
[113] "Syria." United States Agency For International Development. USAID.gov. https://www.usaid.gov/political-transition-initiatives/syria
[114] "U.S. Department of State Daily Press Briefing- April 27, 2016." Mark C. Toner. Deputy Spokesperson. State.Gov. http://www.state.gov/r/pa/prs/dpb/2016/04/256667.htm

Barrel bombs – sometimes filled with chlorine – are the biggest killer of civilians in Syria today. Our unarmed and neutral rescue workers have saved more than 40,823 people from the attacks in Syria, but there are many we cannot reach. There are children trapped in rubble we cannot hear. For them, the UN Security Council must follow through on its demand made last year to stop the barrel bombs, by introducing a 'no-fly zone' if necessary."[115]

Saleh himself is an interesting case. Content to shower Saleh and his organization with millions of dollars and flattering public relations material, the United States apparently does not trust Saleh enough to allow free access to American soil. In April, 2016 Saleh was set to receive another typical back-slapping award in Washington, D.C. However, Saleh's visa was canceled and he was forced to go back to Istanbul. The New York Times reported,

The leader of a Western-backed rescue organization that searches for survivors of bombings in Syria was denied entry into the United States this week, where he was to receive an award recognizing his contributions to humanitarian relief.

Raed Saleh, the head of the Syria Civil Defense, was to accept the award from InterAction, an alliance of aid agencies, at its gala dinner Tuesday night in Washington. The dinner's keynote speaker was Gayle Smith, the administrator of the United States Agency for International Development.

But when Mr. Saleh, who works in Syria and Turkey, arrived Monday at Washington's Dulles International Airport on a flight from Istanbul, the authorities said he could not enter the United States. He was told his visa had been canceled.

It was unclear whether Mr. Saleh's name might have shown up on a database, fed by a variety of intelligence and security agencies and intended to guard against the prospect of terrorism suspects slipping into the country.

The State Department declined to give specifics, but a spokesman, John Kirby, said that "the U.S. government's system of continual vetting means that traveler records are screened against available information in real time."

"While we can't confirm any possible specific actions in this case, we do have the ability to immediately coordinate with our interagency partners when new information becomes available," he added.[116]

State Department Spokesman Mark Toner was also questioned about the details surrounding Saleh's visa but Toner found it difficult to answer any questions regarding this incident in a coherent fashion. According to the State Department's own published transcripts the reporter/spokesman interaction went as follows:

QUESTION: On the last one —

MR TONER: Yes, sir.

---

[115] "Support The White Helmets." WhiteHelmets.org. https://www.whitehelmets.org/ Homepage, accessed on November 18, 2016.

[116] Sengupta, Somini; Barnard, Anne. "Leader of Syria Rescue Group, Arriving In U.S. For Award, Is Refused Entry." New York Times. April 20, 2016. http://www.nytimes.com/2016/04/21/world/middleeast/leader-of-syria-rescue-group-arriving-in-us-for-award-is-refused-entry.html?_r=2

QUESTION: — you commend this group, you're going to continue to support them, and yet you revoked the visa of their leader. I don't – that makes zero sense to me.

MR TONER: Well —

QUESTION: What – what's exactly going on?

MR TONER: Well, I mean, this group, and I would precisely make that —

QUESTION: Yeah, but this is the guy who is the leader of this group who the head of USAID lionized in a – and her – that she lauded him —

MR TONER: Sure. Sure.

QUESTION: — in a speech at the event that he was supposed to be accepting —

MR TONER: Sure.

QUESTION: — an award that he couldn't get here for because the State Department canceled his visa while he was in the middle – while he was in midair, presumably, over the Atlantic so that when he arrived at Dulles, he was promptly thrown on the next plane back to Turkey. And now here you are talking about how wonderful his group is. I just don't understand how it works.

MR TONER: So a couple responses. One is, unfortunately, we can't speak to individual visa cases. I think broadly speaking, though, on any visa case we are constantly looking at new information, so-called continually vetting travel or records. And if we do have new information that we believe this – an individual —

QUESTION: But —

MR TONER: — let me finish – would pose a security risk, we'll certainly act on that. I can't speak again specifically to this case, but what I can talk about is this group. And this group, as I said, has saved some 40,000 lives, that are first responders, they operate in a combat zone, and the fact that they're being singled out and hit by the Syrian regime is, frankly, cause for a concern. And we do support this group. We do support their efforts to save lives in what is admittedly a very complex and convoluted battlefield scene.

And to speak to your broader – to say that this group's – which I think is the implication of your question, that they somehow have ties to —

QUESTION: No, I'm not suggesting that at all.

MR TONER: Then – okay.

QUESTION: I'm saying that it just strikes me as a bit odd that you're saying that this group is wonderful and does such a great job and you're commending them for their heroism, and yet, this – you're doing this just 10 days after the leader of this group, who was supposed to be – who got his visa revoked and wasn't allowed to travel here. I understand there was an attack that killed some of its members, and I know that that's the immediate cause of it —

MR TONER: Right.

QUESTION: — but it just strikes me as being a bit inconsistent if you say that this group is wonderful, and yet, you also ban its leader from coming to the States to collect an award for which – and you say you're going to continue to support the group. I mean, if you have reason to revoke his visa, that he could be a security threat or something like that, why would you continue to support —

MR TONER: But again – but again, I'm trying to separate this individual from the group, which we believe is —

QUESTION: All right. So the guy is – you're saying that basically he is suspect but his group is not?

MR TONER: Well, again, I can't speak to the specific allegations against him, Matt.

QUESTION: Well, not if I —

MR TONER: No, I'm sorry, I – my hands are tied too but —

QUESTION: All right. The other thing —

MR TONER: — but yes, we're not condemning the group in any way whatsoever.

QUESTION: Off —

MR TONER: We believe it's doing good work.

QUESTION: Could I —

QUESTION: (Off-mike.)

QUESTION: If he is the leader of the group, how do you support this group and he is not allowed to get into the States? This is the question.

MR TONER: I understand that and all I can say is that —

QUESTION: How can you separate the leader of the group from the group?

MR TONER: Well, he's one individual in the group.

QUESTION: But the leader of the group.

MR TONER: And any individual – again, I'm broadening my language here for specific reasons, but any individual in any group suspected of ties or relations with extremist groups or that we had believed to be a security threat to the United States, we would act accordingly. But that does not, by extension, mean we condemn or would cut off ties to the group for which that individual works for.

QUESTION: Okay. It just seems a little odd.

QUESTION: Could I just follow up on the group? Which group is —

MR TONER: Sophisticated. (Laughter.)

QUESTION: I mean, they are a civil defense group, right? They are —

QUESTION: The White Helmets?

QUESTION: Who are —

MR TONER: The White Helmets. So this is a group —

QUESTION: White Helmets. Okay, I understand.

MR TONER: So, yeah, this is the Syrian Civil Defense Group. Yeah.

QUESTION: Do you know – I understand about the White Helmets. Do you know who finances them, how they operate, who are they supported by, what kind of organization they have? How do you get your information from them and so on?

MR TONER: Well – well, I can say we provide them with —

QUESTION: We – you do know a little bit.

MR TONER: Well, I can tell you that we provide, through USAID, about $23 million in assistance to them.[117]

---

[117] "U.S. Department of State Daily Press Briefing- April 27, 2016." Mark C. Toner. Deputy Spokesperson. State.Gov. http://www.state.gov/r/pa/prs/dpb/2016/04/256667.htm

Vanessa Beeley also exposes Mosab Obeidat, White Helmets Project Officer and Farouq al-Habib. She writes,

> Mosab Obeidat, previous Assistant Chief of Mission with the Qatar Red Crescent, one of whose officials, Khaled Diab was accused of supplying $ 2.2 m to secure arms for the terrorist groups in Syria. Details of this transaction and its exposure can be found in this Al Akhbar article from June 2013. [118]

> At least three other members of the team were a part of the Syrian "revolution" including Farouq al Habib, one of the 3 most prominent White Helmet leaders who was also a leader of the Homs uprising against the Syrian government and according to his testimony, was tortured by the Syrian "regime" security forces in 2012 for smuggling a journalist into Syria to "cover" the "peaceful protests".[119] [120] Habib was a founder member of the 'Homs Revolutionary Council' (the CIA have been linked to nearly all 'Revolutionary Councils in Syria)[121] before fleeing to Turkey in 2013 (A more in-depth analysis of his anti-Syrian government testimony will be presented in Part II of this article).[122]

Fraudulent Photos: White Helmets And The Propaganda Machine

In addition to calling for the implementation of a "No-Fly Zone," the White Helmets have also gone so far as to post fraudulent photos so as to blame the Syrian military for civilian casualties and intentional targeting of civilians when such is not the case. In October, 2015 White Helmets released pictures on its Twitter account purporting to show the aftermath of the Russian bombing campaign against ISIS and assorted terrorists launched on September 30. "Russia strike in Homs today. 33 civilians killed including 3 children and 1 @SyriaCivilDef volunteer" the caption read.[123] [124]

The picture showed a bleeding girl being held by a "Civil Defense" volunteer and claimed that the child was injured along with a number of other civilians.

---

[118] Mortada, Radwan. "Qatar Red Crescent Funds Syrian Rebel Arms." Al Akhbar English. June 18, 2013. http://english.al-akhbar.com/node/16160

[119] "Our Team." MayDay Rescue. http://www.maydayrescue.org/our-team Accessed on November 18, 2016.

[120] Kolodny, Carina; Kassie, Emily. "A Syrian Revolutionary Speaks Out: Here's What The World Should Know." Huffington Post. November 6, 2014. http://www.huffingtonpost.com/2014/10/03/syrian-revolutionary-speaks-out_n_5914182.html

[121] Lantier, Alex. "The petty bourgeois "left" promotes the war in Syria." World Socialist Web Site. April 12, 2013. https://www.wsws.org/en/articles/2013/04/12/isos-a12.html

[122] Beeley, Vanessa. "White Helmets: War By Way Of Deception Part 1." The Wall Will Fall. October 23, 2015. https://thewallwillfall.org/2015/10/23/white-helmets-war-by-way-of-deception/

[123] Turbeville, Brandon. "Soros-Backed NGO Fakes Photos To Blame Russia For Dead Civilians." Activist Post. October 2, 2015. http://www.activistpost.com/2015/10/soros-backed-ngo-fakes-photos-to-blame-russia-for-dead-civilians.html

[124] Screen shots of tweets were provided by @USDeptOfFear. http://www.activistpost.com/2015/10/soros-backed-ngo-fakes-photos-to-blame-russia-for-dead-civilians.html

Unfortunately for the White Helmets, Twitter users immediately exposed the photos as a fraud, since the pictures were actually taken five days prior on September 25, 2015.

Interestingly enough, the White Helmets, in an attempt to assist drumming up opposition to Vladmir Putin and Russia's attack on jihadists, also managed to tweet about the horror of Russia's air strikes hours before Russia's parliament even granted Putin the authority to use the Air Force in Syria, according to Sputnik.[125]

White Helmets: Anti-Assad Propaganda, Support And Rescue Team For Al-Nusra

Despite being routinely cited as a "humanitarian" organization, however, the White Helmets appear to be much more than even a wolf in sheep's clothing in the NGO world. Not only providing the basis for carefully crafted propaganda opportunities, the organization appears to actually work side by side with terrorist outfits like Jobhat al-Nusra both on the propaganda angle and the battlefield.

For one, it is important to note that the area of operation for the White Helmets is never within territory controlled by the Syrian government. It is without deviation solely located within territory held by "moderate terrorists," Nusra, or other related Western-backed terrorist groups. Obviously, if White Helmets truly represented the Syrian people, they would be operating in both territories. As Rick Sterling wrote in his article "Highly Effective Manipulators,"

> The trainees are said to be 'nonpartisan' but only work in rebel-controlled areas of Idlib (now controlled by Nusra/Al Queda) and Aleppo. There are widely divergent claims regarding the number of people trained by the White Helmets and the number of people rescued. The numbers are probably highly exaggerated especially since rebel-controlled territories have few civilians. A doctor who recently served in a rebel-controlled area of Aleppo described it as a ghost town. The White Helmets work primarily with the rebel group Jabat al Nusra (Al Queda in Syria).[126]

White Helmets: 'Unarmed And Unbiased'

While the White Helmets' tag line is "unarmed and unbiased," nothing could be further from the truth. Indeed, the organization is incredibly biased and visibly armed. In the second part to her expose of White Helmets, "Part II: Syria's White Helmets: War By Way Of Deception," Vanessa Beeley writes,

> As part of the myth-building process, White Helmet members are repetitively described as 'ordinary people', specifically, "bakers, tailors, engineers, pharmacists, painters, carpenters, students", and are relentlessly depicted as heroes, miracle workers, saints and super-humans scaling the "Mount Everest" of war zones with impartiality and neutrality. "Unarmed and unbiased" is their strapline, as they

---

[125] "Homs Airstrike: White Helmets Caught Faking Syria Casualty Reports." Sputnik. September 30, 2015. https://sputniknews.com/middleeast/201509301027807644-ngo-caught-faking-syria-casualties-report/

[126] Sterling, Rick. "Seven Steps Of Highly Effective Manipulators." Dissident Voice. April 9, 2015. http://dissidentvoice.org/2015/04/seven-steps-of-highly-effective-manipulators/

sacrifice themselves for the "Syrian People". Indeed, those same Syrian people who have never heard of them. The myth-making continues…

. . . . .

Can a organisation rightly be called an 'independent relief organisation' when it is being funded by a foreign government who is directly involved in the military over-throw of Syria's government? Most intelligent people should have no problem answering that question.

. . . . . .

This video below reveals a White Helmet operative describing the "throwing of Shabiha bodies in the trash". Shabiha is a derogatory term for Syrian Government militia or state-employed security forces but is liberally applied by terrorist aka "rebel alliance" factions to any member of the Syrian military, irrespective of whether they are Alawite, Sunni, or Shia. Let's remind ourselves of White Helmet claims on their websites of how its 'aid workers' "have risked sniper fire to rescue SAA bodies to give them a proper burial."[127]

. . . . .

This same neutral White Helmet operative goes on to pledge allegiance to the terrorist forces in the region stating:

"They are our role models, the best of people and we have the honour to serve them"

"SERVE THEM [armed terrorists, Al Nusra/Al Qaeda]", curious turn of phrase for a neutral, impartial humanitarian "moderate" organisation?[128]

. . . . .

He also congratulates the Mujahadeen for liberating Jisr al Shugour from Assad's forces.

"Glad tidings have reached us in Jisr al Shugour by the hands of our Mujahadeen brothers. May Allah strengthen them and make them steadfast on the correct way and soon, insh'Allah, the strongholds of the Assad regime in Latakia and Damascus will be liberated."

It should be clear that these alleged "moderates" you are watching here are actually moderate extremists and jihadists, and the western media has been very careful in hiding this fact.[129]

---

[127] "Al-Qaeda-Linked White Helmets "We Throw Syria Soldiers' Corpses In The Trash." Youtube. Posted by Navsteva. October 22, 2015. https://www.youtube.com/watch?v=eOz0jt_wA8w Video shows "White Helmet" terrorist stating that the group collects the bodies of "Shabiha" (derogatory term for pro-Assad militias) and throw them in the trash.

[128] "Syria's White Helmets Express Support For al-Qaeda." Youtube. Posted by Navsteva. Posted on October 22, 2015. https://www.youtube.com/watch?v=5qM0Xu4Sz80 Video shows White Helmet terrorist praising terrorist fighters, specifically the "mujihadeen."

[129] "Syria's White Helmets Celebrating al-Qaeda Takeover of Jisr al-Shughur." Youtube. Posted by Navsteva. Posted on October 22, 2015. https://www.youtube.com/watch?v=EiRquhd50mc Video shows White Helmet terrorist praising the recent victory of al-Qaeda in Jisr al-Shughur and referring to them as "our mujihadeen brothers."

. . . . .

Moving on to another video, this time revealing White Helmet operatives standing on the discarded dead bodies of SAA [Syrian Arab Army] soldiers and giving the victory sign. This display of support for the Al Nusra extremist terrorists who have just massacred these soldiers once again demonstrates where their true allegiances lie.

Numerous photos and large amounts of video footage is available showing the alleged "unarmed" White Helmets parading about with rifles, virtually indistinguishable in their appearance and actions from the terrorists they are working with except for their actual white helmets. In at least on instance, White Helmets members were videotaped apparently taking part in the execution of a man condemned to death by Nusra/ISIS fighters. In this video, the execution of the man who is shot in the head by the terrorists is clearly shown. Before his body is even fully still, the White Helmets arrive at the scene, within seconds, to collect the body as if they were on standby.[130]

Conclusion

With all of the above information taken together, White Helmets should be considered nothing more than a terrorist rescue operation and propaganda wing for al-Nusra Front. This organization is wholly funded, directed, and promoted by Western governments, intelligence agencies and Foundations for the purposes of assisting Western-backed terrorists in destroying secular Syria and replacing it with a collection of impotent religious/ethnicity-based petty squabbling microstates and mini-states.[131] The organization serves as a clever and opportunistic tool to be used by Western media for the purposes of sourcing false claims from "impartial" "activist" groups on the ground in Syria and giving the claims the source and credibility of a "human rights" organization. Clearly, whatever claims are made by the White Helmets should be immediately dismissed as yet another false statement in a long string of lies easily traced directly back to the United States and the UK.

The Real Syria Civil Defense VS. The White Helmets

Despite the failure to award the White Helmets with the Nobel Peace Prize and the pathetic propaganda film that accompanied the run-up to the decision, there remains a continued effort to not only promote the White Helmets as being a humanitarian organization and hide their actual terroristic nature, but also to conceal the real humanitarian heroes in Syria, the Syria Civil Defense.

Indeed, if one searches the web for Syria Civil Defense, he will be met with links to a White Helmets website operating under the domain of SyriaCivilDefense.org. Wikipedia also lists the Syria Civil Defense as "aka" the White Helmets.[132]

---

130 Beeley, Vanessa. "Part II – Syria's White Helmets: War By Way Of Deception – 'Moderate Executioners.'" 21st Century Wire. October 28, 2015.
http://21stcenturywire.com/2015/10/28/part-ii-syrias-white-helmets-war-by-way-of-deception-moderate-executioners/
131 Brzezinski, Zbigniew. The Grand Chessboard: American Primacy And Its Geostrategic Imperatives. Basic Books, 1st Edition. 1998.
132 "Syria Civil Defense." Wikipedia. https://en.wikipedia.org/wiki/Syrian_Civil_Defense

It is, of course, a necessity for the NATO powers to erase the real Syria Civil Defense and replace them with the White Helmets so that the corporate outlets' information sourcing can come from a "respected" humanitarian organization whenever false claims leveled against the Syrian government. Propaganda sounds so much better when it comes from selfless, humanitarian, rescue operations.

Vanessa Beeley, the researcher who has ripped the mask of the White Helmets numerous times before and who may be the person most responsible for preventing the terrorist support group from receiving the Nobel Peace Prize, describes the real Syria Civil Defense in the following way:

> The REAL Syria Civil Defence was established as an organisation, in 1953, some 63 years before the White Helmets were a glimmer in the eyes of CIA and MI6 operatives.

> The REAL Syria Civil Defence is a founding member of the ICDO (International Civil Defence Organisation). Other ICDO partners include the UN Department of Humanitarian Affairs (OCHA), Secretarian of the International Strategy for Disaster Reduction (UNISDR), International Search and Rescue Advisory Group (INSARAG), World Health Organisation (WHO), United Nations of Geneva (UNOG), Red Cross and the Red Crescent.

> To our knowledge and according to the Head Quarters of the REAL Syria Civil Defence in Damascus, the White Helmets are NOT a member of the ICDO. The REAL Syria White Helmets have received awards for their participation in the training of other member states in USAR (Urban Search and Rescue) and for their contributions to the Civil Defence community, prior to the NATO dirty war on Syria that began in earnest, in 2011.

> Later in Part II, we will go into further detail regarding this affiliation with the ICDO and the role the REAL Syria Civil Defence has played in global civil defence developments for the last 63 years – which is tremendous, and something the White Helmets could never lay claim to in reality, despite all the superficial accolades being rained down upon them by the US and NATO fueled organisations, foundations and cosmetic award bodies.

> This is an introduction to the unsung heroes who, unlike the counterfeit White Helmets, do truly risk their lives every day, working not only in government controlled areas, but forging deep into terrorist strongholds to rescue civilians living under the brutal US-NATO-backed terrorist siege and occupation that engulfs all of Syria.

> When Syrian civilians are at risk, injured, or buried under the rubble of homes, schools and hospitals destroyed by terrorist mortar showers, it's not Le Mesurier's White Helmets who rush to their aid – it's the REAL Syria Civil Defence, a real civic organization who, up until the publication of this article, have never been mentioned by any western media outlets.[133]

---

[133] Beeley, Vanessa. "The REAL Syria Civil Defence Exposes Fake 'White Helmets' As Terrorist-Linked Imposters." 21st

Beeley traveled to Syria in 2016 in order to get a firsthand feel for the situation on the ground and to investigate the Syria Civil Defense/White Helmet issue. She traveled all over the country, most notably in Aleppo and Damascus, the latter city being the headquarters of the real Syria Civil Defense. She, along with journalist Eva Bartlett, was able to interview members of the SCD and inspect the organization's equipment and facilities.

Beeley writes,

> On the 15th of August, I entered the work yard of Aleppo's REAL Syria Civil Defence and was greeted by an exhausted team of about fifteen crew-members. That morning from 11am until around 3 pm, just before our visit, they had been fighting a fire in a cement and plastics factory which had been ignited by Al Nusra Front mortar fire.

> They were understandably wary, but they still gathered around us (my colleague and independent journalist, Eva Bartlett and our translator) in the searing arid summer heat. Over the course of this 5 years and 6 months of this dirty war against Syria, not one western media journalist had ever asked to speak to them.

> This extraordinary omission and failure to follow the most rudimentary journalist text book rules by the western media is staggering, but hardly surprising considering the level of spin and propaganda employed daily by the likes of the BBC, CNN, FOX News, The Guardian, New York Times, and Washington Post. Sadly, western media lap dogs end up simply wagging their tails to their masters voice and turning somersaults with the truth to merit reward.

> Unfortunately for the Syrian people, western pundits have only reported on crucial and pivotal events in the war on Syria based largely on 'evidence' supplied by the US-UK-NATO construct, the White Helmets, who are ensconsed only in Al Nusra Front aka Al Qaeda and ISIS held areas.

> As a result of western media outlets not bothering to make contact with the volunteer Syrians in the REAL Syria Civil Defence, western audiences never received a balanced view of the situation. Instead, western media only disseminates what amounts to a biased, one-sided view which mirrors anti-Syrian state and Syrian Arab Army rhetoric issued by the US State Dept and British Foreign Office.

> I explained in detail, why I had come to talk with them, that my objective was to find out who were the real heroes inside Syria, the multi million NATO funded White Helmets created in 2013 or the Syrian Syria Civil Defence established in 1953.

> Aleppo's REAL Syria Civil Defence informed us there are 150 volunteers working across all units in Aleppo, the headquarters are in the Hamadaniya area which is one of the most severely targeted civilian areas, by Al Nusra Front Hell Cannon mortar fire and explosive bullets. The volunteers ages range between 25-45 years old, and the minimum age for training is 18.

> All members of the crew were genuine volunteers. They spoke proudly of the intensive training process they undergo before they can be accepted into the unit. They are fully trained in urban search and rescue techniques (USAR). They are also fully qualified paramedics.

A glance around their yard revealed that their equipment is tired and worn. The fire trucks were gleaming in the sun but showed signs of heavy use. Tattered jackets hung from the fenders and wing mirrors of the trucks and a Syrian flag had been draped across the radiator of one truck, perhaps in honour of our visit.

She adds,

The West Aleppo crew is forced to attend missions without the standard issue equipment and to deal with situations like chemical weapons attacks with only the ineffectual paper breathing masks. This is another result of the EU-US sanctions being enforced against Syria, and effectively against the Syrian people. The REAL Syria Civil Defence is unable to replace equipment or replenish supplies, unlike the NATO White Helmets who enjoy an endless stream of kit and replacement materials via the Turkey supply chain that has remained unbroken for much of the four years that Aleppo has been under terrorist siege.

Beeley's article, "The REAL Syria Civil Defence Exposes Fake 'White Helmets' As Terrorist-Linked Imposters," details firsthand accounts of SCD volunteers risking (and sometimes losing) their lives in order to save the lives of civilians. The article also details stories from volunteers regarding the horrific aftermath of terrorist hell cannons, missiles, and other indiscriminate strikes against civilian areas. I would highly recommend reading the entirety of Beeley's article.

When Beeley asked the volunteers their opinions on the White Helmets, an image was painted that appears much different from the fantasy portrayed by Western media and Hollywood film sets as well as the Nobel Prize committee. She writes,

When we got on to the subject of NATO's White Helmets, the West Aleppo REAL Syrian Civil Defence crew became animated. One of them, stepped forward and began to talk excitedly to our translator. He had been stationed in East Aleppo at a REAL Syrian Civil Defence unit based in an area that has since been overrun by Al Nusra Front and their associate terrorist gangs.

Again, we are unable, as we have said, to provide names of the men we spoke with. They are prime targets for the Al Nusra Front and company in East Aleppo. This crew member, lets call him 'Khaled,' described what happened when the terrorists (western media still call them "opposition" or "moderate rebels") started to invade East Aleppo in 2012.

"They came in and they drove us out of our homes and they came to the Syria Civil Defence yard and they killed some of my comrades, they kidnapped others. They wanted to force me to work with them. I escaped at night. I was forced to leave my teenage sons behind. They burned my house to the ground and they put my name on all the terrorist checkpoints so if I go back, they will kill me."

Khaled went on to explain how those men who later became the White Helmets were among this first wave of terrorists:

"They are terrorists, not rescuers. They stole our ambulances and three of our fire engines. They don't do any rescue work. They drive round with guns in the back of their car like any other terrorist. Some are from East Aleppo, some are from Syria but not from Aleppo and some are even coming in from abroad."

Granted, this might come as a shock to anyone who has already bought into the public relations image of the group that's already been developed over three years by various agencies in New York, Washington DC and London, but these are the real accounts regarding what one might say is the true unmasked nature of the west's White Helmets

Beeley also writes that the volunteers of the SCD had a chance to view some of the White Helmets' "rescue videos" and found a number of oddities if the White Helmets were truly rescuing trapped civilians or even simply retrieving bodies.

Beeley continues,

At this point other crew members interjected and told me that they had watched the White Helmet "rescue" videos.

"They are fake. They don't carry out any correct procedures, either as paramedics or as search and rescue experts."

They described how the White Helmets use a heavy-duty power drill to dig down for civilians buried under the rubble of homes allegedly targeted by "Syrian or Russian airstrikes."

"It's the wrong equipment to use. It is not sensitive enough and because it vibrates powerfully, it can displace the rubble which is dangerous if anyone is genuinely buried beneath it."

They went on to describe other aspects of the White Helmet videos that they believe contravene all standard procedures that are followed by genuine search and rescue experts, paramedics and first responders.

In the following very recent video made by a White Helmet camera crew, men pretending to be genuine rescuers attack an area of rubble where they seem to know where a body buried. They start with a mint condition JCB digger, which attacks the heap of rubble with gusto. Then, alarmingly, they begin to pound the rubble with a heavy duty mallet without employing any devices to actually determine where the body is located, under the impenetrable concrete blocks. Finally, the JCB digger returns to the mound of rubble and enters the teeth of its bucket into the rubble without any hesitation, surely not standard procedure if there is a chance of a body being under the debris.

Miraculously, as with all White Helmet videos, they seem to find exactly where the bodies are, despite having displaced the majority of the rubble in the process. They also, miraculously, avoided staving in the first body's head with the mallet. There is no intention to downplay or belittle the deaths that have obviously occurred but we do ask the questions:

1. How did the White Helmets know the bodies would be exactly where they found them?

2. Where is this rescue being filmed?

3. "Activists", "citizen journalists", the White Helmets and western media would have us believe that East Aleppo is under almost constant Russian or Syrian aerial attack yet the White Helmets make, on average, 4 or 5 films per day and we never see or hear any sign of an attack, only the "aftermath".

4. Where do these bodies come from? Are they victims of air strikes as we are told by these NATO funded "activists" and "first responders" or are they taken from among the thousands of "disappeared" that have been kidnapped by Nusra Front and other terrorist gangs in East Aleppo? Are they gruesome props being used inhumanely, to polish the image of this faux NGO embedded in East Aleppo, HQ for Al Nusra Front.

Indeed, upon my own travels to the Middle East, I spoke with Syrians (not volunteers with the SCD) who had similar questions about White Helmets rescues. How do they always know right where to find the bodies? How do they not kill living victims or damage dead bodies with the equipment they are using in the videos? Why are they always videotaped? These were all questions the individuals that I spoke with were asking about the White Helmets. Another issue was the extraordinary budget this group receives from the U.K. and the U.S., a budget that is more akin to a military coffer than a humanitarian one.

Beeley went further, however, and met with the real Aleppo Medical Association. She asked them about the White Helmets and the alleged work they do in East Aleppo (they only operate in terrorist-held territory). Interestingly enough, according to Dr. Bassem Hayak, the man in charge of the medical teams that assess civilians fleeing East Aleppo to West Aleppo, stated that the White Helmets are unknown to civilians in East Aleppo.

Beeley writes,

> One of the other meetings we had during our time in Aleppo, was with the Aleppo Medical Association. We met with the Director, Dr Zahar Buttal and Dr Bassem Hayak, who is in charge of the medical teams assessing refugees from East Aleppo who fled to West Aleppo via the Russian and Syrian state humanitarian corridors, created on the 29th July, which have allowed over 2000 people to escape the terrorist strongholds to safety, food and medical care in government-protected West Aleppo. These figures were given to us by the Aleppo Medical Association on the 15th August 2016.

> One of the questions I asked Dr Hayak, who spoke good English, was what he knew of the White Helmets. His response was concise and without preamble. His family is still in East Aleppo and although he has not been able to get back into East Aleppo for the last year, his family have told him that the White Helmets are not known in East Aleppo. I asked again to be sure, and was told again, people, civilians do not know of the White Helmets in East Aleppo. Any actual first response work is carried out by foreign workers from various countries, Pakistan and the Gulf region among them. These foreigners work with Syrian people who are not properly trained in first response. They might only receive 2 or 3 months training before being allowed to work.

> Dr Hayak says, "Even with our relationship with WHO (World Health Organisation) and the UN, we still didn't hear about the White Helmets."

> Are the White Helmets, NATO ghosts?

> Dr Hayak also states quite clearly, he has a cousin, working as a surgeon in East Aleppo. ISIS and other terrorist factions have forced her to stay in East Aleppo by threatening to kill her family, should she leave for West Aleppo.

Dr Hayak also said that the majority of civilians in East Aleppo are "hostages" of the NATO/US allied terrorists.

In East Aleppo, civilians living under Al Nusra Front occupation, do not know the White Helmets.

Doctors Without Borders

As fighting continues to rage across Syria, Doctors Without Borders (DWB) is calling for "greater access for humanitarian aid to Syrians suffering in their country's civil war" and urging the international community to show as much urgency in regard to humanitarian aid as it did to the Syrian government's chemical weapons.[134]

Of course, it should be noted immediately that the conflict in Syria is not so much a civil war but an invasion of foreign forces put together from all over the world and funded by the Anglo-American powers. Moreover, it should also be pointed out that, during the international hysteria over Syria's chemical weapons stockpile, there has never been even one shred of evidence suggesting that the Syrian government has used chemical weapons against civilians or even against the deaths squads running rampant and inflicting terror upon the Syrian people.

Regardless, the General Director for Doctors Without Borders Christopher Stokes, stated to AP that,

> You have an industrial-scale war, but you have a very kind of small-scale humanitarian response. There is a recognition that greater humanitarian access is needed for life-saving assistance, but at the same time we don't see the mobilization.

> Although the United Nations council issued a call for immediate access to all areas inside Syria, including in conflict areas and across battle lines, there still exists a number of obstacles to actually getting that aid to the people who may need it.[135]

The AP report continued by stating,

> Stokes said the aid community has long been told that it's impossible to grant full access to all regions affected by the fighting, and that "one side is always blaming the other" for the impasse.

> But the recent agreement to grant international inspectors unfettered access to every site linked to Syria's chemical weapons program "has shown is that it is possible, if the international political willingness is there, to grant access and free movement to aid agencies to go into these enclaves," Stokes said.

> "Cease-fires could be organized as was done to allow chemical weapons inspectors in, they could be organized to allow in medical convoys," he said.[136]

Yet, while Stokes claims that part of the difficulty in providing aid to suffering Syrians is because "one side is always blaming the other" and therefore hindering the delivery, it should be noted that not only does the responsibility for the entire conflict rest on the

---

[134] Sterling, Rick. "The Caesar Photo Fraud That Undermined Syrian Negotiations." Information Clearing House. March 4, 2016. http://www.informationclearinghouse.info/article44369.htm

[135] Lucas, Ryan; Laub, Karin. "Aid Group Calls For Humanitarian Access In Syria." The San Diego Union Tribune. October 15, 2013. http://www.sandiegouniontribune.com/sdut-aid-group-calls-for-humanitarian-access-in-syria-2013oct15-story.html

[136] Lucas, Ryan; Laub, Karin. "Aid Group Calls For Humanitarian Access In Syria." The San Diego Union Tribune. October 15, 2013. http://www.sandiegouniontribune.com/sdut-aid-group-calls-for-humanitarian-access-in-syria-2013oct15-story.html

shoulders of the death squads, but that it is not the Assad government who has captured and kidnapped aid workers – it is only the death squads who have been guilty of this crime. Thus, the responsibility regarding the hindrance of aid deliverability should fall on the shoulders of the death squads as well.[137]

It is true, however, that the Syrian government has not granted DWB permission to operate inside Syria at this time. However, there may be a more justifiable reason for Assad's refusal to allow the organization to set up camp in Syria than first meets the eye.

This is because Doctors without Borders, along with several other internationally recognized and renowned human rights and medical charity organizations, have been clearly implicated in their cooperation with Anglo-American interests in the ginning up of a case for Western military action against Syria by misreporting and even outright lying in regards to massacres having taken place inside the country.

Indeed, DWB is maintaining a highly questionable operation in Syria – with aid distribution almost exclusively established within "rebel controlled" areas, thus allowing the death squads to soak up much of the humanitarian supply line.

Even in the AP report, DWB admits that it is currently operating six "field hospitals" in "rebel-controlled" areas and is supporting medical facilities in both areas that are controlled by the death squads and the government. Still, both the AP report and DWB imply that the Assad government is to blame by suggesting that it is stalling further aid to the Syrian people – despite recent events which prove quite the opposite.

It is important to point out, as Tony Cartalucci has done in his excellent article "'Doctors' Behind Syrian Chemical Weapons Claims are Aiding Terrorists," that, despite media claims that DWB is "independent," the fact is that the organization itself is being bankrolled by many of the financier interests that clearly support Western military action against Syria.

As Cartalucci writes,

> To begin with, Doctors Without Borders is fully funded by the very same corporate financier interests behind Wall Street and London's collective foreign policy, including regime change in Syria and neighboring Iran. Doctors Without Borders' own annual report (2010 report can be accessed here), includes as financial donors, Goldman Sachs, Wells Fargo, Citigroup, Google, Microsoft, Bloomberg, Mitt Romney's Bain Capital, and a myriad of other corporate-financier interests. Doctors Without Borders also features bankers upon its Board of Advisers including Elizabeth Beshel Robinson of Goldman Sachs.[138]

In a telling interview with NPR, which Cartalucci partially quotes in his own article, the Executive Director of DWB, Stephen Cornish, admitted the fact that the organization

---

[137] Hadid, Diaa. "In Syria, four of seven kidnapped Red Cross, Red Crescent Aid Workers Are Released." Washington Post. October 14, 2013. http://www.washingtonpost.com/world/in-syria-four-of-seven-kidnapped-red-cross-red-crescent-aid-workers-are-released/2013/10/14/a3a62f06-34f8-11e3-8a0e-4e2cf80831fc_story.html

[138] Cartalucci, Tony. "Doctors' Behind Syrian Chemical Weapons Claim Are Aiding Terrorists." Land Destroyer Report. August 25, 2013. http://landdestroyer.blogspot.com/2013/08/doctors-behind-syrian-chemical-weapons.html

largely has provided medical aid to the death squads not just as a matter of unbiased Hippocratic Oath-based treatment, but what appears to be a "rebel"-based program.

As Cornish revealed,

> Over the past months, we've had a surgery that was opened inside a cave. We've had another that was opened in a chicken farm, a third one in a house. And these structures, we've tried to outfit them as best as we can with enough modern technology and with full medical teams. They originally were dealing mainly with combatant injuries and people who were - civilians who were directly affected by the conflict.[139]

 Even assuming that the "civilians" Cornish mentions are truly civilians, Cornish's team has also been focused largely on "combatant injuries" which is an interesting focus considering that the teams are mainly located within death squad controlled territory.

Indeed, Cornish removes all doubt about whether or not the death squads are receiving priority care as the interview continues. Cornish states,

> So it is very difficult for civilians to find care. And one of the difficulties also is that a number of smaller surgeries that have been set up are either overwhelmed with combatants or primarily taking care of combatants. And what we would certainly urge is that all surgeries and all health posts also are accommodating the civilian population.
>
> BLOCK: You mean, in other words, that the fighters are getting priority for medical care and the civilians are suffering for that.
>
> CORNISH: Unfortunately, that is sometimes the reality on the ground. Some of the surgeries we visited, you could tell that because not only there were no civilians on the wards, but there were also no beds or toilet facilities for women. So it's kind of a dead giveaway.[140]

Tony Cartalucci expertly responds to the alleged "charity" provided by DWB when he writes,

> In other words, the Wall Street-funded organization is providing support for militants armed and funded by the West and its regional allies, most of whom are revealed to be foreign fighters, affiliated with or directly belonging to Al Qaeda and its defacto political wing, the Muslim Brotherhood.[141] This so-called "international aid" organization is in actuality yet another cog in the covert military machine being turned against Syria and serves the role as a medical battalion.[142]

---

[139] "Doctor: 'We Are Truly Failing The Syrian People." All Things Considered. National Public Radio. May 17, 2013. http://www.npr.org/2013/05/17/184845130/doctor-we-truly-are-failing-the-syrian-people

[140] "Doctor: 'We Are Truly Failing The Syrian People." All Things Considered. National Public Radio. May 17, 2013. http://www.npr.org/2013/05/17/184845130/doctor-we-truly-are-failing-the-syrian-people

[141] Cartalucci, Tony. "US-British Al-Qaeda Airlift: 3,000 Tons Of Weapons Fuel Syria's Destruction." Land Destroyer Report. March 9, 2013. http://landdestroyer.blogspot.com/2013/03/us-british-al-qaeda-airlift-3000-tons.html

[142] Cartalucci, Tony. "Doctors' Behind Syrian Chemical Weapons Claim Are Aiding Terrorists."

Indeed, following in the footsteps of corrupted and compromised "human rights" and "charity" organizations like Human Rights Watch and Amnesty International, Doctors Without Borders is sacrificing whatever legitimacy and trustworthiness it ever had for the benefit of wealthy donors and their Anglo-American imperialist desires.[143] [144] [145] [146]

In polite society, it is incredibly difficult to criticize an organization that uses charity, real or imagined, as a cover for more nefarious means. Although Doctors Without Borders may have done legitimate work in the past, its current position as the medical wing of the Syrian destabilization will forever mar the organization, and it should therefore be discredited as a source of information from this point forward.

Human Rights Watch

Putting its hypocritical and biased nature on full display once again, the alleged human rights organization, Human Rights Watch, was recently caught in an attempt to fabricate "evidence" of Assad's use of barrel bombs in civilian areas for the purposes of further demonizing the secular Syrian government.

On February 25, 2015, HRW posted a photo of a devastated civilian area in Syria with the tagline "Syria dropped barrel bombs despite ban." The "ban" HRW is referring to is the ban on bombing civilian areas that applies to both sides in Aleppo after the United Nations stepped in to save the Western-backed terrorists from annihilation. Assad's forces had surrounded the city and had cut off a major supply route for the death squads from Turkey thus making the ultimate elimination of the jihadist forces a virtual inevitability.[147]

As Somini Sengupta wrote for the New York Times on February 24,

> Human Rights Watch said Tuesday that the Syrian government had dropped so-called barrel bombs on hundreds of sites in rebel-held towns and cities in the past year, flouting a United Nations Security Council measure.
>
> In a report released Tuesday, the group said it relied on satellite images, photos, videos and witness statements to conclude that the Syrian government had bombarded

---

Land Destroyer Report. August 25, 2013. http://landdestroyer.blogspot.com/2013/08/doctors-behind-syrian-chemical-weapons.html

[143] Cartalucci, Tony. "Exposing The International Arbiters." Land Destroyer Report. April 10, 2011. http://landdestroyer.blogspot.com/2011/04/exposing-international-arbiters.html

[144] Lightbown, Richard. "Fabricating 'Facts' About Syria." DesertPeace. September 25, 2013. https://desertpeace.wordpress.com/2013/09/25/fabricating-facts-about-syria/

[145] Jalabi, Raya. "Critics Question Catholic Nun's 'Alternative Story' On Syria Civil War." The Guardian. December 5, 2013. https://www.theguardian.com/world/2013/dec/05/catholic-nun-mother-agnes-syria-civil-war

[146] Cartalucci, Tony. "Amnesty International Is US State Department Propaganda." Land Destroyer Report. August 22, 2012. http://landdestroyer.blogspot.com/2012/08/amnesty-international-is-us-state.html

[147] Turbeville, Brandon. "NATO/UN Desperately Seek Ceasefire To Save ISIS After Syrian Army Encircles Aleppo." Activist Post. February 18, 2015. http://www.activistpost.com/2015/02/natoun-desperately-seek-ceasefire-to.html

at least 450 sites in and around the southern town of Daraa and at least 1,000 sites in Aleppo in the north.[148]

The report focused on the period since Feb. 22, 2014, when the Security Council specifically condemned the use of barrel bombs, which are large containers filled with explosives and projectiles that can indiscriminately hurt civilians and are prohibited under international law.[149] [150]

There was only one problem with HRW's tweet – the photograph the organization provided was not Aleppo.

In fact, the damage that had been wrought upon the civilian area in the photograph was not committed by the Syrian military but by the United States.

The photo was actually a picture of Kobane (Ayn al-Arab), the city which has been the site of heavy US aerial bombardment over several months prior as the US engaged in its program of death squad herding and geographical reformation of sovereign Syrian and Iraqi territory.

But, while HRW was content to use the destruction of the city as a reason to condemn the Assad government and continue to promote the cause for US military action in Syria, the "human rights organization" was apparently much less interested in the exact same destruction wrought by US forces.

In other words, if Assad's forces bomb a civilian area into the Stone Age, it is an atrocity, a war crime, and justification for international military involvement. If the United States bombs a civilian area into the Stone Age, it's no biggie.

Partially funded by George Soros, Human Rights Watch has repeatedly shilled for NATO and America's imperialist aims, particularly in Syria.[151] [152]

For instance, when Western media propaganda had reached a crescendo regarding the outright lie that Assad had used chemical weapons against his own people, HRW stood right beside Barack Obama and John Kerry in their effort to prove Assad's guilt.[153]

---

[148] "Syria: New Spate of Barrel Bomb Attacks." Human Rights Watch. February 24, 2015. http://www.hrw.org/news/2015/02/24/syria-new-spate-barrel-bomb-attacks

[149] Sengupta, Somini. "U.N. Orders Both Sides In Syria To Allow Humanitarian Aid." New York Times. February 22, 2014. http://www.nytimes.com/2014/02/23/world/middleeast/un-orders-both-sides-in-syria-to-allow-humanitarian-aid.html

[150] Sengupta, Somini. "Syria Dropped 'Barrel Bombs' Despite Ban, Report Says." New York Times. February 24, 2015. http://www.nytimes.com/2015/02/25/world/middleeast/syria-dropped-barrel-bombs-despite-ban-report-says.html?_r=1

[151] "George Soros To Give $100 Million To Human Rights Watch." Human Rights Watch. September 7, 2010. https://www.hrw.org/news/2010/09/07/george-soros-give-100-million-human-rights-watch

[152] Jalabi, Raya. "Critics Question Catholic Nun's 'Alternative Story' On Syria Civil War." The Guardian. December 5, 2013. https://www.theguardian.com/world/2013/dec/05/catholic-nun-mother-agnes-syria-civil-war

[153] Turbeville, Brandon. 5 Ways 'Incontrovertible Evidence' On Syria Is Controvertible." Activist Post. September 12, 2015. http://www.activistpost.com/2013/09/5-ways-incontrovertible-evidence-on.html

HRW even went so far as to repeat the lie that the UN report suggested that Assad was the offending party, driving the final nail into the coffin of any credibility HRW may have had.[154] [155]

When a last-minute chemical weapons deal was secured by Russia in an effort to avoid yet another US/NATO invasion of Syria, HRW did not rejoice for the opportunity of peaceful destruction of chemical weapons and a chance to avoid war, it attacked the deal by claiming that it "failed to ensure justice." Of course, the deal did fail to ensure justice. There were no provisions demanding punishment of the death squads who actually used the weapons or the US/NATO apparatus that initiated and controlled the jihadist invasion to begin with.[156]

Regardless, when Mother Agnes Mariam of the Cross released her report that refuted what the US/NATO was asserting in regards to chemical weapons in Syria, HRW embarked upon a campaign of attack against her and her work.[157]

Even as far back as 2009, however, HRW was showing its true colors when it apparently signed off on and supported renditions – the process of kidnapping individuals off the street without any due process and "rendering" them to jails and prisons in other countries where they are often tortured – in secret talks with the Obama administration.[158]

If HRW ever had any credibility in terms of the question of actual human rights, then all of that credibility has assuredly been lost. HRW is nothing more than a pro-US, pro-NATO NGO that acts as a smokescreen for the continuation of the violation of human rights across the world – that is, unless those violations are committed by America's enemies.

Huge Explosion In Latakia Reveals US HRW Hypocrisy

On May 25, when a large explosion took place in Latakia, Syria, a few mainstream media outlets covered the incident from the angle of it being yet one more sign that the Syrian regime was losing its grip on power. This explosion was followed by a huge yellow plume of smoke that caused many informed observers to wonder whether or not the explosion was that of a chemical weapon.

On the chemical weapons question, however, the mainstream Western press was silent.

---

[154] "Syria: Government Likely Culprit In Chemical Attack." Human Rights Watch. September 10, 2013. https://www.hrw.org/news/2013/09/10/syria-government-likely-culprit-chemical-attack
[155] "Syria's Chemical Weapons: The Russia Factor." Human Rights Watch. September 26, 2015. https://www.hrw.org/news/2013/09/26/syrias-chemical-weapons-russia-factor
[156] "UN Syria Resolution 'Fails To Ensure Justice:' HRW." FOX News. September 28, 2013. http://www.foxnews.com/world/2013/09/28/un-syria-resolution-fails-to-ensure-justice-hrw/
[157] "Mother Agnes: Syria's 'Detective' Nun Who Says Gas Attack Film Faked." BBC. October 1, 2013. http://www.bbc.com/news/world-middle-east-24358543
[158] Hayden, Tom. "CIA Secret Rendition Policy Backed By Human Rights Groups?" Huffington Post. March 4, 2009. http://www.huffingtonpost.com/tom-hayden/cia-secret-rendition-poli_b_162916.html

This was despite the fact that the media clearly sees the sign of yellow smoke as the indication of chemical weapons use, which it subsequently uses to blame Bashar al-Assad and gin up support for US invasion when those explosions take place in certain areas or have deleterious results for the death squads. After all, when a missile/explosion was detonated in Dara (Dera'ah), Dr. Annie Sparrow, a "health activist" married to the head of Human Rights Watch, Kenneth Roth, claimed that a chlorine-based chemical weapon had been detonated by the Assad regime (who else?). Sparrow's photograph showed a plume of yellow smoke that looked identical to that in Latakia.[159]

Indeed, her husband's HRW organization has also made statements suggesting that yellow colored smoke was an indication of the use of chlorine-based chemical weapons.[160]

Yet, while there was widespread condemnation (despite a stunning lack of evidence and plenty of evidence to the contrary) of the Assad regime as a result of her claims, why didn't Sparrow or HRW condemning the terrorists who detonated a missile/chlorine based weapon in Latakia? After all, one could see from the pictures posted on Twitter that the explosions were almost identical.

The answer is that, much like the Western press, NATO, and the myriad of NGOS, Foundations, and think tanks across the Western world, Human Rights Watch is nothing more than a misleading front group for the imperialist powers that seek the destruction of sovereign states the world over.

To be clear, it is a matter of intense speculation as to the nature of the explosion. There is no consensus as to what the source or the material of the explosion might be. The possibilities of an improvised chemical weapon, a missile, or even a crashed drone are competing theories.[161]

Still, it must be remembered that HRW was caught in a brazen attempt to use a picture of the US bombing of Ayn al-Arab to claim that Assad had destroyed a Syrian city with barrel bombs.

While the attack in Latakia was clearly the work of Western-backed terrorists (Latakia is firmly in government control), all previous claims of chlorine-based chemical weapons have also been shown to be the work of jihadists.

Avaaz

It's considered one of the globe's largest NGOs, yet the odds are most Americans have never heard of it. Avaaz, (whose name means "voice" in many languages), is a massive "online activist organization" that claims to promote freedom and democracy all across the world in a variety of different means and for a variety of different causes.[162]

---

[159] Mitchell, Heidi. "Health Activist Annie Sparrow's Fight To End Polio." Vogue. Janury 29, 2015. http://www.vogue.com/9070805/health-activist-annie-sparrow-polio-outbreak-syria/

[160] "Syria: Strong Evidence Government Used Chemicals As A Weapon." Human Rights Watch. May 13, 2014. https://www.hrw.org/news/2014/05/13/syria-strong-evidence-government-used-chemicals-weapon

[161] "VIDEO: Syrian Regime Weapon With Orange Smoke May Be Chlorine Gas – Or Just A Missile." Al-Bawaba. May 25, 2015. http://www.albawaba.com/loop/video-syrian-regime-weapon-orange-smoke-may-be-chlorine-gas-%E2%80%94-or-just-missile-699100

According to its own website, since its creation in 2007, Avaaz's mission is to "organize citizens of all nations to close the gap between the world we have and the world most people everywhere want."[163]

It also states,

> Avaaz empowers millions of people from all walks of life to take action on pressing global, regional and national issues, from corruption and poverty to conflict and climate change. Our model of internet organising allows thousands of individual efforts, however small, to be rapidly combined into a powerful collective force. (Read about results on the Highlights page.)[164]

> The Avaaz community campaigns in 15 languages, served by a core team on 6 continents and thousands of volunteers. We take action -- signing petitions, funding media campaigns and direct actions, emailing, calling and lobbying governments, and organizing "offline" protests and events -- to ensure that the views and values of the world's people inform the decisions that affect us all.[165]

While Avaaz's stated goals might sound laudable to many Americans, anyone who has observed the number of "people power" revolutions in Eastern Europe and the Middle East might recognize the language from the Avaaz website as indicative of the color revolution apparatus that has helped inflame the world over the last 5-7 years.

Avaaz is, indeed, part of the color revolution apparatus, having apparently received funds from George Soros' Open Society Foundation to start up in 2007. Avaaz was founded by Res Publica and Moveon.org, both Soros-funded organizations that attempt to co-opt the American left into supporting ideas and campaigns closely associated with the communitarian foundation oligarchs.[166] [167]

---

[162] Avaaz website. https://www.avaaz.org/page/en/

[163] "About Us." Avaaz Website. https://avaaz.org/en/about.php

[164] Highlists. Avaaz Website. https://avaaz.org/en/highlights.php/?aboutus

[165] "About Us." Avaaz Website. https://avaaz.org/en/about.php

[166] "Avaaz." NGO Monitor. March 10, 2013. http://www.ngo-monitor.org/ngos/avaaz/ Website reads: 2007 by "Res Publica, a global civic advocacy group, and Moveon.org," a George Soros-funded organization involved in ideological and political campaigns in the United States."

[167] "Avaaz.org." Discover The Networks. http://www.discoverthenetworks.org/printgroupProfile.asp?grpid=7621   The website reads: Avaaz, or the Avaaz Foundation, is a global "e-advocacy" nonprofit organization whose chief function is to promote leftwing political agendas through Web-based movement-building and campaigns. Its mission is to "organize citizens of all nations to close the gap between the world we have and the world most people everywhere want." Its primary methods of activism are: mass e-mailings, online petitions, videos, "write-your-leader" campaigns, and targeted citizen organizing. The global counterpart of the George Soros-funded MoveOn, Avaaz also seeks to influence elections directly, particularly in Canada, and is a registered a non-profit lobbying organization in the state of Delaware.

The Avaaz Players

In addition, a number of Avaaz founders and board members have close connections to Soros' Open Society Foundations such as Eli Pariser (both a Board Member of OSF and a member of the Open Society US programs as well as Moveon.org) and Pedro Abramovay (the Regional Director For Latin America and the Caribbean at OSF, the Director of Latin America Programs at OSF and a campaign director of Avaaz).[168] [169]

Conservative organization, Discover the Networks, published a summary of the connections between some of the founders of Avaaz. The website writes,

> Ricken Patel: A Canadian, Patel is both the executive director of Res Publica and president/executive director of Avaaz

> Eli Pariser: The executive director of MoveOn, Pariser is Avaaz's board chairman and also serves on the advisory board of Res Publica.

> Tom Perriello: This former U.S. congressman from Virginia co-founded Res Publica and has been a longtime advocacy partner with Ricken Patel.

> Ben Brandzel: Formerly an advocacy director for MoveOn, Brandzel also served as director of new-media campaigns and fundraising for Barack Obama's Organizing for America. In addition, he worked for the presidential campaigns of Howard Dean and John Edwards.[170]

As one might suspect, despite its constant rhetoric regarding "human rights," "freedom," and "democracy," Avaaz has openly supported violence, war, and imperialism. In 2011, Avaaz raised its voice as loudly as it could with demands that the EU, NATO, UN, and all other parties "stop the violent crackdown" on civilians in Libya.[171] Translated: Avaaz called on the EU, NATO, UN, and all other parties to come to the rescue of jihadists that had been unleashed against the government and the people of Libya in order to overthrow Ghaddafi for the benefit of the NATO powers.

Avaaz – Propaganda Against Syria

Avaaz soon after turned its sights on Syria, the next country in line to suffer under NATO's attempt to destroy an uncooperative national government.[172] As a sampling of the drivel Avaaz regularly released regarding Syria, Avaaz posted on its website the

---

[168] "Eli Pariser." Open Society Foundations. "People."
https://www.opensocietyfoundations.org/people/eli-pariser
[169] "Pedro Abramovay." Open Society Foundations. "People."
https://www.opensocietyfoundations.org/people/pedro-abramovay
[170] "Avaaz.org." Discover The Networks.
http://www.discoverthenetworks.org/printgroupProfile.asp?grpid=7621
[171] "Libya: Stop The Crackdown." Avaaz.org.
https://www.avaaz.org/en/libya_stop_the_crackdown_eu/?rc=fb
[172] Engdahl, F. William. "Soros Plays Both Ends In Syria Refugee Chaos." Ron Paul Institute.
December 31, 2015. http://ronpaulinstitute.org/archives/featured-articles/2015/december/31/soros-plays-both-ends-in-syria-refugee-chaos/

following transparent propaganda in an attempt to drum up support for a No Fly Zone in Syria:

> It's inspiring -- over 1 million people from across the world have joined the call to protect Syrian civilians. And an Avaaz-commissioned poll shows a majority of Americans supporting a targeted No Fly Zone to save lives. Right now, the US Congress and the UN are talking about how to protect Syrian civilians -- let's keep the pressure on for life-saving action!
>
> The Syrian air force just dropped chlorine gas bombs on children. Their little bodies gasped for air on hospital stretchers as medics held back tears, and watched as they suffocated to death.
>
> But today there is a chance to stop these barrel bomb murders with a targeted No Fly Zone.
>
> The US, Turkey, UK, France and others are right now seriously considering a safe zone in Northern Syria. Advisers close to President Obama support it, but he is worried he won't have public support. That's where we come in.
>
> Let's tell him we don't want a world that just watches as a dictator drops chemical weapons on families in the night. We want action.
>
> One humanitarian worker said 'I wish the world could see what I have seen with my eyes. It breaks your heart forever.' Let's show that the world cares -- sign to support a life-saving No Fly Zone.[173]

Obviously, the purpose of the post was to drum up support for a "No-Fly Zone" in Syria, tantamount to a direct military invasion of the country on the model of that which destroyed Libya and returned the country to the years shortly prior to the Stone Age.

Also obvious was the glaringly false claim that Assad's troops had dropped chemical weapons on Syrian civilians. The Syrian military has never been implicated in using chemical weapons against the Syrian people except in the pages of the Western mainstream press and the minds of a gullible public. Every use of chemical weapons has been, at some point, traced back to the Western-backed terrorists fighting against the Syrian government.

Avaaz has also pushed for relocating Syrian refugees and "Syrian refugees" to England as a result of "chlorine bombs" "falling from the sky" "in Syria. Avaaz thus used non-existent "chlorine bombs falling from the sky" to justify relocating "refugees" from a war zone that it is partly responsible for creating itself.[174]

Avaaz has posted dubious "calls for help" from "Syrians" such as the one entitled "Cry For Help In Syria," in Homs.[175] Of course, while most Syrians are horrified at the state of war in which they find themselves as a result of the Western destabilization, the overwhelming majority of Syrians support their government and despise the Western-

---

[173] "Safe Zones For Syria, Now!." Avaaz.org.
https://secure.avaaz.org/en/syria_safe_zone_loc/?pv=192&rc=fb
[174] "A Safe Haven For Syrian Refugees." Avaaz.org.
https://secure.avaaz.org/en/syrian_refugees_uk/?pv=66&rc=fb
[175] "Cry For Help From Syria." Avaaz.org.
https://www.avaaz.org/en/syria_ray_of_hope_loc/?pv=80&rc=fb

backed savages raping and beheading their way across the country. If one is interested in reading or listening to the opinion of a real Syrian, feel free to consult the videos and articles of Afraa Dagher, a true victim of the so-called "civil war" that would be more aptly named an invasion.[176] [177] [178]

Vanessa Beeley describes typical Avaaz treachery in her article, "The Propaganda War Against Syria Led By Avaaz And The White Helmets." Beeley is referring to the Avaaz propaganda that emerged in the wake of the Russian attacks against ISIS and other related terrorists in Syria. Avaaz, of course, followed the State Department and NATO line that Russia was bombing the as-yet-undiscovered "moderate rebels."[179] She writes,

> Now let's examine the unsavoury marketing aspect of the propaganda campaign being waged by a frustrated and increasingly infuriated US alliance. Of course the usual triad has leapt into action. HRW, Avaaz and the White Helmets. Avaaz has produced one of its most poisonous and misleading petitions to date.[180] The inevitable eyewitness statements claim that Russia targeted civilian areas utterly free of ISIS operatives. These statements are already rendered questionable by the evidence I have submitted above.

> When we watch the videos, particularly the longer Liveleak version, it is hard to detect the women and children that are being described. The majority of protagonists appear to be male and of fighting age. There is no evidence of "civilian" life among the deserted buildings, the only movement is of males, some on foot, some on scooters and presumably some taking the time to film events even as the bombs are falling. Not the actions of terrified, innocent civilians.*[181]

> There is one other video that does show about 2 seconds of a young boy crying and obviously injured. However this video must be questioned as to its authenticity as the claims are that the initial shot of planes overhead is not even of Russian planes. The

[176] Dagher, Afraa. "Merry Christmas From Syria: A Look From Inside." Activist Post. December 29, 2015. http://www.activistpost.com/2015/12/merry-christmas-from-syria-a-look-from-inside.html

[177] "Brandon Turbeville Interview With Afraa From Syria August 1, 2015, Turkey, Kurds, "ISIL-Free Zone." Youtube. Posted by Brandon Turbeville. Posted on August 2, 2015. https://www.youtube.com/watch?v=7LhrdaWRH2c Brandon Turbeville and Afraa discuss the 2015 declaration of an "ISIL-Free Zone" in Syria, the bombing of the Kurds, US and Turkish support for ISIS, Brookings Institution documents, and more

[178] Dagher, Afraa. "Terror En Estambul Y Rumores Saudies." Syriana Afraa. SyrianaAfrona.wordpress. July 1, 2016. https://syrianaafrona.wordpress.com/ Afraa's work can also be followed at BrandonTurbeville.com, The Duran, Syria News, Activist Post, and her personal website, SyrianaAfrona.wordpress.com.

[179] Beeley, Vanessa. "The Propaganda War Against Syria Led By Avaaz And The White Helmets." The Wall Will Fall. October 1, 2015. http://www.globalresearch.ca/the-propaganda-war-against-syria-led-by-avaaz-and-the-white-helmets/5479307

[180] "Russian Bombing Of Syrian Civilian Neighborhoods Kills Women And Children – Eyewitnesses." Avaaz.org. September 20, 2015. https://secure.avaaz.org/act/media.php?press_id=666

[181] * Please note that Beeley links to a Live Leak video of the Russian bombing of Homs. "Mr-Creoshites Non Syrian, Beastiality practising goat lovers taste some Russian bear jizz." Live Leak. Posted by MacDuff. September 30, 2015. http://www.liveleak.com/view?i=eb9_1443646193

quality of the video is poor and apart from the footage of the one child, again demonstrates that the majority of people involved are men of fighting age in a deserted built up area to the north of Homs.

In this disgusting display of blatant propaganda calling for the long sought after no fly zone, Emma Ruby-Sachs, deputy director of Avaaz makes the extraordinary statement "Russia says it's bombing ISIS, but eyewitnesses say their brutal attacks targeted areas way outside of ISIS control. This will only sow instability and radicalisation and should be an urgent wake-up call to the US and its allies to enforce a targeted no-fly zone to save lives, counter ISIS and alleviate the refugee crisis. Syrians civilians need protection now, not further attacks from Russian bombs."

Speaking to one Damascus resident this morning, I asked for their opinion on this statement. His reply was simple, "I am just relieved that the Russian Air Force is in action". The hypocrisy of this statement from Ruby-Sachs perfectly mirrors the hypocrisy of Congress, Obama's Teflon speech at the UNGA, Pentagon's barefaced obscurantism over the US role in creating exactly this instability and radicalisation in Syria and bringing misery, terror and bloodshed to the people of Syria with the sole aim of securing their interests in the region [and those of their staunchest partner in crimes against Humanity, Israel]

If we wish to speak of civilian casualties perhaps we should turn the spotlight on the pre- existing Coalition bombing campaign. The civilian death rates from these strikes is rarely discussed and often concealed by the Pentagon and US/European associated analysts like the SOHR. Where for example was the Avaaz petition calling for a No Fly Zone when the coalition air strikes resulted in a multitude of non-combatant deaths including children? This report from Airwars reveals the disturbing numbers:

Syria has also seen a number of troubling mass casualty events attributed to Coalition actions. On the first night of bombing on September 23rd 2014, US aircraft killed as many as 15 civilians in the village of Kafar Daryan. On December 28th at least 58 civilians reportedly died when the Coalition struck a temporary Daesh prison at al Bab (see report). And on April 30th 2015, 64 civilians died in a likely Coalition airstrike at Ber Mahli. In these three incidents alone, 106 non-combatant victims have so far been publicly named – 38 of them children. It remains unclear whether any of these events have been investigated by the Coalition.[182]

Syria's civilians need a spanner putting in the spokes of this crushing propaganda vehicle that rides roughshod over their genuine needs with devastating consequences. Those needs are simple: stop lying, stop fabricating and stop creating, funding, arming and incubating the terrorist cancer in Syria.[183]

Yet Avaaz is not merely involved in the propaganda side of the war on national sovereignty and the people living in the countries resisting Anglo-American domination, it is and has been involved directly on the ground, particularly in Syria, in attempts to facilitate the so-called "Arab Spring" color revolution and other forms of "Syrian

---

[182] "Cause For Concern: Civilians Killed In Coalition Airstrikes." Airwars. August, 2015. https://airwars.org/wp-content/uploads/2015/08/airwars-cause-for-concern-civilians-killed-by-coalition.pdf

[183] Beeley, Vanessa. "The Propaganda War Against Syria Led By Avaaz And The White Helmets." The Wall Will Fall. October 1, 2015. http://www.globalresearch.ca/the-propaganda-war-against-syria-led-by-avaaz-and-the-white-helmets/5479307

activism" (read: terrorism funded and supported by the West, the GCC, NATO, and Israel).

Avaaz Role In The Syrian Destabilization

Avaaz was instrumental in providing not only the online propaganda supporting terrorists and color revolution participants in Syria and back home in the West, but it was also helpful in providing material support such as technology, propaganda and tech training, and medical supplies to the terrorists on the ground.

As Ed Pilkington wrote for the Guardian in his March, 2012 article, "Avaaz Faces Questions Over Role At Center Of Syrian Protest Movement,"

Syria has certainly been risky. The group was quicker on the draw in responding to the first signs of the protest movement than most aid organisations, even than most media outlets that pride themselves in getting speedily to difficult places.

To begin with, Avaaz sent a team of staff organisers to Lebanon after spotting the first signs of a nascent protest movement in Syria. Contact was then made with Syrian activists inside the country, and go-betweens recruited, notably Wissam Tarif, a highly respected Syrian pro-democracy leader who is widely consulted by journalists and senior western diplomats.

From there its involvement in the Syrian Arab spring drew it steadily further and further into the conflict. First off Avaaz sent in hundreds of thousands of dollars' worth of communications equipment – satellite phones and internet connections known as BGANs – that gave the protesters a link to the outside world.

As with earlier Arab spring engagements in Tunisia and Libya, they realised that equipment alone was not enough: the protesters needed to know how to use it if they were to be effective. So Avaaz sent in trainers who could give grounding in how to use the smartphones as well as basic training in citizen journalism.

"Verification was a key element," says Patel. "We could get stuff out, but the media didn't know what they were looking at, or couldn't be sure where it had come from. So we began playing the middle man, verifying information. That was in some ways the greatest value we brought to maintaining the oxygen of international attention on these protest movements."

Reports coming from Avaaz-trained citizen journalists in Homs and other key conflict zones, channelled through the Avaaz communications hub outside the country, has been a major source of information on the uprising and the regime's bloody response, used by news outlets around the world.

Getting in the equipment involved opening up smuggling routes across the Syrian border into hotbeds such as Homs and its most badly bombed neighbourhood, Baba Amr, which led Avaaz seemlessly into the next phase of its engagement. With the smuggling routes open, it could help get $2m of blood bags, tetanus shots, respiratory machines and other medical supplies into the country, bringing relief to communities that were desperate for help and that more establishment institutions like the ICRC had failed to reach.

It has also smuggled 34 international journalists into the trouble zones. Marie Colvin, the Sunday Times journalist, entered using another conduit, but the French photographer Remi Ochlik who died with her as a result of Syrian government shelling was helped in by Avaaz.[184]

Thus, Avaaz finds itself among treacherous company – "humanitarian" organizations like Doctors Without Borders, White Helmets, Human Rights Watch, and even Amnesty International.[185]

Conclusion

At the end of the day, Avaaz is just one more tentacle of the color revolution octopus partially funded by George Soros, the U.S. State Department, and the CIA as well as the budgets of other NATO countries both above and below publicly available knowledge. Its worldwide internet organization is nothing more than a hub for dupes and witless participants who are disenchanted with the current system for whatever reason. The human mass is then used as a battering ram against the target government, ushering in a system that is almost always worse than the one the movement helped overthrow.

There is no shortage of color revolution NGOs in Syria or anywhere else in the world. To compile a list of such organizations currently existing would require a full time commitment even as new groups are formed all the time. It is not necessarily the individual organization itself that must be exposed but the methods by which color revolutions and mass movements are created, facilitated, and accomplished that must be understood.

Only by understanding the nature of the color revolution and destabilization can such tragedies be avoided in the future.

---

[184] Pilkington, Ed. "Avaaz Faces Questions Over Role At Centre Of Syrian Protest Movement." The Guardian. March 2, 2012. http://www.theguardian.com/world/2012/mar/02/avaaz-activist-group-syria

[185] O' Colmain, Gearoid. "The Empire's War Against Burundi: War Propaganda In Preparation For An R2P 'Humanitarian Intervention.'" Wrong Kind of Green. December 23, 2015. http://www.wrongkindofgreen.org/2015/12/23/the-empires-war-against-burundi-war-propaganda-in-preparation-for-an-r2p-humanitarian-intervention/

Chapter III: America's Ceasefires

America's ceasefires have the most convenient timing it is scarcely believable that there is even the slightest amount of legitimacy to them. Indeed, every time the Syrian military is poised to make important gains and monumental victories over the terrorists, the United States, France, UK, or the UN rush in with pleas for "ceasefires" and peace plans.

Few can deny that these proposed "truces" are very "convenient" in their timing from the point of view of NATO strategists. As Tony Cartalucci of Land Destroyer writes,

> It is curious because talks of "truces" were completely absent just as recently as 2011, when both organizations, the UN and NATO, backed hordes of terrorists sweeping across Libya, committing abhorrent atrocities including the systematic, genocidal extermination of Libya's black communities.

> Indeed, NATO and UN peace treaties only seem to appear when the NATO terrorist proxies encounter serious trouble on the battlefield.[186]

While peace is no doubt to be desired in Syria, Western powers should not be allowed to use the concept as a weapon against the Syrian government or the Syrian people.

The United States, UK, France, NATO, and the UN do not want peace. They want a reprieve for their proxy forces. Syria, Iran, Hezbollah, and Russia should all know this very well and should thus not be tempted to enter into agreements and deals with a country and an alliance that has demonstrated time and time again that they are neither willing or capable of maintaining their end of the bargain.

If the terrorist "rebels" encircled in Aleppo and embattled throughout the rest of the country want peace, they should have the option of unconditional surrender. Amnesty, upon surrender, could also be discussed at the pleasure of the Syrian government.

Otherwise, the encirclement should continue and the liberation of Aleppo must necessarily follow.

Assad must not "go." NATO and its terrorist proxies must go.

Fake peace agreements and politically based "truces" are no longer acceptable and they are no longer credible in the eyes of any informed observer.

Only true and total peace, stability, and reconstruction are acceptable options for Syria.

Is The Syria Ceasefire Actually A Good Thing?

As the US-Russian-backed "ceasefire" plan took effect in Syria, much of the world held its breath in hopes that all guns would fall silent and that a "political solution" would be found.[187] Despite the fact that virtually everyone expects the ceasefire to fall apart within

---

[186] Cartalucci, Tony. "U.N. Presses For 'Truce' To Save Embattled Terrorists In Aleppo." Land Destroyer. February 18, 2015. http://landdestroyer.blogspot.com/2015/02/uns-presses-for-truce-to-save-embattled.html

[187] "Airstrikes Leave Scores Dead Ahead Of Syria Ceasefire." Deutsche Welle. September 11,

a short amount of time, the Western media hailed the agreement as a diplomatic victory for the United States while many alternative media outlets represented the agreement as a victory for the Russians.

The ceasefire deal, brokered between Russia and the United States, was made up of a number different facets. First, Russia was required to pressure the Syrian government to stop its military combat activities against what is considered "moderate" US-backed rebels. On the other side, if the ceasefire were to have held for at least seven days, the United States was supposed to join Russia in military operations against Jobhat al-Nusra (Jobhat Fatah al-Sham). The U.S. would also have had to be more clear which "rebels" are "moderate" cannibals and which ones are "extremist" cannibals and, as John Kerry admitted, it would have required "some sharing of information" with the Russians.

"This requires halting all attacks, including aerial bombardments, and any attempts to gain additional territory at the expense of the parties to the cessation. It requires unimpeded and sustained humanitarian access to all of the besieged and hard-to-reach areas, including Aleppo," said US Secretary of State John Kerry.[188]

Kerry also stated that the agreement would prevent the Syrian military from flying combat operations against "moderate" rebels and anywhere the "opposition" publicly deemed legitimate by the United States is present. He called this provision the "bedrock of the agreement" and stated that "That should put an end to the barrel bombs, an end to the indiscriminate bombing of civilian neighborhoods."[189] The ceasefire plan was supposed to take effect on a nationwide basis.

But was the ceasefire plan really something that would have benefited the Syrian people? Certainly, the quieting of rifles and artillery are good for many civilians in the short term but it may also be incredibly destructive for all civilians in the long run. Short term peace may quiet the battlefield for now but, in the end, if this ceasefire is the gateway to a "political transition" that sees Western-backed foreign terrorists assume "power-sharing" positions in the government, ushering in tyrannical Sharia law and pro-Western "free-market" globalism then Syria, in the long term, will be the worse for it.

It should also be noted that, as John Kerry stated, this agreement was going to create a de facto No Fly Zone over the entire country. While the agreement admittedly contained no enforcement mechanism for breaking the terms, it undoubtedly provided the West a pretense for military action or further involvement if airstrikes were carried out by the Syrian government. Even if the SAA launched airstrikes in response to a breaking of the ceasefire by ISIS or other US-backed terrorists, the Western media would no doubt have leapt to paint the narrative that the Syrian government is the violating party and thus some type of justification for further American action.

2016. http://www.dw.com/en/airstrikes-leave-scores-dead-ahead-of-syria-ceasefire/a-19542688

[188] Browne, Ryan; Labott, Elise. "Kerry Announces US-Russia Deal On Syrian Ceasefire." CNN. September 10, 2016. http://www.cnn.com/2016/09/09/politics/syria-ceasefire-kerry-lavrov/

[189] Browne, Ryan; Labott, Elise. "Kerry Announces US-Russia Deal On Syrian Ceasefire." CNN. September 10, 2016. http://www.cnn.com/2016/09/09/politics/syria-ceasefire-kerry-lavrov/

Nevertheless, these "ceasefire" agreements have the most convenient timing it is scarcely believable that there is even the slightest amount of legitimacy to them. Indeed, every time the Syrian military is poised to make important gains and monumental victories over the terrorists, the United States, France, UK, or the UN rush in with pleas for "ceasefires" and peace plans.[190]

With the last big ceasefire agreement [at the time of the writing of this book], and the Syrian military having fully encircled Aleppo again, with the manpower and armaments of the terrorists lower than ever, as well as strategic victories by the SAA all over the country, it was thus time for the US to rush in to save their terrorist pets.

Few can deny that the proposed "truces" are very "convenient" in their timing from the point of view of NATO strategists. As Tony Cartalucci of Land Destroyer writes,

> It is curious because talks of "truces" were completely absent just as recently as 2011, when both organizations, the UN and NATO, backed hordes of terrorists sweeping across Libya, committing abhorrent atrocities including the systematic, genocidal extermination of Libya's black communities.[191]

Indeed, NATO and UN peace treaties only seem to appear when the NATO terrorist proxies encounter serious trouble on the battlefield.

While peace is no doubt to be desired in Syria, Western powers should not be allowed to use the concept as a weapon against the Syrian government or the Syrian people.

The United States, UK, France, NATO, and the UN do not want peace. They want a reprieve for their proxy forces. Syria, Iran, Hezbollah, and Russia should all know this very well and should thus not be tempted to enter into agreements and deals with a country and an alliance that has demonstrated time and time again that they are neither willing or capable of maintaining their end of the bargain. If the terrorist "rebels" encircled in Aleppo and embattled throughout the rest of the country want peace, they should have the option of unconditional surrender. Amnesty, upon surrender, could also be discussed at the pleasure of the Syrian government. Otherwise, the encirclement should continue and the liberation of Aleppo must necessarily follow.

Assad must not "go." NATO and its terrorist proxies must go.

Fake peace agreements and politically based "truces" are no longer acceptable and they are no longer credible in the eyes of any informed observer. Only true and total peace, stability, and reconstruction are acceptable options for Syria.

---

[190] Turbeville, Brandon. "NATO/UN Desperately Seek Ceasefire To Save ISIS After Syrian Army Encircles Aleppo." Activist Post. February 18, 2015.
http://www.activistpost.com/2015/02/natoun-desperately-seek-ceasefire-to.html
[191] Cartalucci, Tony. "UN Presses For 'Truce' To Save Embattled Terrorists In Aleppo." Land Destroyer Report. February 18, 2015. http://landdestroyer.blogspot.com/2015/02/uns-presses-for-truce-to-save-embattled.html

Chapter IV: America's Propaganda
Chemical Weapons
The Ghouta Chemical Weapons Attack

On Wednesday August 21, 2013, it was reported by numerous media outlets that a chemical weapons attack took place inside Syria which killed anywhere from 213 to 1300 people in the Damascus suburbs of Ain Tarma, Zamalka, and Jobar. The attacks were allegedly the result of rockets with chemical agents hitting the neighborhoods shortly before dawn. The attacks, if the reports had been accurate, would be the largest and most severe chemical weapons usage since the beginning of the Syrian destabilization campaign in 2011.

As Dominic Evans and Khaled Yacoub Oweis report for Reuters,

> A nurse at Douma Emergency Collection facility, Bayan Baker, said the death toll, as collated from medical centers in the suburbs east of Damascus, was 213.

> "Many of the casualties are women and children. They arrived with their pupil dilated, cold limbs and foam in their mouths. The doctors say these are typical symptoms of nerve gas victims," the nurse said.

> Extensive amateur video and photographs purporting to show victims appeared on the Internet. A video purportedly shot in the Kafr Batna neighborhood showed a room filled with more than 90 bodies, many of them children and a few women and elderly men. Most of the bodies appeared ashen or pale but with no visible injuries. About a dozen were wrapped in blankets.

> Other footage showed doctors treating people in makeshift clinics. One video showed the bodies of a dozen people lying on the floor of a clinic, with no visible wounds. The narrator in the video said they were all members of a single family. In a corridor outside lay another five bodies.

> A photograph taken by activists in Douma showed the bodies of at least 16 children and three adults, one wearing combat fatigues, laid at the floor of a room in a medical facility where bodies were collected.[192]

Deputy Head of the Syrian National Coalition (Western-backed death squad umbrella coalition), George Sabra, has insisted that the death toll is 1,300.[193]

Predictably, the Syrian death squads claimed that the Syrian government was responsible for the chemical attacks and these assertions were repeated with the implication of truth throughout the vast majority of mainstream media outlets. Even the

---

[192] Evans, Dominic; Oweis, Khaled Yacoub; "Activists say more than 200 killed in gas attack near Damascus." Reuters. August 21, 2013. http://www.reuters.com/article/2013/08/21/us-syria-crisis-gas-idUSBRE97K07O20130821

[193] "Syria opposition group claims 1,300 killed in chemical attack in Damascus suburbs." CBS News. August 21, 2013.http://www.cbsnews.com/8301-202_162-57599467/syria-opposition-group-claims-1300-killed-in-chemical-attack-in-damascus-suburbs/

Evans/Oweis article published by Reuters mentioned above, although not openly accusing the Syrian government of committing the atrocity, tacitly implied that this is the case.

Indeed, before the dust from the rockets even settled, corporate media outlets such as the New York Daily News ran the headline "Bashar al-Assad kills 1,300 in Syrian nerve gas attack, activist estimate," clearly suggesting that Assad was the guilty party, despite there being so many loose ends to the story.[194]

However, as has been the case with every other propaganda push against Assad regarding chemical weapons, there was absolutely no evidence to implicate the Syrian government in the launching and use of chemical agents against the Syrian people or even against the death squads themselves. In fact, the accounts published throughout the mainstream media were always very suspect in their own right.

First, although there is some video evidence of chemical weapons usage, the estimates of the extent of the atrocity as well as the blame for the attacks came entirely from the death squads themselves. Both in the title to the Reuters article mentioned above and in nearly all of the mainstream media reports, statistics and information were prefaced by the phrase "activists say." "Activists say," of course, can be translated merely as "death squads" say, as the activists being referred to are indeed nothing more than terrorist killers politically, ideologically, and physically invested in the outcome and presentation of the Syrian crisis. In short, these individuals have a vested interest in the blame for these attacks being placed on Assad, popular opinion being turned against the Syrian government, and some type of condemnation or military action being taken against the Syrian army.

Second, the location of the attack is heavily suspect. The Ghouta region, where the attacks allegedly took place, was an area that was overrun with death squad organizations such as Jabhat al-Nusra and was largely seen to be under death squad control. It is also interesting to note that the attacks came at a time when this area had been under heavy military bombardment, suggesting that the death squads themselves may have detonated chemical weapons as a move of desperation and coordination with NATO/Anglo-American interests seeking to justify military action against Syria.

Third, and even more interesting, was the fact that the chemical weapons attacks came just days after a team of U.N. chemical experts entered Damascus and checked into a hotel a few miles from the targeted area. With this in mind, one must ask "why would Assad order the use of chemical weapons in this area at such an inopportune time?" Given the track record of Assad's cleverness, this seems to be an incredibly foolish move, even as the Syrian army has gained the clear upper hand against the death squads. Why detonate chemical weapons in front of UN chemical experts? Why wait until after they arrive to do so? Why detonate chemical weapons so close to them?

---

[194] Brown, Stephen Rex. "Bashar al-Assad kills 1,300 in Syrian nerve gas attack, activist estimate." New York Daily News. August 21, 2013. http://www.nydailynews.com/news/world/213-feared-dead-syrian-nerve-gas-attack-article-1.1432526

These questionable details have even caused mainstream "experts" to hesitate when commenting on the nature of the alleged chemical attacks. For instance, Charles Lister, an analyst at HIS Jane's Terrorism and Insurgency Center, stated,

> Logically, it would make little sense for the Syrian government to employ chemical agents at such a time, particularly given the relatively close proximity of the targeted towns (to the U.N. team).[195]

Nonetheless, the Ghouta region (where the attacks were reported) is well known for its opposition leanings. Jabhat al-Nusra has had a long-time presence there and the region has borne the brunt of sustained military pressure for months now.

BBC security correspondent Frank Garnder also stated something similar, when he said, "Firstly, the timing is odd, bordering on suspicious. Why would the Assad government, which has recently been retaking ground from the rebels, carry out a chemical attack while UN weapons inspectors are in the country?"[196]

Likewise, Swedish diplomat and former UN weapons inspector Rolf Ekeus stated to Reuters that, "It would be very peculiar if it was the government to do this at the exact moment the international inspectors come into the country….at the least, it wouldn't be very clever."

Another Swede, chemical weapons expert Ake Sellstrom, who led the UN inspection team in Syria, told SVT that the large number of victims being reported sounded "suspicious."[197]

As I have written at length in the past, attempts to blame Assad for chemical weapons attacks[198] have taken place on at least two occasions, both times yielding convincing evidence[199] that it was the death squads, not Assad, who had used chemical weapons. Indeed, plans have been uncovered on several occasions regarding a Western attempt to stage chemical weapons attacks inside Syria which would subsequently be blamed on Assad for the purposes of justifying a Western invasion.

---

[195] "Hundreds Of Syrians Killed In Alleged Chemical Attack By Assad's Forces." The Jerusalem Post. August 21, 2013. http://www.jpost.com/Middle-East/Assad-forces-allegedly-use-chemical-agents-in-bombardment-killing-hundreds-323754

[196] Clabough, Raven. "Syrian Opposition Accuses Assad Of Chemical Attack." The New American. August 21, 2013. http://www.thenewamerican.com/world-news/asia/item/16370-syrian-opposition-accuses-assad-of-a-chemical-attack

[197] "'Poisonous Gas' Attack By Regime Troops Kill At Least 100 In Syria, Activists Say." FOX News. August 21, 2013. http://www.foxnews.com/world/2013/08/21/syrian-opposition-claims-poisonous-gas-attack.html

[198] Turbeville, Brandon. "False Flag Attacks in Syria Pin Atrocities on Assad To Justify 'Red Line' Engagement." Activist Post. March 30, 2013. http://www.activistpost.com/2013/03/false-flag-attacks-in-syria-pin.html

[199] Turbeville, Brandon. "New U.N. Chemical Weapons Report On Syria Blames Assad." Activist Post. June 4, 2013.http://www.activistpost.com/2013/06/new-un-chemical-weapons-report-on-syria.html

While it is important to examine information impartially as it appears, it is also important to speak out against falsehoods and nefarious propaganda. We cannot allow such tired and blatant propaganda to engulf Syria, the Middle East, or the world in war.

With all this in mind, it is thus important to take a step back and take a look at the previous allegations of chemical weapons usage that took place prior to those in Ghouta. After that, Ghouta, since it represented one of the moments where the United States came closest to invading Syria, must be analyzed as well.

The March Chemical Attacks - False Flag Attacks In Syria Pin Atrocities On Assad And Justify "Red Line" Engagement

Only days after the chemical weapons attack inside Syria, the Israeli, US, and NATO governments did everything in their power to not only push the idea that the "red line" of the Obama administration was crossed, but also to maintain the fragile public relations narrative that the attack was launched by the Assad government. Fortunately for everyone involved – except for, perhaps, the death squads wreaking havoc on Syrian soil – such a dual approach is proving very difficult.[200]

This is because the chemical attack was not the work of the Assad regime but of the death squads who have been killing and maiming innocent people since the very beginning of the crisis. Although the Western and Israeli imperialists are clearly always poised to take advantage of a false flag attack such as the use of a chemical weapon by the inappropriately named "rebels" to immediately be blamed on Assad, the openness with which the death squads advertised their possession of and intent to use such weapons proved to be a major hurdle in the attempt to create a successful campaign of public outcry against the Assad government. In short, the false narrative of Assad's use of chemical weapons "against his own people" was so easily dispelled that the public relations push stalled, even if only for a brief time.[201]

Since the ridiculous "red line" talk was repeated in government halls and press conferences since late 2012 by both President Barack Obama and then-Secretary of State Hillary Clinton as well as French President Francois Hollande, the idea that the Syrian government would be the party to actually use chemical weapons was patently absurd from the beginning.

As far back as June 2012, the pieces were clearly seen being moved into place in order to create the environment and subsequent chain of events for a successful false flag attack used to justify an invasion of or, at the very least, some limited military action

---

[200] Bouzid, Salma. "TV Show Renews Controversy Over Tunisian Fighters In Syria." Tunisia Live. March 22, 2013. http://www.tunisia-live.net/2013/03/22/tv-show-renews-controversy-over-tunisian-fighters-in-syria/

[201] Cartalucci, Tony. "Syria Conflict: The Price Of Defying The West." Land Destroyer Report. March 28, 2013. http://landdestroyer.blogspot.com/2013/03/syrian-conflict-price-of-defying-west.html

against Syria. However, the more hidden aspects being used to create infrastructure for such an event could be seen going back even further.

For instance, in November, 2011, it was reported in The Telegraph that the "transitional" government of terrorists, Muslim Brotherhood, and NATO puppets in Libya were offering to send money, personnel (aka terrorists and mercenaries), and weapons to the death squads operating in Syria. It was largely understood, at least after the initial announcement of the weapons deal, that the weapons in question included chemical weapons.[202] [203] [204] [205]

Later, in June of 2012, it was reported by Russia Today that these weapons had indeed found themselves into the hands of the death squads by virtue of their Libyan counterparts now acting as head of the failed Libyan State. RT stated that, "They allegedly plan to use it against civilians and pin the atrocity on the Bashar al-Assad regime."[206]

Thus, it should be noted that the London Guardian reported that the Libya possessed "25 metric tonnes of bulk mustard agent and 1,400 metric tonnes of precursor chemical used to make chemical weapons."[207]

It was also reported in August of 2012 that the death squads had managed to capture a missile site belonging to the Syrian army which contained chemical weapons. The death squads erroneously claimed that the reason for attacking the site was to prevent the Assad government from using the weapons against members of the "opposition." Regardless, one does not have to speculate very much as to the possibilities available here – in June, the death squads gain access to chemical weapons. In August, they gain access to a delivery mechanism in the form of missiles.[208]

It is just such a coincidence that should cause one to examine another event which occurred shortly before the assault on the missile site. In July 2012, Tony Cartalucci of

---

[202] Sherlock, Ruth. "Libya's New Rulers Offer Weapons To Syrian Rebels." The Telegraph. November 25, 2011. http://www.telegraph.co.uk/news/worldnews/middleeast/syria/8917265/Libyas-new-rulers-offer-weapons-to-Syrian-rebels.html

[203] Cartalucci, Tony. "The Libyan Election Farce." Land Destroyer. July 9, 2012. http://www.activistpost.com/2012/07/libyan-election-farce.html

[204] "Libyan Fighters Join 'Free Syrian Army' Forces. Al Bawaba. November 29, 2011. http://www.albawaba.com/news/libyan-fighters-join-free-syrian-army-forces-403268

[205] Watson, Ivan; Razek, Raja. "Faces of the Free Syrian Army." CNN. July 27, 2012. http://edition.cnn.com/2012/07/24/world/meast/northern-syria-violence/index.html

[206] "Syrian Rebels Aim To Use Chemical Weapons, Blame Damascus – Report." RT. June 10, 2012. http://rt.com/news/syria-chemical-weapons-plot-532/

[207] Wintour, Patrick. "Britain Sends Officials To Libya To Help Destroy Chemical Weapons." The Guardian. November 14, 2011. https://www.theguardian.com/world/2011/nov/14/british-officials-help-libya-chemical-weapons

[208] "Turkey's (NATO) FSA Terrorists Storm Into A Missiles Warehouse & Start Propaganda." Youtube. Posted by Arabi Souri. Posted on August 28, 2012. Video shows FSA terrorists storming Aftriss area warehouse where artillery munitions and tanks belonging to the SAA were stored. https://www.youtube.com/watch?v=vRK5SBtdUhg

Land Destroyer Report described "reports of so-called 'Free Syrian Army' militants seen trying on gas masks, along with reports of Libyan chemical weapon caches & equipment being discovered in Damascus."[209]

Together with the acquisition of the missile delivery capability by virtue of the conquering of the Syrian missile site and the possession of the chemical weapons themselves via Libya, the acquisition of gas masks points to the preparation for the launch of an actual chemical attack, or at least the possibility of it, on the part of the death squads.

As one of the death squad members stated to Reuters in April, 2012, "'The rebels are getting better at bomb-making; as you know, desperation is the mother of invention." Reuters also commented that the death squads were now able to develop "more sophisticated bombs" due to "rare outside donations" although Reuters did not attempt to name those mysterious sources.[210]

Moving forward to August 2012, a false flag plot was discovered which had been hatched between NATO and Saudi Arabia that would have staged a chemical weapons deployment in Syria either by mercenary firms or by the NATO-backed death squads, an attack that would subsequently have been blamed on the Assad government, thus serving as a pretext for NATO intervention and the creation of a "buffer zone" in the country.

Here, a source reported an impending attack to Syrian news channel Addounia and stated that a Saudi Arabian firm "had fitted 1400 ambulance vehicles with anti-gas & anti-chemical filtering systems at a cost of $97,000 dollars each, in preparation for a chemical weapons attack carried out by FSA rebels using mortar rounds. A further 400 vehicles have been prepared as troop carriers."[211]

Interestingly enough, the attack was alleged to make use of white phosphorous, sarin and mustard gas. It then stands as yet another questionable "coincidence" that, among the weapons possessed by the Libyan regime and now in the hands of the death squads, was large quantities of bulk mustard agent.

Nevertheless, the potential false flag attack reported by Addounia was allegedly set to be launched on densely populated areas, most likely Daraa, a city on the Syria/Jordan border, after which the newly fitted ambulances would pour into Syria under the guise of humanitarian aid. Although painted with the labels, "Syrian People's Relief," the ambulances would actually be nothing more than armored personnel carriers designed to

---

[209] Cartalucci, Tony. "Syrians: NATO-Backed Militants Seen Donning Gas Masks." July 27, 2012. http://www.activistpost.com/2012/07/syrians-nato-backed-militants-seen.html
[210] Solomon, Erika. "Outgunned Syria Rebels Make Shift To Bombs." Reuters. April 30, 2012. http://www.reuters.com/article/2012/04/30/us-syria-bombs-idUSBRE83T0XY20120430
[211] "French & US Intelligence Chemical Weapons False Flag In Syria Exposed." Youtube. Posted by Arabi Souri. Posted on August 28, 2012. https://www.youtube.com/watch?v=SxKIyk5dgqk
The video shows news reports by Addounia claiming information from a source detailing a plan to carry out a false flag attack against the Syrian government using ambulances. The attack was to be carried out by the Free Syrian Army in concert with some outside force.

capitalize on a manufactured disaster for the purpose of deploying such personnel in order to create the desired buffer zone.

Furthermore, the same company that was accused of manufacturing and fitting the ambulances to be used in the attack is one that is based in Riyadh and was negotiating a contract with the Yemeni government for the manufacture of military vehicles for the Yemeni army.

A source also reported to Addounia that a meeting had taken place between the head of Al Arabiya, the Saudi news channel, and a U.S. diplomat at the U.S. Embassy in the United Arab Emirates. As Paul Joseph Watson writes, "The purpose of the meeting was to agree upon a conditioning program to prepare the public for the likelihood that Bashar Al-Assad's forces would use chemical weapons. Shortly after the meeting, Al Arabiya began running news segments depicting the inevitability of a chemical weapons attack carried out by Assad's forces."[212]

Of course, it was around this same time period that discussions of a "red line" by the French and American Presidents as well as the U.S. State Department and Israeli representatives began their repetition in the mainstream media circles and hence the American public at large.

For instance, in August, President Barack Obama warned that not only the use but merely the transportation of chemical weapons would constitute a "red line" that would result in military intervention. French President Hollande also stated at the time that the use of chemical weapons "Would be a legitimate reason for direct intervention."[213]

Likewise, Israel's Vice Premier Silvan Shalom told media outlets that if Syrian rebels obtained chemical weapons from stockpiles belonging to the Assad regime, such a development would force Israel to resort to "preventive operations," in other words – a military strike on Syria.[214]

The creation of a "buffer zone" inside Syria is also interesting in its own right, not just because of the necessary loss of legitimate territory close to Syria's borders but also because of its inherent nature of destabilization and weakening of the ruling regime in Damascus. Thus, it is interesting to note that, while the false flag chemical attack and the subsequent creation of a buffer zone was designed to use the pretext of humanitarian aid as mentioned above, such a plan follows the roadmap provided by the Brookings Institution in a paper entitled "Saving Syria: Assessing Options for Regime Change," published in March 2012. The paper essentially argued for the use of a humanitarian issue in order to engage in military intervention on the part of NATO in Syria.[215]

---

[212] Watson, Paul Joseph. "NATO Plot To Use Ambulances As Cover For Humanitarian Invasion Of Syria." Infowars.com. August 29, 2012. http://www.infowars.com/nato-plot-to-use-ambulances-as-cover-for-humanitarian-invasion-of-syria/
[213] "France Warns Syria Over Chemical Weapons Use." Reuters. August 27, 2012. http://uk.reuters.com/article/uk-syria-crisis-france-idUKBRE87Q0QZ20120827
[214] "Israel Threatens Syria Strike If Rebels Get Chemical Arms." Reuters. January 27, 2013. http://www.reuters.com/article/us-syria-crisis-israel-idUSBRE90Q03I20130127
[215] Byman, Daniel; Doran, Michael; Pollack, Kenneth, Shaikh, Salman. "Saving Syria: Assessing Options For Regime Change." Saban Center at Brookings. Brookings Institution. March 2012.

Indeed, the paper states, "An alternative is for diplomatic efforts to focus first on how to end the violence and how to gain humanitarian access, as is being done under Annan's leadership. This may lead to the creation of safe-havens and humanitarian-corridors, which would have to be backed by limited military power."[216]

Yet one does not have to go any further afield in order to understand that the plan to stage false flag chemical weapons attack inside Syria in order to see the mass of evidence supporting such a claim.

In December 2012, a video was obtained by the Syria Tribune and subsequently released in their report and posted on YouTube which allegedly shows the NATO-backed death squads testing chemical weapons on "lab" rabbits.[217]

As the Syria Tribune describes the video,

The video (see here)[218] starts with several scenes showing chemical containers with Tekkim labels (Tekkim is a Turkish chemicals company) and some lab equipment, while playing Jihadists chants in the background.[219] [220] A glass box then appears with two rabbits inside, with a poster on the wall behind it reading The Almighty Wind Brigade (Kateebat A Reeh Al Sarsar). A person wearing a lab mask then mixes chemicals in a beaker in the glass box, and we see some gas emitting from the beaker. About a minute later, the rabbits start to have random convulsions and then die. The person says: You saw what happened? This will be your fate, you infidel Alawites, I swear by ALLAH to make you die like these rabbits, one minute only after you inhale the gas.[221]

Memo #21. http://www.scribd.com/doc/108893509/BrookingsSyria0315-Syria-Saban
[216] Byman, Daniel; Doran, Michael; Pollack, Kenneth, Shaikh, Salman. "Saving Syria: Assessing Options For Regime Change." Saban Center at Brookings. Brookings Institution. March 2012. Memo #21. http://www.scribd.com/doc/108893509/BrookingsSyria0315-Syria-Saban
[217] "Syrian Rebels Testing Tekkim Chemicals To Use As Chemical Weapons." Youtube. Posted by Syria Tribune. Posted on December 5, 2012. https://www.youtube.com/watch?v=H-6O-gApVrU The video's description (accurate) reads in the following way:
This video appeared on YouTube yesterday showing what appears to be a rebel group in Syria testing a chemical combination to be used as a chemical weapon (most likely nerve agents as judged by the reaction of lab rabbits in the video) and threatening to use this chem weapon against civilians in Syria on a sectarian basis.
[218] "Syrian Rebels Testing Tekkim Chemicals To Use As Chemical Weapons." Youtube. Posted by Syria Tribune. Posted on December 5, 2012. https://www.youtube.com/watch?v=H-6O-gApVrU The video's description (accurate) reads in the following way:
This video appeared on YouTube yesterday showing what appears to be a rebel group in Syria testing a chemical combination to be used as a chemical weapon (most likely nerve agents as judged by the reaction of lab rabbits in the video) and threatening to use this chem weapon against civilians in Syria on a sectarian basis.
[219] Tekkim.com. Tekkim website. http://www.tekkim.com.tr/
[220] "US, NATO, GCC-Backed Terrorists Preparing Chemical Attack?" Syria Tribune. December 7, 2012. http://landdestroyer.blogspot.com/2012/12/us-nato-gcc-backed-terrorists-preparing.html
[221] "US, NATO, GCC-Backed Terrorists Preparing Chemical Attack?" Syria Tribune. December 7, 2012. http://landdestroyer.blogspot.com/2012/12/us-nato-gcc-backed-terrorists-

The Syria Tribune also comments that "Judging from the rabbits' reaction, the gas must be a nerve agent. The number of containers, if not a bluff, indicates ability to produce a considerable amount of this gas. Deployment could be by means of a smoke generator placed in the target area, an explosion, possibly a suicide one, of a "chemmed" car, or simply by using a humidifier."[222]

In March, 2013, yet another YouTube video was released which contained a clip of a second "test" of chemical weapons on captive rabbits by the death squads.[223]

This is quite an ironic presentation, since the Assad government has repeatedly vowed never to use chemical weapons inside Syria, while the death squads have repeatedly threatened to do just that. Indeed, in direct contrast to the tone and statements of the death squads, the Syrian Foreign Ministry spokesman Jihad Makdissi issued a statement saying, "No chemical or biological weapons will ever be used, and I repeat, will never be used, during the crisis in Syria no matter what the developments inside Syria."[224]

Still, the drums of war and military intervention from the United States, NATO, and Israel nevertheless continue to relentlessly beat.

Regardless, the video mentioned above also contains an alleged audio recording of a phone conversation between two Free Syrian Army fighters discussing the "details of a plan to carry out a chemical weapons attack capable of impacting an area the size of one kilometer."[225]

As Paul Joseph Watson writes,

> The recording of the phone conversation purports to be between two FSA militants, one inside Syria and one outside of the country. Abu Hassan, the militant inside Syria, asks the person on the other end of the line to transmit a message to Sheikh Suleiman, a rebel-seized army base in Aleppo, asking for "two chemical bombs ....phosphoric" in order to "finish this whole thing."[226]

> "I want them to be effective," states Hassan, adding, "The radius of the strike, or reach of the gases, has to be 1km."[227]

---

preparing.html
[222] "US, NATO, GCC-Backed Terrorists Preparing Chemical Attack?" Syria Tribune. December 7, 2012. http://landdestroyer.blogspot.com/2012/12/us-nato-gcc-backed-terrorists-preparing.html
[223] "West Turns A Blind Eye That Their Terrorists In Syria Used WMDs, Against All Evidence." Youtube. Posted by nuts flipped. Posted on March 20, 2013. http://www.youtube.com/watch?feature=player_embedded&v=BLAMVtLq2V0#!
[224] "UN Told Syria Will Never Use WMDs." Press Tv. August 12, 2012. http://www.presstv.com/detail/2012/12/08/276916/un-told-syria-will-never-use-wmds/
[225] "Syria Says Chemical Or Biological Weapons Could Be Used If There Is 'External Aggression.'" CBS News. July 23, 2012. http://www.cbsnews.com/news/syria-says-chemical-or-biological-weapons-could-be-used-if-there-is-external-aggression/
[226] "West Turns A Blind Eye That Their Terrorists In Syria Used WMDs, Against All Evidence." Youtube. Posted by nuts flipped. Posted on March 20, 2013. http://www.youtube.com/watch?feature=player_embedded&v=BLAMVtLq2V0#!

The video also contains a clip of the death squads openly announcing their plans to engage in chemical weapons attacks, all the while surrounded by bottles of nitric acid and other substances.[228]

Again, back in December of 2012, after the death squads managed to capture a chlorine factory inside Syria, the Syrian government actually issued a warning that the death squads might attempt to use chemical weapons of this nature in their battle to overthrow and oppress the government and people of Syria respectively. The Syrian Foreign Ministry stated, "Terrorist groups may resort to using chemical weapons against the Syrian people … after having gained control of a toxic chlorine factory."[229]

Thus, when another alleged chemical weapon attack took place and caused both a frothing and bumbling public relations response from the Anglo-Americans, it is interesting to note that chlorine has been fingered as being one of the major ingredients.

As Alex Thomson of The Telegraph reported,

> The Syrian military is said to believe that a home-made locally-manufactured rocket was fired, containing a form of chlorine known as CL17, easily available as a swimming pool cleaner. They claim that the warhead contained a quantity of the gas, dissolved in saline solution.
>
> . . . . .
>
> CL17 is normal chlorine for swimming pools or industrial purposes. It is rated as Level 2 under the chemical weapons convention, which means it is dual purpose – it can be used as a weapon as well as for industrial or domestic purposes. Level 1 agents are chemicals whose sole use is as weapons, such as the nerve agents sarin or tabun.
>
> There has been extensive experimentation by insurgents in Iraq in the use of chlorine, which is harmful when mixed with water to form hydrochloric acid. It vapourises quickly, meaning that in a big explosion it will evaporate; in a small blast – for instance, one delivered by a home-made rocket – it will turn into airborne droplets before dispersing quickly.
>
> So it is likely only to produce limited casualties. In this case there were only 26 fatalities, far fewer than would be expected from a full chemical weapon attack. In short, it is easily improvised into a chemical device but not one that would be used by an army seeking mass-casualty effects.[230]

---

[227] Watson, Paul Joseph. "Syrian Rebels Caught On Tape Discussing Chemical Weapons Attack." Infowars. March 20, 2013. http://www.infowars.com/syrian-rebels-caught-on-tape-discussing-chemical-weapons-attack/

[228] "West Turns A Blind Eye That Their Terrorists In Syria Used WMDs, Against All Evidence." Youtube. Posted by nuts flipped. Posted on March 20, 2013. http://www.youtube.com/watch?feature=player_embedded&v=BLAMVtLq2V0#!

[229] "Rebels Could Resort To Chemical Weapons, Syria Warns." France 24. December 8, 2012. http://www.france24.com/en/20121208-syria-warns-rebels-may-resort-chemical-weapons-assad-united-nations-islamists

[230] Thomson, Alex. "Syria Chemical Weapons: Finger Pointed At Jihadists." The Telegraph. March 23, 2013. http://www.telegraph.co.uk/news/worldnews/middleeast/syria/9950036/Syria-chemical-weapons-finger-pointed-at-jihadists.html

Reports by the Syrian government coincide with the accounts given by the victims of the chemical weapons attack which one can view in the video clip contained in the YouTube video mentioned above. (See here) It is also important to note that many of the victims allegedly name the Free Syrian Army and the "rebels" as the perpetrators as they are being interviewed while waiting for medical treatment.[231]

"The Free Syrian Army hit us with a rocket," one woman said. "We smelled an odor and everyone fell to the ground. People died where they fell . . . the kids . . . "

A young girl was also interviewed, who said, "My lungs closed and I couldn't breathe or speak. God curse them. Everyone died on the ground. My mom and dad died. I don't know where is my brother. God curse them. May they [FSA] all die. This is the freedom they bring us. They [FSA] want to kill everyone. I hope there remains not a single one of them [FSA] alive."

Let us not forget that the death squads have been responsible for unspeakable atrocities against innocent people ever since the destabilization effort began. In October, 2012, the death squads, in typical terrorist fashion, conducted at least four suicide bombings in Aleppo that killed around 40 innocent civilians.[232]

Receiving more attention in the media, however, at least until the death squads were found to be responsible, was the infamous Houla Massacre of 2011 where approximately 90 people were killed.

Numerous other atrocities have also been documented with videos showing the death squads machine gunning captives, beheading prisoners, and forcing young children to behead them. I, myself, have written an article dealing with reports regarding the death squad's hanging of a young child after murdering his family in front of him. One can also view the videos of the death squad members beating and humiliating the famous elderly "Yellow Man" in Aleppo.[233] [234] [235] [236] [237] [238] [239]

---

[231] "West Turns A Blind Eye That Their Terrorists In Syria Used WMDs, Against All Evidence." Youtube. Posted by nuts flipped. Posted on March 20, 2013. http://www.youtube.com/watch?feature=player_embedded&v=BLAMVtLq2V0#!

[232] Clabough, Raven. "Evidence Shows Syrian Rebels Behind Chemical Attack." The New American. March 27, 2013. http://www.thenewamerican.com/world-news/asia/item/14929-evidence-shows-syrian-rebels-behind-chemical-attack

[233] "Rebels Massacre 11 Prisoners In Saraqib, Syria." Youtube. Posted by SyrianRebelWatch. Posted on November 2, 2012. https://www.youtube.com/watch?v=t5OLmnYpIXs (Accurate) Description of the video:

(01/11/12) At least 11 wounded prisoners are forced to lie down before being beaten and then shot to death by insurgents in the central town of Saraqib. The victims are taunted, insulted and stamped on before a hail of gunfire is directed at their prone bodies.

The men were said to have been captured after Syrian rebels overran a checkpoint.

This is one of hundreds of such mass executions carried out by rebel forces since the conflict in Syria began, the methods varying from shooting to beheading. While such atrocities are arguably far more common than those often falsely attributed to Syria government forces they are often completely ignored by Western journalists and politicians keen to portray the insurgents in a positive light despite all the evidence to the contrary. Numerous other examples of such executions are available on my channel and facebook page.

Indeed, the videos of the torture of prisoners in the hands of the death squads are legion. One need only type the relevant keywords into a YouTube search engine to be greeted with generous results.

Such open acts of terrorism, lack of regard for human life, and outright savagery on the part of the death squads have thus made even coordinated Western media propaganda campaigns rest on shakier ground. Unfortunately, we must never overestimate the intellectual prowess of the population of the television and entertainment-saturated Western populations. After all, it has failed on countless occasions in the past.

Thus, while Obama has himself been forced to approach the Syrian issue with more caution, both he and the War Hawks in Congress as well as their counterparts in the Anglo-American networks of imperialism are still marching forward on the war path. Obama himself refused to admit the fact that the death squads are responsible for the chemical attack.[240] [241]

---

[234] "Syrian Rebels Behead A Man In Aleppo, Syria – 11/08/12." Youtube. Posted by 3TimeToFightBack. Posted on August 13, 2012. https://www.youtube.com/watch?v=FL0uGSBhORc (Accurate) Description of the video: This footage, first posted by a member of the opposition purports to show the beheading of an Assad supporter in Aleppo. The man is beaten and insulted before being executed by a man wielding a small knife who proceeds to cut his throat. His captors suggest that he was a 'Shabiha' a term now frequently used to describe all those deemed loyal to the Syrian government. His killers are heard to laugh and chant 'God Is Great' and 'thanks be to God' as they carry out the atrocity.

[235] "Syrian Rebel Criminals Force Young Child To Behead Prisoner." Youtube. Posted by Mussalaha Reconcilliation. Posted on August 25, 2013. https://www.youtube.com/watch?v=jpDd0ptes1M

[236] Watson, Paul Joseph. "Gruesome Video Shows Syrian Rebel Beheading Civilian." Infowars.com. March 21, 2013. http://www.infowars.com/gruesome-video-shows-syrian-rebel-beheading-civilian/

[237] "Syrian Rebels Use Child In Beheading Unarmed Prisoners In Homs." Youtube. Posted by Human Rights Investigations. Posted on December 11, 2012. https://www.youtube.com/watch?v=yjmH5kU8msc

[238] Turbeville, Brandon. "Iranian News Reports Child Hanged By Syrian 'Rebels.'" Activist Post. August 7, 2012. http://www.activistpost.com/2012/08/iranian-news-reports-child-hanged-by.html

[239] "Salafist Jihadis Beat 'Yellow Man' In Aleppo Syria (Eng Subtitles)." Youtube. Posted by iamforhumanity. Posted on March 8, 2013. https://www.youtube.com/verify_controversy?next_url=/watch%3Ffeature%3Dplayer_embedded%26v%3DEuylhA477x0%26bpctr%3D1364589201 Video shows the elderly "Yellow Man" being beaten, humiliated, spit on, and even having his beard ripped from his face by terrorists before eventually being led to a car where he is loaded and driven off.

[240] Clabough, Raven. "Evidence Shows Syrian Rebels Behind Chemical Attack." The New American. March 27, 2013. http://www.thenewamerican.com/world-news/asia/item/14929-evidence-shows-syrian-rebels-behind-chemical-attack

[241] Cartalucci, Tony. "West Drops Syria WMD Narrative As Evidence Points To Western-Armed Terrorists." Land Destroyer Report. March 24, 2013.

He stated, "I am deeply skeptical of any claim that, in fact, it was the opposition that used chemical weapons. Everybody who knows the facts of the chemical weapon stockpiles inside Syria as well as the Syrian government's capabilities I think would question these claims."[242]

This statement was clearly designed to act as some level of protection for the operations of destabilization and invasion that his undeserved and illogical reputation as a man of peace in the eyes of the American people has been instrumental in assisting.[243]

Others, however, are even less subtle about the desire to invade yet another sovereign nation. House Intelligence Committee Chair Mike Rogers, for instance, stated as much to CBS when he said, "I think that it is abundantly clear that that red line has been crossed. There is mounting evidence that it is probable that the Assad regime has used at least a small quantity of chemical weapons during the course of this conflict." Such "there might be evidence that [insert foreign nation here] might have [insert weapons here] sometime in the undefined future has been used before to a great degree of success.[244]

However, regardless of the insanity of bought-and-paid-for parasites such as Rogers and Obama, the fact is that anyone who has investigated the events transpiring in Syria, particularly the chemical weapons attack, is able to recognize the operation for what it is – a destabilization effort aimed at replacing the Assad government with a more manageable regime to the benefit of the Anglo-American establishment and the detriment of the Syrian people. Such an outcome is direct product of the work of Western Governments and Intelligence agencies, the NATO world army network, and the Mad Dog of the Middle East known as Israel.[245]

In the end, Syria is simply another stop on the Path to Persia. If Americans and other Westerners have any sense of self-preservation left among them, they must do everything they can to steer themselves off of this road before the destination is reached.[246]

---

http://www.activistpost.com/2013/03/west-drops-syria-wmd-narrative-as.html

[242] Clabough, Raven. "Evidence Shows Syrian Rebels Behind Chemical Attack." The New American. March 27, 2013. http://www.thenewamerican.com/world-news/asia/item/14929-evidence-shows-syrian-rebels-behind-chemical-attack

[243] Turbeville, Brandon. "U.S. Under Attack By Globalist Death Squad Experts." Activist Post. May 27, 2012. http://www.activistpost.com/2012/05/syria-under-attack-by-globalist-death.html

[244] Boerma, Lindsay. "'Red Line Has Been Crossed' In Syria, Rogers Says." CBS News. March 24, 2013. http://www.cbsnews.com/news/red-line-has-been-crossed-in-syria-rogers-says/

[245] Cartalucci, Tony. "CONFIRMED: US Shipping Weapons To Syria – Al Nusra's 'Mystery' Sponsors Revealed." Land Destroyer Report. March 25, 2013.
http://www.activistpost.com/2013/03/confirmed-us-shipping-weapons-to-syria.html

[246] Pollack, Kenneth M.; Byman, Daniel L.; Indyk, Martin; Maloney, Suzanne; O'Hanlon, Michael E.; Riedel, Bruce. "Which Path To Persia? Options For A New American Strategy Toward Iran." The Saban Center For Middle East Policy At The Brookings Institution. Analysis Paper Number 20. June, 2009.
http://www.brookings.edu/~/media/research/files/papers/2009/6/iran%20strategy/06_iran_strategy.pdf

5 Ways 'Incontrovertible Evidence' on Syria Chemical Weapons Attack Was Controvertible

Below are just a few reasons to question the "evidence" and "proof" presented by the Administration regarding the use of chemical weapons in Syria by the Assad government:

1.) The Source of the information

Much of the information presented to the American people, where it is enumerated at all, revolved around shadowy "intelligence" in the same way as the Iraqi WMD claims were presented to the public during 2003. That is to say that there is only the statement of the possession of "intelligence" but never a presentation of the actual intelligence itself.

The bulk of the so-called concrete evidence that has been produced, however, is an alleged intercepted phone conversation between a Syrian Ministry of Defense official and a member of a Syrian chemical weapons unit that was obtained by none other than the Israeli Defense Force intelligence unit which goes by the number 8200, the largest unit in the IDF.[247] [248]

The mainstream Western media, of course, has attempted to portray these calls (if they are even authentic) as proof that Assad and Syrian government forces were the responsible party for the chemical attacks in Ghouta. However, a close look at the calls and the content therein reveals several conflicting aspects of the narrative being pushed by Western governments and media outlets.

For instance, the calls are supposed to reveal that these Syrian officials, "exchanged panicked phone calls with a leader of a chemical weapons unit, demanding answers for a nerve agent strike that killed more than 1,000 people," in Ghouta.[249] Without disputing the claim of 1,000 dead, a figure provided by the death squads and Saudi media outlet Al-Arabiya, one should certainly wonder how a government which launches a chemical weapons attack would then be surprised and demand answers regarding the chemical weapons attack it had launched.[250]

---

[247] Griffin, Jennifer; Baier, Bret; Henry, Ed. "Israeli Intelligence First Confirmed Assad Regime Behind Alleged Chemical Attack." FOX News. August 28, 2013.
http://www.foxnews.com/politics/2013/08/28/israeli-intelligence-first-confirmed-assad-regime-behind-alleged-chemical.html
[248] Sherwood, Harriet. "Israeli Intelligence 'Intercepted Syrian Regime Talk About Chemical Attack." The Guardian. August 28, 2013.
https://www.theguardian.com/world/2013/aug/28/israeli-intelligence-intercepted-syria-chemical-talk
[249] Watson, Paul Joseph. "Intelligence Suggests Assad Not Behind Chemical Weapons Attack." Infowars. August 28, 2013. http://www.infowars.com/intelligence-suggests-assad-not-behind-chemical-weapons-attack/
[250] "Syrian Gas Attack Story Has Whiff Of Saudi War Propaganda." RT. August 21, 2012.
https://www.rt.com/op-edge/syria-gas-attack-chemical-propaganda-796/

Why would the official be demanding answers for a chemical attack if the government was responsible for it?

Of course, media outlets such as Foreign Policy, the official news agency of the Council on Foreign Relations, attempted to spin the obvious contradiction as the result of a Syrian military officer going rogue and "overstepping his bounds." Still, if this was the case (and it should be stressed that there is no evidence that it is), it would only go to show that the Syrian government did not order such an attack and that, in order to do so, this rogue officer would have had to violate his chain of command and Syrian military procedure. Thus, the intercepted calls do nothing to build the case for the guilt of the Syrian government, much less a case for war.[251]

It is also important to point out that Israel's IDF and Mossad are no mere innocent and impartial bystanders to the Syrian crisis. Indeed, Israel has, on at least three occasions, attacked Syria by air and is known to have Mossad and Special Forces agents working on the ground inside the country. Indeed, as IPS wrote, even "U.S. intelligence officials have long been doubtful about intelligence from Israeli sources that is clearly in line with Israeli interests."[252]

The only other form of "proof" provided by the Anglo-Americans revolves around highly dubious if not outright faked or non-existent samples allegedly taken from Ghouta by "first responders in East Damascus." Secretary of State John Kerry stated, that "those samples of hair and blood have been tested, and they have reported positive for signatures of sarin." Unfortunately for Kerry, he and the rest of his warmongering ilk were entirely unable to present any real evidence to back up these claims.[253] [254]

Of course, because the UN investigation was hampered by both the death squads and the United States, the White House claims that only the mysterious "samples" taken by shadowy "first responders" which were then tested and analyzed by secret agents of the very government which has been relentless in its push for war against Syria is admissible as justification for military action.[255]

As Zeina Karam and Kimberly Dozier wrote for AP,

---

[251] Shachtman, Noah. "Intercepted Calls Prove Syrian Army Used Nerve Gas, U.S. Spies Say." Foreign Policy. August 27, 2013. http://thecable.foreignpolicy.com/posts/2013/08/27/exclusive_us_spies_say_intercepted_calls _prove_syrias_army_used_nerve_gas
[252] Porter, Gareth. "Obama's Case For Syria Didn't Reflect Intel Consensus." Inter Press Service (IPS News). September 9, 2013. http://www.ipsnews.net/2013/09/obamas-case-for-syria-didnt-reflect-intel-consensus/
[253] Boerma, Lindsey. "U.S. Has Firm Evidence Sarin Gas Was Used In Syria Chemical Weapons Attack, Sec. Kerry Says." CBS News. September 1, 2013. http://www.cbsnews.com/8301-204_162-57600439/chemical-nerve-agents-a-very-toxic-and-horrible-way-to-die/
[254] Jaslow, Ryan. "Chemical nerve agents: A 'very toxic and horrible way to go.'" CBS News. September 1, 2013. http://www.cbsnews.com/news/chemical-nerve-agents-a-very-toxic-and-horrible-way-to-die/
[255] Boerma, Lindsey. "U.S. Has Firm Evidence Sarin Gas Was Used In Syria Chemical Weapons Attack, Sec. Kerry Says." CBS News. September 1, 2013. http://www.cbsnews.com/8301-204_162-57600439/chemical-nerve-agents-a-very-toxic-and-horrible-way-to-die/

The U.S. government insists it has the intelligence to prove it, but the public has yet to see a single piece of concrete evidence produced by U.S. intelligence - no satellite imagery, no transcripts of Syrian military communications - connecting the government of President Bashar Assad to the alleged chemical weapons attack last month that killed hundreds of people.

In its absence, Damascus and its ally Russia have aggressively pushed another scenario: that rebels carried out the Aug. 21 chemical attack. Neither has produced evidence for that case, either. That's left more questions than answers as the U.S. threatens a possible military strike.

[. . .]

Yet one week after Secretary of State John Kerry outlined the case against Assad, Americans - at least those without access to classified reports - haven't seen a shred of his proof.

[. . .]

What's missing from the public record is direct proof, rather than circumstantial evidence, tying this to the regime.

The Obama administration, searching for support from a divided Congress and skeptical world leaders, says its own assessment is based mainly on satellite and signals intelligence, including intercepted communications and satellite images indicating that in the three days prior to the attack that the regime was preparing to use poisonous gas.

But multiple requests to view that satellite imagery have been denied, though the administration produced copious amounts of satellite imagery earlier in the war to show the results of the Syrian regime's military onslaught. When asked Friday whether such imagery would be made available showing the Aug. 21 incident, a spokesman referred The Associated Press to a map produced by the White House last week that shows what officials say are the unconfirmed areas that were attacked.

The Obama administration maintains it intercepted communications from a senior Syrian official on the use of chemical weapons, but requests to see that transcript have been denied. So has a request by the AP to see a transcript of communications allegedly ordering Syrian military personnel to prepare for a chemical weapons attack by readying gas masks.

The U.S. administration says its evidence is classified and is only sharing details in closed-door briefings with members of Congress and key allies.

Yet the assessment, also based on accounts by Syrian activists and hundreds of YouTube videos of the attack's aftermath, has confounded many experts who cannot fathom what might have motivated Assad to unleash weapons of mass destruction on his own people - especially while U.N. experts were nearby and at a time when his troops had the upper hand on the ground.[256]

---

[256] Karam, Zeina; Dozier, Kimberly. "Syria Chemical Weapons Case Remains In Doubt As U.S. Refuses To Release Concrete Evidence." The Associated Press (AP). September 8, 2013. http://news.nationalpost.com/news/syria-chemical-weapons-case-remains-in-doubt-as-u-s-refuses-to-release-concrete-evidence

In short, John Kerry's "strong case" against Assad was no case at all.

2.) The White House Admitted It Had No Concrete Evidence

On September 8, White House Chief of Staff Dennis McDonough went on a number of Sunday talk shows to press the case for war in a coordinated propaganda campaign designed to lead up to the President's speech. Yet, during his appearance on CNN, McDonough admitted that the alleged proof being sold to the American people was based more on what he termed a "common sense test" not "irrefutable, beyond-a-reasonable-doubt evidence."[257]

McDonough stated "We've seen the video proof of the outcome of those attacks. All of that leads to a quite strong common-sense test irrespective of the intelligence that suggests that the regime carried this out. Now do we have a picture or do we have irrefutable beyond-a-reasonable-doubt evidence? This is not a court of law and intelligence does not work that way."[258]

He went on to absurdly claim that "nobody is rebutting the intelligence; nobody doubts the intelligence."[259]

In addition, McDonough stated that, by attacking Syria, the United States would be sending a message to Iran to cease their alleged attempts at developing a nuclear weapon and saying that this military strike would be a chance "to be bold with Iran." This, of course, is in direct contradiction to the propaganda being fed to the American people who have heretofore been told that the reason for the assault is due to a humanitarian tragedy, not merely for political intimidation.[260]

Regardless, as Slate wrote when reporting the McDonough statement,

> The answer highlights how the White House still has not shown the public a concrete piece of intelligence that directly connect Assad's regime to the alleged chemical weapons attack, as the Associated Press points out in a detailed story. Meanwhile, Syria and Russia insist it was the rebels who used chemical weapons, a charge they have also failed to prove with any actual evidence.[261]

---

[257] Politi, Daniel. "White House 'Common Sense Test' And Not 'Irrefutable' Evidence Hold Assad Responsible." The Slate. September 8, 2013.
http://www.slate.com/blogs/the_slatest/2013/09/08/dennis_mcdonough_white_house_says_c ommon_sense_test_links_assad_to_chemical.html

[258] Politi, Daniel. "White House 'Common Sense Test' And Not 'Irrefutable' Evidence Hold Assad Responsible." The Slate. September 8, 2013.
http://www.slate.com/blogs/the_slatest/2013/09/08/dennis_mcdonough_white_house_says_c ommon_sense_test_links_assad_to_chemical.html

[259] Politi, Daniel. "White House 'Common Sense Test' And Not 'Irrefutable' Evidence Hold Assad Responsible." The Slate. September 8, 2013.
http://www.slate.com/blogs/the_slatest/2013/09/08/dennis_mcdonough_white_house_says_c ommon_sense_test_links_assad_to_chemical.html

[260] Politi, Daniel. "White House 'Common Sense Test' And Not 'Irrefutable' Evidence Hold Assad Responsible." The Slate. September 8, 2013.
http://www.slate.com/blogs/the_slatest/2013/09/08/dennis_mcdonough_white_house_says_c ommon_sense_test_links_assad_to_chemical.html

The Daily Caller went even further by writing,

> The Obama administration has selectively used intelligence to justify military strikes on Syria, former military officers with access to the original intelligence reports say, in a manner that goes far beyond what critics charged the Bush administration of doing in the run-up to the 2003 Iraq war.

> According to these officers, who served in top positions in the United States, Britain, France, Israel, and Jordan, a Syrian military communication intercepted by Israel's famed Unit 8200 electronic intelligence outfit has been doctored so that it leads a reader to just the opposite conclusion reached by the original report.[262]

3.) The Evidence presented represents the rush to war, not an actual intelligence assessment.

Clearly, as any observer should understand, the rush to war and the propaganda push toward a stampede in that direction has rendered any reports of "intelligence" by the United States government and the rest of the Anglo-American world and/or Israel highly questionable at best. Recent memories of concrete "intelligence" allegedly proving the presence of WMDs in Iraq should serve as a prompt for the requirement of incontrovertible proof by the American people whenever the discussion of military action enter into the equation.

Yet the intelligence presented to the American people was not only based entirely upon a political motivation, the reality is that the report did not actually represent the true "intelligence" picture of the very intelligence agencies that are tasked with analyzing the facts on the ground. Rather, the report was nothing but the conglomeration of cherry-picked intelligence which was arranged to produce a picture that bolsters the position of the warmongers in the Anglo-American pyramid governing structure.

Even some former intelligence officials have stated this much in an interview with IPS news, claiming that the chemical warfare intelligence summary is not the presentation of intelligence agencies complete with their unbiased professional analysis (assuming that this would even be possible in the first place), but an entirely political document consisting of lies and opinions coming from the White House.

As IPS reports,

> Contrary to the general impression in Congress and the news media, the Syria chemical warfare intelligence summary released by the Barack Obama administration Aug. 30 did not represent an intelligence community assessment, an IPS analysis and interviews with former intelligence officials reveals.

---

[261] Politi, Daniel. "White House 'Common Sense Test' And Not 'Irrefutable' Evidence Hold Assad Responsible." The Slate. September 8, 2013. http://www.slate.com/blogs/the_slatest/2013/09/08/dennis_mcdonough_white_house_says_common_sense_test_links_assad_to_chemical.html

[262] Timmerman, Kenneth. "Verify Chemical Weapons Use Before Unleashing The Dogs Of War." The Daily Caller. August 29, 2013. http://dailycaller.com/2013/08/29/verify-chemical-weapons-use-before-unleashing-the-dogs-of-war/

The evidence indicates that Director of National Intelligence James Clapper culled intelligence analyses from various agencies and by the White House itself, but that the White House itself had the final say in the contents of the document.

Leading members of Congress to believe that the document was an intelligence community assessment and thus represents a credible picture of the intelligence on the alleged chemical attack of Aug. 21 has been a central element in the Obama administration's case for war in Syria.

That part of the strategy, at least, has been successful. Despite strong opposition in Congress to the proposed military strike in Syria, no one in either chamber has yet challenged the administration's characterisation of the intelligence. But the administration is vulnerable to the charge that it has put out an intelligence document that does not fully and accurately reflect the views of intelligence analysts.

Former intelligence officials told IPS that that the paper does not represent a genuine intelligence community assessment but rather one reflecting a predominantly Obama administration influence.

In essence, the White House selected those elements of the intelligence community assessments that supported the administration's policy of planning a strike against the Syrian government force and omitted those that didn't.[263]

Backing up its claims in this regard, IPS also points out numerous subtle giveaways that what Congress is actually viewing is not an intelligence picture but a propaganda piece. IPS writes,

In a radical departure from normal practice involving summaries or excerpts of intelligence documents that are made public, the Syria chemical weapons intelligence summary document was not released by the Office of the Director of National Intelligence but by the White House Office of the Press Secretary.

It was titled "Government Assessment of the Syrian Government's Use of Chemical Weapons on August 21, 2013." The first sentence begins, "The United States government assesses," and the second sentence begins, "We assess".

The introductory paragraph refers to the main body of the text as a summary of "the intelligence community's analysis" of the issue, rather than as an "intelligence community assessment", which would have been used had the entire intelligence community endorsed the document.

A former senior intelligence official who asked not to be identified told IPS in an e-mail Friday that the language used by the White House "means that this is not an intelligence community document".

The former senior official, who held dozens of security classifications over a decades-long intelligence career, said he had "never seen a document about an international crisis at any classification described/slugged as a U.S. government assessment."

---

[263] Porter, Gareth. "Obama's Case For Syria Didn't Reflect Intel Consensus." Inter Press Service (IPS News). September 9, 2013. http://www.ipsnews.net/2013/09/obamas-case-for-syria-didnt-reflect-intel-consensus/

The document further indicates that the administration "decided on a position and cherry-picked the intelligence to fit it," he said. "The result is not a balanced assessment of the intelligence."

Greg Thielmann, whose last position before retiring from the State Department was director of the Strategic, Proliferation and Military Affairs Office in the Bureau of Intelligence and Research, told IPS he has never seen a government document labeled "Government Assessment" either.

"If it's an intelligence assessment," Thielmann said, "why didn't they label it as such?"

Former National Intelligence Officer Paul Pillar, who has participated in drafting national intelligence estimates, said the intelligence assessment summary released by the White House "is evidently an administration document, and the working master copy may have been in someone's computer at the White House or National Security Council."

Pillar suggested that senior intelligence officials might have signed off on the administration paper, but that the White House may have drafted its own paper to "avoid attention to analytic differences within the intelligence community."

Comparable intelligence community assessments in the past, he observed – including the 2002 Iraq WMD estimate – include indications of differences in assessment among elements of the community.[264]

IPS also raises the question of whether or not Director of National Intelligence James Clapper, while involved in the compilation of the document, refused to attach his name to it due to lack of confidence in the report after it was revised and doctored by the White House. Clapper's name is nowhere to be found on the document.[265]

4.) Even members of Congress had serious doubts about the evidence.

While the U.S. Congress has never been particularly known for its ability to examine evidence and make an informed decision on it (absent a powerful financial lobbying campaign), some members, after having viewed the intelligence document, openly stated that they questioned the veracity of the claims therein and were not convinced by what they saw.

For instance, Washington's Blog recently compiled a short list of some of the remarks being made by several U.S. Congressional Representatives which presented statements such as the following:

Congressman Justin Amash said last week:

What I heard in Obama admn briefing actually makes me more skeptical of certain significant aspects of Pres's case for attacking.

---

[264] Porter, Gareth. "Obama's Case For Syria Didn't Reflect Intel Consensus." Inter Press Service (IPS News). September 9, 2013. http://www.ipsnews.net/2013/09/obamas-case-for-syria-didnt-reflect-intel-consensus/

[265] Porter, Gareth. "Obama's Case For Syria Didn't Reflect Intel Consensus." Inter Press Service (IPS News). September 9, 2013. http://www.ipsnews.net/2013/09/obamas-case-for-syria-didnt-reflect-intel-consensus/

He noted yesterday, after attending *another* classified briefing and reviewing more classified materials:

Attended another classified briefing on #Syria & reviewed add'l materials. Now more skeptical than ever. Can't believe Pres is pushing war.

And today, Amash wrote:

If Americans could read classified docs, they'd be even more against #Syria action. Obama admn's public statements are misleading at best.

Congressman Tom Harkin said:

I have just attended a classified Congressional briefing on Syria that quite frankly raised more questions than it answered. I found the evidence presented by Administration officials to be circumstantial.

Congressman Michael Burgess said:

Yes, I saw the classified documents. They were pretty thin.

Yahoo News reports:

New Hampshire Democratic Rep. Carol Shea-Porter, for instance, left Thursday's classified hearing and said she was opposed to the effort "now so more than ever."

"I think there's a long way to go for the president to make the case," she said after the briefing. "It does seem there is a high degree of concern and leaning no."

Senator Joe Manchin announced he was voting "no" for a Syria strike right after hearing a classified intelligence briefing.

One of the most vocal Representatives, however, was Alan Grayson who wrote a scathing criticism of the report presented to Congress which was printed in the New York Times. He wrote,

The documentary record regarding an attack on Syria consists of just two papers: a four-page unclassified summary and a 12-page classified summary. The first enumerates only the evidence in favor of an attack. I'm not allowed to tell you what's in the classified summary, but you can draw your own conclusion.

On Thursday I asked the House Intelligence Committee staff whether there was any other documentation available, classified or unclassified. Their answer was "no."

The Syria chemical weapons summaries are based on several hundred underlying elements of intelligence information. The unclassified summary cites intercepted telephone calls, "social media" postings and the like, but not one of these is actually quoted or attached — not even clips from YouTube. (As to whether the classified summary is the same, I couldn't possibly comment, but again, draw your own conclusion.)

***

And yet we members are supposed to accept, without question, that the proponents of a strike on Syria have accurately depicted the underlying evidence, even though the proponents refuse to show any of it to us or to the American public.

In fact, even gaining access to just the classified summary involves a series of unreasonably high hurdles.

We have to descend into the bowels of the Capitol Visitors Center, to a room four levels underground. Per the instructions of the chairman of the House Intelligence Committee, note-taking is not allowed.

Once we leave, we are not permitted to discuss the classified summary with the public, the media, our constituents or even other members. Nor are we allowed to do anything to verify the validity of the information that has been provided.

And this is just the classified summary. It is my understanding that the House Intelligence Committee made a formal request for the underlying intelligence reports several days ago. I haven't heard an answer yet. And frankly, I don't expect one.

***

By refusing to disclose the underlying data even to members of Congress, the administration is making it impossible for anyone to judge, independently, whether that statement is correct.[266]

5.) The US intelligence document clashes with all of the other evidence.

As I wrote in my article, "New Chemical Weapons Attack In Syria Another False Flag?" it has been the case with every other propaganda push against Assad regarding chemical weapons, that there is absolutely no evidence to implicate the Syrian government in the launching and use of chemical agents against the Syrian people or even the death squads. In fact, the accounts being published throughout the mainstream media are very suspect in their own right.

Although there is some video evidence of chemical weapons usage, the estimates of the extent of the atrocity, as well as the blame for the attacks, are coming entirely from the death squads themselves. It is thus important to point out that statistics and information is prefaced by the phrase "activists say."

"Activists say," of course, can be translated merely to mean "death squads" say, as the activists being referred to are indeed nothing more than terrorist killers - politically, ideologically, and physically - invested in the outcome and presentation of the Syrian crisis. In short, these individuals have a vested interest in the blame for these attacks being placed on Assad, popular opinion being turned against the Syrian government, and some type of condemnation or military action being taken against the Syrian army.

Even more interesting is the fact that the chemical weapons attacks came just days after a team of U.N. chemical experts entered Damascus and checked into a hotel a few miles from the targeted area. With this in mind, one must ask "why would Assad order the use of chemical weapons in this area at such an inopportune time?" Given the track record of Assad's cleverness, this seems to be an incredibly foolish move, even as the Syrian army has gained the clear upper hand against the death squads. Why detonate chemical

---

[266] "Congress Members Who Have Seen Classified Evidence About Syria Say It Fails To Prove Anything." Washington's Blog. September 7, 2013.
http://www.washingtonsblog.com/2013/09/classified-intelligence-doesnt-prove-anything.html

weapons in front of UN chemical experts? Why wait until after they arrive to do so? Why detonate chemical weapons so close to them?

These questionable details have caused even mainstream "experts" to hesitate when commenting on the nature of the alleged chemical attacks. For instance, Charles Lister, an analyst at IHS Jane's Terrorism and Insurgency Center, stated, "Logically, it would make little sense for the Syrian government to employ chemical agents at such a time, particularly given the relatively close proximity of the targeted towns (to the U.N. team)."[267]

Nonetheless, the Ghouta region (where the attacks were reported) is well known for its opposition leanings. Jabhat al-Nusra has had a long-time presence there and the region bore the brunt of sustained military pressure for months.

BBC security correspondent Frank Garnder also stated something similar, when he said, "Firstly, the timing is odd, bordering on suspicious. Why would the Assad government, which has recently been retaking ground from the rebels, carry out a chemical attack while UN weapons inspectors are in the country?"[268]

Likewise, Swedish diplomat and former UN weapons inspector Rolf Ekeus stated to Reuters that, "It would be very peculiar if it was the government to do this at the exact moment the international inspectors come into the country….at the least, it wouldn't be very clever."[269]

Another Swede, chemical weapons expert Ake Sellstrom, who is currently leading the UN inspection team in Syria, told SVT that the large number of victims being reported sounded "suspicious."[270]

In addition, soon after the attacks, Russian Foreign Ministry Spokesman Alexansdr Lukashevich stated that the attacks may have been a "provocation planned in advance" promoted for political purposes by "biased regional media."[271]

Lukashevich also said, "It draws attention to the fact that biased regional media have immediately, as if on command, begun an aggressive information attack, laying all the responsibility on the government."[272]

---

[267] "Hundreds Of Syrians Killed In Alleged Chemical Attack By Assad's Forces." The Jerusalem Post. August 21, 2013. http://www.jpost.com/Middle-East/Assad-forces-allegedly-use-chemical-agents-in-bombardment-killing-hundreds-323754

[268] "Syria Conflict: 'Chemical Attacks Kill Hundreds.'" BBC. August 21, 2013. http://www.bbc.com/news/world-middle-east-23777201

[269] "White House Seeks UN Inquiry On Alleged New Syrian Chemical Site." Nuclear Threat Initiative. (NTI.org). August 21, 2013. http://www.nti.org/gsn/article/white-house-urges-inquiry-syrian-chemical-strike/

[270] "'Poisonous Gas' Attack By Regime Troops Kills At Least 100 In Syria, Activists Say." FOX News. August 21, 2013. http://www.foxnews.com/world/2013/08/21/syrian-opposition-claims-poisonous-gas-attack.html

[271] "Russia Suggests 'Chemical Attack' Was 'Planned Provocation' By Rebels." RT. August 21, 2013. https://www.rt.com/news/russia-syria-chemical-attack-801/

[272] "Russia Suggests 'Chemical Attack' Was 'Planned Provocation' By Rebels." RT. August 21, 2013. https://www.rt.com/news/russia-syria-chemical-attack-801/

When Lukashevich referred to "biased regional media" he most likely means news agencies such as Al-Arabiya who, according to William Engdahl, was the agency who broke the initial story regarding claims of 500 deaths from chemical attacks, reports which were taken almost entirely from "activists" aka death squads. After the initial reports were made by Al-Arabiya the massive wave of Western media picked up the story and ran with it, inflating the numbers of victims almost every hour, finally reaching claims of 1,300 deaths.[273]

As Engdahl writes,

> Al Arabiya, the origin of the story, is not a neutral in the Syrian conflict. It was set up in 2002 by the Saudi Royal Family in Dubai. It is majority-owned by the Saudi broadcaster, Middle East Broadcasting Center (MBC). Saudi Arabia is a major financial backer of the attempt to topple Syria's government. That is a matter of record. So on first glance Saudi-owned media reporting such an inflammatory anti-Assad allegation might be taken with a dose of salt.[274]

In addition, the Russian spokesman also added that "A homemade rocket with a poisonous substance that has not been identified yet – one similar to the rocket used by terrorists on March 19 in Khan al-Assal - was fired early on August 21 [at Damascus suburbs] from a position occupied by the insurgents."[275]

As RT reported in their article "Russia suggests Syria 'chemical attack' was 'planned provocation' by rebels,"

> Lukashevich pointed out that similar reports about Syrian authorities allegedly using chemical weapons have popped up before. However, the information has never been confirmed.

> In Moscow's view, the latest possible "provocation" might be the opposition's attempt to get support from the UN Security Council and undermine the Geneva peace talks on Syria.

> Russia believes the incident should be thoroughly investigated by professionals. It urged everyone who has influence on armed extremists to do everything possible to finally put an end to such provocations involving chemical poisonous substances.[276]

Obviously, Lukashevich and the Russian government had ample reason to suspect that the recent chemical weapons attack in Syria was the handiwork of the death squads instead of the Syrian government.[277]

---

[273] "Syria Gas Attack Story Has Whiff Of Saudi War Propaganda." RT. August 21, 2013. http://rt.com/op-edge/syria-gas-attack-chemical-propaganda-796/

[274] "Syria Gas Attack Story Has Whiff Of Saudi War Propaganda." RT. August 21, 2013. http://rt.com/op-edge/syria-gas-attack-chemical-propaganda-796/

[275] "Russia Suggests 'Chemical Attack' Was 'Planned Provocation' By Rebels." RT. August 21, 2013. https://www.rt.com/news/russia-syria-chemical-attack-801/

[276] "Russia Suggests 'Chemical Attack' Was 'Planned Provocation' By Rebels." RT. August 21, 2013. https://www.rt.com/news/russia-syria-chemical-attack-801/

[277] Turbeville, Brandon. "False Flag Attacks In Syria Pin Atrocities On Assad And Justify 'Red Line' Engagement." Activist Post. March 30, 2015. http://www.activistpost.com/2013/03/false-flag-attacks-in-syria-pin.html

Despite the fact that the ridiculous "red line" talk began being repeated in government halls and press conferences since late 2012 by both President Barack Obama and then-Secretary of State Hillary Clinton as well as French President Francois Hollande, the idea that the Syrian government would be the party to actually use chemical weapons was patently absurd from the beginning.

As far back as June 2012, the pieces were clearly seen being moved into place in order to create the environment and subsequent chain of events for a successful false flag attack used to justify an invasion of or, at the very least, some limited military action against Syria. However, the more hidden aspects being used to create infrastructure for such an event could be seen going back even further.

I would encourage the readers to access my article "Propaganda Overdrive Suggests Syria War Coming Soon," in order to get a glimpse into the false narrative supplied by the Western media regarding a series of propagandized chemical weapons attacks inside Syria as a justification for military action. The issue is also discussed elsewhere within this book. [278]

Add this to the report provided by Dale Gavlak of Mint Press which revealed admission by Syrian death squads that they themselves were responsible for the chemical weapons attack in Ghouta and one can clearly see that the evidence being presented by the United States regarding these attacks is hanging by a thread with much of what is being promoted as fact not existing at all.[279]

It is also important to note that the death squads claimed they were given both the chemical weapons and their salaries by Saudi Prince Bandar bin Sultan, also known as Bandar Bush due to his close ties with the Bush family. The weapons were apparently supposed to have gone directly to al-Qaeda fighters such as Jabhat al-Nusra.

In the end, the "intelligence documents" and alleged proof provided by the Obama administration was nothing more than Iraq 2.0 – a determination to go to war with a Middle Eastern nation which has done absolutely nothing to harm the United States on the basis of fabricated intelligence and propagandized "proof" surrounding lies of "crimes against humanity," and WMDs.

If anyone has the feeling that somehow we have been here before it is because we have. We cannot afford another foreign military adventure where untold numbers of innocent people will be slaughtered for the good of geopolitical concerns, the military-industrial complex, corporations, Wall Street, or esoteric agendas. We cannot afford such a war either financially, physically, or spiritually. It is time to get off the Path to Persia while we still have the ability to do so.[280]

---

[278] Turbeville, Brandon. "Propaganda Overdrive Suggests Syria War Coming Soon." Activist Post. August 24, 2013. http://www.activistpost.com/2013/08/propaganda-overdrive-suggests-syria-war.html

[279] Gavlak, Dale; Ababneh, Yahya. "Syrians In Ghouta Claim Saudi-Supplied Rebels Behind Chemical Attack." Mint Press News. August 29, 2013.
http://www.mintpressnews.com/witnesses-of-gas-attack-say-saudis-supplied-rebels-with-chemical-weapons/168135/

[280] Pollack, Kenneth M.; Byman, Daniel L.; Indyk, Martin; Maloney, Suzanne; O'Hanlon, Michael

Chemical Weapons Victims Were Staged Using Kidnapped Hostages: Report

In the aftermath of the release of the UN report on the Ghouta chemical weapons attack, it was clear that the propaganda push against the Syrian government and Bashar al-Assad was still in full swing.[281] Indeed, with headlines such as "Forensic Details in UN Report Point To Assad's Use of Gas" by the New York Times and "UN report confirms chemical weapons use in Syria" by NBC, Western media outlets attempted to do the thinking for the American people and determine that not only did Assad use chemical weapons but that the UN investigators were responsible for this determination.[282] [283]

Of course, the task of the investigators was not to determine who used the chemical weapons, only to determine whether or not they were used to begin with. Still, Western governments and their media mouthpieces have been adamant in placing the blame on Assad, despite all relevant and available evidence showing that it was, in fact, the death squads running rampant in Syria that used the chemical weapons.[284]

Yet, while so much attention was placed on the UN chemical weapons report (which was not tasked with determining the guilt over who used the chemical weapons), very little attention was paid to another report compiled by the International Support Team for Mussalaha (Consilience) in Syria for the International Institute For Peace, Justice, and Human Rights released on September 15, 2013.

The report, entitled "The Chemical Attacks On East Ghouta: To Justify Military Right To Protect Intervention In Syria," and authored largely by Mother Agnes Mariam of the Cross, who is President of ISTEAMS, not only argues that the chemical weapons attacks

---

E.; Riedel, Bruce. "Which Path To Persia? Options For A New American Strategy Toward Iran." The Saban Center For Middle East Policy At The Brookings Institution. Analysis Paper Number 20. June, 2009.
http://www.brookings.edu/~/media/research/files/papers/2009/6/iran%20strategy/06_iran_st rategy.pdf

[281] "United Nations General Assembly Security Council: A/68/663-S/2013/735" "Agenda Item 33: Prevention of Armed Conflict." "Identical letters dated 13 December 2013 from the Secretary-General addressed to the President of the General Assembly and the President of the Security CouncilDecember 13, 2013.
http://www.un.org/ga/search/view_doc.asp?symbol=A/68/663

[282] Gladstone, Rick; Chivers, C.J.; "Forensic Details In Report Point To Assad's Use of Gas." New York Times. September 16, 2013. http://www.nytimes.com/2013/09/17/world/europe/syria-united-nations.html?_r=0

[283] Dann, Carrie. "UN Report Confirms Chemical Weapons Use In Syria." NBC News. September 17, 2013. http://www.nbcnews.com/news/other/un-report-confirms-chemical-weapons-use-syria-f8C11169027

[284] "Russia Will Give UN 'Proof' Of Syria Rebel Chemical Usage." BBC. September 18, 2013. http://www.bbc.com/news/world-middle-east-24140475
See also,
"5 Ways 'Incontrovertible Evidence' On Syria Is Controvertible." Activist Post. September 12, 2013. http://www.activistpost.com/2013/09/5-ways-incontrovertible-evidence-on.html

were the handiwork of the Syrian death squads, but also that the entire ordeal was a carefully crafted and planned propaganda campaign utilizing kidnapped citizens from Lattakia, Syria as stage props.[285]

Latakia was the area which was invaded and overrun by death squads in early August 2013, with 11 Alawite villages being overrun on August 4and over 150 women and children abducted by Jobhat al Nusra. Allegedly, the Nusra Front was attempting to use them as ransom for the release of jailed detainees.[286]

In addition, shortly before the Ghouta chemical attack, dozens of civilians were abducted in Rabiha and marched through the streets as if they were cattle.[287]

While the whereabouts of these individuals were unknown ever since their disappearance, some of them were identified by virtue of photographs and YouTube videos shown to relatives of the chemical weapons attacks in Ghouta.

In other words, a number of the Lattakia kidnapping victims were later discovered in Ghouta as victims of the chemical weapons attack.[288]

As the ISTEAMS report states,

> On the other hand, we are in close contact with the survivors of the horrendous massacres perpetrated the 4th of August 2013 by Jobhat El Nosra and allies in eleven villages from Lattakiah mountains. As a Reconciliation Committee we are trying to liberate more than 150 women and children, abducted under the pretext to exchange them with detainees. We have been contacted by the families of some abducted women and children. They recognize their relatives in the videos published online that show the alleged victims of the Chemical Attack in East Ghouta.[289]

Of course, unless these kidnapping victims managed to escape and then decided to start their lives over in Ghouta without telling their families back home and, additionally, did

---

[285] "The Chemical Attacks On East Ghouta: To Justify Military Right To Protect Intervention In Syria." International Support Team For Mussahala (Consilience) In Syria. September 15, 2013. http://tarpley.net/docs/20130915-ISTeams-Ghouta-Report.pdf

[286] "Syria Undeniable PROOF SNC & Al Farok Did Chemical Weapons Attack In Syria 8 21 2013." Youtube. Posted by Neveah West. Posted on September 30, 2016. https://www.youtube.com/watch?v=FdF6aSnxhDs&feature=player_embedded#t=130 Video shows film of civilians being kidnapped by terrorist groups and marched away down the street. It also shows terrorists loading and using chemical weapons.

[287] "Syria Undeniable PROOF SNC & Al Farok Did Chemical Weapons Attack In Syria 8 21 2013." Youtube. Posted by Neveah West. Posted on September 30, 2016. https://www.youtube.com/watch?v=FdF6aSnxhDs&feature=player_embedded#t=130 Video shows film of civilians being kidnapped by terrorist groups and marched away down the street. It also shows terrorists loading and using chemical weapons.

[288] "The Chemical Attacks On East Ghouta: To Justify Military Right To Protect Intervention In Syria." International Support Team For Mussahala (Consilience) In Syria. September 15, 2013. http://tarpley.net/docs/20130915-ISTeams-Ghouta-Report.pdf

[289] "The Chemical Attacks On East Ghouta: To Justify Military Right To Protect Intervention In Syria." International Support Team For Mussahala (Consilience) In Syria. September 15, 2013. http://tarpley.net/docs/20130915-ISTeams-Ghouta-Report.pdf

so all at the same time, it is indeed compelling evidence that the death squads were not only responsible for the chemical weapons attack but that they (most likely with Western help) were responsible for a coordinated and planned false flag attack which would subsequently be blamed on the Assad government.

Mother Agnes Mariam and ISTEAMS also showed further evidence that the Ghouta chemical attacks were an entirely scripted event by demonstrating that, prior to the chemical weapons attack, Ghouta was largely a ghost town with residents having fled as a result of both the death squad incursion and the subsequent shelling of the area by the Syrian army. The report states,

> East Ghouta is a distant eastern suburb of Damascus that was until recently a farming community. The urban population came mostly from Damascus and fled there as refugees to family members when rebels seized the town. Ghouta is no longer a community that includes women and children, but rather an armed camp of militant men, including many violent zealots. The social picture represented in insurgent videos is at complete variance with the demographic facts and street scenes of Ghouta under occupation – there are no women or children to be seen at all.[290]

Later the report contains personal testimony indicating the abandoned nature of Ghouta. It states,

> I was in Damascus two days before. There was the heaviest shelling from the Syrian legal army on the East Ghouta. Going out to Lebanon I have seen thousands of refugees fleeing the targeted areas. It means that the area that was already emptied from its population was more emptied during the heavy attack of the Syrian army.[291]

Referring to a young boy that was interviewed about the chemical weapons attack, the report continues by writing, "Hear the little orphan who was interviewed having allegedly lost his parents: 'who else died among your friends and neighbors?' He said 'nobody.' They had already left or are refugees."[292]

Referring to a young boy named Abdullah, the report states,

> This boy, Abdullah, does not say where he lives in East Ghouta. He asserts what everybody in Damascus and its rural area knows: that most of the neighbors had already fled from their houses because the East Ghouta is a semi destroyed area due to the continuous clashes between the rebels and the Syrian army and the violent aerial strikes and shellings of the Syrian army.[293]

---

[290] "The Chemical Attacks On East Ghouta: To Justify Military Right To Protect Intervention In Syria." International Support Team For Mussahala (Consilience) In Syria. September 15, 2013. http://tarpley.net/docs/20130915-ISTeams-Ghouta-Report.pdf

[291] "The Chemical Attacks On East Ghouta: To Justify Military Right To Protect Intervention In Syria." International Support Team For Mussahala (Consilience) In Syria. September 15, 2013. http://tarpley.net/docs/20130915-ISTeams-Ghouta-Report.pdf

[292] "The Chemical Attacks On East Ghouta: To Justify Military Right To Protect Intervention In Syria." International Support Team For Mussahala (Consilience) In Syria. September 15, 2013. http://tarpley.net/docs/20130915-ISTeams-Ghouta-Report.pdf

[293] "The Chemical Attacks On East Ghouta: To Justify Military Right To Protect Intervention In Syria." International Support Team For Mussahala (Consilience) In Syria. September 15, 2013. http://tarpley.net/docs/20130915-ISTeams-Ghouta-Report.pdf

In short, the ISTEAMS report suggests, with relevant evidence, that women and children kidnapped in Lattakia and Rabiha were taken to Ghouta and used as stage props for a false flag attack to be blamed on Assad and used to justify a Western military action against Syria.[294]

The report also mentions photos and videos which were broadcast as photographic evidence of the death of the Ghouta residents early on in the immediate aftermath of the attacks and the propaganda push that followed it. ISTEAMS points out, however, that these photos and videos were not taken in Ghouta or even in Syria at all, but that they were actually photos taken from Cairo Egypt during the Muslim Brotherhood riots. The photos used to show dead bodies of Syrian adults were, in fact, photos of dead Muslim Brotherhood supporters in Egypt.[295] [296]

Such ruthless propaganda efforts hearken back to the earlier efforts to frame the Syrian army for the Houla massacre or even the recent photograph touted by the BBC as evidence of a mass murder by the Assad regime – a child jumping over what appears to be hundreds of dead bodies wrapped in burial shrouds – but what actually turned out to be a photograph taken in Iraq in 2003.[297] [298]

Indeed, the conclusion of the report reads as follows:

> After insurgents murdered the men in these communities, they organized mass abductions of the surviving women and children. ISTEAMS' report includes evidence that links these abductions to the ensuing chemical attacks(s) that killed mainly women, children, and infants in Ghouta, east of Damascus, on August 21, 2013. Women and children who went missing after their families were massacred in Latakia appear to be among the Ghouta victims shown in western propaganda videos.[299]

In the end, the Ghouta chemical attacks were, at best, an example of the Anglo-Americans and Western media seizing upon a crisis for a political purpose. At worst, the attacks were an entirely staged and coordinated event designed to justify military action

---

[294] "The Chemical Attacks On East Ghouta: To Justify Military Right To Protect Intervention In Syria." International Support Team For Mussahala (Consilience) In Syria. September 15, 2013. http://tarpley.net/docs/20130915-ISTeams-Ghouta-Report.pdf

[295] "The Chemical Attacks On East Ghouta: To Justify Military Right To Protect Intervention In Syria." International Support Team For Mussahala (Consilience) In Syria. September 15, 2013. http://tarpley.net/docs/20130915-ISTeams-Ghouta-Report.pdf

[296] Ayah, Aman. "Egypt's Massacre, Viewed From Field Hospital." Al-Monitor. August 16, 2013. http://www.al-monitor.com/pulse/originals/2013/08/egypt-muslim-brotherhood-massacre-sisi.html

[297] "Prime German Paper: Syrian Rebels Committed Houla Massacre." Global Research. June 10, 2012. http://www.globalresearch.ca/breaking-prime-german-paper-syrian-rebels-committed-houla-massacre/31339

[298] "BBC News Uses 'Iraq Photo To Illustrate Syrian Massacre.'" The Telegraph. May 27, 2012. http://www.telegraph.co.uk/news/worldnews/middleeast/syria/9293620/BBC-News-uses-Iraq-photo-to-illustrate-Syrian-massacre.html

[299] "The Chemical Attacks On East Ghouta: To Justify Military Right To Protect Intervention In Syria." International Support Team For Mussahala (Consilience) In Syria. September 15, 2013. http://tarpley.net/docs/20130915-ISTeams-Ghouta-Report.pdf

against Syria. Unfortunately, considering the evidence presented by the ISTEAMS report, the latter seems more likely.

New U.N. Chemical Weapons Report Contradicts The Previous U.N. Report

After having some time to regroup, Western-backed propaganda against the Assad government of Syria regarding the alleged (and erroneous) claims of the use of chemical weapons against rebels death squads and civilians resumed.

As Reuters reported, "United Nations human rights investigators said on Tuesday they had "reasonable grounds" to believe that limited amounts of chemical weapons had been used by government forces in Syria."[300]

Reuters also stated that "In their latest report, based on interviews with victims, medical staff and other witnesses, they said they had received allegations that both Syrian government forces and rebels had used the banned weapons, but that at least four instances related to their use by state forces."[301]

Paulo Pinheiro, chair of the UN Commission of Inquiry, told a news conference in Geneva, Switzerland "There are reasonable grounds to believe that limited quantities of toxic chemicals weapons were used. It has not been possible, on the evidence available, to determine the precise chemical agents used, their delivery systems or the perpetrator."[302]

Pinheiro stated that the information he was reporting came from interviews conducted with "victims, refugees who fled some areas, and medical staff." The interview process, as Reuters reports, involved teams "composed of more than 20 investigators, conducted 430 interviews from January 15 to May 15 among refugees in neighboring countries and by Skype with people still in Syria."[303]

The UN Commission of Inquiry largely contradicted earlier reports by its own UN investigators into the nature of chemical weapons' use in Syria.

For instance, UN investigator Carla del Ponte stated to Western media outlets as far back as March that chemicals weapons were used, not by the Syrian government, but the Syrian death squads that the Western media so desperately attempts to promote as freedom fighters and peaceful protesters.[304]

---

[300] "UN Has "Reasonable Grounds' To Believe Assad Forces Used Chemical Weapons." Haaretz. June 4, 2013. http://www.haaretz.com/news/middle-east/un-has-reasonable-grounds-to-believe-assad-forces-used-chemical-weapons-in-syria-1.527720
[301] "UN Has "Reasonable Grounds' To Believe Assad Forces Used Chemical Weapons." Haaretz. June 4, 2013. http://www.haaretz.com/news/middle-east/un-has-reasonable-grounds-to-believe-assad-forces-used-chemical-weapons-in-syria-1.527720
[302] "UN Has "Reasonable Grounds' To Believe Assad Forces Used Chemical Weapons." Haaretz. June 4, 2013. http://www.haaretz.com/news/middle-east/un-has-reasonable-grounds-to-believe-assad-forces-used-chemical-weapons-in-syria-1.527720
[303] "UN Has "Reasonable Grounds' To Believe Assad Forces Used Chemical Weapons." Haaretz. June 4, 2013. http://www.haaretz.com/news/middle-east/un-has-reasonable-grounds-to-believe-assad-forces-used-chemical-weapons-in-syria-1.527720

Interestingly enough, while media outlets and Western governments cling to whatever brief positive public relations stories surrounding the "rebels" that may exist, those opportunities are few and far between.

In addition, it must be pointed out the inaccurate and intentionally skewed manner in which Western media outlets, "human rights campaigners," and Western governments gather "information" that is later parroted back to the public through those same media outlets. For instance, the reliance on "interviews" conducted with "activists," "human rights organizations," "victims," "medical personnel," and, obviously, "rebel" forces generally translates to mean one thing – interviews and reports with and from the very agents and organizations that are intent on destabilizing and overthrowing the Assad government to begin with.

Organizations like the Syrian Observatory for Human Rights, operated out of the UK by an admitted member of the Syrian death squad cult, Rami Abdul Rahman, are a clear example of the types of "human rights organizations" consulted when "investigators" attempt to "gather information" on the situation on the ground in Syria.

As Tony Cartalucci of Land Destroyer writes,

> In reality, the Syrian Observatory for Human Rights has long ago been exposed as an absurd propaganda front operated by Rami Abdul Rahman out of his house in England's countryside.[305] According to a December 2011 Reuters article titled, "Coventry - an unlikely home to prominent Syria activist," Abdul Rahman admits he is a member of the so-called "Syrian opposition" and seeks the ouster of Syrian President Bashar Al Assad:

> After three short spells in prison in Syria for pro-democracy activism, Abdulrahman came to Britain in 2000 fearing a longer, fourth jail term.

> "I came to Britain the day Hafez al-Assad died, and I'll return when Bashar al-Assad goes," Abdulrahman said, referring to Bashar's father and predecessor Hafez, also an autocrat.[306]

> One could not fathom a more unreliable, compromised, biased source of information, yet for the past two years, his "Observatory" has served as the sole source of information for the endless torrent of propaganda emanating from the Western media. Perhaps worst of all, is that the United Nations uses this compromised, absurdly overt source of propaganda as the basis for its various reports . . . .[307]

---

[304] "UN's del Ponte Says Evidence Syrian Rebels 'Used Sarin." BBC. May 6, 2013. http://www.youtube.com/watch?feature=player_embedded&v=sY_9SrIUVwU#%21

[305] Cartalucci, Tony. "West's Syrian Narrative Based On 'Guy In British Apartment." Land Destroyer Report. June 4, 2012. http://landdestroyer.blogspot.com.au/2012/06/wests-syrian-narrative-based-on-guy-in.html

[306] Abbas, Mohammad. "Coventry – An Unlikely Home To Prominent Syria Activist." Reuters. December 8, 2011. http://uk.reuters.com/article/uk-britain-syria-idUKTRE7B71XG20111208

[307] Cartalucci, Tony. "EXPOSED: Syrian Human Rights Front Is EU-Funded Fraud." Land Destroyer Report. April 12, 2013. http://landdestroyer.blogspot.com/2013/04/exposed-syrian-human-rights-front-is-eu.html

It is also widely known that any mainstream Western media which uses the term "activists say" to preface any transmission of information can easily be understood as having come straight from the death squads themselves. Likewise with many of the selected "victims" and "refugees," a majority of which bring their own political agendas with them which conveniently tends to match up exactly with the agenda of the Western powers seeking to destroy Syria.

Yet, while the report accuses the Assad government of using chemical weapons on the basis of scant, dubious, and even outright erroneous evidence, it also attempts to defend the Syrian death squads. It reads, "It is possible that anti-government armed groups may access and use chemical weapons . . . though there is no compelling evidence that these groups possess such weapons or their requisite delivery systems."[308]

This claim is fundamentally untrue. First, as mentioned above, it directly contradicts the reports by other UN investigators such as Carla Del Ponte.

Second, as mentioned earlier, in December 2012, a video was obtained by the Syria Tribune and subsequently released in their report and posted on YouTube which allegedly showed the NATO-backed death squads testing chemical weapons on "lab" rabbits.[309]

As the Syria Tribune describes the video,

> The video (see here)[310] starts with several scenes showing chemical containers with Tekkim labels (Tekkim is a Turkish chemicals company)[311] and some lab equipment,[312] while playing Jihadists chants in the background. A glass box then appears with two rabbits inside, with a poster on the wall behind it reading *The Almighty Wind Brigade (Kateebat A Reeh Al Sarsar)*. A person wearing a lab mask then mixes chemicals in a beaker in the glass box, and we see some gas emitting from the beaker. About a minute later, the rabbits start to have random convulsions and then die.[313] The person

[308] "UN Has "Reasonable Grounds' To Believe Assad Forces Used Chemical Weapons." Haaretz. June 4, 2013. http://www.haaretz.com/news/middle-east/un-has-reasonable-grounds-to-believe-assad-forces-used-chemical-weapons-in-syria-1.527720

[309] "US, NATO, GCC-Backed Terrorists Preparing Chemical Attack?" Syria Tribune. December 7, 2012. http://landdestroyer.blogspot.com/2012/12/us-nato-gcc-backed-terrorists-preparing.html

[310] "Syrian Rebels Testing Tekkim Chemicals To Use As Chemical Weapons." Youtube. Posted by Syria Tribune. Posted on December 5, 2012. https://www.youtube.com/watch?v=H-6O-gApVrU The video's description (accurate) reads in the following way:
This video appeared on YouTube yesterday showing what appears to be a rebel group in Syria testing a chemical combination to be used as a chemical weapon (most likely nerve agents as judged by the reaction of lab rabbits in the video) and threatening to use this chem weapon against civilians in Syria on a sectarian basis.

[311] Tekkim.com. Tekkim website. http://www.tekkim.com.tr/

[312] "US, NATO, GCC-Backed Terrorists Preparing Chemical Attack?" Syria Tribune. December 7, 2012. http://landdestroyer.blogspot.com/2012/12/us-nato-gcc-backed-terrorists-preparing.html

[313] "US, NATO, GCC-Backed Terrorists Preparing Chemical Attack?" Syria Tribune. December 7, 2012. http://landdestroyer.blogspot.com/2012/12/us-nato-gcc-backed-terrorists-

says: *You saw what happened? This will be your fate, you infidel Alawites, I swear by ALLAH to make you die like these rabbits, one minute only after you inhale the gas.*[314]

The Syria Tribune also comments that "Judging from the rabbits' reaction, the gas must be a nerve agent. The number of containers, if not a bluff, indicates ability to produce a considerable amount of this gas. Deployment could be by means of a smoke generator placed in the target area, an explosion, possibly a suicide one, of a "chemmed" car, or simply by using a humidifier."[315]

In March, 2013, yet another YouTube video was released which contained a clip of a second "test" of chemical weapons on captive rabbits by the death squads.[316]

This is quite an ironic presentation, since the Assad government has repeatedly vowed never to use chemical weapons inside Syria, while the death squads have repeatedly threatened to do just that. Indeed, in direct contrast to the tone and statements of the death squads, the Syrian Foreign Ministry spokesman Jihad Makdissi issued a statement several months ago saying, "No chemical or biological weapons will ever be used, and I repeat, will never be used, during the crisis in Syria no matter what the developments inside Syria."[317]

Regardless, the video mentioned above also contains an alleged audio recording of a phone conversation between two Free Syrian Army fighters discussing the "details of a plan to carry out a chemical weapons attack capable of impacting an area the size of one kilometer."[318]

As Paul Joseph Watson writes,

> The recording of the phone conversation purports to be between two FSA militants, one inside Syria and one outside of the country. Abu Hassan, the militant inside Syria, asks the person on the other end of the line to transmit a message to Sheikh Suleiman, a rebel-seized army base in Aleppo, asking for "two chemical bombs ….phosphoric" in order to "finish this whole thing."[319]

---

preparing.html

[314] "US, NATO, GCC-Backed Terrorists Preparing Chemical Attack?" Syria Tribune. December 7, 2012. http://landdestroyer.blogspot.com/2012/12/us-nato-gcc-backed-terrorists-preparing.html

[315] "US, NATO, GCC-Backed Terrorists Preparing Chemical Attack?" Syria Tribune. December 7, 2012. http://landdestroyer.blogspot.com/2012/12/us-nato-gcc-backed-terrorists-preparing.html

[316] "West Turns A Blind Eye That Their Terrorists In Syria Used WMDs, Against All Evidence." Youtube. Posted by nuts flipped. Posted on March 20, 2013. http://www.youtube.com/watch?feature=player_embedded&v=BLAMVtLq2V0#!

[317] "UN Told Syria Will Never Use WMDs." Press Tv. August 12, 2012. http://www.presstv.com/detail/2012/12/08/276916/un-told-syria-will-never-use-wmds/

[318] "Syria Says Chemical Or Biological Weapons Could Be Used If There Is 'External Aggression.'" CBS News. July 23, 2012. http://www.cbsnews.com/news/syria-says-chemical-or-biological-weapons-could-be-used-if-there-is-external-aggression/

[319] "West Turns A Blind Eye That Their Terrorists In Syria Used WMDs, Against All Evidence." Youtube. Posted by nuts flipped. Posted on March 20, 2013. http://www.youtube.com/watch?feature=player_embedded&v=BLAMVtLq2V0#!

"I want them to be effective," states Hassan, adding, "The radius of the strike, or reach of the gases, has to be 1km."[320]

The video also contains a clip of the death squads openly announcing their plans to engage in chemical weapons attacks, all the while surrounded by bottles of nitric acid and other substances. In addition, even more circumstantial evidence points toward the possession, delivery capabilities, and use of chemical weapons by the death squads.

As detailed earlier, back in December 2012, after the death squads managed to capture a chlorine factory inside Syria, the Syrian government actually issued a warning that the death squads might attempt to use chemical weapons of this nature in their battle to overthrow and oppress the government and people of Syria respectively. The Syrian Foreign Ministry stated, "Terrorist groups may resort to using chemical weapons against the Syrian people ... after having gained control of a toxic chlorine factory."[321]

Thus, with the subsequent chemical weapon attack which has caused both a frothing and bumbling public relations response from the Anglo-Americans, it is interesting to note that chlorine was fingered as being one of the major ingredients.

As Alex Thomson of The Telegraph reported,

> The Syrian military is said to believe that a home-made locally-manufactured rocket was fired, containing a form of chlorine known as CL17, easily available as a swimming pool cleaner. They claim that the warhead contained a quantity of the gas, dissolved in saline solution.
>
> . . .
>
> CL17 is normal chlorine for swimming pools or industrial purposes. It is rated as Level 2 under the chemical weapons convention, which means it is dual purpose - it can be used as a weapon as well as for industrial or domestic purposes. Level 1 agents are chemicals whose sole use is as weapons, such as the nerve agents sarin or tabun.
>
> There has been extensive experimentation by insurgents in Iraq in the use of chlorine, which is harmful when mixed with water to form hydrochloric acid. It vapourises quickly, meaning that in a big explosion it will evaporate; in a small blast - for instance, one delivered by a home-made rocket - it will turn into airborne droplets before dispersing quickly.
>
> So it is likely only to produce limited casualties. In this case there were only 26 fatalities, far fewer than would be expected from a full chemical weapon attack. In short, it is easily improvised into a chemical device but not one that would be used by an army seeking mass-casualty effects.[322]

[320] Watson, Paul Joseph. "Syrian Rebels Caught On Tape Discussing Chemical Weapons Attack." Infowars. March 20, 2013. http://www.infowars.com/syrian-rebels-caught-on-tape-discussing-chemical-weapons-attack/
[321] "Rebels Could Resort To Chemical Weapons, Syria Warns." France 24. December 8, 2012. http://www.france24.com/en/20121208-syria-warns-rebels-may-resort-chemical-weapons-assad-united-nations-islamists
[322] Thomson, Alex. "Syria Chemical Weapons: Finger Pointed At Jihadists." The Telegraph. March 23, 2013. http://www.telegraph.co.uk/news/worldnews/middleeast/syria/9950036/Syria-chemical-weapons-finger-pointed-at-jihadists.html

Reports by the Syrian government coincide with the accounts given by the victims of the chemical weapons attack which one can view in a number of YouTube videos.[323] It is also important to note that many of the victims allegedly name the Free Syrian Army and the "rebels" as the perpetrators as they are being interviewed while waiting for medical treatment.

"The Free Syrian Army hit us with a rocket," one woman said. "We smelled an odor and everyone fell to the ground. People died where they fell . . . the kids . . ."[324]

A young girl was also interviewed, who said, "My lungs closed and I couldn't breathe or speak. God curse them. Everyone died on the ground. My mom and dad died. I don't know where is my brother. God curse them. May they [FSA] all die. This is the freedom they bring us. They [FSA] want to kill everyone. I hope there remains not a single one of them [FSA] alive."[325]

Lastly, the UN report laughably attempted to absolve the death squads of war crimes while shifting the burden of cruelty and savage conduct to that of the Assad government. While asserting that Syrian government forces have been responsible for "committing torture, rape, forcible displacement and enforced disappearance," no credible (and often even no incredible) evidence is ever provided to bolster the claims.[326]

While admitting that the death squads have carried out "sentencing and execution without due process, as well as committing torture, taking hostages and pillaging," the report hilariously states that crimes committed by the death squads "did not, however, reach the intensity and scale of those committed by government forces and affiliated militias."[327]

---

[323] West Turns A Blind Eye That Their Terrorists In Syria Used WMDs, Against All Evidence." Youtube. Posted by nuts flipped. Posted on March 20, 2013. http://www.youtube.com/watch?feature=player_embedded&v=BLAMVtLq2V0#! Video shows terrorists discussing and preparing to launch chemical attacks on Syrian military soldiers and civilians. Video shows terrorists testing these chemicals.

[324] West Turns A Blind Eye That Their Terrorists In Syria Used WMDs, Against All Evidence." Youtube. Posted by nuts flipped. Posted on March 20, 2013. http://www.youtube.com/watch?feature=player_embedded&v=BLAMVtLq2V0#! Video shows terrorists discussing and preparing to launch chemical attacks on Syrian military soldiers and civilians. Video shows terrorists testing these chemicals.

[325] West Turns A Blind Eye That Their Terrorists In Syria Used WMDs, Against All Evidence." Youtube. Posted by nuts flipped. Posted on March 20, 2013. http://www.youtube.com/watch?feature=player_embedded&v=BLAMVtLq2V0#! Video shows terrorists discussing and preparing to launch chemical attacks on Syrian military soldiers and civilians. Video shows terrorists testing these chemicals.

[326] "UN Has "Reasonable Grounds' To Believe Assad Forces Used Chemical Weapons." Haaretz. June 4, 2013. http://www.haaretz.com/news/middle-east/un-has-reasonable-grounds-to-believe-assad-forces-used-chemical-weapons-in-syria-1.527720

[327] "UN Has "Reasonable Grounds' To Believe Assad Forces Used Chemical Weapons." Haaretz. June 4, 2013. http://www.haaretz.com/news/middle-east/un-has-reasonable-grounds-to-believe-assad-forces-used-chemical-weapons-in-syria-1.527720

Perhaps the United Nations Commission was simply unaware of videos showing the death squads machine gunning captives, beheading prisoners and forcing young children to behead them. I, myself, have written an article dealing with reports regarding the death squad's hanging of a young child after murdering his family in front of him. One can also easily view the videos of the death squad members beating and humiliating the famous elderly "Yellow Man" in Aleppo on YouTube.

Indeed, the videos of the torture of prisoners in the hands of the death squads are legion. One need only type the relevant keywords into a YouTube search engine to be greeted with generous results.

So either the United Nations Commission of Inquiry was incredibly inept and incompetent in their inquiry, or they have been actively engaged in covering up the atrocities of the death squads while framing the Assad government for crimes it did not commit thus shoring up popular support for military action by the Anglo-Americans on yet one more sovereign nation. Either way, the UN Commission of Inquiry's report is a total fraud.

Seymour Hersh Confirms Obama Lied About Syria Chemical Weapons Attacks

Almost five months after the chemical weapons attacks that took place in the Ghouta region of Syria, legendary reporter and revealer of American war crimes such as My Lai and Abu Grahib, Seymour Hersh, revealed yet another bombshell of information – specifically that the Obama Administration intentionally misrepresented information that was used to claim Assad and the Syrian government was responsible for the attack.

Hersh's article, "Whose Sarin?" which was notably published in the UK press and not in the American media, claims that the Obama administration is guilty of "cherry picking" intelligence information to suit the goal of military action against Syria. Hersh's accusations come after his conversations with at least two "intelligence and military officials."[328]

Ultimately, Hersh's article rests on the criticism and revelations that the administration intentionally buried information regarding Jobhat al-Nusra operating inside Syria and the clear and documented evidence that the extremist group did, in fact, have access to sarin gas and the means to deliver it via improvised rocket propelling devices. Hersh also criticizes the American media for engaging in "confirmation bias" and riding the wave of propaganda being promoted against the Assad government.

In addition, the respected journalist points out that the administration actually manipulated evidence so as to attempt to portray the Assad forces as the aggressors. Hersh clearly states that the administration's claims shortly after the Ghouta chemical weapons attack were nothing more than a fabrication, echoing the fabrication that famously preceded the tragedy of Iraq.

Hersh also states,

---

[328] Hersh, Seymour. "Whose Sarin?" London Review Of Books. Vol. 35. No. 24. Pp. 9-12. December 19, 2013. http://www.lrb.co.uk/2013/12/08/seymour-m-hersh/whose-sarin

Barack Obama did not tell the whole story this autumn when he tried to make the case that Bashar al-Assad was responsible for the chemical weapons attack near Damascus on 21 August. In some instances, he omitted important intelligence, and in others he presented assumptions as facts. Most significant, he failed to acknowledge something known to the US intelligence community: that the Syrian army is not the only party in the country's civil war with access to sarin, the nerve agent that a UN study concluded – without assessing responsibility – had been used in the rocket attack.[329]

Hersh goes even further when he claims that the administration was well aware of the fact that the Nusra Front had access to Sarin and the means by which to deliver it. He writes,

In the months before the attack, the American intelligence agencies produced a series of highly classified reports, culminating in a formal Operations Order – a planning document that precedes a ground invasion – citing evidence that the al-Nusra Front, a jihadi group affiliated with al-Qaida, had mastered the mechanics of creating sarin and was capable of manufacturing it in quantity. When the attack occurred al-Nusra should have been a suspect, but the administration cherry-picked intelligence to justify a strike against Assad.[330]

According to Hersh, the Defense Intelligence Agency was well aware of Nusra's ability to acquire and deliver chemical weapons as far back as June 20, 2013. He says,

On 20 June a four-page top secret cable summarising what had been learned about al-Nusra's nerve gas capabilities was forwarded to David R. Shedd, deputy director of the Defense Intelligence Agency. 'What Shedd was briefed on was extensive and comprehensive,' the consultant said. 'It was not a bunch of "we believes".' He told me that the cable made no assessment as to whether the rebels or the Syrian army had initiated the attacks in March and April, but it did confirm previous reports that al-Nusra had the ability to acquire and use sarin. A sample of the sarin that had been used was also recovered – with the help of an Israeli agent – but, according to the consultant, no further reporting about the sample showed up in cable traffic.[331]

In addition, Hersh demonstrates that not only the Defense Intelligence Agency, but the Central Intelligence Agency and the Joint Chiefs of Staff were aware of Nusra's chemical weapons capabilities as well. Hersh states,

Independently of these assessments, the Joint Chiefs of Staff, assuming that US troops might be ordered into Syria to seize the government's stockpile of chemical agents, called for an all-source analysis of the potential threat. 'The Op Order provides the basis of execution of a military mission, if so ordered,' the former senior intelligence official explained. 'This includes the possible need to send American soldiers to a Syrian chemical site to defend it against rebel seizure. If the jihadist rebels were going to overrun the site, the assumption is that Assad would not fight us because we were protecting the chemical from the rebels. All Op Orders contain an intelligence threat

---

[329] Hersh, Seymour. "Whose Sarin?" London Review Of Books. Vol. 35. No. 24. Pp. 9-12. December 19, 2013. http://www.lrb.co.uk/2013/12/08/seymour-m-hersh/whose-sarin
[330] Hersh, Seymour. "Whose Sarin?" London Review Of Books. Vol. 35. No. 24. Pp. 9-12. December 19, 2013. http://www.lrb.co.uk/2013/12/08/seymour-m-hersh/whose-sarin
[331] Hersh, Seymour. "Whose Sarin?" London Review Of Books. Vol. 35. No. 24. Pp. 9-12. December 19, 2013. http://www.lrb.co.uk/2013/12/08/seymour-m-hersh/whose-sarin

component. We had technical analysts from the Central Intelligence Agency, the Defense Intelligence Agency, weapons people, and I & W [indications and warnings] people working on the problem … They concluded that the rebel forces were capable of attacking an American force with sarin because they were able to produce the lethal gas. The examination relied on signals and human intelligence, as well as the expressed intention and technical capability of the rebels.'[332]

Yet there was more than simply the ignorance of intelligence pointing toward the death squads' responsibility for the chemical weapons attack; there was a concerted effort to paint the Assad government as the responsible party. Hersh explains,

Once the scale of events on 21 August was understood, the NSA mounted a comprehensive effort to search for any links to the attack, sorting through the full archive of stored communications. A keyword or two would be selected and a filter would be employed to find relevant conversations. 'What happened here is that the NSA intelligence weenies started with an event – the use of sarin – and reached to find chatter that might relate,' the former official said. 'This does not lead to a high confidence assessment, unless you start with high confidence that Bashar Assad ordered it, and began looking for anything that supports that belief.' The cherry-picking was similar to the process used to justify the Iraq war.

[…]

The White House's misrepresentation of what it knew about the attack, and when, was matched by its readiness to ignore intelligence that could undermine the narrative. That information concerned al-Nusra, the Islamist rebel group designated by the US and the UN as a terrorist organisation. Al-Nusra is known to have carried out scores of suicide bombings against Christians and other non-Sunni Muslim sects inside Syria, and to have attacked its nominal ally in the civil war, the secular Free Syrian Army (FSA). Its stated goal is to overthrow the Assad regime and establish sharia law. (On 25 September al-Nusra joined several other Islamist rebel groups in repudiating the FSA and another secular faction, the Syrian National Coalition.)[333]

The misrepresentation and outright fabrication of relevant information regarding who was responsible for the chemical weapons attack, however, did not stop at the White House. In typical fashion, mainstream media outlets joined in on beating the drums of war. Again, typically, the New York Times was at the forefront of pro-war propaganda. As Hersh writes,

An annex to the UN report reproduced YouTube photographs of some recovered munitions, including a rocket that 'indicatively matches' the specifics of a 330mm calibre artillery rocket. The New York Times wrote that the existence of the rockets essentially proved that the Syrian government was responsible for the attack 'because the weapons in question had not been previously documented or reported to be in possession of the insurgency'.[334]

[332] Hersh, Seymour. "Whose Sarin?" London Review Of Books. Vol. 35. No. 24. Pp. 9-12. December 19, 2013. http://www.lrb.co.uk/2013/12/08/seymour-m-hersh/whose-sarin
[333] Hersh, Seymour. "Whose Sarin?" London Review Of Books. Vol. 35. No. 24. Pp. 9-12. December 19, 2013. http://www.lrb.co.uk/2013/12/08/seymour-m-hersh/whose-sarin
[334] Hersh, Seymour. "Whose Sarin?" London Review Of Books. Vol. 35. No. 24. Pp. 9-12. December 19, 2013. http://www.lrb.co.uk/2013/12/08/seymour-m-hersh/whose-sarin

The actual evidence, however, demonstrated quite the opposite. Much like what Tony Cartalucci reported in his article 5 Lies Invented to Spin UN Report on Syrian Chemical Weapons Attack (virtually deconstructing the propaganda narrative in real time), Hersh points out that the information intentionally misrepresented in the New York Times was easily exposed once it was held up to the light. He writes,

> Theodore Postol, a professor of technology and national security at MIT, reviewed the UN photos with a group of his colleagues and concluded that the large calibre rocket was an improvised munition that was very likely manufactured locally. He told me that it was 'something you could produce in a modestly capable machine shop'. The rocket in the photos, he added, fails to match the specifications of a similar but smaller rocket known to be in the Syrian arsenal. The New York Times, again relying on data in the UN report, also analysed the flight path of two of the spent rockets that were believed to have carried sarin, and concluded that the angle of descent 'pointed directly' to their being fired from a Syrian army base more than nine kilometres from the landing zone. Postol, who has served as the scientific adviser to the chief of naval operations in the Pentagon, said that the assertions in the Times and elsewhere 'were not based on actual observations'. He concluded that the flight path analyses in particular were, as he put it in an email, 'totally nuts' because a thorough study demonstrated that the range of the improvised rockets was 'unlikely' to be more than two kilometres. Postol and a colleague, Richard M. Lloyd, published an analysis two weeks after 21 August in which they correctly assessed that the rockets involved carried a far greater payload of sarin than previously estimated. The Times reported on that analysis at length, describing Postol and Lloyd as 'leading weapons experts'. The pair's later study about the rockets' flight paths and range, which contradicted previous Times reporting, was emailed to the newspaper last week; it has so far gone unreported.[335]

While Hersh's revelations are by no means anything new, they go some length in corroborating what many researchers and writers like myself, Tony Cartalucci, Webster Tarpley, Ziad Fadel, and others have been writing ever since the chemical weapons attack took place on August 21, 2013. Hersh's article is particularly important due to its sources of military and intelligence officials and the open admission of the lack of any real evidence which would implicate the Assad government.

Yet, while information such as that provided by Seymour Hersh in "Whose Sarin?" is extremely important, it is also important to remember that such information was widely available at the time of the attacks and was provided by members of the alternative media. Thus, with the choices placed before the American people regarding whether or not to support war, stories such as this should serve as a reminder of just why the corporate media should be viewed as a highly discredited institution.

One must also consider the fact that the information therein came nearly five months after the fact, despite the reality of its wide availability at the time of the controversy and debate. Far too many times, Americans have allowed themselves to be led down the path to war only to find out years or months later that the "intelligence" or information they were given was nothing more than a lie. Had the American people acquiesced to military

---

[335] Hersh, Seymour. "Whose Sarin?" London Review Of Books. Vol. 35. No. 24. Pp. 9-12. December 19, 2013. http://www.lrb.co.uk/2013/12/08/seymour-m-hersh/whose-sarin

action against Syria, the United States would have taken place in yet one more farce that ended as tragedy. Thus, it is important to remember such treachery on the part of the ruling elite and their mouthpiece media when a new propaganda narrative takes shape around Syria or yet more lies are used to pave the Path to Persia.

West Blames Assad For Chemical Weapons Attack, Again

After the initial push for war by the NATO powers was narrowly avoided by a clever act of diplomacy on the part of the Russians – an agreement that Syria would hand over all of its chemical weapons for destruction by the United Nations – another "convenient" usage of chemical weapons took place as the U.N. was attempting to dismantle the existing stockpile. Of course, the United States and the West in general rushed to blame Assad and the Syrian military.

This time, a chlorine-based gas attack in Kfar Zeita prompted the Anglo-European propaganda machine to once again begin greasing up its gears to accuse Bashar al-Assad of crimes against humanity and justify some form of humanitarian intervention in Syria by NATO forces.

The attacks came shortly before the completion of the transfer and destruction of Syria's chemical weapons stockpile.[336]

Predictably, the recent attacks were promoted by Western outlets as an example of how a chemical weapons free Syria is still capable of deploying chemical weapons against civilians due to a loophole allowing for the production of chlorine gas.[337]

State Department spokeswoman Jen Psaki seized upon the reports, having stated "We have indications of the use of a toxic industrial chemical — probably chlorine — in Syria this month in the opposition-dominated village of Kfar Zeita ... We're examining allegations that the government was responsible. We take all allegations of the use of chemicals in combat use very seriously."[338]

However, what was completely ignored by these outlets is both the possibility and high probability that the Syrian government was not responsible for the chlorine gas attacks to being with.[339]

---

[336] McDonnell, Patrick J. "Chemical Weapons Removed From Syria Nearly Complete." Los Angeles Times. April 22, 2014. http://www.latimes.com/world/middleeast/la-fg-syria-chemical-weapons-20140423-story.html

[337] Vinograd, Cassandra. "Syria Chlorine Attack Reports Raise Questions About Loopholes." NBC News. April 23, 2014. http://www.nbcnews.com/news/world/syria-chlorine-attack-reports-raise-questions-about-loopholes-n87666

[338] Labott, Elise. "U.S.: Signs Point To Syria Using Chlorine In Gas Attacks." CNN. April 21, 2014. http://www.cnn.com/2014/04/21/world/meast/syria-chemical-u-s-/

[339] Cartalucci, Tony; Bowie, Nile. "Subverting Syria: How CIA Contra Gangs And NGO's Manufacture, Mislabel, And Market Mass Murder." Progressive Press. September 11, 2012.

Indeed, there are several reasons to doubt the claims made by Western governments and Western media outlets, aside from the fact that both of these institutions have lied on repeated occasions regarding the use of chemical weapons in Syria.

First, after Syria's near miss with the chemical weapons controversy in Ghouta, it would be absolutely foolish for the Syrian government to launch a chemical weapons attack against civilians. Having avoided the catastrophe of a Western invasion in August only due to a deal brokered by the Russians at the very last minute, the Assad government is not likely to be so incompetent as to have put itself in the same position. (Note: The Assad government had not put itself in this position the first time, since it was the death squads who were responsible for the chemical weapons attacks.)[340] [341]

Since the Ghouta chemical weapons attack drew Syria to the brink of war with the United States and NATO. Why would Assad use chemical weapons after that experience?

Why would Assad use chemical weapons when he is clearly winning? Indeed, this was one of the main questions surrounding the flawed reasoning that sought to blame Assad for the Ghouta chemical weapons attack. Yet the Syrian military was even better off militarily this time than it was during the Ghouta controversy, thus making any attempt to blame the Syrian government for the deployment of chemical weapons in Kafr Zeita even more implausible.

Second, although corporate media outlets such as TIME and ABC confidently reported that Assad was the most likely culprit in terms of the Kafr Zeita gas attacks, the fact is that there was no evidence for these claims whatsoever.[342] [343]

Turkish Party Member Claims Syria Chemical Weapons Attacks Were Committed By Jihadists With Help From Turkey

In 2015, two years after the attack, even more evidence emerged which demonstrated that the attacks in Ghouta were not only committed by Western-backed jihadists but were facilitated by NATO itself. According to Turkish opposition party member, Eren Erdem (Republican People's Party [CHP]), a cover-up of Turkish involvement in terms

---

[340] Cartalucci, Tony. "VIDEO: Rockets Used In Damascus Chemical Weapons Attack Fired From Makeshift Flatbeds, Not Military Vehicles." Land Destroyer Report. September 25, 2013. http://www.globalresearch.ca/video-rockets-used-in-damascus-chemical-weapons-attack-fired-from-makeshift-flatbeds-not-military-vehicles/5351533

[341] Gavlak, Dale; Yahya, Ababneh. "Syrians In Ghouta Claim Saudi-Supplied Rebels Behind Chemical Attack." Mint Press News. http://landdestroyer.blogspot.com/2013/08/syrians-in-ghouta-claim-saudi-supplied_29.html

[342] Arrouas, Michelle. "Syrian Government Accused Of New Deadly Gas Attacks On Opposition." TIME. April 23, 2014. http://time.com/73315/syria-gas-attack-chlorine/

[343] Weinberg, Ali. "Bashar al-Assad's Deadly Loophole In Syria Deal." ABC News. April 23, 2014. http://abcnews.go.com/blogs/politics/2014/04/bashar-al-assads-deadly-loophole-in-syria-deal/

of both the foreknowledge and the shipping of chemical weapons materials to terrorists operating in Syria took place soon after the attacks.

Erdem cites evidence from an "abruptly-closed criminal case." He told RT that "There is data in this indictment. Chemical weapon materials are being brought to Turkey and being put together in Syria in camps of ISIS which was known as Iraqi Al Qaeda during that time." The case Erdem is referring to is criminal case number 2013/120, opened by the General Prosecutor's Office in Andana. [344]

According to RT, "The investigation revealed that a number of Turkish citizens took part in negotiations with Islamic State (IS, formerly ISIS/ISIL) representatives on the supply of sarin gas."[345]

Erdem pointed out, by citing evidence in the case mentioned above, that wiretapped phone conversations clearly demonstrated that Hayyam Kasap, an al-Qaeda member and fighter, had acquired Sarin. [346]

"These are all detected. There are phone recordings of this shipment like 'don't worry about the border, we'll take care of it' and we also see the bureaucracy is being used," Erdem stated.[347]

The evidence gathered during the course of the investigation resulted in the ability of the Adana authorities to conduct a number of raids and arrest 13 suspects. However, only a week later, the case was mysteriously and abruptly closed and all the suspects were released. Erdem says they immediately cross the Turkish-Syrian border.[348]

Erdem stated,

About the shipment, Republic prosecutor of Adana, Mehmet Arıkan, made an operation and the related people were detained. But as far as I understand he was not an influential person in bureaucracy. A week after, another public prosecutor was assigned, took over the indictment and all the detainees were released. And they left Turkey crossing the Syrian border.

The phone recordings in the indictment showed all the details from how the shipment was going to be made to how it was prepared, from the content of the labs to the source of the materials. Which trucks were going to be used, all dates etc. From A to Z, everything was discussed and recorded. Despite all of this evidence, the suspects were released.

---

[344] "Sarin Materials Brought Via Turkey And Mixed In Syrian ISIS Camps – Turkish MP To RT." RT. December 14, 2015. https://www.rt.com/news/325825-sarin-gas-syria-turkey/

[345] "Sarin Materials Brought Via Turkey And Mixed In Syrian ISIS Camps – Turkish MP To RT." RT. December 14, 2015. https://www.rt.com/news/325825-sarin-gas-syria-turkey/

[346] "Sarin Materials Brought Via Turkey And Mixed In Syrian ISIS Camps – Turkish MP To RT." RT. December 14, 2015. https://www.rt.com/news/325825-sarin-gas-syria-turkey/

[347] "Sarin Materials Brought Via Turkey And Mixed In Syrian ISIS Camps – Turkish MP To RT." RT. December 14, 2015. https://www.rt.com/news/325825-sarin-gas-syria-turkey/

[348] "Sarin Materials Brought Via Turkey And Mixed In Syrian ISIS Camps – Turkish MP To RT." RT. December 14, 2015. https://www.rt.com/news/325825-sarin-gas-syria-turkey/

And the shipment happened. Because no one stopped them. That's why maybe the sarin gas used in Syria is a result of this.[349]

Erdem also spoke of evidence fingering Turkish Mechanical and Chemical Industry Corporation for being involved in the operation as well, with some "unconfirmed reports" suggesting a government cover-up, specifically with the involvement of Minister of Justice Bekir Bozdag's heavy involvement. Some of Erdem's evidence suggests that Bozdag wanted to know from the Sarin producer whether the jihadists/ISIS fighters would receive the chemical material and if they would use it before the transfer took place. [350]

Erdem stated,

When I read the indictment, I saw clearly that these people have relationships with The Machinery and Chemical Industry Institution of Turkey and they don't have any worries about crossing the border. For example in Hayyam Kasap's phone records, you hear him saying sarin gas many times, saying that the ateliers are ready for production, materials are waiting in trucks which were supposedly carrying club soda.[351]

According to Erdem, he confronted Bozdag who only denied that he wanted to know about the operations before they took place.[352]

Erdem refers to the 2013 Ghouta chemical weapons attack which Western governments attempted to blame on Assad. According to him, the Adana case proves it was not Assad who committed the attacks but the Western-backed jihadists. In addition, he points out that the West, especially Europe, provided the materials necessary to create such a weapon.[353]

Erdem stated to RT,

For example the chemical attack in Ghouta. Remember. It was claimed that the regime forces were behind it. This attack was conducted just days before the sarin operation in Turkey. It's a high probability that this attack was carried out with those basic materials shipped through Turkey. It is said the regime forces are responsible but the indictment says it's ISIS. UN inspectors went to the site but they couldn't find any evidence. But in this indictment, we've found the evidence. We know who used the sarin gas, and our government knows it too.

All basic materials are purchased from Europe. Western institutions should question themselves about these relations. Western sources know very well who carried out the sarin gas attack in Syria. They know these people, they know who these people are

---

[349] "Sarin Materials Brought Via Turkey And Mixed In Syrian ISIS Camps – Turkish MP To RT." RT. December 14, 2015. https://www.rt.com/news/325825-sarin-gas-syria-turkey/

[350] "Sarin Materials Brought Via Turkey And Mixed In Syrian ISIS Camps – Turkish MP To RT." RT. December 14, 2015. https://www.rt.com/news/325825-sarin-gas-syria-turkey/

[351] "Sarin Materials Brought Via Turkey And Mixed In Syrian ISIS Camps – Turkish MP To RT." RT. December 14, 2015. https://www.rt.com/news/325825-sarin-gas-syria-turkey/

[352] "Sarin Materials Brought Via Turkey And Mixed In Syrian ISIS Camps – Turkish MP To RT." RT. December 14, 2015. https://www.rt.com/news/325825-sarin-gas-syria-turkey/

[353] "Sarin Materials Brought Via Turkey And Mixed In Syrian ISIS Camps – Turkish MP To RT." RT. December 14, 2015. https://www.rt.com/news/325825-sarin-gas-syria-turkey/

working with, they know that these people are working for Al-Qaeda. I think is Westerns are hypocrats about the situation.[354]

Regardless of Erdem's new evidence, it was clear long ago that the Assad government had nothing to do with the chemical weapon's attacks in Ghouta or any other chemical weapons attacks in Syria. If Erdem's new evidence is accurate, however, we now have a clear glimpse into not only who used the weapons but who helped provide them. As is the case in virtually every terrorist operation in Syria, such evidence does not paint a positive picture of Turkey and the West.

2016 Chemical Weapons Attack In Ghouta - 'Rebels' Gas Syrian Soldiers

Three years after the infamous Ghouta chemical weapons attack launched by Western-backed terrorists but blamed on the Syrian government by Western mainstream media outlets, Ghouta, in 2016, was once again the scene of another possible chemical weapons attack.

According to a Syrian military source cited by Al-Masdar, "rebels" in Damascus used crudely assembled chemical bombs to attack Syrian soldiers with nerve gas in Ghouta. "Several soldiers suffered breathing difficulties after the attack and were immediately taken to a military hospital. Thankfully, all of them are now in stable conditions," the source stated. [355]

Video evidence was produced which reportedly shows Syrian soldiers suffering the effects of the gas and undergoing treatment.[356]

The attack took place on Wednesday after four days of intense fighting between "rebels" and the Syrian military where the SAA managed to reclaim territory from the Western-backed Islamists. Jaish al-Islam, a terrorist group backed by the U.S. and NATO, denied using the chemical weapons and instead claimed that the Syrian government was the perpetrator. Thus, with both sides claiming that chemical weapons were used, it appears that such an attack did take place.[357]

Video evidence such as that produced by Syrian news agency SANA, however, tends to lend credence to the claims of the Syrian government rather than the terrorist groups.

---

[354] "Sarin Materials Brought Via Turkey And Mixed In Syrian ISIS Camps – Turkish MP To RT." RT. December 14, 2015. https://www.rt.com/news/325825-sarin-gas-syria-turkey/

[355] Adra, Zen. "In Video: Ghouta Rebels Attack Syrian Army With Nerve Gas." Al-Masdar. June 16, 2016. https://www.almasdarnews.com/article/video-ghouta-rebels-attack-syrian-army-nerve-gas/

[356] "Jihadists Use Nerve Toxic Gas Against The Syrian Army In Eastern Ghouta." SANA. Posted to Youtube by Al-Masdar. Posted on June 16, 2016. https://www.youtube.com/watch?v=oTRlkTuNr_l

[357] Adra, Zen. "In Video: Ghouta Rebels Attack Syrian Army With Nerve Gas." Al-Masdar. June 16, 2016. https://www.almasdarnews.com/article/video-ghouta-rebels-attack-syrian-army-nerve-gas/

The 2013 chemical weapons attack was blamed on the Assad government by the United States and its allies despite evidence that it was actually the terrorist proxy forces that committed the attacks. It stands as one of the most intense moments in the Syrian crisis as the United States was preparing to launch a Libya-style invasion before the Russians stepped in and mediated a diplomatic solution that resulted in Syria surrendering its chemical weapons stockpile.

Terrorists in Syria, backed by the West, have used chemical weapons on a number of occasions, even televising proof of their possession of the chemicals and the manufacturing capability needed to produce them.

On the contrary, there has never been any credible evidence to suggest that the Syrian military has used chemical weapons against either civilians or combatants.

Russian Analysis Shows Western-Backed Terrorists Using Chemical Weapons Against Civilians

In yet another blow to the credibility of the Western corporate media and the anti-Syria propaganda blitz it has maintained since early 2011, experts from the Russian Center for Radiological, Chemical, and Biological Defense announced that analysis of the shells fired by terrorists at the 1070 Apartment Complex in Aleppo contained chemical weapons.

This new revelation brings Western propaganda crashing to ground in regards to the claims that it is Assad's government using chemical weapons and that the terrorists have no access to them.[358]

"Rapid sample analysis shows that the toxic substances in the militants' artillery ammunition were chlorine and white phosphorus," an analyst from the center said.[359]

Notably, all of these substances were banned by the Chemical Weapons Convention on January 13, 1993.[360]

The Russian center established a mobile analysis center in Aleppo in order to test samples quickly but the samples were supposed to be sent to the Radiological, Chemical, and Biological Center in Moscow. This center is accredited by the Organization for the Prohibition of Chemical Weapons.[361]

---

[358] "Expert Proves Jihadists Bombarded Aleppo Neighborhood With Chemical Weapons." Al-Masdar. November 11, 2016. https://www.almasdarnews.com/article/expert-proves-jihadists-bombarded-aleppo-neighborhood-chemical-weapons/
[359] "Expert Proves Jihadists Bombarded Aleppo Neighborhood With Chemical Weapons." Al-Masdar. November 11, 2016. https://www.almasdarnews.com/article/expert-proves-jihadists-bombarded-aleppo-neighborhood-chemical-weapons/
[360] "Expert Proves Jihadists Bombarded Aleppo Neighborhood With Chemical Weapons." Al-Masdar. November 11, 2016. https://www.almasdarnews.com/article/expert-proves-jihadists-bombarded-aleppo-neighborhood-chemical-weapons/
[361] "Expert Proves Jihadists Bombarded Aleppo Neighborhood With Chemical Weapons." Al-

Although the 1070 Apartment Complex was liberated by the Syrian government, the terrorists had been repeatedly shelling the area with indiscriminate missiles in order to kill civilians attempting to flee terrorist control as well as firing missiles at Syrian military personnel. Many of these missiles were filled with poisonous gas which the Russian Center has identified as being chlorine and white phosphorous.[362]

Dozens of people were injured as a result of the chemical munitions and were hospitalized for treatment. Chlorine and white phosphorous both cause extremely painful deaths.[363]

Masdar. November 11, 2016. https://www.almasdarnews.com/article/expert-proves-jihadists-bombarded-aleppo-neighborhood-chemical-weapons/

[362] "Expert Proves Jihadists Bombarded Aleppo Neighborhood With Chemical Weapons." Al-Masdar. November 11, 2016. https://www.almasdarnews.com/article/expert-proves-jihadists-bombarded-aleppo-neighborhood-chemical-weapons/

[363] "Expert Proves Jihadists Bombarded Aleppo Neighborhood With Chemical Weapons." Al-Masdar. November 11, 2016. https://www.almasdarnews.com/article/expert-proves-jihadists-bombarded-aleppo-neighborhood-chemical-weapons/

Israel's Chemical Weapons Stockpile Highlights Western Hypocrisy

Unmitigated hysteria continues to be expressed in the Western corporate press regarding the alleged use or possession of chemical weapons by the Syrian government. This continues despite the fact that there is absolutely no evidence tying the Assad government to the deployment of chemical weapons in Syria. The U.S. government and the rest of the Anglo-American network relentlessly demonstrate its unwavering hypocrisy on the chemical weapons and WMD issue.

Syria and Iraq's possession of chemical WMDs have been considered to be situations warranting an immediate military response, while the possibility of a nuclear Iran is used to browbeat the American populace into a state of fear over a nuclear holocaust. Meanwhile, the possession of chemical and biological weapons, as well as hundreds of nuclear warheads by the state of Israel, has been simultaneously denied and ignored. Clearly, some Middle Eastern countries are more equal than others.

Yet, while both Israel and the West have denied the existence of many of these weapons for some time, an article published by the official magazine of the Council on Foreign Relations, *Foreign Policy*, has demonstrated that Israel does indeed possess chemical and biological weapons, as well as its own nuclear stockpile.

The report entitled "Does Israel Have Chemical Weapons Too?" revolves around a document belonging to the Central Intelligence Agency which was apparently found by a friend of Matthew M. Aid, the author of the article, at the Ronald Reagan Library -- a single page had been stapled to an "innocuous unclassified document." The page was attached to a September 15, 1983 report entitled "Implications of Soviet Use of Chemical and Toxin Weapons for US Security Interests."[364]

The unclassified report dealt with unproven claims regarding Soviet chemical and biological weapons usage in Afghanistan and Southeast Asia and was largely declassified in 2009. Interestingly enough, however, while the CIA was willing to declassify the part of the report that dealt with Soviet possession and use of chemical and biological weapons as well as that of some of its client states, the agency was much less willing to declassify the sections of the report dealing with countries outside of the Soviet sphere. Indeed, censors actually removed virtually all of the information related to the Middle East before releasing it to the National Archives. Most notably, all references to what the CIA believed it knew regarding Israel's chemical weapons programs in 1983 were entirely scrubbed.

According to *Foreign Policy*,

> Reports have circulated in arms control circles for almost 20 years that Israel secretly manufactured a stockpile of chemical and biological weapons to complement its nuclear arsenal. Much of the attention has been focused on the research and

---

[364] Aid, Matthew M. "Does Israel Have Chemical Weapons?" Foreign Policy. September 10, 2013. http://foreignpolicy.com/2013/09/10/exclusive-does-israel-have-chemical-weapons-too/

development work being conducted at the Israeli government's secretive Israel Institute for Biological Research at Ness Ziona, located 20 kilometers south of Tel Aviv.

But little, if any, hard evidence has ever been published to indicate that Israel possesses a stockpile of chemical or biological weapons. This secret 1983 CIA intelligence estimate may be the strongest indication yet.[365]

Indeed, according to the document, in 1982, spy satellites uncovered "a probable CW [chemical weapon] nerve agent production facility and a storage facility... at the Dimona Sensitive Storage Area in the Negev Desert. Other CW production is believed to exist within a well-developed Israeli chemical industry."[366]

The report also stated, "While we cannot confirm whether the Israelis possess lethal chemical agents several indicators lead us to believe that they have available to them at least persistent and nonpersistent nerve agents, a mustard agent, and several riot-control agents, marched with suitable delivery systems."[367]

Aid describes the level of knowledge regarding the Israeli chemical weapons by writing,

> The 1983 CIA estimate reveals that U.S. intelligence first became aware of Israeli chemical weapons-testing activities in the early 1970s, when intelligence sources reported the existence of chemical weapons test grids, which are specially instrumented testing grounds used to measure the range and effectiveness of different chemical agents, particularly nerve agents, in simulated situations and in varying climatic conditions. It is almost certain that these testing grids were located in the arid and sparsely populated Negev Desert, in southern Israel.

> But the CIA assessment suggests that the Israelis accelerated their research and development work on chemical weapons following the end of the 1973 Yom Kippur War. According to the report, U.S. intelligence detected "possible tests" of Israeli chemical weapons in January 1976, which, again, almost certainly took place somewhere in the Negev Desert. A former U.S. Air Force intelligence officer whom I interviewed recalled that at about this time, the National Security Agency captured communications showing that Israeli air force fighter-bombers operating from Hatzerim Air Base outside the city of Beersheba in southern Israel had been detected conducting simulated low-level chemical weapons delivery missions at a bombing range in the Negev Desert.

> The U.S. intelligence community was paying an extraordinary amount of attention to Israel in the 1970s, according to a retired CIA analyst I spoke with who studied the region at the time. The possible January 1976 Israeli chemical weapons test occurred a little more than two years after the end of the 1973 war, an event that had shocked

---

[365] Aid, Matthew M. "Does Israel Have Chemical Weapons?" Foreign Policy. September 10, 2013. http://foreignpolicy.com/2013/09/10/exclusive-does-israel-have-chemical-weapons-too/
[366] Aid, Matthew M. "Does Israel Have Chemical Weapons?" Foreign Policy. September 10, 2013. http://foreignpolicy.com/2013/09/10/exclusive-does-israel-have-chemical-weapons-too/
[367] Aid, Matthew M. "Does Israel Have Chemical Weapons?" Foreign Policy. September 10, 2013. http://foreignpolicy.com/2013/09/10/exclusive-does-israel-have-chemical-weapons-too/

the Israeli political and military establishment because it demonstrated for the first time that the Arab armies were now capable of going toe-to-toe on the battlefield with the Israeli military.[368]

There were also a series of leaks in the U.S. press which quoted several intelligence officials from the CIA stating that Israel actually possessed nuclear weapons, a known but unspoken fact even to this day. Aid writes,

> The leak was based on an authorized off-the-record briefing of newspaper reporters by a senior CIA official in Washington, who intimated to the reporters that Israel was also involved in other activities involving weapons of mass destruction, but refused to say anything further on the subject. The CIA official was likely referring to the agency's belief that the Israelis may have conducted a chemical weapons test in January 1976. According to a declassified State Department cable, Israeli foreign minister Yigal Allon called in the U.S. ambassador to Israel and registered a strong protest about the story, reiterating the official Israeli government position that Israel did not possess nuclear weapons. After the protest, all further public mention of Israeli WMD activities ceased and the whole subject was quickly and quietly forgotten.

> Still, the CIA kept an eye on what Israel was actually testing and experimenting with in the wastelands of the Negev desert. What was described as a "probable CW nerve agent production facility and a storage facility" was suspected to actually be located at the Dimona Sensitive Storage Area." Yet the CIA report does not describe exactly where this facility is located.[369]

Aid, however, in compiling his report for *Foreign Policy* did a little digging of his own and managed to come up with a possible location for the facility. He writes,

> At my request, a friend of mine who retired years ago from the U.S. intelligence community began systematically scanning the available cache of commercial satellite imagery found on the Google Maps website, looking for the mysterious and elusive Israeli nerve agent production facility and weapons storage bunker complex near the city of Dimona where Israel stores its stockpile of chemical weapons.

> It took a little while, but the imagery search found what I believe is the location of the Israeli nerve agent production facility and its associated chemical weapons storage area in a desolate and virtually uninhabited area of the Negev Desert just east of the village of al-Kilab, which is only 10 miles west of the outskirts of the city of Dimona. The satellite imagery shows that the heavily protected weapons storage area at al-Kilab currently consists of almost 50 buried bunkers surrounded by a double barbed-wire-topped fence and facilities for a large permanent security force. I believe this extensive bunker complex is the location of what the 1983 CIA intelligence estimate referred to as the Dimona Sensitive Storage Area.

> If you drive two miles to the northeast past the weapons storage area, the satellite imagery shows that you run into another heavily guarded complex of about 40 or 50

---

[368] Aid, Matthew M. "Does Israel Have Chemical Weapons?" Foreign Policy. September 10, 2013. http://foreignpolicy.com/2013/09/10/exclusive-does-israel-have-chemical-weapons-too/
[369] Aid, Matthew M. "Does Israel Have Chemical Weapons?" Foreign Policy. September 10, 2013. http://foreignpolicy.com/2013/09/10/exclusive-does-israel-have-chemical-weapons-too/

acres. Surrounded again by a double chain-link fence topped with barbed wire, the complex appears to consist of an administrative and support area on the western side of facility. The eastern side of the base, which is surrounded by its own security fence, appears to consist of three large storage bunkers and a buried production and/or maintenance facility. Although not confirmed, the author believes that this may, in fact, be the location of the Israeli nerve agent production facility mentioned in the 1983 CIA report.[370]

While Aid writes that it is unknown whether or not Israel maintains the stockpile of chemical and biological weapons, the fact is that if Israel did not continue to possess and maintain such weapons, it would be an abrupt change of position and procedure. Indeed, while Aid can only concede that the US intelligence community "had suspicions about this stockpile for decades, and that the U.S. government kept mum about Israel's suspected possession of chemical weapons just as long," Israel has given the international and intelligence community more than enough reason to believe that it does, in fact, possess these chemical and biological weapons. Aid himself writes that "the Israeli government has a well-known penchant for preserving any asset thought to be needed for the defense of the state of Israel, regardless of the cost or possible diplomatic ramifications."[371]

In fact, the list of Israeli usage of chemical weapons against Palestinians is quite long, going as far back as 1948 and as recently as at least 2004.[372]

Regardless of the lack of information surrounding the location of the weapons facility and the actual knowledge the CIA or other government agencies may have of the Israeli chemical weapons agenda, one thing is clear – there will be no red lines drawn in the sand over this particular program.

The Torture Report – Caesar And The New Holocaust

On January 20, 2014, only two days before negotiations were set to begin over Syria in Switzerland, a now famous report was released claiming to hold photographic evidence of Bashar al-Assad's brutality against his own people and institutional torture programs in place by the Syrian government. The report, whose source was an alleged "defector" going only by the name of "Caesar," and photos he allegedly took at a Syrian government military hospital, was touted as evidence of Assad's cruelty and an example of how the Syrian president was committing war crimes reminiscent of Nazi Germany.

The report was plastered all across Western media, television screens, and internet sites in perfect timing to disrupt any hope of a negotiated end to the Western-backed violence in Syria (at a time when the Syrian government was experiencing serious setbacks). Ever

---

[370] Aid, Matthew M. "Does Israel Have Chemical Weapons?" Foreign Policy. September 10, 2013. http://foreignpolicy.com/2013/09/10/exclusive-does-israel-have-chemical-weapons-too/
[371] Aid, Matthew M. "Does Israel Have Chemical Weapons?" Foreign Policy. September 10, 2013. http://foreignpolicy.com/2013/09/10/exclusive-does-israel-have-chemical-weapons-too/
[372] Brooks, James. "Israel's Chemical Weapons." Antiwar.com. July 8, 2004. http://www.antiwar.com/orig/brooks.php?articleid=2957

since, that report and the related photos have repeatedly crept back into the media spotlight at convenient times when massive propaganda blitzes against the Syrian government were being put in place or when key decisions were being made.

The alleged defector, who only goes by the name "Caesar," spoke in front of a closed-door session of the House Foreign Affairs Committee in late July, 2014.

The photos, which were supposed to number in the tens of thousands were "analyzed" by the Federal Bureau of Investigation at the request of the Ambassador-At-Large for War Crimes, Steven J.Rapp and were in the process of analysis at the time of the flurry of reports Caesar's Congressional testimony.

Rapp stated in an interview that the photos are "horrific — some of them put you in visceral pain. This is some of the strongest evidence we've seen in the area of proof of the commission of mass atrocities."[373]

Rapp, apparently intending to head off any suggestions that the photos may be either fakes or photos of some other atrocity perhaps committed by the death squads armed, trained, funded, and directed by NATO, the Ambassador claimed that the FBI assured him that they think it is impossible that the photographs could be forgeries. Rapp said that the FBI assured that there is no evidence of doctoring. This, of course, is quite a bizarre conclusion to reach since the investigation is not yet over. Thus, one must wonder if the FBI had determined the veracity of the photographs before even opening the packages they came in.[374]

As Michael Isikoff writes for Yahoo! News,

> The story behind the photos begins in March 2011, when Arab Spring protests against the Assad government swept through Syria. As the military began rounding up suspected dissidents, Caesar — a military police officer — was assigned to lead a team of 11 photographers whose job it was to document the deaths of detainees brought to a military hospital from three detention centers around Damascus.

> But by the summer of 2013, Caesar has told investigators, he was so sickened by what he was seeing that he made contact with Syrian rebels. "I can't do this anymore," he told them, according to David Crane, a former war-crimes prosecutor for Sierra Leone who spent hours interviewing Caesar as part of a separate review of the photos commissioned by the government of Qatar.

> […]

> Caesar began smuggling his photos to the rebels, providing them with thumb drives concealed in his shoes, Crane said. To protect his family, Caesar faked his death, staging an elaborate funeral, before he escaped from Syria in August 2013. He is now in hiding in Europe.

---

[373] Isikoff, Michael. "Inside Bashar Assad's Torture Chambers." Yahoo News. October 13, 2014. https://www.yahoo.com/news/bashar-al-assad-s-syrian-torture-chambers-205323124.html?ref=gs

[374] Isikoff, Michael. "Inside Bashar Assad's Torture Chambers." Yahoo News. October 13, 2014. https://www.yahoo.com/news/bashar-al-assad-s-syrian-torture-chambers-205323124.html?ref=gs

The photos, according to Crane, document "an industrial killing machine not seen since the Holocaust." They show corpses, some of them lined up in a warehouse, many appearing to be victims of starvation, their ribs protruding from emaciated bodies.[375]

The Syrian government denied most of the photos as fake and has stated that it believes many of them to be pictures of dead terrorists who were killed in battle. The Syrian government's suggestions are entirely plausible and, indeed, quite likely to be true. Remember, NATO has already attempted to frame the Assad government for a number of war crimes and atrocities that later turned out to be the handiwork of the terrorists funded by NATO itself. The Ghouta chemical weapons attack, the famous Houla massacre, and a number of other atrocities all come to mind instantly.[376]

Unfortunately, in a gross insult to the victims of the Nazis, the Holocaust museum placed a number of these photographs on display for propaganda purposes, an obvious attempt to dredge up memories of the Holocaust and paint Assad as the new Hitler.

Such ridiculous comparisons were made the first and second time this cynical display of propaganda was pushed in mainstream media outlets.

As it was then, there remain a number of reasons to question the photographs, reports, and "defectors" presenting the "smoking gun" against Assad now.

1.) The Gulf State Feudal Monarchy Qatar is the sponsor of one of the main reports and "reviews" of the photographs. Qatar is, of course, one of the major sponsors of the Syrian invasion (aka the Syrian "rebels") and has played a massively important role in financing, training, arming, and directing the death squads currently being mopped up by the Assad government.[377]

2.) The source of the report and photographs. One would be justified in questioning the nature of the reports and photos since the sole source of the material comes by virtue of an allegedly "defected Syrian military police officer" who was apparently fine with photographing thousands of dead victims for over a year up until his "Damascus Road Conversion." Regardless of the possibility for such a "moral" conversion, taking information from a "defected" member of government forces once again returns us to the realm of the "activists say" school of journalism – a notorious method used by Western media outlets to promote the side of the death squads and only the side of the death squads as fact in popular reports. Note that "Caesar" himself claims that he was in touch with the Syrian opposition, meaning terrorist death squads and cannibal savages funded by the West. Apparently, he thought these murderers as a better option than

---

[375] Isikoff, Michael. "Inside Bashar Assad's Torture Chambers." Yahoo News. October 13, 2014. https://www.yahoo.com/news/bashar-al-assad-s-syrian-torture-chambers-205323124.html?ref=gs

[376] Isikoff, Michael. "Inside Bashar Assad's Torture Chambers." Yahoo News. October 13, 2014. https://www.yahoo.com/news/bashar-al-assad-s-syrian-torture-chambers-205323124.html?ref=gs

[377] Isikoff, Michael. "Inside Bashar Assad's Torture Chambers." Yahoo News. October 13, 2014. https://www.yahoo.com/news/bashar-al-assad-s-syrian-torture-chambers-205323124.html?ref=gs

Assad. If so, that perspective tells us much about the allegiances and affiliations of "Caesar."

3.) "Caesar" reminiscent of "Curveball." We cannot forget the famous Codename, "Curveball" that played a major role in the initiation of a previous and still ongoing conflict that was later admitted to be a fabrication. Being fooled by the same type of propaganda twice in eleven years is indeed a humiliation too great for a country to bear.[378]

4.) Past claims of Assad's "Crimes Against Humanity." It is important to remember past experiences with Western charges against Assad for alleged "crimes against humanity," all of which turned out to have been committed by the death squads, not the Syrian government. From the Houla massacre to the Ghouta chemical weapons attacks, the Syrian government has been exonerated by all credible evidence. The death squads, however, have been proven guilty by virtue of their own video tapes and YouTube accounts, of some of the most horrific acts imaginable. While many innocent people have no doubt been killed in the crossfire between the military and the death squads, the Western media has done everything in its power to place the blood of each and every death inside Syria in the hands of the government.

5.) Possibility that the death squads could have killed the victims shown in the photographs, that the death squads are themselves the victims, or that the photographs contain a mix of the two. The victims shown in the report have clearly been abused and starved. However, before jumping to conclusions about just how these unfortunate individuals met their fate, perhaps it would be a good idea to look back at the context of the victims. As mentioned earlier, the death squads operating in Syria are no strangers to crimes against humanity, murder, and torture. In fact, they have been both the initiators of such depravity and overwhelmingly the largest proprietors of it.

Furthermore, the fact that the victims were starved does not necessarily mean that they were starved by the government. Indeed, it is important to remember that, due to the siege of a number of cities by both the military and the death squads as well as due to death squad cruelty and attempted cordoning off of specific areas, food shortage has been a serious concern in some areas for some time.[379] There is also plentiful evidence of death squad groups killing innocent people and shipping their bodies to the places where cameras are set up, waiting for the recording of the propaganda piece. The Ghouta chemical attack is just one instance in which innocent civilians were captured and killed by the death squads and used as stage props for propaganda purposes.[380]

Indeed, it is also important to remember that the death squads themselves are quite adept at keeping prisoners in atrocious conditions. Remember, it was reported that the Syrian military was able to free a number of captive Syrian women from the hands of

---

[378] "Faulty Intel Source 'CurveBall' Revealed." CBS News. November 1, 2007. http://www.cbsnews.com/news/faulty-intel-source-curve-ball-revealed/

[379] Turbeville, Brandon. "Cats On The Menu While Death Squads Halt Food Shipments." Activist Post. November 6, 2013. http://www.activistpost.com/2013/11/syria-cats-on-menu-while-death-squads.html

[380] Turbeville, Brandon. "Syria Chemical Weapons Victims Were Staged Using Kidnapped Hostages: Report." Activist Post. September 25, 2013. http://www.activistpost.com/2013/09/syria-chemical-weapons-victims-were.html

the death squads who had kept them in captivity in underground tunnels for months on end for the purposes of using them as sex slaves.[381]

6.) The photographs were conveniently released just two days before the Geneva II Peace Conference meeting on Syria the first time. Now they are conveniently released as the United States and NATO are considering a "Buffer Zone" in Syria.[382]

After the retraction of an invitation to Iran to attend the peace conference, the Qatari-funded report regarding the photographs was released just two days before the peace conference was scheduled to take place. With such evidence being studied and analyzed and a report being compiled, to believe that it was only a coincidence that the information was released two days before the conference is absurd. If this evidence was real and of such grave importance why did world leaders only learn of it days before the peace conference? If world leaders knew, why did it take so long to hear about it?[383]

Now, as the United States and NATO eye a no-fly zone in Syria, the photographs are being recycled complete with the requisite Hitler references during the run-up to the implementation of the "buffer zone."

The convenience of this report for the NATO and GCC agenda to destroy Syria and overthrow Assad is such that precludes its honesty.

7.) Involvement of Color Revolution NGOs. "Caesar's" entire trip to the United States has been organized and facilitated by the Coalition For A Democratic Syria, an organization that has very close ties with the National Democratic Institute (NDI), a subsidiary of the National Endowment for Democracy, both groups being notorious color revolutions operations.[384] [385] [386] The NDI website states that

> NDI works with a number of established political parties and emerging movements on party development and organizational structure. The Institute's partners include: the Damascus Declaration; the People's Party; Building the Syrian State; the Kurdish Youth Tanseekiyat Union; the Ahrar Party; the Muslim Brotherhood; the Democratic Platform; the National Change Trend; the Syrian Democratic Coalition; and the Yekiti party, as well as many others.[387]

---

[381] Turbeville, Brandon. "Kidnapped Girls Used As Sex Slaves: Report." Activist Post. November 13, 2013. http://www.activistpost.com/2013/11/kidnapped-syrian-girls-used-as-sex.html

[382] "What Is the Geneva II Conference On Syria?" BBC. January 22, 2014. http://www.bbc.com/news/world-middle-east-24628442

[383] Charbonneau, Louis; Hafezi, Parisa. "Iran Invite To Syria Talks Withdrawn After Boycott Threat." Reuters. Jaunary 20, 2014. http://www.reuters.com/article/2014/01/20/us-syria-un-iran-idUSBREA0J01K20140120

[384] Chakraborty, Barnini. "Syrian Defector Testifies, Shows House Lawmakers Graphic Images Of Assad Torture." FOX News. July 31, 2014. http://www.foxnews.com/politics/2014/07/31/syrian-defector-caesar-shows-lawmakers-thousands-pictures-assad-related-torture.html

[385] Coalition For A Democratic Syria website. http://www.coalitionforademocraticsyria.org/

[386] "Syria." National Democratic Institute. https://www.ndi.org/syria

[387] "NDI Syria Program Overview: June 2014."National Democratic Institute. https://www.ndi.org/files/citizen_syria_overview.pdf

It is also notable that the SDC's website contains a number of pictures of Syria with the Green, White and Black flag of the death squads and their smokescreen "moderate" faction instead of the real Red, White, and Black flag of the Syrian government.

The NDI website also admits funding terrorists in Syria albeit through very couched terms. It says,

> NDI has built long-term partnerships with Syrian organizations since 2005, working with more than 1,200 Syrian democrats in an extensive network of civil society leaders and opposition activists. Through 2010, NDI assisted a Damascus-based civil society organization and resource center, Etana Press, in assessing the needs of civil society in Syria and building resources and knowledge to meet those needs. Since the beginning of the Syrian conflict in 2011, NDI has intensified its assistance to opposition activists seeking democratic reform.[388]

A recent report written by Rick Sterling of Syria Solidarity Movement and entitled "The Caesar Photo Fraud That Undermined Syrian Negotiations: 12 Problems With The Story Of Mass Torture And Execution In Syria," expands on these points and provides a detailed deconstruction of the "Caesar" photos over the course of 30 pages.

Sterling provides 12 problems with the "Caesar Torture Photos:"

1. Almost half the photos show the opposite of the allegations.

2. Allegations other photos only show "tortured detainees" are exaggerated or false.

3. The true identity of 'Caesar' is probably not as claimed.

4. The Carter Ruck inquiry was rushed, faulty and politically motivated.

5. The US Central Intelligence Agency (CIA) is involved.

6. Simple administrative procedures are portrayed as mysterious and sinister.

7. The photos have been tampered with.

8. The photo catalog is faulty.

9. Western media has uncritically promoted the story.

10. Politicians have promoted the story for propaganda purposes.

11. The Human Rights Watch assessment is biased.

12. The legal accusations are biased and ignore the supreme crime of aggression.[389]

Sterling wrote an article to go along with his report of the same name that acts as a condensed version of the full report. In that article, he confirms the suspicions this writer

---

[388] "NDI Syria Program Overview: June 2014."National Democratic Institute. https://www.ndi.org/files/citizen_syria_overview.pdf

[389] Sterling, Rick. "The Caesar Photo Fraud That Undermined Syrian Negotiations: 12 Problems With The Story Of Mass Torture And Execution From Syria." Syria Solidarity Movement. March, 2016. http://www.syriasolidaritymovement.org/wp-content/uploads/2016/03/CaesarPhotoFraudReport_v6.compressed.pdf

put forth in 2014. In other words, Sterling demonstrates that the report is constructed for the purpose of blaming the Syrian government for something it did not do. Sterling writes,

> The Carter Ruck Inquiry Team [evaluation of the Caesar story conducted by the Carter-Ruck Law Firm on contract to Qatar] claimed there were about 55,000 photos total with about half of them taken by 'Caesar' and the other half by other photographers. The Carter Ruck team claimed the photos were all 'similar'. Together they are all known as 'Caesar's Torture Photos'.

> The photographs are in the custody of an opposition organization called the Syrian Association for Missing and Conscience Detainees (SAFMCD). In 2015, they allowed Human Rights Watch (HRW) to study all the photographs which have otherwise been secret. In December 2015, HRW released their report titled "If the Dead Could Speak". The biggest revelation is that over 46% of the photographs (24,568) do not show people 'tortured to death" by the Syrian government. On the contrary, they show dead Syrian soldiers and victims of car bombs and other violence (HRW pp2-3). Thus, nearly half the photos show the opposite of what was alleged. These photos, never revealed to the public, confirm that the opposition is violent and has killed large numbers of Syrian security forces and civilians.[390]

Sterling also writes that claims that the "other" photos – meaning the photos other than the ones that demonstrated exactly the opposite of the Caesar story – showed only "abused detainees" are also false. He writes,

> The Carter Ruck report says 'Caesar' only photographed bodies brought from Syrian government detention centers. In their December 2015 report, HRW said, "The largest category of photographs, 28,707 images, are photographs Human Rights Watch understands to have died in government custody, either in one of several detention facilities or after being transferred to a military hospital." They estimate 6,786 dead individuals in the set.

> The photos and the deceased are real, but how they died and the circumstances are unclear. There is strong evidence some died in conflict. Others died in the hospital. Others died and their bodies were decomposing before they were picked up. These photographs seem to document a war time situation where many combatants and civilians are killed. It seems the military hospital was doing what it had always done: maintaining a photographic and documentary record of the deceased. Bodies were picked up by different military or intelligence branches. While some may have died in detention; the big majority probably died in the conflict zones. The accusations by 'Caesar', the Carter Ruck report and HRW that these are all victims of "death in detention" or "death by torture" or death in 'government custody" are almost certainly false.[391]

In addition, Sterling points out that many of the photos were manipulated by using duplicate photos and editing out (and in) information and case numbers, etc. Sterling says,

---

[390] Sterling, Rick. "The Caesar Photo Fraud That Undermined Syrian Negotiations." Information Clearing House. March 4, 2016. http://www.informationclearinghouse.info/article44369.htm
[391] Sterling, Rick. "The Caesar Photo Fraud That Undermined Syrian Negotiations." Information Clearing House. March 4, 2016. http://www.informationclearinghouse.info/article44369.htm

Many of the photos at the SAFMCD website have been manipulated. The information card and tape identity are covered over and sections of documents are obscured. It must have been very time consuming to do this for thousands of photos. The explanation that they are doing this to 'protect identity' is not credible since the faces of victims are visible. What are they hiding?

. . . .

There are numerous errors and anomalies in the photo catalog as presented at the SAFMCD website.

For example, some deceased persons are shown twice with different case numbers and dates.

There are other errors where different individuals are given the same identity number.

Researcher Adam Larson at A Closer Look at Syria website has done detailed investigation which reveals more errors and curious error patterns in the SAFMCD photo catalog.[392]

Sterling highlights the fact that the "inquiry" also claims that simple administrative duties are classified as horrific war crimes in the report. He states,

The Carter Ruck inquiry team falsely claimed there were about 11,000 tortured and killed detainees. They then posed the question: Why would the Syrian government photograph and document the people they just killed? The Carter Ruck Report speculates that the military hospital photographed the dead to prove that the "orders to kill" had been followed. The "orders to kill" are assumed.

A more logical explanation is that dead bodies were photographed as part of normal hospital/morgue procedure to maintain a file of the deceased who were received or treated at the hospital.

The same applies to the body labeling/numbering system. The Carter Ruck report suggest there is something mysterious and possibly sinister in the coded tagging system. But all morgues need to have a tagging and identification system.[393]

The victims shown in the report have clearly been abused and starved. However, before jumping to conclusions about just how these unfortunate individuals met their fate, it is necessary to look back at the context of the victims. After all, the death squads operating in Syria are no strangers to crimes against humanity, murder, and torture. In fact, they have been both the initiators of such depravity and overwhelmingly the largest proprietors of it.

Furthermore, the fact that the victims were starved does not necessarily mean that they were starved by the government. Indeed, it is important to remember that, due to the siege of a number of cities by both the military and the death squads as well as due to death squad cruelty and attempted cordoning off of specific areas, food shortage has been a serious concern in some areas for some time. There is also plentiful evidence of

---

[392] Sterling, Rick. "The Caesar Photo Fraud That Undermined Syrian Negotiations." Information Clearing House. March 4, 2016. http://www.informationclearinghouse.info/article44369.htm

[393] Sterling, Rick. "The Caesar Photo Fraud That Undermined Syrian Negotiations." Information Clearing House. March 4, 2016. http://www.informationclearinghouse.info/article44369.htm

death squad groups killing innocent people and shipping their bodies to the places where cameras are set up, waiting for the recording of the propaganda piece. The Ghouta chemical attack is just one instance in which innocent civilians were captured and killed by the death squads and used as stage props for propaganda purposes.[394]

Indeed, it is also important to remember that the death squads themselves are quite adept at keeping prisoners in atrocious conditions. Remember, it was reported some time ago that the Syrian military was able to free a number of captive Syrian women from the hands of the death squads who had kept them in captivity in underground tunnels for months on end for the purposes of using them as sex slaves.[395]

Nevertheless, Sterling also calls into question the identity of the "defector" going by the name of "Caesar." He writes,

> The Carter Ruck Report says "This witness who defected from Syria and who had been working for the Syrian government was given the code-name 'Caesar' by the inquiry team to protect the witness and members of his family." (CRR p.12) However, if his story is true, it would be easy for the Syrian government to determine who he really is. After all, how many military photographers took photos at Tishreen and Military 601 Hospitals during those years and then disappeared? According to the Carter Ruck report, Caesar's family left Syria around the same time. Considering this, why is "Caesar" keeping his identity secret from the western audience? Why does "Caesar" refuse to meet even with highly sympathetic journalists or researchers?

> The fact that 46% of the total photographic set is substantially the opposite of what was claimed indicates two possibilities:

> * Caesar and his promoters knew the contents but lied about them expecting nobody to look.

> * Caesar and his promoters did not know the contents and falsely assumed they were like the others.

> The latter seems more likely which supports the theory that Caesar is not who he claims to be.[396]

Sterling also presents evidence that "Caesar" himself may have been working for the U.S. Central Intelligence Agency in an effort to create a propaganda campaign against the Syrian government. Sterling uses quotes from Prof. Crane of the Carter Ruck inquiry in order to build his case. Indeed, Crane's statements to France 24 are quite revealing. Sterling writes,

> In an interview on France24,[397] Prof. David Crane of the inquiry team describes how 'Caesar' was brought to meet them by "his handler, his case officer". The expression

---

[394] Turbeville, Brandon. "Syria Chemical Weapons Victims Were Staged Using Kidnapped Hostages: Report." Activist Post. September 25, 2013.
http://www.activistpost.com/2013/09/syria-chemical-weapons-victims-were.html
[395] Turbeville, Brandon. "Kidnapped Syrian Girls Used As Sex Slaves: Report." Activist Post. November 13, 2013. http://www.activistpost.com/2013/11/kidnapped-syrian-girls-used-as-sex.html
[396] Sterling, Rick. "The Caesar Photo Fraud That Undermined Syrian Negotiations." Information Clearing House. March 4, 2016. http://www.informationclearinghouse.info/article44369.htm

'case officer' usually refers to the CIA. This would be a common expression for Prof. Crane who previously worked in the Defense Intelligence Agency. The involvement of the CIA additionally makes sense since there was a CIA budget of $1Billion for Syria operations in 2013.

Prof. Crane's "Syria Accountability Project" is based at Syracuse University where the CIA actively recruits new officers despite student resistance.

Why does it matter if the CIA is connected to the 'Caesar' story? Because the CIA has a long history of disinformation campaigns. In 2011, false reports of viagra fueled rape by Libyan soldiers were widely broadcast in western media as the U.S. pushed for a military mandate. Decades earlier, the world was shocked to hear about Cuban troops fighting in Angola raping Angolan women. The CIA chief of station for Angola, John Stockwell, later described how they invented the false report and spread it round the world. The CIA was very proud of that disinformation achievement. Stockwell's book, "In Search of Enemies" is still relevant.[398]

As I pointed out in my own article in 2014, the Carter Ruck inquiry itself was fraught with conflicts of interest and fraught with the telltale signs of carefully constructed propaganda. The law firm conducting the inquiry having been contracted by Qatar (a GCC member assisting in the funding of al-Qaeda terrorists and the destruction of Syria) and represented Turkey's President Erdogan (another major player in the war against Syria), the Carter Ruck inquiry reveals itself for the hoax that it is. Put together with the apparent intentionally shoddy research conducted by Carter Ruck, Crane's ties to the U.S. intelligence community, and the involvement of color revolution NGOs, the Caesar story simply does not hold water.

Sterling addresses many of these issues in his report when he writes,

> The credibility of the "Caesar" story has been substantially based on the Carter-Ruck Inquiry Team which "verified" the defecting photographer and his photographs. The following facts suggest the team was biased with a political motive:
>
> * the investigation was financed by the government of Qatar which is a major supporter of the armed opposition.
>
> * the contracted law firm, Carter Ruck and Co. has previously represented Turkey's President Erdogan, also known for his avid support of the armed opposition.
>
> * the American on the legal inquiry team, Prof David M. Crane, has a long history working for U.S. Dept of Defense and Defense Intelligence Agency. The U.S. Government has been deeply involved in the attempt at 'regime change' with demands that 'Assad must go' beginning in summer 2011 and continuing until recently.

[397] David M. Crane, Co-author of a report on Syrian prisoners." France 24. The Interview. March 17, 2014. http://www.france24.com/en/20140315-interview-david-michael-crane-co-author-report-on-syrian-prisoners-torture-killing-assad-regime

[398] Sterling, Rick. "The Caesar Photo Fraud That Undermined Syrian Negotiations." Information Clearing House. March 4, 2016. http://www.informationclearinghouse.info/article44369.htm

* Prof Crane is personally partisan in the conflict. He has campaigned for a Syrian War Crimes Tribunal and testified before Congress in October 2013, three months before the Caesar revelations.

* by their own admission, the inquiry team was under "time constraints" (CRR, p.11).

* by their own admission, the inquiry team did not even survey most of the photographs

* the inquiry team was either ignorant of the content or intentionally lied about the 46% showing dead Syrian soldiers and attack victims.

* the inquiry team did their last interview with "Caesar" on January 18, quickly finalized a report and rushed it into the media on January 20, two days prior to the start of UN sponsored negotiations.

The self-proclaimed "rigor" of the Carter Ruck investigation is without foundation. The claims to a 'scientific' investigation are similarly without substance and verging on the ludicrous.[399]

School Bombings

Americans should no longer be shocked at the level of depravity to which Western governments and their media mouthpieces will sink in order to demonize the government of a target nation. While the historical parallels are plentiful, relatively recent events should serve as enough of a reminder that reports circulating from Western media outlets should never be trusted when concerning the situation on the ground inside a country that is slated for NATO intervention. Indeed, Syria has been witness to this fact time and time again.

Thus, as reports began to circulate regarding the alleged Syrian military airstrike against a school in Aleppo, it was and remains vitally important to remember the history of the Anglo-European propaganda machine in regards to so many other "massacres" and "crimes against humanity" that have later turned out to be either completely fabricated or twisted in such a way as to represent a narrative that is 180 degrees different from the truth.[400]

With that in mind, mainstream outlets like Reuters reported that on April 30, 2014, the Syrian military conducted an airstrike on a school in the Al-Ansari District of Aleppo which resulted in the death of at least 18 people, most of them children. The reports presented the bombing of the Ain Jalout School as if it were the target of the Syrian Air Force all along.[401] The pro-death squad organization, the Syrian Observatory for Human Rights, essentially one man located in Britain, claim that the death toll surrounding the school bombing was 18, while the media wing of the death squads, the Aleppo Media Centre, claimed that the death toll was higher, with at least 25 children being killed.[402]

---

[399] Sterling, Rick. "The Caesar Photo Fraud That Undermined Syrian Negotiations." Information Clearing House. March 4, 2016. http://www.informationclearinghouse.info/article44369.htm
[400] Cartalucci, Tony; Bowie, Nile. "Subverting Syria: How CIA Contra Gangs And NGO's Manufacture, Mislable, And Market Mass Murder." Progressive Press. September 11, 2012.
[401] "Air strike on Aleppo School Kills 18: Syrian Activists." Reuters. April 30, 2014.
http://www.reuters.com/article/us-syria-crisis-aleppo-idUSBREA3T0PA20140430

Videos posted by the death squad forces show bodies strewn about the floor along with blood and debris.

The United Nations apparatus then fell over itself to condemn the airstrikes with the United Nations Children's Fund stating that it was "outraged by the latest wave of indiscriminate attacks perpetrated against schools and other civilian targets across Syria."[403]

While indiscriminate bombing campaigns by the Syrian military are certainly not outside the realm of possibility, despite mountains of evidence that Syrian airstrikes a mostly surgical in nature, there are several reasons to doubt the veracity of the claims made by Western media outlets that attempt to imply that Syrian government forces intentionally targeted the school. Indeed, there are also reasons to question whether or not the school was bombed at all. Given the history of the Anglo-European propaganda machine in its rush to war against Syria, we cannot ignore these possibilities.

1.) While mainstream Western media outlets attempt to present the school bombing as if it were the calculated tactic of the Assad government, some level-headed reporters have provided a slightly more sober interpretation of the events in Aleppo. For instance, Jason Ditz of Antiwar.com writes that the bombing, while the fault of the Syrian government, was not an intentional targeting of the school, but an errant bomb that veered off course. He states,

> Underscoring the increasingly inaccurate nature of the Syrian Civil War, a military air strike, involving a barrel bomb, careened off course in a rebel held district of the northern city of Aleppo, hitting an elementary school.

> The bomb tore through the school, ripping the side off of it and killing 25 people within, including several children.[404] Multiple strikes hit the Ansari District of Aleppo,[405] though this was the only one reported to have caused deaths.[406]

2.) The source of the reports paraded across Western screens were from the infamous "activists say" school of journalism. "Activists" in this sense, of course, can be translated to mean "death squads" (aka the "rebels"). These "activists" have provided weak information at best, but have provided unsubstantiated as well as outright fabricated and staged information on numerous occasions.

---

[402] "EXPOSED: Syrian Human Rights Front Is EU-Funded Fraud." Land Destroyer Report. April 12, 2013. http://landdestroyer.blogspot.com/2013/04/exposed-syrian-human-rights-front-is-eu.html

[403] Besheer, Margaret. "Syrian Air Strike Hits School, Killing 18, Many Of Them Children." Voice of America (VOA). April 30, 2014. http://www.voanews.com/content/syrian-air-strike-hits-school-killing-18-many-of-them-children/1904850.html

[404] Yan, Holly; Abedine, Saad. "25 Children Killed In Elementary School Bombing, Syrian Activists Say." CNN. April 30, 2014. http://www.cnn.com/2014/04/30/world/meast/syria-civil-war/

[405] "Air strike on Aleppo School Kills 18: Syrian Activists." Reuters. April 30, 2014. http://www.reuters.com/article/us-syria-crisis-aleppo-idUSBREA3T0PA20140430

[406] Ditz, Jason. "Syria Air Strike Hits Aleppo School, Killing 25." Antiwar.com. April 30, 2014. http://news.antiwar.com/2014/04/30/syria-air-strike-hits-aleppo-school-killing-25/

The Ghouta chemical weapons attack scenario stands as one of the more famous instances of "activists saying" that Assad forces fired sarin gas against Syrian civilians while themselves having staged the entire event with captured civilians from Latakia.

3.) There is also the question of exactly how many civilians remain inside Aleppo to be bombed. Aleppo, particularly the rebel-held areas, has witnessed a massive out flux and evacuation of citizens. This is not only because of the fighting and potential attacks by opposing sides, but also because of the savagery inflicted upon the subject populous once the death squad fighters seize power.

Indeed, the New York Times reported in mid-February, 2014 that hundreds of thousands of civilians had been forced to flee the rebel-held areas of Aleppo.[407] Even more so, Al-Jazeera reports that rebel-held Aleppo is a "ghost town" with whole neighborhoods having been abandoned.[408]

This is the same situation of Ghouta, where most civilians had left their homes in order to escape the fighting and death squads. Still, the Western media ignored the clear evidence that these attacks had been staged and attempted to portray the Ghouta region as heavily populated with civilians.

4.) In keeping with the tradition of both the terrorists operating on the ground and that of the Anglo-American propaganda outlets, there exists the very real possibility that this attack never actually happened in terms of the way it is being portrayed.

Keep in mind that the collusion of Western governments and the death squads have presented numerous instances of Assad's alleged cruelty and war crimes that have all turned out to be those of the death squads themselves. The Ghouta chemical weapons attacks, the Houla Massacre, the Khan al-Assal chemical weapons attacks, and many others have all initially been blamed on the Assad government. Evidence to the contrary, however, subsequently emerged. As in the case of the three specific atrocities mentioned above, reports based on "activists say" and videos provided by death squads were used to justify the possibility of military action by NATO. Indeed, in the case of Ghouta, captives were actually used as stage props in order to pin the attacks on the Syrian government. Likewise, we must remember the documented cases of photographic tampering that have occurred during the course of the Syrian destabilization.

The image, reportedly showing a Syrian orphan child lying between his parents' graves, which was passed around the mainstream media to tug on the

---

[407] Hubbard, Ben. "Bombings In Syria Force Wave of Civilians To Flee." New York Times. February 17, 2014. http://www.nytimes.com/2014/02/18/world/middleeast/bombings-in-syria-force-wave-of-civilians-to-flee.html?_r=0

[408] Gilbert, Ben. "Thousands of Syrian Civilians Flee 'Barrels of Death.'" Al-Jazeera. February 14, 2014. http://america.aljazeera.com/articles/2014/2/14/thousands-of-syrianciviliansfleebarrelsofdeath.html

heartstrings of Westerners, turned out to be nothing more than an art project that was taken in Saudi Arabia. The child was not even an orphan.[409] Another photo, showing a child jumping over a row of dead bodies, and also used for war propaganda turned out to be a photograph of Iraq, not Syria.[410] Likewise, the photo portraying a lost little boy alone in the desert being comforted by UN staff, turned out to be a cleverly cropped photo used to drum up misguided sympathy and promote NATO involvement under the Responsibility to Protect doctrine.[411]

With all of this in mind, it is important to note that another school was bombed in Syria the same week as the Aleppo school. Shortly before the alleged bombing of the Ain Jalout School, a school was bombed by terrorists in Damascus. Although not widely reported, particularly after the mainstream outlets picked up on the propaganda point of the Ain Jalout School, that Tuesday saw four mortar shells fired by terrorists in central Damascus killing approximately 14 people and wounding many others. The CBC reports quoted the Damascus Police Command as having stated that two of those shells hit a school complex.[412] Even the pro-death squad organization, Syrian Observatory for Human Rights, admitted that the attacks occurred, explaining that the school taught students as young as 14.[413] The video of the attack can easily be viewed on YouTube.

Whether or not the bombing in Aleppo was an errant bomb, an intentional strike on death squads holding a military position from the school, or simply never happened, it is imperative that we remember the false narrative that has been provided to the Western public since the beginning of the destabilization. We must remember the fabricated stories repeated ad nauseum regarding Assad's alleged atrocities only to later find that it was the Western-backed death squads who were responsible. In the end, we must observe these events from a logical standpoint and always take whatever comes from NATO media outlets with a large grain of salt.

---

[409] Hooton, Christopher. "'Heartbreaking' Syrian Orphan Photo Wasn't Taken In Syria and Not Of An Orphan." The Independent. January 17, 2014.
http://www.independent.co.uk/news/world/middle-east/heartbreaking-syria-orphan-photo-wasnt-taken-in-syria-and-not-of-orphan-9067956.html

[410] Furness, Hannah. "BBC News Uses 'Iraq Photo To Illustrate Syrian Massacre.'" The Telegraph. May 27, 2012. http://www.telegraph.co.uk/culture/tvandradio/bbc/9293620/BBC-News-uses-Iraq-photo-to-illustrate-Syrian-massacre.html

[411] Sherwood, Harriet; Malik, Shiv. "Image Of Syrian Boy In Desert Triggers Sympathy – And Then A Backlash." The Guardian. February 18, 2014.
https://www.theguardian.com/world/2014/feb/18/image-syrian-boy-desert-un-refugees-tweet

[412] "Syria Attacks In Homs, Damascus Kill 50." Associated Press. CBC News. April 29, 2014.
http://www.cbc.ca/news/world/syria-attacks-in-homs-damascus-kill-50-1.2625305

[413] "Rebel Attack Kills 14 In Damascus." The Sydney Morning Herald. April 29, 2014.
http://www.smh.com.au/world/rebel-attack-kills-14-in-damascus-20140429-zr1hu.html

Hospital Bombings

A Tale Of Two Hospitals: Potentially Fabricated Bombing Incident VS Open Terrorist Targeting Of Facilities In Aleppo

In May, 2016, the Western corporate press kicked into overdrive with reports of hospital bombings, dead civilians, and war crimes all blamed predictably on the secular government of Bashar al-Assad. According to Western governments and their media mouthpieces, Assad's forces have targeted civilian hospitals in order to . . . well . . . no one knows why Assad's forces would logically target civilian hospitals. Still, the Western harpies – both media and "human rights NGOs" – continued to hammer the unsubstantiated claims and misinformation at the tops of their lungs that the SAA is dropping bombs on civilian medical facilities.

The First "Hospital:" al-Quds

The bombing that was attributed to the Syrian military is the destruction of the "al-Quds" hospital, an alleged Medicines Sans Frontieres hospital located in Aleppo. Even officially, however, it is important to note that the alleged "hospital" was not an MSF facility but one which was "supported" by MSF. This might seem like a small technicality but it is actually an important difference since MSF (aka Doctors Without Borders) is well known to be anything but an impartial observer in the Syrian crisis. As Tony Cartalucci wrote in his article, "'Doctors' Behind Syrian Chemical Weapons Claim Are Aiding Terrorists," in 2013,

> While it is often described by the Western media as "independent," nothing could be further from the truth.

> To begin with, Doctors Without Borders is fully funded by the very same corporate financier interests behind Wall Street and London's collective foreign policy, including regime change in Syria and neighboring Iran. Doctors Without Borders' own annual report (2010 report can be accessed here), includes as financial donors, Goldman Sachs, Wells Fargo, Citigroup, Google, Microsoft, Bloomberg, Mitt Romney's Bain Capital, and a myriad of other corporate-financier interests. Doctors Without Borders also features bankers upon its Board of Advisers including Elizabeth Beshel Robinson of Goldman Sachs.

> Complicating further Doctors Without Borders so-called "independent" and "aid" claims is the fact that their medical facilities are set up in terrorist held regions of Syria, especially along Syria's northern border with NATO-member Turkey. In an interview with NPR, Doctors Without Borders' Stephen Cornish revealed the nature of his organization's involvement in the Syrian conflict, where he explains that aid is being sent to regions outside of the Syrian government's control, and that his organization is in fact setting up facilities in these areas. Cornish admits:

> *Over the past months, we've had a surgery that was opened inside a cave. We've had another that was opened in a chicken farm, a third one in a house. And these structures, we've tried to outfit them as best as we can with enough modern*

technology and with full medical teams. They originally were dealing mainly with combatant injuries and people who were – civilians who were directly affected by the conflict.

In other words, the Wall Street-funded organization is providing support for militants armed and funded by the West and its regional allies, most of whom are revealed to be foreign fighters, affiliated with or directly belonging to Al Qaeda and its defacto political wing, the Muslim Brotherhood. This so-called "international aid" organization is in actuality yet another cog in the covert military machine being turned against Syria and serves the role as a medical battalion.[414]

In a telling interview with NPR, which Cartalucci partially quotes in his own article, the Executive Director of DWB, Stephen Cornish, admitted the fact that the organization largely has provided medical aid to the death squads not just as a matter of unbiased Hippocratic Oath-based treatment, but what appears to be a "rebel"-based program.[415]

Again, Cornish revealed,

Over the past months, we've had a surgery that was opened inside a cave. We've had another that was opened in a chicken farm, a third one in a house. And these structures, we've tried to outfit them as best as we can with enough modern technology and with full medical teams. They originally were dealing mainly with combatant injuries and people who were – civilians who were directly affected by the conflict.[416]

Even assuming that the "civilians" Cornish mentions are truly civilians, Cornish's team has also been focused largely on "combatant injuries" which is an interesting focus considering that the teams are mainly located within death squad controlled territory.[417]

Indeed, Cornish removes all doubt about whether or not the death squads are receiving priority care as the interview continues. Cornish states,

So it is very difficult for civilians to find care. And one of the difficulties also is that a number of smaller surgeries that have been set up are either overwhelmed with combatants or primarily taking care of combatants. And what we would certainly urge

---

[414] Cartalucci, Tony. "'Doctors' Behind Syrian Chemical Weapons Claims Are Aiding Terrorists." Land Destroyer Report. August 25, 2013. http://landdestroyer.blogspot.ca/2013/08/doctors-behind-syrian-chemical-weapons.html

[415] "Doctor: We Are Truly Failing The Syrian People." All Things Considered. NPR. May 17, 2013. http://www.npr.org/2013/05/17/184845130/doctor-we-truly-are-failing-the-syrian-people
See also,
Turbeville, Brandon. "Doctors Without Borders Aiding Globalists In Syria." Activist Post. October 17, 2013. http://www.activistpost.com/2013/10/doctors-without-borders-aiding.html

[416] "Doctor: We Are Truly Failing The Syrian People." All Things Considered. NPR. May 17, 2013. http://www.npr.org/2013/05/17/184845130/doctor-we-truly-are-failing-the-syrian-people

[417] "Doctor: We Are Truly Failing The Syrian People." All Things Considered. NPR. May 17, 2013. http://www.npr.org/2013/05/17/184845130/doctor-we-truly-are-failing-the-syrian-people
See also,
Turbeville, Brandon. "Doctors Without Borders Aiding Globalists In Syria." Activist Post. October 17, 2013. http://www.activistpost.com/2013/10/doctors-without-borders-aiding.html

is that all surgeries and all health posts also are accommodating the civilian population.

BLOCK: You mean, in other words, that the fighters are getting priority for medical care and the civilians are suffering for that.

CORNISH: Unfortunately, that is sometimes the reality on the ground. Some of the surgeries we visited, you could tell that because not only there were no civilians on the wards, but there were also no beds or toilet facilities for women. So it's kind of a dead giveaway. [418]

Returning to the question of the al-Quds hospital, however, it should be noted that the facility has been reported to be nothing more than a "field hospital" for terrorists trapped in Aleppo in the past, the bombing of which allegedly killed over 50 death squad fighters, at least according to reports by Ziad Fadel of *Syrian Perspective*.[419] After all, the hospital was being run in the "rebel"-held area of Sukkari.[420]

Some, however, dispute whether or not the hospital was ever actually bombed. Both the Syrian and Russian governments denied bombing the hospital to begin with.[421] The Russians suggested that the "anti-ISIL coalition" was operating fighter jets in the area around the time of the bombing, implying that the bombing may have been conducted by the American forces, but the U.S. denies the Russian claim.[422]

In addition to the question of whether or not the bombed "hospital" was a civilian operation or a combatant one, there is even question as to whether or not the field hospital that was bombed was actually al-Quds and, strangely enough, whether or not al-Quds ever actually existed.

For instance, Dr. Nabil Antaki, a doctor based in western Aleppo called into question the existence of al-Quds. After viewing the Channel 4 video showing the hospital moment before the attack, he responded that "This hospital [Al Quds] did not exist before the war started. It must have been installed in a building after the war began. I don't know anyone in the East of Aleppo who could confirm this hospital is Al Quds."[423] [424]

[418] "Doctor: We Are Truly Failing The Syrian People." All Things Considered. NPR. May 17, 2013. http://www.npr.org/2013/05/17/184845130/doctor-we-truly-are-failing-the-syrian-people

[419] Fadel, Ziad. "Terrorist Apes Target Civilians In Aleppo In Flop Attack On Syrian Army; 34 Dead Rodents With Scores Wounded; Terrorists Leave Their Own Dead To Rot." Syrian Perspective. May 3, 2016. http://syrianperspective.com/2016/05/terrorist-apes-target-civilians-in-aleppo-in-flop-attack-on-syrian-army-34-dead-rodents-with-scores-wounded-terrorists-leave-their-own-dead-to-rot.html

[420] El Deeb, Sarah. "Airstrikes Kill At Least 60 In Syria's Aleppo City, MSF-Backed Al-Quds Hospital Hit." The Star. April 28, 2016. https://www.thestar.com/news/world/2016/04/28/airstrikes-kill-at-least-60-in-syrias-aleppo-city-msf-backed-al-quds-hospital-hit.html

[421] Kourdi, Mohammed Eyad. "Kerry Expresses Outrage After 50 Killed In Strike On Syrian Hospital." CNN. April 30, 2016. http://www.cnn.com/2016/04/28/middleeast/syria-aleppo-hospital-airstrike/

[422] "14 Killed In Hospital Strike In Syria's Aleppo While UN's de Mistura Urges To Protect Ceasefire." RT. April 28, 2016. https://www.rt.com/news/341296-aleppo-hospital-mistura-ceasefire/

[423] Beeley, Vanessa. "Syria: #AleppoIsBurning Campaign Created By US And NATO To Facilitate A

The Second Hospital: al-Dhabeet

Yet if the pinnacle of war crimes and brutality is the bombing of hospitals, the United States was forced to eat its own words when, after only a few days of propagandizing the Western public with reports of SAA hospital bombing, its very own terrorist pets would begin openly firing missiles at another hospital in Aleppo.

Obviously, the United States made no mention of its own bombing of a MSF hospital in Kunduz, Afghanistan earlier this year.[425]

Still, U.S. Secretary of State John Kerry was forced to condemn the rocket attacks aimed at the Syrian hospital by Western-backed terrorists, albeit in a manner which would not directly attribute blame to the U.S. proxy forces.[426]

Indeed, on May 3, *SANA* news agency reported that,

> terrorists fired 65 rocket shells on the neighborhoods of al-Neel Street, al-Siryian, al-Khalidyia, al-Mocambo, al-Sabeel and the surroundings of al-Rahman mosque leaving 11 civilians killed and 37 injured. A source at Aleppo Health Directorate said that most of the wounded civilians are children and women and their injuries are severe as the number of the killed civilians might increase.[427]

Eva Bartlett chronicles the report in her own article "Hospitals Bombed: Aleppo Burning Under 'Moderate' Terrorist Bombs," by writing,

> Later, SANA's correspondent in Aleppo reported that three women were killed, 17 other women and children were wounded and extensive material damage was caused by terrorist organizations' attack with a rocket shell on al-Dhabeet Hospital in al-Mouhafaza neighborhood."

> SANA listed the attacked districts as: al-Midan, al-Furqan, Nile Street, al-Mukambo, al-Khalidiye, Jami'et al-Zahra'a, al-Ameriye, al-Ramousa, al-Masharqa, al-Muhafaza, al-Meridian, al-Serian, al-Sabeel, and al-Jamiliye in Aleppo city.

> SANA's Facebook update included numerous photos of the bombed al-Dhabeet Hospital, noting the number of dead had risen to at least 14, a number which will no doubt rise in the coming hours.

'No Bomb Zone.'" The Wall Will Fall. May 4, 2016. https://thewallwillfall.org/2016/05/04/syria-aleppoisburning-campaign-created-by-us-and-nato-to-facilitate-a-no-bomb-zone/

[424] Antaki, Par Nabil. "Alep – L'information mensongère continue. Par Nabil Antaki." Arret Sur Info. May 1, 2016. http://arretsurinfo.ch/alep-linformation-mensongere-continue-par-nabil-antaki/

[425] "Afghanistan: MSF Demands Explanations After Deadly Airstrikes Hit Hospital In Kunduz." Medecins Sans Frontieres. October 3, 2015. http://www.doctorswithoutborders.org/article/afghanistan-msf-demands-explanations-after-deadly-airstrikes-hit-hospital-kunduz

[426] "U.S.'s Kerry Condemns Rebel Attack On Aleppo Hospital." Reuters. May 3, 2016. http://www.reuters.com/video/2016/05/03/uss-kerry-condemns-rebel-attack-on-alepp?videoId=368345219

[427] "16 Civilians Killed, 68 Wounded In Terrorist Attacks On Aleppo Neighborhoods And A Hospital." Syrian Arab News Agency (SANA). May 3, 2016. http://sana.sy/en/?p=76237

According to SAMA tv, the number of murdered has risen to 28.

Ruptly TV raw footage shows the disastrous impacts of the bombings, and–uncensored–some of the mutilated victims.[428]

A tale of two hospitals indeed, at least from the point of the view of the West and the Anglo-Americans. In the Western media, one hospital bombing (if it actually took place) equals a war crime that warrants the condemnation of the world while the other warrants merely a forced, hesitant, and tepid complaint. Even the painful admission that bombing civilians and civilian hospitals is wrong was barely uttered out of Kerry's mouth before it was accompanied by the requisite condemnation of the Syrian government and the elected President Bashar al-Assad. Yet the recent bombing of al-Dhabeet is nothing new in Syria. Western-backed terrorists have been launching assaults on hospitals since the beginning of the crisis. As Prof. Tim Anderson pointed out,

> Over the past five years the al Qaeda groups have attacked 2/3 of all Syria's hospitals and clinics, plus pharmaceutical factories, many of which were in Aleppo. [Most recent one should read 'al Dabit'] Al Razi General Hospital (state) was also hit by the al Nusra coalition, just days ago."

Anderson also pointed out a number of other attacks on hospitals such as those listed below.

–"al Watani hospital in Qusayr bombed by Farouq FSA, back in 2012." (Video)[429]

-"al Nusra-FSA suicide bomb al Kindi hospital Aleppo, December 2013." (Video)[430]

-"al Qaeda groups bombed Ibn Rushd hospital also in Aleppo, on 26 April." (Video)

-"al Razi general hospital was also hit, just days ago." (Link)[431] [432]

"Unsurprisingly," Eva Bartlett writes, "instead of reporting on these documented instances of terrorists (filming themselves) attacking Syrian hospitals, corporate media and propagandizing "human rights" groups[433] are instead filling front pages and tv

---

[428] Bartlett, Eva. "Hospitals Bombed: Aleppo Burning Under 'Moderate' Terrorists' Bombs." In Gaza. https://ingaza.wordpress.com/2016/05/03/hospitals-bombed-aleppo-burning-under-moderate-terrorists-bombs/

[429] "NATO FSA Mercenaries Bomb The al Watani Hospital In Qusayr, Homs/Syria." Youtube. Posted by OxTRX007. Posted on September 5, 2012. https://www.youtube.com/watch?v=bL1xHEhzPKE Accurate description of the video reads: The Al Farouk brigade (Al Qaeda affiliate) of the "Free Syrian Army" (FSA) terrorists destroy a hospital in Qusayr in the Homs province. At the chants of "Allahu Akbar", these proud terrorists destroy hospitals, an act that only top criminals with no morals at all can manage to do.

[430] "Syria FSA Suicide Attack vs al Kindi Hospital 20 12." Youtube. Posted by WW3. Posted on December 21, 2013. https://www.youtube.com/watch?v=EQ4kPiKiQb4

[431] "VIDEO: 57 Civilians Killed, 150 Injured In Continued Terrorist Attacks On Aleppo." Al-Alam. April 29, 2016. http://en.alalam.ir/news/1812988

[432] Anderson, Tim. Facebook post with infographic. May 3, 2016. https://www.facebook.com/photo.php?fbid=10208173612830985&set=a.10207184336939706.1073741994.1021408357&type=3&theater

[433] Bartlett, Eva. "'Human Rights' Front Groups ('Humanitarian Interventionalists') Warring On Syria." In Gaza. https://ingaza.wordpress.com/syria/human-rights-front-groups-humanitarian-

screens with screaming accusations of the Syrian army and/or Russia having bombed a so-called MSF hospital in Aleppo."[434]

Conclusion

Obviously, the Western indignation over the alleged bombing of the al-Quds non-hospital was never anything more than propaganda aimed at drumming up support for greater U.S. military involvement in Syria and the increased attempt at destroying the secular Syrian government. At best, the information repeated to Western audiences was misconstrued. At worst, it was entirely made up.

A Tale Of Two Cities: Mosul And Aleppo

According to Western governments and their media mouthpieces, Assad's forces and the Russian Air Force have targeted civilian in order to . . . well . . . no one knows why they would logically target civilians or civilian hospitals. Still, the Western harpies – both media and "human rights NGOs" - continue to hammer the unsubstantiated claims and misinformation at the tops of their lungs that the SAA is dropping bombs on civilian medical facilities, civilian homes, "barrel bombing" innocent people, and all around being responsible for every single death in the Syrian war.

Particularly with the campaign to liberate East Aleppo, the Western media has gone into overdrive accusing Assad and Putin of every crime imaginable in order to gin up support for more aggressive and drastic tactics by the U.S. government to protect "civilians" (which really means terrorists) in the embattled part of the city. Never mind that America's rebels had been shelling civilians for days in both Aleppo and Damascus. According to the U.S. State Department, only Assad kills people and all the people he kills are civilians.

Interestingly enough, the U.S. and its media sock puppets are portraying the battle for Aleppo as if battles for major cities can be won without death. For the mainstream media outlets, if anyone is killed in Aleppo during the course of the battle, it is the fault of Assad and Putin and all of the deaths – even those of terrorists – are unjustified murder.

But such a narrative provides us with a Tale of Two Cities indeed. For in Mosul, an attempt to liberate the city is welcomed and no amount of "collateral damage" seems to matter.

The liberation of Mosul is an important and necessary battle but, unfortunately, like most battles, it will be one that results in the deaths of untold numbers of innocent people. Still, because the United States wants to maintain its rotting ties to the Iraqi government and the dependence which the latter still has upon the former as well as the fact that the U.S. wants to engage in "death squad herding," pushing the terrorists into Syria, civilian casualties are acceptable. But, while the U.S. government and Western corporate media justify the battle for Mosul, they do nothing but howl and scream over

---

interventionalists-warring-on-syria/

[434] Bartlett, Eva. "Hospitals Bombed: Aleppo Burning Under 'Moderate' Terrorists' Bombs." In Gaza. https://ingaza.wordpress.com/2016/05/03/hospitals-bombed-aleppo-burning-under-moderate-terrorists-bombs/

the "humanitarian disaster" in East Aleppo, the area held by terrorists supported by the West itself, and decry any attempt to liberate the city.

One need only look at the reports and the glaringly different context and style presented by the very same media outlet in order to see how both cities are being represented in the corporate press. For instance, on October 17, the Guardian posted an article titled, "Mosul Offensive: Forces Launch Mass Attack On Iraqi City In Bid To Oust ISIS," where it merely reported the "facts" about the new offensive. While it admitted that there may be mass casualties, it was characteristic of all reports surrounding U.S. or NATO war operations, i.e. it presented them as being unavoidable. The article reads,

A long-awaited offensive to seize back Mosul after two years of Isis control has begun with columns of armour and military starting to move on the northern Iraqi city.

The start of the offensive, which has been months in the planning, was announced in an address on state television by Iraq's prime minister in the early hours of Monday morning.

. . . . .

After a month-long buildup, the last urban stronghold of Islamic State in Iraq has for several days been almost completely surrounded by a 30,000-strong force.

On Monday morning just before dawn, columns of Kurdish Peshmerga fighters could be seen lined up for the offensive to the north-east of the city. The forces had taken control of seven villages and the main road linking Mosul with the Iraqi Kurdish regional capital, Irbil, by 10am BST, Turkey's state-run news agency reported.

Soldiers had earlier stood by bonfires singing battle hymns while in the distance the sound of airstrikes reverberated along with a regularly artillery barrage.

South of the city, Iraqi forces, which had driven hundreds of miles for what Baghdad has hailed as a last battle against the terrorist group, moved into their final positions on Friday.

Also on the ground are US, British and French special forces, which have been advising the peshmerga and will play a prominent role in calling in airstrikes against Isis targets inside the city.

Skirmishes have flared outside Iraqi's second largest city over the last few days with an airstrike on one of its main bridges on Sunday. It is not clear who was responsible for the strike on the al-Hurriya bridge but Amaq, the news agency associated with Isis, blamed US forces. It is thought that the destruction of the bridge could hinder Isis fighters trying to flee the city.

Early on Monday, a dense, noxious haze hung over the mountains and the plains leading to Mosul – a haze caused by oil fires lit by Isis in anticipation of the attack.

Pehmerga forces are aiming to take three villages and advance up to 12km on the first day of the offensive but insist they will not enter Mosul itself. Isis is believed to have heavily mined the roads leading into its territory with large numbers of improvised devices and the Iraqi government has previously warned Mosul resident to stay in their homes.

Ahead of Abadi's televised statement, thousands of four-page leaflets were dropped across the city telling civilians to avoid certain parts of the city and declaring it was "victory time".

The fight is expected to last weeks, if not months, and if the battles to wrest Falluja and Ramadi from the grip of Isis are any indication, Mosul is predicted to be a protracted and difficult affair.

The assault on the city is the most critical challenge yet to Isis's two-year-old caliphate, which has shredded state authority in the region's heartland, caused a mass exodus of refugees, attempted a genocide of minorities and led to grave doubts over the future of the country.[435]

Virtually the only mention of impending civilian casualties comes when the article merely addresses the possibility and quickly puts the blame solely on ISIS, suggesting also that civilians could have left and those that didn't have made their choices. The latter half of this statement, of course, is merely inferred but it is noteworthy to point out that, in Aleppo, the blame is not place on the terrorists holding out in the Eastern part of the city, but on the Syrian military attempting to dislodge them. Nevertheless, the article reads,

The International Committee of the Red Cross has warned that the battle for the city could result in a humanitarian crisis with up to a million refugees fleeing.

Militants have banned civilians from leaving the city, set up checkpoints on outwards roads and blown up the homes of those who fled.

While leaving can mean trekking through minefields and the risk of discovery and punishment by Isis, those who stay know they face airstrikes, street battles, a potential siege by the Iraqi security forces and the grim possibility of being used as human shields by Isis.[436]

Contrast this article with an article posted by the same outlet on September 26, entitled "'Hell Itself' Aleppo Reels From Alleged Use Of Bunker-Buster Bombs," where the assault is presented as a bloodthirsty march to kill as many civilians as possible. It reads,

Airstrikes have tormented the people of Aleppo's eastern districts for five consecutive days, claiming hundreds of lives and wounding many more, with a ferocity that local

---

[435] Chulov, Martin; Summers, Hannah. "Mosul Offensive: Forces Launch Mass Attack On Iraqi City In Bid To Oust ISIS." The Guardian. October 17, 2016. https://www.theguardian.com/world/2016/oct/17/iraqi-forces-begin-assault-on-isis-stronghold-mosul

[436] Chulov, Martin; Summers, Hannah. "Mosul Offensive: Forces Launch Mass Attack On Iraqi City In Bid To Oust ISIS." The Guardian. October 17, 2016. https://www.theguardian.com/world/2016/oct/17/iraqi-forces-begin-assault-on-isis-stronghold-mosul

people say is unrivalled since the beginning of the revolution turned civil war more than five years ago.

The city, once Syria's bustling commercial capital, is divided into east and west, held by rebels and the government of Bashar al-Assad respectively. The eastern part has been besieged for three months.

The latest campaign comes after the collapse of a brief ceasefire negotiated by Moscow and Washington, and Assad's government has vowed to reclaim the whole city, apparently no matter the cost.

Eastern Aleppo has endured years of destruction, the ruins of districts having been repeatedly bombarded with barrel bombs, and more lately phosphorus and incendiary munitions, which have left them in flames.

The images of the past week have been unrelentingly horrifying. In one, civil defence workers find a mother holding her infant under the rubble, dead and covered in white dust. In another, five bodies from the same family in a rebel-held town just outside Aleppo lie in white shrouds, the child's burial cloth conspicuously smaller.

There is a new awe and horror in residents' voices as they describe the impact of the bunker busters. "We are standing before inhumanity, real massacres, extraordinary weapons whose blasts we never heard before. They make the ground shake beneath our feet," said Mohammad Abu Rajab, a doctor in one of the largest medical centres in eastern Aleppo.

At a UN security council meeting on Sunday, the UK and US condemned the use of bunker busters. Samantha Power, the US envoy, condemned the barbarity with which she said Russia was prosecuting the war on behalf of Assad.

"Bunker-busting bombs, more suited to destroying military installations, are now destroying homes, decimating bomb shelters, crippling, maiming, killing dozens, if not hundreds," said Matthew Rycroft, the UK ambassador to the UN.

Residents of eastern Aleppo have often come up with new solutions to survive the onslaughts on their neighbourhoods. Moving below ground had, until now, been one means of protection.

"I've been in Aleppo for five years and I've seen a lot of bombing, but the destruction of these bombs, I have never seen before," said Omar Arab, a journalist who lives in the Mashhad neighbourhood and witnessed the destruction there and in the neighbourhood of Sukkari, where the opposition says a bunker buster bomb was used.

Even the dreaded barrel bomb, a cylinder packed with explosives that is pushed out of planes and helicopters and is woefully inaccurate, does not inspire as much fear.

. . . . .

For those who continue to brave the assault on eastern Aleppo, it is clear the scorched-earth campaign, including the alleged use bunker busters, has the sole purpose of frightening residents into submission.[437]

[437] Shaheen, Kareem. "'Hell Itself:' Aleppo Reels From Alleged Use Of Bunker-Buster Bombs." The Guardian. Septmber 26, 2016. https://www.theguardian.com/world/2016/sep/26/hell-itself-aleppo-reels-from-alleged-use-of-bunker-buster-bombs

These two reports demonstrate quite a different presentation of what is essentially – at least in terms of military strategy and physical results – the same thing. So why is one assault a liberating cause of celebration and another assault a horrific bloodbath aimed tormenting civilians for torment's sake? The reason is simple: because the first assault is being conducted by the U.S./NATO forces and the second is being conducted by Syria/Russia. The first assault is being conducted as a method of "death squad herding" and the other is ultimately designed to defeat and destroy the death squads, a fate that Washington, London, and Paris find very unpalatable to say the least. Indeed, as the terrorists die in Syria so do the plans of the U.S., NATO, GCC, and Israel.

Regardless, we have reached the point warned about in 1984 so many years ago. The media provides a story and a narrative to go along with it which is then eaten up by the general public. The very next day, or even within a matter of hours, a contrasting narrative and story that is obviously the opposite of the original story is fed to the public yet no one is the wiser. It is as if the latter story was always the truth. When that truth changes yet again, no one notices. In the morning, an assault on a major city in the Middle East is a milestone of liberation. In the evening, it is the epitome of genocide and brutality. On Monday, al-Qaeda is the enemy. On Tuesday, it is our friend.

This Orwellian narrative shift creates, as a side effect, a schizophrenic population, which is, at the same time, both paranoid and trusting, volatile and docile, tribal but isolated. The wiring of the nation's people is short-circuited and the culture has devolved to a level that only drastic measures would ever be able to repair.

As George Orwell, the man who coined the popular label of "doublethink" to be applied to cognitive dissonance, once said about the mainstream media of his day "Journalism is printing what someone else does not want printed: everything else is public relations." If it is not clear by now that America's media is nothing more than a PR firm for the military industrial complex, intelligence agencies, and the national elite, a change of viewing habits is certainly in order.

Western Media Blames Russia, Syria For Attack On UN Convoy; Video And Photos Tell Different Story

Throughout the entirety of the Syrian crisis, Western media outlets have misrepresented facts and presented outright lies to their audiences regarding virtually every aspect of the war but, particularly when it comes to specific occurrences used to gin up support for greater Western intervention in Syria, these outlets kick it up a notch, launching flurries of disinformation and misinformation designed to leave imprints of false narratives in the minds of half attentive audiences. Incidents such as the Ghouta chemical weapons attack, little Omran, and, now the alleged attack on a U.N. convoy are now parts of a larger narrative and, no matter how much they are debunked, confusion and distortion leave behind traces of the narrative embedded in the mind of the consumer.[438] [439]

---

[438] Turbeville, Brandon. "Footage of Boy In Aleppo Is Opportunistic, Vile Propaganda From Western Media." Activist Post. August 20, 2016. http://www.activistpost.com/2016/08/footage-

Still, it is important to point out the false narratives where they do exist in order to deconstruct them as much as possible.

For instance, the hysteria over an alleged attack on a U.N. convoy by "either Syrian or Russian jets" (because it couldn't have been the U.S. of course), has been used as an attempt to paint Russia and Syria as violators of a ceasefire and states so evil that they would dare attack the sacred U.N. who only ever provides food to hungry people and candy to children. Yet the entire incident, which the West is attempting to use as a political hammer, exists only through the channels and pages of Western media. In reality, however, not so much.

The story being peddled to the American people is that, even as the ceasefire was still in effect (from the point of view of the United States despite the fact that its terrorists never abided by one principle or obligation of the ceasefire from the very beginning), either Russia or Syria bombed a U.N. aid convoy on its way to deliver supplies to civilians.

However, further investigation reveals that the aid convoy that was destroyed and the U.N. aid convoy being presented to the American public as being the victim of the attack are two different convoys and two different incidents.

The convoy that was actually attacked, a Syrian Red Crescent aid operation, was attacked outside a warehouse in Urm al-Kubra just west of Aleppo. 20 to 30 trucks were said to be destroyed in this attack which took place shortly after the ceasefire officially ended on September, 19. However, there is no evidence to suggest that the attackers were the Syrian or Russian militaries. Instead, it is most likely America's rebels who attacked the convoy.

Still, the United States claims that, although it doesn't know which military, it is confident that the UN aid convoy was bombed by either Syria or Russia. As the Washington Post reports,

> We know it was an airstrike and not one from the coalition. We don't know if it was Russia or the regime," the only others flying over Syria, a senior administration official said. "In either case, the Russians have a responsibility certainly to avoid doing it themselves, but also to keep restraint on the regime.[440]

But, per the usual method of accusation, the United States never explained exactly how they knew this. Where was the intelligence coming from? Are there satellite images? Anything?

---

of-boy-in-aleppo-is-opportunistic-vile-propaganda-from-western-media.html

[439] Nebehay, Stephanie; Miles, Tom. "U.N. Suspends Aid Convoys In Syria After Hit, ICRC Warns On Impact." Reuters. September 20, 2016. http://www.reuters.com/article/us-mideast-crisis-syria-aid-idUSKCN11Q0W1

[440] DeYoung, Karen; Cunningham, Erin. "At Least 12 Aid Workers Killed In Syria Airstrike." Washington Post. September 19, 2016. https://www.washingtonpost.com/world/syrias-7-day-grace-period-ends-with-no-aid-and-cease-fire-in-tatters/2016/09/19/633ecd72-7dea-11e6-ad0e-ab0d12c779b1_story.html

Russia, however, denied that its planes, or Syrian jets for that matter, were involved in the attack. In addition, the Russian defense ministry pointed out some anomalies suggesting that the convoy was not bombed from the air at all.

"We have studied video footage from the scene from so-called 'activists' in detail and did not find any evidence that the convoy had been struck by ordnance," said Igor Konashenkov of the Russian Defense Ministry. "There are no craters and the exterior of the vehicles do not have the kind of damage consistent with blasts caused by bombs dropped from the air."

Indeed, photographs of the convoy do not line up with the damage that one would expect to see if the trucks had been attacked from the air. As Tom Miles and Angus McDowall reported for the Asia Times,

> He [Igor Konashenkov] said the damage to the convoy visible in footage was caused by its cargo catching fire. It had occurred at the same time as militants from the group formerly called the Nusra Front had started a big offensive in nearby Aleppo, he said, appearing to point the finger at rescue workers from a group called the "White Helmets" who filmed the aftermath.

> "Only representatives of the 'White Helmets' organization close to the Nusra Front who, as always, found themselves at the right time in the right place by chance with their video cameras can answer who did this and why."[441]

Hussein Badawi, head of the White Helmets in the town, said he was 100 meters (yards) from the aid depot when the attack took place and was injured by shrapnel in the hand.

> "There were fires, martyrs, wounded people. We were able to pull out four survivors and five dead bodies at first," Badawi said. "The bombardment was continuous. The rescue teams weren't even able to work. Those who arrived in ambulances couldn't come in."[442]

Despite having immediately claimed that the attacks were the result of airstrikes, the United Nations was forced to walk back its assertions after the Russian response and explanation. Now, the U.N. statement has replaced the word "airstrikes" with the word "attacks." U.N Humanitarian Spokesman Jens Laerke stated that the references were the result of a "clerical error."[443]

"We are not in a position to determine whether these were in fact air strikes. We are in a position to say that the convoy was attacked," he said.[444]

---

[441] Miles, Tom; McDowall, Angus. "UN Rows Back From Describing Syria Convoy Attack As Air Strikes." Asia Times. September 20, 2016. http://www.atimes.com/article/un-halts-aid-after-convoy-attack-kerry-says-ceasefire-not-dead//

[442] Miles, Tom; McDowall, Angus. "UN Rows Back From Describing Syria Convoy Attack As Air Strikes." Asia Times. September 20, 2016. http://www.atimes.com/article/un-halts-aid-after-convoy-attack-kerry-says-ceasefire-not-dead//

[443] Miles, Tom; McDowall, Angus. "UN Rows Back From Describing Syria Convoy Attack As Air Strikes." Asia Times. September 20, 2016. http://www.atimes.com/article/un-halts-aid-after-convoy-attack-kerry-says-ceasefire-not-dead//

[444] Miles, Tom; McDowall, Angus. "UN Rows Back From Describing Syria Convoy Attack As Air

The Russian explanation, photographic evidence, and the intentional confusion that has come as a result of a propaganda push on the part of the Western media apparatus as well as the fact that the White Helmets, a notorious terrorist support group were first on the scene and that al-Nusra fighters were themselves launching an attack in the general area at the same time as the convoy was attacked, all point to the possibility that it was the terrorists who attacked the convoy and not a traditional state actor.

Furthermore, video evidence has been posted appearing to show a jihadist vehicle armed with an artillery/mortar launcher riding beside the convoy.[445]

Still, the western media is intentionally confusing two different convoys – one that never entered Syria and was waiting on the Turkish side of the Turkey-Syria border and one that was traveling from the government held area in West Aleppo into terrorist held areas. The former was a U.N. aid convoy, the latter a Syrian Red Crescent convoy.

It should be noted that the U.N. convoys sitting idle at the border were not allowed in by the Syrian government because the U.N. would not allow the Syrian government to inspect the trucks. The fear on the part of the Syrian government was that the NATO powers were smuggling in more weaponry and supplies for terrorists under the guise of U.N. aid trucks, a fear that has already been realized in the past.[446] [447]

Strikes." Asia Times. September 20, 2016. http://www.atimes.com/article/un-halts-aid-after-convoy-attack-kerry-says-ceasefire-not-dead//

[445] "BREAKING: Russian Army Drone filmes a jihadist military vehicle hiding in Aleppo humanitarian convoy." Youtube. Posted by Russia Insider. Posted on September 20, 2016. https://www.youtube.com/watch?v=lJU_gWkpYJ8 Per the accurate video description:
 The video shows that the UN aid convoy was accompanied by a terrorists' off-road vehicle with a large-caliber mortar launcher, the Russian Defense Ministry spokesman said.
"The examination of the video footage made via drones of the movement of the humanitarian convoy in areas controlled by militants in the province of Aleppo has revealed new details. The video clearly shows how terrorists are redeploying a pickup with a large-caliber mortar on it using the convoy as a cover," Maj. Gen. Igor Konashenkov said. He said that "it is unclear yet who accompanies whom: the [pickup with a] mortar accompanies the convoy with "White Helmets" volunteers or vise versa. And most importantly, where did the mortar disappear near the destination point of the convoy and what was the target of its fire during the convoy's stop and unloading?" On Monday, the United Nations' Office for the Coordination of Humanitarian Affairs (OCHA) said that the aid convoy crossed the conflict line in the Big Orem area of the Syrian city of Aleppo. © AFP 2016/ OMAR HAJ KADOUR Russian, Syrian Jets Did Not Conduct Strikes on UN Aid Convoy in Aleppo - Russian MoD Later in the day, UN officials stated that the convoy had been shelled and there were casualties. Earlier in the day, the Russian Defense Ministry said that neither Russian, not Syria aircraft carried out strikes against the UN aid convoy, emphasizing that the examination of video footage reveals no signs of an ammunition strikes on the convoy and it seems to be set on fire. The ministry emphasized that the perpetrator of the fire, as well as his goal may be known by members of the "White Helmets" organization that allegedly has connection to al-Nusra Front terrorists who have "accidentally" been at the right time and in the right place with cameras. According to the official, al-Nusra Front terrorist group carried out an artillery attack on the southwestern suburb of Aleppo using multiple launch rocket systems.

[446] "Turkey Enhance Weapons And Ammunition Supplies To Militants In Syria Cover Of

We thus witnessed a full on propaganda onslaught in the West attempting to blame Russia and/or Syria for bombing a U.N. aid convoy that was never bombed to begin with while at the same time hiding evidence of terrorists having attacked the one that was. As a result of deceptive reporting and propaganda coming out of official State Department mouths, the American public was fooled into believing that Russia and Syria have committed a tragic war crime despite the evidence showing that the attack on the actual convoy may very well have been committed by America's proxy terrorists. The United States and the West are obviously driving the final few nails into what little credibility they have left.

U.S. Says Russia Bombed Convoy Even If It Didn't

As if to add to the absurdity, Chairman of the Joint Chiefs of Staff, Gen. Joe Dunford lobbed the first nonsensical claim to the Senate Armed Services Committee when he stated that "There is no doubt in my mind that the Russians are responsible, we just don't know whose aircraft dropped the bombs." Dunford even stated, "I don't have the facts." [448]

It's good to know that military policy is decided without facts and that determinations are made regardless of them, isn't it? Dunford's statement was essentially "We want to blame the Russians and, regardless of who bombed this convoy, we will blame the Russians. Fuck the facts."

Yet Secretary of Defense Ashton "Ash" Carter (appropriately named "Ash" since that will be all that is left of the world by the time the U.S. Empire is finished provoking every country in the world including nuclear powers) was not to be outdone by Dunford. "[The] Russians are responsible for this strike whether they conducted it or not because they associated themselves with the Syrian regime," he said. [449]

Now, that's an interesting point. Let's say for the sake of argument that the Syrian "regime" was "killing its own people," "bombing civilians," and "torturing" Syrian civilians as the U.S. government claims it is. To be clear, there is no evidence of any of this but, for the sake of argument, let's say the alternate universe of the Western

---

Humanitarian Aid (video)." RT. (RT Arabic). November 28, 2015.
See also,
"Syria Army Says Turkey Increases Arms Shipment To Rebels." Reuters. November 28, 2015.
http://www.reuters.com/article/us-mideast-crisis-syria-turkey-idUSKBN0TH0KU20151128
[447] Fadel, Leith. "Turkish Intelligence Caught Supplying al-Qaeda Under The Cover Of Humanitarian Aid." Al-Masdar News. May 29, 2015.
https://www.almasdarnews.com/article/turkish-intelligence-caught-supplying-al-qaeda-under-the-cover-of-humanitarian-aid/
[448] Kube, Courtney; Eremenko, Alexey. "Sec. Carter: Russians Responsible For Airstrikes On Aleppo Aid Convoy." NBC News. September 22, 2016.
http://www.nbcnews.com/news/world/gen-dunford-russians-responsible-airstrikes-aleppo-aid-convoy-n652581
[449] Kube, Courtney; Eremenko, Alexey. "Sec. Carter: Russians Responsible For Airstrikes On Aleppo Aid Convoy." NBC News. September 22, 2016.
http://www.nbcnews.com/news/world/gen-dunford-russians-responsible-airstrikes-aleppo-aid-convoy-n652581

corporate media and the State Department is reality for a second. If the Russians are then responsible for the behavior of the Syrian government, wouldn't the United States be responsible for the behavior of the "rebels" because the U.S. is associating itself with them?

Indeed, by the logic of Ashton Carter (an oxymoronic statement to say the least), the United States is responsible for untold executions, implementation of violent Sharia law, genocide, rape, child molestation, beheadings, torture, and, of course, cannibalism. Ironically, whether we follow the logic of Ashton Carter or not, the end result is the same - the United States is indeed responsible for all of these crimes and more in Syria.

The Russians responded with a slight jab at the U.S. government with Igor Konashenkov stating:

> Unlike the chairman of the Joint Chiefs of Staff of the U.S. Armed Forces, we do have the 'facts', that is, data of objective control of the aerial situation in Aleppo on Sept. 19. And these facts unequivocally confirm the presence of an American unmanned fighting air vehicle Predator, launched from the Incirlik air base, in the area of the convoy's passing by Urum al-Kubra.[450]

Unfortunately, Konashenkov must have been unaware that the facts don't matter to the United States government or to the Western corporate media.

If facts mattered, the fact that there is no evidence of Russian or Syrian or any aerial bombardment of the Syrian Red Crescent convoy would be adequately reported. Indeed, evidence that the bombing was an attack against a completely different convoy than what the American media has painted as the actual victim and the fact that the Western-backed terrorists were the most likely culprits would be discussed all over the airwaves right now.

But, of course, if the facts actually mattered, America's "moderate" rebels would have never been labeled "moderate," "peaceful," of "democratic." Nor would America have armed "rebels" in the first place. Or invaded Libya. Or Iraq. Or Afghanistan. Unfortunately, however, facts and logic are an endangered species in America these days.

The Media PSYOP That Never Was

In June, 2012, with the Syrian crisis heating up amidst heightened agitation by NATO powers and the announcement by Russian officials that two military combat divisions and one brigade of Russian troops are being readied in order to support the Assad government, very disturbing reports began to be echoed by reliable sources such as Thierry Meyssan and Webster Griffin Tarpley regarding a potential false flag in the region.

---

[450] Kube, Courtney; Eremenko, Alexey. "Sec. Carter: Russians Responsible For Airstrikes On Aleppo Aid Convoy." NBC News. September 22, 2016.
http://www.nbcnews.com/news/world/gen-dunford-russians-responsible-airstrikes-aleppo-aid-convoy-n652581

The event, which was to take the form of staged massacres, rebellions, and resignations, using television studios and the commandeering of Syrian television, would have served the purpose of both spreading disinformation across the world and a campaign of demoralization against the Syrian people. [451]

Meyssan stated that, although the time and date are not set in stone, the plan, which had been in the works for months, had been accelerated due to the recent announcements made by Vladmir Putin.

Meyssan writes:

> Studio-shot images will show massacres that are blamed on the Syrian government, people demonstrating ministers and generals resigning from their posts, President al-Assad fleeing, the rebels gathering in the big city centers, and a new government installing itself in the presidential palace.[452]

The plan, according to Meyssan, had been largely organized by Ben Rhodes,[453] US Deputy National Security Advisor for Strategic Communication and speechwriter for Barack Obama.

Meyssan stated that the Arab League had officially asked satellite operators Arabsat and Nilesat to stop broadcasting Syrian media, regardless of whether those broadcasts are government-based or private.

However, although Syrian media was to be cut, television broadcasts presenting the staged scenarios mentioned above would have replaced the regularly scheduled programming.

Meyssan wrote that, according to his sources, several international meetings were held where a discussion took place regarding how to coordinate the disinformation operation. He claimed that the first meeting held in Doha, Qatar, was of a technical nature and the third meeting, held in Riyadh, Saudi Arabia dealt with political ramifications.

Meyssan wrote:

> The first meeting assembled PSYOP officers, embedded in the satellite TV channels of Al-Arabiya, Al-Jazeera, BBC, CNN, Fox, France 24, Future TV and MTV. It is known that since 1998, the officers of the US Army Psychological Operations Unit (PSYOP) have been incorporated in CNN. Since then this practice has been extended by NATO to other strategic media as well.

---

[451] Meyssan, Thierry. "Sectarian Genocide In Syria:US-NATO and the GCC Preparing a Coup d'e'tat." Voltaire Net. June 11, 2012. Reposted by Global Research. http://www.globalresearch.ca/sectarian-genocide-in-syria-us-nato-and-the-gcc-preparing-a-coup-d-tat/31373 Accessed on July 27, 2013.

[452] Meyssan, Thierry. "Sectarian Genocide In Syria:US-NATO and the GCC Preparing a Coup d'e'tat." Voltaire Net. June 11, 2012. Reposted by Global Research. http://www.globalresearch.ca/sectarian-genocide-in-syria-us-nato-and-the-gcc-preparing-a-coup-d-tat/31373 Accessed on July 27, 2013.

[453] "Ben Rhodes." Time. http://www.time.com/time/specials/packages/article/0,28804,2023831_2023829_2025191,00.html Accessed on July 16, 2013.

They fabricated false information in advance, on the basis of a 'story-telling' script devised by Ben Rhodes's team at the White House. A procedure of reciprocal validation was installed, with each media quoting the lies of the other media to render them plausible for TV spectators. The participants also decided not only to requisition the TV channels of the CIA for Syria and Lebanon (Barada, Future TV, MTV, Orient News, Syria Chaab, Syria Alghad) but also about 40 religious Wahhabi TV channels to call for confessional massacres to the cry of 'Christians to Beyrouth, Alawites into the grave!'

The second meeting was held for engineers and technicians to fabricate fictitious images, mixing one part in an outdoor studio, the other part with computer generated images. During the past weeks, studios in Saudi Arabia have been set up to build replicas of the two presidential palaces in Syria and the main squares of Damascus, Aleppo and Homs. Studios of this type already exist in Doha (Qatar), but they are not sufficient.

The third meeting was held by General James B. Smith, the US ambassador, a representative of the UK, prince Bandar Bin Sultan (whom former U.S. president George Bush named his adopted son so that the U.S. press called him 'Bandar Bush'). In this meeting the media actions were coordinated with those of the Free 'Syrian' Army, in which prince Bandar's mercenaries play a decisive role.[454]

As Webster Tarpley has pointed out,[455] this plan sounded eerily familiar to the false broadcast of the Green Square in Tripoli, Libya which turned out to be faked film footage[456] created on a film set in Qatar.

It should also be pointed out that Victoria Nuland,[457] Spokesperson for the U.S. State Department, around the same time, predicted more massacres[458] similar to the Houla incident. Indeed, she was quite precise with her predictions, providing the exact locations[459] of the "potential" massacres.

---

[454] Meyssan, Thierry. "Sectarian Genocide In Syria:US-NATO and the GCC Preparing a Coup d'e'tat." Voltaire Net. June 11, 2012. Reposted by Global Research. http://www.globalresearch.ca/sectarian-genocide-in-syria-us-nato-and-the-gcc-preparing-a-coup-d-tat/31373 Accessed on July 27, 2013.

[455] Tarpley, Webster G. "Russia Reportedly Preparing 2 Divisions, Spetsnaz Brigade for Deployment to Syria; Mini-Goebbels Ben Rhodes of Obama White House Runs Colossal Black Propaganda Op to Assist NATO Coup; Massacre of Alawites and Christians Looms; Cass Sunstein Destabilizes Vatican to Muzzle Protest." PressTV. June 12, 2012. http://tarpley.net/2012/06/12/russia-reportedly-preparing-divisions-for-deployment-to-syria/ Accessed on July 16, 2012.

[456] Perreira, Gerald A. "Resistance in Libya: Imperialism will be buried in Africa." Global Research. September 21, 2011. http://www.globalresearch.ca/resistance-in-libya-imperialism-will-be-buried-in-africa/26710 Accessed on July 16, 2013.

[457] Original Source no longer available. http://www.state.gov/r/bios/180394.htm See "Victoria Nuland." Biography. U.S. Department of State. http://www.state.gov/r/pa/ei/biog/bureau/180394.htm Accessed on July 16, 2013.

[458] "US warns of a potential massacre in Syria's Haffa." The Telegraph. June 12, 2012. http://www.telegraph.co.uk/news/worldnews/middleeast/syria/9326541/US-warns-of-a-potential-massacre-in-Syrias-Haffa.html Accessed on July 16, 2013.

Whether or not the plan never came to fruition because it was exposed or because the Syrian government took measures to prevent its effectiveness (likely the latter) might never be fully known. However, the fact that it existed in the first place goes great lengths to demonstrate the depths to which this agenda and those who wish to destroy Syria will sink in conspiracy.

The propaganda blitz did not end with the attempt to commandeer Syrian television stations. However, the media assault did begin to turn inward, focusing more on shoring up support for military action in Syria on the home front, stirring a Western population always psychologically eager and willing for a new war.

Western governments, think tanks, and media outlets attempted everything from faked film footage on behalf of some of the West's largest media outlets, borderline idiotic propaganda narratives geared toward special Western demographics, compromised human rights organizations asserting unsupported claims of human rights violations, and even official hysteria "chemical weapons" and "red lines" that were eerily similar to the "weapons of mass destruction" and "mushroom clouds" repeated over and over in the same media outlets in the run up to the Iraq invasion.

To a vapid Western population obsessed with television, sports, and entertainment, propaganda efforts succeeded the most. These hapless victims remained stunningly unaware of the world that existed all around them while, at the same time, maintaining the opinion that Assad was oppressing his people and that the "death squads" were freedom fighters just like them as if that opinion was their own. To those who did pay marginal attention to news reports (but only through mainstream outlets), the only source of news they would consider credible was providing them with official positions, on the ground reporting, and visual evidence that confirmed their implanted beliefs. Regardless of their inbred political pedigree, the message was Assad=bad, "rebels" = good.

Yet, to even the casual observer not swept up in the false narrative portrayed by Western media outlets, the propaganda was increasingly transparent. The mistakes were becoming more and more obvious.

Consider the case of the temporarily famous "Syria Danny," a young man portrayed as an "activist" in Syria who appeared weekly on the mainstream outlets where he backed up the narratives fed to the Western public and begged for American and even Israeli support against the Syrian government. However, very soon after "Syria Danny's" appearances grew in their popularity, it became known that "Syria Danny" was nothing more than an actor and an agent of destabilization and propaganda efforts when he was caught, on camera, coordinating staged gunfire and explosions to be used in his interview with CNN. The goal, obviously, was to create a clip in which Danny was talking to the Western media while taking heavy fire from government forces. However, the camera had continued to roll as Danny and friends continued to coordinate the soundstage.

---

[459] Tarpley, Webster G. "West seeks annihilation of Syria: Webster Tarpley." PressTV. Youtube. Posted by PressTVGlobalNews. Posted on June 12, 2012. http://www.youtube.com/watch?feature=player_embedded&v=98lln0lS-Ol#! Accessed on July 16, 2013.

As Paul Joseph Watson wrote in his article, "'Syria Danny Caught Staging CNN War Propaganda Stunt:'"

> As we have previously documented,[460] 'Syria Danny' is a 22-year-old British citizen of Syrian descent from Cambridge. After returning from Homs in summer last year, he lived in London for a few months before returning to Syria in December, from which point onwards he became the poster child for a western military intervention in Syria, begging almost daily on CNN for the United States or even Israel to bombard the country.
>
> . . . . .
>
> While waiting to be connected, Danny says, "Well, let the gunfire sound then," before subsequently asking someone off camera, "Did you tell him to get the gunfire ready?" An explosion is heard soon after, but Danny doesn't even flinch.
>
> The person working the camera, Danny himself, and at least one person off camera, clearly appear to be coordinating staged gunfire and explosions to coincide with the CNN interview.
>
> The cameraman then reminds Danny to talk about recovering dead bodies before the interview with Anderson Cooper begins. The talking point about Assad's forces carrying out indiscriminate violence is strongly emphasized.

Watson continues by saying:

> Despite the threat of the violence he claims is occurring all around him, in addition to his high profile as a media-friendly anti-regime activist which would make him a prime target, Danny seems remarkably calm and composed in an environment one would expect to be fraught with tension. At one point, he even appears to be bored, jokingly asking for a mattress.
>
> Observers have noted[461] that Danny's stories about the violence he claims to have witnessed appear to change each time he appears on a different news show, suggesting he is embellishing or outright manufacturing his testimony.
>
> In another clip, footage presented by the mainstream media as depicting "government shelling" of innocent citizens actually shows the camera shot being set up hours beforehand, ready to capture an attack on an oil refinery in the city of Homs which occurred on February 8.[462] There is no evidence of tanks or "shelling" and the clip was likely produced by the same terrorists who blew up the oil refinery.[463]

---

[460] Watson, Paul Joseph. "Global Media Promotes Syrian 'Activist' Begging For Military Invasion." PrisonPlanet. February 13, 2012. http://www.prisonplanet.com/global-media-promotes-syrian-activist-begging-for-military-invasion.html Accessed on July 16, 2013.

[461] Elmassian, Kevork; Kelanee, Hiba; Kardous, Feeda; al Kadri, Zoubaida. "The truth about western media's favourite Syrian 'activist:' Danny Dayem." Lizzie Phelan. February 22, 2012. http://lizzie-phelan.blogspot.com/2012/02/truth-about-western-medias-favourite.html Accessed on July 16, 2013.

[462] "Report: Terrorist group attacks oil refinery in Homs." YNetNews. February 8, 2012. http://www.ynetnews.com/articles/0,7340,L-4187031,00.html Accessed on July 16, 2013.

[463] Watson, Paul Joseph. "'Syria Danny' Caught Staging CNN War Propaganda Stunt." PrisonPlanet.com. March 6, 2012. http://www.prisonplanet.com/syria-danny-caught-staging-

In a subsequent article, after CNN offered a very lame defense of its Syria Danny shtick, Watson writes,

> CNN's attempt to refute claims that dubious activist Danny Dayem, known as 'Syria Danny', was caught staging sounds of gunfire during a recent interview with the network only resulted in further embarrassment, when Dayem admitted that the suspect video "should have been deleted," presumably to hide the evidence of his propaganda stunt. Following our exposé yesterday morning,[464] which documented how Dayem, who has become the establishment media's poster child for a military invasion of Syria, had ordered staged gunfire sounds to be made off camera during an interview, CNN's Anderson Cooper invited him to engage in damage control during last night's show.
>
> During the interview with Cooper, Dayem only succeeds in virtually admitting the fact that the video is suspect. Asked how the footage was leaked, Dayem starts to say 'we should have deleted it' before hastily stating, "this has all been deleted."
>
> "I don't know how they got it, this is all private, we should have, this has all been deleted, we have to delete all this stuff," said Dayem.
>
> Why Dayem is so insistent that the footage should be deleted, unless it contains something incriminating, is not explained. The interview from the footage has already been broadcast globally by CNN, so why the need to delete the rest of the footage? Perhaps because Dayem finds it hard to explain why he tells someone off camera during the clip, "Did you tell him to get the gunfire ready?"
>
> This quote is not even addressed during Dayem's interview with Cooper.[465]

Likewise, the repetitive propaganda that preceded Syria Danny, "Gay Girl in Damascus," an online blogger and social media favorite, particularly among groups and individuals obsessed with specific demographic concerns was also discovered to be an entirely false narrative. In truth, "Gay Girl in Damascus" turned out to be neither gay nor a girl, nor even in Damascus but a straight American male living in Scotland. This hoax came to an abrupt end after the host of the blog attempted to stage "her" arrest at the hands of the Syrian government. As Robert Mackey of the New York Times wrote,

> Six days after a post on a well-known blog called "A Gay Girl in Damascus"[466] triggered panic among its readers by suggesting that the author, who claimed to be a Syrian-American lesbian caught up in the protest movement, had been arrested, a new entry appeared on Sunday that described the entire online diary as a work of fiction by an American man.

---

cnn-war-propaganda-stunt.html Accessed on June 26, 2013.

[464] Watson, Paul Joseph. "'Syria Danny' Caught Staging CNN War Propaganda Stunt." PrisonPlanet. March 6, 2012. http://www.prisonplanet.com/syria-danny-caught-staging-cnn-war-propaganda-stunt.html Accessed on July 16, 2013.

[465] Watson, Paul Joseph. "CNN Botches Effort To Refute 'Syria Danny' Propaganda Scandal." PrisonPlanet.com. March 7, 2012. http://www.infowars.com/cnn-botches-effort-to-refute-syria-danny-propaganda-scandal/ Accessed on June 26, 2013.

[466] "A Gay Girl In Damascus." Website. http://damascusgaygirl.blogspot.com/ Accessed on July 16, 2013.

The post, "Apology to Readers," was signed by Tom MacMaster, who identified himself as a 40-year-old American graduate student and "The sole author of all posts on this blog." That would include four months of diary entries from Amina Abdallah Arraf, a self-described 35-year-old lesbian born and raised in the United States but living in Damascus, and two posts attributed to Rania O. Ismail, a self-described cousin of Ms. Arraf's, who had relayed news of her arrest to the blog's readers last week.

. . . . .

Despite the new post's title, the brief text included no apology, only justifications from the blogger for having disguised fiction as fact. The post began: "I never expected this level of attention. While the narrative voice may have been fictional, the facts on this blog are true and not misleading as to the situation on the ground. I do not believe that I have harmed anyone — I feel that I have created an important voice for issues that I feel strongly about."

Before that post, Mr. MacMaster had denied that he was the blog's author when confronted by an inquiry from a reporter for The Electronic Intifada,[467] a pro-Palestinian[468] Web site, about circumstantial evidence that had linked him to Amina Abdallah Arraf.[469]

Considering the nature of such pathetic and thinly veiled propaganda efforts launched by the Western media/Western military alliance, it should come as no surprise that claims of "torture" and "crimes against humanity," would eventually follow. Baseless claims of torture and other acts of terror against the civilian population by the Assad government began to surface from the compromised Soros-funded Human Rights Watch[470] even as the death squads intensified their campaign of murder and torture against civilians and government forces alike. In essence, these "crimes against humanity," and claims of "torture," produced without one shred of credible evidence, became the "incubator babies" of the Syrian war campaign.

---

[467] The Electronic Intifada. Homepage. http://electronicintifada.net/ Accessed on July 16, 2013.
[468] "The Palestinian Authority." New York Times. http://topics.nytimes.com/topics/reference/timestopics/organizations/p/palestinian_authority/index.html?inline=nyt-classifier Accessed on July 16, 2013.
[469] Mackey, Robert. "'Gay Girl in Damascus' Blog a Hoax, American Says." New York Times. June 13, 2011. http://www.nytimes.com/2011/06/13/world/middleeast/13blogger.html?_r=0 Accessed on June 27, 2013.
[470] Steinberg, Gerald. "Selling Out To Soros: Right's Group's Dubious Record." New York Post. September 12, 2010. http://www.nypost.com/p/news/opinion/opedcolumnists/selling_out_to_soros_iYfn7YXaZg8xE FCp5iEcCJ Accessed on June 27, 2013.

Chapter V: ISIS: Made In The USA

It is important to point out that the Islamic State is not some shadowy force that emerged from the caves of Afghanistan to form an effective military force that is funded by Twitter donations and murky secretive finance deals. ISIS is entirely the creation of NATO and the West and the West remains in control of the organization.

As Tony Cartalucci writes in his article "Implausible Deniability: West's ISIS Terror Hordes In Iraq,"

> Beginning in 2011 – and actually even as early as 2007 – the United States has been arming, funding, and supporting the Muslim Brotherhood and a myriad of armed terrorist organizations to overthrow the government of Syria, fight Hezbollah in Lebanon, and undermine the power and influence of Iran, which of course includes any other government or group in the MENA region friendly toward Tehran.

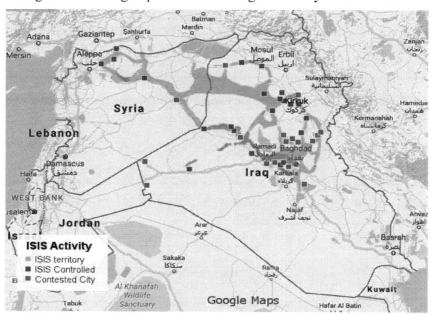

Map Created By Tony Cartalucci of Land Destroyer Report

Billions in cash have been funneled into the hands of terrorist groups including Al Nusra, Al Qaeda in Iraq (AQI), and what is now being called "Islamic State in Iraq and Syria" or ISIS. One can see clearly by any map of ISIS held territory that it butts up directly against Turkey's borders with defined corridors ISIS uses to invade southward – this is because it is precisely from NATO territory this terrorist scourge originated.

ISIS was harbored on NATO territory, armed and funded by US CIA agents with cash and weapons brought in from the Saudis, Qataris, and NATO members themselves. The "non-lethal aid" the US and British sent including the vehicles we now see ISIS driving around in.[471]

They didn't "take" this gear from "moderates." There were never any moderates to begin with. The deadly sectarian genocide we now see unfolding was long ago predicted by those in the Pentagon – current and former officials – interviewed in 2007 by Pulitzer Prize-winning veteran journalist Seymour Hersh. Hersh's 9-page 2007 report, "The Redirection" states explicitly:

> To undermine Iran, which is predominantly Shiite, the Bush
> Administration has decided, in effect, to reconfigure its
> priorities in the Middle East. In Lebanon, the Administration
> has cooperated with Saudi Arabia's government, which is
> Sunni, in clandestine operations that are intended to weaken
> Hezbollah, the Shiite organization that is backed by Iran. The
> U.S. has also taken part in clandestine operations aimed at Iran
> and its ally Syria. A by-product of these activities has been the
> bolstering of Sunni extremist groups that espouse a militant
> vision of Islam and are hostile to America and sympathetic to
> Al Qaeda.[472]

"Extremist groups that espouse a militant vision of Islam" and are "sympathetic to Al Qaeda" – is a verbatim definition of what ISIS is today. Clearly the words of Hersh were as prophetic as they were factually informed, grounded in the reality of a regional conflict already engineered and taking shape as early as 2007. Hersh's report would also forewarn the sectarian nature of the coming conflict, and in particular mention the region's Christians who were admittedly being protected by Hezbollah.

While Hersh's report was written in 2007, knowledge of the plan to use death squads to target Middle Eastern countries, particularly Syria, had been reported on even as far back as 2005 by Michael Hirsh and John Barry for Newsweek in an article entitled "The Salvador Option."[473]

Regardless, Cartalucci states in a separate article, "NATO's Terror Hordes In Iraq A Pretext For Syria Invasion,"

> In actuality, ISIS is the product of a joint NATO-GCC [Gulf Cooperation Council] conspiracy stretching back as far as 2007 where US-Saudi policymakers sought to ignite a region-wide sectarian war to purge the Middle East of Iran's arch of influence stretching from its borders, across Syria and Iraq, and as far west as Lebanon and the coast of the Mediterranean. ISIS has been harbored, trained, armed, and extensively funded by a coalition of NATO and Persian Gulf states within Turkey's (NATO territory) borders and has launched invasions into northern Syria with, at times, both

---

[471] Snyder, Stephen. "This One Toyota Pickup Truck Is At The Top Of The Shopping List For The Free Syrian Army – And The Taliban." PRI's The World And Global Post. April 1, 2014. http://www.pri.org/stories/2014-04-01/one-toyota-pickup-truck-top-shopping-list-free-syrian-army-and-taliban

[472] Hersh, Seymour. "The Redirection." The New Yorker. March 5, 2007. http://www.newyorker.com/magazine/2007/03/05/the-redirection

[473] Hirsch, Michael; Barry, John. "The Salvador Option." Newsweek. January 9, 2005. http://web.archive.org/web/20050110030928/http://www.msnbc.msn.com/id/6802629/site/newsweek/

Turkish artillery and air cover. The most recent example of this was the cross-border invasion by Al Qaeda into Kasab village, Latikia province in northwest Syria.[474]

Cartalucci is referring to a cross-border invasion that was coordinated with NATO, Turkey, Israel, and the death squads where Israel acted as air force cover while Turkey facilitated the death squad invasion from inside its own borders. [475] [476]

Keep in mind also that, prior to the rapid appearance and seizure of territory by ISIS in Syria and Iraq, European media outlets like Der Spiegel reported that hundreds of fighters were being trained in Jordan by Western intelligence and military personnel for the purpose of deployment in Syria to fight against Assad.[477] The numbers were said to be expected to reach about 10,000 fighters when the reports were issued in March, 2013. Although Western and European media outlets would try to spin the operation as the training of "moderate rebels," subsequent reports revealed that these fighters were actually ISIS fighters.[478]

Western media outlets have also gone to great lengths to spin the fact that ISIS is operating in both Syria and Iraq with an alarming number of American weapons and equipment. As Business Insider stated, "The report [study by the London-based small arms research organization Conflict Armament Research] said the jihadists disposed of 'significant quantities' of US-made small arms including M16 assault rifles and included photos showing the markings 'Property of US Govt.'"[479] The article also acknowledged that a large number of the weapons used by ISIS were provided by Saudi Arabia, a close American ally.

It is now common knowledge that the destabilization effort was and continues to be supported by the United States, Britain, France, and the whole of NATO, as well as Saudi Arabia, Qatar, and other feudal monarchies, in addition to the true Mad Dog of the Middle East, Israel. However, the level to which these countries and hence their military and intelligence agencies play a part has been largely shrouded in mystery.

---

[474] Cartalucci, Tony. "NATO's Terror Hordes In Iraq A Pretext For Syria Invasion." Activist Post. June 13, 2014. http://www.activistpost.com/2014/06/natos-terror-hordes-in-iraq-pretext-for.html

[475] Klein, Aaron. "Shock Claim: Israeli Airstrike Coordinated With Al-Qaeda-Linked Rebels. Jihadists Advance Throughout Syria Immediately After Today's Bomb Attack." World Net Daily. May 5, 2013. http://kleinonline.wnd.com/2013/05/05/shock-claim-israeli-airstrike-coordinated-with-al-qaida-linked-rebels-jihadists-advance-throughout-syria-immediately-after-todays-bomb-attack/

[476] Turbeville, Brandon. "Why Aren't ISIS And Al-Qaeda Attacking Israel?" Activist Post. August 7, 2014. http://www.activistpost.com/2014/08/why-arent-isis-and-al-qaeda-attacking.html

[477] Jones, Gareth; Webb, Jason. "Americans Are Training Syria Rebels In Jordan: Spiegel." Reuters. March 10, 2013. http://www.reuters.com/article/us-syria-crisis-rebels-usa-idUSBRE9290FI20130310

[478] Klein, Aaron. "Blowback! U.S. Trained Islamists Who Joined ISIS." World Net Daily. June 17, 2014. http://www.wnd.com/2014/06/officials-u-s-trained-isis-at-secret-base-in-jordan/

[479] "Report: ISIS Has More US Weapons Than Previously Thought." Business Insider. September 8, 2014. http://www.businessinsider.com/report-isis-has-more-us-weapons-than-previously-thought-2014-9

Yet, at times, it is possible for those of us who are aware of the historical treachery and the levels of control over public perception held by both the mainstream media and Western governments to occasionally catch a glimpse of the true mechanisms of "color revolution" and destabilizations and, thus, put the pieces of the puzzle together.

Putting together these pieces is not as hard as one might imagine. After all, the information and evidence of foreign intelligence and military intervention in Syria was publicized several years before the operations began to culminate in the recent "rebellion."

As Tony Cartalucci of Land Destroyer Report has documented on numerous occasions, the plan to invade and destabilize Syria by using hordes of al-Qaeda terrorists and mercenaries has been in existence since at least 2007. Cartalucci writes,

> A 2007 *New Yorker* article written by renowned journalist Seymour Hersh revealed a plan under the Bush Administration to organize, arm, train, and deploy a regional army of terrorists, many with ties directly to Al Qaeda, in a bid to destabilize and overthrow both Syria and Iran. The plan consisted of US and Israeli backing, covertly funneled through Saudi proxies to conceal Washington and Tel Aviv's role, in building the sectarian extremist front.

> According to Seymour Hersh's 2007 article, "The Redirection: Is the Administration's new policy benefiting our enemies in the war on terrorism?," Saudi Arabia, a more credible candidate for openly interfacing with the militants, openly admitted that it was a danger, but that they "created it," and therefore could "control it," in meetings with Washington. The plan called for not only setting up terrorist enclaves in nations neighboring Syria, including Lebanon, Jordan, and US-occupied Iraq, but also for building up the Muslim Brotherhood, both inside Syria's borders and beyond – including in Egypt.[480] [481]

Hersh also pointed out the long history between the Saudi Royals and their funding of religious fanatics for the purposes of destabilization since the 1970s proxy war against the Soviet Union, the Iranians, and to the more recent (in terms of the writing of the article) possibilities of using such types of fighters in Lebanon, Iraq, Jordan, Iran, and Syria. He wrote,

> Nasr went on, "The Saudis have considerable financial means, and have deep relations with the Muslim Brotherhood and the Salafis"—Sunni extremists who view Shiites as apostates. "The last time Iran was a threat, the Saudis were able to mobilize the worst kinds of Islamic radicals. Once you get them out of the box, you can't put them back."

> The Saudi royal family has been, by turns, both a sponsor and a target of Sunni extremists, who object to the corruption and decadence among the family's myriad princes. The princes are gambling that they will not be overthrown as long as they

---

[480] Hersh, Seymour. "The Redirection." The New Yorker. March 5, 2007.
http://www.newyorker.com/magazine/2007/03/05/the-redirection
[481] Cartalucci, Tony. "Extremists Ravaging Syria Created By US In 2007." Land Destroyer Report. March 11, 2012. http://landdestroyer.blogspot.com/2012/05/sunni-extremists-ravaging-syria-created.html

continue to support religious schools and charities linked to the extremists. The Administration's new strategy is heavily dependent on this bargain.

Nasr compared the current situation to the period in which Al Qaeda first emerged. In the nineteen-eighties and the early nineties, the Saudi government offered to subsidize the covert American C.I.A. proxy war against the Soviet Union in Afghanistan. Hundreds of young Saudis were sent into the border areas of Pakistan, where they set up religious schools, training bases, and recruiting facilities. Then, as now, many of the operatives who were paid with Saudi money were Salafis. Among them, of course, were Osama bin Laden and his associates, who founded Al Qaeda, in 1988.[482]

In a more telling passage, however, Hersh describes the connection between the Saudis, Jihadists, and the U.S. government. He wrote,

This time, the U.S. government consultant told me, Bandar and other Saudis have assured the White House that "they will keep a very close eye on the religious fundamentalists. Their message to us was 'We've created this movement, and we can control it.' It's not that we don't want the Salafis to throw bombs; it's who they throw them at—Hezbollah, Moqtada al-Sadr, Iran, and at the Syrians, if they continue to work with Hezbollah and Iran."[483]

Hersh continued by stating that the Israelis, the Saudis, and the Americans have "developed a series of informal understandings about their new strategic direction." In addition to the security of Israel, the weakening of Hamas, and the countering of "Shiite ascendance in the region," there was also a fourth goal of the three entities. Hersh wrote,

Fourth, the Saudi government, with Washington's approval, would provide funds and logistical aid to weaken the government of President Bashir Assad, of Syria. The Israelis believe that putting such pressure on the Assad government will make it more conciliatory and open to negotiations. Syria is a major conduit of arms to Hezbollah. The Saudi government is also at odds with the Syrians over the assassination of Rafik Hariri, the former Lebanese Prime Minister, in Beirut in 2005, for which it believes the Assad government was responsible. Hariri, a billionaire Sunni, was closely associated with the Saudi regime and with Prince Bandar. (A U.N. inquiry strongly suggested that the Syrians were involved, but offered no direct evidence; there are plans for another investigation, by an international tribunal.)[484]

Hersh also quoted Walid Jumblatt, leader of the Druze minority in Lebanon and adamant Assad opponent who stated to Hersh that he had actually traveled to Washington, D.C. to meet with then Vice President Dick Cheney regarding the possibility of weakening and destabilizing the Assad government in Syria. Hersh stated,

Jumblatt then told me that he had met with Vice-President Cheney in Washington last fall to discuss, among other issues, the possibility of undermining Assad. He and his colleagues advised Cheney that, if the United States does try to move against Syria,

---

[482] Hersh, Seymour. "The Redirection." The New Yorker. March 5, 2007.
http://www.newyorker.com/magazine/2007/03/05/the-redirection
[483] Hersh, Seymour. "The Redirection." The New Yorker. March 5, 2007.
http://www.newyorker.com/magazine/2007/03/05/the-redirection
[484] Hersh, Seymour. "The Redirection." The New Yorker. March 5, 2007.
http://www.newyorker.com/magazine/2007/03/05/the-redirection

members of the Syrian Muslim Brotherhood would be "the ones to talk to," Jumblatt said.

The Syrian Muslim Brotherhood, a branch of a radical Sunni movement founded in Egypt in 1928, engaged in more than a decade of violent opposition to the regime of Hafez Assad, Bashir's father. In 1982, the Brotherhood took control of the city of Hama; Assad bombarded the city for a week, killing between six thousand and twenty thousand people. Membership in the Brotherhood is punishable by death in Syria. The Brotherhood is also an avowed enemy of the U.S. and of Israel. Nevertheless, Jumblatt said, "We told Cheney that the basic link between Iran and Lebanon is Syria—and to weaken Iran you need to open the door to effective Syrian opposition."

There is evidence that the Administration's redirection strategy has already benefitted the Brotherhood. The Syrian National Salvation Front is a coalition of opposition groups whose principal members are a faction led by Abdul Halim Khaddam, a former Syrian Vice-President who defected in 2005, and the Brotherhood. A former high-ranking C.I.A. officer told me, "The Americans have provided both political and financial support. The Saudis are taking the lead with financial support, but there is American involvement." He said that Khaddam, who now lives in Paris, was getting money from Saudi Arabia, with the knowledge of the White House. (In 2005, a delegation of the Front's members met with officials from the National Security Council, according to press reports.) A former White House official told me that the Saudis had provided members of the Front with travel documents.[485]

Hersh also spoke with Sheikh Hassan Nasrallah, the Hezbollah leader, who told Hersh that he believed that the United States wished to cause the partitioning of both Lebanon and Syria. Hersh states that, "In Syria, he [Nasrallah] said, the result would be to push the country "into chaos and internal battles like in Iraq."[486]

The Brzezinski Plan A, Kerry Plan B – Federalization Of Syria

The idea that Syria would be partitioned is an interesting concept to say the least since it echoes the typical geopolitical strategy of "Micro States and Mini States" espoused by Neo-Liberal members of the governing class such as Zbigniew Brzezinski. Yet, the ruling regime at the time of the writing of Hersh's article and the interview conducted with Hassan Nasrallah was the Neo-Conservative regime of Bush/Cheney, a branch of the Anglo-American ruling class that typically expresses geopolitical strategy in the manifestation of hard power and ham-fisted warfare.

The Brzezinski method, of course, is not promoted by Brzezinski alone, however. Bernard Lewis, famed Middle Eastern "strategist," wrote for the Council on Foreign Relations' Foreign Policy in 1992 promoting the idea of the "Lebanonization" of states in the Middle East and even Eastern Europe. Lewis wrote that these "Lebanonized"

---

[485] Hersh, Seymour. "The Redirection." The New Yorker. March 5, 2007.
http://www.newyorker.com/magazine/2007/03/05/the-redirection
[486] Hersh, Seymour. "The Redirection." The New Yorker. March 5, 2007.
http://www.newyorker.com/magazine/2007/03/05/the-redirection

states could be precipitated by fundamentalism. In the article, "Rethinking The Middle East," he wrote,

> Another possibility, which could even be precipitated by fundamentalism, is what has of late become fashionable to call "Lebanonization." Most of the states of the Middle East—Egypt is an obvious exception—are of recent and artificial construction and are vulnerable to such a process. If the central power is sufficiently weakened, there is no real civil society to hold the polity together, no real sense of common national identity or overriding allegiance to the nation state. The state then disintegrates—as happened in Lebanon—into a chaos of squabbling, feuding, fighting sects, tribes, regions and parties. If things go badly and central governments falter and collapse, the same could happen, not only in the countries of the existing Middle East, but also in the newly independent Soviet republics, where the artificial frontiers drawn by the former imperial masters left each republic with a mosaic of minorities and claims of one sort or another on or by its neighbours.[487]

The fact that the Brzezinski method of using puppet states, mercenaries, and religious fanatics against target states while "leading from behind" was being planned and orchestrated during a branch of the ruling elite that typically exhibits a different strategy is telling in that it shows both that the plan to partition Syria was developed long before the recent "rebellion" and that the plan crosses not only both political parties but also both factions of the ruling elite. In short, the existence of such a plan during the Bush/Cheney regime and the attempted implementation of the plan by the Obama regime shows that not only are political parties operated by the same (somewhat) hidden forces but even the hidden hand behind the hidden forces are themselves more centralized than what many informed political analysts would choose to believe.

The Syrian partition issue is also interesting considering the fact that a potential false flag attack was discovered by German hackers involving the use of chemical weapons by the Syrian death squads to be blamed on the Assad government and accomplishing this goal. This "attack" would have then been followed by the entrance of ambulances emblazoned with the words "Syrian People's Relief." Although the pretext would have been humanitarian aid, the ambulances would have been, in reality, nothing more than armored personnel carriers designed to create "buffer zones" in the border areas of Syria during the midst of a crisis and the panic that would have resulted.

In his testimony to a U.S. Senate committee regarding the Syria ceasefire agreement brokered by the United States and Russia in 2016, Secretary of State John Kerry didn't express much optimism for the success of the plan.[488] That is not surprising, however, since no informed observer had any real hope for the success of the ceasefire because the agreement seemed to lie largely in the hands of the Western-backed terrorists, none of whom are moderates.

---

[487] Lewis, Bernard. "Rethinking The Middle East." Foreign Policy (News outlet of the Council On Foreign Relations. Fall 1992. https://www.foreignaffairs.com/articles/middle-east/1992-09-01/rethinking-middle-east

[488] "Russia Role Vital To Syrian Truce, But US Has 'Plan B' – Kerry." RT. February 24, 2016. https://www.rt.com/usa/333419-kerry-plan-ceasefire-syria/

Despite the lack of enthusiasm in his presentation, Kerry went through the motions of Congressional testimony when an agreement has already been made and a public show is required for mass consumption. What was telling about his testimony, however, was Kerry's allusion to a mysterious "Plan B" if the ceasefire agreement does not work.

"There is a significant discussion taking place now about a Plan B in the event that we do not succeed at the [negotiating] table," Kerry said. But he did not go into specifics as to exactly what that Plan B would look like. That is, except for a slight comment suggesting that the U.S. may have to shift its policy from the total destruction of the Assad government and Syria as a whole to almost total destruction of the country in the form of partitioning and dividing the country into separate principalities.

To this end, Kerry only stated that it could be "too late to keep as a whole Syria if we wait much longer."

Yet Kerry's "Plan B" sounds very much like the "Plan A" of a number of other strategists, policy makers, and imperialist organs.[489]

Consider the op-ed published by Reuters and written by Michael O'Hanlon, entitled "Syria's One Hope May Be As Dim As Bosnia's Once Was." The article argues essentially that the only way Russia and the United States will ever be able to peacefully settle the Syrian crisis is if the two agree to a weakened and divided Syria, broken up into separate pieces.[490]

O'Hanlon wrote,

> To find common purpose with Russia, Washington should keep in mind the Bosnia model, devised to end the fierce Balkan conflicts in the 1990s. In that 1995 agreement, a weak central government was set up to oversee three largely autonomous zones.

> In similar fashion, a future Syria could be a confederation of several sectors: one largely Alawite (Assad's own sect), spread along the Mediterranean coast; another Kurdish, along the north and northeast corridors near the Turkish border; a third primarily Druse, in the southwest; a fourth largely made up of Sunni Muslims; and then a central zone of intermixed groups in the country's main population belt from Damascus to Aleppo. The last zone would likely be difficult to stabilize, but the others might not be so tough.

> Under such an arrangement, Assad would ultimately have to step down from power in Damascus. As a compromise, however, he could perhaps remain leader of the Alawite sector. A weak central government would replace him. But most of the power, as well as most of the armed forces would reside within the individual autonomous sectors — and belong to the various regional governments. In this way, ISIL could be targeted collectively by all the sectors.

---

[489] Cole, Juan. "Kerry Warns Of Break Up Of Syria; But Is It That Realistic?" Juan Cole.com. February 25, 2016. http://www.juancole.com/2016/02/kerry-warns-of-break-up-of-syria-but-is-that-realistic.html?utm_source=dlvr.it&utm_medium=facebook

[490] O'Hanlon, Michael. "Syria's One Hope May Be As Dim As Bosnia's Once Was." Reuters. October 6, 2015. http://blogs.reuters.com/great-debate/2015/10/06/syrias-one-hope-may-be-as-dim-as-bosnias-once-was/

Once this sort of deal is reached, international peacekeepers would likely be needed to hold it together — as in Bosnia. Russian troops could help with this mission, stationed, for example, along the Alawite region's borders.

This deal is not, of course, ripe for negotiation. To make it plausible, moderate forces must first be strengthened. The West also needs to greatly expand its training and arming of various opposition forces that do not include ISIL or al-Nusra. Vetting standards might also have to be relaxed in various ways. American and other foreign trainers would need to deploy inside Syria, where the would-be recruits actually live — and must stay, if they are to protect their families.

Meanwhile, regions now accessible to international forces, starting perhaps with the Kurdish and Druse sectors, could begin receiving humanitarian relief on a much expanded scale. Over time, the number of accessible regions would grow, as moderate opposition forces are strengthened.

Though it could take many months, or even years, to achieve the outcome Washington wants, setting out the goals and the strategy now is crucial. Doing so could provide a basis for the West's working together with — or at least not working against — other key outside players in the conflict, including Russia, as well as Turkey, the Gulf states and Iraq.[491]

O'Hanlon is no stranger to the Partition Plan for Syria. After all, he was the author the infamous Brookings Institution report "Deconstructing Syria: A New Strategy For America's Most Hopeless War," in June, 2015 where he argued essentially the same thing.

In this article for Brookings, a corporate-financier funded "think tank" that has been instrumental in the promotion of the war against Syria since very early on, O'Hanlon argued for the "relaxation" of vetting processes for "rebels" being funded by the U.S. government, the direct invasion of Syria by NATO military forces, and the complete destruction of the Syrian government. O'Hanlon argued for the creation of "safe zones" as a prelude to these goals.[492]

Yet, notably, O'Hanlon also mentioned the creation of a "confederal" Syria as well. In other words, the breakup of the solidified nation as it currently exists. He wrote,

The end-game for these zones would not have to be determined in advance. The interim goal might be a confederal Syria, with several highly autonomous zones and a modest (eventual) national government. The confederation would likely require support from an international peacekeeping force, if this arrangement could ever be formalized by accord. But in the short term, the ambitions would be lower—to make these zones defensible and governable, to help provide relief for populations within them, and to train and equip more recruits so that the zones could be stabilized and then gradually expanded.[493]

---

[491] O'Hanlon, Michael. "Syria's One Hope May Be As Dim As Bosnia's Once Was." Reuters. October 6, 2015. http://blogs.reuters.com/great-debate/2015/10/06/syrias-one-hope-may-be-as-dim-as-bosnias-once-was/

[492] O'Hanlon, Michael. "Deconstructing Syria: A New Strategy For America's Most Hopeless War." Brookings Institution. June 30, 2015. http://www.brookings.edu/blogs/order-from-chaos/posts/2015/06/30-deconstructing-syria-ohanlon

Such a plan is reminiscent of the Zbigniew Brzezinski method of "micro-states and mini-states." In other words, the construction of a weak, impotent state based upon ethnicity, religion, and other identity politics but without the ability to resist the will of larger nations, coalitions, and banking/industrial corporations.[494]

Thus, it appears that Kerry's "Plan B" is, in actuality, "Plan A" for a number of powerful geopolitical strategists from Brzezinski himself to worker bees at the Brookings Institution. While Syria is gaining ground by the day against the Western-backed proxy terrorists who have run rampant across the country since 2011, the West is clearly not giving up on its plan to eliminate a geopolitical obstacle on its way to establishing world hegemony.

Earlier Hints Of Western Intentions, Western Intelligence Involvement In Syria

Hersh's information, which was published in 2007, was not the first mention of the Syrian destabilization being manufactured by Western powers.

In 2005, for instance, writing about the possible options for defeating the then-powerful insurgency in Iraq, Michael Hirsh and John Barry of *Newsweek* wrote an article entitled, "' The Salvador Option: The Pentagon May Put Special -Forces-led assassination or kidnapping teams in Iraq,'" where the writers acknowledged a plan by the Pentagon to install Special Forces hit teams or death squads made up of religious fanatics to engage in the policy of assassinations and outright terror. This strategy came to be known as "The Salvador Option," after the methods used by the United States in El Salvador in the 1980s which resulted in the deaths of nearly 50,000 innocent civilians.[495]

With this in mind, Hirsh and Barry write tellingly of the plan to use such a strategy in Iraq and Syria. They state,

> [O]ne Pentagon proposal would send Special Forces teams to advise, support and possibly train Iraqi squads, most likely hand-picked Kurdish Peshmerga fighters and Shiite militiamen, to target Sunni insurgents and their sympathizers, even across the border into Syria, according to military insiders familiar with the discussions. It remains unclear, however, whether this would be a policy of assassination or so-called 'snatch' operations, in which the targets are sent to secret facilities for interrogation. The current thinking is that while U.S. Special Forces would lead operations in, say, Syria, activities inside Iraq itself would be carried out by Iraqi paramilitaries.[496]

---

[493] O'Hanlon, Michael. "Deconstructing Syria: A New Strategy For America's Most Hopeless War." Brookings Institution. June 30, 2015. http://www.brookings.edu/blogs/order-from-chaos/posts/2015/06/30-deconstructing-syria-ohanlon

[494] Brzezinski, Zbigniew. *The Grand Chessboard: American Primacy And Its Geostrategic Imperatives*. 1st Edition. Basic Books. 1998.

[495] Hirsh, Michael; Barry, John. "The Salvador Option." Newsweek. January 9, 2005. http://web.archive.org/web/20050110030928/http://www.msnbc.msn.com/id/6802629/site/newsweek/

[496] Hirsh, Michael; Barry, John. "The Salvador Option." Newsweek. January 9, 2005.

It is interesting then, that death squads would be invading and terrorizing the nation of Syria only six years later, attempting to accomplish some of the very goals set forward by the Anglo-Americans as indicated by the aforementioned reports.

Yet, while the majority of the fighting (as well as the looting, beheading, torturing, and raping) is being undertaken by the death squads themselves, one also wonders just what hand actual intelligence agents have played in the foreign-backed destabilization.

It is almost a certainty that the Western intelligence agencies that coordinated so much of the foreign insurgency would not leave the death squads, with their quality of intellect (or more accurately the lack thereof), alone to control the entirety of the operations themselves. The operation itself is much too important to be left in the hands of mere death squad operatives.

It is for this reason that many have suspected for some time that the intelligence agencies and military special ops divisions have themselves been involved in the fighting; or, at the very least, the direct coordination inside Syria.

Without a doubt, U.S. Ambassador Robert Ford has played a major role in the organizing of the Syrian death squads, alongside former CIA Director and U.S. General David Petraeus as I have documented in past articles such as "Syria under Attack by Globalist Death Squad Experts."[497] In addition, serious questions have been raised regarding the role Norwegian General Robert Mood has played in the death squad organization.

The question of direct intervention via actual intelligence agents as opposed to mere coordination, however, has been a murkier question. Yet, although harder to decipher in terms of hard evidence, such a suggestion is not entirely without evidence.

After all, it was reported early on in the Syrian destabilization effort that 13 French military officers acting as mercenaries/death squad participants were captured by the Syrian government, all the while the mainstream Western media reported the events as "peaceful protest" and a grassroots level organic Syrian uprising against an oppressive regime.[498]

Around the same time, hacked emails obtained by Anonymous in December 2011 and released by WikiLeaks in steady drips ever since February 27, 2012, revealed that NATO troops, including those from the U.S., U.K, and France, were likely already operating inside Syria.[499]

---

http://web.archive.org/web/20050110030928/http:/www.msnbc.msn.com/id/6802629/site/newsweek/

[497] Turbeville, Brandon. "Syria Under Attack By Globalist Death Squad Experts." Activist Post. May 27, 2012. http://www.activistpost.com/2012/05/syria-under-attack-by-globalist-death.html

[498] "13 Undercover French Army Officers Seized In Syria – Report." RT. March 5, 2012. https://www.rt.com/news/french-army-officers-syria-893/

[499] "Stratfor Leaks: NATO Commandos In Illegal Special Ops In Syria." RT. March 6, 2012. https://www.rt.com/news/stratfor-syria-secret-wikileaks-989/

The emails were obtained from the private U.S. intelligence firm, Stratfor, and were apparently sent by Stratfor's Director of Analysis, Reva Bhalla (bhalla@stratfor.com) and contain discussion of a December confidential Pentagon meeting which was attended "by senior analysts from the US Air Force, and representatives from its chief allies, France and the United Kingdom.[500]

Tellingly, the email's author stated that US officials "said without saying that SOF [special operation forces] teams (presumably from the US, UK, France, Jordan and Turkey) are already on the ground, focused on recce [reconnaissance] missions and training opposition forces." Later in the email, it was stated that "the idea 'hypothetically' is to commit guerrilla attacks, assassination campaigns, try to break the back of the Alawite forces, elicit collapse from within."[501]

This should come as no surprise since Western troops and intelligence agents maintained a heavy presence inside Libya during the destruction of that nation, increasing their presence as the destabilization and subsequent invasion succeeded.[502]

Regardless of the direct involvement of Western forces inside Syria, however, there is absolutely no doubt that the Syrian conflict is very much the result of Anglo-American treachery, control, and coordination. The entire invasion of secular Syria with religious fanatics, mercenaries, and maniacs was the brainchild of Western governments and Israel, the Mad Dog of the Middle East, along with the usual Gulf state feudal monarchies such as Saudi Arabia, Qatar, and others acting as proxies and puppets.

Indeed, with the recent announcement of even more commitments to openly arm, aid, and assist the death squads, the idea that the Syrian destabilization was organized and is being controlled by Western governments is no longer up for debate.

The only debate yet to be had is whether or not citizens of Western countries will continue to allow their governments to run roughshod over both their rights and the rights of sovereign people in foreign countries.

Clearly, the continued assault on Syria is part of a major agenda that is slowly unfolding before our eyes. It would be wise for Americans and all other Western nations to get off of the Path to Persia before the mutual destruction of the world is the only thing left at the end of the road.[503]

---

[500] "Stratfor Leaks: NATO Commandos In Illegal Special Ops In Syria." RT. March 6, 2012. https://www.rt.com/news/stratfor-syria-secret-wikileaks-989/
[501] "Stratfor Leaks: NATO Commandos In Illegal Special Ops In Syria." RT. March 6, 2012. https://www.rt.com/news/stratfor-syria-secret-wikileaks-989/
[502] Borger, Julian; Chulov, Martin. "Al-Jazeera Footage Captures 'Western Troops On The Ground' In Libya." The Guardian. May 30, 2011. https://www.theguardian.com/world/2011/may/30/western-troops-on-ground-libya
[503] Pollack, Kenneth M.; Byman, Daniel L.; Indyk, Martin; Maloney, Suzanne; O'Hanlon, Michael E.; Riedel, Bruce. "Which Path To Persia? Options For A New American Strategy Toward Iran." The Saban Center For Middle East Policy At The Brookings Institution. Analysis Paper Number 20. June, 2009. http://www.brookings.edu/~/media/research/files/papers/2009/6/iran%20strategy/06_iran_strategy.pdf

While the Western mainstream media and even independent gatekeepers like Noam Chomsky for years spread the lie that any suggestion that the United States and NATO were supporting ISIS was a "conspiracy theory," recently uncovered and declassified documents from the Defense Intelligence Agency have proven the Western press and the likes of Chomsky wrong and, yet again, the so-called "conspiracy theorists" right. [504] [505] [506]

This is because, on May 18, Judicial Watch published a selection of recently declassified documents that were obtained from the US Department of Defense and the US State Department as a result of a lawsuit filed against the US government. The lawsuit and most of the documents contained within the release revolved around the Benghazi scandal but a deeper look into the documents dating back to 2012 reveal an even bigger story – that the US and NATO have admitted in their own documents to supporting al-Qaeda and ISIS in Syria and Iraq.[507]

Docs Show Al-Qaeda Involvement From Beginning – No Moderates

The documents demolish the "official story" of Western governments promoted from the beginning of the Syrian crisis until the present day – that the "rebellion" was organic, grassroots, and made up of moderates and freedom-loving democracy proponents. The document states unequivocally that "The Salafist [sic] the Muslim Brotherhood, and AQI are the major forces driving the insurgency in Syria." It points out that "The West, Gulf countries, and Turkey support the opposition; while Russia, China, and Iran support the regime." Tellingly, the report then states that "AQI supported the Syrian opposition from the beginning, both ideologically and through the media . . ."[508]

Indeed, the documents clearly admit that the crisis unfolding in Syria was never a moderate rebellion fighting for democracy; it was made up of fighters from the Muslim Brotherhood and al-Qaeda (al-Qaeda In Iraq/Al-Nusra Front) from the very beginning.

---

[504] Turbeville, Brandon. "Blowback And The Incompetence Theory." Activist Post. October 31, 2014. http://www.activistpost.com/2014/10/blowback-and-incompetence-theory.html

[505] "14-L-0552/DIA/287 - 293." Defense Intelligence Agency. Judicial Watch. http://www.judicialwatch.org/wp-content/uploads/2015/05/Pg.-291-Pgs.-287-293-JW-v-DOD-and-State-14-812-DOD-Release-2015-04-10-final-version11.pdf

[506] Hoff, Brad. "2012 Defense Intelligence Agency Document: West Will Facilitate Rise Of Islamic State "in order to isolate the Syrian regime." Levant Report. May 19, 2015. https://levantreport.com/2015/05/19/2012-defense-intelligence-agency-document-west-will-facilitate-rise-of-islamic-state-in-order-to-isolate-the-syrian-regime/

[507] "14-L-0552/DIA/287 - 293." Defense Intelligence Agency. Judicial Watch. http://www.judicialwatch.org/wp-content/uploads/2015/05/Pg.-291-Pgs.-287-293-JW-v-DOD-and-State-14-812-DOD-Release-2015-04-10-final-version11.pdf

[508] "14-L-0552/DIA/287 - 293." Defense Intelligence Agency. Judicial Watch. http://www.judicialwatch.org/wp-content/uploads/2015/05/Pg.-291-Pgs.-287-293-JW-v-DOD-and-State-14-812-DOD-Release-2015-04-10-final-version11.pdf

US, Turkey, NATO Supporting ISIS and al-Qaeda – Supporting the Creation of Buffer Zones

The document continues in its revelations by stating that:

> Opposition forces are trying to control the eastern areas (Hasaka and Der Zor), adjacent to the western Iraqi provinces (Mosul and Anbar), in addition to neighboring Turkish borders. Western countries, the Gulf states and Turkey are supporting these efforts. This hypothesis is most likely in accordance with the data from recent events, which will help prepare safe havens under international sheltering, similar to what transpired in Libya when Benghazi was chosen as the command center of the temporary government.[509]

"Opposition forces," of course, are al-Qaeda, al-Nusra Front, and ISIS, as mentioned and defined earlier by the DIA document. Thus, any questions of whether or not the US and its NATO/GCC allies have been supporting jihadists and terrorists, should be answered with the admissions made within these pages.

If al-Qaeda/ISIS = the "opposition," then the US support for the "opposition" = US support for al-Qaeda/ISIS.

What is also well-known but now finally admitted to by the US government itself is the plan to establish "buffer zones" and "safe zones" on the Libyan model inside Syria.[510] [511] Such a plan has been covered extensively by myself and Tony Cartalucci (as well as many others in the alternative media) when the concept was considered a "conspiracy theory."

Dividing Iraq and Syria – Fighting Iran and Shi'ite Expansion

In regards to geopolitical concerns and the breakup and destruction of the Syrian government as well as the Iraqi leadership, the document states:

> If the situation unravels there is the possibility of establishing a declared or undeclared Salafist principality in eastern Syria, (Hasaka and Der Zor), and this is exactly what the supporting powers to the opposition want, in order to isolate the Syrian regime, which is considered the strategic depth of the Shia expansion (Iraq and Iran).[512]

---

[509] "14-L-0552/DIA/287 - 293." Defense Intelligence Agency. Judicial Watch. http://www.judicialwatch.org/wp-content/uploads/2015/05/Pg.-291-Pgs.-287-293-JW-v-DOD-and-State-14-812-DOD-Release-2015-04-10-final-version11.pdf

[510] Turbeville, Brandon. "Right On Schedule: US Eyes 'Buffer Zone' In Syria 'Very Very Closely.'" Activist Post. October 10, 2014. http://www.activistpost.com/2014/10/right-on-schedule-us-eyes-buffer-zone.html

[511] Turbeville, Brandon. "Libya 2.0? US Says 'No Fly Zone' Over Syria A Possibility." Activist Post. September 27, 2014. http://www.activistpost.com/2014/10/right-on-schedule-us-eyes-buffer-zone.html

[512] "14-L-0552/DIA/287 - 293." Defense Intelligence Agency. Judicial Watch.

This "Salafist principality" is obviously the Islamic State, particularly when one visualizes the maps of territory claimed by the jihadist organization. As the DIA document admits, the expansion of the ISIS principality is taking place with the support and assistance of Western powers. This much is evidenced by the fact that the ISIS fighters running rampant across Iraq and especially Syria could never have been able to do so were it not for the support given to them by the GCC and NATO. These fighters certainly could never have held such territory if Western military assistance, Saudi money, and Turkish/Israeli logistics and intelligence had not been provided to them.

Note also the justification provided for such support: not only is the goal to "isolate the Syrian regime," it is to prevent the "Shia expansion," meaning the arc of influence held by Iran, growing daily largely due to Western imperialism, hypocrisy, tyranny, and double standards. Instead of attempting to combat Iran's influence in a race for development and the raising of living standards, the West funds jihadist savages to behead and rape their away across civilized nations. This is because the goal is not merely to disrupt Iranian influence, it is to destroy Iran completely.[513] Even Iran itself is a stepping stone to a greater confrontation with Russia and China.[514]

Tony Cartalucci understands this concept well as he writes in his own article "America Admittedly Behind ISIS 'Surge,'" when he says:

The Syrian war is not a localized conflict with limited goals. It is one leg of a much larger agenda to destroy Iran next, then move on to Russia and China. Combined with the Syrian campaign, the West has attempted to create arcs of destabilization across Eastern Europe, Central Asia, and completely encircling China in Southeast Asia.

What this constitutes is a World War executed through the use of 4th generation warfare. At the same time, the West attempts to seek temporary appeasement and accommodation for itself so that it can more effortlessly advance its plans. Attempts to portray itself as interested in "negotiations" with Iran while it wages a proxy war on its doorstep is a prime example of this.

The corporate-financier special interests that have hijacked the United States and Europe have essentially declared war on all lands beyond their grasp, as well as on any and all among their own ranks who oppose their hegemonic aspirations.

The vile conspiracy now openly unfolding in Syria, seeing to its destruction at the hands of terrorists the US is openly backing after claiming for over a decade to be "fighting" is a harbinger of the destruction that complacency and failure to resist will bring all other nations caught in the path of these special interests. Nations not immediately caught in the grip of chaos created by this conspiracy must use their time wisely, preparing the appropriate measures to resist. They must study carefully what

---

http://www.judicialwatch.org/wp-content/uploads/2015/05/Pg.-291-Pgs.-287-293-JW-v-DOD-and-State-14-812-DOD-Release-2015-04-10-final-version11.pdf

[513] Turbeville, Brandon. "ISIS In Iraq And The Path To Iran." Activist Post. June 20, 2014. http://www.activistpost.com/2014/06/isis-in-iraq-and-path-to-iran.html

[514] Turbeville, Brandon. "The Role Of NATO And The EU On Brzezinski's Grand Chessboard." Activist Post. May 27, 2014. http://www.activistpost.com/2014/05/the-role-of-nato-and-eu-on-brzezinskis.html

has been done in Syria and learn from both the mistakes and accomplishments of the Syrian government and armed forces in fighting back.[515]

ISIS Is al-Qaeda

It is important to remember that the so-called leader of ISIS is Abu Bakr al-Baghdadi. As Voltaire Net describes Baghdadi,

Abu Bakr al-Baghdadi is an Iraqi who joined Al-Qaeda to fight against President Saddam Hussein. During the U.S. invasion, he distinguished himself by engaging in several actions against Shiites and Christians (including the taking of the Baghdad Cathedral) and by ushering in an Islamist reign of terror (he presided over an Islamic court which sentenced many Iraqis to be slaughtered in public). After the departure of Paul Bremer III, al-Baghdadi was arrested and incarcerated at Camp Bucca from 2005 to 2009. This period saw the dissolution of Al-Qaeda in Iraq, whose fighters merged into a group of tribal resistance, the Islamic Emirate of Iraq.

On 16 May 2010, Abu Bakr al-Baghdadi was named emir of the IEI, which was in the process of disintegration. After the departure of U.S. troops, he staged operations against the government al-Maliki, accused of being at the service of Iran. In 2013, after vowing allegiance to Al-Qaeda, he took off with his group to continue the jihad in Syria, rebaptizing it *Islamic Emirate of Iraq and the Levant*. In doing so, he challenged the privileges that Ayman al-Zawahiri had previously granted, on behalf of Al-Qaeda, to the *Al-Nusra Front* in Syria, which was originally nothing more than an extension of the IEI.[516]

Regardless, false assumptions surrounding the true leadership of ISIS would be called into question in January of 2014 when Al-Arabiya, a Saudi-owned and operated news agency, published an article as well as a video of an interrogation of an ISIS fighter who had been captured while operating inside Syria.[517] [518]

When asked why ISIS was following the movement of the Free Syrian Army and who had given him the orders to do so, the fighter stated that he did not know why he was ordered to monitor the FSA's movement but that the orders had come from Abu Faisal, also known as Prince Abdul Rachman al-Faisal of the Saudi Royal Family.[519]

---

[515] Cartalucci, Tony. "America Admittedly Behind ISIS 'Surge.'" Land Destroyer Report. May 25, 2015. http://landdestroyer.blogspot.co.uk/2015/05/america-admittedly-behind-isis-surge.html

[516] "Iraq Under Attack By US, France, Saudi Arabia." Voltaire Net. June 11, 2014. http://webcache.googleusercontent.com/search?q=cache:http://www.voltairenet.org/article184211.html

[517] "Islamic State of Iraq And The Levant Led By Prince Abdul Rahman." Voltaire Net. February 4, 2014. http://webcache.googleusercontent.com/search?q=cache:http://www.voltairenet.org/article182036.html

[518] Cartalucci, Tony; Bowie, Nile. Subverting Syria: How CIA Contra Gangs And NGO's Manufacture, Mislable, And Market Mass Murder." Progressive Press. 2012. https://www.amazon.com/Subverting-Syria-Contra-Manufacture-Mislabel-ebook/dp/B008FTILYA?ie=UTF8&linkCode=wsw&ref_=as_sl_pd_tf_sw&tag=permacultucom-20#navbar

[519] Cartalucci, Tony; Bowie, Nile. "War On Syria: Gateway To WWIII." Tony Cartalucci and Nile

An excerpt from the relevant section of the interrogation reads as follows:

> Interrogator: Why do you (ISIS) monitor the movement of the Free Syrian Army?
>
> ISIS Detainee: I don't know exactly why but we received orders from ISIS command.
>
> Interrogator: Who among ISIS gave the orders?
>
> ISIS Detainee: Prince Abdul Rachman al-Faisal, who is also known as Abu Faisal.[520]

Such revelations, of course, will only be shocking news to those who have been unaware of the levels to which the Saudis have been involved with the funding, training, and directing of death squad forces deployed in Syria.[521] [522] [523] Indeed, the Saudis have even openly admitted to the Russian government that they do, in fact, a number of varied terrorist organizations across the world.[524]

Even tired mainstream media organizations such as Newsweek (aka The Daily Beast) can no longer ignore the facts surrounding the Saudis' involvement with the organization of terrorist groups across the world.[525]

Note also that Voltaire Net describes al-Nusra, a documented al-Qaeda connected group, as merely an extension of the IEI (Islamic Emirate of Iraq) which itself was nothing more than a version of Al-Qaeda in Iraq. Thus, from Al-Qaeda in Iraq, came the IEI, which then became the Islamic Emirate of Iraq and the Levant. IEIL then became ISIS/ISIL which is now often referred to as IS.

In other words, Nusra=Al-Qaeda-IEI=IEIL=ISIL=ISIS=IS.

With the information presented above regarding the nature of the Free Syrian Army and the so-called "moderate rebels," it would be entirely fair to add these "moderate" groups to the list as well.

Bowie. 2012. https://www.scribd.com/document/114889281/War-on-Syria-Cartalucci-Bowie2 see also http://landdestroyer.blogspot.com/p/war-on-syria-gateway-to-wwiii.html

[520] Lehmann, Christof. "ISIS Unveiled: The Identity Of The Insurgency In Syria And Iraq." Nsnbc international. June 15, 2014. http://nsnbc.me/2014/06/15/isis-unveiled-identity-insurgency-syria-iraq/

[521] Nimmo, Kurt; Jones, Alex. "Saudi Arabia, Sunni Caliphate, NATO Run Secret Terror Army In Iraq And Syria." Infowars. June 13, 2014. http://www.infowars.com/saudi-arabia-sunni-caliphate-nato-run-secret-terror-army-in-iraq-and-syria/

[522] Black, Ian. "Syria Crisis: Saudi Arabia To Spend Millions To Train New Rebel Force." The Guardian. November 7, 2013. https://www.theguardian.com/world/2013/nov/07/syria-crisis-saudi-arabia-spend-millions-new-rebel-force

[523] Cartalucci, Tony. "NATO's Terror Hordes In Iraq A Pretext For Syria Invasion." New Eastern Outlook. June 13, 2012. http://journal-neo.org/2014/06/13/nato-s-terror-hordes-in-iraq-a-pretext-for-syria-invasion/

[524] Evans-Pritchard, Ambrose. "Saudis Offer Russia Secret Oil Deal If It Drops Syria." The Telegraph. August 27, 2013. http://www.telegraph.co.uk/finance/newsbysector/energy/oilandgas/10266957/Saudis-offer-Russia-secret-oil-deal-if-it-drops-Syria.html

[525] Rogin, Josh. "America's Allies Are Funding ISIS." The Daily Beast. June 14, 2014. http://www.thedailybeast.com/articles/2014/06/14/america-s-allies-are-funding-isis.html

Although too lengthy of a study to be presented in this book, it is important to point out that al-Qaeda is entirely a creation of the West, created for the purpose of drawing the Soviets into Afghanistan in the 1970s and a host of other geopolitical goals in the middle east and around the world, 9/11 being the most memorable instance of Western intelligence al-Qaeda mobilization.[526] [527]

Consider the interview conducted with Zbigniew Brzezinski by Le Nouvel Observatour Paris as far back as 1998. A telling excerpt from the interview goes as follows:

Question: The former director of the CIA, Robert Gates, stated in his memoirs ["From the Shadows"], that American intelligence services began to aid the Mujahadeen in Afghanistan 6 months before the Soviet intervention. In this period you were the national security adviser to President Carter. You therefore played a role in this affair. Is that correct?[528]

Brzezinski: Yes. According to the official version of history, CIA aid to the Mujahadeen began during 1980, that is to say, after the Soviet army invaded Afghanistan, 24 Dec 1979. But the reality, secretly guarded until now, is completely otherwise Indeed, it was July 3, 1979 that President Carter signed the first directive for secret aid to the opponents of the pro-Soviet regime in Kabul. And that very day, I wrote a note to the president in which I explained to him that in my opinion this aid was going to induce a Soviet military intervention.

Q: Despite this risk, you were an advocate of this covert action. But perhaps you yourself desired this Soviet entry into war and looked to provoke it?

B: It isn't quite that. We didn't push the Russians to intervene, but we knowingly increased the probability that they would.

Q: When the Soviets justified their intervention by asserting that they intended to fight against a secret involvement of the United States in Afghanistan, people didn't believe them. However, there was a basis of truth. You don't regret anything today?

B: Regret what? That secret operation was an excellent idea. It had the effect of drawing the Russians into the Afghan trap and you want me to regret it? The day that the Soviets officially crossed the border, I wrote to President Carter. We now have the opportunity of giving to the USSR its Vietnam war. Indeed, for almost 10 years, Moscow had to carry on a war unsupportable by the government, a conflict that brought about the demoralization and finally the breakup of the Soviet empire.

---

[526] "Interview With Zbigniew Brzezinski, President Jimmy Carter's National Security Adviser." Le Nouvel Observatour, Paris. January 15-21, 1998. Reposted and archived by Global Research in 2001 under the title "The C.I.A.'s Intervention In Afghanistan." Global Research. October 15, 2001. http://www.globalresearch.ca/articles/BRZ110A.html

[527] Tarpley, Webster Griffin. *9/11 Synthetic Terror: Made In USA*. 5th Edition. Progressive Press. 2011.

[528] "Interview With Zbigniew Brzezinski, President Jimmy Carter's National Security Adviser." Le Nouvel Observatour, Paris. January 15-21, 1998. Reposted and archived by Global Research in 2001 under the title "The C.I.A.'s Intervention In Afghanistan." Global Research. October 15, 2001. http://www.globalresearch.ca/articles/BRZ110A.html

Q: And neither do you regret having supported the Islamic fundamentalism, having given arms and advice to future terrorists?

B: What is most important to the history of the world? The Taliban or the collapse of the Soviet empire? Some stirred-up Moslems or the liberation of Central Europe and the end of the cold war?

Q: Some stirred-up Moslems? But it has been said and repeated Islamic fundamentalism represents a world menace today.

B: Nonsense! It is said that the West had a global policy in regard to Islam. That is stupid. There isn't a global Islam. Look at Islam in a rational manner and without demagoguery or emotion. It is the leading religion of the world with 1.5 billion followers. But what is there in common among Saudi Arabian fundamentalism, moderate Morocco, Pakistan militarism, Egyptian pro-Western or Central Asian secularism? Nothing more than what unites the Christian countries.[529]

Video Shows American Soldiers Posing As "Rebels," "Fleeing" Jihadists In Syria

In a series of reports that floated around even some of the mainstream press organs, a video has emerged that reportedly shows U.S. "commandos" fleeing U.S.-backed rebels in the northern part of Syria.

The video shows what appears to be American soldiers riding in the backs of white Toyota pickups leaving the area that Turkish troops, with FSA terrorists in tow, recently conquered from "ISIS" militants. While many of the reports suggest that the soldiers are "fleeing" the scene, the men in the footage seem incredibly nonchalant for those who are trying to escape. Instead, they seem calm, even waving at the FSA terrorists shouting abuse at them as they drive away.[530]

Other reports claim that the commandos entered the town of al-Rai, fighting alongside the Turks and FSA but were soon forced out by the terrorists. But, as mentioned, the Americans do not seem as if they are under attack but as if they are simply leaving the scene.[531]

As Raf Sanchez writes for the Telegraph,

---

[529] "Interview With Zbigniew Brzezinski, President Jimmy Carter's National Security Adviser." Le Nouvel Observatour, Paris. January 15-21, 1998. Reposted and archived by Global Research in 2001 under the title "The C.I.A.'s Intervention In Afghanistan." Global Research. October 15, 2001. http://www.globalresearch.ca/articles/BRZ110A.html

[530] Sanchez, Raf. "American Commadoes 'forced to run away' from US-backed Syrian Rebels." The Telegraph. September 16, 2016. http://www.telegraph.co.uk/news/2016/09/16/american-commandos-forced-to-run-away-from-us-backed-syrian-rebe/

[531] Sanchez, Raf. "American Commadoes 'forced to run away' from US-backed Syrian Rebels." The Telegraph. September 16, 2016. http://www.telegraph.co.uk/news/2016/09/16/american-commandos-forced-to-run-away-from-us-backed-syrian-rebe/

Video footage appears to show US commandos fleeing a Syrian town under a barrage of abuse and insults hurled at them by fighters from the American-backed Free Syrian Army (FSA) rebel group.

The video appears to be the first evidence of US special forces cooperating with Turkish troops in their battle against Islamic State (Isil).

The incident illustrates the complex web of alliances and enmities in Syria, where many of America's allies are fighting each other and some rebel groups that receive US support still harbour strong anti-American sentiments.

The footage shows a crowd of rebel fighters in the town of al-Rai near the Turkish border, which was captured from Isil by Syrian rebel groups with the backing of Turkey. Turkey, which launched a military incursion into Syria in late August, has been backing the FSA.[532]

To be sure, the terrorists in the video are hurling insults at the soldiers. As Sanchez reports,

The fighters scream anti-American chants as a column of pick-up trucks carrying US commandos drives away from them.

"Christians and Americans have no place among us," shouts one man in the video. "They want to wage a crusader war to occupy Syria."

Another man calls out: "The collaborators of America are dogs and pigs. They wage a crusader war against Syria and Islam. "[533]

RT reports similar verbal assaults. It writes,

The footage shows a group of agitated men, gathered in the town square, shouting anti-American slogans in Arabic, as a cavalcade of vehicles passes by.

The chants include: "Down with America," "Get out you dogs," and "They are coming to Syria to occupy it." Voices in the background call the US troops "pigs" and "crusaders."

"We don't want a single American fighting in Syria alongside us," says a man in the second video. "We are Muslims, we are not infidels. Get out!"

Reuters cited a US official and a "senior rebel commander," who confirmed that a protest had taken place, which ended with US troops making their way back towards the Turkish border.[534]

[532] Sanchez, Raf. "American Commadoes 'forced to run away' from US-backed Syrian Rebels." The Telegraph. September 16, 2016. http://www.telegraph.co.uk/news/2016/09/16/american-commandos-forced-to-run-away-from-us-backed-syrian-rebe/
[533] Sanchez, Raf. "American Commadoes 'forced to run away' from US-backed Syrian Rebels." The Telegraph. September 16, 2016. http://www.telegraph.co.uk/news/2016/09/16/american-commandos-forced-to-run-away-from-us-backed-syrian-rebe/
[534] "'Crusaders! Infidels! Dogs! Get Out!' US-Backed Rebels Force US Commandos To Leave Syrian Town." RT. September 16, 2016. https://www.rt.com/news/359591-syria-us-forces-rebels/

While much of the report is largely unsurprising, there are at least two points that must be mentioned. First, we now have visual evidence of the American military fighting alongside the Turkish military in its illegal invasion of Syria and the establishment of a "buffer zone" in the northern portion of the country. Obviously, this "buffer zone" is nothing more than a forward operating base for terrorists to launch attacks even deeper into Syria and Aleppo in particular. The U.S. has now provided the world with documented evidence of its direct involvement in creating this terrorist safe haven.[535]

Second, the United States also now has video footage proving that it has "boots on the ground" (despite the Obama regime's promise otherwise) fighting alongside terrorists in Syria. Although we have known since the beginning of the conflict that the United States Special Forces troops and intelligence agents were fighting alongside terrorists covertly, the recent footage now provides even more evidence in this regard.[536]

In addition, it shows that these American soldiers are acting as the terrorists and not only fighting beside them. One need only take a look at the men in the footage and see that they are dressed in American protective gear but not American uniforms. In fact, they are dressed the same as the FSA terrorists and operating FSA-style vehicles and guns. For all intents and purposes, these soldiers are posing as "moderate rebels." After all, if "moderate" terrorists don't exist, you have to invent them – literally.

The Syrian crisis is thus now more than a mere proxy war against a sovereign state initiated by the United States and NATO. It is a cauldron of mutual and conflicting interests. At the heart of it, however, it should always be remembered that the initiator of aggression was the West who funded proxy terrorists to overthrow the legitimate and secular government of Bashar al-Assad for a wide array of political and geopolitical purposes. In addition to the immoral nature of the conflict to begin with, the U.S. must immediately end its involvement in the campaign to overthrow Assad in Syria before the hubris and psychopathic ruling elite manage to get everyone inside and out of the United States killed in the process.

The United States Funding Terrorists In Syria Since 2006- Wikileaks

On April 18, 2011, in an article written by Ariel Zirulnick of the Christian Science Monitor, it was reported that a number of emails obtained by Wikileaks revealed that the United States had been covertly funding the "Syrian opposition" for at least five years. Zirulnick writes,

> That aid continued going into the hands of the Syrian government opposition even after the US began its reengagement policy with Syria under President Barack Obama in 2009, the Post reports. In January, the US posted its first ambassador to the country since the Bush administration withdrew the US ambassador in 2005 over concerns

---

[535] Cartalucci, Tony. "Beware: Israel The Eager Provocateur." New Eastern Outlook. August 8, 2014. http://journal-neo.org/2014/08/08/beware-israel-the-eager-provocateur/
[536] Zirulnick, Ariel. "Cables Reveal Covert US Support For Syria's Opposition." The Christian Science Monitor. April 18, 2011. http://www.csmonitor.com/World/terrorism-security/2011/0418/Cables-reveal-covert-US-support-for-Syria-s-opposition

about Syria's involvement in the assassination of former Lebanese prime minister Rafik Hariri.

. . . . . .

That is a dilemma that concerned the US government even before the protests began. The author of an April 2009 cable expressed concern that some of the projects being funded by the US, if discovered by the Syrian government, would be perceived as "an attempt to undermine the Asad [sic] regime, as opposed to encouraging behavior reform."

The Post reported that much of the money – as much as $6 million since 2006 – has been funneled through a group of Syrian exiles in London, known as the Movement for Justice and Development. The group is connected to a London-based satellite television station that is broadcast in Syria, known as Barada TV, which has recently expanded its coverage to include the mass protests.

Several other civil society initiatives in Syria received secret US funding, but by 2009, US officials were concerned that the Syrian government had discovered the US funding. The Post was unable to confirm whether programs are still being funded, but cables indicate the funding was planned at least through September 2010.[537]

The Question Of Blowback

Amidst a rash of terror attacks in the Western world, the general public has once again witnessing a discussion playing out in the mainstream media as to the solutions and appropriate responses to international Islamic terror. As usual, these solutions and responses involve the bombing, invasion, or general destruction of a country in Africa or the Middle East, always one which was conveniently placed on the hit list of the United States, NATO, or Israel.

During the course of this discussion, as with terror attacks of the past, the public is also being subjected to a discussion of the nature and causes of such terrorism in the first place. In the pro-war camp, the answer is simple – "They hate us for our freedom." In the anti-war camp, the answer is also simple – "blowback."

Obviously, the pro-war argument can be dismissed out of hand due to its imbecilic nature and the fact that it is nothing more than a pathetic propaganda narrative aimed at Americans with far too much bravado or fear and not nearly enough intelligence. Indeed, if terrorists hated America for its freedoms it is unfortunately the case that they could have stopped hating America a long time ago.

The anti-war camp, however, while its aims may be well-meaning (or not) will argue that such fundamentalist terrorism is the result of the United States and its allies having relentlessly bombed a number of countries in the past, engendering hatred, and thus perpetuating a cycle – simply put, more bombing begets more terror.

---

[537] Zirulnick, Ariel. "Cables Reveal Covert US Support For Syria's Opposition." The Christian Science Monitor. April 18, 2011. http://www.csmonitor.com/World/terrorism-security/2011/0418/Cables-reveal-covert-US-support-for-Syria-s-opposition

These are now the responses being introduced into the discussion yet again after a number of terrorist attacks taking place across the Western world.

The United States, Canada, and Europe, according to the "blowback" camp, are simply reaping the seeds it has sewn for taking part in the NATO destruction of Iraq and Syria.

Predictably, the alternative media has soon followed behind the blowback proponents who are usually mainstream individuals – commentators, theorists, "journalists," hosts, politicians, "activists," etc. – as an attempt to use the alleged credibility of the speaker so as to bolster its own anti-war case. Unfortunately, the blowback position is not only fraught with problems and inconsistencies; it is entirely a cop out.

To argue that terrorist attacks like 9/11, the London 7/7 bombings, Boston Bombings, the Canadian shootings, Paris, Brussels, and Orlando among others are the result of bad American policy is to find oneself arguing a timeline of "who started it" that does not exactly match up with the theory or a cause-and-effect scenario that does not always match up the cause with the effect or the regions in which the cause and effect have taken place.

Blowback proponents must subsequently find themselves arguing against any comprehensive response to terrorism beyond simply ending all current foreign engagements and hoping that extremist sentiment finally settles down and dissipates over time. For those who have died in terrorist attacks in the past and those set to die by them in the future, such logic is bound to ring hollow. The argument to simply pull back, hope for the best, and expect a "cooling down" period to take its course is weak indeed.

Most importantly, however, proponents of the blowback theory, regardless of their good intentions, essentially act as cover-up artists for the world oligarchy. Like 9/11, "incompetence theories," blowbackers are forced to admit that such terrorist organizations are organically organized in response to some perceived injustice. Even blowbackers who are able to admit that groups like al-Qaeda were actually created by the United States intelligence community are subsequently forced to acquiesce to the idea that it is an organization that was abandoned by the U.S., mishandled, or otherwise no longer under the control of the West.

This argument, of course, fundamentally misses the facts surrounding situations like 9/11, 7/7, the 1993 WTC bombing, Libya, Iraq, and Syria.

Indeed, attempting to understand any of the crises mentioned above without understanding that NATO, the United States, Britain, France, Israel, GCC, and other allies not only created but funded, directed, trained, armed, and continue to control these terrorist organizations, is an exercise in futility. That is, such an approach is an exercise in futility if one's goal is to determine the truth surrounding the situation.

For this reason, blowback theory is generally pushed by "gatekeepers" for the establishment. The purpose and method of the gatekeeper is to act as one of the last buffers against an individual's potential to discover the true nature of the conflict. The gatekeeper must present criticism seen as hard-hitting, unpopular, and cutting edge while, at the same time, not going so far as to reveal the actual nature of the situation.

The gatekeeper cannot allow the ardent follower to get too close to reality. Thus, when the ardent follower begins to introduce relevant facts into the discussion that question even the gatekeeper's narrative, the gatekeeper typically responds with catcalls of "conspiracy theory."

The blowback superstars include a small number of politicians but especially include individuals like Noam Chomsky and Glenn Greenwald, two individuals who have repeatedly assailed the 9/11 truth movement despite their inability to adequately address the inconsistencies in the official story or provide adequate solutions to any problem they are forced to address.

Blowback theory presents the 1993 World Trade Center bombing, 7/7, 9/11, and other terrorist attacks as a response to Western aggression and thus completely covers up the fact that these attacks were entirely orchestrated by the very governments who claimed victimhood by them after the fact. Blowback theory presents the emergence of ISIS in Iraq and Syria as an organic creation that appeared due to American interference in Iraq. Blowback theory attempts to portray al-Qaeda as a group that was created (if the theory proponent is even moderately honest) by the U.S. which has come back to bite us.

The truth is that "blowback" has very little, if any, historical precedent.

It is also the truth that "blowback" is nothing more than intellectual gatekeeping, regardless of who espouses it. If one wishes to discover the hidden hand behind international terror, he need look no further than Washington, D.C., London, Riyadh, and Tel Aviv. He may begin looking at the myriad of inconsistencies surrounding virtually every terrorist attack that has occurred in the Western world within recent memory, a search that will lead to precisely the same locations.

The European Rape Crisis: The Cause, The Reasons, The Solutions

The crisis in Syria, entirely created by NATO, the GCC, Israel, and the West, is now having repercussions across the entire globe. These repercussions are coming not only in the form of mass numbers of dead civilians, lowered living standards, dangerous geopolitical chess moves between nuclear powers and tremendous strains on economies but also in terms of mass migration and social upheaval.

The displacement of tens of thousands of Syrians whose lives have been destroyed by NATO and the West is now placing the indigenous people of NATO countries in a moral quandary – whether or not to welcome the victims of the wars their governments have launched without their permission or to turn them back as a threat to the already lowered living standards of the average citizens of the West and to what is left of their culture.

Coupled with the fact that the majority of "refugees" are not refugees at all but immigrants from other locations in the Middle East and North Africa (MENA) who are coming to Europe and America for economic reasons and purposes other than asylum from warfare, assimilation programs in Europe and America are overwhelmed, Western cultures are being destroyed, and economies are facing an even greater low-wage competition for jobs. Already lowered living standards are thus being lowered further.

There is an immense clash of cultures taking place in Europe as masses of "immigrants" from cultures vastly different from those of the West have now been placed directly in the middle of European society. General crime is now increasing in Europe as a result, violent attacks on indigenous Europeans are becoming a regular occurrence, and rape has skyrocketed beyond belief. Indigenous Europeans are even being forced out of their homes to house "refugees" and thousands of years of historical cultural norms are being changed to accommodate foreigners.[538]

Obviously, European governments (save for a few) have done nothing to stem the tide of immigration, to prevent violence against Europeans, or even, at the very least, to ensure that the people entering Europe are assimilated in an orderly way. Instead, these governments have done the opposite – encouraging more immigration and accusing anyone critical of it as xenophobic and racist.

As a result of the increased number of attacks, Europeans are now being forced to take matters into their own hands to protect themselves and their women who are under drastically increased threats of rape and violence. Some are doing whatever they can to avoid public places while others are attempting whatever feeble means left to them in the anti-gun utopias of Europe to defend themselves. Others still are forming groups of their own to patrol the streets and prevent these assaults from taking place. These individuals are then being attacked by the European press and social justice warriors who label them xenophobes and attempt to draw parallels to German fascism of the 1930s.

Yet, unfortunately, some individuals are forming truly racist and anti-Muslim gangs for the purpose of harassing Muslims, Middle Easterners, and immigrants and promoting their own racist agenda of "pure blood" and the like, targeting "Muslim" shops and neighborhoods as par for the course.

The Situation

The fact that rapes and violence against Europeans has increased exponentially ever since the EU has allowed hordes of immigrants and "refugees" to enter Europe is virtually undeniable. Even the most incredible feats of political correctness and collective Anglo-European guilt cannot cover up the fact that such acts have increased. Arguments in opposition to this fact are so inept that silence is the rebuttal of choice.

The number of cases of rapes as a result of Europe's open door policy to any and all immigrants (it must be pointed out once again that most of these individuals are not even from Syria to begin with) are too voluminous to include in one article. However, Germany's experience over New Year's Eve – especially in places like Cologne – are enough to illustrate the cultural and moral clash that is taking place in Germany and much of the rest of Europe as well as the drastically increased danger to European women.

---

[538] Huggler, Justin. "German Woman Threatened With Eviction To Make Way For Refugees." The Telegraph. September 25, 2015.
http://www.telegraph.co.uk/news/worldnews/europe/germany/11891631/German-woman-threatened-with-eviction-to-make-way-for-refugees.html

As Allison Pearson wrote for the Telegraph,

> On New Year's Eve, in the precincts of the beautiful, twin-spired cathedral, up to 1,000 men of Arab or North African appearance sexually assaulted and robbed women who were enjoying the festivities. Around 100 complaints have been made to police so far, including two cases of rape. Eighteen-year-old Michelle said she and her friends were surrounded by 30 men, who molested them and then stole their belongings. Michelle said the men looked angry.

> And there is the crux of the problem. If you are doctrinally commanded to cover up your women then the sight of a woman like the lovely, blonde Michelle, who is both uncovered and happily self-confident, provokes temptation, and this makes you angry. That anger is not directed where it should be – at yourself or at a belief system which forbids a woman to move and dress as she pleases – but at the temptress. (Just as it was in early Christianity.) In order for male pride to be salvaged, the temptress can be humiliated and terrorised, thus restoring power and dominance to where it properly belongs – the man.

> This puts a liberal western society, which values women's rights, and admits men from countries that don't, in a bit of a bind, to put it mildly. It's difficult to raise the issue without being howled down by cries of "Islamophobia". Sensitivities were already running high in Germany following Angela Merkel's open invitation to refugees, which saw more than a million people arrive over the past twelve months.[539] Shamefully, it took several days for the German news media to mention the Cologne assaults. As for the police, they issued a comically self-satisfied report saying that a jolly, peaceful time had been had by all. Apart from the girls who had fingers stuck in their most intimate parts, presumably.[540]

And what was the response of the authorities in Germany, a country who does not think twice about jailing elderly women for Thoughtcrime[541] or legislating and promoting various forms of cultural Marxist ideologies like feminism?[542] It was to suggest that the victims were largely responsible and should conduct themselves in a way that does not invite an assault upon them. This was, of course, after the authorities and the press remained entirely silent on the whole affair for as long as possible before the sheer number of victims reached a level where it could no longer be kept under the rug.

---

[539] Guerot, Ulrike. "Angela Merke's Paying A High Price To Get Her Way." The Telegraph. September 21, 2015. http://www.telegraph.co.uk/news/worldnews/europe/germany/angela-merkel/11880279/Angela-Merkels-paying-a-high-price-to-get-her-way.html

[540] Pearson, Allison. "Cologne Assault: Cultural Difference Is No Excuse For Rape." The Telegraph. January 7, 2016. http://www.telegraph.co.uk/news/worldnews/europe/germany/12087780/Cologne-assault-Cultural-difference-is-no-excuse-for-rape.html

[541] "German 'Nazi Grandma' Sentenced To 10 Months In Prison For Holocaust Denial." The Telegraph. November 13, 2015. http://www.telegraph.co.uk/news/worldnews/europe/germany/11993382/German-Nazi-grandma-sentenced-to-10-months-in-prison-for-Holocaust-denial.html

[542] Beppler-Spahl, Sabine. "Germany's Gender Quota: Illiberal And Divisive." Spiked Online. August 20, 2015. http://www.spiked-online.com/newsite/article/germanys-gender-quota-illiberal-and-divisive/17323#.V6qACPkrKM9

Pearson writes,

> It soon became impossible to ignore the gravity of what had happened. Even then, the authorities' default position was denial. On Tuesday, Henriette Reker, the Mayor of Cologne, made a statement which I sincerely hope will haunt her till her dying day. Asked how women were supposed to cope with this menace, the mayor proposed a new "code of conduct" for young women and girls "so that such things do not happen to them". In particular, she suggested that women maintain an arm's length from strangers. This caused a storm of sarcasm on Twitter where the German for arm's length - #einearmlange – was soon trending. The idea that a woman ambushed by a Moroccan gang should inform them, politely and Germanically, that she was staying at arm's length to avoid sexual harassment would have been a joke, had the threat not been so real and frightening. Meanwhile, reports of similar attacks were coming in from Hamburg, Dusseldorf and Stuttgart.

> Politicians and journalists had previously been reluctant to address stories about rape and child abuse in German refugee camps, where unaccompanied women are apparently seen as "fair game". Reporting the mistreatment of women is seen as playing into the hands of a Right-wing agenda and stoking ethnic tensions. It's hardly surprising that the government's first reaction was to pretend it simply wasn't true. Remember what happened last time in Germany when there was demonization of "the other"?[543]

Pearson was, of course, right in her criticism, tepid as it was. We will return to the latter issue of her argument later. But Germany is not the only country where such massive sexual assaults and rapes have occurred.

Sweden experienced its own "refugee" rape fest at a Stockholm music festival where immigrant gangs leapt upon teenage girls and raped them as well. There were a number of other incidents too which were also covered up by Swedish police because of a desire not to paint immigration, "multiculturalism," and forced "diversity" in a bad light. Too bad for the victims.[544]

While the statistics are murkier than some would prefer to present them, it is notable that, ever since allowing itself to become a paragon of "diversity" and a modern "multicultural" society, rape in Sweden has increased by 1400%.[545] Violent crime has also increased. Of course, neither of these statistics can be blamed on migrants alone but the notable increase of violent attacks and rapes that are occurring in Sweden today are indeed a result of open immigration policies. This is almost undeniable. It is well-known amongst Swedish society but no one dare say it, lest they labeled racist, anti-immigrant, or xenophobic.

---

[543] Pearson, Allison. "Cologne Assault: Cultural Difference Is No Excuse For Rape." The Telegraph. January 7, 2016.
http://www.telegraph.co.uk/news/worldnews/europe/germany/12087780/Cologne-assault-Cultural-difference-is-no-excuse-for-rape.html
[544] Brown, Andrew. "This cover-up of sex assaults in Sweden is a gift for xenophobes." The Guardian. January 13, 2016. https://www.theguardian.com/commentisfree/2016/jan/13/sex-assaults-sweden-stockholm-music-festival
[545] Carlqvist, Ingrid; Hedegaard, Lars. "Sweden: Rape Capital Of The West." The Gatestone Institute. February 14, 2015. https://www.gatestoneinstitute.org/5195/sweden-rape

But these two countries are only two examples. On New Year's Eve alone sexual assaults at the hands of migrant gangs were reported in Switzerland, Austria, and Finland.[546]

In France, the open immigration has become such a problem that highways near Calais resemble a scene Children of Men as opposed to an orderly society.[547] [548] Other videos have surfaced showing "refugees," alongside trendy social justice warriors (SJW), howling at French residents in Calais, chasing them onto their own property and into their homes, all while throwing trash, tires, and bricks at them. [549]

The Resident Response

Not only did many European authorities attempt to cover up the refugee violence and heavy increase in rape but they are essentially refusing to do anything about it even after it was revealed. Indeed, many "officials" are calling for allowing even more immigrants in! Thus, many European residents are being forced to police against rape and assault themselves in the absence of any action and despite much of it taken by government.

While the more trendy leftist members of European society, for whom life is incapable of living without being the victim of some racist, sexist, homophobic, or xenophobic act, scream to allow the "refugees" in and give them "grace" for their own cultural norms, other members of society are more hesitant to allow the mass rape of their women, children, and even men in the service of "cultural sensitivity."

With that, a number of men across Europe have begun to band together and form "vigilante gangs" for the purpose of patrolling the streets and attempting to prevent further attacks on indigenous Europeans. These groups – some legitimate expressions of community solidarity and some actual racists – are, of course, being lumped into one

---

[546] Wyke, Tom; Akbar, Jay. "Migrant rape fears spread across Europe: Women told not to go out at night alone after assaults carried out in Sweden, Finland, Germany, Austria, and Switzerland amid warnings gangs are co-ordinating attacks." The Daily Mail. January 8, 2016. http://www.dailymail.co.uk/news/article-3390168/Migrant-rape-fears-spread-Europe-Women-told-not-night-assaults-carried-Sweden-Finland-Germany-Austria-Switzerland-amid-warnings-gangs-ordinating-attacks.html

[547] "Rioting migrants yesterday – Calais to Dover port." Youtube. Posted on June 8, 2015. https://www.youtube.com/watch?v=syyl0gfNDRE Jukin Media. Video shows hordes of migrants ransacking an eighteen wheeler on the highway in broad daylight.

[548] Slack, James. "Calais Migrants Ambush Britons at knifepoint in terrifying 'highway robberies." The Daily Mail. December 10, 2009. http://www.dailymail.co.uk/news/article-1201039/Calais-migrants-ambush-Britons-knifepoint-terrifying-highway-robberies.html

[549] "France tensions flare as Calais resident points gun at pro-refugee rally." Ruptly Tv. Posted on Youtube January 23, 2016. https://www.youtube.com/watch?v=OdZLMUKJOJg Video shows a confrontation between pro-refugee rally participants and two French men on the sidewalk near the Frenchmen's apparent home. Rally participants begin throwing objects at the men who retreat to their property where rally participants continue to pelt them with objects. One of the men enters the home and returns with a shotgun. The gun is aimed at the rally participants but is quickly put away again despite rally participants continuing to pelt them with objects. The men and their family eventually retreat to the inside of the home and the video ends.

category by the European and Western press. According to the mainstream press reports, anyone who dare show force by which to prevent women from being raped on the streets of Europe is a "racist," "bigot," "xenophobe," "white supremacist," "far-right," or a "Neo-Nazi."

But the designation these groups receive in the press reveal another debilitating aspect of European culture - the collective "German guilt" over the second world war and the holocaust combined with the European obsession with political correctness and "anti-racism" that borderlines an actual mental illness. In an effort to appear "tolerant," Europeans are allowing catcalls of xenophobia to overshadow any suggestion of preventing unfettered immigration policies or the destruction of their own culture. Hence, they are witnessing the literal destruction of European culture before their very eyes.

For this reason, it is difficult to tell which groups are truly racist neo-Nazis and which are legitimate citizens simply fed up with mass rape. According to mainstream media postings, they are all one in the same.

European society has been so overcome with political correctness and "Rightspeech" that the best many European men can do is to march through the streets in women's clothing to express their opposition to rape. But who in their right mind

---

[550] "The Abandoned Front Line Of Europe's Refugee Crisis." Journeyman Pictures. Posted on Youtube on August 24, 2015. https://www.youtube.com/watch?v=wQj1xvQth6Y&feature=youtu.be&t=12m3s Film shows interviews with refugees and locals regarding the refugee crisis. It is clear from these interviews that many of the refugees are not Syrian. The description of the video is as follows, taken from the Youtube posting:

In Leros, a tiny Greek island near the Turkish coast, 2,500 migrants have arrived illegally by boat in the last 3 weeks. The Guardian visits the local volunteers struggling to prevent chaos and humanitarian crisis.

This is the abandoned frontline of the biggest migrant crisis in Europe since World War Two. The entry of thousands of refugees is driving a fragile country, already in profound crisis, to breaking point. Overstretched local authorities are unable to cope, leaving it to volunteers such as Martina to help those who arrive on the shores of Leros: "I feel that we cannot do many things. We try, all day we try. But I think it's so little." For the last four days no food has been provided by the port authorities. Over chaos and shouting as over 100 migrants settle down for the night in a nearby villa, Martina's husband explains: "It's a very difficult night, too many people... We cannot handle them." As the minister for migration policy describes, "We're in a crisis within a crisis." Yet this chaos is infinitely preferable to the kind in the places these migrants have fled. As two Syrian brothers are reunited after years apart, one cries, "I was so terrified. I was so terrified that the regime would kill us." With a continuous flow of migrants, support from Athens and Europe is needed more than ever before.

The Guardian – Ref. 6544

See also,

Greenwood, Phoebe; Payne-Frank Noah; Fotiadis, Apostolis. "The Tiny Greek Island Sinking Under Europe's Refugee Crisis – Video." The Guardian. August 18, 2015. https://www.theguardian.com/world/video/2015/aug/18/greek-island-leros-europe-migrant-crisis-video

would think this is a deterrent? Do these men truly believe that gang rapists are concerned about men wearing women's clothing and merely parading themselves up and down the street in a pathetic demonstration? If anything, does this not send a message of weakness? Unfortunately, in many areas of Europe, the expression of true masculinity is now being equated with the Adolph Hitler regime.

While true racism and anti-Muslim hate groups should be reviled and while gangs of "enforcers" and bullies are indeed a sign of fascism, a decision to form a group of men to escort and protect women from mass rape is not an example of the "return to fascism" in Germany or anywhere else in Europe. The expression of masculinity and a readiness to defend one's women and culture as a reaction to a mass uptick in rape and sexual assault is not the equivalent of a slippery slope to the holocaust. It simply isn't and to suggest that it is, is an insult to those who suffered through it.

Europeans and Germans in particular, had better start dropping this idea of collective "German," "European," or "white" guilt and see things for what they are. Not everything that suggests Germany has a culture of its own and that its people also deserve as much is a return to Hitler's Germany. Likewise, not everything presented as humanitarian is just or humane.

The Myth Of The Syrian Refugee

While social justice warriors, the mainstream media, and western governments continue to push the idea that the massive wave of immigrants flooding into Europe are the result of the "butcher" Assad and the Syrian civil war, the facts on the ground show otherwise. Not only is the ridiculous claim that Assad is the aggressor and responsible party in the tragedy that has befallen the Syrian people entirely false and easily debunked, the truth is that the overwhelming majority of the immigrants marching through Europe are not even Syrian but are coming from a diverse menu of Middle Eastern and African states.[550]

In fact, only one in five immigrants to the EU are "refugees" from Syria.[551] [552]

Pakistanis, Eritreans, Bangladeshis, Afghanis, Nigerians, and refugees from all across the MENA and even sub-Saharan Africa are all heading to Europe in droves, with many claiming Syrian nationality and being granted refugee status once they reach the shore.[553]

Despite the best efforts by Social Justice Warriors to claim otherwise, the majority of "immigrants" rushing into Europe have been demonstrated by numerous reports, videos, and eyewitness testimony to be male.

---

[551] Drury, Ian. "Four out of five migrants are NOT from Syria: EU figures expose the 'lie' that the majority of refugees are fleeing war zone." The Daily Mail. September 18, 2015. http://www.dailymail.co.uk/news/article-3240010/Number-refugees-arriving-Europe-soars-85-year-just-one-five-war-torn-Syria.html

[552] Willis, Amy. "EU Statisticians Claim Only 1 in 5 Migrants Are From Syria." Metro.co.uk. September 19, 2015. http://metro.co.uk/2015/09/19/eu-statisticians-claim-only-1-in-5-migrants-are-from-syria-5398412/

[553] "Why IS EU Struggling With Migrants And Asylum?" BBC. March 3, 2016. http://www.bbc.com/news/world-europe-24583286

In addition, there has been a concerted effort to recruit more fundamentalist elements of foreign societies for relocation in Europe. Sources inside Syria, for instance, told this writer early on that the more fundamentalist Muslims in Syria seem to be given preferential treatment for "refugee" status. Of course, this is not to say that the Syrian refugees are fundamentalist or even that the majority of them are of this variety. We must be careful not to paint with broad brushes. Still, it is difficult to avoid seeing that the more fundamentalist "refugees" seem to be given greater attention and assistance in making their way to European countries. This information has been corroborated by the behavior of many of these "refugees" in the form of mass rape, sexual assault, and general violence.[554] [555] [556] [557]

The Reason For The Immigration Push

Why the sudden influx of immigrants and refugees into Europe now?

With the ability of Assad to hold out for as long as he has in the face of the Anglo-American onslaught, the need for greater use of Western military power in addition to terrorist proxies has become apparent. The creation of a "safe zone" in Syria by the United States and Turkey was one major step toward greater direct military involvement in Syria and the re-creation of the destruction of Libya, this time in version 2.0.[558]

The Russian involvement in Syria and the upcoming vote on the Iranian nuclear deal in the US Congress, however, created the need to accelerate the attack on Syria before the Russians became too entrenched and before Iranian money and supplies began to flow even freer to the SAA.

Hence, we are provided the "debate" as to whether or not certain European countries should engage in greater bombing in Syria or troop deployment, under the guise of fighting ISIS but, in reality, targeting the Syrian government.

Thus, we see that the influx of "refugees" into Europe is being used to frighten the European public with images of Muslim fanatics, hordes of people chanting "Allahu Akbar!" and "Fuck you!" into supporting a bombing campaign against the Syrian government. The European public, already witnessing their countries and cultures being destroyed under waves of immigration and now being confronted with the physical violence of dislocation of themselves as well as the immigrants, are likely to simply

---

[554] "Muslim Refugees Chant 'Fuck You' And 'Allahu Akbar" In Budapest." Posted on Youtube by Immigration Disaster. September 5, 2015. https://www.youtube.com/watch?v=tl16QDk2sig Footage shows hordes of immigrants in the streets chanting "fuck you" and "allahu akbar."
[555] Messia, Hada; Borghese, Livia; Hanna, Jason. "Italian Police: Muslim Migrants Threw Christians Overboard." CNN. April 19, 2015. http://www.cnn.com/2015/04/16/europe/italy-migrants-christians-thrown-overboard/
[556] Leiken, Robert S. "Europe's Angry Muslims." Foreign Affairs (Council On Foreign Relations). July/August 2005. http://www.cfr.org/religion/europes-angry-muslims/p8218
[557] "15% Of French People Back ISIS Militants, Poll Finds." RT. August 18, 2014. https://www.rt.com/news/181076-isis-islam-militans-france/
[558] Turbeville, Brandon. "A 'No-Fly Zone' By Any Other Name - The 'ISIL-Free Zone' In Syria." Activist Post. July 29, 2015. http://www.activistpost.com/2015/07/a-no-fly-zone-by-any-other-name-isil.html

throw up their hands in frustration and accept the bombing campaign as a solution. They will simply say "Do whatever you have to do stop ISIS and/or Assad. Just get these people out of here!"

The waves of immigrants arriving from a war-torn country, fresh with images of drowned children, thirsty adults, and general misery will be used by the Responsibility To Protect (R2P)/Humanitarian Bomber crowds of the left liberal variety in order to bring the second half of the false political dichotomy on board with a bombing campaign right conservatives were already vociferously supporting.

The second aspect of this latest wave of immigration, and perhaps the most important, is the destruction of European culture with diverse and often "opposing" cultures and the creation of an easy "divide and conquer" strategy in order to break the European people using the already broken immigrant population. Already, Europe has been overwhelmed with massive waves of immigration from Middle Eastern and African nations as well as other "third world" countries, even before the Syrian crisis.

Under a number of guises – economic, ethical, etc. – the ruling class has opened the floodgates to immigration from countries whose culture is vastly different from that of the host country and where the majority of citizens of European countries are themselves struggling to make ends meet. The influx of immigrants has only worsened the economic situation of the European countries who have taken them in, creating another underclass of low-wage low skill workers who are then played off against the indigenous Europeans. Anger at second class status is directed at Europeans from immigrants while anger at the lowering of wages and living standards are directed at immigrants from Europeans. Neither group ever understands that it is the oligarchical elements of their societies that have created such conditions at home and abroad and thus turn their pent up anger on one another.

Furthermore, any society that no longer maintains a common culture is one that begins to break apart at the seams, only finding connection with members of small specialized groups – race, religion, gender, etc. – and further subgroups and groupiscules. Such a society is no longer able to unify against an aggressor since it is, by nature, fractured. There is no unified culture and thus no unified people. It is thus ripe for the picking by any oligarchy, corporation, bank, or government that seeks to dominate it. Like the Brzezinski method of micro-states and mini-states, the resulting population will be nothing more than a grouping of weak, impotent, squabbling identity cliques.

An invading horde of immigrants that contains substantial elements of criminals, rapists, and religious fanatics will be a perfect spark for the fire of tension that will be necessary to initiate a major culture clash – intellectually and physically.

Solutions

The immigration crisis being experienced in Europe today is entirely one of Europe's own making. By engaging in war after war in the Middle East and North Africa, it is Europe that bears the responsibility (along with Israel and the United States) for killing millions of innocent people and displacing millions more. It is thus the responsibility of

Europe and other guilty parties to engage in policies that will eliminate the source of displacement.

Yet the same sources of so much destruction in the Middle East and Africa are responsible for not only creating the conditions in those countries where so many would want to leave, they are also responsible for bringing hordes of immigrants to Europe.

Of course, the European oligarchs know well that they are responsible for the mass displacement and are working to exploit that displacement to their own ends. Regardless, it is important to mention a number of rational solutions that would solve an ensuing tragedy in the hopes that activists and the general public may force their implementation.

1.) End Illegal and Unfettered Immigration To Europe

It is clear that Europe cannot continue to accept such unfettered immigration. Immigration policies such as the ones discussed above have already wrought economic and cultural havoc upon a number of European nations. The average European, of course, is as entitled to his own country, culture, and opportunities as any other human being. However, while Europe should refuse to allow such waves of immigration, legitimate immigrants themselves should never be blamed for seeking a better life or for seeking to escape the hell that the West has visited upon them. That being said, sexual assault, rape, and other criminal behavior should never be given a pass because of fears of "racism" or attempts to be "culturally sensitive."

Thus, Europe must immediately cease accepting any new immigrants from entering the EU. If the EU is incapable of preventing the influx, individual nations must act on their own and reassert their own national sovereignty.

2.) Enact A Program Of Repatriation Of Immigrants

If the "refugees" are indeed from Syria and are indeed seeking refuge from warfare and violence, then, with the stabilization of the Western and Northwestern portions of Syria by the SAA and the Russians, there should be no ethical or logistical issue with allowing them to return to their homelands. Such a program must be enacted immediately to ensure that Syrians return to Syria.

If other individuals have come to Europe under the false pretenses or claiming to be Syrian, they must be deported to their home countries immediately.

Europe must begin the process of returning illegal immigrants and immigrants who have not begun the process of naturalization by legal methods. A freeze on all further immigration might also be enacted for a set period of time, allowing for a period of assimilation to take place.

3.) End The Bombing, Destabilization, and Economic Attack On Syria, Iraq, And Other Target Countries In The Middle East And North Africa

The third step must be an immediate cessation of any and all bombing of Syria and other related nations. There must be an immediate cessation of support for ISIS, FSA, Nusra, or any other "moderate" cannibals operating in the Middle East. The Syrian government must be allowed to wipe these terrorists off its territory, preferably with assistance and intelligence provided by Europe and the United States. If the United States refuses to change its position on Syria, then the E.U. must go it alone.

Remember, legitimate Syrian immigrants who are truly seeking refuge from warfare are not going to Europe because they dream of debating gender politics, sipping coffee in French cafes, or kneeling at the feet of the queen. They are going to Europe because their homes have been destroyed, their families have been killed, and their country is overrun with savages.

4.) Begin Investing In International Development, Rebuilding, And Scientific Progress In The Middle East and Africa

Europe would also be well served to assist in the rebuilding of Syria with a comprehensive plan of foreign investment and credit extended from various European central banks (nationalized banks) and a nationalized Federal Reserve for the purpose of rebuilding civilian infrastructure, hospitals, schools, sanitation, roads, and industry. Credit can be made available for the procurement of products, materials, equipment, and even services so that no actual money changes hands – only materials – in order to avoid fears of corruption or reckless use of finances. Europe and the United States should extend civilized cooperation with Syria in this regard. The goal should be to bring the various countries up to the standards of the First World and Western societies, improving public health, transportation, communications, drinking water, food supplies, and the like.

5.) End The Obsession With Political Correctness

There is an ideology and a mindset that is destroying Europe but it is not Islam or even Islamic fundamentalism - it is political correctness and the obsession with collective European guilt. The European brainwashing of its citizens to view any critique of immigration policies as "racist" "xenophobic," or even a return to fascism has now led to a situation in which many legitimate critics are dismissed as luddites, the majority are afraid to speak out for fear of being labeled, and a significant portion of European society adamantly support the destruction of their own culture. For that reason, Europe must immediately abandon the historically alien concept of "multiculturalism" and "political correctness."

While in staunch opposition to the will of the world oligarchy, the above solutions are the only hope of the Syrian and the European peoples. If unheeded, both Syrian and European culture and national identities will be erased and the living standards of all continue to be eviscerated.

The United States, now beginning to witness immigration from the same countries producing immigrants to Europe, must heed these warning as well and it must immediately take part in the solutions.

Clearly, European oligarchs and their American counterparts do not want to see a peaceful end to the crisis in Syria nor do they desire to see a peaceful and humanitarian end to the immigration crisis. It is for that reason that the European and American people must begin to build coalitions amongst themselves and, indeed, amongst immigrant communities, in order to force these oligarchs to do so.

The Supply Line Question

Tony Cartalucci of the excellent geopolitical website, Land Destroyer, asks what is perhaps the most pertinent question regarding ISIS' alleged strength and fighting capacity. He writes,

> If rebels are being directly supplied across the Turkish-Syrian border by a multinational coalition, how is it possible that ISIS forces are somehow better equipped and able to overwhelm these forces? The length of any ISIS logistical line supporting its fighters in this alleged battle - if not also extending over the Turkish-Syrian border in the immediate vicinity of the fighting, must be hundreds of miles long and in itself an immense strain on ISIS' fighting capacity.

> It would be rather remarkable, in fact, unbelievable for ISIS to somehow not be being aided and abetted from directly across the Turkish-Syrian border where allegedly "foreign-backed insurgents" are allegedly receiving aid from nations like the US, Turkey, Saudi Arabia, and Qatar.[559]

Indeed. But to add to that question, how is it considered possible that the most advanced surveillance state in the entire world, currently occupying Iraq and watching the Syrian crisis carefully would not be able to notice such a massive organization and rally of ISIS fighters, marching in caravans across the desert with no camouflage until it was too late?

At one point, the Kurds had seized and largely maintained control of an area that spans the Turkey-Syria border from its western to eastern extremities all except for one small pocket in the middle – from Jarablus in the East to Dabiq in the West. Others have described the zone in slightly different dimensions as being from Jarablus in the East to Afrin or Azaz in the West. Regardless, this corridor, also known as a potential "safe zone," is about the exact dimensions of the ISIS supply lines coming in from Turkey to Syria and, if either the Syrian military or the Kurds were able to capture this small section of land on the border, ISIS supply lines would be entirely cut from the North. With Assad's forces tightening their grip in the South and Southwestern portions of the country and the SAA/Hezbollah forces cracking down on any ISIS movements on the Syria-Lebanon border, and most notably the Russian bombing campaign aiding the Syrian military in retaking full control of Aleppo and other parts of northern Syria, ISIS would essentially be cut off from most avenues of outside assistance.*

Even mainstream media outlets have recognized the fact that Turkey effectively operates as a transit zone for ISIS. Consider the article written for the Guardian in

---

*This description should be understood in terms of battlefield conditions which are continuing to shift and change even as this book is being written. Such are the obstacles to writing a book about a war in the midst of a war. The most important aspect of this paragraph is to understand that the "Jarablus Corridor" extends[ed] from Jarablus in the East to Afrin/Azaz in the West and al-Bab in the South.

[559] Cartalucci, Tony. "Syrian Border Chaos as NATO Aims To Win Proxy War." Land Destroyer. May 31, 2016. http://landdestroyer.blogspot.com/2016/05/syrian-border-chaos-as-nato-aims-to-win.html

November, 2015 by David Graeber entitled "Turkey Could Cut Off Islamic State's Supply Lines. So Why Doesn't It?" Graeber writes,

> It might seem outrageous to suggest that a Nato member like Turkey would in any way support an organisation that murders western civilians in cold blood. That would be like a Nato member supporting al-Qaida. But in fact there is reason to believe that Erdoğan's government does support the Syrian branch of al-Qaida (Jabhat al-Nusra) too, along with any number of other rebel groups that share its conservative Islamist ideology.[560] The Institute for the Study of Human Rights at Columbia University has compiled a long list of evidence of Turkish support for Isis in Syria.[561]

> How has Erdoğan got away with this? Mainly by claiming those fighting Isis are 'terrorists' themselves

> And then there are Erdoğan's actual, stated positions. Back in August, the YPG, fresh from their victories in Kobani and Gire Spi, were poised to seize Jarablus, the last Isis-held town on the Turkish border that the terror organisation had been using to resupply its capital in Raqqa with weapons, materials, and recruits – Isis supply lines pass directly through Turkey.[562] [563] [564]

> Commentators predicted that with Jarablus gone, Raqqa would soon follow. Erdoğan reacted by declaring Jarablus a "red line": if the Kurds attacked, his forces would intervene militarily – against the YPG. So Jarablus remains in terrorist hands to this day, under de facto Turkish military protection.[565]

> How has Erdoğan got away with this? Mainly by claiming those fighting Isis are "terrorists" themselves.[566]

Dr. Nafeez Ahmed has recently summed up many (but certainly not all) of the Turkey's connection to ISIS in his recent article for Insurge Intelligence, "NATO Is Harbouring The Islamic State," when he writes,

---

[560] Edelman, Eric S. "America's Dangerous Bargain With Turkey." New York Times. August 27, 2015. http://www.nytimes.com/2015/08/27/opinion/americas-dangerous-bargain-with-turkey.html?_r=2

[561] Phillips, David L. "Research Paper: ISIS-Turkey Links." The Huffington Post. March 7, 2016. http://www.huffingtonpost.com/david-l-phillips/research-paper-isis-turke_b_6128950.html

[562] Mahmood, Mona. "'We Are So Proud' – The Women Who Died Defending Kobani Against ISIS." The Guardian. January 30, 2015. https://www.theguardian.com/world/2015/jan/30/kurdish-women-died-kobani-isis-syria

[563] Youtube. "YPG Start Cleaning Up Gire Spi From ISIS 15.6.2015. footage from ANHA. https://www.youtube.com/watch?v=sFurbdijiRw Footage shows Kurdish/YPG combat action against ISIS.

[564] "Jarablus." Wikipedia. https://en.wikipedia.org/wiki/Jarabulus

[565] Tastekin, Fehim. "Erdogan Looks For Military Victory To Avenge Electoral Defeat." Al-Monitor. July 2, 2015. http://www.al-monitor.com/pulse/originals/2015/07/turkey-syria-erdogan-lost-election-want-win-as-army-chief.html

[566] Graeber, David. "Turkey Could Cut Off Islamic State's Supply Lines. So Why Doesn't It?" The Guardian. November 18, 2015. https://www.theguardian.com/commentisfree/2015/nov/18/turkey-cut-islamic-state-supply-lines-erdogan-isis

President Hollande wants European Union leaders to suspend the Schengen Agreement on open borders to allow dramatic restrictions on freedom of movement across Europe.[567] He also demands the EU-wide adoption of the Passenger Name Records (PNR) system allowing intelligence services to meticulously track the travel patterns of Europeans, along with an extension of the state of emergency to at least three months.

Under the extension, French police can now block any website, put people under house arrest without trial, search homes without a warrant, and prevent suspects from meeting others deemed a threat.[568]

Mass surveillance at home and endless military projection abroad are the twin sides of the same coin of national security, which must simply be maximized as much as possible.

Conspicuously missing from President Hollande's decisive declaration of war however, was any mention of the biggest elephant in the room: state-sponsorship.

Syrian passports discovered near the bodies of two of the suspected Paris attackers, according to police sources, were fake, and likely forged in Turkey.[569]

Earlier this year, the Turkish daily Today's Zaman reported that "more than 100,000 fake Turkish passports" had been given to ISIS. Erdogan's government, the newspaper added, "has been accused of supporting the terrorist organization by turning a blind eye to its militants crossing the border and even buying its oil… Based on a 2014 report, Sezgin Tanrıkulu, deputy chairman of the main opposition Republican People's Party (CHP) said that ISIL terrorists fighting in Syria have also been claimed to have been treated in hospitals in Turkey."[570]

This barely scratches the surface. A senior Western official familiar with a large cache of intelligence obtained this summer told the Guardian that "direct dealings between Turkish officials and ranking ISIS members was now 'undeniable.'"[571]

---

[567] Foster, Peter. "Paris Attacks: France To Call For Effective Suspension Of Schengen Open Borders." The Telegraph. November 16, 2015. http://www.telegraph.co.uk/news/worldnews/europe/france/11998301/Paris-attacks-France-to-call-for-effective-suspension-of-Schengen-open-borders.html

[568] Griffin, Andrew. "France State Of Emergency Declared For Three Months, Allowing Authorities To Shut Down Websites And Giving Police Sweeping New Powers." The Independent. November 19, 2015. http://www.independent.co.uk/news/world/europe/france-state-of-emergency-declared-for-three-months-allowing-authorities-to-shut-down-websites-and-a6740886.html

[569] Atkinson, Mary. "Syrian Passports Found At Paris Attacks Scene Were Fakes Made In Turkey." Middle East Eye. November 15, 2015. http://www.middleeasteye.net/news/syrian-passports-found-scene-paris-attacks-fakes-made-turkey-police-520642631

[570] Sayfa, Ana. "Report: More Than 10,000 Fake Turkish Passports Given To ISIL." Today's Zaman. http://www.todayszaman.com/anasayfa_report-more-than-100000-fake-turkish-passports-given-to-isil_377534.html

[571] Chulov, Martin. "Turkey Sends In Jets As Syria's Agony Spills Over Every Border." The Guardian. July 25, 2015. https://www.theguardian.com/world/2015/jul/26/isis-syria-turkey-us

The same official confirmed that Turkey, a longstanding member of NATO, is not just supporting ISIS, but also other jihadist groups, including Ahrar al-Sham and Jabhat al-Nusra, al-Qaeda's affiliate in Syria. "The distinctions they draw [with other opposition groups] are thin indeed," said the official. "There is no doubt at all that they militarily cooperate with both."

In a rare insight into this brazen state-sponsorship of ISIS, a year ago Newsweek reported the testimony of a former ISIS communications technician, who had travelled to Syria to fight the regime of Bashir al-Assad.[572]

The former ISIS fighter told Newsweek that Turkey was allowing ISIS trucks from Raqqa to cross the "border, through Turkey and then back across the border to attack Syrian Kurds in the city of Serekaniye in northern Syria in February." ISIS militants would freely travel "through Turkey in a convoy of trucks," and stop "at safehouses along the way."

The former ISIS communication technician also admitted that he would routinely "connect ISIS field captains and commanders from Syria with people in Turkey on innumerable occasions," adding that "the people they talked to were Turkish officials... ISIS commanders told us to fear nothing at all because there was full cooperation with the Turks."

In January, authenticated official documents of the Turkish military were leaked online, showing that Turkey's intelligence services had been caught in Adana by military officers transporting missiles, mortars and anti-aircraft ammunition via truck "to the al-Qaeda terror organisation" in Syria.[573]

There is no "self-sustaining economy" for ISIS, contrary to the fantasies of the Washington Post and Financial Times in their recent faux investigations, according to Martin Chulov of the Guardian. As a senior ISIS member recently revealed to him:

"They need the Turks. I know of a lot of cooperation and it scares me. I don't see how Turkey can attack the organization too hard. There are shared interests."[574]

Meanwhile, NATO leaders feign outrage and learned liberal pundits continue to scratch their heads in bewilderment as to ISIS' extraordinary resilience and inexorable expansion.

Some officials have spoken up about the paradox, but to no avail. Last year, Claudia Roth, deputy speaker of the German parliament, expressed shock that NATO is allowing Turkey to harbour an ISIS camp in Istanbul, facilitate weapons transfers to Islamist militants through its borders, and tacitly support IS oil sales.[575]

---

[572] Guiton, Barney. "'ISIS Sees Turkey As Its Ally': Former Islamic State Member Reveals Turkish Army Cooperation." Newsweek. November 7, 2014. http://www.newsweek.com/isis-and-turkey-cooperate-destroy-kurds-former-isis-member-reveals-turkish-282920

[573] Tastekin, Fehim. "Erdogan Looks For Military Victory To Avenge Electoral Defeat." Al-Monitor. July 2, 2015. http://www.al-monitor.com/pulse/originals/2015/07/turkey-syria-erdogan-lost-election-want-win-as-army-chief.html

[574] Chulov, Martin. "Turkey Sends In Jets As Syria's Agony Spills Over Every Border." The Guardian. July 25, 2015. https://www.theguardian.com/world/2015/jul/26/isis-syria-turkey-us

[575] "German Deputy Speaker: NATO Must Stop Turkey Support For ISIS." Rudaw. December 10, 2014.

Nothing happened.

Instead, Turkey has been amply rewarded for its alliance with the very same terror-state that wrought the Paris massacre on 13th November 2015. Just a month earlier, German Chancellor Angela Merkel offered to fast-track Turkey's bid to join the EU, permitting visa-free travel to Europe for Turks.[576]

In his testimony before the Senate Armed Services Committee in September 2014, General Martin Dempsey, then chairman of the US Joint Chiefs of Staff, was asked by Senator Lindsay Graham whether he knew of "any major Arab ally that embraces ISIL"?[577]

General Dempsey replied:

"I know major Arab allies who fund them.

In other words, the most senior US military official at the time had confirmed that ISIS was being funded by the very same "major Arab allies" that had just joined the US-led anti-ISIS coalition.

These allies include Saudi Arabia, Qatar, the UAE, and Kuwait in particular—which for the last four years at least have funneled billions of dollars largely to extremist rebels in Syria. No wonder that their anti-ISIS airstrikes, already miniscule, have now reduced almost to zero as they focus instead on bombing Shi'a Houthis in Yemen, which, incidentally, is paving the way for the rise of ISIS there.[578]

ISIS, in other words, is state-sponsored—indeed, sponsored by purportedly Western-friendly regimes in the Muslim world, who are integral to the anti-ISIS coalition.

Which then begs the question as to why Hollande and other Western leaders expressing their determination to "destroy" ISIS using all means necessary, would prefer to avoid the most significant factor of all: the material infrastructure of ISIS' emergence in the context of ongoing Gulf and Turkish state support for Islamist militancy in the region.

There are many explanations, but one perhaps stands out: the West's abject dependence on terror-toting Muslim regimes, largely to maintain access to Middle East, Mediterranean and Central Asian oil and gas resources.[579]

Tony Cartalucci has also written extensively about Turkish connections to ISIS such as in his article "Implausible Deniability: West's ISIS Terror Hordes In Iraq,"

---

[576] Tattersall, Nick; Carrel, Paul. "Merkel, In Bind On Migrants, Ready To Back Faster Turkish EU Bid." Reuters. October 18, 2015. http://www.reuters.com/article/us-europe-migrants-germany-turkey-idUSKCN0SC08B20151019#uCAxJZqVkTjZIkEk.97

[577] "General Dempsey Acknowledges U.S. Arab Allies Funding ISIS." CSPAN. September 16, 2014. https://www.c-span.org/video/?c4509231/general-dempsey-acknowledges-us-arab-allies-funding-isis

[578] Crowcroft, Orlando. "ISIS: Who Is Behind The Islamic State's Latest Franchize In War Torn Yemen?" International Business Times. April 27, 2015. http://www.ibtimes.co.uk/isis-who-behind-islamic-states-latest-franchise-war-torn-yemen-1498532

[579] Ahmed, Nafeez. "NATO Is Harbouring The Islamic State." Insurgent Intelligence (Medium.com). November 19, 2015. https://medium.com/insurge-intelligence/europe-is-harbouring-the-islamic-state-s-backers-d24db3a24a40#.cuf3b9ag1

Beginning in 2011 – and actually even as early as 2007 – the United States has been arming, funding, and supporting the Muslim Brotherhood and a myriad of armed terrorist organizations to overthrow the government of Syria, fight Hezbollah in Lebanon, and undermine the power and influence of Iran, which of course includes any other government or group in the MENA region friendly toward Tehran.

Billions in cash have been funneled into the hands of terrorist groups including Al Nusra, Al Qaeda in Iraq (AQI), and what is now being called "Islamic State in Iraq and Syria" or ISIS. One can see clearly by any map of ISIS held territory that it butts up directly against Turkey's borders with defined corridors ISIS uses to invade southward – this is because it is precisely from NATO territory this terrorist scourge originated.

ISIS was harbored on NATO territory, armed and funded by US CIA agents with cash and weapons brought in from the Saudis, Qataris, and NATO members themselves. The "non-lethal aid" the US and British sent including the vehicles we now see ISIS driving around in.[580] [581]

Cartalucci states in a separate article, "NATO's Terror Hordes In Iraq A Pretext For Syria Invasion,"

In actuality, ISIS is the product of a joint NATO-GCC [Gulf Cooperation Council] conspiracy stretching back as far as 2007 where US-Saudi policymakers sought to ignite a region-wide sectarian war to purge the Middle East of Iran's arch of influence stretching from its borders, across Syria and Iraq, and as far west as Lebanon and the coast of the Mediterranean. ISIS has been harbored, trained, armed, and extensively funded by a coalition of NATO and Persian Gulf states within Turkey's (NATO territory) borders and has launched invasions into northern Syria with, at times, both Turkish artillery and air cover. The most recent example of this was the cross-border invasion by Al Qaeda into Kasab village, Latakia province in northwest Syria.[582]

Cartalucci was referring to a cross-border invasion that was coordinated with NATO, Turkey, Israel, and the death squads where Israel acted as air force cover while Turkey facilitated the death squad invasion from inside its own borders.[583] [584]

---

[580] Cartalucci, Tony. "Implausible Deniability: West's ISIS Terror Hordes In Iraq." Land Destroyer Report. August 8, 2014. http://landdestroyer.blogspot.com/2014/08/implausible-deniability-wests-isis.html#more

[581] Snyder, Stephen. "This One Toyota Pickup Truck Is At The Top Of The Shopping List For The Free Syrian Army – And The Taliban." PRI. April 1, 2014. http://www.pri.org/stories/2014-04-01/one-toyota-pickup-truck-top-shopping-list-free-syrian-army-and-taliban

[582] Cartalucci, Tony. "NATO's Terror Hordes In Iraq A Pretext For Syria Invasion." New Eastern Outlook. June 13, 2014. http://journal-neo.org/2014/06/13/nato-s-terror-hordes-in-iraq-a-pretext-for-syria-invasion/

[583] Klein, Aaron. "Shock Claim: Israeli Airstrike Coordinated With al-Qaeda-Linked Rebels. Jihadists Advance Throughout Syria Immediately After Today's Bomb Attack." Klein Online. May 5, 2013. http://kleinonline.wnd.com/2013/05/05/shock-claim-israeli-airstrike-coordinated-with-al-qaida-linked-rebels-jihadists-advance-throughout-syria-immediately-after-todays-bomb-attack/

[584] Turbeville, Brandon. "Why Aren't ISIS And al-Qaeda Attacking Israel?" Activist Post. August 7, 2014. http://www.activistpost.com/2014/08/why-arent-isis-and-al-qaeda-attacking.html

Keep in mind also that, prior to the rapid appearance and seizure of territory by ISIS in Syria and Iraq, European media outlets like Der Spiegel reported that hundreds of fighters were being trained in Jordan by Western intelligence and military personnel for the purpose of deployment in Syria to fight against Assad.[585] The numbers were said to be expected to reach about 10,000 fighters when the reports were issued in March, 2013. Although Western and European media outlets would try to spin the operation as the training of "moderate rebels," subsequent reports revealed that these fighters were actually ISIS fighters. Those fighters were ultimately funneled into Syria via Turkey.[586]

In addition, on October 2, 2014, Turkey's parliament passed a resolution to allow the Turkish military to enter the sovereign territory of Iraq and Syria under the pretext of battling Western-backed IS militants.

The resolution also allowed foreign troops to use Turkish territory for the same purpose suggesting that the Incirlik air base may soon be used by the United States for its airstrikes against Syria. Only recently, it was reported by Turkish media that a formal agreement was reached between the United States and Turkey for the use of Incirlik in the faux American campaign against ISIS.[587]

The vote on the resolution regarding foreign troops on Turkish soil (to be used in Syria) was 298 in favor of the motion and 98 opposed.

---

[585] Jones, Gareth; Webb, Jason. "Americans Are Training Syria Rebels In Jordan: Spiegel." Reuters. March 10, 2013. http://www.reuters.com/article/us-syria-crisis-rebels-usa-idUSBRE9290FI20130310

[586] Klein, Aaron. "Blowback! U.S. Trained Islamists Who Joined ISIS." World Net Daily. June 17, 2014. http://www.wnd.com/2014/06/officials-u-s-trained-isis-at-secret-base-in-jordan/

[587] "Turkey's Key Air Base Posed To Host anti-ISIL Coalition Aircraft." Hurriyet Daily News. July 23, 2015. http://www.hurriyetdailynews.com/turkeys-key-air-base-poised-to-host-anti-isil-coalition-aircraft.aspx?pageID=238&nid=85811

Chapter VI: Who Benefits?
Turkey

Despite its claims that the vote was centered around defeating ISIS on its borders, Turkish Prime Minister Recep Erdogan, perhaps inadvertently, admitted that the real target of NATO aggression is the Syrian government.

As the BBC reports,

Speaking in parliament earlier on Wednesday, President Recep Tayyip Erdogan urged the West to find a long-term solution to the crises in Syria and Iraq, pointing out that dropping "tonnes of bombs" on IS militants would only provide a temporary respite.

While he said "an effective struggle" against IS would be a priority for Turkey, "the immediate removal of the administration in Damascus" would also continue to be its priority.

Erdogan also called for a "buffer zone" on the Turkey/Syria border – which would be enforced by a no-fly zone – to "ensure security."[588]

Turkey has also been front and center in the promotion of Uyghur terrorism both in Syria and Asia as well as other locations.[589] Turkey has repeatedly violated Syrian territory and engaged in "limited" military action against the Syrian military in support of ISIS terrorists and jihadist connected to some of the hundreds of smaller groups and factions.[590]

Turkey has long advocated for a "No-Fly Zone" over Syria. A buffer zone, of course, has been part of the NATO agenda against Syria since the beginning of the Western-controlled crisis in the country. Remember, it was under the guise of a humanitarian corridor or buffer zone in Libya, that NATO bombing took place which ultimately led to the destruction of the Libyan government, the murder of Ghaddaffi, and the subsequent expansion of chaos, anarchy, and genocide across the entire North African country.[591]

Turkey or, more specifically Recep Erdogan is apparently attempting to re-establish a neo-Ottoman empire, a foolish and dangerous quest that might very well lead to the eventual breakup of Turkey itself in the near future.

---

[588] "Islamic State: Turkish MPs Back Iraq-Syria Deployment." BBC. October 2, 2014. http://www.bbc.com/news/world-middle-east-29455204

[589] Turbeville, Brandon. "From Syria To Asia To Russia – Terror Network Organized By NATO And Turkey." Activist Post. October 1, 2015. http://www.activistpost.com/2015/10/from-syria-to-asia-to-russia-terror-network-organized-by-nato-and-turkey.html

[590] Turbeville, Brandon. "Turkey's Invasion Of Syria Shows Turkey's Connection To ISIS; NATO Agenda." Activist Post. February 24, 2015. http://www.activistpost.com/2015/02/turkeys-invasion-of-syria-shows-turkish.html

[591] "Security Council Approves 'No-Fly Zone' Over Libya, Authorizing 'All Necessary Measures' to Protect Civilians, by vote of 10 in Favour with 5 Abstentions." United Nations website, UN.org. March 17, 2011. http://www.un.org/press/en/2011/sc10200.doc.htm

In August, 2016, however, Turkey launched a cross-border invasion of Syria. As Turkey deepened its push into Syrian territory, numerous geopolitical interests began colliding with one another in what appeared to be a war worthy of the reputation the Middle East has for political and geopolitical complexity. Having had its immediate expedition across the Turkey-Syria border condemned by the Syrian government, Turkey also faced some public criticism from the United States in regards to its military efforts against Kurdish forces east of the Euphrates who are themselves aligned with the United States, partially against ISIS and the Syrian government as well as staunch enemies of the Turkish government.[592]

The United States stated publicly (although public statements do not always mirror behind the scenes agendas) that fighting between Turkey, Turk-supported "rebels" (aka ISIS, al-Qaeda, FSA), and Kurdish forces were "unacceptable" and that the clashes must stop. The U.S. envoy to the anti-ISIS coalition, Brett McGurk, stated that fighting in areas where ISIS was not present is "a source of deep concern."[593]

According to the BBC,

Turkish forces have attacked what they say are Kurdish "terrorists" since crossing the border last week.

But the Kurdish YPG militia says Turkey just wants to occupy Syrian territory.

Ankara says it aims to push both IS and Kurdish fighters away from its border.

Turkish forces and allied factions of the rebel Free Syrian Army (FSA) forced IS out of the Syrian border city of Jarablus on Tuesday and have since pounded neighbouring villages held by Kurdish-led, US-backed Syria Democratic Forces (SDF).

The Turkish military carried out 61 artillery strikes around Jarablus over the past 24 hours Reuters news agency reported on Monday,

Turkey has insisted Kurdish militia, which it regards as terrorists, retreat east across the Euphrates river.[594]

For its part, Turkey refused to buckle to the public statements of the United States with Omer Celik stating that "No one has the right to tell us which terrorist organization we can fight against."[595]

---

[592] Barrington, Lisa; Bektas, Umit. "Turkish Forces Deepen Push Into Syria, Draw U.S. Rebuke Over Their Target." Reuters. August 29, 2016. http://www.reuters.com/article/us-mideast-crisis-syria-idUSKCN11305C

[593] Brett McGurk Twitter Feed. "DOD: We want to make clear that we find these clashes -- in areas where #ISIL is not located -- unacceptable and a source of deep concern." August 29, 2016. https://twitter.com/brett_mcgurk/status/770185546756919296

[594] "Syria War: US Warns Over Turkish-Syria Violence." BBC. August 29, 2016. http://www.bbc.com/news/world-middle-east-37212256

[595] Barrington, Lisa; Bektas, Umit. "Turkish Forces Deepen Push Into Syria, Draw U.S. Rebuke Over Their Target." Reuters. August 29, 2016. http://www.reuters.com/article/us-mideast-crisis-syria-idUSKCN11305C

Turkish Foreign Minister Mevlut Cavusoglu stated that the YPG was attempting to seize territory where Kurds have not had a tradition of making up a large ethnic bloc. This much, at least, is undeniably true. "The YPG is engaged in ethnic cleansing, they are placing who they want to in those places," he said.[596]

The YPG, while denying that its forces were west of the Euphrates, responded by saying that the Turks merely wanted a pretext to annex Syrian land.

In terms of Turkish military progress, Reuters reports:

On Monday, Turkish-backed forces had advanced on Manbij, a city about 30 km (20 miles) south of Turkey's border captured this month by the SDF with U.S. help. The Turkish military said it was also shifting operations westwards, which would take it into territory still under Islamic State control.

Sources on the ground inside Ayn al-Arab (Kobane) are reporting that the Turkish military has reached the outskirts of the city. Claims are now being made that the Turks are considering building a wall to separate the two countries.[597]

What Is Turkey Doing?

The Turkish invasion was predicated on the basis of "fighting ISIS," a wholly unbelievable goal since Turkey itself has been supporting, training, and facilitating ISIS since day one.[598] Not only that, but Turkey arrived in Syria with terrorists in tow since, as the BBC reported, "Between nine and 12 tanks crossed the frontier, followed by pick-up trucks believed to be carrying hundreds of fighters from Turkish-backed factions of the rebel Free Syrian Army (FSA)."[599] If Turkey was interested in stopping terrorism, why would they lead the charges for more terrorists to enter Syria? Indeed, if stopping terrorism was truly Turkey's goal, it is capable of sealing the border from its own side without any need for invasion so why the war the party?

Turkey' interests do not lie in stopping terrorism. Far from it. Turkey's foreign policy and military decision to invade Syria was based along three lines; its desire for more territory (which it believes was stolen from it long ago), its willingness to continue working with NATO in its attempt to destroy the secular government of Syria, and its concern over the Kurdish expansion.

With this invasion, Turkey solidified its willingness to risk outright war with Syria and perhaps even Russia in order to fulfill the goals of NATO and Anglo-American powers who have sought to destroy Syria from the beginning. Part of this strategy is the

---

[596] Susli, Maram. "Why A Kurdish Enclave Is A Very Bad Idea." Global Independent Analytics. April 6, 2016. https://gianalytics.org/690-why-a-kurdish-enclave-in-syria-is-a-very-bad-idea
[597] Antonopolous, Paul. "Photos: Turkey Penetrates Into Kobane, Hundreds Protest." Al-Masdar News. August 29, 2016. https://www.almasdarnews.com/article/photos-turkey-penetrates-kobane-hundreds-protest/
[598] Turbeville, Brandon. "The Turkish Invasion of Syria: Who Is Behind It And Why?" Activist Post. August 25, 2016. http://www.brandonturbeville.com/2016/08/the-turkish-invasion-of-syria-who-is.html
[599] "IS Conflict: Turkey-Backed Syrian Rebels Take Jarablus." BBC. August 24, 2016. http://www.bbc.com/news/world-europe-37171995

creation of "buffer zones" and "safe zones" in the north, precisely the concepts that were re-floated and discussed by the United States and U.K. only days before the invasion. Note that the invasion and operations centered around Jarablus, the eastern border of the famed Jarablus corridor which, bordered by Afrin and Azaz in the West, make up the last fully functioning terrorist supply routes coming in from Turkey. These were precisely the dimensions that were discussed by Western think tanks and NGOs in regards to what a "safe zone" in Syria should look like. Although argued on the basis of "giving civilians somewhere to go" the zones were supposed to be controlled by "moderate" Western-backed terrorists and were clearly designed to prevent the Syrian government and Russian forces from closing the supply routes coming from the Turkish side of the border into Syria.[600]

This "safe haven" is also a way for the neo-Ottoman Erdogan to lay claim to more territory in order to placate his dream of becoming the 21st Century equivalent of the leader of the Turkish Empire. At the very least, this desire for more land under the Turkish flag will lead to a situation similar to that of the Golan Heights, which Israel has illegally occupied for decades but which there is frequent threat of military action and controversy.

Erdogan is also incredibly concerned about the growing Kurdish movement both inside Turkey and in Syria.[601] With the Kurds gaining more and more territory in the north of Syria, in large part because of support being given by the United States, as well as Kurds in Iraq becoming more and more willing to work with YPG Kurds in Syria and the growing interest of dissent and military operations inside Turkey by the PKK, Erdogan is undoubtedly concerned that the Kurds could decide to unite and initiate a massive campaign for autonomy and independence or, at the very least, inspire Turkish Kurds to launch a revolution.[602] [603]

Carving Out Kurdistan

While the wheels of the propaganda machine is turning on the screens of Westerners in the US and Europe, the plan to carve out a Kurdistan is taking a much more violent form in Syria and Iraq. The ability to remove all forces within the borders of what would be called Kurdistan (except for the Kurdish forces) has been the result of constant U.S. bombing and death squad herding around towns like Ayn al-Arab (Kobane),Tal Abyad, and others where the Kurds have been able to outline their territory by virtue of military prowess.[604]

---

[600] Turbeville, Brandon. "U.S. Renews Calls For Attack On Syria Air Force, U.K. Calls For Safe Zones, Military Action." Activist Post. August 23, 2016. http://www.activistpost.com/2016/08/u-s-renews-calls-for-attack-on-syria-air-force-u-k-calls-for-safe-zones-military-action.html

[601] Turbeville, Brandon. "Clashes Between Syrian Army, Kurds Pushes Brzezinski Plan In Syria." Activist Post. July 11, 2016. http://www.activistpost.com/2016/07/clashes-between-syrian-army-kurds-pushes-brzezinski-plan-forward-in-syria.html

[602] Turbeville, Brandon. "Carving Out Kurdistan – The US/NATO Plan To Break Up Syria And Iraq." Activist Post. July 3, 2015.

[603] "Brandon Turbeville On The Corbett Report – April 3, 2016 – 'Federalizing Syria' And The NATO 'Plan A' For The Region." BrandonTurbeville.com. April 3, 2016. Interview with James Corbett of The Corbett Report (CorbettReport.com).

After all, the US bombing has done nothing but strengthen ISIS at every other location in Syria and Iraq, while even bombing Syrian infrastructure and Iraqi military forces directly, and "accidentally" airdropping of support to ISIS. In the Kurdish areas, however, such bombing seems to be functioning as a primitive and violent method of border shaping that will outline the Kurdish territory from the Syrian and Iraqi territories. Increasing ISIS forces in Ayn al-Arab (Kobane) significantly hampers the ability of the Syrian Army to respond to defeat those forces in these specific areas, thus cutting off Ayn al-Arab from the Syrian Army and leaving the Kurdish areas to the devices of the Kurds as the ISIS forces are beaten back from inside the borders of the developing Kurdistan.[605] [606] [607] [608]

Leaving the question of the legitimacy of a Kurdistan aside for a while and acknowledging the heroism of the Kurds in their fight against ISIS, Nusra, and other terrorist forces, it should be noted that the Kurds have found some very unsavory allies in the process. Most notably, those unsavory allies turn out to be the United States and the Free Syrian Army (proxy terrorists of the US and NATO).[609]

For instance, the United States has been tacitly supporting the Kurdish fighters in Iraq for some time under the pretext of assisting them in their fight against ISIS, despite the fact that the United States has armed, trained, funded, facilitated, and directed ISIS from the beginning. The United States has allegedly stopped short of directly arming the Kurds but it has maintained very close ties with them. Some would even argue that, with the exception of the ISIS fighters themselves – the Kurds have more friendly relations with the U.S. than the Iraqi government.[610]

The US government has been attempting to pass legislation to directly arm the Kurdish and Sunni forces in Iraq for some time, recently passing part of that legislation in the form of the National Defense Authorization Act of 2016 (although differences in the House and Senate version are currently being worked out).[611]

---

[604] "Syrian Kurds Regain Control Of Tal Abyad After IS Attack." Middle East Institute. http://www.mei.edu/content/news/syria-kurds-regain-control-tal-abyad-after-attack

[605] Winter, Charlie. "America's Bombs Are Only Making ISIS Stronger, And al-Qaeda Has Just Proven It." The Independent. October 17, 2014. http://www.independent.co.uk/voices/comment/americas-bombs-are-only-making-isis-stronger-and-al-qaeda-has-just-proven-it-9802325.html

[606] Turbeville, Brandon. "Libya 2.0? US Says 'No-Fly Zone' Over Syria A Possibility." Activist Post. September 27, 2014. http://www.activistpost.com/2014/09/libya-20-us-says-no-fly-zone-over-syria.html

[607] Turbeville, Brandon. "Middle East Officials Question 'Convenient Mistakes' Of US Airdrops To al-Qaeda." Activist Post. January 6, 2015. http://www.activistpost.com/2015/01/middle-east-officials-question.html

[608] "First US Airstrikes In Syria Kills Civilians." TeleSur. September 23, 2014. http://www.activistpost.com/2015/01/middle-east-officials-question.html

[609] Turbeville, Brandon. "Carving Out Kurdistan – The US/NATO Plan To Break Up Syria And Iraq." Activist Post. July 3, 2015. http://www.activistpost.com/2015/07/carving-out-kurdistan-usnato-plan-to.html

[610] Turbeville, Brandon. "The Roots Of ISIS." Activist Post. September 11, 2014. http://www.activistpost.com/2014/09/the-roots-of-isis.html

The arming of the Kurds directly in Iraq, along with the Sunni forces, would thus create the perception of fully separate and independent principalities, free from the control of the Iraqi central government, leading to the breakup of the country as a whole into three separate entities – a Kurdish segment, Sunni segment, and Shiite segment. Such a plan has long been in the works for Iraq and, if the US continues its support of Kurds in Syria, the situation is ripe for the appearance of a Kurdistan entity across the borders of Iraq and Syria. Indeed, much like the plan to break up Iraq into three separate parts in Iraq, a similar plan was devised for Syria in the absence of total destruction in the same vein as Libya.

While the question of accepting arms may easily be explained by the "gold is where you find it" motive, the fact that the YPG is now working directly with the Free Syrian Army (FSA) is further evidence of collusion between NATO/US and the YPG. While presented as moderate by the mainstream western press, the FSA is nothing more than al-Qaeda, ISIS, and Nusra.[612] Indeed, there is no such thing as a moderate rebel in Syria and there never has been.[613] [614] The FSA is documented to have committed massive atrocities and the groups – directed, armed, controlled and funded by the US – are intent upon implementing Sharia law on the subjugated populations.[615] [616] As I and other researchers have documented, the FSA is nothing more than a wing of al-Qaeda/ISIS and has even publicly stated that it was working with the terrorist organizations (also funded, trained, armed, and directed by the West) in the past.[617] [618]

The fact that the YPG would be willing to cooperate with the FSA is telling but the fact that the FSA would be willing to cooperate with the YPG is even more telling. After all, the Iraqi Kurds have long been connected to US intelligence and military operations in the past.[619] [620] With an increase of signs of cooperation between the YPG and their

[611] "H.R. 1735 – National Defense Authorization Act For Fiscal Year 2016." Congress.gov. https://www.congress.gov/bill/114th-congress/house-bill/1735/text

[612] Banco, Eric. "Free Syrian Army Rebels Join Forces With Kurds To Fight ISIS In Kobane." International Business Times. October 9, 2014. http://www.ibtimes.com/free-syrian-army-rebels-join-forces-kurds-fight-isis-kobane-1702500

[613] Hubbard, Ben. "Islamist Rebels Create Dilemma On Syria Policy." New York Times. April 27, 2013. http://www.nytimes.com/2013/04/28/world/middleeast/islamist-rebels-gains-in-syria-create-dilemma-for-us.html?pagewanted=all&_r=2

[614] Cartalucci, Tony. "In Syria, There Are No Moderates." Land Destroyer. September 20, 2013. http://landdestroyer.blogspot.com/2013/09/in-syria-there-are-no-moderates.html#more

[615] Turbeville, Brandon. "False Flag Attacks Pin Atrocities On Assad And Justify 'Red Line' Engagement." Activist Post. March 20, 2013. http://www.activistpost.com/2013/03/false-flag-attacks-in-syria-pin.html

[616] Turbeville, Brandon. ISIS Agrees To Work With Itself – US Calls For Panic, Attack On Assad." Activist Post. November 15, 2014. http://www.activistpost.com/2014/11/isis-agrees-to-work-with-itself-us.html

[617] Knutsen, Elise. "Frustration Drives Arsal's FSA Into ISIS Ranks." The Daily Star. September 8, 2014. http://www.dailystar.com.lb/News/Lebanon-News/2014/Sep-08/269883-frustration-drives-arsals-fsa-into-isis-ranks.ashx

[618] "'I Am Not Fighting Against al-Qa'ida . . . It's Not Our Problem' Says West's Last Hope In Syria." The Independent. http://www.handsoffsyriasydney.com/articles/i-am-not-fighting-against-al-qaida-its-not-our-problem-says-wests-last-hope-in-syria/?print=pdf

Iraqi counterparts, one can only wonder if the events transpiring on the ground in relation to the Kurds in Syria, Iraq, and Turkey are part of an overarching US plan to finally carve out a pound of geographic flesh out of Iraq and Syria.

Unfortunately for the Kurds, the history of their community and the US has been one of short-term usefulness and treachery. Seldom have the Kurds benefited from supporting American actions or working in the service of US geopolitical agendas, whether wittingly or unwittingly. In almost every single circumstance, the Kurds have provided yeomen's service in the name of destabilization and the strategy of tension but have been left holding the bag in the end. That bag almost always contains horrific slaughter and subsequent oppression of the Kurdish people.

The legitimacy of anything resembling a Kurdistan in Syria, however, is easily disproven as a justifiable option. As Maram Susli wrote in her article "Why A Kurdish Enclave In Syria Is A Bad Idea," for Global Independent Analytics,

> The region of Al Hasakah, which the Kurdish Nationalist Party (PYD) and its military wing YPG have declared a Kurdish federal state, does not have a Kurdish majority. Al Hasakah Governorate is a mosaic of Assyrian Christians, Armenians, Turkmen, Kurds and Bedouin Arabs. Of the 1.5 million population of Al Hasakah, only 40% are ethnically Kurdish. [621] [622] Moreover, parts of Al Hasakah Governorate, such as Al Hasakah district, is less than 15% Kurdish (!). Among the other large minorities in the area the Arabs and Assyrian Christians form a majority. Declaring a small area with a wide array of ethnic groups as belonging to a specific ethnic minority is a recipe for oppression. [623]

> The Kurdish population of Al Hasakah has also been heavily infiltrated by illegal Kurdish immigration from Turkey. Kurdish immigration to Syria began in the 1920's and occurred in several waves after multiple failed Kurdish uprisings against Turkey. [624] It continued throughout the century. In 2011 the Kurdish population in Syria reached between 1.6 to 2.3 million, [625] but 420,000 of these left Syria for Iraq [626] and Turkey as

[619] Myre, Greg. "Why Does The U.S. Like Iraq's Kurds But Not Syria's?" NPR. September 23, 2014. http://www.npr.org/sections/parallels/2014/09/23/350579007/why-does-the-u-s-like-the-kurds-in-iraq-but-not-in-syria

[620] Zunes, Stephen. "The United States And The Kurds: A Brief History." CommonDreams. October 26, 2007. http://www.commondreams.org/views/2007/10/26/united-states-and-kurds-brief-history

[621] Heras, Nicholas A. "The Battle For Syria's Al-Hasakah Province." Combatting Terrorism Center. October 24, 2013. https://www.ctc.usma.edu/posts/the-battle-for-syrias-al-hasakah-province

[622] Bozbuga, Rasim. "Kurdish Population In Syria." Sahipkiran. August 5, 2014. http://sahipkiran.org/2014/08/05/kurdish-population-in-syria/

[623] Bozbuga, Rasim. "Kurdish Population In Syria." Sahipkiran. August 5, 2014. http://sahipkiran.org/2014/08/05/kurdish-population-in-syria/

[624] Fakhr, Saqr Abu. "Christian Decline In The Middle East: A Historical View." Notes On Arab Orthodoxy. ArabOrthodoxy.blogspot.com. December 22, 2013. http://araborthodoxy.blogspot.com.au/2013/12/as-safir-on-history-of-persecution-of.html

[625] "Who Are The Kurds?" BBC.com. March 14, 2016. http://www.bbc.com/news/world-middle-east-29702440

a result of the current conflict.[627] Some Syrian Kurds have lived in Homs and Damascus for hundreds of years and are heavily assimilated into the Syrian society. However, Kurdish illegal immigrants who mostly reside in north Syria, and who could not prove their residence in Syria before 1945, complain of oppression when they were not granted the rights of Syrian citizens.[628] Syrian law dictates that only a blood born Syrian whose paternal lineage is Syrian has a right to Syrian citizenship.[629] No refugee whether Somali, Iraqi or Palestinian has been granted Syrian citizenship no matter how long their stay. In spite of this, in 2011 the Syrian President granted Syrian citizenship to 150,000 Kurds.[630] This has not stopped the YPG from using illegal Kurdish immigrants who were not granted citizenship as a rationale for annexing Syrian land. Those who promote Federalism are imposing the will of a small minority - that is not of Syrian origin - on the whole of Al Hasakah's population and the whole of Syria.

. . . . .

PYD did not bother to consult with other factions of Syrian society before its unilateral declaration of Federalism. The other ethnicities that reside in Al Hasake governate, which PYD claims is now an autonomous Kurdish state, have clearly rejected federalism. An assembly of Syrian clans and Arab tribes in Al Hasaka[631] and the Assyrian Democratic Organization (ADO) rejected PYD's federalism declaration.[632] In Geneva, both the Syrian government and the opposition rejected PYD's federalism declaration.[633] Furthermore, PYD does not represent all of Syria's Kurdish population. The Kurdish faction of Syrian national coalition condemned PYD's federalism declaration.[634] Most of Syria's Kurds do not live in Al Hasakah and many

---

[626] Sood, Anubha; Seferis, Louisa. "Syrians Contributing To Kurdish Economic Growth." Forced Migration Review. http://www.fmreview.org/syria/sood-seferis.html

[627] Syrian Refugees.EU. http://syrianrefugees.eu/?page_id=80 Original source used by author unable to be retrieved.

[628] Tejel, Jordi. "Syria's Kurds: History, Politics, And Society." Routlege Advances In Middle East Islamic Studies Series. Routlege Taylor and Francis Group. 2009.
https://books.google.com.au/books?id=g4f54qsU618C&pg=PA51&lpg=PA51&dq=census+kurds&source=bl&ots=-
ZV9mYrveX&sig=NXovGH3KSQROmiQJKhhQ3UjKzfM&hl=en&sa=X&ved=0ahUKEwivkPuAt_LLAh
XCNxQKHUqpDyE4FBDoAQgdMAE#v=onepage&q=census%20kurds&f=false

[629] Osborne, Louise; Russell, Ruby. "Refugee Crisis Creating Stateless Generation Children In Limbo Experts Say." The Guardian. December 27, 2015.
https://www.theguardian.com/world/2015/dec/27/refugee-crisis-creating-stateless-generation-children-experts-warn

[630] "Syrian Kurds Granted Nationality." Xinhua.net. March 7, 2011.
http://news.xinhuanet.com/english2010/world/2011-04/07/c_13817925.htm

[631] "Assembly Of Syrian Tribes And Clans In Hasaka Reject So-Called 'Federal Region In Northern Syria." SANA. March 19, 2016. http://sana.sy/en/?p=72431

[632] "ADO: Unilateral Kurdish Federalism Unacceptable." Assyria TV. March 24, 2011.
http://www.assyriatv.org/2016/03/ado-unilateral-kurdish-federalism-unacceptable/

[633] "Syria Government, Opposition Reject Federal System: De Mistura." Press TV. May 17, 2016.
http://www.presstv.ir/Detail/2016/03/17/456328/Syria-UN-Mistura-Daesh/

[634] Wilgenberg, Wladmir Van. "Kurdish National Council In Syria Condemns Federalism Declaration By Kurdish Rival." ARA News. March 19, 2016. http://aranews.net/2016/03/kurdish-

that do work outside it. Thousands of Kurds have joined ISIS and are fighting for an Islamic State not a Kurdish one.[635]

A unilateral declaration of federalism carries no legitimacy since federalism can only exist with a constitutional change and a Referendum. Federalism is unlikely to garner much support from the bulk of Syria's population, 90-93% of whom is not Kurdish.[636] Knowing this, PYD has banned residents of Al Hasakah from voting in the upcoming Parliamentary elections to be held across the nation.[637] This shows the will of the people in Al Hasakah is already being crushed by PYD. It is undemocratic to continue to discuss federalism as a possibility when it has been rejected by so many segments of Syrian society. Ironically we are told the purpose of the US' Regime change adventure in Syria is to bring democracy to the middle east.

. . . . . .

While Kurds make up only 7-10% of Syria's total population, PYD demands 20% of Syria's land.[638] What's more, the region of Al hasakah, which YPG wants to annex has a population of only 1.5 million people.[639] Much of Syria's agriculture and oil wealth is located in Al Hasakah and is shared by Syria's 23 million people. Al Hasakah province produces 34% of Syria's wheat[640] and much of Syria's oil.[641] The oil pumping stations are now being used by ISIS and YPG's Kurds to fund their war efforts while depriving the Syrian people.[642]

While headlines abound about Syria's starving population, there is little talk of how federalising Syria could entrench this starvation into law for generations to come.[643]

---

national-council-syria-condemns-federalism-declaration-kurdish-rival/

[635] Kaplan, Michael. "Kurds Joining Islamic State? ISIS Finds Unlikely Supporters Among Turkey's Disgruntled Kurds." International Business Times. July 30, 2015. http://www.ibtimes.com/kurds-joining-islamic-state-isis-finds-unlikely-supporters-among-turkeys-disgruntled-2029924

[636] "Who Are The Kurds?" BBC. March 14, 2016. http://www.bbc.com/news/world-middle-east-29702440

[637] "Kurds Vow To Prevent Assad Regime From Holding Parliamentary Elections In Rojova." April 2, 2016. ARA News. http://aranews.net/2016/04/kurds-vow-prevent-assad-regime-holding-parliamentary-elections-rojava/

[638] "Who Are The Kurds?" BBC. March 14, 2016. http://www.bbc.com/news/world-middle-east-29702440

[639] Heras, Nicholas A. "The Battle For Syria's Al-Hasakah Province." Combatting Terrorism Center. October 24, 2013. https://www.ctc.usma.edu/posts/the-battle-for-syrias-al-hasakah-province

[640] "Syria: Crop Progress Report." FAS – Office Of Global Analysis (OGA), United States Department of Agriculture (USDA), International Operational Agriculture Monitoring Program. January 24, 2009. http://www.pecad.fas.usda.gov/pdfs/Syria/Syria_January2009_Monthly_Report.pdf

[641] Sheikho, Youssef. "Syrian Kurds Bank On Big Oil Reserves." Al-Akhbar English. March 6, 2015. http://english.al-akhbar.com/node/15221

[642] "ISIS, Kurds Deprive Syrian State Of Revenues." The Arab Weekly. June 5, 2015. http://www.thearabweekly.com/?id=661

[643] "Syria: Starvation As A Weapon Of War." Al Jazeera. January 16, 2016. http://www.aljazeera.com/programmes/upfront/2016/01/syria-starvation-weapon-war-160115084832001.html

Instead, promoters of Federalism talk about how giving the resources shared by 23 million people to 1.5 million people will lead to peace.

. . . . . .

Since the majority of Syria's population and Syria's government oppose Kurdish annexation claims, PYD will not be able to achieve federalism through legal means. The only way the PYD and YPG can achieve federalism is through brute force. This brute force may backed by the US air force and an invasion by special forces which contradicts international law. Head of PYD Saleh Islam has already threatened to attack Syrian troops if they attempt to retake Raqqa from ISIS.[644] A Kurdish state in Syria as the Iraqi Kurdistan ensures US hegemony in the region. Like the KRG[645] the YPG are already attempting to build a US base on Syrian soil. Russia, which has been an ally of Syria for a long time, will be further isolated as a result.[646] This will once again tip the balance of power in the world.

All of Syria's neighbouring countries are also opposed to an ethnocentric Kurdish state in Syria. The YPG is linked to the PKK, which is active in Turkey and which the United Nations has designated a terrorist organisation.[647] Turkey will see YPG's federalism claims as strengthening the PKK. Turkey may invade Syria as a result, guaranteeing at least a regional war. This regional war could involve Iran, Syria, Hezbollah and Israel.

Israel wants to establish a Kurdistan, as a Sunni-Iranian rival to Shi'ite Iran. They hope such a Sunni state will block Iran's access to Syria and will also prevent Lebanese resistance against Israeli invasion. This was all outlined in Israel's Yinon Plan published in 1982.[648] Israel is an extension of US influence and hegemony in the region, the Israeli lobby holds much sway over US politics. Strengthening Israel in the region will strengthen US influence over the region, once again shrinking Russian influence and pushing the nuclear power into a corner. Journalists who show a sense of confusion about the reason the West is supportive of Kurdish expansionism should consider this point.[649]

Finally, a designated 'Kurdish area' in Syria is deeply rooted in ethnocentric chauvinism. A US state strictly designated for Hispanic, White or Black ethnicity

---

[644] "Salih Muslim: We Will Not Allow The Syrian Army To Enter [Territory] If Democracy Restored." (Translation approximate from Google Translate). Sham Times. http://www.shaamtimes.net/news-detailz.php?id=52261 see original http://www.shaamtimes.net/news-detailz.php?id=52261
[645] The Kurdish Regional Government in Iraq. (Footnote provided by Maram Susli)
[646] Akulov, Andrei. "US To Illegally Build Military Base In Syria In Preparation Of Ground War." Strategic Culture Foundation. January 23, 2016. http://m.strategic-culture.org/news/2016/01/23/us-illegally-build-military-base-syria-preparation-ground-war.html
[647] "List of Designated Terror Organizations." Wikipedia.org. https://en.wikipedia.org/wiki/List_of_designated_terrorist_groups
[648] Susli, Maram. "Kerry's Plan At Balkanizing Syria." New Eastern Outlook. March 29, 2016. http://journal-neo.org/2016/03/29/kerry-s-plan-at-balkanising-syria/
[649] "Why Should The Kurds Have A Federal Region In Syria." GIA Analytics. https://gianalytics.org/653-why-should-the-kurds-have-a-federal-region-in-syria

would be outrageous to suggest and would be considered racist. But the use of ethnicity as a means to divide and conquer is the oldest and most cynical form of imperialism. Syria must remain for all Syrians, not just for one minority. Voices who oppose this should be discouraged. The Syrian Constitution should continue to resist all ethnocentric religious-based parties. If there is a change to the Syrian constitution, it should be the removal of the word Arab from Syrian Arab Republic. In spite of the fact that the vast majority Syrians speak the Arabic language, the majority of Syrian are historically not ethnically Arab.[650] All sections of Syrian society should be treated equally under the Syrian flag.[651]

One can scarcely argue with the points made by Susli. In addition to those listed above, however, Susli also draws attention to the question of Kurdish ethnic cleansing campaigns that could be potentially launched against Assyrians and Christians. She writes,

Since the Kurdish population is not a majority in the areas PYD are trying to annex, the past few years have revealed that PYD/YPG are not beyond carrying out ethnic cleansing of non-Kurdish minorities in an attempt to achieve a demographic shift. The main threat to Kurdish ethnocentric territorial claims over the area are the other large minorities, the Arabs and the Assyrian Christians.

Salih Muslim, the leader of PYD, openly declared his intention to conduct an ethnic cleansing campaign against Syrian Arabs who live in what he now calls Rojava.[652] "One day those Arabs who have been brought to the Kurdish areas will have to be expelled," said Muslim in an interview with Serek TV. Over two years since that interview he has fulfilled his word, as YPG begun burning Arab villages around Al Hasakah Province hoping to create a demographic shift.[653] It is estimated that ten thousand Arabs have been ethnically cleansed from Al Hasake province so far.[654] The villages around Tal Abayad have suffered the most as Kurdish expansionists seek to connect the discontiguous population centres of Al Hasakah and Al Raqqa. "The YPG burnt our village and looted our houses," said Mohammed Salih al-Katee, who left Tel Thiab Sharki, near the city of Ras al-Ayn, in December.

In addition, Susli points out that such campaigns are not without precedent. She continues,

---

[650] Landis, Joshua. "The Assyrians Of Syria: History And Prospets by Mardean Isaac." JoshuaLandis.com December 20, 2015. www.joshualandis.com/blog/the-assyrians-of-syria-history-and-prospets-by-mardean-isaac/

[651] Susli, Maram. "Why A Kurdish Enclave In Syria Is A Very Bad Idea." Gia Analytics. April 6, 2016. http://www.globalresearch.ca/why-a-kurdish-enclave-in-syria-is-a-very-bad-idea/5519109

[652] "PYD Leader Warns Of War With Arab Settlers In Kurdish Areas." Rudaw.net. December 24, 2013. http://rudaw.net/english/middleeast/syria/24112013

[653] YPG Hopes To 'Change The Demographic Map' In Al-Hasakah." SyriaDirect.org March 24, 2015. http://syriadirect.org/news/ypg-hopes-to-%E2%80%98change-the-demographic-map%E2%80%99-in-al-hasakah/

[654] "Arabs Driven Out By Kurdish Ethnic Cleansing In Syria." The Australian. http://www.theaustralian.com.au/news/world/the-times/10000-arabs-driven-out-by-kurdish-ethnic-cleansing-in-syria/news-story/49a7e1c8241248964a65535fb6d97377

YPG have also begun a campaign of intimidation, murder and property confiscation against the Assyrian Christian minority. The YPG and PYD made it a formal policy to loot and confiscate the property of those who had escaped their villages after an ISIS attack, in the hope of repopulating Assyrian villages with Kurds.[655] The Assyrians residents of the Khabur area in Al Hasaka province formed a militia called the Khabour Guard in the hope of defending their villages against ISIS attacks. The Khabur Guard council leaders protested the practice of looting by Kurdish YPG militia members who looted Assyrian villages that were evacuated after ISIS attacked them.[656] Subsequently, the YPG assassinated the leader of the Khabur Guard David Jindo and attempted to Assassinate Elyas Nasser.[657] At first, the YPG blamed the assassination on ISIS but Elyas Nasser, who survived, was able to expose the YPG's involvement from his hospital bed.[658] Since the assassination YPG has forced the Khabour Guard to disarm and to accept YPG 'protection.' Subsequently, most Assyrian residents of the Khabour who had fled to Syrian Army controlled areas of Qamishli City could not return to their villages.[659]

The Assyrian Christian community in Qamishli has also been harassed by YPG Kurdish militia. YPG attacked an Assyrian checkpoint killing one fighter of the Assyrian militia Sootoro and wounding three others.[660] The checkpoint was set up after three Assyrian restaurants were bombed on December 20, 2016 in an attack that killed 14 Assyrian civilians. Assyrians suspected that YPG was behind these bombings in an attempt to assassinate Assyrian leaders and prevent any future claims of control over Qamishli.[661] [662]

It would be foolish to ignore the signs that more widely spread ethnic cleansing campaigns may occur if Kurdish expansionists are supported, especially since other ethnic groups are not on board with their federalism plans. It has only been 90 years since the Assyrian genocide which was conducted by Turks and Kurds.[663] This

---

[655] "Assyrians, Armenians In Syria Protest Kurdish Confiscation Of Property." Assyrian International News Agency (AINA). November 2, 2015.
http://www.aina.org/news/20151102170051.htm
[656] "Assyrian Military Commander Assassinated By YPG, Tells American Mesopotamian Org. (AMO)." Liveleak. May 13, 2015. http://www.liveleak.com/view?i=256_1431537234
[657] "Assyrian Military Commander Assassinated By YPG, Tells American Mesopotamian Org. (AMO)." Liveleak. May 13, 2015. http://www.liveleak.com/view?i=256_1431537234
[658] "Assyrians, Armenians In Syria Protest Kurdish Confiscation Of Property." Assyrian International News Agency (AINA). November 2, 2015.
http://www.aina.org/news/20151102170051.htm
[659] Fadel, Leith. "Official Statement From The Khabour Assyrian Council of Guardians." Al-Masdar News. August 6, 2015. http://www.almasdarnews.com/article/official-statement-from-the-khabour-assyrian-council-of-guardians/
[660] Antonopolous, Paul. "Revisiting Kurdish Tolerance: YPG Attacks Assyrian Militia." December 1, 2016. https://www.almasdarnews.com/article/revisiting-kurdish-tolerance-ypg-attacks-assyrian-militia/
[661] "Assyrian Restaurants Bombed In Qamlishi, Syria, 16 Killed." Assyrian International News Agency (AINA). December 30, 2015. http://www.aina.org/news/20151230181909.htm
[662] "Kurdish YPG Forces Attack Assyrians In Syria, 1 Assyrian, 3 Kurds Killed." Assyrian International News Agency (AINA). January 12, 2015.
http://www.aina.org/news/20160112034707.htm

history should not be allowed to be repeated. Assyrians have enjoyed safety and stability in the Syrian state since this time. Forcing the Assyrians to accept federalism is not going to ensure their safety. Establishment of a Kurdish federal state in Iraq has not protected Assyrian villages from attacks by Kurdish armed groups either.[664] The campaign of ethnic cleansing against both Assyrians and Arabs in Al Hasakah has already begun and may now only escalate.

The Difference Between ISIS and FSA

So what's the big difference between the "moderate" terrorists and the extremist terrorists running rampant in Syria today? At one time, we were told there were no terrorists at all. Then, we were told terrorists were indeed present but that there were also moderate, secular, democracy-loving freedom fighters in the country. Now, after the nature of the so-called "rebels" has been revealed ad infinitum by the alternative and independent press, it is admitted that the "fighters" in Syria are terrorists but, apparently, some are moderate and some are extreme.[665]

Of course, they all have the same goal of Sharia. They all hate minorities, Christians, Alawites, Shiites, etc. They all torture. They all rape. We could go on and on. In the world of the West's "rebels," there is not one shred of difference between any of the armed groups fighting against the secular Syrian government besides the names they call themselves.[666] [667]

Still, we are told there are clear differences and that the U.S. State Department knows just what they are. Only, they aren't telling the American people. Or the Russians. Or the Syrians. Or anybody. The "moderate" terrorists are thus a very mysterious force, a group of which we may speak but also one that never shows itself.

Of course, there are groups that the United States admits are brutal killers but somehow rationalizes to the public that they are "our" brutal killers. The U.S. can, at times, be forced to admit that the groups it supports as "freedom fighters" have committed atrocities, rapes, murders, torture, and establishment of Islamic theocracy upon unwilling inhabitants. Essentially, the U.S. can admit (when pressured) that these groups have the same ideology as ISIS, although the State Department will never say these exact words.

Thus, it is clear that any designation of terrorist groups as "extremist" or "moderate" is obviously based on political motivation and geopolitical designs, not the nature or action

---

[663] "Assyrian Genocide." Wikipedia.org

[664] Antonopolous, Paul. "Questioning Kurdish Secularism." Al-Masdar News. November 22, 2015. https://www.almasdarnews.com/article/questioning-kurdish-secularism/

[665] Turbeville, Brandon. "What's The Big Difference Between NATO's Moderates And Extremists In Syria?" Activist Post. May 25, 2016. http://www.activistpost.com/2016/05/whats-the-big-difference-between-natos-moderates-and-extremists-in-syria.html

[666] Hubbard, Ben. "Islamist Rebels Create Dilemma On Syria Policy." New York Times. April 27, 2013. http://www.nytimes.com/2013/04/28/world/middleeast/islamist-rebels-gains-in-syria-create-dilemma-for-us.html?_r=0

[667] Turbeville, Brandon. "The Roots Of ISIS." Activist Post. September 11, 2014. http://www.activistpost.com/2014/09/the-roots-of-isis.html

of the terrorist group in question. If that were the case, then Ahrar al-Sham, Jaish al-Islam, and other groups would easily be listed as terrorist organizations that would subsequently not be covered under the "ceasefire" agreement. After all, there is no distinguishing characteristic that sets these groups apart from ISIS or Nusra other than a name.

But when the Russians attempted to remove these groups from the list of non-protected terrorists in Syria (terrorists protected at the insistence of the West), the United States, Britain, France, and Ukraine rushed to their rescue and blocked the Russian proposal.[668] This is, of course, despite the fact that both of these groups, which make up around half of the "Syrian opposition forces" thanks to Western name changes, have repeatedly worked together with Nusra and ISIS forces. Jaish al-Islam and Ahrar al-Sham have both worked so closely with ISIS and Nusra that the groups themselves are virtually interchangeable. Nevertheless, the U.S. is only digging its own international public relations grave with its refusal to designate known and obvious terrorists as precisely that, particularly when it has launched campaigns of destruction and death across the world on the basis of allegedly "fighting terror."

The fact is that there never has been a difference between these organizations and this reality has been exposed time and time again in growing numbers of outlets in the alternative and independent media.[669]

As Tony Cartalucci wrote in his article, "In Syria, There Are No Moderates,"

> . . . . . there were never, nor are there any "moderates" operating in Syria. The West has intentionally armed and funded Al Qaeda and other sectarian extremists since as early as 2007 in preparation for an engineered sectarian bloodbath serving US-Saudi-Israeli interests. This latest bid to portray the terrorists operating along and within Syria's borders as "divided" along extremists/moderate lines is a ploy to justify the continued flow of Western cash and arms into Syria to perpetuate the conflict, as well as create conditions along Syria's borders with which Western partners, Israel, Jordan, and Turkey, can justify direct military intervention.[670]

Indeed, even the New York Times has been forced to admit that there are, as Cartalucci expertly argues in his article, no moderates in the ranks of the Syrian death squads. As Ben Hubbard writes,

> In Syria's largest city, Aleppo, rebels aligned with Al Qaeda control the power plant, run the bakeries and head a court that applies Islamic law. Elsewhere, they have seized government oil fields, put employees back to work and now profit from the crude they produce.

---

[668] Tomson, Chris. "Western U.N. Bloc Rejects Russian Bid To Blacklist Islamist Groups In Syria." Al-Masdar News. December 5, 2016. https://www.almasdarnews.com/article/western-u-n-bloc-rejects-russian-bid-blacklist-islamist-groups-syria/

[669] Turbeville, Brandon. "Terrorists Wage War On Each Other In Syria; New Round of Propaganda Begins." Activist Post. September 27, 2013. http://www.activistpost.com/2013/09/terrorists-wage-war-on-each-other-in.html

[670] Cartalucci, Tony. "In Syria, There Are No Moderates." Land Destroyer. September 20, 2013. http://landdestroyer.blogspot.com/2013/09/in-syria-there-are-no-moderates.html#more

Across Syria, rebel-held areas are dotted with Islamic courts staffed by lawyers and clerics, and by fighting brigades led by extremists. Even the Supreme Military Council, the umbrella rebel organization whose formation the West had hoped would sideline radical groups, is stocked with commanders who want to infuse Islamic law into a future Syrian government.

Nowhere in rebel-controlled Syria is there a secular fighting force to speak of.[671]

Other Interests

While some may suggest that Turkey is getting off the reservation and simply acting on its own interests (i.e. rolling back the Kurds), Erdogan has long acted as a major tool of the NATO agenda against Syria. The very fact that the United States has aided Turkish operations with airstrikes of its own should go some length in demonstrating that the NATO powers are in full support of the Turkish military incursion in Syria.

Still, others have a different perspective. Andrew Korybko of Katehon argues that the Syrians, Iranians, and Russians are tacitly supporting the incursion because it alleviates them of the responsibility of cleansing ISIS and Kurdish battalions from northern Syria. Korybko points to increased political talks between Syria and Turkey in the days leading up to the military operation as well as the domestic climate of Russia in terms of support for increased military operations. Korybko suggests that the United States has been duped by Turkey into falling in line with the incursion which is, in reality, an agreement on strategy and policies related to Syria by the "multipolar bloc."[672] Korybko writes,

> . . . . . Damascus and Ankara have been engaged in secret talks for months now in the Algerian capital of Algiers, as has been repeatedly confirmed by many multiple media sources ever since this spring.[673] Moreover, Turkey just dispatched one of its deputy intelligence chiefs to Damascus a few days ago to meet with his high-level Syrian counterparts, so this might explain the reason why Russia and Iran aren't condemning Turkey's incursion into Syria, nor why the Syrian officials aren't loudly protesting against it either.[674] More and more, the evidence is pointing to Turkey's operation being part of a larger move that was coordinated in advance with Syria, Russia, and Iran.

> Nevertheless, for domestic political reasons within both Syria and Turkey, neither side is expected to admit to having coordinated any of this, and it's likely that bellicose rhetoric might be belched from Ankara just as much as it's predictable that Damascus will rightfully speak about the protection of its sovereignty.

---

[671] Hubbard, Ben. "Islamist Rebels Create Dilemma On Syria Policy." New York Times. April 27, 2013. http://www.nytimes.com/2013/04/28/world/middleeast/islamist-rebels-gains-in-syria-create-dilemma-for-us.html?_r=0

[672] Korybko, Andrew. "Turkey Crosses Into Syria: Unipolar Conspiracy Or Multipolar Coordination?" Katehon. August 24, 2016. http://katehon.com/article/turkey-crosses-syria-unipolar-conspiracy-or-multipolar-coordination

[673] "Turkish, Syrian Governments Hold Secret Meeting In Algeria: El-Watan." Al-Masdar News. March 11, 2015. https://www.almasdarnews.com/article/turkish-syrian-governments-hold-secret-meeting-algeria-el-watan/

[674] "Ankara Sent Deputy Intel Chief To Damascus, Reports." Al-Masdar News. August 22, 2016. https://www.almasdarnews.com/article/ankara-sent-deputy-intel-chief-damascus-reports/

What's most important, though, isn't to listen so much to Turkey and Syria, but to watch and observe what Russia and Iran say and do, since these are the two countries most capable of defending Syria from any legitimate aggression against its territory and which have been firmly standing behind it for years now, albeit to differing qualitative extents though with complementary synergy (i.e. Russia's anti-terrorist air operation and Iran's special forces ground one). This isn't in any way to 'excuse', 'apologize for', or 'explain away' the US' opportunistic and illegal inadvertent contribution to this coordinated multipolar campaign, but to accurately document how and why it decided to involve itself in this superficially Turkish-led venture, namely because it was cleverly misled by Erdogan into thinking that this is a precondition for the normalization of relations between both sides.

Russia lacks the political will to cleanse the Wahhabi terrorists and Kurdish separatists from northern Syrian itself, and for as much as one may support or condemn this, it's a statement of fact that must be taken into account when analyzing and forecasting events. With this obvious constraint being a major factor influencing the state of affairs in Syria, it's reasonable then that Syria, Russia, and Iran wouldn't vocally object too much to Turkey tricking the US into doing this instead out of the pursuit of its own self-interests vis-à-vis the attempted normalization with Ankara. The major qualifying variable that must be mentioned at this point is that serious Russian and Iranian condemnation of Turkey's ongoing operation would signal that something either went wrong with their multilaterally coordinated plan, or that Turkey was just a backstabbing pro-American Trojan Horse this entire time and the skepticism surrounding Moscow and Tehran's dedicated efforts to coax Ankara into a multipolar pivot was fully vindicated as the correct analysis all along.[675]

Still, with all that in mind, it should be remembered that Washington has essentially led Erdogan by the nose through most of the Syrian crisis. Only in 2016 has the neo-Ottoman shown signs of moving away from U.S. influence but, even those apparent moves are being questioned by researchers and analysts. At this point, we still do not definitively know if the United States was behind the coup in Turkey or if it was an inside job/false flag staged by Erdogan and the U.S. in order to justify a clampdown on Erdogan's opponents. Judging by the fact that no diplomatic staff was recalled, Incirlik continues to be used by the United States, and joint military operations are taking place between the United States and Turkey, it is difficult to believe that Turkey truly believes the U.S. was behind an attempted coup against Erdogan.[676]

Regardless, Turkish incursions into Syrian territory on the basis of a false flag, all the while being supported by the West, are nothing new. For instance, in 2014, Turkey was exposed for planning to use an alleged attack on the tomb of Suleiman Shah as well as a false flag attack on Turkish territory in order to justify an invasion of Syria.

In its article, "Turkey YouTube Ban: Full Transcript Of Leaked Syria 'War' Conversation Between Erdogan Officials," the International Business Times released the

---

[675] Korybko, Andrew. "Turkey Crosses Into Syria: Unipolar Conspiracy Or Multipolar Coordination?" Katehon. August 24, 2016. http://katehon.com/article/turkey-crosses-syria-unipolar-conspiracy-or-multipolar-coordination
[676] Turbeville, Brandon. "What The Hell Is Happening In Turkey?" Activist Post. July 19, 2016. http://www.activistpost.com/2016/07/what-the-hell-is-happening-in-turkey.html

transcript of a conversation between members of Turkish leadership planning a false flag using their terrorist proxies in order to justify an invasion:

> Ahmet Davutoğlu: "Prime Minister said that in current conjuncture, this attack (on Suleiman Shah Tomb) must be seen as an opportunity for us."

> Hakan Fidan: "I'll send 4 men from Syria, if that's what it takes. I'll make up a cause of war by ordering a missile attack on Turkey; we can also prepare an attack on Suleiman Shah Tomb if necessary."

> Feridun Sinirlioğlu: "Our national security has become a common, cheap domestic policy outfit."

> Yaşar Güler: "It's a direct cause of war. I mean, what're going to do is a direct cause of war."[677]

With this in mind, it is interesting to note that an eerily similar type of "opportunity" took place right before the recent invasion. As the New York Times described,

> A bombing on Saturday night at a Kurdish wedding in Gaziantep, a Turkish town near the Syrian border, was one of the deadliest in a string of terrorist attacks that have struck Turkey. Since June 2015, Kurdish and Islamic State militants have staged at least 15 major attacks across Turkey, killing more than 330 people.[678]

The New Atlas also sees the Turkish invasion as part of the NATO goal of destroying the secular government of Bashar al-Assad. The website writes,

> Thus, Turkey's government and a complicit Western media have helped place the blame equally on both the Islamic State and Kurdish militants ahead of the now ongoing cross-border operation.

> The above mentioned BBC article would also note:

> Turkey has vowed to "completely cleanse" IS from its border region, blaming the group for a bomb attack on a wedding that killed at least 54 people in Gaziantep on Saturday.[679]

> In the aftermath of the July coup, many were hopeful Turkey would realign itself geopolitically and play a more constructive and stabilising role in the region.

> Instead, while citing the threat of the Islamic State and Kurdish forces along its border, a threat that its own collusion with US and Persian Gulf States since 2011 helped create, Turkey has decisively helped move forward a crucial part of US plans

---

[677] Moore, Jack. "Turkey Youtube Ban: Full Transcript Of Leaked Syria 'War' Conversation Between Erdogan Officials." International Business Times. March 27, 2014.
http://www.ibtimes.co.uk/turkey-youtube-ban-full-transcript-leaked-syria-war-conversation-between-erdogan-officials-1442161
[678] "Wedding Bombing Is The Latest In A Series Of Deadly Terror Attacks In Turkey." New York Times. August 21, 2016.
http://www.nytimes.com/interactive/2016/06/28/world/middleeast/turkey-terror-attacks-bombings.html
[679] "IS Conflict: Turkey-Backed Syrian Rebels Take Jarablus." August 24, 2016.
http://www.bbc.com/news/world-europe-37171995

to dismember Syria and move its campaign of North African and Middle Eastern destabilisation onward and outward.

The response by Syria and its allies in the wake of Turkey's cross-border foray has so far been muted. What, if any actions could be taken to prevent the US and its allies from achieving their plans remain to be seen.

While the toppling of the government in Damascus looks unlikely at the moment, the Balkanisation of Syria was a secondary objective always only ever considered by US policymakers as a mere stop gap until eventually toppling Damascus as well. Conceding eastern and parts of northern Syria to US-led aggression will only buy time.[680]

Buffer Zones

The idea of establishing a "safe zone" in Syria is, of course, not a new concept.[681] In July, 2015, the agreement being discussed would have effectively created a "buffer zone" that would have spanned from the Turkish border line into Syria.[682] It would have extended from Azaz in the West to Jarablus in the East and as far south as al-Bab. The width of the zone would have been about 68 miles and would have extended around 40 miles deep into Syria, right on the doorstep of Aleppo.[683] [684]

The zone would have much smaller than that which Turkey and the United States have called for in the years prior and wouldn't have necessarily stretched the length of the Turkey-Syria border. But it would have been a start.

True to form, the US and Turkey attempted to obfuscate the fact that their agreement was the creation of a no-fly zone by renaming it an "ISIL-free zone."[685] This is the same tactic used when the term "no-fly zone" and "buffer zone" began to draw too much ire from observers only a year ago. Then, the term became "safe zone." [686]

---

[680] "Turkey Invades Northern Syria – Truth Of 'Turkish' Coup Revealed?" The New Atlas. August 24, 2016. http://www.thenewatlas.org/2016/08/turkey-invades-northern-syria-truth-of.html
[681] Byman, Daniel L.; Doran, Michael; Pollack, Kenneth M.; Shaikh, Salman. "Saving Syria: Assessing Options For Regime Change." Brookings Institution. March 15, 2012. https://www.brookings.edu/research/saving-syria-assessing-options-for-regime-change/
[682] DeYoung, Karen; Sly, Liz. "U.S. – Turkey Deal Aims To Create De Facto 'Safe Zone' In Northwest Syria." New York Times. Washington Post. July 26, 2015. https://www.washingtonpost.com/world/new-us-turkey-plan-amounts-to-a-safe-zone-in-northwest-syria/2015/07/26/0a533345-ff2e-4b40-858a-c1b36541e156_story.html?tid=sm_tw
[683] Turbeville, Brandon. "U.S. Renews Call For Attack On Syria Air Force, U.K. Calls For Safe Zones, Military Action." Activist Post. August 23, 2016. http://www.activistpost.com/2016/08/u-s-renews-calls-for-attack-on-syria-air-force-u-k-calls-for-safe-zones-military-action.html
[684] Turbeville, Brandon. "A 'No-Fly Zone' By Any Other Name – The 'ISIL-Free Zone' In Syria." Activist Post. July 29, 2015. http://www.activistpost.com/2015/07/a-no-fly-zone-by-any-other-name-isil.html
[685] Dagher, Sam. "Syrian Rebels Make Fresh Gains." The Wall Street Journal. July 28, 2015. http://www.wsj.com/articles/syrian-rebels-make-fresh-gains-1438116530
[686] Dermitas, Serkan. "Turkey, US To Create 'ISIL-Free Zone' Inside Syria." Hurriyet Daily News. July 25, 2015.

Semantics have served NATO and the United States well over the years. After all, a simple name change of terrorist organizations has made the Anglo-American powers able to produce "moderate rebels" and the most frightening terrorist organization the world has ever seen while using the same group of terrorists.[687]

The description of the "ISIL-free zone" of 2015 was that it would be a distinguished area in which the Turkish and U.S. military would engage in aggressive operations against ISIS. It was floated that this area would have also functioned as a place where civilians displaced by the Syrian crisis may run to for safe haven and where "moderate rebel" forces can maintain a higher presence free from the battles with ISIS.

"Once the area is cleared, the plan is to give control to as-yet-unidentified moderate Syrian rebel groups. The United States and Turkey have differing interpretations as to which groups can be defined as 'moderate,'" the Washington Post reported.[688]

The reality, however, is that the "ISIL-free zone" would have been nothing more than a Forward Operating Base deeper into Syrian territory, working under the direct protection of the U.S. military and Turkish air force. That is exactly what the British and the U.S. are arguing for today.[689]

Going further back, public discussion of the implementation of a "buffer zone" began as far back as 2012 when the Brookings Institution, in their memo "Assessing Options For Regime Change" stated

> An alternative is for diplomatic efforts to focus first on how to end the violence and how to gain humanitarian access, as is being done under Annan's leadership. This may lead to the creation of safe-havens and humanitarian corridors, which would have to be backed by limited military power. This would, of course, fall short of U.S. goals for Syria and could preserve Asad in power. From that starting point, however, it is possible that a broad coalition with the appropriate international mandate could add further coercive action to its efforts.[690]

---

[687] Cartalucci, Tony. "NATO's Terror Hordes In Iraq A Pretext For Syria Invasion." Land Destroyer Report. June 13, 2014. http://www.activistpost.com/2014/06/natos-terror-hordes-in-iraq-pretext-for.html
See also,
Cartalucci, Tony. "Implausible Deniability – West's ISIS Terror Hordes In Iraq." Land Destroyer Report. August 8, 2014. http://landdestroyer.blogspot.com/2014/08/implausible-deniability-wests-isis.html#more
See also,
Turbeville, Brandon. "Turkey's Call For 'Safe Zones' In Syria Are Based On Problem Turkey Helped Create." Activist Post. July 28, 2015.
http://landdestroyer.blogspot.com/2014/08/implausible-deniability-wests-isis.html#more
[688] DeYoung, Karen; Sly, Liz. "U.S. – Turkey Deal Aims To Create De Facto 'Safe Zone' In Northwest Syria." New York Times. Washington Post. July 26, 2015.
https://www.washingtonpost.com/world/new-us-turkey-plan-amounts-to-a-safe-zone-in-northwest-syria/2015/07/26/0a533345-ff2e-4b40-858a-c1b36541e156_story.html?tid=sm_tw
[689] Cartalucci, Tony. "Beware Israel: The Eager Provocateur." New Eastern Outlook. August 8, 2014. http://journal-neo.org/2014/08/08/beware-israel-the-eager-provocateur/
[690] Byman, Daniel L.; Doran, Michael; Pollack, Kenneth M.; Shaikh, Salman. "Saving Syria:

The Brookings Institution went further, however, describing a possible scenario that mirrors the one currently unfolding in Syria where Turkey, in coordination with Israel, could help overthrow Assad by establishing a "multi-front war" on Syria's borders. Brookings writes,

> In addition, Israel's intelligence services have a strong knowledge of Syria, as well as assets within the Syrian regime that could be used to subvert the regime's power base and press for Asad's removal. Israel could posture forces on or near the Golan Heights and, in so doing, might divert regime forces from suppressing the opposition. This posture may conjure fears in the Asad regime of a multi-front war, particularly if Turkey is willing to do the same on its border and if the Syrian opposition is being fed a steady diet of arms and training. Such a mobilization could perhaps persuade Syria's military leadership to oust Asad in order to preserve itself. Advocates argue this additional pressure could tip the balance against Asad inside Syria, if other forces were aligned properly.[691]

Of course, the establishment of a "No-Fly Zone" is tantamount to a declaration of war.[692] Such has even been admitted by top U.S. Generals when explaining exactly what a No Fly Zone would entail. As General Carter Ham stated,

> We should make no bones about it. It first entails killing a lot of people and destroying the Syrian air defenses and those people who are manning those systems. And then it entails destroying the Syrian air force, preferably on the ground, in the air if necessary. This is a violent combat action that results in lots of casualties and increased risk to our own personnel.[693]

General Philip Breedlove also echoed this description when he said,

> I know it sounds stark, but what I always tell people when they talk to me about a no-fly zone is . . . it's basically to start a war with that country because you are going to have to go in and kinetically take out their air defense capability.[694]

Assessing Options For Regime Change." Brookings Institution. March 15, 2012. https://www.brookings.edu/research/saving-syria-assessing-options-for-regime-change/

[691] Byman, Daniel L.; Doran, Michael; Pollack, Kenneth M.; Shaikh, Salman. "Saving Syria: Assessing Options For Regime Change." Brookings Institution. March 15, 2012. https://www.brookings.edu/research/saving-syria-assessing-options-for-regime-change/

[692] Turbeville, Brandon. "As Russia Bombs Terrorists In Syria, NATO Members Repeat Calls For 'No-Fly Zone' And War." Activist Post. February 18, 2016. http://www.activistpost.com/2016/02/as-russia-bombs-terrorists-in-syria-nato-members-repeat-calls-for-no-fly-zone-and-war.html

[693] "Face The Nation Transcripts September 28, 2014: Blinken, Kaine, Flournoy." CBS News. September 28, 2014. http://www.cbsnews.com/news/face-the-nation-transcripts-september-28-2014-blinken-kaine-flournoy/

[694] "Face The Nation Transcripts September 28, 2014: Blinken, Kaine, Flournoy." CBS News. September 28, 2014. http://www.cbsnews.com/news/face-the-nation-transcripts-september-28-2014-blinken-kaine-flournoy/

Conclusion

Regardless of the fact that the Anglo-American empire may very well be risking a direct military confrontation with another nuclear power, the NATO forces are intent on moving forward in their attempt to destroy Syria and its government. The major victories by the Syrian military that have taken place in over 2016 as well as the inability of the West's terrorists to roll back SAA gains have obviously convinced NATO that more drastic measures are needed and that proxies are simply not enough to defeat a committed military supported by its people. Thus, we now see the plan so heavily promoted by Western think tanks and military industrial complex firms being implemented.

Clearly, the Turkish agenda is not focused on combating ISIS. If it was, the Turks would have long ago sealed their borders with Syria as well as ceased their training and facilitation of terrorist groups flowing into Syria from Turkish territory.[695]

The Turks do not need NATO Buffer Zones to end terrorism within their own country. They need to seal the borders with Syria, immediately cease funding, training, and facilitation of terrorists operating inside Turkish borders alongside a massive sting operation netting and eliminating these organizations. Turkey would also greatly benefit by backing away from Erdogan, his idiotic policies, and his equally idiotic Islamist government. Turkey must put aside "political Islam" and return to a culture of secular governance. Lastly, Turkey must pursue a reasonable and fair policy toward the Kurds in its Southeast.

Of course, Turkey has sent every signal possible to announce that they intend to stick with the NATO line of destroying the secular government of Bashar al-Assad and replacing it with a government or governments beholden and favorable to Washington and the Anglo-American oligarchy.

Obviously, a "buffer zone" and/or a "no-fly zone," of course, is tantamount to war and an open military assault against the sovereign secular government of Syria because the implementation of such a zone would require airstrikes against Assad's air defense systems.

With the establishment of this "buffer zone," a new staging ground will be opened that allows terrorists such as ISIS and others the ability to conduct attacks even deeper inside Syria. While one wishes for the best of all possible worlds – the roll back of Western-backed terrorists and Kurdish fanaticism while, at the same time, seeing the Syrian government regain control over all of its territory – we cannot wish away the facts. Amidst the tangled web of political and geopolitical interests at play in regards to this invasion, the fact is that neither the United States, the Kurdish militias, nor the Turks have the best interest of Syria or the Syrian people at heart.

---

[695] Turbeville, Brandon. "Turkey's Call For 'Safe-Zones' In Syria Are Based On Problem Turkey Helped Create." Activist Post. July 28, 2015. http://www.activistpost.com/2015/07/turkeys-call-for-safe-zones-in-syria.html

The Race For Raqqa

The Syrian military is slowly closing in on Raqqa, one of the last ISIS strongholds in the country, and a major battle between government and terrorist forces is inevitable. Already, the Syrian military liberated a number of areas in eastern Syria near the Taqba airbase, another site that is expecting liberation in the future.[696] The Syrian military has already reached the edge of Raqqa province.[697]

Raqqa has acted as the ISIS capital since the mysterious appearance of the group two years ago and has gone virtually untouched as the Syrian military has been bogged down in major cities and western/central areas of the country in their fight against the Western-backed terrorists. Notably, despite its rhetoric of fighting to "degrade and destroy" ISIS, the U.S.-led coalition has not seen fit to heavily bomb the city.

Fresh on the heels of a major public relations victory in Palmyra, however, the Syrian military is now marching toward Raqqa and, if successful, it will score one of the biggest victories in the five-year war. This is not only because the *de facto* ISIS capital will be eliminated or because the SAA will gain more territory, it is because the liberation of Raqqa will be yet another example of how the Syrian military will have accomplished in weeks what the United States and coalition members have claimed may take a decade to do. It will be another instance where the lack of will on the part of the United States to actually destroy Daesh is put on display for the rest of the world, either causing the U.S. to look weak in the eyes of the world or exposing it for actually supporting the terrorist organization to begin with. Regardless, the victory for the Syrian government will be twofold.[698]

That is, unless the U.S. gets there first . . . .

The U.S. Interest In Raqqa – A Sudden Shift

The U.S. has been using the presence of ISIS in Syria as an excuse to bomb, send Special Forces, publicly support terrorists, and possibly invade since the Western-backed terror group appeared on the scene two years ago. Yet, despite its rhetoric, the United States and its coalition have barely bombed Raqqa and have largely abstained from bombing any other terrorist group.[699] [700] [701] Instead, the U.S. has focused on

---

[696] Fadel, Ziad. "Syrian Army Continues Approach To Al-Raqqa And Tabqa; First Woman Speaker Of The House Elected By Firm Majority; Jordan Struck By Jordanian Rebel! Many Rat Leaders Eliminated Today." Syrian Perspective. June 6, 2016. https://www.rt.com/news/345394-raqqa-syria-kurds-army/

[697] "Onslaught On ISIS: Syrian Army Enters Raqqa Province As Kurds, Rebels Advance." RT. June 4, 2016. https://www.rt.com/news/345394-raqqa-syria-kurds-army/

[698] Dagher, Afraa. "The Liberation of Palmyra: US Narratives And NATO Terrorists Defeated In The Syrian Desert." Activist Post. March 28, 2016. http://www.activistpost.com/2016/03/the-liberation-of-palmyra-us-narratives-and-nato-terrorists-defeated-in-the-syrian-desert.html

[699] Turbeville, Brandon. "US Gives ISIS 45 Minute Warning Before Bombs, 'Runs Out of Ammo' Against ISIS Targets." Activist Post. December 2, 2015. http://www.activistpost.com/2015/12/us-gives-isis-45-minute-warning-before-bombs-runs-out-of-ammo-against-isis-targets.html

bombing Syrian military targets, civilians and civilian infrastructure (see here also), and acting as a deterrent to the Syrian military's movement in many "rebel-held" areas of the country.[702] [703] [704]

Now, however, the United States seems to have great interest in Raqqa as it aids its loose collection of terrorists, fanatical Kurds, and Arabs known as the Syrian Democratic Forces (SDF) in "battles" around the ISIS capital.[705]

So why the sudden interest in Raqqa? It's fairly simple. The United States sees clearly that the Syrian military and its Russian allies are going to liberate Raqqa soon enough and the U.S. does not want to suffer another public relations setback. A defeat for ISIS is thus a humiliation for the United States. That fact alone should raise some eyebrows.

Regardless, the United States would like to have its own "victory" in Raqqa before the Syrians and the Russians can have theirs. If the SDF is able to "take" Raqqa, the U.S. will then be able to shout from the rooftops that America has liberated Raqqa and defeated ISIS in its own capital.

The U.S. also has another goal in Raqqa – the theft of more Syrian territory by using its proxy forces going by the name of the SDF. Whether or not ISIS proper is in control of Raqqa is merely a secondary concern for the United States. If the SDF succeeds in imposing control over the city and the province, then the West will have succeeded in cementing control over the area in the hands of its proxy terrorists once again, but with yet another incarnation of the same Western-backed jihadist fanaticism. The U.S. can then use the "moderate rebel" label to keep Russia and Syria from bombing the fighters who merely assumed a position handed to them, albeit through some level of violence, by ISIS.

---

[700] Jones, Susan. "US Planes Left ISIS Fuel Tankers Unharmed Because "They Ran Out Of Ammunition." CNSNews. November 24, 2015. http://cnsnews.com/news/article/susan-jones/us-planes-left-isis-fuel-tankers-unharmed-because-they-ran-out-ammunition

[701] Durden, Tyler. "'Get Out Of Your Trucks And Run Away': US Gives ISIS 45 Minute Warning On Oil Tanker Strikes." Zero Hedge. November 23, 2015. http://www.zerohedge.com/news/2015-11-23/get-out-your-trucks-and-run-away-us-gives-isis-45-minute-warning-oil-tanker-strikes

[702] Turbeville, Brandon. "The Real Reasons For U.S. Airstrikes In Syria – Breaking The Assad Regime." Activist Post. September 24, 2014. http://www.activistpost.com/2014/09/the-real-reasons-for-us-airstrikes-in.html

[703] Turbeville, Brandon. "As Russia Bombs ISIS, US Bombs Syrian Civilian Power Stations." Activist Post. October 13, 2015. http://www.activistpost.com/2015/10/as-russia-bombs-isis-us-bombs-syrian-civilian-power-stations.html

[704] "Two U.S. Led Coalition F16 Aircrafts Violate Syrian Airspace, Target Electric Power Plants In Aleppo." SANA (Syrian Arab News Agency). October 10, 2015. http://www.globalresearch.ca/two-us-led-coalition-f16-aircrafts-violate-syrian-airspace-target-electric-power-plants-in-aleppo/5481464

[705] Al-Khalidi, Suleiman. "US-Backed Syrian Alliance Launches New Attack Near Islamic State Capital." Reuters. May 24, 2016. http://www.reuters.com/article/us-mideast-crisis-syria-raqqa-idUSKCN0YF2IS

The Meeting In The Middle

With the situation as it stands, there is now the very real possibility of some type of major confrontation taking place in Raqqa that could very well have international ramifications. On one hand, there is the Syrian military, backed by the Russian Air Force and Russian Special Forces heading East to Raqqa while, on the other side, there is the SDF, backed by the U.S. Air and Special Forces, heading West toward Raqqa.[706] Both sides are in a race to gain control over the ISIS capital, gain territory, and declare a victory for the world to see. But what if they arrive in Raqqa at the same time?

In other words, there is a distinct potential that, in the race for Raqqa, the Syrian/Russian alliance might find itself face to face with the possibility of direct military conflict with the U.S. /SDF (terrorist) alliance. At that point, the question will be who, if either, will back down? If both forces decide to push forward, the result could be devastating not only for Syria but for the rest of the world.

Regardless of what happens, it is important to remember that the Syrian military is acting entirely in self-defense both against the terrorists posing as "rebels" and the United States. Russia, Iran, and Hezbollah have all been invited in to Syria, acting legally and with the assent of the Syrian government, while the United States and its coalition are once again acting completely outside of international law in an attempt to shore up its terrorist proxies; and, once again, the United States and its coalition of the willing is pushing the patience of the rest of the world.

Israel

With the recent slaughter of Palestinians taking place on television screens across the world, only the grossly misinformed would believe that Israel's Palestinian extermination program is actually "self-defense."

Yet for all of Israel's whining about how it is being targeted by "Islamic extremists" and "terrorists," (which should be translated to mean Palestinians, Iran, or any other secular or nationalist Arab government in the region) there is a curious and deafening silence when it is confronted with actual terrorists and Muslim fanatics such as ISIS, al-Nusra, and the myriad of other fundamentalist groups waging jihad in Syria and Iraq.[707]

This bizarre silence has yet to raise the eyebrows of the somnambulant general public.

Of course, Israel's lack of concern regarding legitimate terrorist groups is not bizarre at all when one understands the perspective and goals held by the settler state toward its neighbors in the region or its connections to the very groups who espouse Israel as their number one enemy.

---

[706] Al-Khalidi, Suleiman. "Syrian Army Presses Offensive Against Islamic State." Reuters. June 4, 2016. http://www.reuters.com/article/us-mideast-crisis-syria-raqqa-idUSKCN0YQ0B8

[707] Cartalucci, Tony; Bowie, Nile. "Subverting Syria: How CIA Contra Gangs And NGOs Manufacture, Mislabel and Market Mass Murder." Progressive Press. September 11, 2012. https://www.amazon.com/Subverting-Syria-Contra-Manufacture-Mislabel/dp/1615775579?ie=UTF8&linkCode=wsw&ref_=as_sl_pd_tf_sw&tag=permacultucom-20

But while Israel does not respond with its usual apoplectic frothing of victimhood and danger regarding these terrorist groups that have now so infested the Middle East as to make the entire region a general war zone, it is important to point out that these same terrorist groups do not launch coordinated military attacks in Tel Aviv, they launch them in Damascus and Mosul – cities belonging to secular nations seen by Israel as the enemy.

The question then is "Why?" Why does Israel not share the concern it has over Palestinians, Iranians, Syrians, and Lebanese with al-Nusra, ISIS, and al-Qaeda? Why do these groups wage jihad against Israel's enemies but not against Israel itself?

Indeed, this curious fact was also raised by Nabil Na'eem, the former al-Qaeda commander who gave an interview to Al-Maydeen where he stated that these organizations of Islamic terror were in fact controlled by the CIA.[708] Na'eem stated in regards to Issam Hattito, the Muslim Brotherhood leader,

> For instance, Issam Hattito, head of Muslim Brotherhood responsible for leading the battles against Bashar Assad, where does he reside? Is he in Beirut? Riyadh or Cairo? He's residing in Tel Aviv.

> Ahmad Jarba, does he stay in Riyadh, Cairo or Tehran? He's moving between New York, Paris and London, his employers, who pay his expenses . . .[709]

Na'eem is right to point out these odd bedfellows because it provides one small piece of a larger puzzle – that Israel, along with its cohorts in the West (the United States and Europe) are not victims of Islamic terror, they are sponsors of it.

From providing medical aid, military training, and outright military assistance, the so-called state of Israel has been a much better friend to Muslim terrorists than any of the regimes it claims as its enemy.

For instance, it has been well-known for quite some time that Israel has been providing wounded Syrian rebels with medical treatment inside Israel so that they can continue the Jihad against the secular government of Bashar al-Assad. According to Colum Lynch of The Cable (the news wing of the Council on Foreign Relations *Foreign Policy*),

> In the past three months, battle-hardened Syrian rebels have transported scores of wounded Syrians across a cease-fire line that has separated Israel from Syria since 1974, according to a 15-page report by U.N. Secretary-General Ban Ki-moon on the work of the U.N. Disengagement Observer Force (UNDOF).[710] Once in Israel, they

---

[708] Chossudovsky, Michel. "America's 'War On Terrorism.'" 2nd edition. Global Research. 2005. https://www.amazon.com/Americas-War-Terrorism-Michel-Chossudovsky/dp/0973714719?ie=UTF8&linkCode=wsw&ref_=as_sl_pd_tf_sw&tag=permacultu com-20

[709] Turbeville, Brandon. "Former Al-Qaeda Operative Claims Qaeda/ISIS Run By The CIA." Activist Post. July 24, 2014. http://www.activistpost.com/2014/07/former-al-qaeda-operative-claims.html#!bwvBwS

[710] "Supervising Ceasefire and Disengagement Agreement." United Nations Disengagement Observer Force. United Nations Websites, UN.org. http://www.un.org/en/peacekeeping/missions/undof/

receive medical treatment in a field clinic before being sent back to Syria, where, presumably, some will return to carry on the fight.

U.N. blue helmets responsible for monitoring the decades-old cease-fire report observing armed opposition groups "transferring 89 wounded persons" from Syrian territory into Israel, where they were received by members of the Israel Defense Forces, according to the report. The IDF returned 21 Syrians to armed opposition members back in Syria, including the bodies of two who died.[711]

Later in the article, the writer mentions the fact that Israel has provided such medical assistance to Syrian rebels since at least as far back as February. Realistically, however, such assistance was being provided even further back. Lynch writes that Israel provided the medical treatment for at least a year.

Indeed, in February, 2014, Prime Minister Benjamin Netanyahu actually visited one of the medical facilities in which the Syrian rebels were being treated and even posed for a photo op shaking hands with a death squad fighter.[712]

More notable than even the medical services, is the fact that Israel has provided military support to the terrorist death squads in the form of artillery and air force bombing campaigns. These attacks have generally come after the Assad government seems to be making considerable gains on the ground against the Western-backed fighters.

For instance, on October 30, 2013, Israel attacked and completely destroyed a Syrian air defense base in Snobar Jableh, Syria which is located near Latakia, a port city on the coast of the Mediterranean.[713] The base was alleged to have housed a surface to air missile battery. [714]

Of course, this was not the only time where Israel inflicted an injury against the enemies of Islamic extremists during the course of the Syrian conflict. It is known that Israel launched attacks against Syrian forces and military convoys at least four times prior to the October 30 attack.[715]

As recently as June, 2014, Israel launched a series of airstrikes against Syrian military positions under the pretext of retaliation for a cross-border attack which was almost certainly initiated by death squad fighters whose logistical inadequacy spilled

---

[711] Lynch, Colum. "Exclusive: Israel Is Tending To Wounded Syrian Rebels." The Cable (Foreign Policy). June 11, 2014. http://foreignpolicy.com/2014/06/11/exclusive-israel-is-tending-to-wounded-syrian-rebels/

[712] Cohen, Gilli. "Israeli Military Sheds Light On Its Humanitarian Aid To Syrians." Haaretz. February 24, 2014. http://www.haaretz.com/israel-news/.premium-1.575981

[713] Turbeville, Brandon. "Confirmed: Israeli Attack On Syria Air Defense Facility." Activist Post. October 31, 2013. http://www.activistpost.com/2013/10/developing-possible-israeli-attack-on.html#!bwx4VU

[714] Okbi, Yasser. "Reports: Syrian Air Base Destroyed In Missile Attack From Sea." Jerusalem Post. October 31, 2013. http://www.jpost.com/Middle-East/Reports-Syrian-air-base-destroyed-in-missile-attack-from-sea-330232

[715] Gordon, Michael R. "Israel Airstrike Targeted Advanced Missiles That Russia Sold To Syria, U.S. Says."

over into Israeli occupied territory in the Golan Heights. Given the questionable circumstances surrounding the justifying incident – the killing of yet another Israeli teenager by an alleged anti-tank missile – one would be justified in questioning the Israeli story.[716]

While the occasional attack on Syrian territory is bad enough, the fact is that Israel has apparently coordinated these attacks with the death squad directors on the ground so as to provide cover fire and diversions for death squad "swarming" and jihadist invasions.

For instance, in May 2013, WABC host and best-selling author Aaron Klein stated that an Israeli airstrike in Syria was closely coordinated with Turkey which, in turn, helped coordinate the death squad attacks to occur at the exact same time as the Israeli airstrikes. The sources speaking to Klein came from Jordanian and Egyptian intelligence agencies.

Klein wrote,

> Israel's air strike in Syria today was coordinated with Turkey, which in turn coordinated rebel attacks throughout Syria timed to coincide with the Israeli strike, according to Egyptian and Jordanian intelligence sources speaking to KleinOnline. The sources said the rebels did not know about the Israeli strike in advance but instead were given specific instructions for when to begin today's major assaults against the regime of President Bashar al-Assad. "Almost the moment the Israel Air Force departed was the moment the rebel advance began," added the Egyptian intelligence source. Multiple reports have noted how the Syrian rebels consist in large part of al-Qaida-linked jihad groups. The Egyptian and Jordanian sources described how immediately after today's Israeli air strike the jihadist rebels used access roads to advance toward Damascus and began heavy clashes with Syrian military forces throughout the country.[717]

Israel was even documented in 2011 as hosting and directing a terrorist mercenary training camp inside the country in order to produce mercenaries tailor-made to be used in the Arab world.

What's more, the Israeli establishment does not seem to feel the need to hide its support for terrorism which, in this specific instance, tends to take the form of mercenaries. Indeed, the Israeli terrorist trainers actually appear to be quite open about their efforts.[718]

---

[716] "Syria: 4 Killed, 9 Wounded In Israeli Airstrikes." Reuters. June 23, 2014. http://www.foxnews.com/world/2014/06/23/israel-bombs-targets-in-syria-in-response-to-boy-death.html

[717] Klein, Aaron. "Shock Claim: Israeli Airstrike Coordinated With al-Qaeda-Linked Rebels. Jihadists Advance Through Syria Immediately After Today's Bomb Attack." Klein Online. May 5, 2013. http://kleinonline.wnd.com/2013/05/05/shock-claim-israeli-airstrike-coordinated-with-al-qaida-linked-rebels-jihadists-advance-throughout-syria-immediately-after-todays-bomb-attack/

[718] Turbeville, Brandon. "Israel's Undisputed Role In Training Middle East Terrorists." Activist Post. August 13, 2013. http://kleinonline.wnd.com/2013/05/05/shock-claim-israeli-airstrike-coordinated-with-al-qaida-linked-rebels-jihadists-advance-throughout-syria-immediately-after-todays-bomb-attack/

In a 2011 report conducted by The Media Line, an international news organization which focuses on the Middle East, Arieh O'Sullivan was able to film an Israeli-run terrorist mercenary training camp, complete with interviews, on-scene narration, and ample video footage of actual training taking place.[719]

As the report begins, one can see a multicultural group of men –Arabs, Africans, Europeans, etc. – dressed in typical Arab clothing, riding camels, and taking part in tactical training.

"The men on these camels have been training for the past week to operate in the Arab world," O'Sullivan says. "They dress as Arabs, even take a ride on a desert Ferrari [camel] and learn rudimentary phrases that will allow them to do their job. They have come to Israel to learn from former members of the country's secret services."

The report continues by saying,

> On this training base, run by the International Security Academy Israel, they are tapping into Israel's unique experience in dealing with these threats and learning counterterrorism techniques in convoy and [VIP?] protection. The changes in the Middle East may be dubbed the Arab Spring but, to continue with another metaphor, it's about to get hot.

> Out here far away from prying eyes, a group of personal protection specialists have come to Israel to learn about the Israeli tactics. Their background is diverse – from police to military officers – even a former French Legionnaire. They will go on to work for governments and private security contractors.[720]

In an interview with one of the "students," the future mercenary stated, "Only the best can train here with the best. I have this feeling that I was . . . something like was bringing me here . . . something was like 'Go. Go and do it now.'"

Another mercenary who was interviewed, stated, "Well, I learn a lot because Israel have bring up a standard of training that everyone in the world will have to emulate from

---

[719] "Arab & Western Mercenaries Train at an Israeli Security Academy." YouTube. Posted by AnonMI SR. Posted on December 30, 2011. Footage shows report conducted by Media Line. The video description reads: " A report published by the BBC on 26 May 2011, and other news networks, claims that in the post Arab Spring Middle East, Arab youth have been training at a dubious institution called the International Security Academy (ISA), run by ex-Israeli Secret Service Officer Mirza David, and located in Negev Desert (al-Naqab) near Gaza, on the Egyptian-Israeli border, close to where the last border clashes killed three Egyptian Officers in August 2011." The footage shows mercenaries training at an Israeli security facility with narration, interviews, and commentary. https://www.youtube.com/watch?v=P0ZWijzG6qQ

[720] "Arab & Western Mercenaries Train at an Israeli Security Academy." YouTube. Posted by AnonMI SR. Posted on December 30, 2011. Footage shows report conducted by Media Line. The video description reads: " A report published by the BBC on 26 May 2011, and other news networks, claims that in the post Arab Spring Middle East, Arab youth have been training at a dubious institution called the International Security Academy (ISA), run by ex-Israeli Secret Service Officer Mirza David, and located in Negev Desert (al-Naqab) near Gaza, on the Egyptian-Israeli border, close to where the last border clashes killed three Egyptian Officers in August 2011." The footage shows mercenaries training at an Israeli security facility with narration, interviews, and commentary. https://www.youtube.com/watch?v=P0ZWijzG6qQ

them. And, with this, as I'm going back, I think I will take what I have learned in Israel, to impart on my fellow colleagues."

The narrator then adds, "But it's an expensive program, costing upwards of $2,000 Euros a week. But this can be a lucrative profession, earning thousands of Euros a day. Just don't call them mercenaries." Still, O'Sullivan ends by saying, "This line of work is one of the oldest in the world. Still, it seems like it is always in demand."

A mercenary who appeared to be from Singapore, named Venky Raman, also chimed in. "Some of those dictatorships governments have fallen basically. And that's going to create new chaos and confusion in the market. And that's also going to create some instability in the market. So that's why I think we're getting more of these incidents and terrorist attacks and such going to happen."[721]

While the individuals seen in the clip mentioned above are largely mercenaries who train the dupes and deviants who take on the role as cannon fodder for Jihad, only engaging in limited combat operations themselves, it is clear the only allegiance they have is to the almighty dollar.

Ironically, however, the individuals who make up the bulk of death squad invasions across the Arab world – religious fanatics, savages, and the criminally insane – maintain an open hatred for Israel. That is, those death squad members at the bottom who are either ignorant of the fact that Israel itself is a major backer of their own movement or those wholly incapable of understanding anything other than what their faction leader has told them are caught somewhere between tragedy and farce.

Yet Israel is not only involved in directed and implementing Islamic terrorism in other countries. On its own soil, Israel has been documented as creating "fake" al-Qaeda groups to justify its treatment of the Palestinian people.[722]

Israel's arch nemesis, Hamas, was created by Israel itself for the purpose of splitting the PLO (Palestinian Liberation Organization) and Fatah, the leading outfit for the Palestinian freedom and resistance movement.

Robert Dreyfuss, a veteran journalist for The Nation, even wrote that,

> In the decades before 9/11, hard-core activists and organizations among Muslim fundamentalists on the far right were often viewed as allies for two reasons, because they were seen a fierce anti-communists and because the opposed secular nationalists such as Egypt's Gamal Abdel Nasser, Iran's Mohammed Mossadegh.

---

[721] "Arab & Western Mercenaries Train at an Israeli Security Academy." YouTube. Posted by AnonMI SR. Posted on December 30, 2011. Footage shows report conducted by Media Line. The video description reads: " A report published by the BBC on 26 May 2011, and other news networks, claims that in the post Arab Spring Middle East, Arab youth have been training at a dubious institution called the International Security Academy (ISA), run by ex-Israeli Secret Service Officer Mirza David, and located in Negev Desert (al-Naqab) near Gaza, on the Egyptian-Israeli border, close to where the last border clashes killed three Egyptian Officers in August 2011." The footage shows mercenaries training at an Israeli security facility with narration, interviews, and commentary. https://www.youtube.com/watch?v=P0ZWijzG6qQ
[722] "Israel 'faked al-Qaeda presence." BBC. December 8, 2002.
http://news.bbc.co.uk/2/hi/middle_east/2550513.stm

***

In Syria, the United States, Israel, and Jordan supported the Muslim Brotherhood in a civil war against Syria. And … Israel quietly backed Ahmed Yassin and the Muslim Brotherhood in the West Bank and Gaza, leading to the establishment of Hamas.[723]

As Justin Raimondo of AntiWar.com wrote in his 2006 article "Hamas, Son of Israel,"

Amid all the howls of pain and gnashing of teeth over the triumph of Hamas in the Palestinian elections, one fact remains relatively obscure, albeit highly relevant: Israel did much to launch Hamas as an effective force in the occupied territories.[724] If ever there was a clear case of "blowback," then this is it. As Richard Sale pointed out in a piece for UPI:

Israel and Hamas may currently be locked in deadly combat, but, according to several current and former U.S. intelligence officials, beginning in the late 1970s, Tel Aviv gave direct and indirect financial aid to Hamas over a period of years. Israel 'aided Hamas directly – the Israelis wanted to use it as a counterbalance to the PLO (Palestinian Liberation Organization),' said Tony Cordesman, Middle East analyst for the Center for Strategic [and International] Studies.Israel's support for Hamas 'was a direct attempt to divide and dilute support for a strong, secular PLO by using a competing religious alternative,' said a former senior CIA official.[725]

Middle East analyst Ray Hanania concurs:

In addition to hoping to turn the Palestinian masses away from Arafat and the PLO, the Likud leadership believed they could achieve a workable alliance with Islamic, anti-Arafat forces that would also extend Israel's control over the occupied territories.[726]

In a conscious effort to undermine the Palestine Liberation Organization and the leadership of Yasser Arafat, in 1978 the government of then-Prime Minister Menachem Begin approved the application of Sheik Ahmad Yassin to start a "humanitarian" organization known as the Islamic Association, or Mujama. The roots of this Islamist group were in the fundamentalist Muslim Brotherhood, and this was the seed that eventually grew into Hamas – but not before it was amply fertilized and nurtured with Israeli funding and political support.[727]

It is important to note here that the Muslim Brotherhood, in addition to this close connection to the predecessor of Hamas and thus Mossad and other forms of Israeli

---

[723] "Israel and the U.S. CREATED Hamas, Hezbollah and al-Qaeda." Washington's Blog. November 18, 2012. http://www.washingtonsblog.com/2012/11/israel-and-the-u-s-created-hamas-hezbollah-and-other-terrorists-via-blowback.html

[724] Sale, Richard. "Analysis: Hamas History Tied To Israel." UPI. June 18, 2002. http://www.upi.com/Business_News/Security-Industry/2002/06/18/Analysis-Hamas-history-tied-to-Israel/UPI-82721024445587/

[725] Raimondo, Justin. "Hamas, Son of Israel." Antiwar.com. January 28, 2006. http://original.antiwar.com/justin/2006/01/27/hamas-son-of-israel/

[726] Hanania, Ray. "Sharon and Hamas." Counterpunch. January 18, 2003. http://www.counterpunch.org/2003/01/18/sharon-and-hamas/

[727] Raimondo, Justin. "Hamas, Son of Israel." January 28, 2006. Antiwar.com. http://original.antiwar.com/justin/2006/01/27/hamas-son-of-israel/

intelligence, also contains close and historical ties to Western intelligence, most notably the British and the American versions.[728]

With that in mind, Raimondo's article continues by stating that,

> Begin and his successor, Yitzhak Shamir, launched an effort to undercut the PLO, creating the so-called Village Leagues, composed of local councils of handpicked Palestinians who were willing to collaborate with Israel – and, in return, were put on the Israeli payroll. Sheik Yassin and his followers soon became a force within the Village Leagues. This tactical alliance between Yassin and the Israelis was based on a shared antipathy to the militantly secular and leftist PLO: the Israelis allowed Yassin's group to publish a newspaper and set up an extensive network of charitable organizations, which collected funds not only from the Israelis but also from Arab states opposed to Arafat.

> Ami Isseroff, writing on MideastWeb, shows how the Israelis deliberately promoted the Islamists of the future Hamas by helping them turn the Islamic University of Gaza into a base from which the group recruited activists – and the suicide bombers of tomorrow. As the only higher-education facility in the Gaza strip, and the only such institution open to Palestinians since Anwar Sadat closed Egyptian colleges to them, IUG contained within its grounds the seeds of the future Palestinian state.[729] When a conflict arose over religious issues, however, the Israeli authorities sided with the Islamists against the secularists of the Fatah-PLO mainstream. As Isseroff relates, the Islamists encouraged Israeli authorities to dismiss their opponents in the committee in February of 1981, resulting in subsequent Islamisation of IUG policy and staff (including the obligation on women to wear the hijab and thobe and separate entrances for men and women), and enforced by violence and ostracization of dissenters. Tacit complicity from both university and Israeli authorities allowed Mujama to keep a weapons cache to use against secularists. By the mid 1980s, it was the largest university in occupied territories with 4,500 students, and student elections were won handily by Mujama.[730]

> Again, the motive was to offset Arafat's influence and divide the Palestinians. In the short term, this may have worked to some extent; in the longer term, however, it backfired badly – as demonstrated by the results of the recent Palestinian election.

***

> Israel's relentless offensive against its perceived enemies – first Fatah, now Hamas and Islamic Jihad – has created a backlash and solidified support for fundamentalist extremist factions in the Palestinian community.[731]

---

[728] Draitser, Eric. "Unmasking The Muslim Brotherhood: Syria, Egypt, and Beyond." Global Research. December 12, 2012. http://www.globalresearch.ca/unmasking-the-muslim-brotherhood-syria-egypt-and-beyond/5315406

[729] Isseroff, Ami. "A History Of The Hamas Movement: Introduction." Mideastweb.org. http://www.mideastweb.org/hamashistory.htm

[730] Isseroff, Ami. "A History Of The Hamas Movement: Introduction." Mideastweb.org. http://www.mideastweb.org/hamashistory.htm

[731] Raimondo, Justin. "Hamas, Son of Israel." Antiwar.com. January 28, 2006. http://original.antiwar.com/justin/2006/01/27/hamas-son-of-israel/

What Raimondo refers to as "backlash", however, has revealed itself to be more of a cleverly written script designed to play out years later.

Still, The Wall Street Journal concurred with Raimondo's analysis in an article published in 2009. In this article, entitled "How Israel Helped To Spawn Hamas," Andrew Higgins wrote (emphasis added),

> "Hamas, to my great regret, is Israel's creation," says Mr. Cohen, a Tunisian-born Jew who worked in Gaza for more than two decades. Responsible for religious affairs in the region until 1994, Mr. Cohen watched the Islamist movement take shape, muscle aside secular Palestinian rivals and then morph into what is today Hamas, a militant group that is sworn to Israel's destruction.

> Instead of trying to curb Gaza's Islamists from the outset, says Mr. Cohen, Israel for years tolerated and, in some cases, encouraged them as a counterweight to the secular nationalists of the Palestine Liberation Organization and its dominant faction, Yasser Arafat's Fatah. Israel cooperated with a crippled, half-blind cleric named Sheikh Ahmed Yassin, even as he was laying the foundations for what would become Hamas. Sheikh Yassin continues to inspire militants today; during the recent war in Gaza, Hamas fighters confronted Israeli troops with "Yassins," primitive rocket-propelled grenades named in honor of the cleric.

> ***

> When Israel first encountered Islamists in Gaza in the 1970s and '80s, they seemed focused on studying the Quran, not on confrontation with Israel. The Israeli government officially recognized a precursor to Hamas called Mujama Al-Islamiya, registering the group as a charity. It allowed Mujama members to set up an Islamic university and build mosques, clubs and schools. Crucially, Israel often stood aside when the Islamists and their secular left-wing Palestinian rivals battled, sometimes violently, for influence in both Gaza and the West Bank.

> ***

> When it became clear in the early 1990s that Gaza's Islamists had mutated from a religious group into a fighting force aimed at Israel — particularly after they turned to suicide bombings in 1994 — Israel cracked down with ferocious force. But each military assault only increased Hamas's appeal to ordinary Palestinians. The group ultimately trounced secular rivals, notably Fatah, in a 2006 election supported by Israel's main ally, the U.S.

> ***

> In Gaza, Israel hunted down members of Fatah and other secular PLO factions, but it dropped harsh restrictions imposed on Islamic activists by the territory's previous Egyptian rulers.

> ***

> The Muslim Brotherhood, led in Gaza by Sheikh Yassin, was free to spread its message openly. In addition to launching various charity projects, Sheikh Yassin collected money to reprint the writings of Sayyid Qutb, an Egyptian member of the

Brotherhood who, before his execution by President Nasser, advocated global jihad. He is now seen as one of the founding ideologues of militant political Islam.

Mr. Cohen, who worked at the time for the Israeli government's religious affairs department in Gaza, says he began to hear disturbing reports in the mid-1970s about Sheikh Yassin from traditional Islamic clerics. He says they warned that the sheikh had no formal Islamic training and was ultimately more interested in politics than faith. "They said, 'Keep away from Yassin. He is a big danger,'" recalls Mr. Cohen.

Instead, Israel's military-led administration in Gaza looked favorably on the paraplegic cleric, who set up a wide network of schools, clinics, a library and kindergartens. Sheikh Yassin formed the Islamist group Mujama al-Islamiya, which was officially recognized by Israel as a charity and then, in 1979, as an association. Israel also endorsed the establishment of the Islamic University of Gaza, which it now regards as a hotbed of militancy.

***

Gen. Yitzhak Segev, who took over as governor in Gaza in late 1979, says he had no illusions about Sheikh Yassin's long-term intentions or the perils of political Islam. As Israel's former military attache in Iran, he'd watched Islamic fervor topple the Shah. However, in Gaza, says Mr. Segev, "our main enemy was Fatah," and the cleric "was still 100% peaceful" towards Israel. Former officials say Israel was also at the time wary of being viewed as an enemy of Islam.

Mr. Segev says he had regular contact with Sheikh Yassin, in part to keep an eye on him. He visited his mosque and met the cleric around a dozen times. It was illegal at the time for Israelis to meet anyone from the PLO. Mr. Segev later arranged for the cleric to be taken to Israel for hospital treatment. "We had no problems with him," he says.

In fact, the cleric and Israel had a shared enemy: secular Palestinian activists. After a failed attempt in Gaza to oust secularists from leadership of the Palestinian Red Crescent, the Muslim version of the Red Cross, Mujama staged a violent demonstration, storming the Red Crescent building. Islamists also attacked shops selling liquor and cinemas. The Israeli military mostly stood on the sidelines.

***

A leader of Birzeit's Islamist faction at the time was Mahmoud Musleh, now a pro-Hamas member of a Palestinian legislature elected in 2006. He recalls how usually aggressive Israeli security forces stood back and let conflagration develop. He denies any collusion between his own camp and the Israelis, but says "they hoped we would become an alternative to the PLO."

A year later, in 1984, the Israeli military received a tip-off from Fatah supporters that Sheikh Yassin's Gaza Islamists were collecting arms, according to Israeli officials in Gaza at the time. Israeli troops raided a mosque and found a cache of weapons. Sheikh Yassin was jailed. He told Israeli interrogators the weapons were for use against rival Palestinians, not Israel, according to Mr. Hacham, the military affairs expert who says he spoke frequently with jailed Islamists. The cleric was released after a year and continued to expand Mujama's reach across Gaza.[732]

---

[732] Higgins, Andrew. "How Israel Helped To Spawn Hamas." The Wall Street Journal. January 24,

Taking into consideration the fact that Israel has provided military and medical support to the most bloodthirsty and brutal Islamic extremist terrorists in the world and the fact that it has created Hamas from the very beginning, the answer to the question of "Why aren't organizations like Nusra, al-Qaeda, and ISIS attacking Israel?" is quite simple – because Israel is partly responsible for funding and directing them.

With all of this in mind, any claims of victimhood by Israel should immediately be discarded. Indeed, this portrayal of self-defense and endangerment should especially be discarded when one considers the history of the state itself.

Israel has made its own enemies by virtue of its colonial nature, its foreign and domestic policy, and even by direct organization and funding. It is thus wholly accurate to say that Israel's enemies are literally those of its own making.

In the end, the information presented in this article is simply one more window into the realm of the Anglo-European-American-Israeli intelligence apparatus and the depths to which the rabbit hole goes in terms of international terrorism. The script which is being acted out across the Middle East and the rest of the world is clearly being directed by a force unseen by the vast majority of the world's population.

Still, the players act out their roles according to the predetermined narrative provided to them, despite the fact that they have no idea they are actually acting out the will of a shadowy "other" who does not have their best interests at heart.

In this game, virtually all of those acting out their parts on the ground are merely players unaware of their roles.

The fact that Anglo-American powers have acted as directors of the death squads in terms of organization, funding, training, and supply has been known for some time. I, myself, have written several articles on this topic as well as on the fact that the intent to organize death squads to destabilize Syrian on behalf of the Anglo-American powers was known to exist at least as far back as 2005.[733]

The Israeli desire to destroy Syria has also been readily apparent through the numerous attempts by the Mad Dog of the Middle East to encourage bombing, military action, and outright invasion of Syria whenever the opportunity to ride the coattails of some engineered propaganda blitz presents itself.[734] Indeed, Israel, always ready to fight to the last American, continually promotes and threatens to engage in unilateral military assaults against any number of its neighbors or other regional nations, even approving the direct bombing of Syrian targets on more than one occasion.[735]

2009. http://www.wsj.com/news/articles/SB123275572295011847?mg=reno64-wsj&url=http%3A%2F%2Fonline.wsj.com%2Farticle%2FSB123275572295011847.html

[733] Turbeville, Brandon. "Globalist Hidden Hand Revealed in Destabilization of Syria." Activist Post. April 8, 2013

[734] "Act of War: Israel Attacks Syrian Weapons Depot Containing Advanced Russian Arms." Global Research. July 15, 2013.http://www.globalresearch.ca/act-of-war-israel-attacks-syrian-weapons-depot-containing-advanced-russian-arms/5341940

[735] "Israel Airstrike Targeted Advanced Missiles That Russia Sold To Syria, U.S. Says." New York Times. July 13, 2013.http://www.nytimes.com/2013/07/14/world/middleeast/israel-airstrike-targeted-advanced-missiles-that-russia-sold-to-syria-us-says.html?_r=0

Yet, in addition to such brazen warmongering and rogue behavior, Israel has also become instrumental in the funding and facilitation of death squad terrorists in both Syria and the rest of the Arab world.

What's more, the Israeli establishment does not seem to feel the need to hide its support for terrorism which, in this specific instance, tends to take the form of mercenaries. Indeed, the Israeli terrorist trainers actually appear to be quite open about their efforts.

For instance, in a 2011 report conducted by The Media Line, an international news organization which focuses on the Middle East, Arieh O'Sullivan was able to film an Israeli-run terrorist mercenary training camp, complete with interviews, on-scene narration, and ample video footage of actual training taking place.[736]

As the report begins, one can see a multicultural group of men –Arabs, Africans, Europeans, etc. – dressed in typical Arab clothing, riding camels, and taking part in tactical training.

"The men on these camels have been training for the past week to operate in the Arab world," O'Sullivan says. "They dress as Arabs, even take a ride on a desert Ferrari [camel] and learn rudimentary phrases that will allow them to do their job. They have come to Israel to learn from former members of the country's secret services."

The report continues by saying,

On this training base, run by the International Security Academy Israel, they are tapping into Israel's unique experience in dealing with these threats and learning counterterrorism techniques in convoy and [VIP?] protection. The changes in the Middle East may be dubbed the Arab Spring but, to continue with another metaphor, it's about to get hot.

Out here far away from prying eyes, a group of personal protection specialists have come to Israel to learn about the Israeli tactics. Their background is diverse – from police to military officers – even a former French Legionnaire. They will go on to work for governments and private security contractors.[737]

In an interview with one of the "students," the future mercenary stated, "Only the best can train here with the best. I have this feeling that I was . . . something like was bringing me here . . . something was like 'Go. Go and do it now.'"[738]

---

[736] "Arab & Western Mercenaries Train at an Israeli Security Academy." YouTube. Posted by AnonMI SR. Posted on December 30, 2011. https://www.youtube.com/watch?v=P0ZWijzG6qQ
[737] "Arab & Western Mercenaries Train at an Israeli Security Academy." YouTube. Posted by AnonMI SR. Posted on December 30, 2011. Footage shows report conducted by Media Line. The video description reads: " A report published by the BBC on 26 May 2011, and other news networks, claims that in the post Arab Spring Middle East, Arab youth have been training at a dubious institution called the International Security Academy (ISA), run by ex-Israeli Secret Service Officer Mirza David, and located in Negev Desert (al-Naqab) near Gaza, on the Egyptian-Israeli border, close to where the last border clashes killed three Egyptian Officers in August 2011." The footage shows mercenaries training at an Israeli security facility with narration, interviews, and commentary. https://www.youtube.com/watch?v=P0ZWijzG6qQ
[738] "Arab & Western Mercenaries Train at an Israeli Security Academy." YouTube. Posted by

Another mercenary who was interviewed, stated, "Well, I learn a lot because Israel have bring up a standard of training that everyone in the world will have to emulate from them. And, with this, as I'm going back, I think I will take what I have learned in Israel, to impart on my fellow colleagues."

The narrator then adds, "But it's an expensive program, costing upwards of $2,000 Euros a week. But this can be a lucrative profession, earning thousands of Euros a day. Just don't call them mercenaries." Still, O'Sullivan ends by saying, "This line of work is one of the oldest in the world. Still, it seems like it is always in demand."

A mercenary who appeared to be from Singapore, named Venky Raman, also chimed in. "Some of those dictatorships governments have fallen basically. And that's going to create new chaos and confusion in the market. And that's also going to create some instability in the market. So that's why I think we're getting more of these incidents and terrorist attacks and such going to happen."

While the individuals seen in the clip mentioned above are largely mercenaries who themselves either train the dupes and deviants who take on the role as cannon fodder for Jihad, only engaging in limited combat operations, it is clear the only allegiance they have is to the almighty dollar.

Ironically, however, the individuals who make up the bulk of death squad invasions across the Arab world – religious fanatics, savages, and the criminally insane – maintain an open hatred for Israel. That is, those death squad members at the bottom who are either ignorant of the fact that Israel itself is a major backer of their own movement or those wholly incapable of understanding anything other than what their faction leader has told them are caught somewhere between tragedy and farce.

In the end, the Syrian people are the real victims. But even the death squad members, with fantastic dreams of a caliphate, Sharia law, and fanatical paradise, are nothing more than victims of a much bigger agenda, as Israel and the West laugh all the way to the bank.

The UN Report And Israel's Connections To Terrorists In Syria

Ever since the Western-backed attack on the secular government of Bashar al-Assad began in earnest in late 2010, Israel had been clearly implicated in providing assistance to the fundamentalist death squad organizations running rampant across Syria. This aid

---

AnonMI SR. Posted on December 30, 2011. Footage shows report conducted by Media Line. The video description reads: " A report published by the BBC on 26 May 2011, and other news networks, claims that in the post Arab Spring Middle East, Arab youth have been training at a dubious institution called the International Security Academy (ISA), run by ex-Israeli Secret Service Officer Mirza David, and located in Negev Desert (al-Naqab) near Gaza, on the Egyptian-Israeli border, close to where the last border clashes killed three Egyptian Officers in August 2011." The footage shows mercenaries training at an Israeli security facility with narration, interviews, and commentary. https://www.youtube.com/watch?v=P0ZWijzG6qQ

was provided despite an alleged mutual hatred between the Zionist settler state and Islamic fundamentalists.

As the crisis continued to unfold, Israel's connections to the terrorists (backed by NATO and the GCC) began to grow more and more apparent.

Now, a series of reports (March 2013 – November 2014) released by the United Nations observers in the Golan Heights and submitted to the United Nations Security Council apparently corroborates those connections. Indeed, the reports claim that, at least for the past 18 months, the Israel Defense Forces have been in regular contact with "Syrian rebels," including members of the Islamic State.[739]

According to Israeli news agency Haaretz, the UN reports detailed several instances where close ties between the Syrian death squads and the Israeli military have been demonstrated.[740]

As the International Business Times writes,

> According to the UN reports, a person wounded on 15 September "was taken by armed members of the opposition across the ceasefire line, where he was transferred to a civilian ambulance escorted by an IDF vehicle."

> Moreover, from 9-19 November, the "UNDOF observed at least 10 wounded persons being transferred by armed members of the opposition from the Bravo side across the ceasefire line to IDF.

> As per the details released by the Israel's health ministry, so far some 1,000 Syrians have been treated in four Israeli hospitals. Besides the civilians, some are members of the secular Free Syrian Army rebel group. [741]

Although initially claiming that it only treated civilians, Israel was forced to walk back from those claims somewhat after the release of the UN report. When asked by i24news whether or not Israel had treated members of ISIS or al-Nusra, an Israeli spokesman stated "In the past two years the Israel Defence Forces have been engaged in humanitarian, life-saving aid to wounded Syrians, irrespective of their identity."[742]

---

[739] UNDOF: United Nations Disengagement Observer Force. Reports Of The Secretary General. UN.org. March 2013-November 2014.
http://www.un.org/en/peacekeeping/missions/undof/reports.shtml

[740] Ravid, Barak. "UN Reveals Israeli Links With Syrian Rebels: Reports By UN Observers In The Golan Submitted To 15 Members Of Security Council Detail Regular Contact Between IDF Officers And Armed Syrian Opposition Figures At Border." Haaretz. December 7, 2014.
http://www.haaretz.com/news/diplomacy-defense/.premium-1.630359?v=4AC46632C7C0D296D80E936AFCEA3D59

[741] Varghese, Johnlee. "UN Reports: Israel In Regular Contact With Syrian Rebels Including ISIS." International Business Times. December 7, 2014. http://www.ibtimes.co.in/un-report-israel-regular-contact-syrian-rebels-including-isis-616404#IQyaLMvSFEH7vgKw.97

[742] Ahronheim, Annie. "Regular Contact Between Israel And Syrian Rebels: UN Report." I24 News. December 7, 2014. http://www.i24news.tv/en/news/international/middle-east/53651-141207-regular-contact-between-israel-and-syrian-rebels-un-report

Of course, the assistance provided by Israel to the death squads was not isolated to mere medical treatment according to the report. As Haaretz reports,

> Observers remarked in the report distributed on June 10 that they identified IDF soldiers on the Israeli side handing over two boxes to armed Syrian opposition members on the Syrian side.

> The last report distributed to Security Council members, on December 1, described another meeting between IDF soldiers and Syrian opposition members that two UN representatives witnessed on October 27 some three kilometers east of Moshav Yonatan. The observers said they saw two IDF soldiers on the eastern side of the border fence opening the gate and letting two people enter Israel. The report, contrary to previous ones, did not note that the two exiting Syria were injured or why they entered Israel.

> This specific event is of particular interest in light of what happened on the Syrian side of the border in the exact same region. According to the report, UN observers stated that tents were set up about 300 meters from the Israeli position for some 70 families of Syrian deserters. The Syrian army sent a letter of complaint to UNDOF in September, claiming this tent camp was a base for "armed terrorists" crossing the border into Israel.[743]

Of course, it has been well known for quite some time that Israel has been providing wounded Syrian rebels with medical treatment inside Israel so that they can continue the Jihad against the secular government of Bashar al-Assad.[744] According to Colum Lynch of The Cable (the news wing of the Council on Foreign Relations Foreign Policy),

> In the past three months [April-June 2014], battle-hardened Syrian rebels have transported scores of wounded Syrians across a cease-fire line that has separated Israel from Syria since 1974, according to a 15-page report by U.N. Secretary-General Ban Ki-moon on the work of the U.N. Disengagement Observer Force (UNDOF).[745] Once in Israel, they receive medical treatment in a field clinic before being sent back to Syria, where, presumably, some will return to carry on the fight.

> U.N. blue helmets responsible for monitoring the decades-old cease-fire report observing armed opposition groups "transferring 89 wounded persons" from Syrian territory into Israel, where they were received by members of the Israel Defense Forces, according to the report. The IDF returned 21 Syrians to armed opposition members back in Syria, including the bodies of two who died.[746]

---

[743] Ravid, Barak. "UN Reveals Israeli Links With Syrian Rebels: Reports By UN Observers In The Golan Submitted To 15 Members Of Security Council Detail Regular Contact Between IDF Officers And Armed Syrian Opposition Figures At Border." Haaretz. December 7, 2014. http://www.haaretz.com/news/diplomacy-defense/.premium-1.630359?v=4AC46632C7C0D296D80E936AFCEA3D59

[744] Turbeville, Brandon. "Why Aren't ISIS And Al-Qaeda Attacking Israel?" Activist Post. August 7, 2014. http://www.activistpost.com/2014/08/why-arent-isis-and-al-qaeda-attacking.html

[745] "Supervising Ceasefire And Disengagement Agreement. United Nations Disengagement Observer Force. http://www.un.org/en/peacekeeping/missions/undof/

[746] Lynch, Colum. "Exclusive: Israel Is Tending To Wounded Syrian Rebels." The Cable (Foreign Policy). June 11, 2014. http://foreignpolicy.com/2014/06/11/exclusive-israel-is-tending-to-wounded-syrian-rebels/

Later in the article, the writer mentions the fact that Israel has provided such medical assistance to Syrian rebels since at least as far back as February 2014. Realistically, however, such assistance was being provided even further back. Lynch writes that Israel provided the medical treatment for at least a year even at the time of the writing of his article, i.e. as far back as at least June 2013.

Even more telling is that, in February, 2014, Prime Minister Benjamin Netanyahu actually visited one of the medical facilities in which the Syrian rebels were being treated and even posed for a photo op shaking hands with a death squad fighter.[747]

While the connections between Israel and Islamic terrorism, particularly the terrorists wreaking havoc across Syria, is by no means a new revelation, it is becoming much harder for the settler state to hide its complicity as well as its direct involvement in the funding, directing, arming, training, and control of terrorism across the Middle East including such terrorism within its own borders.[748] [749]

The New Ulster: The Nature And Purpose Of The State Of Israel

Since the inception of the Israeli state and its official formalization in 1948, Israel has baffled the world with its seeming irrational aggression, hypocrisy, brutality, and willingness to entirely ignore international law. Indeed, Israel is well-known for thumbing its nose at even the basic etiquette for international relations.

Israel's sordid history – that of its connections to mega-rich banking families like the Rothschilds, racism, double-edged alliances, and genocide – has caused it to, therefore, be the target of many researchers and activists that see it as the sole source of evil upon the earth. Zionist Christians (mostly those in the West), have generally pledged religious allegiance to Israel under the pretext of supporting "God's Chosen People" and Biblical prophecy. Still others pretend that Israel is the absolute pinnacle of the power structure and condemn Jews as responsible for all the horrors of the world.

Of course, none of these representations are accurate.

Yet, with virtually the entire Middle East erupting in flames, it is important to understand the purpose of the Israeli state as well as the reasons for its seeming irrationality and unmitigated aggression against its immediate and regional neighbors.

In his article entitled, "Beware: Israel the Eager Provocateur," Tony Cartalucci, points out that Israel "is a stunted, militaristic faux-state that depends entirely on the West for its continued existence." Cartalucci also accurately describes Israel as a "Forward Operating Base" for a greater power above it.[750]

---

[747] Cohen, Gili. "Israeli Military Sheds Light On Its Humanitarian Aid To Syrians." Haaretz. February 24, 2014. http://www.haaretz.com/israel-news/.premium-1.575981

[748] Turbeville, Brandon. "The New Ulster: The Nature And Purpose Of The State Of Israel." Activist Post. August 18, 2014. http://www.activistpost.com/2014/08/the-new-ulster-nature-and-purpose-of.html

[749] Turbeville, Brandon. "Why Aren't ISIS And al-Qaeda Attacking Israel?" Activist Post. August 7, 2014. http://www.activistpost.com/2014/08/why-arent-isis-and-al-qaeda-attacking.html

Cartalucci writes,

> As such, Israel's constant and otherwise irrational belligerence makes perfect sense. An FOB's priorities are not prosperity and peace as would a nation's, but rather to engage forward into enemy territory. The trick over the years has been to portray Israel as a nation, while propping up its constant belligerence and aggression as "self-defense." To keep this illusion in motion, Israel and its regional and Western collaborators have even created full-time enemies, including Hamas itself - a creation of Israeli intelligence and to this day primarily propped up by Saudi Arabia and Qatar, both of which are defacto regional partners with the West and of course Israel itself.[751]

While a Forward Operating Base (FOB) is one way to describe Israel, it is also much more than simply a territorial staging ground for Western imperialist motives. It is, in fact, a carefully constructed destabilization organ that was planned an implemented long ago for the purpose of dividing and conquering the entire Middle East as well as for the purpose of fostering and initiating a global military confrontation between major world powers and the world's three major religions – Judaism, Islam, and Christianity.

As Conn Hallinan wrote for Foreign Policy In Focus, "When British Foreign Secretary Arthur James Balfour issued his famous 1917 Declaration guaranteeing a "homeland" for the Jewish people in Palestine, he was less concerned with righting a two thousand year old wrong than creating divisions that would serve growing British interests in the Middle East."[752]

Indeed, the righting of an alleged two-thousand-year-old wrong was not even a consideration among the British aristocrats, bankers, and the equivalent parties of other governments and institutions. This mythical righting of a wrong was merely a cover story provided to the public for propaganda purposes. This propaganda was aimed particularly at those of religious backgrounds.

It is important to note, of course, that the narrative being provided by the architects of Israel were entirely new to these religions and that it was not a philosophy that was adhered to or acknowledged in any of these faiths, at least not in the way it was presented.[753]

For instance, Sir Ronald Storrs, the first governor of Jerusalem for the British Empire wrote in his memoirs in 1937 that Israel and the mythical "Jewish Homeland" would be nothing more than a pit of destabilization. Storrs stated that "Even though the land could not yet absorb sixteen millions, nor even eight, enough could return, if not to form The Jewish State (which a few extremists publicly demanded), at least to prove that the enterprise was one that blessed him that gave as well as him that took by forming for England "a little Jewish Ulster" in a sea of potentially hostile Arabism."[754]

---

[750] Cartalucci, Tony. "Beware: Israel The Eager Provocateur." Land Destroyer. August 8, 2014. http://landdestroyer.blogspot.com/2014/08/beware-israel-eager-provocateur.html

[751] Cartalucci, Tony. "Beware: Israel The Eager Provocateur." Land Destroyer. August 8, 2014. http://landdestroyer.blogspot.com/2014/08/beware-israel-eager-provocateur.html

[752] Hallinan, Conn. "Divide And Conquer As Imperial Rules." Foreign Policy In Focus. October, 1, 2005. http://fpif.org/divide_and_conquer_as_imperial_rules/

[753] Sizer, Rev. Dr. Stephen. "Christian Zionism: The Heresy That Undermines Middle East Peace." Information Clearing House. http://www.informationclearinghouse.info/article35747.htm

Ulster, of course, was the original Israel.

Ulster was a place in Northern Ireland where, in 1609, the English King Charles I concocted a plan (presumably not on his own) to further weaken the Irish by the tried and true "divide and conquer" mechanism. He marched forward with this plan by removing the O'Donnell and O'Neill clans from the area and moving in around 20,000 Scottish and English Protestants and forming the plantation of Ulster in overwhelmingly Catholic Ireland.

Because of the structure of Ulster, religious tension became inflamed. Division between religious denominations and sects became the order of the day, while the true enemy – Britain – took a back seat in the minds of those squabbling over religious differences and those who received preferential beggar status compared to those who did not.

Ulster was essentially divided into two societies - the Protestants who were "first class" and the native Catholics who were considered and treated as "second class." The class difference was, of course, sanctioned and enforced by the Crown. Although, after a bit of time, native Irish Catholics were allowed to enter Ulster for purposes of working the land, their presence was entirely labor-based.

Protestants were also granted the "Ulster Privilege," which afforded them special access to land and lower rent. Ulster Privilege, incidentally, was a concept that was quite similar to the Israeli/Palestinian arrangement today.

In Ireland, resentment between the religious groups could not help but arise as the result of the mandated social structure in Ulster and that, of course, is precisely what happened.

Finally, the religious divisions that resulted from the establishment of Ulster were codified into law with the enactment of the Penal Laws of 1692. These laws denied Catholics any civil rights, removed their ability to sign contracts, become lawyers, or hire more than two apprentices. It is also important to note that the laws were extended to Protestants who intermarried with Catholics.

"In essence," Hallinan writes, "they insured that Catholics would remain poor, powerless, and locked out of the modern world." These laws had reverberations that are still being felt in Ireland today.

Even Edmund Burke once commented that the laws were "A machine of wide and elaborate contrivance and as well fitted for the oppression, impoverishment and degradation of a people as ever proceeded from the perverted ingenuity of man."

Nevertheless, once the British implemented the plan of religious tension and division, it was only a matter of time before the nation of Ireland was subdued and the conquest of the country was solidified. It was a tactic that the British would use successfully throughout its empire across the world.

Of course, these laws, as well as a number of other mandates and societal practices are themselves very similar to the current mechanics of Israel. As Conn Hallinan writes,

---

[754] Storrs, Sir Ronald. The Memoirs of Sir Ronald Storrs. GP Putnam's Sons. New York. 1937. P. 364. https://archive.org/stream/memoirsofsirrona001290mbp#page/n7/mode/2up

It would appear the Israelis have paid close attention to English colonial policy because their policies in the Occupied Territories bear a distressing resemblance to Ireland under the Penal Laws.

The Israeli Knesset recently prevented Palestinians married to Arab Israelis from acquiring citizenship, a page lifted almost directly from the 1692 laws. Israeli human rights activist Yael Stein called the action "racist," and Knesset member Zeeva Galon said it denied "the fundamental right of Arab Israelis to start families." Even the U.S. is uncomfortable with the legislation. "The new law," said U.S. State Department spokesman Phillip Reeker, "singles out one group for different treatment than others."

Which, of course, was the whole point.

[...]

As the penal laws impoverished the Irish, so do Israeli policies impoverish the Palestinians and keep them an underdeveloped pool of cheap labor. According to the United Nations, unemployment in the West Bank and Gaza is over 50 percent, and Palestinians are among the poorest people on the planet.

Any efforts by the Palestinians to build their own independent economic base are smothered by a network of walls, settler-exclusive roads and checkpoints. It is little different than British imperial policy in India, which systematically dismantled the Indian textile industry so that English cloth could clothe the sub-continent without competition.

Divide and conquer was 19th and early 20th century colonialism's single most successful tactic of domination. It was also a disaster, one which still echoes in civil wars and regional tensions across the globe. This latter lesson does not appear to be one the Israelis have paid much attention to. As a system of rule, division and privilege may work in the short run, but over time it engenders nothing but hatred.[755]

Hallinan is correct to draw such parallels between Ulster and Israel. However, it is incorrect to assert that the Israelis have not paid attention to the fact that "divide and rule" is a strategy that ends in civil and sometimes regional wars. This, unfortunately, is the goal of Israel's existence.

In the end, and with all of this in mind, the purpose and nature of the settler state of Israel is more easily understood. Simply put, Zionism is not the center of the conspiratorial spider web; it is just another strand of it.

The sole purpose of Israel is not to create a "Jewish" state, but to create a "Jewish" Ulster for the purposes of dividing Christians, Muslims, and Jews against one another and creating a center of constant tension in the Middle East.

By enacting its own reign of terror against Palestinians, controlling and directing fanatical Muslim extremist groups throughout the Middle East, conning Western Christians into supporting military action in the Middle East under the guise of "protecting Israel against its hostile enemies," and, all the while, doing so under the

---

[755] Hallinan, Conn. "Divide And Conquer As Imperial Rules." Foreign Policy In Focus. October, 1, 2005. http://fpif.org/divide_and_conquer_as_imperial_rules/

cover of a "Jewish" state, Israel stands as the greatest destabilizing force in the entire Middle East.

Saudi Arabia

As ISIS marches across the sands of Iraq, the vast majority of Americans are no doubt convinced yet again that what amounts to a coordinated fighting army is merely the product of bearded fanatics hiding in caves hating America "for its freedoms."

Although the overwhelming majority of the American public will never look any closer than a variant of the cleverly crafted description provided above, those that do pay some modicum of attention to current events will discover that, according to the mainstream media and Western governments, the leader of ISIS is none other than Abdullah al-Rashid al-Baghdadi, the alleged creator of al-Qaeda in Iraq.

However, upon further study, it is revealed that the true leader is not Baghdadi at all. Indeed, the leader is not even an Iraqi.

The commander of ISIS is none other than Saudi Prince Abdul Rachman al-Faisal, the brother of Prince Saud al-Faisal and Prince Turki al-Faisal.

Of course, information regarding Faisal's control over ISIS has been known for some time, yet the Western media has conveniently neglected to report on it.

In a 2007 article published by Reuters entitled "Senior Qaeda Figure In Iraq A Myth: U.S. Military," Dean Yates writes that a senior al-Qaeda operative informed U.S. Military interrogators that the Islamic State of Iraq was nothing more than a front for another organization and that its leader, Abdullah al-Rashid al-Baghdadi was himself a fictional person.[756]

In fact, Brigadier General Kevin Bergner told a news conference that Baghdadi did not exist and that "he" was merely an attempt to put an Iraqi face on what was a "foreign-driven network.

Bergner stated that "In his [Khalid al-Mashadani – the captured al-Qaeda fighter] words, the Islamic State of Iraq is a front organization that masks the foreign influence and leadership within al Qaeda in Iraq in an attempt to put an Iraqi face on the leadership of al Qaeda in Iraq."

Bergner further stated that Mashadani informed the U.S. Military that the fictional leader Baghdadi was played by an actor whenever his character surfaced on the Internet.

Yet, while Mashadani confessed that Baghdadi was indeed a fictional character, very little was revealed regarding the true leader of the group, at least nothing that was reported by Reuters.

However, while this may lead many to believe that Mashadani and his Egyptian colleague Abu Ayyab al-Masri were the masterminds behind al-Qaeda in Iraq or the Islamic State of Iraq (ISIS), the rabbit hole goes somewhat deeper.

---

[756] Yates, Dean. "Senior Qaeda Figure In Iraq A Myth: U.S. Military." Reuters. July 18, 2007. http://www.reuters.com/article/us-iraq-qaeda-idUSL1820065720070718?rpc=92

Still, Baghdadi does apparently have some real history pointing to the fact that, at least at some point, he may have truly existed. As Voltaire Net has reported,

> Abu Bakr al-Baghdadi is an Iraqi who joined Al-Qaeda to fight against President Saddam Hussein. During the U.S. invasion, he distinguished himself by engaging in several actions against Shiites and Christians (including the taking of the Baghdad Cathedral) and by ushering in an Islamist reign of terror (he presided over an Islamic court which sentenced many Iraqis to be slaughtered in public). After the departure of Paul Bremer III, al-Baghdadi was arrested and incarcerated at Camp Bucca from 2005 to 2009. This period saw the dissolution of *Al-Qaeda in Iraq*, whose fighters merged into a group of tribal resistance, the Islamic Emirate of Iraq.

> On 16 May 2010, Abu Bakr al-Baghdadi was named emir of the IEI, which was in the process of disintegration. After the departure of U.S. troops, he staged operations against the government al-Maliki, accused of being at the service of Iran. In 2013, after vowing allegiance to Al-Qaeda, he took off with his group to continue the jihad in Syria, rebaptizing it Islamic *Emirate of Iraq and the Levant*. In doing so, he challenged the privileges that Ayman al-Zawahiri had previously granted, on behalf of Al-Qaeda, to the Al-Nusra Front in Syria, which was originally nothing more than an extension of the IEI.[757]

Of course, all of the information above could indeed be nothing more than information dreamed up and served to a gullible public for the purposes of a propaganda narrative as well as the creation of a leader for prospective members of ISIS.

Regardless, false assumptions surrounding the true leadership of ISIS would be called into question in January of 2014 when Al-Arabiya, a Saudi-owned and operated news agency, published an article as well as a video of an interrogation of an ISIS fighter who had been captured while operating inside Syria.[758]

When asked why ISIS was following the movement of the Free Syrian Army and who had given him the orders to do so, the fighter stated that he did not know why he was ordered to monitor the FSA's movement but that the orders had come from Abu Faisal, also known as Prince Abdul Rachman al-Faisal of the Saudi Royal Family.

An excerpt from the relevant section of the interrogation reads as follows:

> Interrogator: Why do you (ISIS) monitor the movement of the Free Syrian Army?

> ISIS Detainee: I don't know exactly why but we received orders from ISIS command.

> Interrogator: Who among ISIS gave the orders?

> ISIS Detainee: Prince Abdul Rachman al-Faisal, who is also known as Abu Faisal.[759]

---

[757] "Iraq Under Attack By US, France, Saudi Arabia." Voltaire Network. June 11, 2014. http://webcache.googleusercontent.com/search?q=cache:http://www.voltairenet.org/article18 4211.html

[758] "Islamic State Of Iraq And The Levant Led By Prince Abdul Rahman." Voltaire Network. February 4, 2014. http://webcache.googleusercontent.com/search?q=cache:http://www.voltairenet.org/article18 2036.html

[759] Lehmann, Christof. "ISIS Unveiled: The Identity Of The Insurgency In Iraq and Syria." NSNBC

Such revelations, of course, will only be shocking news to those who have been unaware of the levels to which the Saudis have been involved with the funding, training, and directing of death squad forces deployed in Syria.[760] [761] [762] Indeed, the Saudis have even openly admitted to the Russian government that they do, in fact, a number of varied terrorist organizations across the world.[763]

Even tired mainstream media organizations such as Newsweek (aka The Daily Beast) can no longer ignore the facts surrounding the Saudis' involvement with the organization of terrorist groups across the world.[764]

Clearly, the American public would do well to ignore the typically peddled stories handfed to them by the American corporate media outlets. The narratives suggesting that terrorism is made up of cave-dwelling religious lunatics is not simply insufficient to explain current developments, it is inaccurate and entirely misleading.

With the close relationship held between the United States and Saudi Arabia, if the U.S. wishes to stop the spread of terrorism in Iraq, it will immediately demand that the Saudis cease funding it.

Unfortunately, however, for a number of reasons, such a request is not likely to happen.

International. June 15, 2014. http://nsnbc.me/2014/06/15/isis-unveiled-identity-insurgency-syria-iraq/

[760] Nimmo, Kurt; Jones, Alex. " Saudi Arabia, Sunni Caliphate, NATO Run Secret Terror Army In Iraq and Syria." Infowars. June 13, 2014. http://www.infowars.com/saudi-arabia-sunni-caliphate-nato-run-secret-terror-army-in-iraq-and-syria/

[761] Black, Ian. "Syria Crisis: Saudi Arabia To Spend Millions To Train New Rebel Force." The Guardian. November 7, 2013. https://www.theguardian.com/world/2013/nov/07/syria-crisis-saudi-arabia-spend-millions-new-rebel-force

[762] Cartalucci, Tony. "NATO's Terror Hordes In Iraq A Pretext For Syria Invasion." New Eastern Outlook. June 13, 2014. http://journal-neo.org/2014/06/13/nato-s-terror-hordes-in-iraq-a-pretext-for-syria-invasion/

[763] Evans-Pritchard, Ambrose. "Saudis Offer Russia Secret Oil Deal If It Drops Syria." The Telegraph. August 27, 2013. http://www.telegraph.co.uk/finance/newsbysector/energy/oilandgas/10266957/Saudis-offer-Russia-secret-oil-deal-if-it-drops-Syria.html

[764] Rogin, Josh. "America's Allies Are Funding ISIS." The Daily Beast. June 14, 2014. http://www.thedailybeast.com/articles/2014/06/14/america-s-allies-are-funding-isis.html

Chapter VII: Back To The Beginning
The Beginning

In late 2010, the first expressions of what would come to be called the Arab Spring began manifesting themselves on the ground in the Arab world, very quickly becoming regular images on Western television sets. Allegedly beginning shortly after a local merchant attempted to immolate himself in a dispute with police and other authorities in Tunisia, demonstrations, protests, riots, and eventually open violence began to take shape in Tunisia and rapidly spread across the Middle East and Africa.[765] One by one, Arab nations found themselves embroiled in widespread protests and violent clashes between demonstrators and police thus initiating a circle of violence spurned by an intensified crackdown by authorities and thus an intensified violence of the protestors.

As national governments began to topple one by one, however, many demonstrators legitimately desiring greater freedom and better government began to realize that they had been played like fiddles. They had functioned as cannon fodder for a cause but, unbeknownst to them, it was a cause that was not their own. After the tyrants they so despised had been deposed in Tunisia and Egypt, the people of those countries and the participants in those movements woke up to find that an even greater tyranny had replaced what they worked so hard to overthrow. They found that military juntas now replaced what was once at least the appearance of a civilian government, sectarians and Islamists replaced what was once a secular (if embattled)government, and that the new boss was much the same as the old boss. In these cases, however, the new boss was much more willing to initiate violent crackdowns to maintain power and to implement drastic austerity measures to placate the IMF, the World Bank, and the international banking cartels and their representatives that had brought these new leaders to power.[766]

Yet, as the Arab Spring wore on, the veneer of organic social demonstrations grew thinner and thinner until it disappeared entirely in Libya and the open Western-backed nature of the insurrection became apparent. There were no longer massive protests and hoards of mindless youth confronting a government all too willing to dish out repressive responses. Instead, the Libyan situation was never a protest; it was an invasion and insurrection – violent from the word "go" – and intent on the destruction of both Libya as a power and Ghaddaffi as a symbol of Arab nationalism and African defiance.

When the "Arab Spring" rolled around to Syria, anyone capable of exercising even a modicum of analytical observation was aware that the disruption in that country was nothing more than Western agitation, a destabilization effort organized, funded, trained, and directed by the traditional Anglo-American NATO powers – the United States,

---

[765] Fahim, Kareem. "Slap to a Man's Pride Set Off Tumult in Tunisia." New York Times. January 21, 2011.
http://www.nytimes.com/2011/01/22/world/africa/22sidi.html?pagewanted=all&_r=0
Accessed on July 9, 2013.

[766] Ahmed, Nafeez. "Egypt's new age of unrest is a taste of things to come." The Guardian. July 4, 2013. http://www.guardian.co.uk/environment/earth-insight/2013/jul/04/egypt-muslim-brotherhood-morsi-unrest-protests   Accessed on July 9, 2013.

Britain, and France as well as the rest of the gaggle of European nations. Like Libya, the Syrian "spring" was violent from the very beginning, with death squad assassins aiming their sniper rifles not only at security personnel but at women and children simply trying to go to and from work, school, or the market.[767] The sectarian and fundamentalist nature of what was then deemed by the Western media (in true Orwellian fashion) "peaceful protestors" was seen early on as was the fact that there was never a period in which the outrageous Islamist demands of the "rebels" were presented as peaceful protest or anything but a series of indiscriminate killings.

The events unfolding in Libya helped shed light on those taking place in Syria as the destruction of Libya was peaking as that of Syria was only beginning to take off. Thus, the Syrian situation could clearly be viewed as nothing more than Libya 2.0. Indeed, as the United Nations passed Resolution 1973 in March 2011, establishing a "no-fly zone" and authorizing "all necessary measures to protect civilians,"[768] the first reports of violent insurrection began appearing in the press. While the mainstream corporate Western media attempted to spin the violent organized rebellion as "peaceful demonstrations," the alternative press was more forthcoming. Nevertheless, the mainstream outlets continued to spin, lie, and deceive in regards to the nature of the violence, blaming all deaths and killings on the alleged and unfounded claims of "Assad's cruelty" and ascribing none to the so-called "rebels."

These early reports of systematic violence on the part of the "rebels" (more aptly named "death squads"), came from the Syrian city of Daraa where "rebels" destroyed parked cars lining the streets and destroyed Ba'ath Party headquarters. In the city of Latakia, these "rebels" attempted to burn down yet another government building. As Tony Cartalucci and Nile Bowie write in their book *War on Syria: Gateway to WWIII*, "It is difficult to understand how any responsible government should be expected to allow foreign-funded mobs to commit widespread arson and vandalism with the expressed goal of removing the standing government from power."[769] Indeed, one can scarcely imagine the Obama administration sitting idly by as Obamacare opponents, Tea Party participants, anti-war protestors, civil libertarians, or gun rights activists stormed government buildings, engaged in riots, and repeatedly stated that their goals were to overthrow the U.S. government and establish a new system of rule based upon their own

---

[767] Tarpley, Webster G.; Jones, Alex. The Alex Jones Show. November 15, 2011. See "SYRIA: Webster Tarpley, in Syria for Infowars English (St-Fr) Part 1." Youtube. Uploaded on November 26, 2011. http://www.youtube.com/watch?v=pnkPSYSRmA8 Accessed on June 24, 2013.

[768] United Nations Security Council. SC/10200. 'Security Council Approves 'No-Fly Zone' Over Libya, Authorizing 'All Necessary Measures' To Protect Civilians, By Vote Of 10 In Favor With 5 Abstentions." Department of Public Information, News and Media Division, New York. March 17, 2011. http://www.un.org/News/Press/docs/2011/sc10200.doc.htm Accessed on June 24, 2013.

[769] Cartalucci, Tony; Bowie, Nile. War on Syria: Gateway to WWIII." November 2012. http://www.scribd.com/doc/114889281/War-on-Syria-Cartalucci-Bowie2 or https://docs.google.com/file/d/0Bzf5hXPESLSdbTd0V2dIY3hvVGM/edit?pli=1 or http://landdestroyer.blogspot.com/p/war-on-syria-gateway-to-wwiii.html Accessed on June 24, 2013.

ideology. One need only remember the brutal manner in which largely benign Occupy protestors or G20 protestors were dispersed in order to gain an idea of how the U.S. government would have handled acts of open insurrection.

Very soon after the violent acts in Daraa and Latakia came the reports of indiscriminate rooftop snipers and their shooting of both civilians and Syrian military soldiers in Homs. While many, due to Western media propaganda, were apt to dismiss claims made by the Syrian government that the "rebels" were responsible for the killings, journalists such as Webster Griffin Tarpley were able to gather firsthand evidence of the rooftop shootings.

Tarpley, who took part in a week-long fact-finding mission in Syria at the onset of the open violence, toured the entire country, particularly those areas considered to be trouble spots. What Tarpley discovered was indeed a large amount of violence; but it was violence perpetrated by the so-called "rebels" and not by the Syrian government as Western media outlets were reporting. Tarpley encountered exactly what was being claimed by the Syrian government – shooters on the rooftops of buildings in Homs who were not only sniping at Syrian soldiers, but also at innocent civilians, - men, women, children who were simply going about their daily business such as going to school, work, or the market.

In an interview with The Alex Jones Show, Tarpley recounted what he experienced in Syria:

> Tarpley: I just spent the day in the city of Homs (H-O-M-S) and if you watch any of this coverage that the U.S. and the European media are putting out, they're telling everybody that Homs is the great center of this rebellion, the democracy revolt that supposed to be going on in Syria. And I've just been walking all over this place and I can tell you that this is a complete big lie. It is one big lie. And of course it's important for people to know this because the people in NATO, right, be it Obama, Sarkozy, Cameron of Britain, they're really willing to go towards some kind of a general war. At least in the Middle East. In the name of this destabilization of Syria.
>
> So let me just set the stage. Starting from Damascus this morning, we drove North on a four-lane highway. And one of the first things you notice when you come to Syria is that is very different from Libya in that there are no checkpoints. I mean, you come into the international airport, Damascus International Airport, it's functioning normally. There's no special security. It looks pretty much like a normal airport. You drive in to the city, the first thing you see – no checkpoints.
>
> Alex Jones: But we now have, but we're told this is a great tyranny. We now have internal checkpoints where the TSA grabs your breasts and genitals on the highway. So is that why we've got to invade? Because pedophiles don't get to grope Syrian children?
>
> Tarpley: Well, let me just try to continue. The idea is the other thing you notice is that there are no checkpoints. Well, I guess we went by two. One is at the entrance to the city of Homs. There's a very kind of low key checkpoint. Kind of looking at cars but nothing much. And then if you want to go visit the Governor of this province which we did. We went and visited the Governor. And I want you to know this was the first delegation of foreign journalists that was allowed to go to the city of Homs. And it was some people from other newspapers. In particular, some Catholic journalists from Europe. From Belgium and from France were there. So we got to meet the Governor

of the city of Homs and he's accompanied by a group of religious leaders. And you've got to remember, Syria is a place that has 15% Christians in the population. That's more than Egypt. Egypt is 10%. Here, it's 15%. So it's more. So you have your Greek Orthodox Metropolitan. You have your Greek Catholic or Catholics that are more or less connected to Rome with the Pope. And also Syrian Catholics. The Patriarchate of Antioch. That's a very old and a very influential one and that's right here in Syria.

Jones: Sure. That's the church set up by Paul. So, continuing....

Tarpley: Yea. Look, now that you mention it, I stayed overnight very close to the place where St. Paul was converted on the Damascus road. And this is a place you can go and visit. So, the Governor tells us there's a huge plot, a huge conspiracy against Syria and the religious leaders basically say the same thing. So now we wanted to go and see with the help of some of the people of the . . . the patriarchs of these Christian churches. [We wanted to] go and see the neighborhood which is supposed to be the great center of this rebellion. That the BBC talks about all the time. It's a neighborhood called Zahra (Z-A-H-R-A). Zahra is the place. This is the area. It's a couple of square miles. Homs is a city of about 1 million. That makes it smaller than Damascus. Damascus has about 6 million. So we go to the neighborhood of Zahra and they tell us "There's a demonstration going on. You're right at the proper time." So we go to see this demonstration, expecting to see people attacking Assad and attacking the government, right? Because that's what the international media has told you is actually going on. This is a demonstration which is pro-Assad! It's true that they don't like the Governor, the guy that we had just met for various local reasons. And the principal complaint they have is there's not enough heating oil for the people to heat their homes now that the winter is coming because it's getting rather chilly here.

Jones: And of course the sanctions are helping...

Tarpley: Well, sanctions, exactly. That's the reason why. It's not really the Governor's fault. It's because of these sanctions. So then we . . . after talking to these people for a while, we go to the local hospital. Now, this should be the place where everything is made clear. You know, because you're talking about the Zahra neighborhood hospital. In Homs. In the great center of this revolution. And a lot of people. Like a spontaneous demonstration forms when this busload of Western correspondent's parks in front of the hospital of Zahra. And people tell us this. They say, "Today we had seven wounded and 5 killed." So, we ask "Who did it?" And they say, "Snipers." Well, who are they? "Well, we don't know." Many many theories. I'll tell you about that. And obviously they have some facts. But today in this one neighborhood , seven wounded, five dead. But it's not like this is going on everywhere. This is supposedly THE center, along with maybe one other or two other places in the entire country.

Jones: And by the way, you have made a beeline to right where the snipers are. We should point out Tarpley's very brave. But, I mean, Webster, to be clear here, because I just do the research, I just go off the facts. And it's just like al-Qaeda being put in to the east of Libya and now taking over and flying the al-Qaeda flag and saying they're going to put in al-Qaeda law and all this stuff. And thousands of shoulder-fired surface to air missiles are gone and our media just says "Ah, ignore that." But I've gone and looked up even what Voice of America admits. It is armed groups that pop up sometimes in clear Western CIA uprisings, shoot people, and our media calls them democracy activists. So clearly this is not an excuse to attack Syria, but now they've got the Arab league to come, in a miscreant fashion, to start calling for sanctions, further sanctions. So I guess they're all afraid. But as long as they back all this I guess they won't be the next person to be taken down.

Tarpley: But what the people say is this. In other words, I've spent the last couple of hours in the middle of a crowd of a couple hundred people who wanted to be heard. And anybody who could speak a little French or a little English would come to the fore and they wanted to be heard because there were some television cameras and people were asking questions. So this was their chance to be heard. Again, it's the first group of foreign journalists to come into the city of Homs. Anybody that claims that they had been here, be it al-Jazeera, they never were here. The BBC was never here. Today we were there. So then we tried to ask them, "Who is doing this? Who are these snipers?" Well, the first thing is, see, it's a series of random killings. It's blind terrorism. It's agent provocateur. And they say, "Look, the thing that we're afraid of is, when we go out, we're afraid of snipers shooting at us from the rooftops."

Jones: It's the classic thing where it's just a projection. These hired terror groups just create violence to point at it and say "See! There's a conflict." So it's Full Spectrum Dominance where they create just a conflict and then project on to it whatever they want.

. . . . .

Jones: Webster Tarpley is in Syria. He's in the area where they say the uprising is originating from. He's right there where the snipers are shooting people everyday. No one knows what side they're on. It's all fluid. Webster is an expert on false flag provocateurs. Continuing, because, I know you're there and you can tell people what's really happening, but separately Webster, let's look at the larger geopolitical [picture] of why this is happening now and what the endgame is. Please continue . . .

Tarpley: Let me just tell you what these people say because this is what's really unique about this. You talk to these people, right? And I've talked to all kinds of people, right? An English teacher, a couple of doctors in the hospital, a couple of nurses, French, English, whatever it is, . . . and you ask them "Who's doing this?" And, again, it's random killings. So, first of all, they say, "There's no pattern to what they do. They kill Christians. They kill Muslims. Among the Muslims, they kill Sunnis. They kill Alawites. They kill others. They kill people who don't have any particular religious identity. They kill members of the army. 5 terrorists today killed one soldier in this Zahra neighborhood." And I keep pressing them and I say, "Alright, who's doing it? Who's doing it?" And here's where they think it comes from. The Governor says that most of the killers he sees are actually Syrians. But, when you talk to the people, they say, "Yea, it's true there are Syrians who are doing the shooting, but behind them there's more." And then you say, "Well, who are they?" And they say, "Saudi Arabia is providing the money. Turkey is providing a lot of the help." Turkey is not that far from here. How about some more? They say, "Qatar," right? The wonderful homeland of al-Jazeera television. That Qatar is heavily involved.

Jones: So it's the same crew that NATO used to soften things up with Ghaddafi.

Tarpley: In Libya. Exactly. United Arab Emirates, important. They also say the Hariri faction of Lebanon. Rafik Hariri the younger. And they say, "Watch out for Hariri. His mother is from Saudi Arabia. This is a bad apple. Rafik Hariri is also a part of it." And of course Lebanon is very very very very close. And then, some of them if you keep prodding will say, "Yea, and the CIA of course. And Mossad." And others, right? NATO. Other forces in Europe. So they'll also tell you that "These people are the Muslim Brotherhood. They are people who may have been in al-Qaeda. Or they're Salafists." Salafist is just another brand of this extreme religious fundamentalism. Some of them just say "These are fundamentalists and anathematizers." In other words, they're religious sectarians who say that everybody's bad except them. The Governor talked a lot about mafia, organized crime, and, you got the idea, drug pushers. It looks to me like this has been thrown together. But the defining that I would have to make at this point after having heard a lot of really important first person testimony is that this problem is in the hundreds. It's not more than several hundred of these killers. With a certain amount of backup. Now, how much that is, is hard to say. I asked a lot of very intelligent people in this hospital today, "What should the Syrian government do?" And they say, "Simple. Send more army troops." They say, "We want soldiers on the roofs of the houses." In other words, on the top floors of apartment houses. "We'd like to have some tanks in the streets. But, above all, we'd like to have some soldiers on the roof because if the soldiers get up on the roof then the snipers can't go there and they can't do it." Now, I was talking to a young woman doctor who was about to walk home. And as she walks home, she's got to worry about getting shot. I was shown a picture of a three or four-year old girl who was shot dead in an automobile with her mother and some other little girls. Now there is one exception to this sniper rule. That is, that kidnappings do go on and there are significant kidnappings going on. Kidnapping is often prelude to a murder. I visited with this group, a bereaved family. And their son had been killed. Their son was a taxi driver. And they were Alawites. They belonged to the same ethno-religious group as the Assad family but these were people, right? The guy was a taxi driver. He was kidnapped by, as they said, these fundamentalists, people with beards is often what you hear too, he was kidnapped and then he was murdered. In other cases, bodies have been dismembered. They've been cut into dozens of parts. There are also stories that I won't go into now but about the mutilation of women victims . . . .[770]

Tarpley reiterated his statements on *The Alex Jones Show* in an interview with *RT* where he stated,

Tarpley: I've just completed a one week fact-finding tour of the country. I've been in Homs. I've been in Tartus. I've been in Banas. I've been in the military hospital here in Baghdad and I can tell you what average everyday Syrians of all ethnic groups – Christian, Alawite, Sunni, Shiite, Druze – what they say about this is that they are being shot at by snipers. In Homs in particular. People complained that there are terrorist snipers who are shooting at civilians, men women and children. Blind terrorism. Random killing. Simply for the purpose of destabilizing the country. I

---

[770] Tarpley, Webster G.; Jones, Alex. The Alex Jones Show. November 15, 2011.
See "SYRIA: Webster Tarpley, in Syria for Infowars English (St-Fr) Part 1." Youtube. Uploaded on November 26, 2011. http://www.youtube.com/watch?v=pnkPSYSRmA8 Accessed on June 24, 2013.

would not call this a civil war by any stretch of the imagination. I think that's a very very misleading term in the following sense: What you're dealing with here are death squads. You're dealing here with terror commandoes. The kind of thing that everybody remembers from Argentina and Central America. This is a typical CIA method. In this case, it's a joint production of CIA, MI-6, Mossad, the DGSE of the French. It's got money coming from Saudi Arabia, the United Arab Emirates and Qatar and it has a couple of interesting manager[s]. . . [771]

Tarpley's findings as well as his analysis proved to be 100% accurate as time wore on. Unfortunately, however, the "hundreds" of al-Qaeda killers present in Syria early on would turn to thousands and, eventually, tens of thousands, threatening to overrun the country and its military forces.[772]

Still, the Western media absurdly attempted to lay all the blame for dead civilians at the feet of Assad. As a general rule, the mainstream media treated any death in Syria as perpetrated by Assad – never by the death squads running rampant in the cities and the countryside alike. Early on, however, even cleverly crafted and edited reports coming from the mainstream press began to show signs that it was becoming harder to cover up for the death squads. For instance, in an Al-Jazeera article entitled, "'Nine killed' at Syria funeral processions," the Qatari-owned news agency claimed that government forces opened fire at innocent civilians attending a funeral service. While trying to frame the story as if the aggressors were government soldiers, Al-Jazeera was forced to admit the presence of snipers on rooftops who had fired into the crowd. However, the agency again cleverly framed the story in such a way as to imply that government soldiers had taken positions on the tops of buildings for this purpose.

The article stated, 'Four people have been killed in the Syrian town of Douma,' a witness told Al Jazeera, after security forces on the ground and snipers on rooftops opened fire on a crowd of thousands of mourners gathered to bury protesters killed on Friday." It very shortly after stated, "Snipers on Saturday had taken up positions on the top of a Baath Party building in the vicinity of the privately-run Hamdan Hospital, where residents had overnight formed a human shield around the main gate, in order to prevent security forces from arresting those who were injured and being treated inside."[773]

Thus, the authors are attempting to paint a picture of government forces murdering innocent civilians attending a funeral with the government firing into the crowd from both the ground and the rooftops as snipers. But the author of the article shoots for a bit too much at one time. This is because the writer also attempts to suggest that, due to mass support of the "rebels" and similar opposition to the Assad regime, civilians

[771] Tarpley, Webster G. RT. "Mossad vs Assad? 'CIA death squads behind Syria bloodbath?" Youtube. Uploaded on November 21, 2011.
https://www.youtube.com/watch?feature=player_embedded&v=5L49L6iZSSg#at=243 Accessed on June 24, 2013.
[772] Turbeville, Brandon. "Foreign Death Squad Network in Syria Larger Than Stated by West." Activist Post. June 19, 2013. http://www.activistpost.com/2013/06/foreign-death-squad-network-in-syria.html Accessed on July 9, 2013.
[773] "'Nine killed' at Syria funeral processions." Al-Jazeera. April 23, 2011.
http://www.aljazeera.com/news/middleeast/2011/04/20114231169587270.html Accessed on June 24, 2012.

surrounded the hospital and formed a human shield in order to prevent security forces from arresting the "protestors" being treated inside. However, if civilians were forming a human shield to protect those inside the hospital, how did government forces obtain positions on top of the building? If they were intent on arresting individuals inside the hospital, why did they remain on top? Why not come down the way they went up? Clearly, the snipers on the roof of the hospital firing into the crowd were members of the death squads themselves.

The article also states,

> [People marching on an overpass] were met with a hail of gunfire, many people certainly wounded directly in front of us, cars turned around, and I can tell you it was an incredibly chaotic scene, and it seems as though pretty much everyone down here in the southern part of the country is now carrying weapons. It is unclear who was firing at whom, that's part of the confusion ... but clearly a very violent incident now being carried out here in the south of the country," he reported.[774]

Yet, again, Al-Jazeera seems to reveal its hand a bit too much. As Cartalucci and Bowie state, "Though cryptic, this description seemed to corroborate the Syrian government's assertion that they weren't the only ones with guns."[775]

It is important to remember, even as only a side note, that the use of snipers during mass protest to further stir up protestors against the national government and provoke international outcry has been tried before. Indeed, the CIA is most likely to blame for the murder of Neda Agha-Soltan, the teenage girl who was shot by a sniper in Iran during a failed "color revolution" directed and controlled by the same forces now attempting to destabilize Syria. The Iranian government itself was astute enough, whatever its real and legitimate civil liberties failings, to recognize both a color revolution and a murder committed for propaganda purposes.[776] It was for this reason alone that the destabilization effort was effectively put down.

Indeed, in Syria, snipers would continue to play a pivotal role in the destabilization. As Cartalucci and Bowie write,

> In the Syrian context, reports of mystery gunmen and "death squads" escalated the situation dramatically, at the expense of thousands of civilian casualties. Reports issued by Iran's Al-Alam Arabic Language News Network described how snipers linked to Saudi Arabia and the American CIA were operating in Syria to purposefully assassinate protesters in order to expand unrest. The reports describe a motorcycle

---

[774] "'Nine killed' at Syria funeral processions." Al-Jazeera. April 23, 2011. http://www.aljazeera.com/news/middleeast/2011/04/20114231169587270.html Accessed on June 24, 2012.

[775] Cartaclucci, Tony; Bowie, Nile. War on Syria: Gateway to WWIII." November 2012. http://www.scribd.com/doc/114889281/War-on-Syria-Cartalucci-Bowie2 or https://docs.google.com/file/d/0Bzf5hXPESLSdbTd0V2dlY3hvVGM/edit?pli=1 or http://landdestroyer.blogspot.com/p/war-on-syria-gateway-to-wwiii.html Accessed on June 24, 2013.

[776] Malcolm, Andrew. "Iran ambassador suggests CIA could have killed Neda Agha-Soltan." Los Angeles Times. June 25, 2009. http://latimesblogs.latimes.com/washington/2009/06/neda-cia-cnn-killing.html Accessed on June 24, 2013.

driver delivering a sniper to a building before speeding off. Once in position, the sniper fires on protesters. Syrian security forces surround the building and a shootout allegedly takes place. The text concludes stating that the sniper is injured and taken to a hospital.

Al-Alam's report and footage would corroborate both government and eyewitness accounts cited by international media, stating that "snipers on rooftops" were shooting at protesters. While "rights activists" assume the snipers are security forces, the government maintains that gunmen have opened fire on protesters and security forces alike. A CNN report from April 2011 cited a Syrian official who stated that, "an unknown 'armed group on rooftops shot at protestors and security forces."[777] . . . . . "China's XinhuaNet reported multiple incidents across Syrian where armed gangs had clashed with security forces killing members on both sides. One attack claimed the lives of 8 bystanders. Official state media in Syria presented evidence that groups had been caught with non-Syrian SIM cards in their phones along with equipment used to stage acts of violence.[778]

In addition, Webster Tarpley's analysis of the Syrian destabilization as resembling the "typical CIA method" harkening back to the days of Central America are also quite accurate. The use of death squads for the purpose of destabilizing national governments, both in the Middle East and in Central and South America has been used effectively for some time.

Western Funding

The connections between Western nations, NATO, and the Anglo-American establishment do not end or begin with the players listed in previous pages, however. The direct involvement of Western agents, both military and financial, have been present for quite some time with many of them becoming increasingly visible as the Syrian destabilization campaign wore on. Indeed, the plan to destabilize Syria via the funding and direction of death squads, religious fanatics, and mercenaries existed long before 2010.

For instance, in an interview with television program LCP, former French Foreign Minister Roland Dumas stated that he had been made aware of preparations for war with Syria by the UK government two years before the violence began taking place in 2011.

Dumas stated,

Dumas: I want to tell you something. Roughly two years before the hostilities started in Syria, I was in England for other things, not related to Syria. I met with English officials and some of them, who are my friends, admitted to me by asking [my opinion], that they are preparing something in Syria. This was in England, and not in the United States. England was preparing the invasion of the rebels in Syria. They even asked me, as a former foreign minister, whether I would participate in this as it .

---

[777] Maktabi, Rima. "Reports of funeral, police shootings raise tensions in Syria." CNN. April 5, 2011. http://www.cnn.com/2011/WORLD/meast/04/05/syria.unrest/index.html Accessed on June 24, 2013.

[778] "Mobile Phones Using non-Syrian SIM Cards." SANA News Agency. April 23, 2011. http://sana.sy/eng/21/2011/04/22/342898.htm Accessed on June 24, 2013.

. . Of course, I said otherwise. I'm French. It does not interest me. This is to say that this operation comes from far away [from Syria]. It was prepared, conceived, and organized . . .

Host: For what purpose?

Dumas: I will tell you . . . in the simple purpose of removing the Syrian government, because, in the region, it is important to know that this Syrian regime . . . has anti-Israeli remarks. Consequently, everything that moves in the region around . . . I'm judging the confidence of the Israeli Prime Minister who had told me a while ago: "We will try to get along with the neighboring states, and those who don't get along, we will take them down." It is a policy. It is a conception of history. Why not, after all? But we need to know it. [779]

Yet, while Dumas provided important and credible information regarding the premeditated nature of the destabilization effort as well as the foreign direction that the death squads have received, to say that the Syrian destabilization campaign began two years before the insurrection and invasion manifested itself on the television screens of the general public is a vast understatement. The fact that plans were made in 2009, while evidence of at least two years' worth of preparation, organization, and direction, is only a small portion of the story. Indeed, the documented history of the outside assault on Syria goes back at least as far as 2005, bridging two presidential administrations. Of course this fact should not be considered surprising to even the casual observer of the current crisis.

For instance, in an article published by the Washington Post, entitled, "U.S. secretly backed Syrian opposition groups, cables released by Wikileaks show," Craig Whitlock wrote,

The U.S. money for Syrian opposition figures began flowing under President George W. Bush after he effectively froze political ties with Damascus in 2005. The financial backing has continued under President Obama, even as his administration sought to rebuild relations with Assad. In January, the White House posted an ambassador to Damascus for the first time in six years.

The cables, provided by the anti-secrecy Web site WikiLeaks,[780] show that U.S. Embassy officials in Damascus became worried in 2009 when they learned that Syrian intelligence agents were raising questions about U.S. programs. Some embassy officials suggested that the State Department reconsider its involvement, arguing that it could put the Obama administration's rapprochement with Damascus at risk.

Syrian authorities "would undoubtedly view any U.S. funds going to illegal political groups as tantamount to supporting regime change," read an April 2009 cable[781]

---

[779] "France's Former Foreign Minister: UK Government Prepared War In Syria Two Years Before 2011 Protests." Youtube. Posted on June 15, 2013. Uploaded by Eretz Zen. http://www.youtube.com/watch?feature=player_embedded&v=Kz-s2AAh06I Accessed on June 25, 2013.

[780] http://www.wikileaks.ch/

[781] "Behavior Reform: Next Steps For A Human Rights Strategy." Washington Post. http://www.washingtonpost.com/wp-srv/special/world/wikileaks-syria/cable1.html Accessed on July 10, 2013.

signed by the top-ranking U.S. diplomat in Damascus at the time. "A reassessment of current U.S.-sponsored programming that supports anti-[government] factions, both inside and outside Syria, may prove productive," the cable said.

It is unclear whether the State Department is still funding Syrian opposition groups, but the cables indicate money was set aside at least through September 2010. While some of that money has also supported programs and dissidents inside Syria, The Washington Post is withholding certain names and program details at the request of the State Department, which said disclosure could endanger the recipients' personal safety.

. . . . .

Edgar Vasquez, a State Department spokesman, said the Middle East Partnership Initiative has allocated $7.5 million for Syrian programs since 2005. A cable from the embassy in Damascus, however, pegged a much higher total — about $12 million — between 2005 and 2010.

The cables report persistent fears among U.S. diplomats that Syrian state security agents had uncovered the money trail from Washington.

A September 2009 cable[782] reported that Syrian agents had interrogated a number of people about "MEPI operations in particular," a reference to the Middle East Partnership Initiative.

"It is unclear to what extent [Syrian] intelligence services understand how USG money enters Syria and through which proxy organizations," the cable stated, referring to funding from the U.S. government. "What is clear, however, is that security agents are increasingly focused on this issue."[783]

Likewise, in a report by the AFP in 2001, entitled, "US trains activists to evade security forces," Michael Posner, the assistant US Secretary of State for Human Rights and Labor, was quoted as saying, "We are trying to stay ahead of the curve and trying to basically provide both technology, training, and diplomatic support to allow people to freely express their views."[784]

The report continued by stating,

The chief US diplomat has said the protests in Egypt and Iran fueled by Facebook, Twitter and YouTube reflected "the power of connection technologies as an accelerant of political, social and economic change."

---

[782] "Show Us The Money! Sarg Suspects 'Illegal' USG Funding." Washington Post. http://www.washingtonpost.com/wp-srv/special/world/wikileaks-syria/cable3.html Accessed on July 10, 2013.

[783] Whitlock, Craig. "U.S. secretly backed Syrian opposition groups, cables released by Wikileaks show." Washington Post. April 17, 2011. http://www.washingtonpost.com/world/us-secretly-backed-syrian-opposition-groups-cables-released-by-wikileaks-show/2011/04/14/AF1p9hwD_story.html Accessed on June 25, 2013.

[784] "US trains activists to evade security forces." AFP. Activist Post. April 8, 2011. http://www.activistpost.com/2011/04/us-trains-activists-to-evade-security.html Accessed on June 25, 2013.

The US government, Posner said, has budgeted $50 million in the last two years to develop new technologies to help activists protect themselves from arrest and prosecution by authoritarian governments.

And it has organized training sessions for 5,000 activists in different parts of the world.

A session held in the Middle East about six weeks ago gathered activists from Tunisia, Egypt, Syria and Lebanon who returned to their countries with the aim of training their colleagues there.

"They went back and there's a ripple effect," Posner said.

State Department officials said one of the new technologies under development is the "panic button," which allows activists to erase contact lists on their cell phones if they are arrested.

"If you can get the panic button that wipes that (list) clean before they get locked up, you're saving lives," said Posner.

The new technology has not yet been made available to pro-democracy campaigners but it will prove useful in places like Syria, where the authorities simply go out and arrest activists who use their mobile phones.

The State Department said it has already funded efforts by private firms, mainly from the United States, to develop a dozen different technologies to circumvent government censorship firewalls.

"One of them has been very successful in Iran. It's being used extensively. and we have the download numbers," a State Department official said on condition of anonymity.

"It's going viral and now that technology is spreading all over the Middle East," said the official, who declined to name the technology in order not to endanger the people who are using it.

The State Department is also funding efforts to prevent governments from launching attacks -- known as denial of service -- aimed at shutting down websites that might publish an investigative report or other critical material.[785]

The funding of "opposition groups" and "opposition figures" by the U.S. State Department is a common theme within nations who have managed to find themselves on the Anglo-American target list. Particularly, the process of funding of NGOs such as the National Endowment for Democracy (NED), the International Republican Institute (IRI), and the National Democratic Institute (NDI) and the hidden subsidiaries on the ground inside the target country has served NATO very well over the years. More will be discussed in this regard in later chapters. However, the very fact that the United States has openly funded "opposition groups" inside Syria since at least 2005 serves to demonstrate that the Western world has not acted merely as an interested spectator at the

---

[785] "US trains activists to evade security forces." AFP. Activist Post. April 8, 2011. http://www.activistpost.com/2011/04/us-trains-activists-to-evade-security.html Accessed on June 25, 2013.

events transpiring in Syrian but, at the very least, as an active participant in the facilitation of destabilization.

Western Methods

The deployment of death squads amongst the population of the target country is not an end in and of itself. Clearly, the funding, organization, and support of death squads and the religious fanaticism that makes of the overwhelming majority of their ranks should not be misconstrued as an ideological sympathy but as an expedient tactic of destabilization. The death squads are nothing more than a convenient spearhead, and one which is virtually incapable of biting the hands that feed them. This is not because of a lack of will and desire, but a lack of mental capacity, cognitive skills, self-preservation, and the ability to unify for a common goal. The majority of death squads running rampant in Syria (as of the writing of this book) are entirely incapable of sustained cooperation and coordination due to the obsessive, psychopathic, and fundamentalist nature of the members and the leaders of these various groups and organizations. They are an army whose purpose (from the standpoint of the Western powers that fund them) is to destabilize and divide yet, as a force; they remain unstable and divided themselves.

Thus, after destroying whatever government they have been unleashed upon and possibly instituting a regime of their own, they are incapable of mounting any real resistance to Anglo-American forces either militarily or politically.

The death squad method, color revolution, and the combination of the two are more successful, the weaker the target state may be. Thus, Tunisia and Egypt were relatively easily overcome. Libya, however, posed a bigger problem, and thus new tactics were introduced.

Syria, although not a first world powerhouse like the United States, Russia, the UK, etc., is a nation with both stable and secular political figures and, likewise, a stable and religiously tolerant population. Syria's governing structure was and still is relatively well-established and capable of withstanding both physical assaults and propaganda campaigns. Syria, also, is not without friends on the world stage. Russia has actively proven that, unlike Ghaddaffi's Libya, Syria was not politically isolated.

With this in mind, simple methods such as "swarming adolescents" and even the deployment of death squads were not likely to have the desired effect without continued support, direction, aid, arming, training, and assistance by NATO powers. In addition, merely releasing death squads to ravage the Syrian countryside were not likely to bring down the Assad government on their own. Even when combined with Western sanctions, the Syrian government, along with the support of the Syrian people, has continued to weather the storm. Thus, the Anglo-Americans have simultaneously employed more sophisticated methods of destabilizing the country.

As stated, the Syrian government alone could have (and has, at least at the time of the writing of this book) survived the invasion of the death squads alone. Politically and militarily, the Syrian government is far superior to the hordes of mentally damaged fanatics running rampant amongst the secular and civilized Syrians.

In terms of politics, the Syrian government also found that it had friends in much the same way as it found support from Russia on the international scene. Unlike other nations whose citizens lived under clear dictatorships and police states of epic proportions to begin with, generations of Syrians had enjoyed a nation of religious tolerance, secularism, and stability that a number of other national populations could scarcely imagine. Although many Syrians passionately opposed Bashar al-Assad and his methods of governance, these detractors and opponents became supporters of the Assad government when it became clear that not only was the insurrection occurring in Syria a western-backed destabilization but that the success of the Western assault would have produced results immeasurably worse than anything they had been resisting previously. Provided with the choice between Assad's continued rule and the ascendance of Islamists to national power, the Syrian people rallied behind their government.

Thus, with the government remaining formidable and enjoying the support of the people, something had to be done in order to break the spirit of the people and to instill a sense of hopelessness and inevitability on the scale of what had been done in Libya only several months prior. Together with their allies in the Gulf State feudal monarchies (Saudi Arabia, Qatar, etc.), a plan was then hatched to actually stage death squad victories, government resignations, and military defeats on the screens of millions of Syrians for the purpose of psychologically softening up the population.

It is important to remember that similar Psychological Operations (PSYOPs) have taken place over the years, most notably in Libya, during the Anglo-American destabilization campaign launched against Col. Ghaddafi.

Out of the many PSYOPs aimed at Libya, perhaps the most extensive was the doctoring, editing, and even creation of various bits of footage that seemed to indicate mass celebrations at the fall of Ghaddafi and mass protests against the regime. The most famous episode among these attempts (among informed observers) was the footage allegedly filmed in the Green Square in Tripoli, Libya. Here, Western media outlets attempted to feed the international community, Libyans, and the Western populations an image of victorious rebels celebrating in the Green Square in order to further instill the sense of inevitability of Ghaddafi's defeat and lack of confidence in the Libyan government. In reality, the scenes being repeated across millions of television screens across the world was not footage from the Green Square but from a television set in Doha, Qatar. The entire scene was nothing more than a television studio production and an elaborate hoax. Unfortunately, this hoax bore real world consequences.

Early reports of this PSYOP were made by the highly credible Thierry Meyssan of the Voltaire Network (Voltairenet.org). Subsequently, these reports were investigated and explained in further detail by Webster Tarpley and a number of other alternative media outlets.

As Tarpley stated in an interview with PressTV:

> And then to cap this thing off, most amazing, was this sound stage that NATO with the help of Doha and Qatar created the equivalent of a Hollywood set, which was designed to mimic the appearance of the Green Square.

> Those green square buildings are very old, some of them go back to the Roman Empire - but they created that in Doha and if you look there is a very interesting

comparison on the Internet where they show you what the Green Square really looks like and what this 'fake set' looks like and it's quite similar, but there were enough giveaways to see that this was also faked.

So this is a tremendous campaign of mass brainwashing and psychological warfare and it had a stunning affect. [786]

Likewise, Michel Chossudovsky of Global Research also demonstrated that the video footage provided by the Western media was faked. He wrote:

Green Square Tripoli. Libyans are seen celebrating the victory of Rebel forces over Ghadaffi in this BBC News Report (see below)

Examine the footage: Its not Green Square and its not the King Idris Flag (red, black green) of the Rebels.

Its the Indian flag (orange, white and green) and the people at the rally are Indians. Perhaps you did not even notice it.

And if you did notice, "it's probably a mistake".

Sloppy journalism at the BBC or outright Lies and Fabrications?

Recognize the flags?

This is not the first time images have been manipulated or switched.

In fact it seems to be a routine practice of the mainstream media.

There is no celebration. It is a NATO sponsored massacre which has resulted in several thousand deaths.

But the truth cannot be shown on network television. The impacts of NATO bombings have been obfuscated.

The rebels are heralded as liberators.

NATO bombing is intended to save civilian lives.

The images must be switched to conform to the "NATO consensus".

Death and destruction is replaced by fabricated images of celebration and liberation.[787]

More specifically, Gerald A. Perriera, also of Global Research, wrote an article entitled, "Imperialism Will Be Buried In Africa – Resistance in Libya," where he detailed the PSYOP as follows:

The corporate media have been accessories to this invasion, and I deliberately use the word accessories, because BBC, CNN and Al Jazeera have most definitely relinquished their right to name themselves news organizations. They have in fact been contracted as "weapons of mass deception", consciously collaborating with

---

[786] "'NATO playing dirty tricks in Libya war.'" PressTV. August 26, 2011. http://www.presstv.com/detail/195942.html Accessed on June 26, 2013.

[787] Chossudovsky, Michel. "Manipulating Video Images: Sloppy Journalism or War Propaganda?" Global Research. PrisonPlanet.com. September 5, 2011. http://www.prisonplanet.com/manipulating-video-images-sloppy-journalism-or-war-propaganda.html Accessed on June 26, 2013.

NATO to present a fictitious version of events. They have fought this war alongside NATO – "embedded" (in bed with) NATO all the way. Their agitation and propaganda (agit/prop) techniques have been a major weapon in NATO's armor and there can be no doubt that they are accomplices to the war crimes committed in Libya. They all have blood on their hands.

Al Jazeera has been the most rabid because, like BBC and CNN, they too dance to the tune of their master, the Emir of Qatar, who has championed this invasion of Libya. It is no secret that Libya is crawling with Qatari troops.

'War is Peace, Freedom is Slavery, Ignorance is Strength' – George Orwell, '1984'

The psych-ops aspect of this war reached whole new levels of deception. Investigative journalist Webster Tarpley has cited irrefutable evidence that a set of Tripoli's Green Square was constructed in Doha and people dressed as Libyan rebels were filmed taking over Green Square. This was the fake footage zoomed into living rooms all over the world.

A set of Tripoli's Green Square was constructed in Doha and people dressed as Libyan rebels were filmed taking over Green Square. This was the fake footage zoomed into living rooms all over the world.

. . . . .

In order to show the world a scene of victorious rebels celebrating the conquest of Tripoli in Green Square, a set resembling Green Square was built in Doha, Qatar, but some significant details in the architecture of its ancient buildings were omitted. Unfortunately, the images in this collage have been "stretched" to fit a rectangular frame. An "unstretched" photo of the real Green Square is shown beneath the videos at the end of this story.[788]

Considering the history of such military/media Psychological Operations, it is also interesting to note the contents of the Washington Post article mentioned earlier. In addition to backing "opposition groups" inside Syria to the tune of tens of millions of dollars (this does not include "black budget" sums and those not reported by the Washington Post), the U.S. State Department was also involved in the funding of a Syrian satellite television channel, Barada TV, which specializes in broadcasting "anti-government" and anti-Assad programming.

As the Washington Post article stated:

The State Department has secretly financed Syrian political opposition groups and related projects, including a satellite TV channel that beams anti-government programming into the country, according to previously undisclosed diplomatic cables.

The London-based satellite channel, Barada TV, began broadcasting in April 2009 but has ramped up operations to cover the mass protests in Syria[789] as part of a long-

---

[788] Perriera, Gerald A. "Imperialism will be buried in Africa – Resistance in Libya, Part 2/2." September 28, 2011. Global Research. Reposted by OleAfrica.com. http://oleafrica.com/politics/imperialism-will-be-buried-in-africa-resistance-in-libya-part-2-2/3239 Accessed on June 26, 2013.

[789] Bahrampour, Tara. "In Syria, protestors push to end decades of isolation." Washington Post. April 16, 2011. http://www.washingtonpost.com/world/inspired-by-neighbors-and-technology-

standing campaign to overthrow the country's autocratic leader, Bashar al-Assad. Human rights groups say scores of people have been killed by Assad's security forces[790] since the demonstrations began March 18[791]; Syria has blamed the violence on "armed gangs."

Barada TV is closely affiliated with the Movement for Justice and Development, a London-based network of Syrian exiles. Classified U.S. diplomatic cables show that the State Department has funneled as much as $6 million to the group since 2006 to operate the satellite channel and finance other activities inside Syria.[792] The channel is named after the Barada River, which courses through the heart of Damascus, the Syrian capital.

. . . . .

It is unclear when the group began to receive U.S. funds, but cables show U.S. officials in 2007 raised the idea of helping to start an anti-Assad satellite channel.

. . . . .

Other dissidents said that Barada TV has a growing audience in Syria but that its viewer share is tiny compared with other independent satellite news channels such as al-Jazeera and BBC Arabic. Although Barada TV broadcasts 24 hours a day, many of its programs are reruns. Some of the mainstay shows are "Towards Change," a panel discussion about current events, and "First Step," a program produced by a Syrian dissident group based in the United States.

Ausama Monajed, another Syrian exile in London, said he used to work as a producer for Barada TV and as media relations director for the Movement for Justice and Development but has not been "active" in either job for about a year. He said he now devotes all his energy to the Syrian revolutionary movement, distributing videos and protest updates to journalists.[793]

Eventually, a similar media PSYOP to that of the Libyan Green Square was planned and attempted in Syria. However, the Syrian government, having more resources than Ghaddafi and having learned from the fate of Libya, were not to be caught with their pants down. During the lead up to the deployment of the media assault, Syrian officials and media outlets were broadcasting warnings of the coming propaganda. Media outlets

---

syrians-join-in-revolution/2011/04/16/AF3JPjqD_story.html Accessed on July 10, 2013.

[790] Bahrampour, Tara. "13 killed as protests continue despite Assad's pledge to lift Syria's emergency rule." Washington Post. April 17, 2011.
http://www.washingtonpost.com/world/syria_protests_continue_despite_presidents_promises_to_lift_emergency_laws/2011/04/17/AFw0fMuD_story.html Accessed on July 10, 2013.

[791] "Syrians Take To The Streets." Washington Post.
http://primary.washingtonpost.com/world/syrians-protest-demanding-freedom/2011/04/08/AFmKI82C_gallery.html Accessed on July 10, 2013.

[792] "Country Guides: Syria." Washington Post. http://www.washingtonpost.com/wp-srv/world/countries/syria.html Accessed on July 10, 2013.

[793] Whitlock, Craig. "U.S. secretly backed Syrian opposition groups, cables released by Wikileaks show." Washington Post. April 17, 2011. http://www.washingtonpost.com/world/us-secretly-backed-syrian-opposition-groups-cables-released-by-wikileaks-show/2011/04/14/AF1p9hwD_story.html Accessed on June 25, 2013.

began advertising the possible nature of the propaganda to be expected and informing viewers where to go in case the stations went dark completely.[794]

Foreign Elements

The fact that the Syrian people were essentially immune to propaganda efforts designed to instill the fear of the inevitable collapse of the government or to insight rebellion, demonstrates at least two things. First, that the propaganda directed back home regarding the nature of the Syrian government and its citizens is largely false. Second, it shows that the information present on the ground inside Syria is readily visible to anyone open to seeing it. As a result, the fundamentalist nature of the death squads sweeping throughout the country is apparent to any Syrian citizen.

Of course, one of the reasons the death squads are so transparent (in addition to their fundamentalist rantings and brutal violence) to native Syrians is the fact that the overwhelming majority of the members of such groups are not Syrian at all. As mentioned earlier, when Webster Tarpley toured Syria for a week as a part of a fact finding mission, the reports he received from Syrian citizens and, indeed, his own firsthand accounts revealed that many of the "rebels" were not native to the country. This raises an interesting question as to how one can rebel against the laws of a nation in which he does not reside. How one can be considered an insurgent while he is fighting in a foreign nation? Obviously, the situation is Syria is not a rebellion, insurgency, or insurrection. It is an invasion.

Indiscriminate Violence

The open savagery of the death squads being organized, trained, funded, armed, and directly supported by NATO powers are shocking both in their brutality and in their creativity for inventing new and surprising methods of cruelty against their victims. It is this one factor that has contributed to what little awareness of the true nature of these so-called "rebels" exists in the public sphere today.

Far from the secular, freedom-and-democracy-loving young people Americans were propagandized to imagine were in Syrian streets, these individuals neither look nor act like the character portrayal of "Syria Danny" or the fantasized appearance of "Gay Girl in Damascus." Instead, they dress and behave much like the "savage muslim" meme that was repeated incessantly in the days and years after 9/11 in order to terrify the American public into surrendering their rights. These individuals look and act like the great big boogeyman – al Qaeda – because that is what they are.

---

[794] "Syrian people warned against 'fake TV channel." PressTV. July 21, 2012. http://www.presstv.com/detail/2012/07/21/251984/syrians-warned-against-fake-tv-channel/ Accessed on July 10, 2013.
See also,
"FLOW OF WISDOM RADIO: Mass Vaccinations, Syria, and Staged Attacks." Brandon Turbeville interview with Sean Anthony of Flow of Wisdom Radio. Youtube. Uploaded by FLowofWisdomTv. Uploaded on July 30, 2012. https://www.youtube.com/watch?feature=player_embedded&v=-xMVeyTGAnY#at=2039 Accessed on June 26, 2013.

Everything sold to the Western public regarding al-Qaeda as a means to terrify them into submission is present with the Syrian death squads. Religious fundamentalism is a prerequisite for membership. Heartless killing is a necessary skill. Likewise a hatred of women and other religions (even their own) is required. In addition, the practice of rape, torture, and cannibalism is ever present among the more adventurous members.

As the Syrian destabilization follows the same roadmap as that which was aimed at Libya, it is thus important to note that, with the victory of the Libyan "rebels," the savagery of the death squads were unleashed upon entire segments of the population with a vengeance. After the capture and cruel killing of Colonel Ghaddaffi, who was sodomized with a metal rod (perhaps even a bayonet), beaten, and then shot in the head,[795] Libyan death squads began the systematic genocide of black Libyans and black African immigrants.[796]

After the fall of Ghaddafi, the death squads ran amok throughout the entire country, rounding up blacks, placing them in concentration camps,[797] torturing them,[798] or simply slaughtering them wholesale. Racist taunts followed close behind as ghost towns, formerly full of black Libyans, were ransacked and the Arabic word for "slave" painted on the empty buildings. As Webster Tarpley wrote of the Libyan "rebels" in March 2011,

> Glen Ford's *Black Agenda Report* has correctly sought to show the racist and reactionary character of the Libyan insurrection. The tribes of southern Libya, known as the Fezzan, are dark skinned. The tribal underpinning of the Gaddafi regime has been an alliance of the tribes of the West, the center, and the southern Fezzan, against the Harabi and the Obeidat, who identify with the former monarchist ruling class. The Harabi and Obeidat are known to nurture a deep racist hatred against the Fezzan. This was expressed in frequent news reports from the pro-imperialist media at the beginning of the rebellion evidently inspired by Harabi accounts, according to which black people in Libya had to be treated as mercenaries working for Gaddafi — with the clear implication that they were to be exterminated. These racist inventions are still being repeated by quackademics like Dean Slaughter of the Woodrow Wilson

---

[795] Hanrahan, Mark. "Gaddafi Sodomized? Video Shows Libya Leader Attacked By Captors." Huffington Post. October 24, 2011. Revised on December 24, 2011. http://www.huffingtonpost.com/2011/10/24/gaddafi-sodomized-video_n_1028970.html Accessed on June 28, 2013.

[796] Newman, Alex. "Libyan Rebels Accused of 'Ethnic Cleansing,' Black Genocide." The New American. September 15, 2011. http://www.thenewamerican.com/world-news/africa/item/8351-libyan-rebels-accused-of-ethnic-cleansing-black-genocide Accessed on June 28, 2013.

[797] Hubbard, Ben. "Libyan rebels round up Black Africans." Associated Press. September 1, 2011. Reposted at MediaTakeOut.com. http://mto.mediatakeout.com/external/50907 Accessed on June 28, 2013.

[798] "US/Al Qaida Genocidal Oil Dictatorship Torturing Black Libyans: Obama And NY Times Say Rigged Election was Cool." FireDogLake. July 8, 2012. Posted by normanb. http://my.firedoglake.com/normanb/2012/07/08/us-backed-al-qaida-manned-oil-dictatorship-genociding-torturing-black-libyans-obama-ny-times-say-rigged-election-was-cool/ Accessed on June 28, 2013.

School at Princeton. And in fact, large numbers of black Africans from Chad and other countries working in Libya have been systematically lynched and massacred by the anti-Gaddafi forces. The Obama White House, for all its empty talk of not wanting to repeat the massacre in Rwanda, has conveniently ignored this shocking story of real genocide at the hands of its new racist friends in Cyrenaica.[799]

Much like their brethren in Libya (many Libyan fighters make up the ranks of Syrian death squads),[800] Syrian death squads have committed unspeakable atrocities against the people of Syria with special attention toward Christians. For instance, it was reported by the Daily Mail on December 30, 2012 that Syrian death squads had captured and killed a Christian taxi driver, Andrei Arbashe, because his brother was overheard criticizing the "rebels." The death squads then fed his dead body to the dogs. As Nick Fagge wrote,

> Sister Agnes-Mariam de la Croix said: 'His only crime was his brother criticised the rebels, accused them of acting like bandits, which is what they are.'

> There have been a growing number of accounts of atrocities carried out by rogue elements of the Syrian Free Army, which opposes dictator Bashar al-Assad and is recognised by Britain and the West as the legitimate leadership.

> Sister Agnes-Miriam, mother superior of the Monastery of St James the Mutilated, has condemned Britain and the west for supporting the rebels despite growing evidence of human rights abuses. Murder, kidnapping, rape and robbery are becoming commonplace, she says.

> 'The free and democratic world is supporting extremists,' Sister Agnes-Miriam said from her sanctuary in Lebanon. 'They want to impose Sharia Law and create an Islamic state in Syria.'

> The 60-year-old Carmelite nun claims the west has turned a blind eye to growing evidence of a 'fifth column' of fanatics within the rag-tag ranks that make up the Free Syrian Army that they back to oust Assad.

> One of the most effective fighting forces is the Jabat Al-Nusra, which has an ideology similar to Al Qaeda.

> . . . . . .

> The rebel attacked the northern town of Ras Al-Ayn, on the Turkish border, last month. The fighters entered the Christian quarter, ordering civilians to leave and leaving their homes.

> 'More than 200 families were driven out in the night,' Sister Agnes-Miriam says. 'People are afraid. Everywhere the deaths squads stop civilians, abduct them and ask for ransom, sometimes they kill them.'

---

[799] Tarpley, Webster G. "The CIA's Libya Rebels: The Same Terrorists Who Killed US, NATO Troops In Iraq." Tarpley.net. March 24, 2011. http://tarpley.net/2011/03/24/the-cia%E2%80%99s-libya-rebels-the-same-terrorists-who-killed-us-nato-troops-in-iraq/ Accessed on June 28, 2011.

[800] Turbeville, Brandon. "Foreign Death Squad Network in Syria Larger Than Stated By West." Activist Post. June 19, 2013. http://www.activistpost.com/2013/06/foreign-death-squad-network-in-syria.html Accessed on July 11, 2013.

Militants wearing black bandanas of Al Qaeda recently laid siege to the Monastery of St James the Mutilated, located between Damascus and Homs, for two days in an attempt to prevent Christmas celebrations, the nun claims.

An estimated 300,000 Christians have been displaced in the conflict, with 80,000 forced out of the Homs region alone, she claims.

Many have fled abroad raising fears that Syria's Christian community may vanish - like others across Middle East, the birthplace of Christianity.[801]

Such fears are not without firm grounds in reality. The killing of a Christian taxi driver is not an isolated event as Christians have actually been targeted en masse by the rebels wherever the death squads were able to gain the upper hand. On May 29, 2013, the Assyrian International News Agency reported that death squads affiliated with the Free Syrian Army (FSA) attacked a Christian populated village, al-Duvair, in Reef on the outskirts of Homs which is located near the border of Syria and Lebanon. After the initial assault, the death squads then massacred all the inhabitants of the village killing men, women, and children and leaving none alive. The Syrian army, although unable to prevent the massacre, did engage the terrorists, leaving at least ten death squad members dead as well.[802]

Yet Christians are not the only targets of the death squads. Fellow Muslims fare no better unless they are of the same Salafist and/or fundamentalist brand as that of the "rebels." For instance, in June 2013, death squads attacked Deir el-Zour and murdered at least 60 Shiites which the compromised Syrian Observatory for Human Rights (SOHR) described as being mostly "pro-regime fighters." Still, even the SOHR was forced to admit that many of the victims were indeed civilians. After the killings, videos were posted that showed death squad members attacking Hatla and vowing vengeance for Qusayr (the recently liberated Syrian city) and raising the black al-Qaeda flag over the homes. One of the rebels is filmed referring to Shiites by saying "We will crush them under our feet." In another video, one can see burning homes as a "rebel" states "All the homes of the Shiites have been set on fire." Shafi al-Ajmi, a fundamentalist Kuwaiti Sunni cleric subsequently praised the killing of the Shiites.[803]

In late March 2013, "rebels" killed famed Muslim cleric and religious scholar Sheikh Mohammad Said Ramadan al-Buti when they detonated a suicide bomb at the Eman Mosque in the Mazraa district of Damascus. Buti was 84 years old and was killed as he gave lessons to students in the mosque.[804] He had been a supporter of Assad in the

---

[801] Fagge, Nick. "Syria rebels 'beheaded a Christian and fed him to the dogs' as fears grow over Islamist atrocities." Daily Mail. December 30, 2012. http://www.dailymail.co.uk/news/article-2255103/Syria-rebels-beheaded-Christian-fed-dogs-fears-grow-Islamist-atrocities.html Accessed on June 28, 2013.

[802] "Armed Rebels Massacre Entire Population of Christian Village in Syria." Assyrian International News Agency. May 29, 2013. http://www.aina.org/news/20130529024056.htm Accessed on June 29, 2013.

[803] Dagher, Sam. "Rebels Kill Dozens in Syrian Shiite Village." LA Times. June 12, 2013. http://online.wsj.com/article/SB10001424127887323734304578541084096054330.html Accessed on July 11, 2013.

[804] Karam, Zeina. "Sheikh Mohammed Said Ramadan Al-Buti Syrian Pro-Assad Cleric, Killed in

conflict and had also been widely recognized as someone who exhibited religious tolerance and acted as a bridge between the Islamic sects and the different religions in Syria.

There have been almost innumerable accounts of brutal executions of civilians and Syrian Army soldiers, Syrian police, or government supporters carried out by the death squads. Videos such as the one surfacing from Saraqib, showing death squads executing 11 men are legion and have become all too common. In this particular video, the prisoners are beaten, insulted, mocked, and forced to lie down before being shot.[805] Just the YouTube account which posted the video mentioned above, SyrianRebelWatch provides numerous similar videos on their channel. Indeed, detailed search is not required in order to uncover the crimes against humanity perpetrated by the death squads on a regular basis.

Other such videos show death squads capturing, beating, and humiliating the famous elderly Yellow Man of Aleppo, an old man who merely dresses in yellow, takes pictures with tourists, and is otherwise an endearing local figure to the townspeople of Aleppo. The 70 year old man was such a tourist attraction that the municipality of Aleppo actually offered him a salary to simply continue doing what he did. However, after the city was overrun with death squads, the man became a victim of their typical savagery, being beaten and humiliated by the "rebels" shortly before being kidnapped, all of which is viewable on video.[806] The death squad members can be seen placing their feet on the Yellow Man's head, itself an insult, and forcing him to bark as a dog and insult Shiites, Assad, as well as himself.[807] After repeated slaps to the face, the old man's mustache was plucked out. The last seconds of the video show the man being placed into a car and being driven away.

Beheadings have also become a staple of the death squads. For some time, the "rebels" have been filmed[808] engaging in executions via beheadings by sword,[809] in some

---

Damascus Bombing." Huffington Post. March 21, 2013.
http://www.huffingtonpost.com/2013/03/21/sheikh-mohammad-said-ramadan-al-buti-killed_n_2925898.html Accessed on July 11, 2013.

[805] "Rebels Massacre 11 Prisoners in Saraquib, Syria." Youtube. Posted on November 2, 2012. Posted by SyrianRebelWatch. https://www.youtube.com/watch?v=t5OLmnYpIXs Accessed on July 11, 2013.

[806] "Salfist Jihadi's Beat 'Yellow Man' In Aleppo Syria (Eng Subtitles)." Youtube. Posted by iam4humanity. Posted on March 8, 2013.
http://www.youtube.com/verify_controversy?next_url=/watch%3Ffeature%3Dplayer_embedded%26v%3DEuylhA477x0%26bpctr%3D1364589201%26bpctr%3D1373564419%26bpctr%3D1373564456%26bpctr%3D1373564465 Accessed on July 11, 2013.

[807] "Foreign-backed militants humiliate Yellow Man in Aleppo." PressTV. May 15, 2013.
http://www.presstv.com/detail/2013/05/15/303617/militants-humiliate-old-man-in-aleppo/ Accessed on July 11, 2013.

[808] "Syrian Rebels Behead A Man in Aleppo, Syria 11/08/12." Youtube. Posted by 3TimeToFightBack. Posted on August 13, 2012.
https://www.youtube.com/watch?v=FL0uGSBhORc July 11, 2013.

[809] Watson, Paul Joseph. "Gruesome Video Shows Syrian Rebel Beheading Civilian." Infowars. March 21, 2013. http://www.infowars.com/gruesome-video-shows-syrian-rebel-beheading-

instances forcing young children to behead the prisoners.[810] Others, however, simply sawed through the throats of their victims with dull hunting knives as the hapless captive squirmed and gasped for breath. The jihadis, proud of their work, often hold up the head of the victim for the camera to see.[811] All of these crimes occurred to the constant background of mindless chants of "Alahu Akbar."

None of the above incidents are isolated, nor are they abnormal behavior for the inappropriately named "rebels." Indiscriminate killings, executions, torture, beheadings, humiliation, and even cannibalism are now hallmarks of the death squads funded, organized, and supported the Anglo-American West.

---

civilian/ Accessed on July 11, 2013.
[810] Watson, Paul Joseph. "Video: Syrian Rebels Make Child Behead Prisoner." Infowars. December 10, 2012. http://www.infowars.com/video-syrian-rebels-make-child-behead-prisoner/ Accessed on July 11, 2013.
[811] "Syria: Rebels Behead Two Civilians In Aleppo Province." Youtube. Posted by SyrianRebelWatch2. Posted on June 27, 2013. https://www.youtube.com/watch?v=P6nXt-P22AM Accessed on July 11, 2013.

Chapter VIII: Al-Qaeda: The CIA's Arab Legion

The fact that the overwhelming majority of the Syrian death squads are of foreign nationalities serves to prove that the inappropriately-named "rebellion" is no organic uprising. As I mentioned earlier, the very fact that the soldiers who make up the majority of a rebellion are mostly foreign precludes that movement from being classified as a rebellion. An armed attack upon the people of a nation and the government of that nation by individuals who are citizens of another nation can only be described as an invasion.

Yet even the foreign nature of the invasion cannot be explained away as merely an organic vacuum of terroristic opportunity sucking in religious fanatics, mercenaries, and lunatics to central location. Indeed, the very fact that mercenaries have been attracted to the battlefield suggests the organized bankrolling of the invasion by powerful individuals and organizations to begin with.

In the lead up to the summer of 2013, it was increasingly revealed in an overt and open manner that the United States, Britain, France (and much of the Anglo-American NATO Empire) were supporting the Syrian death squads financially and by shipments of "non-lethal" aid.[812] After the absurd and fabricated claims that the Assad government had used chemical weapons against death squads and civilians and thus had crossed the "red line" set by Obama and the Israeli government, announcements were made to the public that support for the al-Qaeda death squads would both increase and expand to include lethal aid.[813] This new aid would involve the shipment of weapons as well as other forms of unspecified aid, which most likely refers to training, financing, and coordination.

However, the debate over whether or not to "step up" aid, whether in the form of lethal or nonlethal aid, is nothing more than a farce. There has never been any question as to whether or not the Anglo-Americans would support, train, and/or arm the death squads. After all, this is precisely what was happening ever since the very beginning of the destabilization.[814] Although the precise nature of CIA involvement inside the borders of Syria are relatively unknown, what is known is that Anglo-American intelligence networks are indeed working inside of Syria and have been doing so for quite some time. Remember, it was reported early on in the Syrian destabilization effort that 13 French military officers acting as mercenaries/death squad participants were captured by the Syrian government, all the while the mainstream Western media reported the events

---

[812] Turbeville, Brandon. "Globalist Hidden Hand Revealed in Destabilization of Syria." Activist Post. April 8, 2013. http://www.activistpost.com/2013/04/globalist-hidden-hand-revealed-in.html Accessed on July 11, 2013.

[813] Delmore, Erin. "Arming Syrian Rebels: Too Little, Too Late?" NBCNews.com. June 19, 2013. http://www.nbcnews.com/id/52210825/t/arming-syrian-rebels-too-little-too-late/ Accessed on June 29, 2013.

[814] Turbeville, Brandon. "Globalist Hidden Hand Revealed in Destabilization of Syria." Activist Post. April 8, 2013. http://www.activistpost.com/2013/04/globalist-hidden-hand-revealed-in.html Accessed on July 11, 2013.

as "peaceful protest" and a grassroots level organic Syrian uprising against an oppressive regime.[815]

As RT reported on March 5, 2012,

> Thirteen French officers have been captured by the Syrian Army, according to Lebanon's Daily Star newspaper. It claims it received the information from a pro-Syrian Palestinian in Damascus.
>
> According to the source, the officers were taken captive in the city of Homs – the heart of the internal conflict between forces loyal to President Bashar al-Assad, and insurrectionists – and are being held in a field hospital there. The source claims the French and Syrian governments are locked in negotiations over the fate of the men.
>
> If confirmed, it would be an embarrassment to France. However the French Foreign Ministry has categorically stated that there are no French soldiers in Syria. Perhaps more intriguingly, the Ministry of Defense has not issued an outright denial, saying instead that it has no knowledge of the situation.
>
> Official Damascus has similarly refused to comment.[816]

Even at the time, RT speculated that the French officers "could have been giving military guidance to the rebels, who floundered when fighting the better-organized army forces."[817]

Still, even as far back as December, 2011, reports were made by former FBI whistleblower, Sibel Edmonds, regarding an American military troop buildup on the borders of Syria inside Jordan for the purposes of a U.S. invasion.[818] While the open invasion has yet to take place, American forces remain massed inside Jordan as of the time of the writing of this book. This lends credence to the idea that the U.S. is planning direct military involvement in Syria in the event of a significant weakening of the Assad government and its military forces. In addition to the hundreds of military troops now stationed in Jordan on the Jordanian/Syrian border, the United States has also relocated at least one and possibly two patriot missile batteries to Jordan from an as of yet unspecified country. Likewise, the United States has also deployed a squadron of 12 to 24 F-16 jet fighters.[819]

In addition to the massing of NATO troops on the border of Syria from inside Jordan, Edmonds also revealed that "the US had been training the Syrian opposition in neighboring Turkey and supplying arms to the country from Incirlik military base close

---

[815] "13 Undercover French Army officers seized in Syria – report." RT. March 5, 2012. http://rt.com/news/french-army-officers-syria-893/ Accessed on June 30, 2013.

[816] "13 Undercover French Army officers seized in Syria – report." RT. March 5, 2012. http://rt.com/news/french-army-officers-syria-893/ Accessed on June 30, 2013.

[817] "13 Undercover French Army officers seized in Syria – report." RT. March 5, 2012. http://rt.com/news/french-army-officers-syria-893/ Accessed on June 30, 2013.

[818] "US troops surround Syria on the eve of invasion?" RT. December 13, 2011. http://rt.com/usa/us-nato-syria-edmonds-709/ Accessed on June 30, 2013.

[819] Halaby, Jamal. "900 U.S. Troops In Jordan To Boost Security In Wake Of Syrian Conflict." Huffington Post. June 22, 2013. http://www.huffingtonpost.com/2013/06/22/us-troops-in-jordan_n_3484024.html Accessed on June 30, 2013.

to the Turkish-Syrian border."[820] On her own blog, Boiling Frogs Post, Edmonds wrote that,

> Col. Riad al-Assad has been in Turkey, working with U.S. & NATO, right inside the US Incirlik Base in Turkey, to do exactly what he vehemently denies: smuggle US weapons into Syria, participate in US psychological and information warfare inside Syria as the middle-man whom Syrian protesters tend to trust, and help with funneling intelligence and military operators across the border and night-time drop offs by air.

> The joint US-NATO secret training camp in the US air force base in Incirlik, Turkey, began operations in April- May 2011 to organize and expand the dissident base in Syria. Since then, in addition to Col. Riad al-Assad, several other high-ranking Syrian military and intelligence officials have been added to operations' headquarters in the US base. Weekly weapons smuggling operations have been carried out with full NATO-US participation since last May. The HQ also includes an information warfare division where US-NATO crafted communications are directed to dissidents in Syria via the core group of Syrian military and Intelligence defectors.[821]

Almost one year later, the mainstream media managed to report on the Incirlik connection to Western support for the Syrian death squads. However, these reports were highly sanitized and they attempted to cover up NATO participation, seeking to shift the responsibility of training and weapons shipments to Saudi Arabia, Qatar, and Turkey. For instance, the report by Reuters in July 2012, read,

> News of the clandestine Middle East-run "nerve centre" working to topple Syrian President Bashar al-Assad underlines the extent to which Western powers - who played a key role in unseating Muammar Gaddafi in Libya[822] - have avoided military involvement so far in Syria.[823]

> . . . . .

> The centre in Adana, a city in southern Turkey[824] about 100 km (60 miles) from the Syrian border, was set up after Saudi Deputy Foreign Minister Prince Abdulaziz bin Abdullah al-Saud visited Turkey and requested it, a source in the Gulf said. The Turks liked the idea of having the base in Adana so that they could supervise its operations, he added.

> A Saudi foreign ministry official was not immediately available to comment on the operation.

---

[820] "13 Undercover French Army officers seized in Syria – report." RT. March 5, 2012. http://rt.com/news/french-army-officers-syria-893/ Accessed on June 30, 2013.

[821] Edmonds, Sibel. "BFP Exclusive: Syria-Secret US-NATO Training & Support Camp to Oust Current Syrian President." BoilingFrogsPost. November 21, 2011. http://www.boilingfrogspost.com/2011/11/21/bfp-exclusive-syria-secret-us-nato-training-support-camp-to-oust-current-syrian-president/ Accessed on June 30, 2013.

[822] "Libya." Reuters. http://www.reuters.com/places/libya?lc=int_mb_1001 Accessed on July 11, 2013.

[823] "Syria." Reuters. http://www.reuters.com/places/syria Accessed on July 11, 2013.

[824] "Turkey." Reuters. http://www.reuters.com/places/turkey?lc=int_mb_1001 Accessed on July 11, 2013.

Adana is home to Incirlik, a large Turkish/U.S. air force base which Washington has used in the past for reconnaissance and military logistics operations. It was not clear from the sources whether the anti-Syrian "nerve centre" was located inside Incirlik base or in the city of Adana.

Qatar, the tiny gas-rich Gulf state which played a leading part in supplying weapons to Libyan rebels, has a key role in directing operations at the Adana base, the sources said. Qatari military intelligence and state security officials are involved.

"Three governments are supplying weapons: Turkey, Qatar and Saudi Arabia,[825]" said a Doha-based source.[826]

Yet, as in Libya, there is evidence that Western military forces have been on the ground in Syria, at least in the early stages of the arming and organizing of the death squads. Citing a report by Israeli news agency Debkafile, RT wrote in February, 2012, that British and Qatari military soldiers were in fact on the ground inside Syria and were directing arms shipments to the death squads. The article stated,

British and Qatari troops are directing rebel ammunition deliveries and tactics in the bloody battle for Homs, according to an Israeli website known for links to intelligence sources.

Four centers of operation have been established in the city with the troops on the ground paving the way for an undercover Turkish military incursion into Syria.

The debkafile site said the presence of British and Qatari troops in Homs topped the agenda of Tuesday's talks between Assad's officials and head of Russia's Foreign Intelligence Service Mikhail Fradkov.[827]

The article explained the parallels between the Syrian situation as it was unfolding with that of the NATO destruction of Libya. It read,

The scenario painted by the report closely resembles Libya's collapse into anarchy. UN Security Council resolution 1973 forbade any ground troops from intervening in Libya while creating a pretext for NATO to launch a bombing campaign against Muammar Gaddafi's troops.

However Qatar, Britain and France later confirmed they had sent units to assist the Libyan rebels. Secret French weapons drops were discovered after they fell into the wrong hands. There were also unconfirmed reports that Western special forces directed air strikes from forward frontline positions and directed combat tactics.

The Pentagon and its allies have proposed the creation of a humanitarian corridor in Syria with a view to delivering supplies and humanitarian aid to Syrian civilians. However, critics have cast doubts on the plans, likening them to the no-fly zone in Libya which preceded military intervention in the country.[828]

---

[825] "Saudi Arabia." Reuters. http://www.reuters.com/places/saudi-arabia?lc=int_mb_1001 Accessed on July 11, 2013.
[826] Doherty, Regan; Bakr, Amena. "Exclusive: Secret Turkish Nerve Center Leads aid to Syrian Rebels." Reuters. July 27, 2012. http://www.reuters.com/article/2012/07/27/us-syria-crisis-centre-idUSBRE86Q0JM20120727 Accessed on June 30, 2013.
[827] "British, Qatari troops already waging secret war in Syria?" RT. February 9, 2012. http://rt.com/news/britain-qatar-troops-syria-893/ Accessed on June 30, 2012.

Commenting on the US's proposal for the creation of a "humanitarian corridor," journalist Carla Stea told RT its "opening could easily become distorted and used for other purposes."[829]

Shortly after this information was made public via RT and other alternative media outlets, the Russian Foreign Ministry stated that British MI-6 agents were indeed on the ground in Syria.[830]

The French weekly *La Canarde Enchaine* and Turkish daily *Milliyet* also confirmed the presence of French intelligence working in the region for the purposes of arming the death squads and training them in the art of urban guerrilla warfare. The camps appear to have been located in the Tripoli, Libya, southern Turkey, and northern Lebanon regions.[831]

Turkish officers were also caught red-handed by the Syrian forces inside the Syrian border not only "supporting" the death squads but actively carrying out terrorist and "insurgent" activities. These officers admitted to being trained by Israeli Special Forces for this specific purpose.[832]

In addition, death squad fighters and weaponry have been flooding across the borders of Iraq into Syria. These fighters were part of the brutal and notorious forces of the organizations known as al-Qaeda in Iraq.[833]

In regards to NATO intelligence agents on the ground inside Syria, it is also important to remember that, around the same time, hacked emails obtained by Anonymous in December 2011 and released by WikiLeaks in steady drips ever since February 27, 2012, revealed that NATO troops, including those from the U.S., U.K, and France, were likely already operating inside Syria.[834] [835]

The emails were obtained from the private U.S. intelligence firm, Stratfor, and were apparently sent by Stratfor's Director of Analysis, Reva Bhalla (bhalla@stratfor.com) and contain discussion of a December confidential Pentagon meeting which was

---

[828] "British, Qatari troops already waging secret war in Syria?" RT. February 9, 2012. http://rt.com/news/britain-qatar-troops-syria-893/ Accessed on June 30, 2012.

[829] "British, Qatari troops already waging secret war in Syria?" RT. February 9, 2012. http://rt.com/news/britain-qatar-troops-syria-893/ Accessed on June 30, 2012.

[830] "Made in Jordan: Thousands of gunmen preparing to enter Syria?" RT. February 21, 2012. http://rt.com/news/jordan-syria-intelligence-training-859/ Accessed on June 30, 2013.

[831] "Made in Jordan: Thousands of gunmen preparing to enter Syria?" RT. February 21, 2012. http://rt.com/news/jordan-syria-intelligence-training-859/ Accessed on June 30, 2013.

[832] "Made in Jordan: Thousands of gunmen preparing to enter Syria?" RT. February 21, 2012. http://rt.com/news/jordan-syria-intelligence-training-859/ Accessed on June 30, 2013.

[833] "Purported head of Al Qaeda in Iraq refuses to end Syria merger." Associated Press. Reposted by FOX News. June 15, 2013. http://www.foxnews.com/world/2013/06/15/in-message-purported-head-al-qaida-in-iraq-defies-order-to-end-merger-with/ Accessed on June 30, 2013.

[834] Turbeville, Brandon. "Globalist Hidden Hand Revealed in Destabilization of Syria." Activist Post. April 8, 2013. http://www.activistpost.com/2013/04/globalist-hidden-hand-revealed-in.html Accessed on July 11, 2013.

[835] "Stratfor Leaks: NATO Commandos In Illegal Special Ops In Syria." RT. March 6, 2012. https://www.rt.com/news/stratfor-syria-secret-wikileaks-989/

attended "by senior analysts from the US Air Force, and representatives from its chief allies, France and the United Kingdom.[836]

Tellingly, the email's author stated that US officials "said without saying that SOF [special operation forces] teams (presumably from the US, UK, France, Jordan and Turkey) are already on the ground, focused on recce [reconnaissance] missions and training opposition forces." Later in the email, it was stated that "the idea 'hypothetically' is to commit guerrilla attacks, assassination campaigns, try to break the back of the Alawite forces, elicit collapse from within."[837]

This should come as no surprise since Western troops and intelligence agents maintained a heavy presence inside Libya during the destruction of that nation, increasing their presence as the destabilization and subsequent invasion succeeded.[838] [839]

It is also important to note that, despite the claims of Western nations regarding their hesitance to arm the Syrian death squads, the United States, Britain, and France have been doing so since the very beginning of the invasion. Yet, these arms are no mere civilian style weaponry or even military rifles. Reports provided by RT indicate that these death squads have been receiving anti-aircraft rocket launchers and other sophisticated weaponry long before the statements announcing the shipments of heavier arms. As RT reported,

> A general in the opposition militia known as the Free Syria Army has told journalists that the rebels have received French and American military assistance, amid reports of worsening violence in the stricken nation.

> In Homs on Tuesday, a general claiming to be from the rebel group appeared on camera and told a journalist from Reuters news agency that *"French and American assistance has reached us and is with us."* When asked to elaborate on the nature of the assistance he added, "*We now have weapons and anti-aircraft missiles and, God willing, with all of that we will defeat Bashar* [President Assad]."[840]

Thus, it must be recorded here, as well as with the announcement by any Western government official who openly arms or supports arming death squad killers in Syria

---

[836] Turbeville, Brandon. "Globalist Hidden Hand Revealed in Destabilization of Syria." Activist Post. April 8, 2013. http://www.activistpost.com/2013/04/globalist-hidden-hand-revealed-in.html Accessed on July 11, 2013.

[837] Turbeville, Brandon. "Globalist Hidden Hand Revealed in Destabilization of Syria." Activist Post. April 8, 2013. http://www.activistpost.com/2013/04/globalist-hidden-hand-revealed-in.html Accessed on July 11, 2013.

[838] Jamal, Akthar. "US, UK, French forces land in Libya." Pakistan Observer. http://pakobserver.net/detailnews.asp?id=78009 Accessed on July 11, 2013.
See also,
Watson, Paul Joseph. "Report: US Special Forces Arrive In Libya." Infowars. March 1, 2011. http://www.infowars.com/report-us-special-forces-arrive-in-libya/ Accessed on July 11, 2013.

[839] Borger, Julian; Chulov, Martin. "Al-Jazeera Footage Captures 'Western Troops On The Ground' In Libya." The Guardian. May 30, 2011.
https://www.theguardian.com/world/2011/may/30/western-troops-on-ground-libya

[840] "France, US arming Syrian rebels with anti-aircraft missiles – report." RT. February 29, 2013. http://rt.com/news/syria-arms-us-france-531/ Accessed on June 30, 2013.

that, in the event of a terrorist attack against a civilian airliner or related civilian target by members of al-Qaeda, it is these very lawmakers, policy directors, and heads of state who must be held accountable for creating the conditions for such an attack in full knowledge such a scenario could be the result of their decisions.

Since the beginning of the Western-backed foreign invasion of jihadist terrorists into Syria in late 2010, the American and Western mainstream media has attempted to present the death squad fighters on the ground as two-sided – one group being Islamist extremists and the other being "moderate rebels." As I have documented extensively, this characterization is entirely inaccurate as there is no such thing as a moderate rebel in Syria.[841] Still, this information has not stopped major media outlets from producing presentations in stark contrast to the facts.

In the months surrounding this incident, however, as more and more evidence surfaced proving the official narrative of the existence of "moderate rebels" to be false, the corporate media outlets have took to yet more propaganda-based name-changes and distortion surrounding the proxy forces fighting on the ground inside Syria.

For instance, al-Nusra Front forces began to be referred to as "Al-Qaeda-linked" fighters and were painted as if they were a mixture of moderate agents who were also willing to work with anyone that has similar objectives as themselves, even al-Qaeda.

The truth, however, is that al-Nusra is not merely "al-Qaeda-linked" but that it is al-Qaeda itself.

In the orbit of the "Levant" and the Syria/Iraq areas, al-Nusra was merely the Syrian branch of al-Qaeda while Al-Qaeda in Iraq was the Iraqi version. Later AQII was rebaptized The Islamic Emirate of Iraq and the Levant. All of these groups were subsidiaries of the same overarching terrorist organization, al-Qaeda proper.[842]

Eventually, both of these groups were renamed "ISIS" because the West, who funds, controls, and directs these terrorists, needed a name change for propaganda purposes. Due to logistical constraints and because of Western-propaganda needs, the names of the various individual groups, (i.e. al-Nusra, al-Qaeda, al-Qaeda in Iraq, etc.) were retained. However, the fact remains that there is no difference between ISIS, al-Nusra, or al-Qaeda nor is there any difference in the source of their funding, training, weapons, and direction – the United States, Israel, and NATO.

The Western propaganda needs mentioned above revolve around the requirement that the US/NATO have forces on the ground that they can at least present as moderate to a gullible public so as to justify the aid provided to them. There is also the need to present the "opposition" as multi-faceted in the sense that there is no centralized control over the hordes of terrorists running rampant across Syria. [843]

---

[841] Turbeville, Brandon. "The Roots Of ISIS." Activist Post. September 11, 2014. http://www.activistpost.com/2014/09/the-roots-of-isis.html

[842] Turbeville, Brandon. "The Roots Of ISIS." Activist Post. September 11, 2014. http://www.activistpost.com/2014/09/the-roots-of-isis.html

[843] Turbeville, Brandon. "Syria Under Attack By Globalist Death Squad Experts." Activist Post. May 27, 2012. http://www.activistpost.com/2012/05/syria-under-attack-by-globalist-death.html

Even mainstream outlets were forced to admit that the organizations were one in the same – albeit accidentally – by stating that all of the groups mentioned above are merely offshoots of al-Qaeda.[844] In the tangled web of Western propaganda and false narratives, the constant debate over whether this group or that is either working together or fighting with one another reveals that the command and control structure remains the same for all of these organizations and that any disagreement between the leaders of these organizations is the result of logistical, public relations, or strategic advantages posed as a result of the presentation of division and conflict– not a true lack of cooperation or where their ultimate orders originate.[845]

In this regard, it must be remembered that one of the principle direct-employers of extremist terrorists in Syria – Qatar – recently offered to provide al-Nusra with an even greater supply of money and weapons than is currently being provided to them by the US/NATO/GCC conglomerate on condition that Nusra publicly renounce their affiliation with al-Qaeda. This renunciation was not based on the methods or actions of the terrorist group but merely on the verbal denouncement for public relations purposes. In a telling response, Nusra refused to play along.[846]

See also,
Hubbard, Ben. "Islamist Rebels Create Dilemma On Syria Policy." New York Times. April 27, 2013. http://www.nytimes.com/2013/04/28/world/middleeast/islamist-rebels-gains-in-syria-create-dilemma-for-us.html?pagewanted=all&_r=1
See also,
Turbeville, Brandon. "Globalist Hidden Hand Revealed In Destabilization Of Syria." Activist Post. April 9, 2013. http://www.activistpost.com/2013/04/globalist-hidden-hand-revealed-in.html
See also,
Turbeville, Brandon. "More Alleged Moderates Join ISIS/al-Qaeda – Bring TOW Missiles With Them." Activist Post. March 3, 2015. http://www.activistpost.com/2015/03/more-alleged-moderates-join-isisal.html
See also,
Turbeville, Brandon. "West Re-Arms Nusra – Mainstream Media Continues Coverup." Activist Post. November 6, 2014.
See also,
Sly, Liz. "U.S.-Backed Syria Rebels Routed By Fighters Linked To al-Qaeda." Washington Post. November 2, 2014. https://www.washingtonpost.com/world/us-backed-syria-rebels-routed-by-fighters-linked-to-al-qaeda/2014/11/02/7a8b1351-8fb7-4f7e-a477-66ec0a0aaf34_story.html
[844] Dettmer, Jamie. "ISIS And Al-Qaeda Read To Gang Up On Obama's Rebels." The Daily Beast. November 11, 2014. http://www.thedailybeast.com/articles/2014/11/11/al-qaeda-s-killer-new-alliance-with-isis.html
[845] Atassi, Basma. "Qaeda Chief Annuls Syrian-Iraqi Jihad Merger." Al-Jazeera. June 9, 2013. http://www.aljazeera.com/news/middleeast/2013/06/2013699425657882.html
[846] Turbeville, Brandon. "Qatar/West Says Public Statement By Al-Nusra Will Wipe Away Jihadist Sins." Activist Post. March 12, 2015. http://www.activistpost.com/2015/03/qatarwest-says-public-statement-by-al.html
See also,
Porter, Tom. "Syria: Qatar Plotting For Al-Nusra Front To Dump Al Qaeda And Challenge ISIS." International Business Times. March 5, 2015. http://www.ibtimes.co.uk/syria-qatar-plotting-al-nusra-front-dump-al-qaeda-challenge-isis-1490425

Of course, why should it? It will continue to receive weapons, intelligence, training, and money regardless of whether or not it repudiates al-Qaeda. It has done so since its formation and continues to do so today.

The representation of al-Nusra or any other terrorist fighting group in Syria as merely having "links" to al-Qaeda is thus nothing more than a propaganda motif designed to perpetuate the lie that there is such a thing as a moderate fighting force opposing the Assad government.

Al-Nusra Vs. Al-Qaeda

Since the beginning of the Syrian crisis in late 2010, I have been writing repeatedly that there are no "moderate rebels" in Syria.[847] Many other credible researchers and even mainstream news organizations, albeit significantly after the fact, have made similar statements in their own writings.[848] In fact, I have even gone so far as to suggest that, if such a thing as a moderate rebel in Syria actually exists, then he must be brought forward for analysis.

After all, such a rare and mysterious being must be thoroughly studied so as to determine if he is a freak of nature or if there are more than just one of him.

Apparently, however, neither myself nor the other researchers mentioned above ever fully understood the process in which one becomes an alleged "rebel" and/or a moderate one.

Thankfully, that question has been answered by the Obama White House and the mainstream media organizations that work as domestic propaganda outlets.

The process by which one becomes a "moderate rebel" vs. a radical jihadist is not by the common sense messages of radical clerics or by taking a firm stand against a totalitarian government. Nor does one become a moderate rebel by joining al-Qaeda, committing atrocities, and imposing Sharia Law. One becomes a moderate rebel by joining al-Qaeda, committing atrocities, imposing Sharia Law and subsequently stating that you do not belong to al-Qaeda. At that point, you are fit to receive all the funding available from the coffers of the GCC and NATO.

Of course, the logic above is incredibly ridiculous. Yet it is, in fact, this very logic that the State Department, NATO, and its puppet governments in the Gulf expect the American people and the people of the Western world to believe.

This is because Qatar is now attempting to rebrand Jobhat al-Nusra as a "moderate rebel" brigade operating inside Syria and thus openly provide the al-Qaeda branch with relatively sophisticated weaponry and training. That is, even more so than is already being provided and in a much more blatant fashion.

The requirement for receiving such weaponry openly? That Nusra "disavow" its connections with al-Qaeda.

Of course, the suggestion that al-Nusra is actually a separate organization to begin with is an absolute falsehood. After all, Al-Nusra Front is merely the Syrian branch of al-

---

[847] Turbeville, Brandon. "Congress Votes To Fight ISIS By Funding ISIS To Fight Assad." Activist Post. September 19, 2014. http://www.activistpost.com/2014/09/congress-votes-to-fight-isis-by-funding.html
See also,
Cartalucci, Tony. "In Syria, There Are No Moderates." Land Destroyer Report. September 20, 2013. http://landdestroyer.blogspot.com/2013/09/in-syria-there-are-no-moderates.html#more
[848] Hubbard, Ben. "Islamist Rebels Create Dilemma On Syria Policy." New York Times. April 27, 2013. http://www.nytimes.com/2013/04/28/world/middleeast/islamist-rebels-gains-in-syria-create-dilemma-for-us.html?pagewanted=all&_r=0

Qaeda in the same way in which al-Qaeda in Iraq functioned as the Iraqi branch of al-Qaeda in that country. Even the CFR's Foreign Policy was forced to admit that al-Nusra is simply Al-Qaeda in Syria.[849]

There are a few establishment critics of the plan, however.[850] The Soufan Group, a global security NGO, stated,

> An Al Nusra removed from Al Qaeda on paper wouldn't mean an anti-Al Qaeda Al Nusra at heart. The history of attempts to turn extremist groups into non-extremist, well-behaved proxies is riddled with failures and devastating blowbacks.
>
> Al Nusra was formed to spread bin Ladinism into Syria, and its members are true adherents of that ideology.[851]

The truth, of course, is that the GCC (which includes Qatar) as well as the United States and NATO have been supporting al-Nusra all along so there was never any need for al-Nusra to "break away" from al-Qaeda to reap the benefits of Western aid, which it refused to do.[852] After all, al-Qaeda in Iraq and al-Qaeda proper have also been receiving Western funding from the very beginning of the Syrian crisis.[853] Al-Qaeda was created by the US and NATO as far back as the late 1970s.[854]

Thus, al-Nusra has refused to abandon al-Qaeda even on the surface. As AFP reports,

---

[849] Mendelsohn, Barak. "Accepting Al-Qaeda: The Enemy Of The United States' Enemy." Foreign Affairs. March 9, 2015. https://www.foreignaffairs.com/articles/middle-east/2015-03-09/accepting-al-qaeda

[850] Porter, Tom. "Syria: Qatar Plotting For Al-Nusra Front To Dump Al Qaeda And Challenge ISIS." International Business Times. March 5, 2015. http://www.ibtimes.co.uk/syria-qatar-plotting-al-nusra-front-dump-al-qaeda-challenge-isis-1490425

[851] "The Challenge Of Removing al-Nusra From al-Qaeda." TSG Intel Brief. The Soufan Group. March 5, 2015. http://soufangroup.com/tsg-intelbrief-the-challenge-of-removing-al-nusra-from-al-qaeda/

[852] Turbeville, Brandon. "The Roots Of ISIS." Activist Post. September 11, 2014. http://www.activistpost.com/2014/09/the-roots-of-isis.html
See also,
Cartalucci, Tony. "Implausible Deniability – West's ISIS Terror Hordes In Iraq." Land Destroyer Report. August 8, 2014. http://landdestroyer.blogspot.com/2014/08/implausible-deniability-wests-isis.html#more
See also,
Cartalucci, Tony. "NATO's Terror Hordes In Iraq A Pretext For Syria Invasion." New Eastern Outlook. June 13, 2014. http://journal-neo.org/2014/06/13/nato-s-terror-hordes-in-iraq-a-pretext-for-syria-invasion/
See also,
Hersh, Seymour M. "The Redirection." The New Yorker. March 5, 2007. http://www.newyorker.com/magazine/2007/03/05/the-redirection

[853] Turbeville, Brandon. "West Re-Arms Nusra – Mainstream Media Continues Coverup." Activist Post. November 6, 2014. http://www.activistpost.com/2014/11/west-re-arms-nusra-mainstream-media.html

[854] "The CIA's Intervention In Afghanistan: Interview with Zbigniew Brzezinski, President Jimmy Carter's National Security Adviser." Le Nouvel Observateur. Paris. January 15-21. 1998. Posted at Global Research. http://www.globalresearch.ca/articles/BRZ110A.html

Al-Qaeda's Syrian affiliate Al-Nusra Front on Monday reaffirmed its allegiance to the global extremist network and denied any plan to break away and become a more internationally acceptable rebel force.

The angry statement followed weeks of speculation on Internet social networks of a split between the jihadist allies.

Al-Nusra "completely denies reports of a break-up with Al-Qaeda," the group said in a statement released on Twitter.

It said Al-Nusra "remains the backbone of jihadists" in Syria, "the first into battle, dedicated to unifying the ranks around sharia (Islamic law)... righting injustice and defending the disadvantaged".[855]

Indeed, the idea that a mere verbal denunciation or formal declaration of opposition will change the fact that Nusra and Qaeda are the same organization is fundamentally irrational.

For those who may have been easily confused in regards to events taking place in Syria by the frequent name changes and allegedly shifting alliances, it is important to remember that, not only are there no moderate rebels operating inside the country, but those jihadist forces that are operating in Syria are nothing more than small branches of the same organization which is, itself, a creation of the United States and NATO.

DOD Admits Supporting ISIS, Buffer Zones In Syria

While the Western mainstream media and even independent gatekeepers like Noam Chomsky for years spread the lie that any suggestion that the United States and NATO were supporting ISIS was a "conspiracy theory," recently uncovered and declassified documents from the Defense Intelligence Agency have proven the Western press and the likes of Chomsky wrong and, yet again, the so-called "conspiracy theorists" right.[856] [857] [858]

This is because, on May 18, Judicial Watch published a selection of recently declassified documents that were obtained from the US Department of Defense and the US State Department as a result of a lawsuit filed against the US government. The lawsuit and most of the documents contained within the release revolved around the Benghazi scandal but a deeper look into the documents dating back to 2012 reveal an

---

[855] "Qaeda In Syria Denies Plan To Break Away." Reuters. AFP. March 9, 2015. https://www.yahoo.com/news/qaeda-syria-denies-plan-break-away-194745608.html?soc_src=mediacontentstory&soc_trk=tw&ref=gs

[856] Turbeville, Brandon. "Blowback And The Incompetence Theory." Activist Post. October 31, 2014. http://www.activistpost.com/2014/10/blowback-and-incompetence-theory.html

[857] "14-L-0552/DIA/287 - 293." Defense Intelligence Agency. Judicial Watch. http://www.judicialwatch.org/wp-content/uploads/2015/05/Pg.-291-Pgs.-287-293-JW-v-DOD-and-State-14-812-DOD-Release-2015-04-10-final-version11.pdf

[858] Hoff, Brad. "2012 Defense Intelligence Agency document: West will facilitate rise of Islamic State 'in order to isolate the Syrian regime." The Levant Report. May 19, 2015. https://levantreport.com/2015/05/19/2012-defense-intelligence-agency-document-west-will-facilitate-rise-of-islamic-state-in-order-to-isolate-the-syrian-regime/

even bigger story – that the US and NATO have admitted in their own documents to supporting al-Qaeda and ISIS in Syria and Iraq.[859]

Docs Show Al-Qaeda Involvement From Beginning – No Moderates – Revisited

The documents demolish the "official story" of Western governments promoted from the beginning of the Syrian crisis until the present day – that the "rebellion" was organic, grassroots, and made up of moderates and freedom-loving democracy proponents. The document states unequivocally that "The Salafist [sic] the Muslim Brotherhood and AQI are the major forces driving the insurgency in Syria." It points out that "The West, Gulf countries, and Turkey support the opposition; while Russia, China, and Iran support the regime." Tellingly, the report then states that "AQI supported the Syrian opposition from the beginning, both ideologically and through the media . . ."[860]

Indeed, the documents clearly admit that the crisis unfolding in Syria was never a moderate rebellion fighting for democracy; it was made up of fighters from the Muslim Brotherhood and al-Qaeda (al-Qaeda in Iraq/Al-Nusra Front) from the very beginning.[861]

US, Turkey, NATO Supporting ISIS and al-Qaeda – Supporting the Creation of Buffer Zones – Revisited

The document continues in its revelations by stating that:

> Opposition forces are trying to control the eastern areas (Hasaka and Der Zor), adjacent to the western Iraqi provinces (Mosul and Anbar), in addition to neighboring Turkish borders. Western countries, the Gulf states and Turkey are supporting these efforts. This hypothesis is most likely in accordance with the data from recent events, which will help prepare safe havens under international sheltering, similar to what transpired in Libya when Benghazi was chosen as the command center of the temporary government.[862]

---

[859] "Judicial Watch: Defense, State Department Documents Reveal Obama Administration Knew That al Qaeda Terrorists Had Planned Benghazi Attack 10 Days In Advance." Judicial Watch. May 18, 2015. http://www.judicialwatch.org/press-room/press-releases/judicial-watch-defense-state-department-documents-reveal-obama-administration-knew-that-al-qaeda-terrorists-had-planned-benghazi-attack-10-days-in-advance/

[860] "14-L-0552/DIA/287 - 293." Defense Intelligence Agency. Judicial Watch. http://www.judicialwatch.org/wp-content/uploads/2015/05/Pg.-291-Pgs.-287-293-JW-v-DOD-and-State-14-812-DOD-Release-2015-04-10-final-version11.pdf

[861] "14-L-0552/DIA/287 - 293." Defense Intelligence Agency. Judicial Watch. http://www.judicialwatch.org/wp-content/uploads/2015/05/Pg.-291-Pgs.-287-293-JW-v-DOD-and-State-14-812-DOD-Release-2015-04-10-final-version11.pdf

[862] "14-L-0552/DIA/287 - 293." Defense Intelligence Agency. Judicial Watch. http://www.judicialwatch.org/wp-content/uploads/2015/05/Pg.-291-Pgs.-287-293-JW-v-DOD-and-State-14-812-DOD-Release-2015-04-10-final-version11.pdf

"Opposition forces," of course, are al-Qaeda, al-Nusra Front, and ISIS, as mentioned and defined earlier by the DIA document. Thus, any questions of whether or not the US and its NATO/GCC allies have been supporting jihadists and terrorists should be answered with the admissions made within these pages.

If al-Qaeda/ISIS = the "opposition," then the US support for the "opposition" = US support for al-Qaeda/ISIS.

What is also well-known but now finally admitted to by the US government itself is the plan to establish "buffer zones" and "safe zones" on the Libyan model inside Syria.[863] [864] Such a plan has been covered extensively by myself and Tony Cartalucci (as well as many others in the alternative media) when the concept was considered a "conspiracy theory."[865]

Dividing Iraq and Syria – Fighting Iran and Shi'ite Expansion – Revisited

In regards to geopolitical concerns and the breakup and destruction of the Syrian government as well as the Iraqi leadership, the document states:

> If the situation unravels there is the possibility of establishing a declared or undeclared Salafist principality in eastern Syria, (Hasaka and Der Zor), and this is exactly what the supporting powers to the opposition want, in order to isolate the Syrian regime, which is considered the strategic depth of the Shia expansion (Iraq and Iran).[866]

This "Salafist principality" is obviously the Islamic State, particularly when one visualizes the maps of territory claimed by the jihadist organization. As the DIA document admits, the expansion of the ISIS principality is taking place with the support and assistance of Western powers. This much is evidenced by the fact that the ISIS fighters running rampant across Iraq and especially Syria could never have been able to do so were it not for the support given to them by the GCC and NATO. These fighters certainly could never have held such territory if Western military assistance, Saudi money, and Turkish/Israeli logistics and intelligence had not been provided to them.

Note also the justification provided for such support: not only is the goal to "isolate the Syrian regime," it is to prevent the "Shia expansion," meaning the arc of influence held

---

[863] Turbeville, Brandon. "Right On Schedule: US Eyes 'Buffer Zone' In Syria 'Very Very Closely.'" Activist Post. October 10, 2014. http://www.activistpost.com/2014/10/right-on-schedule-us-eyes-buffer-zone.html

[864] Turbeville, Brandon. "Libya 2.0? U.S. Says 'No-Fly Zone' Over Syria A Possibility." Activist Post. September 27, 2014. http://www.activistpost.com/2014/09/libya-20-us-says-no-fly-zone-over-syria.html

[865] Byman, Daniel L.; Doran, Michael; Pollack, Kenneth M.; Shaikh, Salman; "Saving Syria: Assessing Options For Regime Change." Brookings Institution. March 15, 2012. https://www.brookings.edu/research/saving-syria-assessing-options-for-regime-change/

[866] "14-L-0552/DIA/287 - 293." Defense Intelligence Agency. Judicial Watch. http://www.judicialwatch.org/wp-content/uploads/2015/05/Pg.-291-Pgs.-287-293-JW-v-DOD-and-State-14-812-DOD-Release-2015-04-10-final-version11.pdf

by Iran, growing daily largely due to Western imperialism, hypocrisy, tyranny, and double standards. Instead of attempting to combat Iran's influence in a race for development and the raising of living standards, the West funds jihadist savages to behead and rape their away across civilized nations. This is because the goal is not merely to disrupt Iranian influence; it is to destroy Iran completely.[867] Even Iran itself is a stepping stone to a greater confrontation with Russia and China.[868]

Tony Cartalucci understands this concept well as he writes in his own article "America Admittedly Behind ISIS 'Surge,'" when he says:

> The Syrian war is not a localized conflict with limited goals. It is one leg of a much larger agenda to destroy Iran next, then move on to Russia and China. Combined with the Syrian campaign, the West has attempted to create arcs of destabilization across Eastern Europe, Central Asia, and completely encircling China in Southeast Asia.
>
> What this constitutes is a World War executed through the use of 4th generation warfare. At the same time, the West attempts to seek temporary appeasement and accommodation for itself so that it can more effortlessly advance its plans. Attempts to portray itself as interested in "negotiations" with Iran while it wages a proxy war on its doorstep is a prime example of this.
>
> The corporate-financier special interests that have hijacked the United States and Europe have essentially declared war on all lands beyond their grasp, as well as on any and all among their own ranks who oppose their hegemonic aspirations.
>
> The vile conspiracy now openly unfolding in Syria, seeing to its destruction at the hands of terrorists the US is openly backing after claiming for over a decade to be "fighting" is a harbinger of the destruction that complacency and failure to resist will bring all other nations caught in the path of these special interests. Nations not immediately caught in the grip of chaos created by this conspiracy must use their time wisely, preparing the appropriate measures to resist. They must study carefully what has been done in Syria and learn from both the mistakes and accomplishments of the Syrian government and armed forces in fighting back.[869]

---

[867] Turbeville, Brandon. "ISIS In Iraq And The Path To Iran." Activist Post. June 20, 2014. http://www.activistpost.com/2014/06/isis-in-iraq-and-path-to-iran.html

[868] Turbeville, Brandon. "The Role of NATO And The EU On Brzezinski's Grand Chessboard." Activist Post. May 27, 2014. http://www.activistpost.com/2014/05/the-role-of-nato-and-eu-on-brzezinskis.html
See also,
Brzezinski, Zbigniew. *The Grand Chessboard: American Primacy And Its Geostrategic Imperatives*. Basic Books. 1997.

[869] Cartalucci, Tony. "America Admittedly Behind ISIS 'Surge.'" Land Destroyer Report. May 25, 2015. http://landdestroyer.blogspot.co.uk/2015/05/america-admittedly-behind-isis-surge.html

U.S. Attacks Syrian Military, Protects ISIS In Deir Al-Zour, Thardeh Mountains

If there was ever any doubt that the United States was supporting and protecting the most feared terrorist organization in the world, that doubt should have been erased as a result of the U.S. strike on Syrian military forces in Deir al-Zour on Saturday.

The attack took place as a battle between the Syrian military and ISIS forces was raging in Deir al-Zour when the United States swooped in with air strikes against Syrian military forces killing "dozens" of Syrian soldiers, allowing ISIS to advance. Some outlets put the death toll as high as 80 while others suggest 62 soldiers were killed.

The United States claims that it did not knowingly strike the Syrian military and that it confused the SAA with ISIS fighters. However, illegal violations of Syrian national sovereignty aside, claims that the United States could not decipher SAA forces from ISIS forces is hardly plausible since the former is easily identified by the fact that it is in battle with the latter.

Either the United States is incredibly incompetent or it intentionally targeted the Syrian military in order to act as the ISIS Air Force such as it has been since the terror group's creation.

This time, the U.S. bombing allowed ISIS to take control of the Thardeh Mountains. As *al-Masdar* reported at the time:

> The U.S.' airstrikes on the Syrian Arab Army's positions allowed the Islamic State of Iraq and Al-Sham (ISIS) to capture the strategic Thardeh Mountains that were originally under government control.

> According to local activists, the U.S. attacked the Syrian Arab Army's positions with phosphorous bombs, killing several soldiers and paving the way for the Islamic State to capture the whole area.

> The attack was conducted by 4 U.S. warplanes that were flying west from the Iraqi border.

> This is the second time this year that the U.S. Air Force has attacked the Syrian Arab Army in the Deir Ezzor Governorate.[870]

Thankfully, the Syrian military via the al-Qassem forces (Special Forces) have managed to recapture a number of areas seized by ISIS by virtue of the U.S. intervention.[871]

The U.S. subsequently claimed that it halted its strikes against the Syrian military after the Russians informed them of the SAA presence. The U.S. reiterated that it would not knowingly strike the Syrian military (despite the fact that it has done so before).

---

[870] Fadel, Leith. "US Jets Attack Syrian Army As ISIS Captures Strategic Mountain In Deir Ezzor." Al-Masdar News. September 17, 2016. https://www.almasdarnews.com/article/us-jets-attack-syrian-army-isis-captures-strategic-mountain-deir-ezzor/

[871] Fadel, Leith. "Syrian Army Recovers Territory In Deir Ezzor After US Attacks Their Positions." Al-Masdar News. Setptember 17, 2016. https://www.almasdarnews.com/article/syrian-army-recovers-territory-deir-ezzor-us-attacks-positions/

The *BBC* reported:

> The US Central Command statement said the coalition believed it was attacking positions of so-called Islamic State and the raids were "halted immediately when coalition officials were informed by Russian officials that it was possible the personnel and vehicles targeted were part of the Syrian military".

> It said the "Combined Air Operations Center had earlier informed Russian counterparts of the upcoming strike".

> It added:

> Syria is a complex situation with various military forces and militias in close proximity, but coalition forces would not intentionally strike a known Syrian military unit. The coalition will review this strike and the circumstances surrounding it to see if any lessons can be learned.[872]

The Russians have stated that, even if the U.S. bombing was an actual error, it would be because the U.S. has refused to cooperate with Russia in terms of reporting military positions.

Russia has officially stated that the U.S. action jeopardizes the ceasefire agreement and is now calling for a United Nations Security Council meeting.

"If the American side does not take the necessary measures to carry out its obligations… a breakdown of the ceasefire will be on the United States," said Russian General Viktor Poznikhir.

The United States and the so-called moderate groups they control have not met a single obligation they assumed in the framework of the Geneva agreement.

Syrian Government Says It Has Audio Recording Of U.S. Conversation With ISIS Before Attack On Syrian Military

According to a report from Russian news agency, Sputnik, Syrian intelligence possesses an audio recording of a conversation that took place between the United States military and ISIS fighters shortly before the U.S. airstrikes on Syrian government positions in Deir el-Zour that.[873]

Likewise, the speaker of the People's Council of Syria stated as much. [874]

---

[872] "Syria Conflict: US Air strikes 'Kill Dozens of Government Troops.'" BBC. September 18, 2016. http://www.bbc.com/news/world-middle-east-37398721

[873] "Damascus Has Audio Of Daesh Talks With US Military Before Strike Syrian Army." Sputnik. September 26, 2016. https://sputniknews.com/middleeast/201609261045706456-us-airstrike-daesh-army/

[874] Antonopoulos, Paul. "Reports: Audio Recording Between ISIS And US Before Deir Ezzor Massacre Found." Al-Masdar News. September 26, 2016. https://www.almasdarnews.com/article/reports-audio-recording-isis-us-deir-ezzor-massacre-found/

"The Syrian Army intercepted a conversation between the Americans and Daesh before the air raid on Deir ez-Zor," said Hadiya Khalaf Abbas as quoted by Al Mayadeen.

These statements appear to suggest that the conversation recorded by the Syrian government will definitively show coordination between the U.S. and ISIS against the Syrian military.

Indeed, during her visit to Iran, the head of the Syrian Parliament stated that, after the coalition airstrikes on Syrian government troops, the U.S. military directed the ISIS attack on the Syrian army that saw the terrorist organization temporarily gain territory surrounding Deir el-Zour.

That the United States has been responsible for the creation, support, direction, arming, and facilitation of ISIS has long been known in informed circles. However, an audio recording of cooperation between the U.S. and ISIS would effectively drive the last nail in the coffin of American credibility any semblance of honesty and logic in is "war on terror" that is, in reality, nothing but a "war of terror" against the world's people.[875]

If there was ever any doubt that the United States was supporting and protecting the most feared terrorist organization in the world, that doubt is now erased as a result of the U.S. strike on Syrian military forces in Deir al-Zour on September 17.

The U.S. bombing all but ended the fragile "ceasefire" plan (terrorists never once abided by any obligation of the agreement) and prompted a war of words between Russian and American diplomats as well as an emergency United Nations Security Council Meeting.[876] [877] [878] [879]

Conclusion

While the Western mainstream press and other "independent" gatekeepers were attempting to paint the suggestion that the United States was supporting ISIS in Iraq and Syria as a "conspiracy theory," the US government was indeed supporting ISIS in Iraq and Syria but hiding behind a narrative of democracy-loving freedom fighters and "moderate rebels" as it did so. This narrative was disseminated by the same Western press that labeled the alternative media as a collection of paranoid schizophrenics for

---

[875] Turbeville, Brandon. "The Roots Of ISIS." Activist Post. September 11, 2014. http://www.activistpost.com/2014/09/the-roots-of-isis.html

[876] "Russia, US Exchange Verbal Attacks After Coalition Airstrike In Deir ez-Zour." Sputnik. September 18, 2016. https://sputniknews.com/world/201609181045445774-russia-us-verbal-attacks/

[877] Turbeville, Brandon. "War Of Words Between Russia, US After Emergency UNSC Meeting." Activist Post. September 21, 2016. http://www.activistpost.com/2016/09/war-of-words-between-russia-u-s-after-emergency-unsc-meeting.html

[878] "'US Is Defending ISIS': Russia Convenes UNSC Meeting After US Coalition Strike On Syrian Army." RT. September 17, 2016. https://www.rt.com/news/359686-un-security-urgent-meeting/

[879] Turbeville, Brandon. "Russia Calls For 'Emergency' UN Security Council Meeting Regarding US Bombing Of Syrian Military." Activist Post. September 18, 2016. http://www.activistpost.com/2016/09/russia-calls-for-emergency-un-security-council-meeting-regarding-us-bombing-of-syrian-military.html

reporting what has now been confirmed by the DIA document release a full four to ten years ago.

 The truth is that the United States has been funding ISIS all along and that the terrorist organization would not exist were it not for its being created by American intelligence agencies as far back as the 1970s under the name Al-Qaeda and Mujahadeen.[880]

 While the DIA document release is only news in terms of the confirmation of US support for ISIS, it can be chalked up as one more reason the mainstream and traditional media outlets have become entirely irrelevant and overwhelmingly discredited.

---

[880] "The CIA's Intervention In Afghanistan: Interview with Zbigniew Brzezinski, President Jimmy Carter's National Security Adviser." Le Nouvel Observateur. Paris. January 15-21. 1998. Posted at Global Research. http://www.globalresearch.ca/articles/BRZ110A.html

Chapter IX: The Nature Of Destabilization

The fact that Anglo-American powers, most notably the United States and Britain, would train, organize, and arm al-Qaeda forces for the purposes of destroying an enemy, no matter how reviled, will no doubt be viewed as heresy by the vast majority of the Western public. This is because Americans and Europeans have been force fed propaganda regarding the existence of an organic fundamentalist Islamic movement dedicated to the destruction of the West and the establishment of an Islamic caliphate. This movement is projected as one that is self-organized and powerful enough to accomplish its goals if it is not countered by the constant action of the Western military and intelligence apparatus. Images of stone-age era culture and fantastic tales of cave-dwellers overcoming the most advanced military security state in world history are produced and repeated on television screens, radio programs, newspapers, universities, and, eventually, in discourse between average citizens. Al-Qaeda thus stands as the eternal boogeyman, one which lurks in the shadows and provides the justification for the evisceration of every Constitutional, civil, or human right the Western population may have believed it ever had.

While there are clearly those individuals who have been poisoned with hatred and fundamentalist indoctrination and crippled by their own mental shortcomings who do wish to cause harm to secular societies, it is high time that citizens of the West stop absorbing the ridiculous propaganda dished out to them regarding the "external threat" that is always used to justify a police state. It is time that Americans and Europeans alike recognize al-Qaeda for what it truly is – the CIA Arab Legion.

As Webster Tarpley explains in his article, "The CIA's Libya Rebels: The Same Terrorists Who Killed US, NATO Troops In Iraq,"

> Al Qaeda is not a centralized organization, but rather a gaggle or congeries of fanatics, dupes, psychotics, misfits, double agents, provocateurs, mercenaries, and other elements. As noted, Al Qaeda was founded by the United States and the British during the struggle against the Soviets in Afghanistan. Many of its leaders, such as the reputed second-in-command Ayman Zawahiri and the current rising star Anwar Awlaki, are evidently double agents of MI-6 and/or the CIA. The basic belief structure of Al Qaeda is that all existing Arab and Moslem governments are illegitimate and should be destroyed, because they do not represent the caliphate which Al Qaeda asserts is described by the Koran. This means that the Al Qaeda ideology offers a ready and easy way for the Anglo-American secret intelligence agencies to attack and destabilize existing Arab and Muslim governments as part of the ceaseless need of imperialism and colonialism to loot and attack the developing nations. This is precisely what is happening in Libya today.

> Al Qaeda emerged from the cultural and political milieu of the Moslem Brotherhood or *Ikhwan*, itself a creation of British intelligence in Egypt in the late 1920s. The US and the British used the Egyptian Muslim Brotherhood to oppose the successful anti-imperialist policies of Egyptian President Nasser, who scored immense victories for his country by nationalizing the Suez Canal and building the Aswan High Dam,

without which modern Egypt would be simply unthinkable. The Muslim brotherhood provided an active and capable fifth column of foreign agents against Nasser, in the same way that the official website of Al Qaeda in the Islamic Maghreb is trumpeting its support for the rebellion against Colonel Qaddafi.

I have discussed the nature of Al Qaeda at some length in my recent book entitled *9/11 Synthetic Terrorism: Made in USA*, and that analysis cannot be repeated here. It is enough to say that we do not need to believe in all the fantastic mythology which the United States government has spun around the name of Al Qaeda in order to recognize the basic fact that militants or patsies who spontaneously join al Qaeda are often sincerely motivated by a deep hatred of the United States and a burning desire to kill Americans, as well as Europeans. The Bush administration policy used the alleged presence of Al Qaeda as a pretext for direct military attacks on Afghanistan and Iraq. The Obama administration is now doing something different, intervening on the side of a rebellion in which Al Qaeda and its co-thinkers are heavily represented while attacking the secular authoritarian government of Colonel Gaddafi. Both of these policies are bankrupt and must be abandoned.[881]

Tarpley describes where he mentions the difference in methodology employed by the Bush and Obama regimes is actually the methodology of the Presidential controllers, loosely identified as Neo-Cons (Neo-Conservatives such as the Project For A New American Century, Rumsfeld, Wolfowitz, Cheney, Kissinger, Carlucci, Baker, etc.) and the Neo Liberals (Brzezinski, Trilateral Commission, etc.). While the Neo-Con geopolitical strategists prefer the method of using al-Qaeda to conduct false flag terror attacks which are then used to justify direct American military force, the Neo-Liberal Brzezinski-ites favor the method of using al-Qaeda as a battering ram against their enemies, weakening nation-states and playing them off of one another in the process. The first method provides quick results, justification of military invasion and thus the effectiveness of Western tactical superiority; the second provides political cover and the ability to avoid direct military confrontation, using one's enemies against one's enemies. This latter method is that which is currently being utilized in Syria, although the former is increasingly becoming a reality. Hence, the Brzezinski method is also described as "leading from behind." This Brzezinski method also involves the creation of "micro states and mini states" in an effort to weaken potential future resistance to Anglo-American agendas as well as provide useful puppet regimes which can then be used against the next set of enemies. These territorially smaller and politically weakened states are also incapable, due to the very nature of these circumstances, of resisting Anglo-American, international financier, or major international corporate assaults.

Tarpley writes,

For those who attempt to follow the ins and outs of the CIA's management of its various patsy organizations inside the realm of presumed Islamic terrorism, it may be useful to trace the transformation of the LIFG-AQIM from deadly enemy to close ally. This phenomenon is closely linked to the general reversal of the ideological

---

[881] Tarpley, Webster G. "The CIA's Libya Rebels: The Same Terrorists Who Killed US, NATO Troops In Iraq." Tarpley.net. March 24, 2011. http://tarpley.net/2011/03/24/the-cia%E2%80%99s-libya-rebels-the-same-terrorists-who-killed-us-nato-troops-in-iraq/ Accessed on July 18, 2013.

fronts of US imperialism that marks the divide between the Bush-Cheney-neocon administrations and the current Obama-Brzezinski-International Crisis Group regime. The Bush approach was to use the alleged presence of Al Qaeda as a reason for direct military attack. The Obama method is to use Al Qaeda to overthrow independent governments, and then either Balkanize and partition the countries in question, or else use them as kamikaze puppets against larger enemies like Russia, China, or Iran. This approach implies a more or less open fraternization with terrorist groups, which was signaled in a general way in Obamas famous Cairo speech of 2009. The links of the Obama campaign to the terrorist organizations deployed by the CIA against Russia were already a matter of public record three years ago.[882] [883]

The Brzezinski method was largely used in Egypt, Tunisia, and Libya, with Libya requiring the movement of "swarming adolescents" and youthful protesters to be replaced with swarming fundamentalists, violence, and, eventually NATO air, ground, and intelligence support. The important factor in the discussion of Libya is that the West was a bankroller and supporter as well as comrade in arms against the Ghaddafi regime with Islamic fundamentalists, mercenaries, death squads, and open al-Qaeda forces.

Tarpley writes in his article, "Al Qaeda: Pawns of CIA Insurrection from Libya to Yemen,"

The Libyan insurrection has four components. The first is provided by the British, and consists of the monarchist and racist Harabi and Obeidat tribes of the Benghazi-Darna-Tobruk corridor, whose traditional culture is that of the obscurantist Senussi Order. During the resistance to Italian colonialism, these tribes allied with the British and were rewarded by seeing the head of the Senussi Order placed on the throne in the person of King Idris I, overthrown by Qaddafi in 1968. Deprived of their role as the monarchist ruling class, these tribes hate the black or dark-skinned pro-Qaddafi Fezzan tribes of southwest Libya, and this has fed into the lynching and massacre of many black Africans from Chad, Mali, and Sudan working in Libya, which the western media have ignored. Enan Obeidi, the woman who claims she was raped by Qaddafi forces, is an Obeidat from Benghazi, and this puts her story into question. For the media, she is a new edition of the Kuwait incubator babies hoax of 1990, made to order to whip up war hysteria against Qaddafi.

Two ingredients come from the CIA. These are Al Qaeda itself, founded as the CIA's own Arab Legion against the USSR by then CIA deputy director Robert Gates – the current Defense Secretary– in Afghanistan in 1981-82. Another CIA ingredient is the Libyan National Salvation Front, based first in Sudan and then in Northern Virginia,

[882] Webster G. Tarpley, "Obama Campaign Linked To Chechen Terrorism: Grant Of Taxpayer-Funded U.S. Asylum For Chechen Terror Envoy Gave Obama Foreign Policy Guru Zbigniew Brzezinski 'One Of The Happiest Days Of My Life,'" February 2, 2008, *Obama the Postmodern Coup: The Making of a Manchurian Candidate* (Joshua Treet CA: Progressive Press, April 2008), pp. 97-115, online at http://tarpley.net/2008/02/03/obama-campaign-linked-to-chechen-terrorism/

[883] Tarpley, Webster G. "The CIA's Libya Rebels: The Same Terrorists Who Killed US, NATO Troops In Iraq." Tarpley.net. March 24, 2011. http://tarpley.net/2011/03/24/the-cia%E2%80%99s-libya-rebels-the-same-terrorists-who-killed-us-nato-troops-in-iraq/ Accessed on July 1, 2013.

which is supposedly sending the CIA asset Khalifa Hifter to lead the rebel military, most likely also to cover the presence of the Al Qaeda types.

A fourth component is contributed by the French, who arranged the defection of top Qaddafi associate Nouri Mesmari last fall, as reported by Maghreb Confidential. A clique of generals around Mesmari helped foment the military mutinies against Qaddafi in northeast Libya.

And Libya is not unique. In Yemen, al Qaeda operatives are decisive components of the CIA putsch attempt against President Saleh, which US is promoting in order to fragment Yemen into two or more rump states. Here the Al Qaeda leader is al-Shihri, a Saudi who was freed along with several other Guantánamo inmates and sent to Yemen by the Bush administration, allegedly as a humanitarian gesture, but in reality to provide leadership for the coming destabilization. Also in Yemen is the American-born Anwar Awlaki, known in the trade as Awlaki the CIA lackey, an obvious US double agent who has been used to give the Al Qaeda seal of approval to dozens of terrorists including the Fort Dix six, Major Hasan of Fort Hood, and Mutallab of Nigeria, the Christmas 2009 underwear bomber.

In Syria, the CIA goal is to deprive Iran of an ally, to isolate Hezbollah, to oust Russia from the Tartus naval station, and to build the power of the Muslim Brotherhood, which is the principal force promoting the insurrection so far.

. . . . .

Under Bush and Cheney, the alleged presence of Al Qaeda was used as a pretext for bombings and invasions. Under Obama, an overstretched and moribund US-UK imperialism is using al Qaeda as its own irregular infantry in the effort to harass and cripple the nation-states of the world, causing them to disintegrate into a tribal, sectarian, criminal, and warlord chaos. In the current phase, al Qaeda has resumed its original status as CIA guerrillas. As a result, civilization itself is threatened across vast areas of the globe. If you are skeptical, just take a look at the city council of Darna, Libya.[884]

Attempts to assassinate Ghaddafi and destabilize Libya by using al-Qaeda terrorist proxies are by no means new. In 1995, for instance, an MI-5 agent named David Shayler discovered that his counterpart at MI-6 had paid £100,000 to an al-Qaeda operative for the purpose of assassinating Ghaddafi. This assassination attempt actually went forward but Ghaddafi escaped unscathed, although several innocent bystanders were wounded and killed. According to Shayler, the goal was to eliminate Ghaddaffi, an act which would send Libya into chaos, civil war, and tribal conflict, with an opening for al-Qaeda itself to seize power. With Ghaddaffi gone and al-Qaeda now in control of the country, the door would be opened for a British invasion of Libya, possibly and probably coupled with American military support and/or a "coalition of the willing" made up of other nations. These international forces would then be able to seize control over the oil fields, pipelines, and the strategic coast. [885]

---

[884] Tarpley, Webster G. "Al Qaeda: Pawns Of CIA Insurrection From Libya To Yemen." Tarpley.net. April 3, 2011. http://tarpley.net/2011/04/03/al-qaeda-pawns-of-cia-insurrection-from-libya-to-yemen/ Accessed on July 1, 2013.
[885] Norton-Taylor, Richard. "Government looks desperately for way out from Shayler affair." The

In addition, MI-6 and other Western intelligence agencies stirred up a sizeable and open insurrection in Northeast Libya, which were precisely the same problem areas where Libya experienced the most violence early on in the destabilization of 2010-2011.[886]

Tarpley recounts the David Shayler events as follows:

> In 1995, David Shayler, an official of the British counterintelligence organization MI-5, became aware that his counterpart at the British foreign espionage organization MI-6 had paid the sum of £100,000 to an Al Qaeda affiliate in exchange for the attempt to assassinate Qaddafi. The assassination attempt did occur, and killed several innocent bystanders, but failed to eliminate the Libyan ruler. As Shayler understood the MI-6 scenario, it included the liquidation of Gaddafi, followed by the descent of Libya into chaos and tribal warfare, with a possible option for a direct seizure of power by al Qaeda itself. This situation would then provide a pretext for Britain, probably but not necessarily acting together with the United States or other countries, to invade Libya and seize control of the oil fields, probably establishing a permanent protectorate over the oil regions, the pipelines, and the coast.[887] This remains the goal today.

> Timed to coincide with the attempt to assassinate Qaddafi, MI-6 and other Western secret intelligence agencies fomented a considerable insurrection in northeast Libya, almost precisely in the same areas which are in rebellion today. Its insurrection was successfully crushed by Qaddafi's forces by the end of 1996. The events of 2011 are simply a *reprise* of the imperialist attack on Libya 15 years ago, with the addition of outside intervention..[888]

In his highly important work regarding the 9/11 attacks, *9/11 Synthetic Terror: Made In USA*, Tarpley recalls the previous attempts to assassinate Ghaddaffi by the West using al-Qaeda fighters, thus opening a window into the true nature of control over these fundamentalists that have been used to terrorize the Western public into surrendering most of their Constitutional, Civil, and Human rights.

Tarpley writes,

> Muammar Qaddafi of Libya, who had been bombed by the US in the mid-1980s, not coincidentally became a target of al-Qaeda. In March 1994, bin Laden supporters killed two German agents in Libya. In November 1996, there was an MI-5

Guardian. April 10, 2000.
http://www.guardian.co.uk/uk/2000/apr/10/davidshayler.richardnortontaylor Accessed on July 1, 2013.
[886] Tarpley, Webster G. "The CIA's Libya Rebels: The Same Terrorists Who Killed US, NATO Troops In Iraq." Tarpley.net. March 24, 2011. http://tarpley.net/2011/03/24/the-cia%E2%80%99s-libya-rebels-the-same-terrorists-who-killed-us-nato-troops-in-iraq/ Accessed on July 1, 2013.
[887] Norton-Taylor, Richard. "Government looks desperately for way out from Shayler affair." The Guardian. April 10, 2000.
http://www.guardian.co.uk/uk/2000/apr/10/davidshayler.richardnortontaylor Accessed on July 1, 2013.
[888] Tarpley, Webster G. "Al Qaeda: Pawns Of CIA Insurrection From Libya To Yemen." Tarpley.net. April 3, 2011. http://tarpley.net/2011/04/03/al-qaeda-pawns-of-cia-insurrection-from-libya-to-yemen/ Accessed on July 1, 2013.

assassination attempt against the Libyan dictator with the help of the local bin Laden organization, in which several people were killed. Here is a prime example of al Qaeda being employed by UK intelligence for purposes of state-sponsored terrorism with the goal of eliminating a political leader who was not appreciated by London. The conclusion is clear: al Qaeda is a subsidiary of Anglo-American intelligence.

According to the French authors Brisard and Dasquie', bin Laden's controllers had been using him to cause trouble for Qaddafi since the early 1980s, when bin Laden demanded permission to set up a base of operations in Libya, but was rebuffed by Qaddafi. "Enraged by Libya's refusal, bin Laden organized attacks inside Libya, including assassination attempts against Qaddafi," Dasquie' told IPS press service. The French authors cited the Islamic Fighting Group, head-quartered in London, as the Libyan opposition group most closely allied with bin Laden. Author Dasquie' told IPS, "Qaddafi even demanded that Western police institutions, such as Interpol, pursue the IFG and bin Laden, but never obtained co-operation. Until this very day [late 2001], members of the IFG openly live in London." In 1998, former MI-5 officer David Shayler told reporters that the British secret services had financed the assassination attempt against Qaddafi.

A rare moment of truth about the infrastructure of international terrorism was provided in October 2001 by Qaddafi, who was aware of al Qaeda's track record of attempting to eliminate him in the service of the US and UK. In an appearance on the popular al-Jazeera program "The Opposite Direction," Qaddafi condemned the 9/11 attacks, and referred to bin Laden's Arab Afghans as "stray dogs" and terrorists. But then Qaddafi began to talk about the support network for al Qaeda:

I am actually puzzled. I mean, if American were serious about eliminating terrorism, the first capital it should rock with cruise missiles is London.

Interviewer: London?

Qaddafi: London. It is the center of terrorism. It gives safehousing to the terrorists. I mean, as long as America does not bomb London, I think the US is not serious, and is using a double standard. I mean, on the contrary. London is far more dangerous than Kabul. How could it rock Kabul with missiles and leave London untouched?

The interviewer, a former BBC employee, quickly changed the subject before the mercurial dictator could say more. At this time, al Jazeera was closely monitored by all the international wire services, since it had the best reporting from inside Afghanistan. But none of them reported these illuminating remarks from Qaddafi.[889]

Tarpley expounds upon the British connection as the "center of terrorism" where Qaddafi left off. He writes,

The role of London as the leading center of Islamic radicalism has been an open secret for many years, but has never been reported by the US controlled corporate media. In the nineteenth century, when Mazzini and Marx operated out of London, the slogan was that "England supports all revolutions but her own." In the post-colonial world, the British have found it to their advantage to encourage violent movements which could be used for destabilizations and assassinations in the former

---

[889] Tarpley, Webster G. 9/11 Synthetic Terror: Made In USA. 4th Edition. 2007. Progressive Press. Pp. 156-157.

colonies, which their ex-masters did not want to see become strong and effective modern states. Between 1995 and 1999, protests were lodged by many countries concerning the willingness of the British government to permit terror groups to operate from British territory. Among the protestors were: Israel, Algeria, Turkey, Libya, Yemen, India, Egypt, France, Peru, Germany, Nigeria, and Russia. This is a list which, if widely known, might force certain US radio commentators to change their world picture about who is soft on terrorism.

A number of groups which were cited as terrorist organizations by the US State Department had their headquarters in London. Among them were the Islamic Group of Egypt, led by bin Laden's current right-hand man, Zawahiri, who was a known participant in the plot to assassinate Egyptian President Sadat; this was also the group which had murdered foreign tourists at Luxor in an attempt to wreck the Egyptian tourist industry. Also present in London were Al Jihad of Egypt, Hamas of Palestine, the Armed Islamic Group (GIA) of Algeria (responsible for large-scale massacres in that country), the Kurdish Worker's Party (PKK), which attacked targets in Turkey, and the Liberation Tigers of Tamil Eelam (Tamil Tigers) of Sri Lanka, who assassinated Indian Prime Minister Rajiv Ghandi. Sheikh Bakri, a bin Laden spokesman, was openly active in London into mid-1998 and later; he gave a press conference after the bombings of the US East African embassies. The killings of figures like Sadat and Rajiv Ghandi should indicate the scale of the destabilization in developing countries of which some of these groups are capable.

Non-Anglo-Saxon press organs have from time to time pointed up the role of London in worldwide subversion. "The track of . . . the GIA leader in Paris leads to Great Britain. The British capital has served as logistical and financial base for the terrorists," wrote Le Figaro on Nov. 3, 1995, in the wake of a murderous terror attack carried out in France. A report by the French National Assembly in October 2001 alleged that London played the key role as clearinghouse for money laundering of criminal and terrorist organizations. On March 3, 1996: Hamas a bombed a market in Jerusalem, leaving 12 Israelis dead. A British newspaper reported soon after: "Israeli security sources say the fanatics . . . are funded and controlled through secret cells operating here . . . Military chiefs in Jerusalem detailed how Islamic groups raised £7 million in donations from British organizations."

In the midst of a campaign of destabilization against Egypt in the mid-1990s, the semi-official organ of the Egyptian government pointed out that "Britain has become the number one base in the world for international terrorism." Egyptian President Hosni Mubarak noted that " . . . some states, like Britain, give political asylum to terrorists, and these states will pay the price for that." British newspapers were also alarmed by the level of Islamic extremist activity they saw around them. By the late 1990s, there were so many Islamic extremists in London that the city had acquired the nickname of "Londonistan."

The leading right-wing paper in the UK wrote, "Britain is now an international center for Islamic militancy on a huge scale . . . and the capital is home to a bewildering variety of radical Islamic movements, many of which make no secret of their commitment to violence and terrorism to achieve their goals." President Putin of Russia saw a direct link between the London Islamic scene and terrorism in his own country. He said in an interview with a German news magazine: "In London, there is a recruitment station for people wanting to join combat in Chechnya. Today − not officially, but effectively in the open – they are talking there about recruiting volunteers to go to Afghanistan."

Brixton Mosque was one of the notorious centers for terrorist recruitment in the heart of London. This was the home base of Zacarias Moussaoui, the French citizen put on trial in Alexandria, Va. It was also the home of Richard Reid, the shoe bomber of December 2001. Imam Qureshi of Brixton and others were allowed by the British authorities to preach anti-US sermons to the some 4,000 Muslim inmates in British prisons, and thus to recruit new patsies for the world-wide terror machine. According to bin Laden's spokesman Bakri, 2,000 fighters were trained yearly during the late 1990s, including many in the US because of the lax firearms legislation. The rival of Brixton Mosque was the equally redoubtable Finsbury Mosque, home of the Saudi demagogue al Masri, who was finally taken into custody in the spring of 2004. There is every reason to believe that London is one of the main recruiting grounds for patsies, dupes, fanatics, double agents, and other roustabouts of the terrorist scene.[890]

The American connection to the creation, organization, and manipulation of fundamentalist groups such as al-Qaeda goes at least as far back as the 1970s when the United States, spearheaded by the work of Zbigniew Brzezinski, created al Qaeda itself in Afghanistan under the auspices of goading the Soviet Union to invade the Eurasian nation. Indeed, in an interview conducted in 1998, Brzezinski admitted to creating al Qaeda for these purposes thus demonstrating that al Qaeda as a fighting force has always been nothing more than a Western controlled battering ram – the CIA's Arab Legion.

The short but telling interview is as follows:

Q: The former director of the CIA, Robert Gates, stated in his memoirs ["From the Shadows"], that American intelligence services began to aid the Mujahadeen in Afghanistan 6 months before the Soviet intervention. In this period you were the national security adviser to President Carter. You therefore played a role in this affair. Is that correct?

Brzezinski: Yes. According to the official version of history, CIA aid to the Mujahadeen began during 1980, that is to say, after the Soviet army invaded Afghanistan, 24 Dec 1979. But the reality, secretly guarded until now, is completely otherwise: Indeed, it was July 3, 1979 that President Carter signed the first directive for secret aid to the opponents of the pro-Soviet regime in Kabul. And that very day, I wrote a note to the president in which I explained to him that in my opinion this aid was going to induce a Soviet military intervention.

Q: Despite this risk, you were an advocate of this covert action. But perhaps you yourself desired this Soviet entry into war and looked to provoke it?

Brzezinski: It isn't quite that. We didn't push the Russians to intervene, but we knowingly increased the probability that they would.

Q: When the Soviets justified their intervention by asserting that they intended to fight against a secret involvement of the United States in Afghanistan, people didn't believe them. However, there was a basis of truth. You don't regret anything today?

[890] Tarpley, Webster G. 9/11 Synthetic Terror: Made In USA. 4th Edition. 2007. Progressive Press. Pp.154-156.

Brzezinski: Regret what? That secret operation was an excellent idea. It had the effect of drawing the Russians into the Afghan trap and you want me to regret it? The day that the Soviets officially crossed the border, I wrote to President Carter: We now have the opportunity of giving to the USSR its Vietnam war. Indeed, for almost 10 years, Moscow had to carry on a war unsupportable by the government, a conflict that brought about the demoralization and finally the breakup of the Soviet empire.

Q: And neither do you regret having supported the Islamic [integrisme], having given arms and advice to future terrorists?

Brzezinski: What is most important to the history of the world? The Taliban or the collapse of the Soviet empire? Some stirred-up Moslems or the liberation of Central Europe and the end of the cold war?

Q: Some stirred-up Moslems? But it has been said and repeated: Islamic fundamentalism represents a world menace today.

Brzezinski: Nonsense! It is said that the West had a global policy in regard to Islam. That is stupid. There isn't a global Islam. Look at Islam in a rational manner and without demagoguery or emotion. It is the leading religion of the world with 1.5 billion followers. But what is there in common among Saudi Arabian fundamentalism, moderate Morocco, Pakistan militarism, Egyptian pro-Western or Central Asian secularism? Nothing more than what unites the Christian countries.[891]

The quote above, along with ample evidence to support Brzezinski's own admissions, clearly demonstrate the control wielded over al Qaeda/Islamic Fundamentalist organizations in the late 1970s by Western intelligence and military agencies. That control has been maintained to this day and is now being utilized once again in Syria.

Indeed, as Brzezinski states, there is no real "global Islam," to speak of. Yet, the ability to unify a global movement of death squads coming from such a vast number of countries across the world must necessarily be capable of exceptional organizational capability and meticulous selection of participants. The Muslim world is not unified under fanatical fundamentalist demagogues. Yet, if one pays attention to MSNBC, FOX, and NPR, it would be hard not to believe that such is the case. The point is that, in order to organize and deploy hordes of fundamentalist terrorists as if they were invading army brigades, an organizing force and an organizing structure is required. But if that organizing structure is not the terrorists themselves and the organizing force or principle is not "global Islam," then what is it? The answer to this question is clear – not only through investigative and empirical historical analysis, but also through the admissions of characters like Brzezinski. The organizing force/principle and structure are the Anglo-American intelligence and military agencies that often appear in the form of NGOs, foundations, corporations, and banks, and who use these witless groups as nothing more than covert cannon fodder.

More importantly, however, is the question of continued control over Islamic fundamentalist terror groups.

---

[891] Cockburn, Alexander; St. Clair, Jeffrey. "How Jimmy Carter and I Started the Mujahideen." Counterpunch. January 15, 1998. http://www.counterpunch.org/1998/01/15/how-jimmy-carter-and-i-started-the-mujahideen/ Accessed on July 2, 2013.

The answer, of course, is that they have used it again. From assassination attempts against Ghaddaffi in Libya, terrorist groups in Chechnya, and the Mujahedeen in Afghanistan, to 9/11, the London bombings, the fall of Libya, and the assault on Syria, the CIA Arab legion has been effectively used to mold public opinion, justify wars, destabilize and destroy sovereign nations, and make incredible strategic power plays upon the geopolitical chessboard.

It is important to note that, in Brzezinski's own book, *The Grand Chessboard: American Primacy* and Its Geostrategic Imperatives, Eurasia is described as the key to global power. Central Asia, he argues, is the key to controlling Eurasia due to its massive oil reserves, natural resources, and geostrategic location. Interestingly enough, Brzezinski also writes in this book that "The attitude of the American public toward the external projection of American power has been much more ambivalent. The public supported America's engagement in World War II largely because of the shock effect of the Japanese attack on Pearl Harbor."[892] He goes on to state that this Central Asia-based strategy of control could not be implemented due to resistance of American military imperialism, "except in the circumstance of a truly massive and widely perceived direct external threat."[893] He reiterates this concept by stating elsewhere that, "the pursuit of power is not a goal that command popular passion, except in the conditions of a sudden threat or challenge to the public's sense of domestic well-being."[894] In the book, he also "prophetically" suggests that the US may possibly be attacked by Afghan terrorists that would then lead to an invasion of Afghanistan and, eventually, Iran.[895]

The very fact that Brzezinski, one of the individuals responsible for the creation and manipulation of al Qaeda, would "predict" an attack on the United States which is blamed on Afghan terrorists resulting in the invasion and conquest of Afghanistan, Central Asia, and Iran - as well as that the latter goal could not be achieved absent some catalyzing event and external enemy - should call into question everything one thought one knew in regards to al Qaeda, terrorism, and the official story of 9/11.

In addition, Tarpley explains Brzezinski's approach and outlook toward geopolitics and the global structure in his book, *Obama: The Postmodern Coup*, where he writes,

> Brzezinski's ancestors worked with the British to incite the subject nationalities of the Russian, Austro-Hungarian, and German Empires to rebel against St. Petersburg, Vienna, and Berlin, not in their own interests, but rather for the greater glory of London. Now Zbigniew wants to pose as the modern Mazzini, who wanted to make Italy turbulent – which was bad for Vienna – without making her united and strong, which would have posed problems for the imperial lifeline to India through the

---

[892] Brzezinski, Zbigniew. The Grand Chessboard: American Primacy And Its Geostrategic Imperatives. Basic Books. 1997. Pp. 24-25.

[893] Brzezinski, Zbigniew. The Grand Chessboard: American Primacy And Its Geostrategic Imperatives. Basic Books. 1997. P. 211.

[894] Brzezinski, Zbigniew. The Grand Chessboard: American Primacy And Its Geostrategic Imperatives. Basic Books. 1997. Pp. 35-36.

[895] "Context of 'October 1997: Brzezinski Highlights the Importance of Central Asia to Achieving World Domination." History Commons. http://www.cooperativeresearch.org/context.jsp?item=a1097chessboard#a1097chessboard Accessed on July 2, 2013.

central Mediterranean. Brzezinski's method would lead quickly to an economically depressed, impoverished and desolate world of squabbling, impotent petty states, presided over by Anglo-American finance oligarchs and their all-important eastern European émigré' advisors.

Naturally, Zbigniew is a fanatical opponent of Third World economic development; he once said that the US would never tolerate any more Japans in Asia – in other words, no more successful transitions from backwardness to a modern full-set economy. A basic tenet of counter-insurgency is that when you are confronted with broadly supported economic and political demands, play the card of divide and conquer in the form of local control, tribal, racial, ethnic, and religious divisions, etc. Zbig claims that the real goal of the world-wide awakening is "dignity." By dignity he means respect for every minute parochial or particularist trait of every real or imagined ethnic group and sub-group. It is the kind of dignity that reduces those who enjoy it from the status of independent nations to mere ethnographic material. Such dignity as Zbig imagines can only be attained by the smallest possible political units – by the thorough balkanization, partition, and subdivision of the existing national states. It is the kind of dignity the British Empire had in mind when it played the Mazzini card of national self-determination against the Austro-Hungarian, Russian, and Ottoman Empires. Woodrow Wilson played the same card at Versailles. This kind of dignity is congenial and compatible with the Bernard Lewis Plan for carving and balkanizing every nation in the Middle East – three Iraqs, six or seven Irans, four or five Pakistans, two Sudans, multiple Lebanons, with Turkey, Syria, and other mutilated and chopped up as well. Think of the kind current tragic status of Iraqi Kurds, Sunnis, and Shiites, and you will see the kind of dignity that Zbig is selling. Zbig obviously intends to apply this recipe in the ethnic labyrinth of the Caucasus and Trans-Caucasus with a view to starting the ethnic disintegration of all of Russia – a lunatic ploy if there ever was one. . . . . . Zbig, one of the cheerleaders for the bombing of Serbia in the spring of 1999, cares as little about international law as any neocon.[896]

Elsewhere in the book, Tarpley writes something similar. He writes,

Brzezinski's influence is not limited merely to issues of war and peace in the foreign policy sphere, critical though that obviously is. The entire profile exhibited by Obama during his campaign would appear to derive from the theoretical elaborations of Brzezinski. The key piece of evidence in this regard is Brzezinski's latest book, *Second Chance*. Here Brzezinski repeats his thesis that a worldwide political awakening is now taking place, and that the goal of this movement is "dignity." Brzezinski's notion of dignity, once all the obfuscation is peeled away, boils down to the quest for cultural and political self-determination and extreme identity politics on the smallest possible scale, with everything shaped by the cultural, ethnic, religious, and social peculiarities and parochialisms of the smallest possible groups. Brzezinski wants mini-states and micro-states with the dimensions of the local control and community control project which have so long been in vogue for counterinsurgency purposes. There is no doubt that Brzezinski's "dignity" thesis represents a declaration of war, not against this or that nation-state, but against the institution of the nation-state itself as we have known it for the last 500 to 650 years, going back to the

---

[896] Tarpley, Webster G. Obama: The Postmodern Coup. Progressive Press. 2008. Pp. 106-108..

Visconti of Milan c. 1380 in the Italian Renaissance. If respecting the tiniest peculiarities of every conceivable group is the order of the day, then a massive wave of secession, Balkanization, subdivision, and partition of the existing nation-states will be the unavoidable result. And this is exactly what Brzezinski wants. The most obvious example is the secession of Kosovo province from Serbia (under KLA terrorist auspices), opening a superpower crisis between Washington and Moscow. For Africa, Brzezinski recommends the so-called "micro-nationalities" concept, which means that the national boundaries established in the 19th century should be swept aside in favor of a crazy quilt of petty tribal entities, each one so small that it could not hope to resist even a medium-sized oil multinational.

In the Middle East, knowledgeable observers have long been familiar with the Bernard Lewis Plan, which contemplates the breakup of the existing nation-states into impotent, squabbling principalities, each on an easy prey for J.P. Morgan Chase, Halliburton, Blackwater, Exxon-Mobil, and other neo-feudal corporate predators. The case of Iraq is already before the eyes of the world: instead of one Iraq, we now have three – the Kurdish entity in the north, the central Sunni region, and the Shiastan in the south. Still, according to the Bernard Lewis Plan, Iran is one day to be divided into six or seven subdivisions, Sudan into at least two parts, and Lebanon into a checkerboard of petty enclaves, while Turkey, Syria, and other Middle East states are destined to be carved and mutilated to create an independent greater Kurdistan and other will-o'-the-wisps that have populated the diseased imagination of Anglo-American geopoliticians going back to Versailles in 1918.[897]

Returning to the British connection, however, it is important to understand that creation, control, and manipulation of extremist groups the world over has been a staple of British imperialism since the early 1800s. From the creation of the Young Societies by Mazzini and the incitement to revolt and destabilize to the continuation of these policies by Thomas E. Lawrence, the use of extremists as a battering ram against the nation-state or competing ideology made up a large portion of the British approach to expansion of its Empire.[898] In current times, nothing has significantly changed.

The Arab Spring In A Different Light – The Color Revolution

The precise techniques of regime change, balkanization, and the weakening of nation-states for political and/or geopolitical purposes are too lengthy to enter into a detailed expose' in the course of this book. However, it is important to understand the basics of these controlled social movements and how they work so that some guard may be erected against their continued occurrence and, at the very least, provide a mechanism for understanding a contrived revolution when it appears.

---

[897] Tarpley, Webster G. Obama: The Postmodern Coup. Progressive Press. 2008. Pp. 57-58.
[898] Daniel, John. "The Crusades: 1099-1314. The Muslim Excuse For . . . The 'Secret Society' Behind Osama bin Laden And His al Qaeda." Bibliotecapleyades.net.
http://www.bibliotecapleyades.net/sociopolitica/sociopol_middleeast04.htm Accessed on July 2, 2013.

The destruction of the modern nation-state or the implementation of regime change can take a variety of forms. The open war method, a favorite of the Neo-Con factions of the ruling elite, usually relies on manipulating death squads, dupes, fanatics, or the mentally handicapped and criminally insane into committing or attempting to commit (acting as a patsy will suffice) a terrorist act of violence, thus justifying a response from the victim nation. The Brzezinski method, as discussed previously, may often involve the outright organization, arming, funding, and direction of death squads such as the method employed in Libya and Syria in order to stir up as much tension and stress as possible within the country, weaken the national government, and directly seize power. Lastly, there is the strategy of the "color revolution" which is largely nonviolent in terms of organized assaults but is massive in scale, politically motivated, and made up of largely genuine participants although the movement itself is directed by the most disingenuous agents of powerful interests.

In dividing up the three methods of destabilization, it should not be assumed that these are the only three available methods of eviscerating the self-determination of a people or sovereign nations or that these methods are mutually exclusive. Indeed, these methods often bleed over into one another, blending aspects of two or even all three.

The agenda of destruction aimed at Afghanistan and Iraq used only the first method (direct military aggression) initially. Iraq subsequently required the invocation of the second method (death squads) in order to divide the Iraqi opposition to American occupation. The efforts against Tunisia and Egypt largely involved the third method (color revolution) with a sprinkling of the second (death squad). Likewise, the failed destabilization of Iran involved both the color revolution and the death squad motive. Libya was attacked by the death squad method but eventually required direct military intervention. Being a special case where the national government is much stronger and the civilian population stalwart against foreign invasion, the Syrian situation called for a combination of both color revolution and death squads and, quite possibly in the near future, direct military invasion.

While color revolutions have tended to be vastly more successful in the Baltic states and Eastern Europe than in the Middle East, what is important to understand, whether color revolution or death squad organization, is that the NGOs (Non-Governmental Organizations), Foundations, and "Human Rights" organizations are always acting as on-the-ground trainers, manipulators, and propagandists of and for the "revolutionaries."

As Eric Pottenger and Jeff Frieson of *Color Revolutions and Geopolitics* described the color revolution process,

> Color revolutions are, without a doubt, one of the main features of global political developments today. . . . . .

> It's a fact that Western governments (especially the US government) and various non-governmental organizations (NGOs) spend millions of dollars to co-opt and "channel" local populations of targeted countries against their own political leadership.

> Empty democracy slogans and flashy colors aside, we argue that color revolutions are good old-fashioned regime change operations: destabilization without the tanks.

The secret ingredient is a sophisticated science used to manipulate emotions and circumvent critical thinking. History shows that, too much of the power elite, humanity is seen as a collection of nerve endings to be pushed and pulled one way or the other, sometimes made to tremble in fear, sometimes made to salivate like Pavlov's dogs. These days the manipulation is so pervasive, so subtle, so effective, that even critical individuals at times must necessarily fail to recognize how often--or in what context--they have fallen prey.

Of course fear is the most obvious emotion played upon to effect massive social change. One need only to reflect upon the last ten years, since 9/11, to know that fear is a primary instrument used to initiate and justify dangerous shifts in public policy.

But as humanity has been physiologically equipped with a *range* of emotions, and is *not merely arrested and controlled by fear alone*, a strata of behavioral and political science also found it useful to master the flip-side of the emotional spectrum, and by that we mean *desire*, and all that drives groups of individuals to act, even in the face of fear, in pursuit of something worthwhile.

Many are the professions that utilize this type of understanding, including (but not limited to) marketing, advertising, public relations, politics and law-making, radio, television, journalism and news, film, music, general business and salesmanship; each of them selling, branding, promoting, entertaining, sloganeering, framing, explaining, creating friends and enemies, arguing likes and dislikes, setting the boundaries of good and evil: in many cases *using their talents to circumvent their audiences' intellect, the real target being emotional, oftentimes even subconscious*.

Looking beneath the facade of the color revolutionary movement we also find a desire-based behavioral structure, in particular one that has been built upon historical lessons offered by social movements and periods of political upheaval.

It then makes sense that the personnel of such operations include perception managers, PR firms, pollsters and opinion-makers in the social media. Through the operational infrastructure, these entities work in close coordination with intelligence agents, local and foreign activists, strategists and tacticians, tax-exempt foundations, governmental agencies, and a host of non- governmental organizations.

Collectively, their job is to make a palace coup (of their sponsorship) seem like a social revolution; to help fill the streets with fearless demonstrators advocating on behalf of a government of *their* choosing, which then legitimizes the sham governments with the authenticity of popular democracy and revolutionary fervor.

Because the operatives perform much of their craft in the open, their effectiveness is heavily predicated upon their ability to veil the influence backing them, and the long-term intentions guiding their work.

Their effectiveness is predicated on their ability to deceive, targeting both local populations and foreign audiences with highly-misleading interpretations of the underlying causes provoking these events.[899]

---

[899] Pottenger, Eric; Frieson, Jeff. ColorRevolutionsAndGeopolitics.blogspot.com. Homepage. Accessed on July 3, 2013.

With this explanation in mind, consider the description provided by Ian Traynor of the *Guardian* regarding the "revolutions" and "mass movements" taking place in Ukraine, Serbia, Belarus, and Georgia in 2004. Traynor writes,

> With their websites and stickers, their pranks and slogans aimed at banishing widespread fear of a corrupt regime, the democracy guerrillas of the Ukrainian Pora youth movement have already notched up a famous victory - whatever the outcome of the dangerous stand-off in Kiev.
>
> Ukraine, traditionally passive in its politics, has been mobilised by the young democracy activists and will never be the same again.
>
> But while the gains of the orange-bedecked "chestnut revolution" are Ukraine's, the campaign is an American creation, a sophisticated and brilliantly conceived exercise in western branding and mass marketing that, in four countries in four years, has been used to try to salvage rigged elections and topple unsavoury regimes.
>
> Funded and organised by the US government, deploying US consultancies, pollsters, diplomats, the two big American parties and US non-government organisations, the campaign was first used in Europe in Belgrade in 2000 to beat Slobodan Milosevic at the ballot box.
>
> Richard Miles, the US ambassador in Belgrade, played a key role. And by last year, as US ambassador in Tbilisi, he repeated the trick in Georgia, coaching Mikhail Saakashvili in how to bring down Eduard Shevardnadze.
>
> Ten months after the success in Belgrade, the US ambassador in Minsk, Michael Kozak, a veteran of similar operations in Central America, notably in Nicaragua, organised a near identical campaign to try to defeat the Belarus hard man, Alexander Lukashenko.
>
> That one failed. "There will be no Kostunica in Belarus," the Belarus president declared, referring to the victory in Belgrade.
>
> But experience gained in Serbia, Georgia and Belarus has been invaluable in plotting to beat the regime of Leonid Kuchma in Kiev.
>
> The operation - engineering democracy through the ballot box and civil disobedience - is now so slick that the methods have matured into a template for winning other people's elections.[900]

Traynor's article represents a rare moment of candor allowed to seep through the iron curtain of the mainstream Western media regarding the nature of the Eastern European protests. Even so, Traynor's depiction of the methodology used by the Foundations, NGOs, and government agencies stirring up dissent and popular revolt is equally illuminating. He writes,

> In the centre of Belgrade, there is a dingy office staffed by computer-literate youngsters who call themselves the Centre for Non-violent Resistance. If you want to know how to beat a regime that controls the mass media, the judges, the courts, the security apparatus and the voting stations, the young Belgrade activists are for hire.

---

[900] Traynor, Ian. "US campaign behind the turmoil in Kiev." The Guardian. November 25, 2004. http://www.guardian.co.uk/world/2004/nov/26/ukraine.usa Accessed on July 3, 2013.

They emerged from the anti-Milosevic student movement, Otpor, meaning resistance. The catchy, single-word branding is important. In Georgia last year, the parallel student movement was Khmara. In Belarus, it was Zubr. In Ukraine, it is Pora, meaning high time. Otpor also had a potent, simple slogan that appeared everywhere in Serbia in 2000 - the two words "gotov je", meaning "he's finished", a reference to Milosevic. A logo of a black-and-white clenched fist completed the masterful marketing.

In Ukraine, the equivalent is a ticking clock, also signaling that the Kuchma regime's days are numbered.

Stickers, spray paint and websites are the young activists' weapons. Irony and street comedy mocking the regime have been hugely successful in puncturing public fear and enraging the powerful.

Last year, before becoming president in Georgia, the US-educated Mr. Saakashvili travelled from Tbilisi to Belgrade to be coached in the techniques of mass defiance. In Belarus, the US embassy organised the dispatch of young opposition leaders to the Baltic, where they met up with Serbs travelling from Belgrade. In Serbia's case, given the hostile environment in Belgrade, the Americans organised the overthrow from neighbouring Hungary - Budapest and Szeged.

In recent weeks, several Serbs travelled to the Ukraine. Indeed, one of the leaders from Belgrade, Aleksandar Maric, was turned away at the border.

The Democratic party's National Democratic Institute, the Republican party's International Republican Institute, the US state department and USAid are the main agencies involved in these grassroots campaigns as well as the Freedom House NGO and billionaire George Soros's open society institute.

US pollsters and professional consultants are hired to organise focus groups and use psychological data to plot strategy.

The usually fractious oppositions have to be united behind a single candidate if there is to be any chance of unseating the regime. That leader is selected on pragmatic and objective grounds, even if he or she is anti-American.

In Serbia, US pollsters Penn, Schoen and Berland Associates discovered that the assassinated pro-western opposition leader, Zoran Djindjic, was reviled at home and had no chance of beating Milosevic fairly in an election. He was persuaded to take a back seat to the anti-western Vojislav Kostunica, who is now Serbian prime minister.

In Belarus, US officials ordered opposition parties to unite behind the dour, elderly trade unionist, Vladimir Goncharik, because he appealed to much of the Lukashenko constituency.

Officially, the US government spent $41m (£21.7m) organising and funding the year-long operation to get rid of Milosevic from October 1999. In Ukraine, the figure is said to be around $14m.

Apart from the student movement and the united opposition, the other key element in the democracy template is what is known as the "parallel vote tabulation", a counter to the election-rigging tricks beloved of disreputable regimes.

There are professional outside election monitors from bodies such as the Organisation for Security and Cooperation in Europe, but the Ukrainian poll, like its predecessors, also featured thousands of local election monitors trained and paid by western groups.

Freedom House and the Democratic party's NDI helped fund and organise the "largest civil regional election monitoring effort" in Ukraine, involving more than 1,000 trained observers. They also organised exit polls. On Sunday night those polls gave Mr. Yushchenko an 11-point lead and set the agenda for much of what has followed.

The exit polls are seen as critical because they seize the initiative in the propaganda battle with the regime, invariably appearing first, receiving wide media coverage and putting the onus on the authorities to respond.

The final stage in the US template concerns how to react when the incumbent tries to steal a lost election.

In Belarus, President Lukashenko won, so the response was minimal. In Belgrade, Tbilisi, and now Kiev, where the authorities initially tried to cling to power, the advice was to stay cool but determined and to organise mass displays of civil disobedience, which must remain peaceful but risk provoking the regime into violent suppression.

If the events in Kiev vindicate the US in its strategies for helping other people win elections and take power from anti-democratic regimes, it is certain to try to repeat the exercise elsewhere in the post-Soviet world.[901]

Jonathan Mowat adds to the recent historical understanding of the controlled-coup and color revolutions in his article, "The New Gladio In Action: 'Swarming Adolescents,'" also focusing on the players and the methods of deployment. Mowat writes,

Much of the coup apparatus is the same that was used in the overthrow of President Fernando Marcos of the Philippines in 1986, the Tiananmen Square destabilization in 1989, and Vaclav Havel's "Velvet revolution" in Czechoslovakia in 1989. As in these early operations, the National Endowment for Democracy (NED), and its primary arms, the National Democratic Institute for International Affairs (NDI) and International Republican Institute (IRI), played a central role. The NED was established by the Reagan Administration in 1983, to do overtly what the CIA had done covertly, in the words of one its legislative drafters, Allen Weinstein. The Cold War propaganda and operations center, Freedom House, now chaired by former CIA director James Woolsey, has also been involved, as were billionaire George Soros' foundations, whose donations always dovetail those of the NED.

What is new about the template bears on the use of the Internet (in particular chat rooms, instant messaging, and blogs) and cell phones (including text-messaging), to rapidly steer angry and suggestible "Generation X" youth into and out of mass demonstrations and the like—a capability that only emerged in the mid-1990s. "With the crushing ubiquity of cell phones, satellite phones, PCs, modems and the Internet," Laura Rosen emphasized in Salon Magazine on February 3, 2001,"the information age is shifting the advantage from authoritarian leaders to civic groups." She might have mentioned the video games that helped create the deranged mindset of these

[901] Traynor, Ian. "US campaign behind the turmoil in Kiev." The Guardian. November 25, 2004. http://www.guardian.co.uk/world/2004/nov/26/ukraine.usa Accessed on July 3, 2013.

"civic groups." The repeatedly emphasized role played by so-called "Discoshaman" and his girlfriend "Tulipgirl," in assisting the "Orange Revolution" through their aptly named blog, "Le Sabot Post-Modern," is indicative of the technical and sociological components involved.

The emphasis on the use of new communication technologies to rapidly deploy small groups, suggests what we are seeing is civilian application of Secretary Donald Rumsfeld's "Revolution in Military Affairs" doctrine, which depends on highly mobile small group deployments "enabled" by "real time" intelligence and communications. Squads of soldiers taking over city blocks with the aid of "intelligence helmet" video screens that give them an instantaneous overview of their environment constitute the military side. Bands of youth converging on targeted intersections in constant dialogue on cell phones constitute the doctrine's civilian application.

This parallel should not be surprising since the US military and National Security Agency subsidized the development of the Internet, cellular phones, and software platforms. From their inception, these technologies were studied and experimented with in order to find the optimal use in a new kind of warfare. The "revolution" in warfare that such new instruments permit has been pushed to the extreme by several specialists in psychological warfare. . . . . .

The new techniques of warfare include the use of both lethal (violent) and nonlethal (nonviolent) tactics. Both ways are conducted using the same philosophy, infrastructure, and modus operandi. It is what is known as Cyberwar. For example, the tactic of swarming is a fundamental element in both violent and nonviolent forms of warfare. This new philosophy of war, which is supposed to replicate the strategy of Genghis Khan as enhanced by modern technologies, is intended to aid both military and non-military assaults against targeted states through what are, in effect, "high tech" hordes. In that sense there is no difference, from the standpoint of the plotters, between Iraq or Ukraine, if only that many think the Ukraine-like coup is more effective and easier.[902]

Mowat then goes on to demonstrate how this theory of destabilization fits with that endorsed by military-industrial theoreticians like Dr. Peter Ackerman who wrote the aptly-named book *Strategic Nonviolent Conflict*. For instance, when Ackerman spoke at the "Secretary's Open Forum" at the State Department in June 29, 2004, Ackerman did not quibble with the imperialist goals of the Bush administration, only the methods used to achieve them. In his speech, "Between Hard and Soft Power: The Rise of Civilian-Based Struggle and Democratic Change," Ackerman suggested that youth movements, not American military might, could be used to bring down North Korea and Iran and that they could have been used to bring down Iraq. Ackerman also stated in his speech that

[902] Mowat, Jonathan. "A New Gladio In Action." Online Journal. Reposted by ColorRevolutionandGeoPolitics.blogspot.com.
http://colorrevolutionsandgeopolitics.blogspot.com/2011/04/from-archives-jonathan-mowat-new-gladio.html Accessed on July 3, 2013.
See also,
Tarpley, Webster G. Obama: The Postmodern Coup. Mowat, Jonathan. "A New Gladio In Action: 'Swarming Adolescents.'" Progressive Press. 2008. Pp. 243-270.

he was working with Lawrence Livermore Laboratories, the U.S. weapons designer, for the purpose of creating new communications technologies that might be used by these "youth insurgencies."[903]

As Mowat points out, Ackerman is the founding Chairman of the International Center on Nonviolent Conflicts of Washington, D.C. where Jack Duvall, a former U.S. Air Force officer, is President. Ackerman is also co-director with former CIA Director James Woolsey of the Arlington Institute (AI) of Washington, D.C. The AI was created by John L. Peterson, in 1989 who is the former Chief of Naval Operations, for the stated purpose of helping "redefine the concept of national security in much larger, comprehensive terms" by introducing "social value shifts into the traditional national defense equation."[904]

Yet the theory of "youth insurgencies" in no way began with Ackerson. As far back as 1967, the Tavistock Institute, the major psychological experimentation wing of the military industrial complex, was studying the effects of using "swarming adolescents" as an instrument of governmental disruption and regime change. As Jonathan Mowat summarizes,

> As in the case of the new communication technologies, the potential effectiveness of angry youth in postmodern coups has long been under study. As far back as 1967, Dr. Fred Emery, then director of the Tavistock Institute, and an expert on the "hypnotic effects" of television, specified that the then new phenomenon of "swarming adolescents" found at rock concerts could be effectively used to bring down the nation-state by the end of the 1990s. This was particularly the case, as Dr. Emery reported in "The next thirty years: concepts, methods and anticipations," in the group's "Human Relations," because the phenomena was associated with "rebellious hysteria." The British military created the Tavistock Institute as its psychological warfare arm following World War I; it has been the forerunner of such strategic planning ever since. Dr. Emery's concept saw immediate application in NATO's use of "swarming adolescents" in toppling French President Charles De Gaulle in 1967.[905]

---

[903] Mowat, Jonathan. "A New Gladio In Action." Online Journal. Reposted by ColorRevolutionandGeoPolitics.blogspot.com.
http://colorrevolutionsandgeopolitics.blogspot.com/2011/04/from-archives-jonathan-mowat-new-gladio.html Accessed on July 3, 2013.
See also,
Tarpley, Webster G. Obama: The Postmodern Coup. Mowat, Jonathan. "A New Gladio In Action: 'Swarming Adolescents.'" Progressive Press. 2008. Pp. 243-270.
[904] Mowat, Jonathan. "A New Gladio In Action." Online Journal. Reposted by ColorRevolutionandGeoPolitics.blogspot.com.
http://colorrevolutionsandgeopolitics.blogspot.com/2011/04/from-archives-jonathan-mowat-new-gladio.html Accessed on July 3, 2013.
See also,
Tarpley, Webster G. Obama: The Postmodern Coup. Mowat, Jonathan. "A New Gladio In Action: 'Swarming Adolescents.'" Progressive Press. 2008. Pp. 243-270.
[905] Mowat, Jonathan. "A New Gladio In Action." Online Journal. Reposted by ColorRevolutionandGeoPolitics.blogspot.com.
http://colorrevolutionsandgeopolitics.blogspot.com/2011/04/from-archives-jonathan-mowat-new-gladio.html Accessed on July 3, 2013.

Of course, the publicly acknowledged and published studies and theoretical applications of using "swarming adolescents" for the purposes of destabilizing one's enemy continued on through the years becoming more and more refined as it moved forward in both theory and practice. As mentioned earlier, the use of death squads and mass movements against the nation state or rival movements is nothing new. This much is evidenced by the work T.E. Lawrence. However, the details and techniques of the manipulation of mass numbers of people have only continued to become more and more advanced and sophisticated. Mowat further describes the research and theory behind color revolutions:

In November 1989, Case Western Reserve in Cleveland, Ohio, under the aegis of that university's "Program for Social Innovations in Global Management," began a series of conferences to review progress towards that strategic objective, which was reported on in "Human Relations" in 1991. There, Dr. Howard Perlmutter, a professor of "Social Architecture" at the Wharton School, and a follower of Dr. Emery, stressed that "rock video in Kathmandu," was an appropriate image of how states with traditional cultures could be destabilized, thereby creating the possibility of a "global civilization." There are two requirements for such a transformation, he added, "building internationally committed networks of international and locally committed organizations," and "creating global events" through "the transformation of a local event into one having virtually instantaneous international implications through mass-media."

Mowat goes on to describe what he deems to be the "final" aspect of color revolutions and destabilizations - the implementation of polling operations providing false "exit poll" data, confidence in government, satisfaction with the current regime, support for the opposition, etc. This method serves to create the perception both inside the target country and outside of it in the form of world public opinion that conditions were abominable before the "revolution" (which may or may not be true), that the overwhelming majority of the citizens within the target country support the coup, and that the regime is failing. In short, the goal is to create a self-fulfilling prophecy of governmental collapse.

After a short propaganda blitz citing these "poll watchers," "freedom and democracy organizations," and "human rights organizations," the door is opened to the implementation of international pressure against the target governments, covert action inside and outside of the nation, and the defection of pre-planned agents planted within the governmental and military structure.

Mowat writes,

This brings us to the final ingredient of these new coups—the deployment of polling agencies' "exit polls" broadcast on international television to give the false (or sometimes accurate) impression of massive vote-fraud by the ruling party, to put targeted states on the defensive. Polling operations in the recent coups have been overseen by such outfits as Penn, Schoen and Berland, top advisers to Microsoft and Bill Clinton. Praising their role in subverting Serbia, then Secretary of State

See also,

Tarpley, Webster G. Obama: The Postmodern Coup. Mowat, Jonathan. "A New Gladio In Action: 'Swarming Adolescents.'" Progressive Press. 2008. Pp. 243-270.

Madeleine Albright (and later Chairman of NDI) , in an October 2000 letter to the firm quoted on its website, stated: "Your work with the National Democratic Institute and the Yugoslav opposition contributed directly and decisively to the recent breakthrough for democracy in that country . . . This may be one of the first instances where polling has played such an important role in setting and securing foreign policy objectives." Penn, Schoen, together with the OSCE, also ran the widely televised "exit poll" operations in the Ukrainian elections.

In the aftermath of such youth deployments and media operations, more traditional elements come to the fore. That is, the forceful, if covert, intervention by international institutions and governments threatening the targeted regime, and using well placed operatives within the targeted regime's military and intelligence services to ensure no countermeasures can be effectively deployed. Without these traditional elements, of course, no postmodern coup could ever work. Or, as Jack DuVall put it in Jesse Walker's "Carnival and conspiracy in Ukraine," in Reason Online, November 30, 2004, "You can't simply parachute Karl Rove into a country and manufacture a revolution."[906]

Because color revolutions, destabilizations, and coups require much more than propaganda inside or outside the country, it is necessary to organize, train, indoctrinate, and mobilize with "boots on the ground" inside the target nation. Since the movement will not be an organic one, the "swarming adolescents" must be organized by the agents directing the destabilization. With this in mind, Mowat's excellent article then goes in to the recent history of color revolution tactics along with a brief discussion regarding the history of some of its individual and organizational players, most notably Gene Sharp, Bob Helvey, and The Albert Einstein Institution. Still, it is important to understand that these individuals and organizations are by no means the pinnacle of international destabilizations and color revolutions nor are they the sole facilitators of it.[907] Regardless, Mowat explains,

The creation and deployment of coups of any kind requires agents on the ground. The main handler of these coups on the "street side" has been the Albert Einstein Institution, which was formed in 1983 as an offshoot of Harvard University under the impetus of Dr. Gene Sharp, and which specializes in "nonviolence as a form of warfare." Dr. Sharp had been the executive secretary of A.J. Muste, the famous U.S.

---

[906] Mowat, Jonathan. "A New Gladio In Action." Online Journal. Reposted by ColorRevolutionandGeoPolitics.blogspot.com.
http://colorrevolutionsandgeopolitics.blogspot.com/2011/04/from-archives-jonathan-mowat-new-gladio.html Accessed on July 3, 2013.
See also,
Tarpley, Webster G. Obama: The Postmodern Coup. Mowat, Jonathan. "A New Gladio In Action: 'Swarming Adolescents.'" Progressive Press. 2008. Pp. 247-248.
[907] Mowat, Jonathan. "A New Gladio In Action." Online Journal. Reposted by ColorRevolutionandGeoPolitics.blogspot.com.
http://colorrevolutionsandgeopolitics.blogspot.com/2011/04/from-archives-jonathan-mowat-new-gladio.html Accessed on July 3, 2013.
See also,
Tarpley, Webster G. Obama: The Postmodern Coup. Mowat, Jonathan. "A New Gladio In Action: 'Swarming Adolescents.'" Progressive Press. 2008. Pp. 243-270.

Trotskyite labor organizer and peacenik. The group is funded by Soros and the NED. Albert Einstein's president is Col. Robert Helvey, a former US Army officer with 30 years of experience in Southeast Asia. He has served as the case officer for youth groups active in the Balkans and Eastern Europe since at least 1999.

Col. Helvey reports, in a January 29, 2001, interview with film producer Steve York in Belgrade, that he first got involved in "strategic nonviolence" upon seeing the failure of military approaches to toppling dictators—especially in Myanmar, where he had been stationed as military attaché—and seeing the potential of Sharp's alternative approach. According to B. Raman, the former director of India's foreign intelligence agency, RAW, in a December 2001 paper published by his institute entitled, "The USA's National Endowment For Democracy (NED): An Update," Helvey "was an officer of the Defence Intelligence Agency of the Pentagon, who had served in Vietnam and, subsequently, as the US Defence Attache in Yangon, Myanmar (1983 to 85), during which he clandestinely organised the Myanmar students to work behind Aung San Suu Kyi and in collaboration with Bo Mya's Karen insurgent group. . . . He also trained in Hong Kong the student leaders from Beijing in mass demonstration techniques which they were to subsequently use in the Tiananmen Square incident of June 1989" and "is now believed to be acting as an adviser to the Falun Gong, the religious sect of China, in similar civil disobedience techniques." Col. Helvey nominally retired from the army in 1991, but had been working with Albert Einstein and Soros long before then.

Reflecting Albert Einstein's patronage, one of its first books was Dr. Sharp's "Making Europe Unconquerable: The Potential of Civilian-Based Deterrence and Defense," published in 1985 with a forward by George Kennan, the famous "Mr. X" 1940's architect of the Cold War who was also a founder of the CIA's Operations division. There, Sharp reports that "civilian-based defense" could counter the Soviet threat through its ability "to deter and defeat attacks by making a society ungovernable by would be oppressors" and "by maintaining a capacity for orderly self-rule even in the face of extreme threats and actual aggression." He illustrates its feasibility by discussing the examples of the Algerian independence in 1961 and the Czechoslovakian resistance to Soviet invasion in 1968-9. In his forward, Kennan praises Sharp for showing the "possibilities of deterrence and resistance by civilians" as a "partial alternative to the traditional, purely military concepts of national defense." The book was promptly translated into German, Norwegian, Italian, Danish, and other NATO country languages. See the link to the Italian translation of the book (Verso un'Europa Inconquistabile. 190 pp. 1989 Introduction by Gianfranco Pasquino) that sports a series of fashionable sociologists and "politologists" prefacing the book and calling for a civil resistance to a possible Soviet invasion of Italy.

Such formulations suggest that Albert Einstein activities were, ironically, coherent (or, possibly updating) the infamous NATO's "Gladio" stay-behind network, whose purpose was to combat possible Soviet occupation through a panoply of military and nonmilitary means. The investigations into Gladio, and those following the 1978 assassination of former Prime Minister Aldo Moro, also shed some light (immediately switched off) on a professional apparatus of destabilization that had been invisible for several decades to the public.

It is noteworthy that the former deputy chief of intelligence for the US Army in Europe, Major General Edward Atkeson, first "suggested the name 'civilian based defense' to Sharp," John M. Mecartney, Coordinator of the Nonviolent Action for National Defense Institute, reports in his group's CBD News and Opinion of March 1991. By 1985, Gen. Atkeson, then retired from the US Army, was giving seminars at Harvard entitled "Civilian-based Defense and the Art of War.

The Albert Einstein Institution reports, in its "1994-99 Report on Activities," that Gen. Atkeson also served on Einstein's advisory board in those years. Following his posting as the head of US Army intelligence in Europe, and possibly concurrently with his position at the Albert Einstein Institution, the Washington-based Center for Strategic and International Studies (CSIS) reports that Gen. Atkeson, who also advised CSIS on "international security." served as "national intelligence officer for general purpose forces on the staff of the director of Central Intelligence."

A 1990 variant of Sharp's book, "Civilian-Based Defense: A Post-Military Weapons System," the Albert Einstein Institution reports, "was used in 1991 and 1992 by the new independent governments of Estonia, Latvia, and Lithuania in planning their defense against Soviet efforts to regain control."

As we shall see below, with such backing, Col. Helvey and his colleagues have created a series of youth movements including Otpor! in Serbia, Kmara! in Georgia, Pora! in Ukraine, and the like, which are already virally replicating other sects throughout the former Soviet Union, achieving in civilian form what had not been possible militarily in the 1980s. The groups are also spreading to Africa and South America.[908]

If one were to desire a case study in the art of color revolution and destabilization, then the case of Milosevic's Serbia could easily be provided. Indeed, Michael Dobbs of the Washington Post wrote an article in 2000 entitled, "U.S. Advice Guided Milosevic Opposition: Political Consultants Helped Yugoslav Opposition Topple Authoritarian Leader," where he peripherally outlined the tactics used by the United States and NGOs in order to accomplish the desired regime change and the weakening of yet another target nation. This successful destabilization resulted in what Mowat deems "The Serbian Virus," a domino effect of color revolutions in the Eastern European and Slavic countries.[909] Dobbs wrote,

---

[908] Mowat, Jonathan. "A New Gladio In Action." Online Journal. Reposted by ColorRevolutionandGeoPolitics.blogspot.com.
http://colorrevolutionsandgeopolitics.blogspot.com/2011/04/from-archives-jonathan-mowat-new-gladio.html Accessed on July 3, 2013.
See also,
Tarpley, Webster G. Obama: The Postmodern Coup. Mowat, Jonathan. "A New Gladio In Action: 'Swarming Adolescents.'" Progressive Press. 2008. Pp. 248-250.

[909] Mowat, Jonathan. "A New Gladio In Action." Online Journal. Reposted by ColorRevolutionandGeoPolitics.blogspot.com.
http://colorrevolutionsandgeopolitics.blogspot.com/2011/04/from-archives-jonathan-mowat-new-gladio.html Accessed on July 3, 2013.
See also,
Tarpley, Webster G. Obama: The Postmodern Coup. Mowat, Jonathan. "A New Gladio In Action: 'Swarming Adolescents.'" Progressive Press. 2008. Pp. 243-270.

U.S.-funded consultants played a crucial role behind the scenes in virtually every facet of the anti-Milosevic drive, running tracking polls, training thousands of opposition activists and helping to organize a vitally important parallel vote count. U.S. taxpayers paid for 5,000 cans of spray paint used by student activists to scrawl anti-Milosevic graffiti on walls across Serbia, and 2.5 million stickers with the slogan "He's Finished," which became the revolution's catchphrase.

Some Americans involved in the anti-Milosevic effort said they were aware of CIA activity at the fringes of the campaign, but had trouble finding out what the agency was up to. Whatever it was, they concluded it was not particularly effective. The lead role was taken by the State Department and the U.S. Agency for International Development, the government's foreign assistance agency, which channeled the funds through commercial contractors and nonprofit groups such as NDI and its Republican counterpart, the International Republican Institute (IRI).

While NDI worked closely with Serbian opposition parties, IRI focused its attention on Otpor, which served as the revolution's ideological and organizational backbone. In March, IRI paid for two dozen Otpor leaders to attend a seminar on nonviolent resistance at the Hilton Hotel in Budapest a few hundred yards along the Danube from the NDI-favored Marriott.

During the seminar, the Serbian students received training in such matters as how to organize a strike, how to communicate with symbols, how to overcome fear and how to undermine the authority of a dictatorial regime. The principal lecturer was retired U.S. Army Col. Robert Helvey, who has made a study of nonviolent resistance methods around the world, including those used in modern-day Burma and the civil rights struggle in the American South.[910]

Mowat summarily documents the rest of the Serbian story by writing,

Helvey, who served two tours in Vietnam, introduced the Otpor activists to the ideas of American theoretician Gene Sharp, whom he describes as "the Clausewitz of the nonviolence movement," referring to the renowned Prussian military strategist.

Peter Ackerman, the above-mentioned coup expert, analyzed and popularized the methods involved in a 2001 PBS documentary-series and book, "A Force More Powerful: A Century of Nonviolent Conflict," together with retired US Airforce officer Jack DuVall. Focusing on youth organizing, they report:

After the NATO bombing, which had helped the regime suppress opposition, Otpor's organizing took hold with a quiet vengeance. It was built in some places around clubhouses where young people could go and hang out, exercise, and party on the weekends, or more often it was run out of dining rooms and bedrooms in activists' homes. These were "boys and girls 18 and 19 years old" who had lived "in absolute poverty compared to other teenagers around the world," according to Stanko Lazendic, an Otpor activist in Novi Sad. "Otpor offered these kids a place to gather, a place where they could express their creative ideas." In a word, it showed them how to empower themselves.

---

910 Dobbs, Michael. "U.S. Advice Guided Milosevic Opposition; Political Consultants Helped Yugoslav Opposition Topple Authoritarian Leader." The Washington Post. December 11, 2000. http://www.highbeam.com/doc/1P2-565855.html Accessed on July 4, 2013.

Otpor's leaders knew that they "couldn't use force on someone who . . . had three times more force and weapons than we did," in the words of Lazendic. "We knew what had happened in. Tiananmen, where the army plowed over students with tanks." So violence wouldn't work—and besides, it was the trademark of Milosevic, and Otpor had to stand for something different. Serbia "was a country in which violence was used too many times in daily politics," noted Srdja Popovic, a 27 year-old who called himself Otpor's "ideological commissar." The young activists had to use nonviolent methods "to show how superior, how advanced, how civilized" they were.

This relatively sophisticated knowledge of how to develop nonviolent power was not intuitive. Miljenko Dereta, the director of a private group in Belgrade called Civic Initiatives, got funding from Freedom House in the U.S. to print and distribute 5,000 copies of Gene Sharp's book, "From Dictatorship to Democracy: A Conceptual Framework for Liberation." Otpor got hold of Sharp's main three-volume work, "The Politics of Nonviolent Action," freely adapting sections of it into a Serbian-language notebook they dubbed the "Otpor User Manual." Consciously using this "ideology of nonviolent, individual resistance," in Popovic's words, activists also received direct training from Col. Robert Helvey, a colleague of Sharp, at the Budapest Hilton in March 2000.

Helvey emphasized how to break the people's habits of subservience to authority, and also how to subvert: the regime's "pillars of support," including the police and armed forces. Crucially, he warned them against "contaminants to a nonviolent struggle," especially violent action, which would deter ordinary people from joining the movement: and alienate the international community, from which material and financial assistance could be drawn. As Popovic put it: "Stay nonviolent and you will get the support of the third party."

That support, largely denied to the Serbian opposition before, now began to flow. Otpor and other dissident groups received funding from the National Endowment for Democracy, affiliated with the U.S. government, and Otpor leaders sat down with Daniel Server, the program director for the Balkans at the U.S. Institute for Peace, whose story of having been tear-gassed during an anti-Vietnam War demonstration gave him special credibility in their eyes. The International Republican Institute, also financed by the U.S. government, channeled funding to the opposition and met with Otpor leaders several times. The U.S. Agency for International Development, the wellspring for most of this financing, was also the source of money that went for materials like t-shirts and stickers.[911]

 With Serbia now under control and a successful destabilization having taken place, a large portion of the Slavic world and Eastern European bloc was now in the crosshairs of the Anglo-Americans.[912] Mowat describes this situation as follows:

---

[911] Mowat, Jonathan. "A New Gladio In Action." Online Journal. Reposted by ColorRevolutionandGeoPolitics.blogspot.com.
http://colorrevolutionsandgeopolitics.blogspot.com/2011/04/from-archives-jonathan-mowat-new-gladio.html Accessed on July 3, 2013.
See also,
Tarpley, Webster G. Obama: The Postmodern Coup. Mowat, Jonathan. "A New Gladio In Action: 'Swarming Adolescents.'" Progressive Press. 2008. Pp. 251-253.
[912] Mowat, Jonathan. "A New Gladio In Action." Online Journal. Reposted by

In the aftermath of the Serbian revolution, the National Endowment for Democracy, Albert Einstein Institution, and related outfits helped establish several Otpor-modeled youth groups in Eastern Europe, notably Zubr in Belarus in January 2001; Kmara in Georgia, in April 2003; and Pora in Ukraine in June 2004. Efforts to overthrow Belarus President Alexsander Luschenko failed in 2001, while the US overthrow of Georgian President Eduard Schevardnadze was successfully accomplished in 2003, using Kmara as part of its operation.

Commenting on that expansion, Albert Einstein staffer Chris Miller, in his report on a 2001 trip to Serbia found on the group's website, reports:

Since the ousting of Milosevic, several members of Otpor have met with members of the Belarusian group Zubr (Bison). In following developments in Belarus since early this year, It is clear that Zubr was developed or at least conceptualized, using Otpor as a model. Also, [Albert Einstein's report] From Dictatorship to Democracy is available in English on the Zubr website at www.zubr-belarus.com. Of course, success will not be achieved in Belarus or anywhere else, simply by mimicking the actions taken in Serbia. However the successful Serbian nonviolent struggle was highly influenced and aided by the availability of knowledge and information on strategic nonviolent struggle and both successful and unsuccessful past cases, which is transferable.

Otpor focused on building their human resources, especially among youth. An Otpor training manual to "train future trainers" was developed, which contained excerpts from The Politics of Nonviolent Action, provided to Otpor by Robert Helvey during his workshop in Budapest for Serbs in early 2000. It may be applicable for other countries.

And with funding provided by Freedom House and the US government, Otpor established the Center for Nonviolent Resistance, in Budapest, to train these groups. Describing the deployment of this youth movement, Ian Trainor, in the above cited Guardian November 2004 article, reports:

In the centre of Belgrade, there is a dingy office staffed by computer-literate youngsters who call themselves the Centre for Non-violent Resistance. If you want to know how to beat a regime that controls the mass media, the judges, the courts, the security apparatus and the voting stations, the young Belgrade activists are for hire.

They emerged from the anti-Milosevic student movement, Otpor, meaning resistance. The catchy, single-word branding is important. In Georgia last year, the parallel student movement was Kmara. In Belarus, it was Zubr. In Ukraine, it is Pora, meaning high time.

Stickers, spray paint and websites are the young activists' weapons. Irony and street comedy mocking the regime have been hugely successful in puncturing public fear and enraging the powerful.

ColorRevolutionandGeoPolitics.blogspot.com.
http://colorrevolutionsandgeopolitics.blogspot.com/2011/04/from-archives-jonathan-mowat-new-gladio.html Accessed on July 3, 2013.
See also,
Tarpley, Webster G. Obama: The Postmodern Coup. Mowat, Jonathan. "A New Gladio In Action: 'Swarming Adolescents.'" Progressive Press. 2008. Pp. 243-270.

Last year, before becoming president in Georgia, the US-educated Mr. Saakashvili traveled from Tbilisi to Belgrade to be coached in the techniques of mass defiance. In Belarus, the US embassy organized the dispatch of young opposition leaders to the Baltic, where they met up with Serbs traveling from Belgrade. In Serbia's case, given the hostile environment in Belgrade, the Americans organized the overthrow from neighboring Hungary—Budapest and Szeged.

In recent weeks, several Serbs traveled to the Ukraine. Indeed, one of the leaders from Belgrade, Aleksandar Maric, was turned away at the border. The Democratic party's National Democratic Institute, the Republican party's International Republican Institute, the US State Department and USAID are the main agencies involved in these grassroots campaigns as well as the Freedom House NGO and billionaire George Soros' Open Society Institute.

An Associated Press article by Dusan Stojanovic, on November 2, 2004, entitled "Serbia's export: Peaceful Revolution," elaborates:

"We knew there would be work for us after Milosevic," said Danijela Nenadic, a program coordinator of the Belgrade-based Center for Nonviolent Resistance. The nongovernmental group emerged from Otpor, the pro-democracy movement that helped sweep Milosevic from power by organizing massive and colorful protests that drew crowds who never previously had the courage to oppose the former Yugoslav president. In Ukraine and Belarus, tens of thousands of people have been staging daily protests—carbon copies of the anti-Milosevic rallies—with "training" provided by the Serbian group.

The group says it has "well-trained" followers in Ukraine and Belarus. In Georgia, Ukraine and Belarus, anti-government activists "saw what we did in Serbia and they contacted us for professional training," group member Sinisa Sikman said. Last year, Otpor's clenched fist was flying high on white flags again—this time in Georgia, when protesters stormed the parliament in an action that led to the toppling of Shevardnadze.

Last month, Ukrainian border authorities denied entry to Alexandar Maric, a member of Otpor and an adviser with the U.S.-based democracy watchdog Freedom House. A Ukrainian student group called Pora was following the strategies of Otpor.

James Woolsey's Freedom House "expressed concern" over Maric's deportation, in an October 14, 2004, press release which reported that he was traveling to Ukraine as part of "an initiative run by Freedom House, the National Democratic Institute, and the International Republican Institute to promote civic participation and oversight during the 2004 presidential and 2006 parliamentary elections in Ukraine." In a related statement, it added that it hoped the deportation was not a sign of the Ukrainian government's "unwillingness to allow the free flow of information and learning across borders that is an integral and accepted part of programs to encourage democratic progress in diverse societies around the world."[913]

---

[913] Mowat, Jonathan. "A New Gladio In Action." Online Journal. Reposted by ColorRevolutionandGeoPolitics.blogspot.com. http://colorrevolutionsandgeopolitics.blogspot.com/2011/04/from-archives-jonathan-mowat-new-gladio.html Accessed on July 3, 2013.
See also,

Mowat also provides an interesting timeline regarding the Serbian, Slovac, and Eastern European color revolutions:

Timeline:

Otpor! founded in Belgrade, Serbia in October 1998. Postmodern Coup overthrows Slobodan Milosevic on October 5, 2000. Subsequently forms Center for Nonviolent Resistance to spread !!! revolutions.

Clinton Administration's Community of Democracies launched in Warsaw, Poland, in June 2000.

Zubr! founded in Minsk, Belarus, on January 14, 2001. Election-Coup efforts fail in September 9, 2001.

Mjaft! founded in Tirana, Albania, on March 15, 2003.

Kmara! founded in Tblisi, Georgia in April 2003. "Rose revolution" overthrows President Eduard Shevardnadze on November 23, 2003.

Pora! founded in Kiev, Ukraine in June 2004. "Orange revolution" installs Victor Yushchenko into power on December 26, 2004.

Kmara! overthrows Abashidze of Ajaria (western Georgian secessionist

province) May 5, 2004[914]

Eastern European, Slovac, and Middle Eastern nations are not the only targets of Anglo-American destabilization campaigns and color revolutions in recent years. South America, Asia, and even Russia have been and continue to be subject to Western meddling in their own internal affairs, with some of these mass mobilizations being more successful than others.

As mentioned previously, the entire "Arab Spring" uprising was nothing more than a Western-backed color revolution bolstered my many legitimate complaints of the subject populations but instigated and guided by Anglo-Americans who have no interest in bringing these people real democracy or freedom. Instead, the teeming masses are nothing more than battering rams for an agenda they do not understand or even know exists.

As in the color revolutions of Eastern Europe and the Slovac world, the "Arab Spring" was engineered and controlled from the very beginning, with "freedom-spreading" organizations working on the ground to recruit, organize, train, and assist participants

Tarpley, Webster G. Obama: The Postmodern Coup. Mowat, Jonathan. "A New Gladio In Action: 'Swarming Adolescents.'" Progressive Press. 2008. Pp. 254-256.
[914] Mowat, Jonathan. "A New Gladio In Action." Online Journal. Reposted by ColorRevolutionandGeoPolitics.blogspot.com. http://colorrevolutionsandgeopolitics.blogspot.com/2011/04/from-archives-jonathan-mowat-new-gladio.html Accessed on July 3, 2013.
See also,
Tarpley, Webster G. Obama: The Postmodern Coup. Mowat, Jonathan. "A New Gladio In Action: 'Swarming Adolescents.'" Progressive Press. 2008. P. 256.

for the upcoming protests and destabilization. As Cartalucci and Bowie write in *War on Syria*,

> One of the organizations involved in recruiting, training, and supporting youth activists ahead of the "Arab Spring" was described in an April 2011 New York Times article.[915] The organization, Movements.org, or Alliance of Youth Movements, would later be described admitting to US funding and involvement in the "Arab Spring" uprisings. The article implicates Freedom House, the National Endowment for Democracy, and two of its satellite organizations, the International Republican Institute, and the National Democratic Institute, in recruiting, training, and supporting the unrest starting as early as 2008. While the New York Times article doesn't mention the organization by name, it links to an official US State Department announcement titled, "Announcement on Alliance of Youth Movements Summit," that most certainly does.[916] The Alliance of Youth Movements is a corporate-sponsored[917] "coup college" of sorts, training activists to subvert and topple governments on the US State Department's behalf.[918]

 Indeed, while the aforementioned New York Times article still attempts to obfuscate and cover for the NGOs in their role in the Arab Spring, and therefore does not reveal the extent to which they were responsible, it is surprisingly open regarding the role played by Western NGOs in the movement. Ron Nixon writes,

> But as American officials and others look back at the uprisings of the Arab Spring, they are seeing that the United States' democracy-building campaigns played a bigger role in fomenting protests than was previously known, with key leaders of the movements having been trained by the Americans in campaigning, organizing through new media tools and monitoring elections.

> A number of the groups and individuals directly involved in the revolts and reforms sweeping the region, including the April 6 Youth Movement in Egypt, the Bahrain Center for Human Rights and grass-roots activists like Entsar Qadhi, a youth leader in Yemen, received training and financing from groups like the International Republican Institute, the National Democratic Institute and Freedom House, a nonprofit human rights organization based in Washington, according to interviews in recent weeks and American diplomatic cables obtained by WikiLeaks.

> The work of these groups often provoked tensions between the United States and many Middle Eastern leaders, who frequently complained that their leadership was being undermined, according to the cables.

> The Republican and Democratic institutes are loosely affiliated with the Republican and Democratic Parties. They were created by Congress and are financed through the National Endowment for Democracy, which was set up in 1983 to channel grants for

---

[915] Nixon, Ron. "U.S. Groups Helped Nurture Arab Uprisings." The New York Times. April 14, 2011. http://www.nytimes.com/2011/04/15/world/15aid.html?pagewanted=all&_r=0 Accessed on July 5, 2013.

[916] "Announcement on Alliance of Youth Movements Summit." America.gov Archive, November 20, 2008.

[917] "Supporters." Movements.org. http://www.movements.org/pages/sponsors Accessed on July 5, 2013.

[918] Cartalucci, Tony; Bowie, Nile. War On Syria: Gateway to WWIII. 2012.

promoting democracy in developing nations. The National Endowment receives about $100 million annually from Congress. Freedom House also gets the bulk of its money from the American government, mainly from the State Department.

. . . . .

Some Egyptian youth leaders attended a 2008 technology meeting in New York, where they were taught to use social networking and mobile technologies to promote democracy. Among those sponsoring the meeting were Facebook, Google, MTV, Columbia Law School and the State Department.

"We learned how to organize and build coalitions," said Bashem Fathy, a founder of the youth movement that ultimately drove the Egyptian uprisings. Mr. Fathy, who attended training with Freedom House, said, "This certainly helped during the revolution."

Ms. Qadhi, the Yemeni youth activist, attended American training sessions in Yemen.

"It helped me very much because I used to think that change only takes place by force and by weapons," she said.

But now, she said, it is clear that results can be achieved with peaceful protests and other nonviolent means.

. . . . .

Diplomatic cables report how American officials frequently assured skeptical governments that the training was aimed at reform, not promoting revolutions.

Last year, for example, a few months before national elections in Bahrain, officials there barred a representative of the National Democratic Institute from entering the country.

In Bahrain, officials worried that the group's political training "disproportionately benefited the opposition," according to a January 2010 cable.

In Yemen, where the United States has been spending millions on an anti-terrorism program, officials complained that American efforts to promote democracy amounted to "interference in internal Yemeni affairs."

But nowhere was the opposition to the American groups stronger than in Egypt.

Egypt, whose government receives $1.5 billion annually in military and economic aid from the United States, viewed efforts to promote political change with deep suspicion, even outrage.

Hosni Mubarak, then Egypt's president, was "deeply skeptical of the U.S. role in democracy promotion," said a diplomatic cable from the United States Embassy in Cairo dated Oct. 9, 2007.[919]

At one time the United States financed political reform groups by channeling money through the Egyptian government.

---

[919] Nixon, Ron. "U.S. Groups Helped Nurture Arab Uprisings." The New York Times. April 14, 2011. http://www.nytimes.com/2011/04/15/world/15aid.html?pagewanted=all&_r=0 Accessed on July 5, 2013.

But in 2005, under a Bush administration initiative, local groups were given direct grants, much to the chagrin of Egyptian officials.

According to a September 2006 cable, Mahmoud Nayel, an official with the Egyptian Ministry of Foreign Affairs, complained to American Embassy officials about the United States government's "arrogant tactics in promoting reform in Egypt."

The main targets of the Egyptian complaints were the Republican and Democratic institutes. Diplomatic cables show that Egyptian officials complained that the United States was providing support for "illegal organizations."

Gamal Mubarak, the former president's son, is described in an Oct. 20, 2008, cable as "irritable about direct U.S. democracy and governance funding of Egyptian NGOs."

The Egyptian government even appealed to groups like Freedom House to stop working with local political activists and human rights groups.[920]

The 5 Necessary Ingredients For A Color Revolution

In his book, *Obama: The Postmodern Coup*, Webster G. Tarpley describes the five necessary ingredients for a color revolution or, as some may describe it, a "people power coup." In addition to large sums of money needed for bribes and the funding of the networks needed to carry out such an overthrow, Tarpley lists the Media, "rent-a-mobs" or gullible cannon fodder, symbols and slogans, fake polling, and a "suitable demagogue" as necessities to the successful color revolution.[921]

Tarpley writes,

In order to carry out a color revolution, large sums of money are required to pay bribes and buy support. Beyond that, the following ingredients are necessary:

1. Media

It is essential to control the key television channels, or at least one major network. In less developed societies, a well-known radio station might suffice, but here in the US it takes a broadcast network and one or more cable networks, backed up by news magazines, daily newspapers, and various Internet sites. These organs must attempt to create a collective hysteria or mania in the whole society in favor of the people power coup. . . . . .

2. Rent-a-mobs.

This term became widespread during Brzezinski's 1978 overthrow of the Shah of Iran in favor of Ayatollah Khomeini. No self-respecting anti-Shah politician in Tehran could venture outdoors without a numerous rent-a-mob. In Kiev, large numbers of young people camped out in the central square of the city to dive home their demand that the pro-Moscow government be replaced with Brzezinski's pro-NATO puppets,

---

[920] Nixon, Ron. "U.S. Groups Helped Nurture Arab Uprisings." The New York Times. April 14, 2011. http://www.nytimes.com/2011/04/15/world/15aid.html?pagewanted=all&_r=0 Accessed on July 5, 2013.

[921] Tarpley, Webster G. "Obama: The Postmodern Coup." Progressive Press. 2008. Pp. 82-85.

although many of them were too naïve to realize that this was the issue. In more prosperous countries, such as the US, the dupe-a-mob offers a more economical equivalent. In any case, the mobs must be big enough to be shown on television, thus creating the illusion that the coup leader is riding a wave of overwhelming popular support and truly represents the Collective Will in Rousseau's sense. . . . . . One modish technical term for these procedures is swarming, but the idea is as old as the mob itself. As Bill Engdahl has noted, "The Pentagon and US intelligence have refined the art of such soft coups to a fine level. RAND planners call it 'swarming,' referring to the swarms of youth, typically linked by short message services and weblogs, who can be mobilized on command to destabilize a target regime."

3. Symbols and slogans.

Ukraine had the orange revolution; Georgia had the rose revolution. The Prague velvet revolution was an earlier pilot project for the same thing. The cedars revolution in Lebanon did not fare so well; here the groups of well-heeled and privileged young people could not match the actual organized power of the Hezbollah mass base. A similar attempt in Belorussia also collapsed in failure. Jeans, tulips, the colors blue and purple, and even bulldozers have been mobilized, as mindless symbols. In addition to the catchy color or symbol, an effective slogan is also required. In Belgrade, at the start of the current series, that was "Gotov je" – "he is finished," meaning that Milosevic had to go. Other slogans have included "It's enough" and "It's time!" For Obama, the solution in this regard was "Change We Can Believe In."

4. Fake Polling

Since the color revolution usually takes place under the cover of an election, faked polling for mass manipulation purposes is indispensable. In Ukraine, the pro-Moscow candidate Yanukovich was declared the winner by the official government vote count, but the rent-a-mobs and dupe-a-mobs in the streets began yelling that this was vote fraud. How could they prove it? Project Democracy had thought of everything: the polling firm of Penn, Schoen and Berland Associates was on the scene, and had carried out an exit poll of voters leaving the polling places. The results of this faked and doctored exit poll, a masterpiece of NATO intelligence, were the basis of the accusation of vote fraud, which was then endorsed by international observers from the European Union, the NED, and the Helsinki CSCE watchdog groups. . . . . . .

5. A suitable demagogue.

In Serbia and Georgia, these were young and attractive oligarchical politicians, often western trained, and always on the make. In Ukraine, the coup candidate was Yushchenko, something of a tired retread and therefore not entirely plausible for the purpose at hand. To drum up sympathy for Yuschenko, he was apparently submitted to some form of disfiguring chemical or biological attack, and this was blamed on the Russians.[922]

[922] Tarpley, Webster G. "Obama: The Postmodern Coup." Progressive Press. 2008. Pp. 82-85.

NGOs At Work In Syria
National Endowment for Democracy

An organization that can be described as the left wing of the CIA, the NED is financed by the US government and other sources and has been a key figure in the color revolution, destabilization campaigns, and regime change efforts in foreign nations for at least three decades. The NED describes itself as "private, nonprofit foundation dedicated to the growth and strengthening of democratic institutions around the world. Each year, with funding from the US Congress, NED supports more than 1,000 projects of non-governmental groups abroad who are working for democratic goals in more than 90 countries."[923] One of those many projects is, of course, Syria as the NED proudly admits on its own website. The NED is active in Syria directly as well as through its subsidiary organizations such as the IRI and the NDIIA.[924]

The NED, since it is considered a private, nonprofit, organization is thus able to accept money from a variety of sources and act independently of any legitimate oversight by Congress or the American people. Its status as "private" allows intelligence agencies to use public funds for their own projects without openly accepting responsibility or consequences for their enacted policies. In most cases, the cover of organizations such as the NED is helpful simply in keeping the role of intelligence agencies under wraps from the dupes and "swarming adolescents" that are being mobilized.

The Institute for Policy Studies describes the NED as follows:[925]

> The National Endowment for Democracy (NED) was created by the Reagan administration in the early 1980s to push democratic reforms and roll back Soviet influence in various parts of the globe. In his 1983 speech inaugurating NED, President Ronald Reagan said: "I just decided that this nation, with its heritage of Yankee traders, ought to do a little selling of the principles of democracy."[926]

> The private, congressionally funded NED has been a controversial tool in U.S. foreign policy because of its support of efforts to overthrow foreign governments. As the writers Jonah Gindin and Kirsten Weld remarked in the January/February 2007 NACLA Report on the Americas: "Since [1983], the NED and other democracy-promoting governmental and nongovernmental institutions have intervened successfully on behalf of 'democracy'—actually a very particular form of low-intensity democracy chained to pro-market economics—in countries from Nicaragua to the Philippines, Ukraine to Haiti, overturning unfriendly 'authoritarian'

---

[923] National Endowment for Democracy, *About Us*, accessed in www.ned.org.

[924] "Syria." NED.org. http://www.ned.org/where-we-work/middle-east-and-northern-africa/syria Accessed on July 5, 2013.

[925] "National Endowment For Democracy." Institute For Policy Studies. March 2, 2012. http://rightweb.irc-online.org/profile/National_Endowment_for_Democracy Accessed on July 18, 2013.

[926] This citation was provided by the author of the block quote Ronald Reagan, "Remarks at a White House Ceremony Inaugurating the National Endowment for Democracy," NED, December 16, 1983.

governments (many of which the United States had previously supported) and replacing them with handpicked pro-market allies."[927]

NED works principally through four core institutes: the National Democratic Institute for International Affairs (NDIIA or NDI), the International Republican Institute (IRI)[928], the American Center for International Labor Solidarity (ACILS), and the Center for International Private Enterprise—representing, respectively, the country's two major political parties, organized labor, and the business community.

Funded almost entirely by the U.S. government, NED claims on its website to be "guided by the belief that freedom is a universal human aspiration that can be realized through the development of democratic institutions, procedures, and values. Governed by an independent, nonpartisan board of directors, the NED makes hundreds of grants each year to support pro-democracy groups in Africa, Asia, Central and Eastern Europe, Eurasia, Latin America, and the Middle East."

The war on terror and subsequent democratic uprisings in the Middle East and North Africa have led to expanded NED programs in Iran, Syria, Iraq, Afghanistan, Egypt, Lebanon, Turkey, Morocco, and the Palestinian territories, according to NED's website.[929] Although many of these programs have performed relatively non-controversial functions like monitoring elections, NED's support for civil society organizations active in their respective countries' politics has not been without controversy.

In early 2012, for example, as part of a broader crackdown on international non-governmental organizations, Egypt's military government enacted a travel ban on several representatives from NDI and IRI, preventing them from leaving the country. As of February 2012, the Egyptian government was planning to prosecute at least 19 Americans, including representatives from NDI and IRI, on charges of illegally operating unlicensed foreign NGOs in the country.[930] The government lifted the travel ban on February 29 under pressure from the United States and amid a series of resignations by Egyptian judges who refused to hear the case, although it was unclear whether the charges would be dropped.[931]

---

[927]This citation was provided by the author of the block quote Jonah Gindin and Kirsten Weld, "Benevolence or Intervention? Spotlighting U.S. Soft Power," NACLA Report on the Americas, January/February 2007.

[928] This citation was provided by the author of the block quote "International Republican Institute." Institute For Policy Studies. February 27, 2012. http://www.rightweb.irc-online.org/profile/International_Republican_Institute Accessed on July 18, 2013.

[929] This citation was provided by the author of the block quote NED, Middle East and North Africa Programs, http://www.ned.org/where-we-work/middle-east-and-northern-africa.

[930] This citation was provided by the author of the block quote Associated Press, "Egypt NGO Trial: Sam LaHood, Ray LaHood's Son, Among 19 Under Investigation," Huffington Post, February 6, 2012, http://www.huffingtonpost.com/2012/02/06/egypt-ngo-trial-sam-lahood_n_1257432.html

[931] This citation was provided by the author of the block quote AP, "Egyptian officials say travel ban on US employees of pro-democracy groups is lifted," *Washington Post*, February 5, http://www.washingtonpost.com/world/middle_east/egyptian-officials-say-travel-ban-on-us-employees-of-pro-democracy-groups-is-lifted/2012/02/29/gIQAJ6JRiR_story.html.

The incident marked a period of considerable tension for the U.S.-Egyptian relationship, with the U.S. government threatening to cut off aid to Egypt if the U.S. detainees were not released. However, some observers have argued that the Egyptian government had reason to be wary of the targeted organizations. UN Human Rights Rappoteur Richard Falk, while criticizing the military regime for using "licensing and funding technicalities as a pretext for a wholesale crackdown on dissent and human rights," added that "these Washington shrieks of wounded innocence, as if Cairo had no grounds whatsoever for concern, are either the memory lapses of a senile bureaucracy or totally disingenuous. In the past it has been well documented that IRI and DNI were active in promoting the destabilisation of foreign governments that were deemed to be hostile to the US foreign policy agenda."[932]

Inter Press Service contributor Emad Mekay argued that NED-backed groups in Egypt were supporting a "small circle of sloganeering politicians on the take from the U.S. government who are unpopular and discredited among their own people." He added, "When these U.S.-funded politicians ran for office in Egypt's first real and democratic elections last month, they lost, leaving Washington with no leverage in the new Egypt. If Washington delivers on its threats to cut aid to Egypt, it is undermining whatever remains of U.S. influence."[933]

Other NED grantees in recent years have included the World Uyghur Congress,[934] neoconservative writer Kenneth Timmerman's[935] Foundation for Democracy in Iran,[936] and South Korean radio broadcasters[937] to the North.

NED's chairman is former Democratic Rep. Dick Gephardt. Its president is Carl Gershman,[938] a longtime figure in U.S. sectarian politics dating back to the 1970s. The NED Board of Directors includes former chairman Vin Weber,[939] a high-profile

---

[932]This citation was provided by the author of the block quote Richard Falk, "When an 'NGO' is not an NGO: Twists and turns under Egyptian skies," Al Jazeera Online, February 21, 2012, .

[933]This citation was provided by the author of the block quote Emad Mekay, "U.S. shouldn't support Egypt's democracy backers," *San Francisco Gate*, February 10, 2012, http://www.sfgate.com/cgi-bin/article.cgi?f=/c/a/2012/02/10/ED9J1N3RN0.DTL

[934]This citation was provided by the author of the block quote Engdahl, F. William. "Is Washington Playing a Deeper Game With China?" The Market Oracle. July 11, 2009. http://www.marketoracle.co.uk/Article11961.html Accessed on July 18, 2013.

[935] This citation was provided by the author of the block quote "Kenneth Timmerman." Institute for Policy Studies. http://www.rightweb.irc-online.org/profile/timmerman_kenneth Accessed on July 18, 2013.

[936] This citation was provided by the author of the block quote "Foundation for Democracy in Iran." Institute For Policy Studies. January 12, 2012. http://www.rightweb.irc-online.org/profile/foundation_for_democracy_in_iran Accessed on January 18, 2013.

[937]This citation was provided by the author of the block quote Johnson, Tim. "U.S.-funded broadcasters in S. Korea bombard North." McClatchy Washington Bureau. September 19, 2007. http://www.mcclatchydc.com/2007/09/20/v-print/19826/us-funded-broadcasters-in-s-korea.html Accessed on July 18, 2013.

[938] This citation was provided by the author of the block quote "Carl Gershman." Institute for Policy Studies. June 19, 2007. http://www.rightweb.irc-online.org/profile/Gershman_Carl Accessed on July 18, 2013.

[939]This citation was provided by the author of the block quote "Vin Weber." Institute For Policy

Washington lobbyist who has supported the work of the Project for the New American Century[940] along with a host of other neoconservative outfits; former U.S. ambassador to the UN and neoconservative activist Zalmay Khalilzad;[941] Will Marshall[942] of the Progressive Policy Institute;[943] Anne-Marie Slaughter, a noted liberal hawk who served as the director of Policy Planning for the U.S. State Department during the Obama administration; and Francis Fukuyama,[944] an erstwhile supporter of the neoconservative political faction and well-known political scientist.[945]

F. William Engdahl adds to the brief history provided by the IRC in his article, "The Shady National Endowment for Democracy & The Prime Agenda of 'Whoever' Is Next US President,"[946] where he states,

> Helping youth engage in political activism is precisely what the same NED did in Egypt over the past several years in the lead up to the toppling of Mubarak. The same NED was instrumental by informed accounts in the US-backed "Color Revolutions" in 2003-2004 in Ukraine and Georgia that brought US-backed pro-NATO surrogates to power. The same NED has been active in promoting "human rights" in Myanmar, in Tibet, and China's oil-rich Xinjiang province.[947]

> As careful analysts of the 2004 Ukraine "Orange revolution" and the numerous other US-financed color revolutions discovered, control of polling and ability to dominate international media perceptions, especially major TV such as CNN or BBC is an essential component of the Washington destabilization agenda. The Levada Center

---

Studies. December 5, 2012. http://www.rightweb.irc-online.org/profile/Weber_John_Vincent_Vin Accessed on July 18, 2013.

[940] This citation was provided by the author of the block quote "Project for the New American Century." Institute for Policy Studies. March 21, 2013. http://www.rightweb.irc-online.org/profile/Project_for_the_New_American_Century Accessed on July 18, 2013.

[941] This citation was provided by the author of the block quote "Zalmay Khalilzad." Institute For Policy Studies. July 1, 2011. http://www.rightweb.irc-online.org/profile/Khalilzad_Zalmay Accessed on July 18, 2013.

[942] "Will Marshall." Institute For Policy Studies. February 14, 2013. http://www.rightweb.irc-online.org/profile/Marshall_Will Accessed on July 18, 2013.

[943] This citation was provided by the author of the block quote "Progressive Policy Institute." Institute for Policy Studies. January 31, 2013. http://www.rightweb.irc-online.org/profile/progressive_policy_institute Accessed on July 18, 2013.

[944] This citation was provided by the author of the block quote "Francis Fukuyama." Institute for Policy Studies. March 13, 2007. http://www.rightweb.irc-online.org/profile/Fukuyama_Francis Accessed on July 18, 2013.

[945] "National Endowment For Democracy." Institute For Policy Studies. March 2, 2012. http://rightweb.irc-online.org/profile/National_Endowment_for_Democracy Accessed on July 18, 2013.

[946] Engdahl, F. William. "The Shady National Endowment for Democracy & The Prime Agenda of 'Whoever' Is Next US President." Engdahl.OilGeopolitics.net. Reposted January 10, 2012. PrisonPlanet.com. http://www.prisonplanet.com/the-shady-national-endowment-for-democracy-the-prime-agenda-of-%E2%80%98whoever%E2%80%99-is-next-us-president.html Accessed on July 5, 2013.

[947] This citation was provided by the author of the block quote F. William Engdahl, *Full Spectrum Dominance: Totalitarian Democracy in the New World Order*, 2010, edition.engdahl press.

would likely be in a crucial position in this regard to issue polls showing discontent with the regime.

By their description, the National Endowment for Democracy (NED) is a "private, nonprofit foundation dedicated to the growth and strengthening of democratic institutions around the world. Each year, with funding from the US Congress, NED supports more than 1,000 projects of non-governmental groups abroad who are working for democratic goals in more than 90 countries."[948]

It couldn't sound more noble or high-minded. However, they prefer to leave out their own true history. In the early 1980's CIA director Bill Casey convinced President Ronald Reagan to create a plausibly private NGO, the NED, to advance Washington's global agenda via other means than direct CIA action. It was a part of the process of "privatizing" US intelligence to make their work more "effective." Allen Weinstein, who helped draft the legislation establishing NED, said in a *Washington Post* interview in 1991, "A lot of what we do today was done covertly 25 years ago by the CIA."[949] Interesting. The majority of funds for NED come from US taxpayers through Congress. It is in every way, shape and form a US Government intelligence community asset.

The NED was created during the Reagan Administration to function as a *de facto* CIA, privatized so as to allow it more freedom of action. NED board members are typically drawn from the Pentagon and US intelligence community. It has included retired NATO General Wesley Clark, the man who led the US bombing of Serbia in 1999. Key figures linked to clandestine CIA actions who served on NED's board have included Otto Reich, John Negroponte, Henry Cisneros and Elliot Abrams. The Chairman of the NED Board of Directors in 2008 was Vin Weber, founder of the ultraconservative organization, Empower America, and campaign fundraiser for George W. Bush. Current NED chairman is John Bohn, former CEO of the controversial Moody's rating agency which played a nefarious role in the still-unraveling US mortgage securities collapse. As well today's NED board includes neo-conservative Bush-era ambassador to Iraq and to Afghanistan, Afghan-American Zalmay Khalilzad.[950][951]

Note: As of 2016, Martin Frost is the current chairman of the NED.[952]

---

[948] This citation was provided by the author of the block quote National Endowment for Democracy, *About Us*, accessed in www.ned.org.

[949] This citation was provided by the author of the block quote David Ignatius, *Openness is the Secret to Democracy*, Washington Post National Weekly Edition, 30 September-6 October,1991, 24-25.

[950]*This citation was included in the quote by F. William Engdahl, *Full Spectrum Dominance: Totalitarian Democracy in the New World Order*, 2010, edition.engdahl press.

[951] This citation references the source for the entire block quote. Engdahl, F. William. "The Shady National Endowment for Democracy & The Prime Agenda of 'Whoever' Is Next US President." Engdahl.OilGeopolitics.net. Reposted January 10, 2012. PrisonPlanet.com. http://www.prisonplanet.com/the-shady-national-endowment-for-democracy-the-prime-agenda-of-%E2%80%98whoever%E2%80%99-is-next-us-president.html Accessed on July 5, 2013.

[952] "Martin Frost is new Chairman of National Endowment for Democracy." PRNewswire. March 12, 2013. http://www.prnewswire.com/news-releases/martin-frost-is-new-chairman-of-

The IRC further elaborates on the purpose of the NED in that it is designed largely to conceal US government funding. The IRC description continues by stating[953],

> When it was created in 1983, NED's core agenda was to support political groups in target countries that would contest communist or otherwise left-of-center organizations and political parties. In announcing its creation, President Ronald Reagan said that the NED would achieve this goal by supporting "the infrastructure of democracy—the system of a free press, unions, political parties, and universities— which allows a people to choose their own way, to develop their own culture, to reconcile their own differences through peaceful means."[954]

> Allen Weinstein, a member of the U.S. Agency for International Development (USAID) working group known as the Democracy Group, which first proposed the formation of a quasi-governmental group to channel U.S. political aid, served as NED's acting president during its first year. Talking about the role of NED, Weinstein told the *Washington Post* in 1991 that "a lot of what we do today was done covertly 25 years ago by the CIA."[955]

> Under NED's elaborate structure, designed to veil U.S. government funding, U.S. Information Agency (USIA) and USAID funding did not flow directly to foreign political parties, unions, business associations, and civic groups, but was instead routed through the AFL-CIO, the International Chamber of Commerce, and the IRI and NDIIA. NED's origins go back to a bipartisan commission called the American Political Foundation established by the State Department that began to address the problem of having U.S.-funded "soft-side" overseas operations perceived as CIA fronts.[956] [957]

Gerald Sussman reinforces the explanation provided by the IRC when he wrote the following for *Monthly Review*:

> While most people in these former single-party authoritarian states no doubt welcome the possibilities of open, multiparty politics, there remains a widespread suspicion and sensitivity to foreign sponsorship of domestic political institutions. Even when NED's funding of Chile's 1988 election helped bring down the Pinochet regime, the opposition parties that benefited nonetheless expressed resentment against U.S. interference. And such suspicion is not unwarranted. The center-right politics of CIPE

---

national-endowment-for-democracy-197514971.html Accessed on July 13, 2013.

[953] "National Endowment For Democracy." Institute For Policy Studies. March 2, 2012. http://rightweb.irc-online.org/profile/National_Endowment_for_Democracy Accessed on July 18, 2013.

[954]This citation was provided by the author of the block quote Beth Sims, "National Endowment for Democracy: A Foreign Policy Branch Gone Awry," Interhemispheric Resource Center, March 1990.

[955] This citation was provided by the author of the block quote David Ignatius, "Innocence Abroad: The New World of Spyless Coups," Washington Post, September 22, 1991.

[956] This citation was provided by the IRC. Beth Sims, "National Endowment for Democracy: A Foreign Policy Branch Gone Awry," Interhemispheric Resource Center, March 1990.

[957] This citation refers to the entire block quote."National Endowment For Democracy." Institute For Policy Studies. March 2, 2012. http://rightweb.irc-online.org/profile/National_Endowment_for_Democracy Accessed on July 18, 2013.

and the AFL-CIO's Solidarity Center are clear. One look at the backgrounds and links of the members of the National Democratic Institute and especially the International Republican Institute—listing sixty-four corporate and foundation "benefactors"—reveals a formidable intersection of bureaucrat-capitalists with representatives from the American Enterprise Institute and Fortune 500 energy, automobile, media, and defense sectors. Although corporations such as Chevron-Texaco, Exxon Mobil, and Enron help fund both NDI and IRI, but their influence, particularly in major NED target countries such as Venezuela, Iraq, and the rest of the Middle East, extends much farther than their relatively small direct contributions would suggest. What makes NED a particularly useful instrument is that although federally funded, the activities of its institutes are not reported to Congress.[958] [959]

Essentially, funding is provided to the NED via government agencies which is then transferred to subsidiaries like the IRI and the NDIIA who either distribute the money further into yet more subsidiaries or work directly on the ground with the masses who will act as the cannon fodder for the destabilization campaign.

The NED and its subsidiaries have had their hands in coup attempts, regime change, destabilizations, and color revolutions all over the world. However, an area of particular interest for the NED/IRI team is Latin America where the organizations worked tirelessly in Venezuela to remove President Hugo Chavez from power. Whatever the negative aspects of Chavez, it was clear that he was a staunch opponent of Anglo-American imperialism and acted somewhat as a fly in the ointment of many of the West's plans in Latin America. Chavez was, in short, the Latin American Ghaddafi.

In this regard, the IRC states,[960]

> Many observers have also accused Washington of having been behind the attempted ouster of Venezuela's President Hugo Chávez in April 2002, although the Bush administration denied any U.S. involvement. Before the coup attempt, millions of U.S. taxpayer dollars were channeled through the IRI and other U.S. organizations that funded groups opposed to Chávez. Writer Mike Ceaser reported that in an April 12, 2002 fax sent to news media, IRI President George A. Folsom rejoiced over Chávez's removal from power. "The Venezuelan people rose up to defend democracy in their country," Folsom wrote. "Venezuelans were provoked into action as a result of systematic repression by the government of Hugo Chávez." With NED funding, IRI had been sponsoring political party-building workshops and other anti-Chávez activities in Venezuela. "IRI evidently began opposing Chávez even before his 1998 election," wrote Ceaser. "Prior to that year's congressional and presidential elections,

---

[958] This citation was provided by the author of the block quote. Barbara Conry, Loose cannon: The National Endowment for Democracy (Cato Institute, 1993), http://www.cato.org; IRI, 2003, http://www.iri.org.

[959] This citation refers to the entire block quote. Sussman, Gerald. "The Myths of 'Democracy Assistance': US Political Intervention In Post-Soviet Eastern Europe." Monthly Review. Volume 58. Issue 7. December, 2006. http://monthlyreview.org/2006/12/01/the-myths-of-democracy-assistance-u-s-political-intervention-in-post-soviet-eastern-europe Accessed on July 5, 2013.

[960] "National Endowment For Democracy." Institute For Policy Studies. March 2, 2012. http://rightweb.irc-online.org/profile/National_Endowment_for_Democracy Accessed on July 18, 2013.

the IRI worked with Venezuelan organizations critical of Chávez to run newspaper ads, TV, and radio spots that several observers characterize as anti-Chávez."[961]

According to NED's website, the largest single 2002 NED grant in Latin America went to ACILS. NED gave this USAID-supported branch of the AFL-CIO $775,000 "to implement a program to reinforce the capacity of labor unions to promote economic and political reform and build alliance with civil society at community and national levels." ACILS did the same in Venezuela, where it worked with anti-Chávez worker groups that formed an alliance with business, civil society, and political parties that engineered the attempted coup in April 2002. The same year, ACILS received $116,000 to "support the Venezuelan trade movement, represented by the Confederation of Venezuelan Workers, in developing a program to extend organization, training, and representation to the informal sector."

In 2004, after Hugo Chávez easily won a referendum in August on his presidency, fresh accusations emerged about the NED's role in supporting anti-Chávez groups. When the government arrested leaders of these groups, Gershman denounced the action, saying: "In the spectrum between democracy and dictatorship, the prosecution against the activists would be moving ... closer to the authoritarian end." Regarding Chávez's claims that the NED was part of a CIA effort to undermine his government, Gershman said: "That's propaganda."[962] Venezuelan congresswoman María Corina Machado, a leading 2012 rival of Chávez, accepted NED funds in as the head of Súmate, a civil society organization that led the petition drive against Chávez that year.[963] [964]

While never a subject of popular debate, the NED has been a center of controversy by relatively informed circles since the days of its inception. The IRC explains:[965]

Although promoted as idealistically oriented programs aimed at encouraging democratic development, NED's work has been repeatedly criticized by observers from all political backgrounds for being potentially detrimental to U.S. relations with other countries and an inappropriate use of taxpayer money.

---

[961] This citation was provided by the author of the block quote Tom Barry, "Aristide's Fall: The Undemocratic U.S. Policy in Haiti," IRC America's Program, February 27, 2004.
See also,
Mike Ceaser, "As Turmoil Deepens in Venezuela, Questions Regarding NED Activities Remain Unanswered," Americas Program, December 9, 2002.
[962] "Venezuela is Inching Toward Dictatorship, Says U.S. Group," Irish Times, November 11, 2004.
[963] This citation was provided by the author of the block quote. Jennifer Barreto-Leyva, "How Venezuela's Opposition Candidates Stack Up Against Hugo Chavez," February 9, 2012, Fox News Latino, http://latino.foxnews.com/latino/politics/2012/02/09/how-venezuelas-opposition-candidates-stack-up-against-hugo-chavez/#ixzz1nobCblc8.
[964] This citation refers to the entire block quote. "National Endowment For Democracy." Institute For Policy Studies. March 2, 2012. http://rightweb.irc-online.org/profile/National_Endowment_for_Democracy Accessed on July 18, 2013.
[965] "National Endowment For Democracy." Institute For Policy Studies. March 2, 2012. http://rightweb.irc-online.org/profile/National_Endowment_for_Democracy Accessed on July 18, 2013.

For instance, Rep. Ron Paul, a Republican from Texas, lambasted NED in an October 2003 op-ed, arguing: "The misnamed National Endowment for Democracy (NED) is nothing more than a costly program that takes U.S. taxpayer funds to promote favored politicians and political parties abroad. What the NED does in foreign countries, through its recipient organizations the National Democratic Institute (NDI) and the International Republican Institute (IRI), would be rightly illegal in the United States. The NED injects 'soft money' into the domestic elections of foreign countries in favor of one party or the other. Imagine what a couple of hundred thousand dollars will do to assist a politician or political party in a relatively poor country abroad. It is particularly Orwellian to call U.S. manipulation of foreign elections 'promoting democracy.' How would Americans feel if the Chinese arrived with millions of dollars to support certain candidates deemed friendly to China? Would this be viewed as a democratic development?"[966]

Some notable observers have defended NED's work, including the British historian Timothy Garton Ash, who in a January 2004 article for the *Guardian* highlighted what he viewed as the positive role NED and other like-minded organizations have played in world affairs. He wrote: "I've seen the impact of the National Endowment for Democracy, together with our own Westminster Foundation for Democracy and other semi- and wholly non-governmental organizations in eastern Europe and the Balkans. Without their work, Slobodan Milosevic might not have been toppled by a revolution in Serbia. Add the clear message that corrupt, oil-bloated Arab elites no longer enjoy Washington's unconditional support, and we could see some fireworks. Not laser-guided American military fireworks from the sky, but emancipatory Arab fireworks from the ground. The fact that this support for would-be democrats is tainted by its association with the United States, the neo-imperialist occupier of Arab lands, will, I suspect, dampen but not extinguish the fuse."[967]

NED's work in Latin America, particularly in the 1980s, roused criticism from both Reagan-era diplomats and some on the libertarian right. During the 1984 elections in Panama, for example, NED supported a candidate associated with the military, Nicholas Ardito Barletta, despite the fact that the United States was purportedly opposed to military rule in the country. The NED's actions prompted an angry response from the U.S. ambassador, who wrote in a secret cable: "The embassy requests that this hair-brained project be abandoned before it hits the fan."

"An even more dubious initiative," wrote Barbara Conry for a 1993 Cato Institute report, "was NED's involvement in Costa Rica. Not only is Costa Rica a well-established democracy—former president George Bush visited the country in 1989 to celebrate 100 years of democracy there—it is the only stable democracy in Central America. But Costa Rican president Oscar Arias had opposed Ronald Reagan's policy in Central America, especially his support of the Nicaraguan Contras. Arias received the Nobel Peace Prize for his efforts to dampen conflicts in the region, but he incurred the wrath of right-wing NED activists. So from 1986 to 1988 NED gave money to Arias's political opposition, which was also strongly supported by Panamanian

---

[966] This citation was provided by the author of the block quote Ron Paul, "National Endowment for Democracy: Paying to Make Enemies of America," AntiWar.com, October 11, 2003.
[967] This citation was provided by the author of the block quote Timothy Garton Ash, "Washington's Post-9/11 War on Terror is Finished," *Guardian*, January 21, 2004.

dictator Manuel Noriega. As Rep. Stephen Solarz (D-NY) commented: 'They may technically have been within the law, but I felt this clearly violated the spirit. ... The whole purpose of NED is to facilitate the emergence of democracy where it doesn't exist and preserve it where it does exist. In Costa Rica, neither of these [conditions] applies.'"[968]

These and other activities have led many observers to question the value of the NED, as well as to highlight the potential danger it poses to U.S. interests. Concluded Conry: "Promoting democracy is a nebulous objective that can be manipulated to justify any whim of the special-interest groups—the Republican and Democratic parties, organized labor, and the U.S. Chamber of Commerce—that control most of NED's funds. As those groups execute their own foreign policies, they often work against American interests and meddle needlessly in the affairs of other countries, undermining the democratic movements NED was designed to assist."

Others have faulted the NED and its affiliates emphasizing only one particular form of democracy, pro-market democracy. Wrote Jonah Gindin and Kirsten Weld in the January/February 2007 NACLA Report on the Americas: "By combining cooptation, coercion, and deep pockets, groups like the NED and the U.S. Agency for International Development (USAID) have at times allied themselves with antidemocratic elites, and at other times capitalized on movements and individuals that were genuinely dedicated to democratizing their countries, setting the parameters of the debate by positioning a particular definition of pro-market representative democracy as the only antiauthoritarian option. U.S. and European organizations have disbursed massive amounts of money, funding some groups and projects while ignoring others, favoring those who share their general ideological conceptions while isolating those that do not."[969]

International Republican Institute

The International Republican Institute (IRI) functions more or less as a subsidiary of the NED and a conduit for the United States Agency for International Development (USAID). The IRI which often works directly on the ground in countries slated by the West for destabilization, coups, or regime change, is also closely associated with the Republican Party and the usual coterie of Neo-Conservatives.[970] According to the Institute for Policy Studies,[971]

---

[968] This citation was provided by the author of the block quote Barbara Conry, "Loose Cannon: The National Endowment for Democracy," Cato Institute Foreign Policy Briefing, November 1993.

[969] "National Endowment For Democracy." Institute For Policy Studies. March 2, 2012. http://rightweb.irc-online.org/profile/National_Endowment_for_Democracy Accessed on July 18, 2013.

[970] "International Republican Institute." Institute For Policy Studies. February 27, 2012. http://www.rightweb.irc-online.org/profile/International_Republican_Institute Accessed on July 19, 2013.

[971] "International Republican Institute." Institute For Policy Studies. February 27, 2012. http://www.rightweb.irc-online.org/profile/International_Republican_Institute Accessed on July 19, 2013.

The International Republican Institute (IRI), a 501(c)(3) nonprofit organization that serves as a vehicle for the National Endowment for Democracy (NED)[972] and the U.S. Agency for International Development, was created by the Ronald Reagan administration in 1983 to push democratization efforts and roll back the influence of the Soviet Union. More recently, the taxpayer-funded IRI has claimed to play a role preventing global terrorism, though some of its interventions since 9/11 have been criticized for undermining democracy. A 2006 IRI brochure declared, "When IRI began its work in 1983, advancing democracy was seen as a noble endeavor; today, it is recognized as a defense against terrorism."[973]

IRI's activities have included funding clandestine opinion surveys in Cuba (2008),[974] monitoring the controversial and violence-tainted elections in Kenya (2007),[975] and undertaking public opinion polls in Pakistan after President Pervez Musharraf declared a state of emergency (2007).[976] More controversially, its "democracy building" program in Haiti was accused of undermining both U.S. State Department diplomacy efforts and the government of President Jean-Bertrand Aristide.[977] IRI also channeled funds to forces in Venezuela that sought to overthrow the controversial but democratically elected President Hugo Chavez in 2002. IRI has also been criticized for supporting and monitoring the 2009 elections in Honduras after the Organization for American States refused to send observers, seeing the election as an attempt to legitimize a right-wing coup that removed a democratically elected progressive government from power.

Along with its Democratic-aligned counterpart, the National Democratic Institute (NDI), the IRI has been active in monitoring elections in Egypt and other countries in the Middle East following a surge of democratic revolutions in the region in 2011. In early 2012, however, as part of a broader crackdown on international non-governmental organizations, Egypt's military government enacted a travel ban on several representatives from both NDI and IRI, preventing them from leaving the country. As of February 2012, the Egyptian government was planning to prosecute at least 19 Americans, including IRI members, on charges of illegally operating unlicensed foreign NGOs in the country.[978]

---

[972] This citation was provided by the author of the quote. "National Endowment For Democracy." Institute For Policy Studies. March 2, 2012. http://rightweb.irc-online.org/profile/National_Endowment_for_Democracy Accessed on July 18, 2013.

[973] This citation was provided by the author of the quote. International Republican Institute brochure, 2006, http://www.iri.org/pdfs/2006IRIBrochure.pdf.

[974] Marc Lacey, "In Rare Study, Cubans Put Money Worries First," New York Times, June 5, 2008.

[975] Maini Kiai and L. Muthoni Wanyeki, "A Deal We Can Live With," New York Times, February 12, 2008.

[976] David Rohde and Carlotta Gall, "Most Want Musharraf to Quit, Poll Shows," New York Times, December 13, 2007.

[977] New York Times editorial, "No Help to Democracy in Haiti," February 3, 2006.

[978] This citation refers to the entire block quote. "International Republican Institute." Institute For Policy Studies. February 27, 2012. http://www.rightweb.irc-online.org/profile/International_Republican_Institute Accessed on July 19, 2013.

Not surprisingly, war hawk (at virtually every opportunity) John McCain has been directly associated with the IRI, having served as its Chairman since 1993. The Institute for Policy Studies describes the IRI as follows:[979]

Although officially nonpartisan, IRI is closely aligned with the Republican Party, just as its sister organization, the National Democratic Institute (NDI), is aligned with the Democratic Party. Sen. John McCain[980] (R-AZ) has served as IRI chairman since 1993, and Lorne Craner, the former assistant secretary of state for democracy and human rights and labor in the George W. Bush administration, is IRI's president.

A July 2008 *New York Times* article described IRI as "McCain's institute" and highlighted the connections between the IRI, the McCain presidential campaign, and various lobbying interests. Reporter Mike McIntire described a 2006 IRI event: "First up that night in September 2006 was the institute's vice chairman, Peter T. Madigan, a McCain campaign fund-raiser and lobbyist whose clients span the globe, from Dubai to Colombia. He thanked Timothy P. McKone, an AT&T lobbyist and McCain fund-raiser, for helping with the dinner arrangements and then introduced the chairman of AT&T, Edward E. Whitacre Jr., whose company had donated $200,000 for the event. AT&T at the time was seeking political support for an $80 billion merger with BellSouth—another Madigan client—and Mr. Whitacre lavished praise on Mr. McCain, a senior member of the Senate Commerce Committee. When Mr. McCain finally took the podium, he expressed 'profound thanks' to AT&T before presenting the institute's Freedom Award to the president of Liberia, a lobbying client of Charlie Black, an institute donor and McCain campaign adviser."[981]

McIntire reported, "The institute is also something of a revolving door for lobbyists and out-of-power Republicans that offers big donors a way of helping both the party and the institute's chairman, who is the second sitting member of Congress—and now candidate for president—ever to head one of the democracy groups. Operating without the sort of limits placed on campaign fund-raising, the institute under Mr. McCain has solicited millions of dollars for its operations from some 560 defense contractors, lobbying firms, oil companies and other corporations, many with issues before Senate committees Mr. McCain was on."[982]

Accompanying the *Times* story was a list of IRI directors and their connections to corporate interests, lobbying groups, and the Republican Party, as well as the amount of money they donated to McCain's presidential campaign—a total of $36,700.[983] The list indicated IRI board members who are also involved in McCain's presidential

---

[979] "International Republican Institute." Institute For Policy Studies. February 27, 2012. http://www.rightweb.irc-online.org/profile/International_Republican_Institute Accessed on July 19, 2013.

[980] This citation was provided by the author of the quote. "John McCain." Institute for Policy Studies. May 9, 2013. http://www.rightweb.irc-online.org/profile/mccain_john Accessed on July 21, 2013.

[981] Mike McIntire, "Democracy Institute Gives Donors Access to McCain," New York Times, July 28, 2008.

[982] Mike McIntire, "Democracy Institute Gives Donors Access to McCain," New York Times, July 28, 2008.

[983] This citation was provided by the author of the quote. McCain's Institute," New York Times, July 28, 2008.

campaign: Craner, IRI president; Gahl Hodges Burt, former White House social secretary; Janet Grissom, automaker lobbyist; Madigan, IRI vice chairman and a lobbyist for foreign governments; Alec Poitevint, Republican committeeman; Randy Scheunemann,[984] head of the lobbying firm Orion Strategies, a campaign adviser on foreign policy and national security to Senator McCain, and a former member of the Project for the New American Century[985] and the Committee for the Liberation of Iraq;[986] Joseph Schmuckler, senior executive at Mitsubishi Securities; and Richard Williamson, lobbyist for AT&T. Other IRI board members include L. Paul Bremer,[987] former special envoy to Iraq; Alison Fortier, vice president of Lockheed Martin; Frank Fahrenkopf, head of the American Gaming Association and former Republican National Committee chairman; Michael Kostiw, a Senate aide to McCain and former Texaco lobbyist; and John Rogers, managing director of Goldman Sachs.[988] The article also featured photos of McCain presenting IRI's "Freedom Award" to Vice President Dick Cheney[989] in 2001, National Security Adviser Condoleezza Rice[990] in 2004, and George W. Bush in 2005.[991]

Despite this, the IRI seems hesitant to acknowledge its partisanship. For instance, in response to the July 2008 *New York Times* article, the institute released a statement saying, "While some IRI staff are Republicans, some are also Democrats and some are not members of any political party. ... Some of IRI's board members have chosen to support Senator McCain's candidacy, just as some of NDI's member's [sic] have chosen to support Barack Obama's."[992] [993]

---

[984] This citation was provided by the author of the quote. "Randy Scheunemann." Institute For Policy Studies. January 15, 2013. http://www.rightweb.irc-online.org/profile/Scheunemann_Randy Accessed on July 21, 2013.

[985] This citation was provided by the author of the quote. "Project For The New American Century." Institute for Policy Studies. March 21, 2013. http://www.rightweb.irc-online.org/profile/Project_for_the_New_American_Century Accessed on July 21, 2013.

[986] This citation was provided by the author of the quote. "Committee for the Liberation of Iraq." Institute for Policy Studies. August 27, 2008. http://www.rightweb.irc-online.org/profile/Committee_for_the_Liberation_of_Iraq Accessed on July 21, 2013.

[987] "L. Paul Bremer." Institute for Policy Studies. May 7, 2012. http://www.rightweb.irc-online.org/profile/Bremer_L_Paul Accessed on July 21, 2013.

[988] This citation was provided by the author of the quote. McCain's Institute," New York Times, July 28, 2008.

[989] "Dick Cheney." Institute for Policy Studies. February 18, 2013. http://www.rightweb.irc-online.org/profile/Cheney_Dick Accessed on July 21, 2013.

[990] "Condoleeza Rice." Institute for Policy Studies." February 19, 2013. http://www.rightweb.irc-online.org/profile/Rice_Condoleezza Accessed on July 21, 2013.

[991] This citation was provided by the author of the quote. Mike McIntire, "Democracy Institute Gives Donors Access to McCain," New York Times, July 28, 2008.

[992] This citation was provided by the author of the quote. International Republican Institute, "IRI Statement Responding to The New York Times Article 'McCain's Lobbyist-Laden Group,'" July 28, 2008, http://www.iri.org/newsreleases/2008-07-28-IRI-NYT.asp.

[993] This citation refers to the entire block quote. "International Republican Institute." Institute For Policy Studies. February 27, 2012. http://www.rightweb.irc-online.org/profile/International_Republican_Institute Accessed on July 19, 2013.

With a large portion of its focus is on polling data, election monitoring, and public opinion polls, the IRI thus recalls the issue of concocting "fake polling data" for propaganda purposes which was raised both by Ian Traynor of *The Guardian* and Jonathan Mowat in his article, "The New Gladio." The IRC summarizes this aspect of the IRI in this manner:

> The IRI has actively supported the "war on terror" with programs in at least 10 countries in the Greater Middle East region, as well as the occupied Palestinian territories. During the Bush administration, the institute was accused repeatedly of using misleading polling data to push the Bush agenda, both at home and abroad. "During the Afghan presidential election of October 2004," reports Raw Story, "IRI's pre-election poll showed Hamid Karzai with a strong lead, and its exit poll, released immediately after the vote and well before the ballots were counted, also gave him over 50% of the vote. The British Helsinki Human Rights Group subsequently suggested that these polls might have helped head off scrutiny of an election that had initially been met with well-founded suspicions of fraud. IRI's polls also serve to influence public opinion in the United States. A year ago, Media Matters pointed out that the *Washington Post* had cited an IRI poll showing that '60% of Iraqis believed the country is headed in the right direction' without indicating the partisan nature of its source. In September 2004, President Bush had cited a similar IRI poll at a press conference, saying, 'I saw a poll that said the right track/wrong track in Iraq was better than here in America. It's pretty darn strong. I mean, the people see a better future.'"[994]

IRI has continued to carry out polls purporting to show, for example, a "fresh burst of optimism" in Afghanistan in 2009,[995] as well as a sharp decline in public support for Pakistan's government in 2008.[996]

IRI's efforts to fund democracy activities in the Middle East have at times backfired. In a June 2007 article for the *New York Times Magazine*, Negar Azimi recounted how efforts to funnel money to Iranian groups through the Office of Iranian Affairs, an outfit established in 2006 within the State Department's Bureau of Near Eastern Affairs and at one point overseen by Elizabeth Cheney,[997] were facing criticism "not only from Iranian officials but also from some of the very people whose causes it aims to advance."

Reported Azimi: "For the Iranian government, the democracy fund is just one more element in an elaborate Bush administration regime-change stratagem. ('Is there even

---

[994] Muriel Kane, "GOP Organization Linked to Dirty Politics, Attempted Coups, 'Building Democracy' for US," Raw Story, June 9, 2006.

[995] This citation was provided by the author of the quote. O'Hanlon, Michael; Riedel, Bruce. "Measuring progress towards peace." Washington Times. September 1, 2009. http://www.washingtontimes.com/news/2009/sep/01/measuring-progress-toward-peace/ Accessed on July 21, 2013.

[996] This citation was provided by the author of the quote. Bukhari, Irfan. "88pc feel Pakistan heading in wrong direction." The Nation. December 30, 2008. http://www.nation.com.pk/pakistan-news-newspaper-daily-english-online/Politics/20-Dec-2008/88pc-feel-Pakistan-heading-in-wrong-direction Accessed on July 21, 2013.

[997] "Elizabeth Cheney." Institute for Policy Studies. April 8, 2010. http://www.rightweb.irc-online.org/profile/cheney_elizabeth Accessed on July 21, 2013.

a perception that the American government has democracy in mind?' Iran's ambassador to the United Nations, Javad Zarif, asked me recently in New York. 'Except among a few dreamers in Eastern Europe?') In recent months, Tehran has upped the pressure on any citizens who might conceivably be linked to the democracy fund and, by extension, on civil society at large, making the mere prospect of American support counterproductive, even reckless. ... It is particularly telling, perhaps, that some of the most outspoken critics of the Iranian government have been among the most outspoken critics of the democracy fund. Activists from the journalist Emadeddin Baghi to the Nobel laureate Shirin Ebadi to the former political prisoner Akbar Ganji have all said thanks but no thanks. Ganji has refused three personal invitations to meet with Bush."

Head of the Office of Iranian Affairs at the time was David Denehy, who according to Azimi is "a veteran of democracy promotion programs in Eastern Europe and Central Asia with the International Republican Institute and a close associate of [former] Deputy Secretary of Defense Paul Wolfowitz.[998] During the Iraq War, he served in Baghdad from June to October 2003, where his focus was on civil-society development."[999 and 1000]

In tandem with the NED, the IRI was also highly active in the attempted overthrow of Venezuelan President Hugo Chavez.[1001] As the IRC explains:

Although the Bush administration steadfastly denied any involvement, many observers accused Washington of being behind the failed April 2002 coup against Venezuela's President Hugo Chávez. However, a relatively clear connection emerged between the U.S. government and the anti-Chávez movement: millions of dollars in U.S. taxpayer money channeled through the IRI and other U.S. organizations to groups opposed to Chávez during the years preceding the April coup.

Via NED funding, IRI had been sponsoring political party-building workshops and other anti-Chávez activities in Venezuela. "IRI evidently began opposing Chávez even before his 1998 election," reported journalist Mike Ceaser. "Prior to that year's congressional and presidential elections, the IRI worked with Venezuelan organizations critical of Chávez to run newspaper ads, TV, and radio spots that several observers characterize as anti-Chávez." Further, according to Ceaser, "The IRI has ... flown groups of Chávez opponents to Washington to meet with U.S. officials. In March 2002, a month before Chávez's brief ouster, one such group of politicians, union leaders, and activists traveled to D.C. to meet with U.S. officials, including members of Congress and State Department staff. The trip came at the time that several military officers were calling for Chávez's resignation and talk of a possible coup was widespread." An opposition figure who benefited from IRI support told

---

[998] "Paul Wolfowitz." Institute for Policy Studies. March 19, 2013. http://www.rightweb.irc-online.org/profile/wolfowitz_paul Accessed on July 21, 2013.

[999] Negar Azimi, "Hard Realities of Soft Power," New York Times Magazine, June 24, 2007.

[1000] This citation refers to the entire block quote. "International Republican Institute." Institute For Policy Studies. February 27, 2012. http://www.rightweb.irc-online.org/profile/International_Republican_Institute Accessed on July 19, 2013.

[1001] "International Republican Institute." Institute For Policy Studies. February 27, 2012. http://www.rightweb.irc-online.org/profile/International_Republican_Institute Accessed on July 19, 2013.

Ceaser that bringing varied government opponents together in Washington accelerated the unification of the opposition. "The democratic opposition began to become cohesive," he said. "We began to become a team."

In an April 12, 2002, written statement to the media, IRI President George A. Folsom rejoiced prematurely over Chávez's removal: "The Venezuelan people rose up to defend democracy in their country," he wrote. "Venezuelans were provoked into action as a result of systematic repression by the government of Hugo Chávez."[1002] [1003]

This open attempt at regime change by the IRI as a proxy for the NED and thus the US government was also repeated in Haiti against President Arisitide. As the IRC writes, it is clear that not only was the IRI involved in the destruction of the Haitian government, it is clear that the IRI's work did not begin during an organic controversy. Indeed, the organization had been involved in Haiti since at least 1987 in its buildup to the coup of 2004.[1004] The IRC writes,

In the first year of the George W. Bush administration, IRI received USAID funding for a new "party-building project" in Haiti, where it had been involved in since 1987. In 2004, the Aristide government collapsed. Before IRI closed its Haiti office in 2007, IRI's USAID-funded party-building activities focused on working with and training the political opposition.[1005]

According to Robert Maguire, director of the Haiti Program at Trinity College in Washington, D.C., IRI was the key U.S. actor in Haiti for several years. In 2004 he said, "NED and USAID are important, but actually the main actor is the International Republican Institute (IRI), which has been very active in Haiti for many years but particularly in the past three years. IRI has been working with the opposition groups. IRI insisted, through the administration, that USAID give it funding for its work in Haiti. And USAID has done so but kicking and screaming all the way. IRI has worked exclusively with the Democratic Convergence groups in its party-building exercises and support. The IRI point person is Stanley Lucas who historically has had close ties with the Haitian military. ... The IRI ran afoul with Aristide right from the beginning since it has only worked with opposition groups that have challenged legitimacy of the Aristide government. Mr. Lucas is a lightning rod of the IRI in Haiti. The United States could not have chosen a more problematic character through which to channel its aid."[1006]

[1002] Mike Ceaser, "As Turmoil Deepens in Venezuela, Questions Regarding NED Activities Remain Unanswered," Americas Program, December 9, 2002.

[1003] This citation refers to the entire block quote. "International Republican Institute." Institute For Policy Studies. February 27, 2012. http://www.rightweb.irc-online.org/profile/International_Republican_Institute Accessed on July 19, 2013.

[1004] . "International Republican Institute." Institute For Policy Studies. February 27, 2012. http://www.rightweb.irc-online.org/profile/International_Republican_Institute Accessed on July 19, 2013.

[1005] 29. International Republican Institute, "Facts about IRI's Work in Haiti," updated July 2008, http://www.iri.org/newsreleases/2008-07-18-Haiti-faq.asp.

[1006] Tom Barry, "Aristide's Fall: The Undemocratic U.S. Policy in Haiti," IRC America's Program, February 27, 2004.

As the *New York Times* reported, "what emerges from the events in Haiti is a portrait of how the effort to nurture democracy became entangled in the ideological wars and partisan rivalries of Washington."

"The Bush administration has said that while Mr. Aristide was deeply flawed, its policy was always to work with him as Haiti's democratically elected leader," the *Times* reported. "But the administration's actions in Haiti did not always match its words. Interviews and a review of government documents show that [the IRI,] a democracy-building group close to the White House and financed by American taxpayers, undercut the official United States policy and the ambassador assigned to carry it out."[1007]

The Raw Story reported: "The secretive aspect to some of IRI's activities, combined with its repeated involvement in subverting left-leaning politicians and parties, creates the appearance that it may be acting as one more tool in the Bush administration's arsenal for regime change by any means available. The recent increase in IRI's federal funding—which almost tripled, from $26 million to $75 million, between 2003 and 2005—adds grounds to this suspicion."[1008] [1009]

National Democratic Institute for International Affairs

The National Democratic Institute for International Affairs (NDI) is a subsidiary of the NED and was created alongside the NED and the IRI. Whereas the IRI functions as the "right wing" Republican branch of the NED, the NDI functions as the "left wing" Democrat branch. Thus the NDI is loosely affiliated with the Democratic Party.[1010] Among a coterie of warmongers and collection of imperialists who are of both a covert and an overt nature, it should be noted that Susan Rice, one of the most openly rabid warmongers of the Obama administration in regards to military action and outlandish propaganda against both Libya and Syria, was listed as a member of the Board of Directors for the NDI in 2006. In addition, the architect of many of the destabilization programs put in place by the Anglo-Americans the world over, Zbigniew Brzezinski, was once the Director of the NDI.[1011]

[1007] Walt Bogdanich and Jenny Nordberg, "Mixed U.S. Signals Helped Tilt Haiti Toward Chaos," New York Times, January 29, 2006.
[1008] Muriel Kane, "GOP Organization Linked to Dirty Politics, Attempted Coups, 'Building Democracy' for US," Raw Story, June 9, 2006.
[1009] This citation refers to the entire block quote. "International Republican Institute." Institute For Policy Studies. February 27, 2012. http://www.rightweb.irc-online.org/profile/International_Republican_Institute Accessed on July 19, 2013.
[1010] "National Democratic Institute: Working To Strengthen And Expand Democracy Worldwide." NDI Brochure. http://web.archive.org/web/20061026072531/http://www.ndi.org/about/ndibrochure03.pdf Accessed on July 5, 2013.
[1011] Sussman, Gerald; Krader, Sascha. "Template Revolutions: Marketing U.S. Regime Change in Eastern Europe." Westminster Papers In Communication and Culture. 5 (3). Portland State University. 2008. Pp.1744-6716. http://www.westminster.ac.uk/__data/assets/pdf_file/0011/20009/006WPCC-Vol5-No3-Gerald_Sussman_Sascha_Krader.pdf Accessed on July 5, 2013.
For easier online access to source article, see the reposted version at

Much like its "right wing" counterpart, the IRI, the NDI is heavily involved in the propaganda method of "exit polling." As Gerald Sussman and Sascha Krader write in their article, "Template Revolutions: Marketing U.S. Regime Change in Eastern Europe,"

> One of the keys to defeating what the United States considered an unworthy leader was the unification of the disparate opposition behind a single political candidate. NED's affiliated institutes, especially IRI and NDI, moved freely throughout Eastern Europe carrying this message of consolidation. The first template application was in Bulgaria in 1996, where NED and IRI 'discovered' that 'NGOs could tilt an election in favor of America's preferred candidate' (MacKinnon 2007, 30) by unifying the opposition and then creating and funding exit polls. NDI contributed to this project by financing the Bulgarian Association for Fair Elections and Civil Rights to oversee exit polls that year (NDI, 2001). Exit polling was next arranged in Romania in 1997 through support to the Pro Democracy Association (Pro Democracy Association 2004); Slovakia in 1998, where the IRI conducted a 'parallel vote tabulation'; and Croatia in 1999, with USAID, NED, Freedom House, and other international financing of a poll watching group, Citizens Organized to Monitor Elections (GONG) (Jašić 2000; MacKinnon 2007, 31-33).

> When Milošević looked vulnerable to election defeat in Serbia, NDI flew the Serbian opposition party leadership to Poland in the late 1990s to solicit advice from Polish party activists (Roelofs 2003, 186). The U.S. polling firm Penn, Schoen and Berland entered the picture and determined that the anti-communist constitutional lawyer Vojislav Koštunica was the most likely person to beat him (Dobbs 2000). Acting on this, U.S. secretary of state Madeleine Albright and German foreign minister Joschka Fischer brought presidential contenders Belgrade mayor Zoran Djindjic and opposition party leader Vuk Draskovic to Budapest where the Serbian politicians were pressured to drop out of the race. IRI and NDI had issued similar counsel in Bulgaria and Romania, getting pro-Western leaders to defer to Washington's preference (MacKinnon 2007, 31, 44).[1012]

Network of Democrats in the Arab World

Another non-profit NGO, NDAW was created in 2006 and, although it states that its goals are to "strengthen democratic transformation in the Arab World by facilitating

---

ColorRevolutionsAndGeopolitics.blogspot.com.
http://colorrevolutionsandgeopolitics.blogspot.com/2011/07/template-revolutions-marketing-us.html Accessed on July 5, 2013.

[1012] Sussman, Gerald; Krader, Sascha. "Template Revolutions: Marketing U.S. Regime Change in Eastern Europe." Westminster Papers In Communication and Culture. 5 (3). Portland State University. 2008. Pp.1744-6716.
http://www.westminster.ac.uk/__data/assets/pdf_file/0011/20009/006WPCC-Vol5-No3-Gerald_Sussman_Sascha_Krader.pdf Accessed on July 5, 2013.
For easier online access to source article, see the reposted version at
ColorRevolutionsAndGeopolitics.blogspot.com.
http://colorrevolutionsandgeopolitics.blogspot.com/2011/07/template-revolutions-marketing-us.html Accessed on July 5, 2013.

member interaction, capacity building, representation and access to information," the organization is registered in the UK.[1013] Although the NGO is relatively new and, accordingly, much less is known about its methods of operations, the NED is funding the NDAW to the sum of $160,000.[1014] Not only that, but George Soros' Open Society Foundations are listed as an official donor to the NDAW as well as The International Center For Not-For-Profit Law, The Fund For Global Human Rights, The Anna Lindh Foundation, The Middle East Partnership Initiative, and Foundation For The Future.[1015]

Nonviolence International

Nonviolence International is a perfect example of an NGO appearing to operate under otherwise noble pretenses – i.e. nonviolence, promotion of freedom and democracy, international peace, etc. – yet acting as an agent of destabilization and regime change. In this context, it is important to remember the writings of Peter Ackerman (referenced earlier) and organizations such as his International Center on Nonviolent Conflicts. Nonviolent protest, while conjuring up memories of the Civil Rights movement in the United States in the 1960's, can be used for good or ill. The fact that the NED is funneling $37,500 for its operations in Syria should serve as a red flag to all who are concerned with the effects such "nonviolent" action would produce in this instance.

Samir Kassir Foundation

Also founded in 2006 and named after a murdered journalist Samir Kassir, the Samir Kassir Foundation operates in Syria, Lebanon, Jordan, and Palestine and claims to work toward the "promotion of cultural freedom and freedom of expression."[1016] Although a noble goal if the work of the organization is truly dedicated to these ideals, the NED has allocated $34,400 to the Foundation for the purpose of

> enhanc[ing] the skills of young citizen journalists in conflict. SKF will develop content for 20 instructional videos. Each two-three minute video will provide hands-on training to journalists to report on local developments throughout the country. Specific topics will include accuracy and credibility of citizen journalism, safety of citizen journalists in times of trouble, reporting during armed conflict, and mobile journalism. SKF's project coordinator will provide one-on-one mentoring and assistance to practicing citizen journalists as they use skills in daily reports.

Work such as that designated above more likely than not marks the beginning of the development of a training program that will culminate in the propaganda efforts

---

[1013] "Our Goals." Network of Democrats in the Arab World.
http://www.ndaworld.org/en/index.php?option=com_content&view=article&id=191&Itemid=2
43 Accessed on July 5, 2013.

[1014] "Syria." National Endowment for Democracy." http://www.ned.org/where-we-work/middle-east-and-northern-africa/syria Accessed on July 5, 2013.

[1015] "Donor Organizations." Network of Democrats in the Arab World.
http://www.ndaworld.org/en/index.php?option=com_content&view=category&layout=blog&id=75&Itemid=249 Accessed on July 5, 2013.

[1016] "Samir Kassir Foundation: Lebanon." Insight on Conflict.
http://www.insightonconflict.org/conflicts/lebanon/peacebuilding-organisations/samir-kassir-foundation/ Accessed on July 5, 2013.

spearheaded by "citizen journalists." This type of "reporting" will be used to justify greater pressure on Assad, greater support for death squads, and possibly even direct military action based on the claims made by "journalists" inside Syria.[1017]

[1017] "Syria." National Endowment for Democracy." http://www.ned.org/where-we-work/middle-east-and-northern-africa/syria Accessed on July 5, 2013.

Chapter X: Russia And World War Three
6 Reasons Why Russia Cares So Much About Syria

As the potential for direct military confrontation between the United States/NATO and Russia in Syria escalates by the day, the vast majority of Americans have little clue why the Russians would have ever become involved in the crisis to begin with. Undoubtedly, most of them believe what they are told through the mainstream media – that Russia is yet again acting aggressively in its plans for total world domination and the establishment of the Fourth Reich.

For many observers in the alternative media, the understanding of the Russian move is somewhat more sophisticated but still substantially lacking. For instance, while some simply oppose the Russian involvement on the basis of not wanting to see any further escalation, others heap lavish praise upon Putin for his decisions and present the Russian president as the potential leader for the world. At times, the adulation borders on the cult of personality, a dangerous situation regardless of the pure motives of the individual at the center of worship. That being said, it is hard not to praise Putin for his courageous stance against U.S./NATO imperialism in Syria, Ukraine, and against Russia itself.

It is true that, in the recent geopolitical back and forth that has been taking place between Russia and the West, the Russians have acted entirely in self-defense and that is has been entirely the West that has provoked the current tensions. Indeed, in the context of Syria, Iran, and Ukraine, Russia has clearly stood on the right side of history while the United States and NATO move further and further in the opposite direction.

However, while Russia has indeed acted and continues to act as a savior in Syria, Iran, and Ukraine, it is important to note that Russian foreign policy is not an act of charity and that, ultimately, Putin's concern is centered with the fate of Russia. Whatever the world wishes to see Putin do in Syria will be subject to the geopolitical, national, and domestic interest of Russia, a stance once can scarcely criticize any national leader for maintaining.

Below are a number of reasons that Putin and Russia are so concerned with the fate of Syria.

1.) The Pipeline

The West has long desired a Qatari pipeline project that would stem from the oil fields of Qatar and traverse Saudi Arabia, Jordan, Syria, and Turkey before making its way to Europe. Besides the obvious benefits for Qatar and the basic addition of another source of oil and gas for Europe, the pipeline would represent a substantial reduction in the amount of leverage Russia currently holds over Europe. As of today, Russia is the main provider of the majority of Europe's oil and gas. If the EU decides to act too provocative in its eastern regions, Ukraine, or other areas of the Russian sphere of influence, Russia has the trump card of being able to turn off the oil and gas spicket, leaving Europe in the dark and cold. Europe would then be left with few options in the short to medium term other than to come around to Russia's way of thinking. With the development of the Qatari pipeline, however, that trump card would be removed as Europe would then simply open the Qatari spicket further to make up for what was lost when the Russians cut there's off. In that event, Russia would also be deprived of a substantial amount of oil and gas-related income.[1018]

Assad nixed the Qatari pipeline idea back in 2009 in favor of the Iran-Iraq-Syria pipeline that would have seen oil and gas coming from Iran through Iraq and Syria and on into Europe. While not directly beneficial to Russia's oil company Gazprom, the pipeline is one that is owned and operated by Russian allies who are generally beholden to Russian support in the United Nations Security Council and military support when faced with NATO/American war efforts. The Russian leverage over Europe would thus largely still exist and the "out" provided by Qatar would be prevented.[1019]

2.) The Warm Water Port

The quest for warm water ports has long played a major role in Russian foreign policy history. Currently, Russia boasts of a number of those ports - Sevastopol, Crimea, and Tartus.[1020]

The Syrian port of Tartus has no doubt been a major force behind Russian support of Assad and Syria throughout the crisis. Up until the crisis, however, the Russians only controlled a portion of the Tartus port. Yet, in concert with Russian military involvement, Russia now controls virtually the entire port. The control of the entirety of the Tartus port most certainly sweetened the deal in terms of Russian involvement. This new development has caused many to wonder whether or not Russia was able to squeeze greater control of the Tartus port out of Assad at a critical moment when Syria needed Russian help the most. It is also worth mentioning of the development of a Russian airbase in Latakia, a port city in its own right.[1021]

[1018] Turbeville, Brandon. "Big Oil, Qataris, Saudis Lick Lips As US 'Fights ISIS' By Bombing Syrian Pipelines." Activist Post. October 26, 2014. http://www.activistpost.com/2014/10/big-oil-qataris-saudis-lick-lips-as-us.html
See also,
Ahmed, Nafeez. "Syria Intervention Plan Fueled By Oil Interests, Not Chemical Weapon Concern." The Guardian. August 30, 2013. https://www.theguardian.com/environment/earth-insight/2013/aug/30/syria-chemical-attack-war-intervention-oil-gas-energy-pipelines
[1019] Turbeville, Brandon. "Big Oil, Qataris, Saudis Lick Lips As US 'Fights ISIS' By Bombing Syrian Pipelines." Activist Post. October 26, 2014. http://www.activistpost.com/2014/10/big-oil-qataris-saudis-lick-lips-as-us.html
See also,
Ahmed, Nafeez. "Syria Intervention Plan Fueled By Oil Interests, Not Chemical Weapon Concern." The Guardian. August 30, 2013. https://www.theguardian.com/environment/earth-insight/2013/aug/30/syria-chemical-attack-war-intervention-oil-gas-energy-pipelines
[1020] Delman, Edward. "The Link Between Putin's Military Campaigns In Syria and Ukraine." The Atlantic. October 2, 2015. http://www.theatlantic.com/international/archive/2015/10/navy-base-syria-crimea-putin/408694/
[1021] Ben-Yishai, Ron. "What Putin's Syria Strategy Means For Israel." YNet News. September 29,

3.) Strategic Influence

Strategic influence plays a major role in the Russian decision as well. Syria has been in its "sphere of influence" for quite some time, but it has also acted one of the last Russian outposts in the Middle East after the fall of the Soviet Union. Russia does not want to lose this asset, with its pipeline potential, buffering qualities against Western aggression, and, of course, the warm water port. Furthermore, a closer alliance with Syria portends a closer alliance with Iran, the last country on the chessboard to fall before the assault begins on Russia and China proper. Russia's alliance with Iran is a separate discussion but, suffice it to say that a greater alliance with Iran is to Russia's distinct advantage and the close alliance with Syria facilitates that needed alliance with Iran. Likewise, with its entrance into the fight against ISIS, Russia has solidified good relationships with Iran, Iraq, Syria, and Hezbollah.

4.) The Domino Theory

As mentioned above, Russia is presumably aware of the strategy being used against it – i.e. the attempt to chip away at all nations that resist the dictates of the NATO power structure and, in particular, areas of Russian alliance and influence before finally turning its sights directly on Russia itself. The creeping moves to gradually surround Russia cannot go unnoticed. If Syria falls, so falls Hezbollah. Iran will be isolated. Once Iran falls, there is little else left beyond Russia itself. Putin will then see the increase of terrorism in Russian territories and a greater push east by NATO in Ukraine. In essence, Russia is attempting to prevent the dominoes from falling.

5.) Fighting Terrorism Abroad

The use of Islamic fundamentalists as proxy fighters in Syria long ago raised the eyebrows of Russian leaders because, if for no other reason, that a number of Chechen fighters were flocking to the Middle East in order to engage in Jihad. The fear was not only that they would return to Russia and begin launching terror attacks but that the networks that control both Middle Easter jihadists and the Chechen variety would begin directing their proxies to attack Russia inside Russia, i.e. Chechnya and even further inside the country. With the constant threat of Western-backed Chechen fighters in Russia launching attacks inside the country in the forefront, Turkey and the puppet government of Ukraine collaborated in the creation of "Muslim brigades" to be used against Russia in Crimea and other areas surrounding or in Russia. Thus, Russia is attempting to "fight ISIS abroad so they don't have to fight them at home" by destroying an organized structure that may exist in Syria and hopefully reducing the number of dupes, fanatics, and psychopaths in absolute number. [1022] [1023]

2015. http://www.ynetnews.com/articles/0,7340,L-4705256,00.html

[1022] Turbeville, Brandon. "Chechen Terrorist Networks Trace Back To The US State Department." Activist Post. April 20, 2013. http://www.activistpost.com/2013/04/chechen-terrorist-networks-trace-back.html

[1023] Turbeville, Brandon. "Turkey And Ukraine Prepare Terrorist Brigades Aimed At Russia." Activist Post. August 24, 2015. http://www.activistpost.com/2015/08/turkey-and-ukraine-prepare-terrorist-brigades-aimed-at-russia.html

7.) Turkish Expansion

While perhaps not the most extensive threat by any means, Turkey is attempting to spread its influence across the Middle East and Asia, a theatre that includes Russia as a target as well. While Turkey has provided Yeomen's service in the agenda of NATO and the Anglo-Americans, it is clear that megalomaniacs like Erdogan have pipe dreams of re-establishing the Ottoman Empire. These dreams are, in reality, delusions. However, these dreams make Turkey dangerous in the meantime, particularly to Russia. The attempt to promote Uyghur terrorism in Asia, in and around Russia's Asian/Eurasian borders, and Tatar terror in Crimea is reason enough for Russia to attempt to crush Turkey's plan for Syria.[1024]

While Russia's position in Syria is, without a doubt beneficial to the Syrian people, it should not be romanticized that the Russian government is simply sitting at home watching the crisis unfold, overcome with concern for the victims of the war. The truth is that many factors have come into play in this regard. We should not allow ourselves to naively assume that world leaders are concerned with all of the same issues as the people they "lead."

Still, it is without question that, in regards to Syria, Ukraine, and virtually the entire geopolitical angle, Russia finds itself on the right side of history. As observers, activists, and people of the world, we must support these efforts where they match up with our own agenda and principles, and be prepared to oppose them when they do not.

Does Russia-U.S. Tension in Syria Foreshadow Military Confrontation?

The Western-backed plot to overthrow the secular government of Bashar al-Assad has now placed the world in a precarious position where two nuclear powers are acting in such close proximity to one another militarily that one trigger happy soldier could now plunge the globe into a nuclear holocaust. If the general public of Russia and the West are not aware of the dangers of further meddling in the Middle East by the United States and NATO, the state actors of the two sides are clearly aware of the potential ramifications. Of course, it cannot go without mentioning that the entire confrontation now taking place in Syria between the United States, NATO, and Russia is entirely the making of the West since it was NATO and the U.S. that created the crisis to begin with.

As the military chess pieces continue to be set across the world, Russian Foreign Minister Sergei Lavrov stated early on that the United States should engage in bi-lateral military-to-military communication with Russia over military operations in Syria in order to avoid "unintended incidents." While Lavrov did not spell out exactly what he meant by "unintended incidents," his meaning was clear – "unintended incidents" are a direct military confrontation between the United States/NATO and Russian forces.[1025]

[1024] Turbeville, Brandon. "From Syria To Asia To Russia – Terror Network Organized By NATO And Turkey." Activist Post. October 1, 2015. http://www.activistpost.com/2015/10/from-syria-to-asia-to-russia-terror-network-organized-by-nato-and-turkey.html
[1025] Lowe, Christian; Edwards, Julia. "Russia to U.S.: Talk To Us On Syria Or Risk 'Unintended Consequences.'" Reuters. September 11, 2015.

"We are always in favor of military people talking to each other in a professional way. They understand each other very well," Lavrov added. "If, as (U.S. Secretary of State) John Kerry has said many times, the United States wants those channels frozen, then be our guest."[1026]

The Western mainstream press, of course, pounced upon the statement as if it were a veiled threat to the United States. Lavrov, however, made his statement in the course of explaining the importance of military-to-military communication so as to avoid such incidents in the course of simultaneous operations on the same field. In other words, it was not a threat but it was a cautionary warning.

Still, Lavrov's words address a very real possibility of direct military confrontation between Russian and American forces in the skies or on the ground in Syria. As I mentioned in my article, "Are Russians Sending Military Support To Syria? Potential Conflict With NATO?," while a Russian military presence in the Syrian capital undoubtedly provides an important boost to the Syrian military's battle against ISIS and other Western-backed terrorists, it also provides the world with the potential for direct military confrontation between the two major world powers, both of them armed with nuclear weapons.

But, while the western press seized upon Lavrov's statement as provocative, it should be pointed out that ISIS Czar General John Allen went much further in terms of hinting at the potential for a real fight to break out between the US and Russia over Syria.

In an interview with Jake Tapper of CNN, Allen was asked about the recent Russian involvement in Syria. Part of that interaction is provided below:

QUESTION: The Russian foreign ministry just finally acknowledged that they do have some personnel in Syria aiding Assad, aiding Bashar al-Assad's regime in its fight against ISIS. Do you have a problem with Russian forces in Syria on Assad's side, but fighting ISIS?

GENERAL ALLEN: We've been watching this closely over the last several days, watching the buildup to see what it might mean.

QUESTION: So we don't know whether or not it's a good thing or a bad thing?

GENERAL ALLEN: Well, I think it's a bad thing —

QUESTION: Okay.

GENERAL ALLEN: — if the Russians use combat forces to prop up the regime of Bashar al-Assad.

QUESTION: Okay.

GENERAL ALLEN: Bashar al-Assad is singularly responsible for the death of tens of thousands of his people. Much of the instability in the region is a direct result of the actions of Bashar al-Assad, and to prop him up with military force creates an

---

http://www.reuters.com/article/2015/09/11/us-mideast-syria-russia-idUSKCN0RB0ZD20150911

[1026] Lowe, Christian; Edwards, Julia. "Russia to U.S.: Talk To Us On Syria Or Risk 'Unintended Consequences.'" Reuters. September 11, 2015.
http://www.reuters.com/article/2015/09/11/us-mideast-syria-russia-idUSKCN0RB0ZD20150911

additional crisis in the region, and in fact, could bring Russian forces in confrontation with Coalition forces that are fighting Daesh in Syria."[1027]

Notice Allen stated that, amidst absurd and ridiculous claims that fighting in the Middle East is largely attributable to Assad (in reality, it is attributable to the United States, NATO, GCC, Israel and people like Allen himself), he states that the Russian involvement in Syria "could bring Russian forces in confrontation with Coalition forces." Allen's rhetoric is not only disingenuous, it is incredibly dangerous. It was also largely unreported in the media in contrast to Lavrov's statement.

Yet the disagreements between Russia and the United States (the anti-ISIS coalition vs the anti-anti-ISIS coalition) have gone beyond mere words. While the United States has committed money, arms, training, Special Forces personnel, and air cover for terrorists, Russia has supplied the Syrian government with arms, missiles, military vehicles and fighter jets. Russia provided Assad with a number of sophisticated missile defense systems and Russian made jets for the purpose of fighting the Western-backed terrorists. Russia has also begun construction of a military base inside Syria, particularly in Latakia that will most likely be used as a Forward Operating Base for operations against ISIS. In addition, Russia has recently committed 2,000 troops to Latakia as part of the "first phase" of its operations against ISIS.

According to the Financial Times,

> Russia is to deploy 2,000 military personnel to its new air base near the Syrian port city of Latakia, signalling the scale of Moscow's involvement in the war-torn country.
>
> The deployment "forms the first phase of the mission there," according to an adviser on Syria policy in Moscow.
>
> The force will include fighter aircraft crews, engineers and troops to secure the facility, said another person briefed on the matter.
>
> Three western defence officials agreed that the Russian deployment tallied with the numbers needed to establish a forward air base similar to those built by western militaries in Afghanistan.[1028]

The New York Times also reported the Russian deployment. It reported

> The deployment of some of Russia's most advanced ground attack planes and fighter jets as well as multiple air defense systems at the base near the ancestral home of President Bashar al-Assad appears to leave little doubt about Moscow's goal to establish a military outpost in the Middle East. The planes are protected by at least

---

[1027] "Interview of General John Allen With Jake Tapper, CNN On Counter-ISIL Coalition Anniversary." U.S. Department of State. September 10, 2015. http://www.state.gov/s/seci/246798.htm

[1028] "Russia To Deploy 2,000 In Syria Air Base Mission's 'First Phase.'" Financial Times. See also,

Durden, Tyler. "2,000 Russian Troops Head To Syria For 'First Phase' Of Mission To Support Assad." Zero Hedge. September 22, 2015. http://www.zerohedge.com/news/2015-09-22/2000-russian-troops-head-syria-first-phase-mission-support-assad

two or possibly three SA-22 surface-to-air, antiaircraft systems, and unarmed Predator-like surveillance drones are being used to fly reconnaissance missions.

"With competent pilots and with an effective command and control process, the addition of these aircraft could prove very effective depending on the desired objectives for their use," said David A. Deptula, a retired three-star Air Force general who planned the American air campaigns in 2001 in Afghanistan and in the 1991 Persian Gulf war.

In addition, a total of 15 Russian Hip transport and Hind attack helicopters are also now stationed at the base, doubling the number of those aircraft from last week, the American official said. For use in possible ground attacks, the Russians now also have nine T-90 tanks and more than 500 marines, up from more than 200 last week.

"The equipment and personnel just keep flowing in," said the American official, who spoke on condition of anonymity to discuss confidential intelligence reports. "They were very busy over the weekend.[1029]

Around the same time and shortly after the deployment, the Russian embassy in Damascus came under a mortar attack from jihadists, an interesting maneuver since the Russians are obviously aware of who is actually controlling the death squads in Syria. In other words, the mortar attack represents a proxy attack on the Russian state apparatus as punishment for entering Syria on the side of Assad and the Syrian people.

The Russian embassy issued a statement which alluded to the fact that the West was responsible for these attacks, stating that "We expect a clear position with regard to this terrorist act from all members of the international community, including regional players. This requires not just words but concrete action." The Ministry stated that the ultimate responsibility was with the fighters' "foreign sponsors" who used their influence on the fighters for such purposes.[1030]

Notorious warmonger Secretary of State John Kerry then decided to one-up ISIS Czar Allen by stating that continued Russian action against ISIS could risk a confrontation with the "anti-ISIS" coalition. In an interview with La Stampa, Kerry stated that "These actions could provoke a further escalation of the conflict and lead to the loss of more innocent lives, increasing the flow of refugees and risking a confrontation with the anti-ISIS (Islamic State) coalition operating in Syria."[1031]

At about the same time, Leith Fadel of Al-Masdar news (the Arab Source), reported that China had decided to commit troops and military aircraft to Syria within the next six

---

[1029] Schmitt, Eric; MacFarquhar, Neil. "Russia Expands Fleet In Syria With Jets That Can Attack Targets On Ground." New York Times. September 21, 2015. http://www.nytimes.com/2015/09/22/world/middleeast/russia-deploys-ground-attack-aircraft-to-syrian-base.html?_r=0

[1030] Durden, Tyler. "2,000 Russian Troops Head To Syria For 'First Phase' Of Mission To Support Assad." Zero Hedge. September 22, 2015. http://www.zerohedge.com/news/2015-09-22/2000-russian-troops-head-syria-first-phase-mission-support-assad

[1031] "Kerry Says Russian Support For Assad Risks Confrontation." Reuters. September 23, 2015. http://www.reuters.com/article/2015/09/23/us-mideast-crisis-russia-kerry-idUSKCN0RN0NK20150923

weeks. Although the reports were not independently confirmed, the outlet cited a senior Syrian officer in the Syrian military for the claims regarding the Chinese plans. Fadel's information has proven accurate many times in the past.

Fadel writes,

On Tuesday morning, a Chinese naval vessel reportedly traveled through Egypt's Suez Canal to enter the Mediterranean Sea; its destination was not confirmed.

However, according to a senior officer in the Syrian Arab Army (SAA) that is stationed inside the Syrian coastal city of Latakia, Chinese military personnel and aerial assets are scheduled to arrive in the coming weeks (6 weeks) to the port-city of Tartous – he could not provide any more detail.

Russia has made it abundantly clear that they are taking an active role in this conflict, but the news of the Chinese military to Syria provides more insight into their contingency.[1032]

The French, always willing to sink to the levels of the absurd while in the midst of a propaganda campaign, even suggested that it will begin "reconnaissance" flights over Syria and retain the option to launch airstrikes against Syrian targets presented as "Daesh" but, in reality, are much more likely to be Syrian infrastructure. After all, the French airstrikes, as part of NATO, will be directed in the same manner as those conducted by the United States. All of this offensive bombing, of course, is only "self-defense."[1033]

French President Francois Hollande stated,

"We received specific intelligence indicating that the resent terrorist attacks against France and other European nations were organized by Daesh [Arabic derogatory term for IS] in Syria. Due to this threat we decided to start reconnaissance flights to have the option for airstrikes, if that would be necessary. This is self-defense."[1034]

Such ridiculous claims of self-defense harken back to the days of France standing together and supporting "free speech" after the Charlie Hebdo bombing, an institution that has not existed in France for decades.[1035]

Secretary of Defense Ashton Carter's ridiculous "Gasoline" statements were also of a warning nature, although not to the extent of Kerry and Allen in threats of "confrontation." On September 24, Carter stated that "To pursue the defeat of ISIL without at the same time pursuing a political transition is to fuel the very kind of extremism that underlies ISIL, and if that's the Russian view that's a logical

---

[1032] Fadel, Leith. "Chinese Military Personnel Expected To Arrive In Syria." Al-Masdar News. September 23, 2015. http://www.almasdarnews.com/article/chinese-military-personnel-expected-to-arrive-in-syria/

[1033] "France Ready To Bomb Syria 'in self-defense' – foreign minister." RT. September 22, 2015. https://www.rt.com/news/316163-france-bomb-syria-defense/

[1034] "France Ready To Bomb Syria 'in self-defense' – foreign minister." RT. September 22, 2015. https://www.rt.com/news/316163-france-bomb-syria-defense/

[1035] Turbeville, Brandon. "Je Suis Charlie Or Je Suis Hypocrite?" Activist Post. January 22, 2015. http://www.activistpost.com/2015/01/je-suis-charlie-or-je-suis-hypocrite.html

contradiction. And the way out of that contradiction is to pursue both of those in parallel. And on that basis I think we're prepared to discuss a way ahead with Russia where the political and the military move in parallel."[1036]

He also stated that to avoid a political transition (i.e. the removal of Assad from power) is to "pour gasoline on the ISIL phenomenon rather than to lead to the defeat of ISIL. At another point he suggested that a "military-only Russian approach" would be the same as "pouring gasoline on the civil war in Syria."[1037]

Of course, the stream of Russian logic is easily able to be followed – in order to defeat ISIS, work with all parties currently fighting ISIS. The American logic presented by Carter is quite the opposite – in order to defeat ISIS, first defeat the enemy of ISIS and oppose interested parties who are having success against ISIS.

Russian President Vladmir Putin expressed this logic when he said that destroying Assad's government "will create a situation which you can witness now in the other countries of the region, ... where all the state institutions are disintegrated." He also added, "There is no other solution to the Syrian crisis than strengthening the effective government structures and rendering them help in fighting terrorism."[1038]

The American logic as it presented publicly, however, is quite different from the reality of the situation. The truth is that the United States does not want to defeat ISIS; it is responsible for the creation, funding, training, arming, and directing of that organization and it aims to continue to use it for foreign policy, geopolitical, and domestic purposes.

Thus, with Russian pilots flying Russian planes in combat missions against ISIS in Syria, there is the very real potential that rogue nations like the United States and its "coalition" aircraft may find themselves in direct confrontation with Russian air forces. Considering the aggressive manner in which NATO powers have engaged in military provocations in places like Ukraine, an "accidental" brush with Russian fighter jets could not be ruled out in Syria, as dangerous and potentially destructive as such an act might be.

With the United States engaging in airstrikes all across Syria, there exists the real possibility that lines of communications may become crossed – intentionally or unintentionally – between the United States and Russian forces, resulting in the downing of one or the other's jets. If that happens, the level of tensions between the two powers will be increased to unprecedented levels, leaving open the question of whether or not the "victim" of the incident will opt to show restraint or engage in retaliatory measures.

[1036] Burns, Robert; Baldor, Lolita C. "US Cautions Russia Against Fanning Flames Of Syria War." Associated Press. September 24, 2015. http://news.yahoo.com/officials-russia-begins-drone-flights-syria-180100996.html

[1037] Burns, Robert; Baldor, Lolita C. "US Cautions Russia Against Fanning Flames Of Syria War." Associated Press. September 24, 2015. http://news.yahoo.com/officials-russia-begins-drone-flights-syria-180100996.html

[1038] Burns, Robert; Baldor, Lolita C. "US Cautions Russia Against Fanning Flames Of Syria War." Associated Press. September 24, 2015. http://news.yahoo.com/officials-russia-begins-drone-flights-syria-180100996.html

Likewise with the Israeli forces that continually launch bombing missions in Syria, and act as air cover for death squad fighters operating on the ground. The Israelis are notoriously provocative in their military adventures, encouraged by the fact that they have the United States military to back them up whenever they find themselves in trouble. Both destabilizing and unpredictable, the Israelis always stand as a potential trigger for dragging the United States into a war. While the Russians are fully supportive of an Israeli (Zionist) settler state, by supporting the Syrians against the Israeli-supported terrorists on the ground, the Russians run the risk of an "accidental" (or otherwise) confrontation with Israeli aircraft.

With the question of Syria only one part of the Russia/Western divide, international peace and security – from Asia to Syria to Ukraine – is becoming increasingly destabilized by Western behavior. There are now two theatres where two nuclear powers have the distinct potential to be forced into direct conflict with one another, a confrontation that very well could end in thermonuclear war. The entire fate of the world could thus rest in the finger of a single soldier who may either prevent or cause a devastating conflagration that will alter life on this planet forever. Unless, of course, that was the plan all along . . .

Brzezinski Calls For 'Retaliation' Against Russia For Fighting ISIS

The leading anti-Russian figure of the Anglo-American establishment and geopolitical chess player, Zbigniew Brzezinski declared in an op-ed for the Financial Times that the United States should "retaliate" against Russia for its actions in Syria, even going so far as military action to do so.[1039]

Brzezinski argued that the recent Russian involvement in Syria puts American credibility and global reputation at stake and suggests that such a situation is intolerable. Brzezinski wrote that Russian attacks against what he and the U.S. State Department have labeled as the "non-ISIS" targets and "rebels backed by the United States" at best reflects "Russian military incompetence" and at worst signals "evidence of a dangerous desire to highlight American political impotence."[1040]

"In these rapidly unfolding circumstances the U.S. has only one real option if it is to protect its wider stakes in the region: to convey to Moscow the demand that it cease and desist from military actions that directly affect American assets," he wrote. "But, better still, Russia might be persuaded to act with the U.S. in seeking a wider accommodation to a regional problem that transcends the interests of a single state," he added later.[1041]

[1039] Gass, Nick. "Brzezinski: Obama Should Retaliate If Russia Doesn't Stop Attacking U.S. Assets." Politico. October 5, 2015. http://www.politico.com/story/2015/10/zbigniew-brzezinski-financial-times-op-ed-obama-retaliate-russia-214438

[1040] Gass, Nick. "Brzezinski: Obama Should Retaliate If Russia Doesn't Stop Attacking U.S. Assets." Politico. October 5, 2015. http://www.politico.com/story/2015/10/zbigniew-brzezinski-financial-times-op-ed-obama-retaliate-russia-214438

[1041] Gass, Nick. "Brzezinski: Obama Should Retaliate If Russia Doesn't Stop Attacking U.S. Assets." Politico. October 5, 2015. http://www.politico.com/story/2015/10/zbigniew-brzezinski-

Brzezinski hinted that Russia was engaged in a "new form of neocolonial domination" and offered up his assessment of the geopolitical situation when he stated

> China would doubtless prefer to stay on the sidelines. It might calculate that it will then be in a better position to pick up the pieces. But the regional chaos could easily spread northeastward, eventually engulfing central and northeastern Asia. Both Russia and then China could be adversely affected. But American interests and America's friends — not to mention regional stability — would also suffer. It is time, therefore, for strategic boldness.[1042]

It is, indeed, a strange kind of "neocolonial domination" that sees the "dominated" country invite the "dominator" in for support with the "dominator" incredibly resistant to doing so for years. It is also incredibly hypocritical to suggest that Russia is the state actor representing a "neocolonial domination" when the United States has marched its blood drenched boots all across the globe for decades, slaughtering, draining, and oppressing the hapless civilians that have been unfortunate enough to have been born in a country with natural wealth or strategic positioning.

Of course, the idea that U.S. credibility is on the line as a result of the Russian involvement is without question. Unfortunately for the United States, however, that ship has already sailed a long time ago and what little shred of American credibility that was left is being eaten up by every sortie flown against ISIS by the Russian military.

Indeed, it is quite amazing what one can accomplish when one bombs the actual terrorist organization it claims is the enemy. The Russians have clearly demonstrated that either the United States military is not capable of fighting itself out of a wet paper bag, or the U.S. government never wanted to fight ISIS to begin with. Considering the trail of destruction the United States has left behind in its wake, it is safe to say that the latter is the logical conclusion.

Turkey and Ukraine Prepare Terrorist Brigades Aimed At Russia

On August 1-2, a meeting was convened at the Hotel Billkent in Ankara, Turkey labeled the Second World Congress of the Tatars. This meeting brought together over 200 Tatar NGOs and associations from all over the world. The event was also attended by Ukrainian Foreign Minister Pavlo Klimkin and Turkish Deputy Prime Minister Numan Kurtulmus. Both officials participated in the event as well.[1043]

As Zaman reports,

---

financial-times-op-ed-obama-retaliate-russia-214438

[1042] Gass, Nick. "Brzezinski: Obama Should Retaliate If Russia Doesn't Stop Attacking U.S. Assets." Politico. October 5, 2015. http://www.politico.com/story/2015/10/zbigniew-brzezinski-financial-times-op-ed-obama-retaliate-russia-214438

[1043] Dobriansky, Andrij. "World Congress of Crimean Tatars held in Turkey." The Ukrainian Weekly. August 14, 2015. http://www.ukrweekly.com/uwwp/world-congress-of-crimean-tatars-held-in-turkey/

Nearly 200 Crimean Tatar nongovernmental organizations and civil society groups gathered in Ankara as part of the Second World Crimean Tatar Congress to discuss the ongoing crisis in Ukraine and the situation of their brethren in Crimea, which was annexed by Russia in February of last year.

The meeting took place on Saturday at Ankara Bilkent Hotel and Congress Center and focused on the dire conditions under which Crimean Tatars have to live in the face of encroaching Russian pressure on their cultural life. The gathering offered an opportunity for lengthy discussions about how to resolve the prolonged conflict in Ukraine and to maintain Tatars' threatened community rights under the new administration in Crimea.[1044]

But, while Russia and the annexation of Crimea were the focus of the meeting, a foolish and potentially dangerous decision was made between Ukraine and Turkey. At the meeting, it was announced by Mustafa Abdulcemil Cemiloglu, acting leader of the Crimean Tatars as decreed by Ukrainian President Poroshenko, announced the creation of a "Muslim Brigade" to oppose "Crimean separatism," as well as "human trafficking" and the "transportation of goods near conflict zones." In other words, the creation of a terrorist brigade to combat Russian involvement in Crimea and pro-Russian sentiment and activism in the area. [1045]

It should be noted that Cemiloglu was a notorious CIA asset and collaborator throughout the years of the Reagan Administration. He was also the former leader of the Crimea Tatar Majlis.[1046]

After the announcement was made by Cemiloglu, he was received by Turkish Recep Erdogan, who assured him of Turkey's full support for the Tatars against Russia. Turkey has been vocal about the "territorial integrity" of Ukraine and has, like the rest of NATO, taken a strong anti-Russian stance on the issue of Ukraine.[1047]

The "Muslim Brigade" will apparently be based at Herson, near the Crimean border and will include volunteers and jihadists from a number of other locations in the region – "Tatarstan," Uzbekistan, Azerbaijan, Chechnya, and Georgia.[1048]

[1044] "Crimean Tatars Gather In Ankara To Discuss Ukrainian Crisis." Today's Zaman. http://www.todayszaman.com/anasayfa_crimean-tatars-gather-in-ankara-to-discuss-ukrainian-crisis_395398.html
See also,
https://www.thefreelibrary.com/Crimean+Tatars+gather+in+Ankara+to+discuss+Ukrainian+crisis-a0424026329
[1045] "Crimean Tatars Gather In Ankara To Discuss Ukrainian Crisis." Today's Zaman. http://www.todayszaman.com/anasayfa_crimean-tatars-gather-in-ankara-to-discuss-ukrainian-crisis_395398.html
See also,
https://www.thefreelibrary.com/Crimean+Tatars+gather+in+Ankara+to+discuss+Ukrainian+crisis-a0424026329
[1046] "Ukraine and Turkey Create An International Muslim Brigade." VoltaireNet. August 5, 2015. http://www.voltairenet.org/article188381.html
[1047] "Erdogan: Turkey Will Not Recognize Crimea's Reunification With Russia." Sputnik. August 3, 2015. http://sputniknews.com/politics/20150803/1025364190.html

Turkey will not be left out of the mix, however, since it will be committing a number of the jihadists currently operating within its own borders for the purposes of destroying the government of Syria to the new Muslim Brigade in Ukraine. Indeed, in December 2013, Turkish intelligence sent a number of Tatar jihadists to Ukraine so they would be able to assist the Western color revolution in Kiev where the terrorists acted as "security" for pro-European and anti-Russian protests in the Maidan, often suspected of being the culprits behind a number of violent acts resulting in the violent crackdown by police.[1049]

As the Voltaire Network reported in its article "Jihadists In Charge of Crowd Control In Kiev Protests,"

> They are members of the "Azatlyk" (freedom) movement led by young Naïl Nabiullin, and campaign for a Greater Turkey. They are backed by Trotskyist parties such as the Russian Left Front of Sergei Udaltsov, as well as the Turkish government of Recep Tayyip Erdoğan. They've just come back from Syria, through Turkey, where they had gone to practice jihad against the Syrian government. They seem to be behind the provocations that have led the Riot Police to commit excesses.[1050]

With this in mind, it is very concerning that Turkey and Ukraine are moving towards greater provocations against Russia – this time using jihadist terrorists on and inside Russian borders. Such moves clearly increase the likelihood that Russia will be forced to engage NATO and its proxies in a direct military fashion at some point.

After all, color revolutions, if caught early, can be eliminated by removing the NGOs and Foundations responsible for organizing the "golden youth" but repeated acts of suicidal terrorism must be cut off at the source or it will continue to take place indefinitely. If Russia finds itself surrounded by US/NATO military bases and missile systems while, at the same time, being faced with economic warfare and sanctions, it may view its current position of non-intervention as untenable when faced with cross-border terrorist attacks openly supported by NATO countries.

Indeed, it appears that Vladmir Putin is already well aware of the attempts by NATO and Turkey in particular to use terrorism against Russia inside the Russian borders. According to a report by Press TV, in recent visit to the Crimea, Putin stated "It's obvious that a risk remains from outside forces to destabilize the situation on the [Crimean] peninsula in one way or another. In certain capitals they talk openly about … the need to carry out subversive activities. Personnel are being recruited and trained to carry out subversion, acts of sabotage to conduct radical propaganda."[1051]

[1048] "Crimean Tatars Gather In Ankara To Discuss Ukrainian Crisis." Today's Zaman. http://www.todayszaman.com/anasayfa_crimean-tatars-gather-in-ankara-to-discuss-ukrainian-crisis_395398.html
See also,
https://www.thefreelibrary.com/Crimean+Tatars+gather+in+Ankara+to+discuss+Ukrainian+crisis-a0424026329
[1049] "Ukraine and Turkey Create An International Muslim Brigade." VoltaireNet. August 5, 2015. http://www.voltairenet.org/article188381.html
[1050] "Jihadists In Charge Of Crowd Control In Kiev Protests." Voltaire Network. December 5, 2013. http://www.voltairenet.org/article181380.html

Turkey's move also bolsters the assertions made by others such as Webster Tarpley that the Turkish bombing of ISIS – on the rare instances where ISIS forces are actually targeted – is nothing more than an attempt to push some ISIS forces East towards Iran and, eventually, Russia.[1052]

Increasing tensions between the United States, NATO and Russia over Syria, Iran, Ukraine, and the current sanctions can only be increased further by Turkey's support of terrorism aimed at Russia. Erdogan's fantasies of becoming the next Ottoman emperor have apparently become so great that he believes challenging Russia is a legitimate means to this end. It is time for both Erdogan and the rest of the Western world to realize the folly of these attempts and to immediately back off of further provocation.

NATO Provokes Russia In Crimea As Syria Tensions Rise

After "mysterious" blasts that took place in the Kherson region of Ukraine over the weekend of November 21-22, 2015, leaving nearly two million citizens without power in the recently annexed Russian territory, the Ukrainian government officially halted aid shipments as "activists" inside Crimea blocked the repair of the power lines. The Kherson region is located in Southeastern Ukraine and on the border with Crimea.[1053]

The blasts brought down electricity pylons that serve Crimea although the intended target was a currency exchange located in Kherson. A man apparently demanded cash before detonating the bomb in the building, with another bomb being found shortly thereafter outside. A separate explosion took place in Odessa, another city in the Southeastern Ukraine region. Explosives were later found near the power lines according to officials, preventing crews from being able to repair them. Shortly thereafter, groups of "activists" made up of Crimean Tatars took to protest and blocked the repair crews from restoring power to the areas suffering from the outage. The demands of the "activists" were that a tougher line be taken against Moscow. This "tougher line" essentially means doing more to "restore" Crimea to Ukraine and to "take it back" from Russia.[1054]

[1051] "Russia's Putin Warns Of 'Sabotage' Plots Against Crimea." PRESS TV. August 19, 2015. http://www.presstv.ir/Detail/2015/08/19/425469/Russia-President-Vladimir-Putin-Crimea

[1052] Tarpley, Webster Griffin. "Faction Fight In The Pentagon: Fox News Signal Piece Reveals Anger Of Loyal US Officers Against ISIS Czar Gen. Allen And His Seditious Clique; July 24 Bait And Switch By Turkey's Erdogan Endangered Lives Of US Special Forces Training Kurds, ISIS Will Grow, Followed By Calls For US Infantry Divisions; Join The #FireAllen4ISIS Social Media Campaign Now!" Tarpley.net. August 13, 2015. INN World Report with Tom Kiely Interview. Tarpley expounds upon this theory during the course of the interview. http://tarpley.net/faction-fight-in-pentagon-fox-news-reveals-anger-of-loyal-us-officers-against-isis-czar-gen-allen/

[1053] Mills, Laura. "Ukraine Escalates Confrontation Over Crimea." Wall Street Journal. November 23, 2015. http://www.wsj.com/articles/russia-confident-ukraine-will-restore-crimean-power-swiftly-1448275201

[1054] Mills, Laura. "Ukraine Escalates Confrontation Over Crimea." Wall Street Journal. November 23, 2015. http://www.wsj.com/articles/russia-confident-ukraine-will-restore-crimean-power-

This is not the first political act groups of Tatars have committed in this regard. Ever since September, Tatar "activists" have stalked the border between Crimea and mainland Ukraine and have attempted to block commercial trucks from entering the peninsula. The Ukrainian fascist government responded by decreeing that all vehicles hauling goods to and from Crimea be temporarily halted. As Laura Mills writes for the Wall Street Journal,

> Prime Minister Arseniy Yatsenyuk asked his cabinet to formalize the decree by drafting a law that would "take into account the interests of our brotherly Crimean Tatar people."

> "We aren't satisfied with today's status quo, when an occupying power neglects the basic rights of the Crimean Tatar people," said President Petro Poroshenko after a meeting with three European foreign ministers. "Crimea is Ukrainian territory. We will defend the rights of the Crimean Tatar people and all Ukrainians who are living on occupied territory."[1055]

While it is unclear whether or not the bombing itself was engineered by Ukrainian, Western, or NATO forces or if it was some coordinated and bizarre robbery plan gone wrong, given the history and methodology of the aforementioned nations and organizations, the circumstances surrounding the bombings are highly suspect. After all, with the bombings coming so close together, succeeding in knocking out civilian power in a highly convenient manner at a highly convenient time, and the resulting measures coming from the "activist" Tatars and the Ukrainian government, it would be reasonable to suggest that a leadership that would allow pro-Moscow activists to be burned to death in a trade union hall would indeed carry out bombings to achieve a much greater geopolitical goal.

Tensions Rising Between Russia, U.S. - Do Drills And Bases Signal Troop Placement?

While most individuals assume that both historical and future events arise as a result of a series of massive and seismic actions, the truth is often that a whimper precedes the bang. While many events are indeed sparked by a single definitive act, it is also true that, in the events leading up to the defining moment, rarely does the general public realize that they are walking along the path to such an event. Even rarer is the individual who realizes that this path was already carved out by high-level players in the halls of banks, corporations, governments, and secret societies long before the destination is ever reached.

For instance, most scholars present the events leading up to World War I as an immediate reaction to the assassination of Franz Ferdinand by a shadowy semi-secret society that was not fundamentally connected to any other secret establishment. The truth, however, is that not only was the Black Hand a part of a Revolutionary

---

swiftly-1448275201

[1055] Mills, Laura. "Ukraine Escalates Confrontation Over Crimea." Wall Street Journal. November 23, 2015. http://www.wsj.com/articles/russia-confident-ukraine-will-restore-crimean-power-swiftly-1448275201

Freemasonic structure and the war itself a carefully orchestrated plot that involved the personal attention and assembly of King Edward VII as well as British and French Freemasonic Lodges, but it was not solely a reaction to the assassination of Ferdinand.[1056] [1057]

Interestingly enough, for thirty days after the assassination, life, for the most part, continued on without any apparent changes in the lives of the general public. Indeed, in the month after the assassination of Ferdinand, the majority of the world's population had returned to what has been described as a "dreamlike trance" of ignorance even as the declarations of war were being prepared behind the scenes.[1058]

The time of this "dreamlike trance" – July 1914 – may very well bear relevance to the time in which we find ourselves today. While we must do our best to avoid sensationalism, the question of US-Russia relations, US imperialism, and the geopolitical imperatives of the US, Russia, China, and NATO compounded by the overwhelming ignorance of the general public is one that should cause some concern as to whether or not we find ourselves in a similar situation today.

In March, 2015, I wrote an article entitled "Do Russia/NATO Military Drills Signal Something Ominous?" where I listed and discussed a number of "military drills" and acts of strategic positioning that pointed toward the potential for direct military confrontation between the two powers. It is now over a year later and that cataclysmic confrontation never took place. Unfortunately, signs and indications that it is a possibility remain.

The Polish Drills

The drills involving U.S., British, and Polish troops, dubbed Anaconda, were some of the largest NATO drills of its kind and they did nothing to ease the tensions with Russia over the deployment of the missile defense system aimed at Russia and being placed essentially at its doorstep.

As Reuters reports,

> US, British and Polish soldiers parachuted to the ground in Poland on Tuesday in a mass show of force as NATO launched its biggest war games in eastern Europe since the Cold War.

> The exercises -- staged against the backdrop of a military and diplomatic standoff between Russia and the West -- have rattled the Kremlin.

[1056] "Webster Tarpley On Assassination Of Archduke Ferdinand." Youtube. Posted by jabarbadi. Posted on june 30, 2014. https://www.youtube.com/watch?v=3_5GbPBfzOM Webster Tarpley interview with Richard Syrrett of Coast to Coast.

[1057] Tarpley, Webster Griffin. "King Edward VII of Great Britain: Evil Demiurge Of The Triple Entente And World War 1." Tarpley.net. *Against Austerity.* http://tarpley.net/online-books/against-oligarchy/king-edward-vii-of-great-britain-evil-demiurge-of-the-triple-entente-and-world-war-1/

[1058] Tarpley, Webster Griffin. "US, Pakistan Near Open War; Chinese Ultimatum Warns Washington Against Attack." Tarpley.net. May 20, 2011. http://tarpley.net/2011/05/21/us-pakistan-near-open-war-chinese-ultimatum-warns-washington-against-attack/

NATO says the 10-day Anaconda manoeuvres involving 31,000 troops are intended to shore up security on the alliance's eastern flank, where member states have been spooked by Russia's increasingly assertive actions.

"There's no reason to be nervous," Ben Hodges, Commanding General, US Army Europe, told reporters, insisting the exercises were purely "defensive".

They are being held a month ahead of a NATO summit in Warsaw set to seal its largest revamp since the Cold War by deploying more troop rotations to eastern European members deeply wary of Russia after its 2014 annexation of Crimea from Ukraine.

Moscow fiercely opposes the NATO moves, billed by the US-led alliance as part of its "deterrence and dialogue" strategy.

And the Kremlin reacted angrily to the start of the manoeuvres, NATO's biggest since the Trident drills last year involving 36,000 troops in Italy, Spain and Portugal.

"The exercises... do not contribute to an atmosphere of trust and security," said spokesman Dmitry Peskov.

"Unfortunately we are still witnessing a deficit in mutual trust."

Anaconda involves troops from 24 states, including 14,000 from the US, as well as ex-Soviet "Partnership for Peace" states like Ukraine.[1059]

The New Russian Base

It is very strange logic to consider a military base built inside one's own country as an act of aggression. However, it can be considered an act of strategic positioning and it cannot be argued that Russia is not being forced to respond to U.S. provocation and encirclement. For this reason, it appears that the Russians are building a new base on the Russian/Ukrainian border in an effort to protect itself from the growing potential of a direct confrontation with NATO troops.

Reuters also reports on the new Russian initiative by writing,

Russia is building an army base near its border with Ukraine, the latest in a chain of new military sites along what the Kremlin sees as its frontline in a growing confrontation with NATO.

While there have been no clashes between the former Cold War rivals, Russia is building up forces on its western frontiers at a time when the NATO alliance is staging major military exercises and increasing deployments on its eastern flank.

A Reuters reporter who visited the Russian town of Klintsy, about 50 km (30 miles) from Ukraine, saw a makeshift army camp, large numbers of newly-arrived servicemen and military vehicles.

. . . . .

[1059] Siberski, Mary. "NATO Irks Russia With Massive War Games In Poland." AFP. June 7, 2016. https://www.yahoo.com/news/poland-hold-biggest-nato-manoeuvres-amid-russia-tensions-171355952.html

Last year, Reuters also reported on construction of two other bases further to the south on Russia's border with Ukraine.[1060]

It is rare for a mainstream media outlet to utter anything resembling reality these days but Anton Zverev did manage to do so when he wrote for Reuters that "Each side says it is only responding to steps taken by the other, but the build-up risks locking NATO and Russia into a spiral of measure and counter-measure from which it will be difficult to escape." Of course, the article did not point out that American/NATO aggression is indeed the reason why Russia feels the need to shore up its defenses.[1061]

The U.S. Aircraft Carrier In The Mediterranean

After the small draw down of Russian troops and aircraft from Syria, the Western media could not contain itself from making claims that the Russians were running scared from their battle with ISIS, despite the fact that the Russian-Syrian alliance had done more to destroy the group in weeks than the U.S. had done in years.

But, while the Russian draw down was itself limited and merely a change in strategy after the initial phase of Russian involvement had been completed, Russia ordered another round of military equipment to Syria.

This time, instead of committing planes and personnel to land bases inside Syria, Russia sent the aircraft carrier, Admiral Kuznetsov, to the Mediterranean.[1062]

Even as that aircraft carrier was scheduled to appear in the Mediterranean, the United States made an "unplanned diversion" of its own as the USS Harry S. Truman was also sent to the Mediterranean.

As Tamer El-Ghobashy of Market Watch wrote,

> This 20-story-tall aircraft carrier with a crew of 5,000 made an unplanned diversion from the Gulf to the eastern Mediterranean last week — a quick pivot intended to send a clear message to Russia.
>
> . . . . .
>
> Rear Adm. Bret Batchelder, the highest-ranking officer on the carrier, told visiting reporters this week that moving the "capital ship" of the U.S. Navy from the Gulf through the Suez Canal is a flexing of muscle meant to reassure North Atlantic Treaty

---

[1060] Zverev, Anton. "Russia Deploys Troops Westward As Standoff With NATO Deepens." Reuters. June 8, 2016. http://www.reuters.com/article/us-russia-base-bryansk-idUSKCN0YT1PN

[1061] Zverev, Anton. "Russia Deploys Troops Westward As Standoff With NATO Deepens." Reuters. June 8, 2016. http://www.reuters.com/article/us-russia-base-bryansk-idUSKCN0YT1PN

[1062] Vasilescu, Valentin. "Russian Planes Soon To Return To Syria, This Time Ship-Based." Russia Insider. May 18, 2016. http://russia-insider.com/en/russian-planes-soon-return-syria-time-ship-based/ri14403?utm_source=Russia+Insider+Daily+Headlines&utm_campaign=2da090567a-Russia_Insider_Daily_Headlines11_21_2014&utm_medium=email&utm_term=0_c626db089c-2da090567a-179259473&ct=t%28Russia_Insider_Daily_Headlines11_21_2014%29&mc_cid=2da090567a&mc_eid=c0e6c3f616

Organization allies of the American commitment to maintaining the balance of naval power in the Mediterranean.

"It is a demonstration of capability. That's for sure," he said. "There are undoubtedly folks who are watching that and this is just a graphic representation of what we're capable of."

A military official in Washington said the Truman's shift was a signal to Moscow and a demonstration of the Navy's operational flexibility and reach.[1063]

The Race For Raqqa

The Syrian military is gradually closing in on Raqqa, one of the last ISIS strongholds in the country, and is eventually expected to reach the city and a major battle between government and terrorist forces is inevitable. The Syrian military has already liberated a number of areas in eastern Syria near the Taqba airbase, another site that is expecting liberation in the next few days. The Syrian military has already reached the edge of Raqqa province.[1064] [1065] [1066]

Raqqa has acted as the ISIS capital since the mysterious appearance of the group two years ago and has gone virtually untouched as the Syrian military has been bogged down in major cities and western/central areas of the country in their fight against the Western-backed terrorists. Notably, despite its rhetoric of fighting to "degrade and destroy" ISIS, the U.S.-led coalition has yet to bomb Raqqa with the earnestness one would expect from a country truly devoted to fighting ISIS.

Fresh on the heels of a major public relations victory in Palmyra, however, the Syrian military is now marching toward Raqqa and, if successful, it will score one of the biggest victories in the five-year war.[1067] This is not only because the de facto ISIS capital will be eliminated or because the SAA will gain more territory, it is because the

---

[1063] El-Ghobashy, Tamer. "U.S. Sends Message To Russia, Moves Aircraft Carrier To Mediterranean." The Wall Street Journal. Market Watch. June 8, 2016. http://www.marketwatch.com/story/us-sends-message-to-russia-moves-aircraft-carrier-to-mediterranean-2016-06-08?siteid=yhoof2

[1064] Turbeville, Brandon. "The Race For Raqqa – Could Two World Powers Meet In Battle Over ISIS HQ?" Activist Post. June 7, 2016. http://www.activistpost.com/2016/06/the-race-for-raqqa-could-two-world-powers-meet-in-battle-over-isis-hq.html

[1065] Fadel, Ziad. "Syrian Army Continues Approach To Al-Raqqa And Taqba: First Woman Speaker Of The House Elected By Firm Majority; Jordan Struck By Jordanian Rebel! Many Rat Leaders Eliminated Today." Syrian Perspective. June 6, 2016. http://syrianperspective.com/2016/06/syrian-army-continues-approach-to-al-raqqa-and-tabqa-first-woman-speaker-of-the-house-elected-by-firm-majority-jordan-struck-by-jordanian-rebel-many-rat-leaders-eliminated-today.html

[1066] "Onslaught On ISIS: Syrian Army Enters Raqqa Province As Kurds, Rebels Advance." RT. June 4, 2015. https://www.rt.com/news/345394-raqqa-syria-kurds-army/

[1067] Turbeville, Brandon. "The Liberation Of Palmyra: US Narratives And NATO Terrorists Defeated In The Syrian Desert." Activist Post. March 28, 2016. http://www.activistpost.com/2016/03/the-liberation-of-palmyra-us-narratives-and-nato-terrorists-defeated-in-the-syrian-desert.html

liberation of Raqqa will be yet another example of how the Syrian military will have accomplished in short order and with a fraction of the resources what the United States and coalition members have claimed may take a decade to do. It will be another instance where the lack of will on the part of the United States to actually destroy Daesh is put on display for the rest of the world, either causing the U.S. to look weak in the eyes of the world or exposing it for actually supporting the terrorist organization to begin with. Regardless, the victory for the Syrian government will be twofold.

That is, unless the U.S. gets there first . . . .

The U.S. has been using the presence of ISIS in Syria as an excuse to bomb, send Special Forces, publicly support terrorists, and possibly invade since the Western-backed terror group appeared on the scene two years ago. Yet, despite its rhetoric, the United States and its coalition has largely abstained from bombing any terrorist groups. Instead, the U.S. has focused on bombing Syrian military targets, civilians and civilian infrastructure (see here also), and acting as a deterrent to the Syrian military's movement in many "rebel-held" areas of the country.[1068] [1069] [1070] [1071] [1072] [1073] Now, however, the United States seems to have great interest in Raqqa as it aids its loose collection of terrorists, fanatical Kurds, and Arabs known as the Syrian Democratic Forces (SDF) in "battles" around the ISIS capital.

So why the sudden interest in Raqqa? It's fairly simple. The United States sees clearly that the Syrian military and its Russian allies are going to liberate Raqqa soon enough and the U.S. does not want to suffer another public relations setback. A defeat for ISIS is thus a humiliation for the United States. That fact alone should raise some eyebrows. Regardless, the United States would like to have its own "victory" in Raqqa before the Syrians and the Russians can have theirs. If the SDF is able to "take" Raqqa, the U.S. will then be able to shout from the rooftops that America has liberated Raqqa and defeated ISIS in its own capital.

[1068] Turbeville, Brandon. "US Gives ISIS 45 Minute Warning Before Bombs, 'Runs Out Of Ammo' Against ISIS Targets." Activist Post. December 2, 2015. http://www.activistpost.com/2015/12/us-gives-isis-45-minute-warning-before-bombs-runs-out-of-ammo-against-isis-targets.html

[1069] Jones, Susan. "US Planes Left ISIS Fuel Tankers Unharmed Because 'They Ran Out Of Ammunition." CNS News. November 24, 2015. http://www.cnsnews.com/news/article/susan-jones/us-planes-left-isis-fuel-tankers-unharmed-because-they-ran-out-ammunition

[1070] Durden, Tyler. "'Get Out Of Your Trucks And Run Away:' US Gives ISIS 45 Minute Warning On Oil Tanker Sites." Zero Hedge. November 23, 2015. http://www.zerohedge.com/news/2015-11-23/get-out-your-trucks-and-run-away-us-gives-isis-45-minute-warning-oil-tanker-strikes

[1071] Turbeville, Brandon. "The Real Reason For U.S. Airstrikes In Syria – Breaking The Assad Regime." Activist Post. September 24, 2014. http://www.activistpost.com/2014/09/the-real-reasons-for-us-airstrikes-in.html

[1072] "As Russia Bombs ISIS, US Bombs Syrian Civilian Power Stations." Activist Post. October 13, 2015. http://www.activistpost.com/2015/10/as-russia-bombs-isis-us-bombs-syrian-civilian-power-stations.html

[1073] "Two US Led Coalition F16 Aircrafts Violate Syrian Airspace, Target Electric Power Plants In Aleppo." SANA. October 10, 2015. http://www.globalresearch.ca/two-us-led-coalition-f16-aircrafts-violate-syrian-airspace-target-electric-power-plants-in-aleppo/5481464

The U.S. also has another goal in Raqqa – the theft of more Syrian territory by using its proxy forces going by the name of the SDF. Whether or not ISIS proper is in control of Raqqa is merely a secondary concern for the United States. If the SDF succeeds in imposing control over the city and the province, then the West will have succeeded in cementing control over the area in the hands of its proxy terrorists once again, but with yet another incarnation of the same Western-backed jihadist fanaticism. The U.S. can then use the "moderate rebel" label to keep Russia and Syria from bombing the fighters who merely assumed a position handed to them, albeit through some level of violence, by ISIS.

With the situation as it stands, there is now the very real possibility of some type of major confrontation taking place in Raqqa that could very well have international ramifications. On one hand, there is the Syrian military, backed by the Russian Air Force and Russian Special Forces heading East to Raqqa while, on the other side, there is the SDF, backed by the U.S. Air and Special Forces, heading West toward Raqqa. Both sides are in a race to gain control over the ISIS capital, gain territory, and declare a victory for the world to see. But what if they arrive in Raqqa at the same time?[1074]

In other words, there is a distinct potential that, in the race for Raqqa, the Syrian/Russian alliance might find itself face to face with the possibility of direct military conflict with the U.S. /SDF (terrorist) alliance. At that point, the question will be who, if either, will back down? If both forces decide to push forward, the result could be devastating not only for Syria but for the rest of the world.

Conclusion

It is now legitimate to wonder whether or not Russia and NATO are engaging in troop placement under the guise of drills for the purposes of preparing for and eventually launching a real war. Indeed, one would be entirely justified in wondering whether or not we are seeing the chess pieces being set for a major military confrontation beginning in Eastern Europe but finding its way to North America and eventually enveloping the entire world.

Given the track record of both governments, it is entirely plausible to believe that, if both nations were indeed placing their military personnel in strategic positions, the cover of "drills" could and would be used so as not to forewarn the general public or cause panic in society and hamper the war effort. In addition, the cover of military drills and exercises is obviously a tactic available to governments whereby they are able to position military personnel in prime locations before any actual combat has taken place.[1075]

With all of this in mind, we must begin to ask ourselves, "Are the American people in a dreamlike trance?"

"Are we in July, 1914?"

[1074] Al-Khalidi, Suleiman. "Syrian Army Presses Offensive Against Islamic State." Reuters. June 4, 2016. http://www.reuters.com/article/us-mideast-crisis-syria-raqqa-idUSKCN0YQ0B8

[1075] Stalin: The First In-depth Biography Based on Explosive New Documents from Russia's Secret Archives, Anchor, (1997) ISBN 0-385-47954-9, pages 454-459

Russia's "No-Fly Zone" Prevents U.S., Israel, UK From Bombing Syria

After a few weeks of Russian bombing in Syria, a new kind of "no-fly zone" seems to have been established. However, this "no-fly zone" is not focused on preventing Syrian planes and military forces from operating inside the country. Instead, it functions as a barrier, at least partially, to Israeli and American air forces seeking to enter Syria through the Mediterranean Sea in order to support terrorists and jihadists against the secular government of Bashar al-Assad.

This is because of Russia's naval presence in the port of Tartus and its new presence just off the coast of Latakia, particularly with ships like the guided missile cruiser Moscow. The ship left Crimea on September 24 and is part of what Russian media is referring to as training exercises.

The Russian Ministry of Defense has stated,

> In the course of the training activity, the Russian ships will practice organization of anti-submarine, anti-ship, and air defense, as well as search-and-rescue activities and rendering assistance to distressed vessels.

> During the exercise, the military seamen are to perform over 40 different combat, tasks including missile and artillery firings at surface and aerial targets.[1076]

Clearly, the ship is in the Mediterranean for more than simple maneuvers. But its presence is also being bemoaned by the obsessively pro-Israeli, pro-NATO, and pro-war crowds howling in the pages of mainstream media outlets about being prevented from being able to cross national borders at will and rain death and destruction down upon innocent civilians and the primary force fighting ISIS and other jihadists in Syria.

As pro-Israeli writer "Eli" from SOFREP wrote in an article that was reposted by Business Insider,

> By positioning the Moskva, a cruiser armed with S300 missiles, west of Latakia, the Russians have endangered the IAF's favorite corridor of flight into Syria. The IAF has no stealth capabilities to circumvent this anti-access/area denial — A2/AD — bubble, nor any other air force in the area.

> Russian President Vladimir Putin managed to do in several days what US President Barack Obama failed to do in the last three years: He's created a true no-fly zone. Putin's actions suggest, in my opinion, that he's willing to force the coalition and the Israel air force into reporting and coordinating their flights in the region — an act I'm sure no one is in favor of or willing to comply with.

> The Moskva carries an estimated 64 S-300 missiles, according to foreign sources), and could intercept multiple targets up to 150 miles away, making it a serious threat in addition to other Russian assets in the region.

[1076] "Eli" SOFREP. "Russian Warships May Be Shutting Out Israel's Air Force Access To Syria." Business Insider. October 26, 2015. http://www.businessinsider.com/it-looks-like-russian-warships-may-be-shutting-out-israels-air-force-access-to-syria-2015-10?r=UK&IR=T

The presence of the Moskva essentially locks down British air assets in Cyprus, American F-16s in the southern part of Turkey, and the Israeli air force, which likes to use that particular flight corridor for penetration into Syria, or alternatively when flying over the western part of Lebanon. Any flights in or around the country will now be tricky for the IAF to accomplish.[1077]

"Eli" made an astute observation. Unless the Israelis and NATO powers are truly willing to risk World War 3, the ability to simply fly in through and over the Mediterranean has been severely hampered by the Russian presence. NATO and Israel could indeed identify themselves and their intentions but they could be denied overflight permission to do so. They would then be forced with the choice between simply stepping back or risking a direct confrontation with Russian jets in the air.

Furthermore, "Eli" concluded that danger is indeed present. He writes,

So what happens to coalition surveillance flights? What about airdrops to parties in the region supported by the coalition? This will become another complicated situation which will require the precision of a surgeon and the creativity of artists. One thing is certain: The Kremlin's recent move is dangerous and places us all in danger. It may be time to dust off the old Cold War books.[1078]

Yet, while "Eli" lamented the Russian presence in the Mediterranean and Syria and attempted to suggest that Russia is simply expanding its empire, his thesis is concerning for three reasons. First, it is perhaps the case that the United States and Israel have violated human rights and national borders for so long that neither their citizens nor their cheerleaders have any grasp of the difference between imperialism and self-defense.

Second, "Eli" laments the Russian presence because he views the Western support of savages raping and beheading their way across Syria as legitimate and justified. He implicitly argues that the Israeli Air Force, along with the U.S. Air Force, has and should continue to have the divine right to cross national borders at will, drop bombs on civilians and national governments as they choose, and be free from any and all consequences of doing so. The "exceptional" people and the "chosen" people thus make a very good team, complete with the blessings of God and the rest of the world.

There is one major problem, however – the fact that Israel and the United States no longer have the blessing of the world to continue their slaughter unabated. Russia has had enough and so have many other nations.

Which brings us to the most concerning aspect of "Eli's" position – that he and those he represents are willing to risk World War 3 to continue settlement and colonization of the Middle East and other "non-compliant" nations. "Eli's" article would not be so concerning if it were not for the fact that it represents the viewpoint of a ruling elite that is so committed to world hegemony that it very well might risk the literal destruction of

---

[1077] "Eli" SOFREP. "Russian Warships May Be Shutting Out Israel's Air Force Access To Syria." Business Insider. October 26, 2015. http://www.businessinsider.com/it-looks-like-russian-warships-may-be-shutting-out-israels-air-force-access-to-syria-2015-10?r=UK&IR=T
[1078] "Eli" SOFREP. "Russian Warships May Be Shutting Out Israel's Air Force Access To Syria." Business Insider. October 26, 2015. http://www.businessinsider.com/it-looks-like-russian-warships-may-be-shutting-out-israels-air-force-access-to-syria-2015-10?r=UK&IR=T

the world in search of those aims. While "Eli" describes the "Kremlin's recent moves" as "dangerous" and having placed us all in danger, the Kremlin is only acting in a way that defends its own self-interests.

If "Eli" is concerned with the danger that we all face, he would do well to warn the White House and the Knesset.

U.S./NATO Edge The Planet Closer To World War Three In Syria

With the U.S. bombing of Syrian government soldiers in Deir ez Zour and the subsequent sabre rattling of the United States and Russia, it is clear to anyone paying attention that the world is edging closer to the possibility of a major confrontation between two world nuclear powers. Such a confrontation would spell disaster not only for the populations of those countries but also for the entire earth if the full military power of Russia and the United States are ever set loose.

While panic is never the best option and constantly proclaiming that the end of the world is nigh is often an attempt to promote products and attract attention, we cannot ignore signs that the world is marching toward an abyss which, if pushed too far, it may not be able to step back from.

The Kirby Warning

In the wake of the collapse of the ceasefire agreement in Syria during which neither the United States nor its terrorist pets abided by any of the terms of the agreements and where the United States ended up bombing Syrian military soldiers in Deir ez Zour in support of ISIS, a war of words ensued between the State Department spokesman, Samantha Power, and Russia's Foreign Ministry Spokeswoman, Maria Zhakarova.[1079] [1080] [108

Yet U.S. State Department spokesman, John Kirby was not to be outdone in rhetoric and threats when he issued a thinly veiled warning to Russia by essentially saying that, if Russia did not knuckle under and play ball with the United States on Syria, the consequences would be terrorism in Russian cities and more Russian soldiers coming home in body-bags.

"Extremist groups will continue to exploit the vacuums that are there in Syria to expand their operations, which could include attacks against Russian interests, perhaps even Russian cities. Russia will continue to send troops home in body bags, and will continue to lose resources, perhaps even aircraft," he said.[1082]

[1079] Fadel, Leith. "US Jets Attack Syrian Army As ISIS Captures Strategic Mountain In Deir Ezzor." Al-Masdar News. September 17, 2016. https://www.almasdarnews.com/article/us-jets-attack-syrian-army-isis-captures-strategic-mountain-deir-ezzor/

[1080] "Russia, US Exchange Verbal Attacks After Coalition Airstrike In Deir ez-Zor." Sputnik. September 18, 2016. https://sputniknews.com/world/201609181045445774-russia-us-verbal-attacks/
See also,
Turbeville, Brandon. "U.S. Attacks Syrian Military, Protests ISIS In Deir Al-Zour, Thardeh Mountains." Activist Post. September 18, 2016. http://www.activistpost.com/2016/09/u-s-attacks-syrian-military-protects-isis-in-deir-al-zour-thardeh-mountains.html
See also,
Turbeville, Brandon. "War Continues Between U.S., Russia Diplomats Over American Aggression, U.K. Joins The Fray." Activist Post. September 28, 2016. http://www.activistpost.com/2016/09/war-continues-between-u-s-russia-diplomats-over-american-aggression-u-k-joins-the-fray.html

Zhakarova hit back on social media by writing,

> And those [acts of terrorism] will be perpetrated by 'moderate' [Syrian opposition groups]? Just the ones that Washington has been unable to separate from Al-Nusra for as long as six months?

> [What about] Terrorist attacks in France, America and other countries; the beheadings of people of all nationalities by Islamic State militants in Syria – is this all kind of a different paradigm? Perhaps another 'parallel reality?'

> Don't you think that such ventriloquism about 'body bags,' 'terrorist attacks in Russian cities' and 'loss of aircraft,' sounds more like a 'get 'em' command, rather than a diplomatic comment?[1083] [1084]

Indeed, it seems that the U.S. took a page out of the Saudi book in terms of its threats. The Kirby statement is eerily reminiscent of the statements made by Saudi Arabia that, if Russia did not abandon Syria, the terrorist groups that KSA controls would be set loose to commit attacks on Russian soil. Kirby's statement was certainly a more veiled threat, but only veiled with the slightest of nuance.[1085] [1086]

U.S. Suspends Bilateral Talks With Russia

Shortly after Kirby's statement and threats to cut bilateral talks with Russia over the Syrian crisis, the United States did, in fact, sever those talks. While military-to-military communication and official government-to-government communications remain intact, all discussions over the ceasefire agreement and diplomatic solutions to the crisis were officially ended.

As Ryan Browne of CNN reported on October 4,

[1082] "Russia Will Continue To Send Troops Home [from Syria] 'In Bodybags' – U.S. State Department. " Youtube. Posted by RT. Posted on September 29, 2016. https://www.youtube.com/watch?v=6wRXncGsktE "Diplomacy In Crisis" segment from RT news broadcast. An accurate description of the video reads: "US Secretary of State John Kerry threatens to cut off all cooperation with Moscow over Syria, unless attacks on Aleppo are stopped and the ceasefire is restored. That's as his spokesperson warns of even worse consequences..."

[1083] Christoforou, Alex. "US State Department John Kirby Warns Russia. Russian Foreign Ministry Maria Zhakarova Warns John Kirby." The Duran. September 29, 2016. http://theduran.com/us-state-department-john-kirby-warns-russia-russian-foreign-ministry-maria-zakharova-warns-john-kirby/

[1084] "Russian FM Spox: US Talks of "attacks in Russia, body bags, downing jets,' sounds like a 'get em' call." RT. September 29, 2016. https://www.rt.com/news/361032-zakharova-kirby-syria-body-bags-attacks/

[1085] "Russian President, Saudi Spy Chief Discussed Syria, Egypt." Al-Monitor. August 22, 2013. http://www.al-monitor.com/pulse/politics/2013/08/saudi-russia-putin-bandar-meeting-syria-egypt.html#ixzz2d5UVLSNv

[1086] "'Saudi Arabia' Trying To Blackmail 'Russia"!" Youtube. Posted by Zeropoint. Posted on August 8, 2013. https://www.youtube.com/watch?v=l1Ut-wyrpxY Video shows a Press TV report detailing the offer from Saudi Arabia to Russia. The offer was to buy huge amounts of Russian weapons in exchange for Russia abandoning Syria. Interview with Zayd al-Isa.

The US announced Monday it is "suspending its participation in bilateral channels with Russia" that had come about as part of the short-lived cessation of hostilities in Syria.

"This is not a decision that was taken lightly," State Department spokesman John Kirby said in a statement announcing the suspension.

Secretary of State John Kerry, who spent months negotiating with his Russian counterpart in order to bring about a ceasefire in Syria, spoke Tuesday about the end of bilateral talks and emphasized that the US was not giving up on peace or the Syrian people.

"Yesterday, as most of you saw, the United States announced our decision to suspend the bilateral discussions with Russia on the re-institution of the cessation of the hostilities agreement. A decision that, believe me, does not come lightly," Kerry told an audience in Brussels, Belgium, while speaking on Transatlantic relations.

The head of Russia's Foreign Affairs Committee, Konstantin Kosachev, stated that "Russia has striven for continuing dialogue with the US on Syria until the last moment, and only our position was keeping the chance to launch a stable peace process alive."[1087]

The U.S. decision to halt talks was largely as a result of the Russian military assistance being given to the Syrian military such as the bombing of terrorist positions in Aleppo, a move that has angered Washington since it has been supporting the terrorist forces since day one.[1088]

Russia Suspends Plutonium Deal With U.S.

In another response to increased anti-diplomatic behavior of the United States, Russia announced that it was suspending the Plutonium Disposition Pact, a nuclear accord between the two countries that was, at one time, seen as a symbol of a new era of cooperation between Russia and the U.S. This accord is a mutual pact requiring both parties to destroy excess weapons grade plutonium by recycling 34 tons of the material per year on the march toward nuclear non-proliferation. The agreement had been signed in 2000.[1089]

Russian President Vladimr Putin stated the reason for the ending of Russian participation in the agreement was due to "the emergence of a threat to strategic stability and as a result of unfriendly actions by the United States of America towards the Russian Federation" and "inability of the United States to ensure the implementation of its obligations to utilize surplus weapons-grade plutonium."[1090]

[1087] Browne, Ryan. "US Suspends Talks With Russia Over Syria." CNN. October 4, 2016. http://www.cnn.com/2016/10/03/politics/us-suspends-talks-with-russia-over-syria/index.html

[1088] "Syria Conflict: US Suspends Talks With Russia." BBC. October 4, 2016. http://www.bbc.com/news/world-middle-east-37546354

[1089] Horner, Daniel. "Russia, US Sign Plutonium Pact." Arms Control Association. May 5, 2010. https://www.armscontrol.org/act/2010_05/Plutonium

[1090] Filipov, David. "Russia Suspends Plutonium Deal With U.S." Washington Post. October 3, 2016. https://www.washingtonpost.com/world/russia-suspends-plutonium-deal-with-us/2016/10/03/c502e628-8980-11e6-8cdc-4fbb1973b506_story.html

As David Filipov writes for the Washington Post,

> Citing "unfriendly actions" by the United States, the Kremlin announced Monday that Russia would suspend a landmark agreement to dispose of surplus weapons-grade plutonium, yet another sign of deteriorating relations between the two countries.

> In a decree released by the Kremlin, President Vladimir Putin said Moscow would consider a resumption of the accord only if Washington agreed to several sweeping conditions. Among them: reducing the American military presence in NATO countries near Russia's border, canceling all sanctions against Russia and compensating Moscow for losses resulting from those sanctions.[1091]

The largely symbolic move reversed an agreement once hailed as an example of successful U.S.-Russian cooperation, and comes at a low point in post-Cold War relations between Moscow and Washington. Following President Putin's statement the Russian Foreign Ministry added that the United States "done all it could to destroy the atmosphere encouraging cooperation."[1092]

U.S. Considering Striking The Syrian Military

Shortly after the suspension of bilateral talks, the U.S. media began reporting on the possibility that the United States would launch strikes against the Syrian military, particularly in Aleppo where the SAA is engaged in a fierce battle to liberate the largest city in Syria. The justification for the strikes would be the need to "make Assad pay a price" for his alleged violations of the ceasefire. The reports came as the result of "leaks" and information provided to mainstream news organizations by anonymous official sources. Some believe these "leaks" were simply a method of suggesting a strike on Syrian forces to gauge the Russian response without officially committing to the intent to launch airstrikes.

Josh Rogin of the Washington Post put forward a standard mainstream report of the possibility of a U.S. airstrike campaign on October 4. He wrote,

> U.S. military strikes against the Assad regime will be back on the table Wednesday at the White House, when top national security officials in the Obama administration are set to discuss options for the way forward in Syria. But there's little prospect President Obama will ultimately approve them.

> Inside the national security agencies, meetings have been going on for weeks to consider new options to recommend to the president to address the ongoing crisis in Aleppo, where Syrian and Russian aircraft continue to perpetrate the deadliest bombing campaign the city has seen since the five-year-old civil war began. A meeting of the Principals Committee, which includes Cabinet-level officials, is scheduled for Wednesday. A meeting of the National Security Council, which could include the president, could come as early as this weekend.

[1091] Filipov, David. "Russia Suspends Plutonium Deal With U.S." Washington Post. October 3, 2016. https://www.washingtonpost.com/world/russia-suspends-plutonium-deal-with-us/2016/10/03/c502e628-8980-11e6-8cdc-4fbb1973b506_story.html
[1092] Filipov, David. "Russia Suspends Plutonium Deal With U.S." Washington Post. October 3, 2016. https://www.washingtonpost.com/world/russia-suspends-plutonium-deal-with-us/2016/10/03/c502e628-8980-11e6-8cdc-4fbb1973b506_story.html

Last Wednesday, at a Deputies Committee meeting at the White House, officials from the State Department, the CIA and the Joint Chiefs of Staff discussed limited military strikes against the regime as a means of forcing Syrian dictator Bashar al-Assad to pay a cost for his violations of the cease-fire, disrupt his ability to continue committing war crimes against civilians in Aleppo, and raise the pressure on the regime to come back to the negotiating table in a serious way.

The options under consideration, which remain classified, include bombing Syrian air force runways using cruise missiles and other long-range weapons fired from coalition planes and ships, an administration official who is part of the discussions told me. One proposed way to get around the White House's long-standing objection to striking the Assad regime without a U.N. Security Council resolution would be to carry out the strikes covertly and without public acknowledgment, the official said.

The CIA and the Joint Chiefs of Staff, represented in the Deputies Committee meeting by Vice Chairman Gen. Paul Selva, expressed support for such "kinetic" options, the official said. That marked an increase of support for striking Assad compared with the last time such options were considered.

"There's an increased mood in support of kinetic actions against the regime," one senior administration official said. "The CIA and the Joint Staff have said that the fall of Aleppo would undermine America's counterterrorism goals in Syria."[1093]

Russia Threatens To Shoot Down American Jets

But the Russians quickly responded to the unofficial official American preparations for airstrikes against the Syrian military. Very soon after the mainstream reports were posted, the Russian Defense Ministry responded that Russia would consider any missiles or airstrikes launched against Syrian government-held territory as threat to Russian personnel and would respond in an appropriate manner, i.e. shoot the missile/planes down.

Russian Defense Ministry spokesman Gen. Igor Konashenkov stated,

Therefore, any missile or air strikes on the territory controlled by the Syrian government will create a clear threat to Russian servicemen.

Russian air defense system crews are unlikely to have time to determine in a 'straight line' the exact flight paths of missiles and then who the warheads belong to.

And all the illusions of amateurs about the existence of 'invisible' jets will face a disappointing reality.

Of particular concern is information that the initiators of such provocations are representatives of the CIA and the Pentagon, who in September reported to the [US] President on the alleged controllability of 'opposition' fighters, but today are lobbying for 'kinetic' scenarios in Syria," he said.[1094]

[1093] Rogin, Josh. "Obama Administration Considering Strikes On Assad, Again." Washington Post. October 4, 2016. https://www.washingtonpost.com/news/josh-rogin/wp/2016/10/04/obama-administration-considering-strikes-on-assad-again/?utm_term=.c3d72af36587

[1094] Milanian, Keyan. "'We'll Shoot Down US Warplanes': Russia Warns Coalition Jets Carrying Out Air Strikes Over Syria Will Be Targeted." Mirror. October 6, 2016.

Konashenkov went on to say that the Russian military has ordered the deployment of not only S-300 but also S-400 units in Syria in order to protect its forces on the ground. Russia has also reportedly sent an additional number of S-300 units as well as Antei-2500 units to Syria as well as more bombers and attack planes. In addition, Russia Beyond The Headlines reports that Russia was planning to send two missile ships to the Mediterranean in mid-October.[1095] Konashenkov also pointed out that the Syrian air defense systems have been updated as well with the implementation of Russian technology.[1096]

Mortar Attack On The Russian Embassy

While a single mortar attack on an embassy might not be the greatest indication of World War 3 when taken on its own merit, when one considers the ominous warning (or thinly veiled threat) coming from State Department Spokesman John Kirby that Russia may see terror attacks in its cities and Russian soldiers coming home in body bags if it does cooperate on Syria, the fact that a mortar attack would take place at the Russian embassy shortly after the statement was uttered is thus a monumental development.

Reuters reported:

> One of the mortar shells, fired from a district controlled by rebels, exploded close to the guard post in front of the embassy, while another detonated near the entrance to the consular office, the ministry said in a statement.

> The embassy compound was strewn with shrapnel, but none of embassy staff were hurt, it said. It said material damage was being assessed.[1097]

Chinese Involvement In Syria

While the United States, NATO, Israel, and the GCC are clearly maintaining a unified front, the Russians, Iranians, Hezbollah, and Syria have been brought together in an apparent loose coalition of mutual interest. Despite all the military might of the Russians and the determination of the Syrians, the latter military coalition has long seemed at a disadvantage considering the condition and prowess of the former as well as the economic disadvantage of the latter. However, with the recent entrance of China to the Syrian scene, tepid as it may be, the balance of power seems to be shifting to that of a more even playing field.

As Sputnik reported,

---

http://www.mirror.co.uk/news/world-news/well-shoot-down-warplanes-russia-8994035

[1095] Litovkin, Nikolai. "Russia: We Will Shoot Down U.S. Jets In Syria That Threaten Our Servicemen." Russia Beyond The Headlines." October 10, 2016. https://rbth.com/defence/2016/10/10/russia-we-will-shoot-down-us-jets-in-syria-that-threaten-our-servicemen_637291

[1096] Rogin, Josh. "Obama Administration Considering Strikes On Assad, Again." Washington Post. October 4, 2016. https://www.washingtonpost.com/news/josh-rogin/wp/2016/10/04/obama-administration-considering-strikes-on-assad-again/?utm_term=.c3d72af36587

[1097] "Russia Says Damascus Embassy Targeted In Mortar Attack, No Staff Hurt." Reuters. October 13, 2016. http://www.reuters.com/article/us-mideast-crisis-syria-russia-diplomacy-idUSKCN12D0OF

On Monday, Chinese Deputy Foreign Minister Li Baodong said that the positions of Beijing and Moscow coincide on the Syrian issue. Speaking to Sputnik, Chinese and Russian analysts confirmed that recent events have demonstrated that the two countries are quickly building a sustainable strategic partnership in their response to the Syrian crisis.

Speaking at a briefing in Beijing, Li said that "China and Russia hold the same position on the most important international and regional issues," including the conflicts in Syria and Afghanistan. "The two countries, being permanent members of the UN Security Council, continue to cooperate closely on international and regional issues," Li added, noting that President Xi Jinping looks forward to meeting with President Vladimir Putin on the sidelines of the upcoming BRICS summit in Goa later this week to discuss the most pressing issues of regional and international politics. Li's words on Russian-Chinese cooperation in Syria were confirmed in practice on Saturday, when China voted in favor of a Russian draft resolution aimed at resolving the Syrian crisis at the UN Security Council. China justified its vote by explaining that the Russian proposal would be the surest way to ensure a cessation of hostilities, humanitarian access, and a more effective joint fight against terror. Chinese UN envoy Liu Jieyi expressed regret that the Russian proposal was not adopted after being blocked by the US and its allies.[1098]

According to the South China Morning Post, the Chinese military was supposed to begin providing assistance and aid to the Syrian government, an agreement which was made on August 14.[1099]

The decision was made after a rare visit by special envoy Xie Xiaoyan, the former Chinese Ambassador to Iran, in March. In addition, the Chinese military delegation to Syria, which was headed by Chinese rear admiral Guan Youfei, the Director of International Cooperation at the Central Military Commission, met with the Syrian Vice Prime Minister, Fahd Jassem al-Freij, and the Syrian Minister of Defense. "They reached consensus on enhancing personnel training, and Chinese military offering humanitarian aid to Syria," said a report by Xinhua news agency.[1100] [1101]

Al-Freij thanked the Chinese government as well as the Chinese military which stated, via Guan, that the Chinese PLA is willing to continue cooperation with the Syrian military.[1102] According to the South China Post, "Guan also met Lieutenant General Sergei Chvarkov, chief of the Russian centre for reconciliation of opposing sides in Syria on Monday."[1103]

[1098] "Russia, China Quickly Forming 'Strategy of Synergy' In Syria." Sputnik. October 10, 2016. https://sputniknews.com/politics/201610101046199510-russia-china-strategy-of-synergy/

[1099] Zhen, Liu. "Chinese Military To Provide 'aid and training assistance' To Syrian Government." South China Morning Post. August 16, 2016. http://www.scmp.com/news/china/diplomacy-defence/article/2004676/chinese-military-provide-aid-and-training-assistance

[1100] "China Says Seeks Closer Military Ties With Syria." Reuters. August 16, 2016. http://www.reuters.com/article/us-mideast-crisis-syria-china-idUSKCN10R10R

[1101] "China Says Seeks Closer Military Ties With Syria." Reuters. August 16, 2016. http://www.reuters.com/article/us-mideast-crisis-syria-china-idUSKCN10R10R

[1102] "China Says Seeks Closer Military Ties With Syria." Reuters. August 16, 2016. http://www.reuters.com/article/us-mideast-crisis-syria-china-idUSKCN10R10R

China sets to benefit by an end to the Syrian crisis or at least the ability of the Syrian government to continue to attrite terrorists fighting on its territory due to its concerns over the Uighur element fighting not only in Syria but also in Chinese territory.[1104] Uighur separatists have long been fighting for "independence" from the oppressive Chinese government. However, the Uighurs are themselves fanatical in nature and maintain ties to Turkey's Grey Wolves terrorist organization as well as NATO's Operation Gladio.[1105]

Regardless, Chinese cooperation with Syria is no doubt welcomed by the Syrian government that is currently mopping up terrorists all across the country but can still use all the help it can get.

Conclusion

The United States is clearly marching itself toward a confrontation with not one but two world powers. China has its own goals of empire and the Russians have given every indication that, while they are willing to stay within their own borders and concern themselves only with Russia, they are not going to allow their country to be encircled and broken apart nor are they willing to let every single ally and strategic interest be pulled out from under them in a death of a thousand cuts.

It is now time for the United States to back away from its plans to destroy Syria and, at the very least, have some sense of self-preservation and realize when it is time to pull back. The U.S. must not allow itself to continue to act as the battering ram for the Anglo-American agenda of world hegemony and empirical harmonization. Aside from the legal and moral implications of the war on Syria, it is becoming more and clearer that there are other powers in the world who are not willing to go see easily into that dark night this time around.

[1103] Zhen, Liu. "Chinese Military To Provide 'aid and training assistance' To Syrian Government." South China Morning Post. August 16, 2016. http://www.scmp.com/news/china/diplomacy-defence/article/2004676/chinese-military-provide-aid-and-training-assistance

[1104] Dagher, Afraa. "Displacement of Syrians For Uyghur Terrorists?" BrandonTurbeville.com. September 28, 2015. http://www.brandonturbeville.com/2015/09/displacement-of-syrians-for-uyghur.html

[1105] Turbeville, Brandon. "From Syria To Asia To Russia – Terror Network Organized By NATO And Turkey." Activist Post. October 1, 2015. http://www.brandonturbeville.com/2015/10/from-syria-to-asia-to-russia-terror.html

Chapter XI: The Inevitable End Of The Empire

The Decline Of The United States And The End Of The American Empire

Ever since 9/11, it has been apparent that the American empire is living on borrowed time. In more recent years, the inevitable collapse of American world hegemony and the unipolar world is one that very few informed observers can continue to ignore.

Riddled with massive unemployment, an overextended military, entrenched police state, crumbling infrastructure, and the ever-present threat to the US dollar, it is clear that the United States is merely the shell of its former self. Indeed, in 2014, the concept of long-term American primacy is only a fantasy maintained by the mainstream media with its constant repetition of meaningless and absurd notions of recoveries, humanitarian interventions, and national security.

More credible researchers, however, are well aware of the fact that the United States, as an empire as well as a nation, is headed the way of every empire before it. There is little doubt that the United States will soon run out of steam in its march across the world and a crackdown at home while reckless economic policy continues to be dictated from the halls of Wall Street.

Yet the decline of the United States is not simply the result of a few years of stupid mistakes made by the ruling class. The truth is that the end of America is nothing more than a waypoint in a script that was written long ago.

In order to gain a deeper grasp of the level to which the fall of the United States is a scripted development, it is worth consulting the work of Zbigniew Brzezinski, the infamous geopolitical strategist, architect of al-Qaeda,[1106] former US government official, and current advisor to Barack Obama.[1107] Particularly, it is important to consult Brzezinski's book, The Grand Chessboard: American Primacy And Its Geostrategic Imperatives.[1108]

It should be remembered that it was in this very book that Brzezinski uttered the famous statement that "America is too democratic at home to be autocratic abroad. This limits the use of America's power, especially its capacity for military intimidation. Never before has a populist democracy attained international supremacy. But the pursuit of

---

[1106] "The CIA's Intervention In Afghanistan: Interview with Zbigniew Brzezinski, President Jimmy Carter's National Security Adviser." Le Nouvel Observateur. Paris. January 15-21. 1998. Posted at Global Research. http://www.globalresearch.ca/articles/BRZ110A.html

[1107] Tarpley, Webster Griffin. Obama: The Postmodern Coup. Progressive Press. June. 2008.http://www.amazon.com/Obama-Postmodern-Making-Manchurian-Candidate/dp/0930852885/ref=pd_bbs_2?ie=UTF8&s=books&qid=1215453402&sr=8-2

[1108] Brzezinski, Zbigniew. *The Grand Chessboard: American Primacy And Its Geostrategic Imperatives*. Basic Books. 1997.

power is not a goal that commands popular passion, except in conditions of a sudden threat or challenge to the public's sense of domestic well-being."[1109]

In addition, Brzezinski also wrote that "as America becomes an increasingly multicultural society, it may find it more difficult to fashion a consensus on foreign policy issues, except in the circumstances of a truly massive and widely perceived direct external threat."[1110]

He went on to write that,

> In the absence of a comparable external challenge [to the Cold War and WWII], American society may find it much more difficult to reach agreement regarding foreign policies that cannot be directly related to central beliefs and widely shared cultural-ethnic sympathies and that still require and enduring and sometimes costly imperial engagement.[1111]

The book, written in 1997, seemed to lament the fact that the public would not support such blatant imperialism unless they truly viewed the crusade to be in their own immediate self-interest. Only four year later, the public would receive such a "sudden threat or challenge" to their "sense of domestic well-being" as well as that "widely perceived direct external threat" in the form of the 9/11 attacks.

The ultimate decline of the United States, however, is dealt with in Brzezinski's concluding section of the book which it tellingly titled "Beyond The Last Global Superpower." Here, Brzezinski opens with the announcement that, not only will American hegemony soon come to an end, but that there will never be another superpower to emerge as powerful as the United States is at the time of the writing of the book, in 1997. He writes,

> In the long run, global politics are bound to become increasingly uncongenial to the concentration of hegemonic power in the hands of a single state. Hence, America is not only the first, as well as the only, truly global superpower, but is also likely to be the very last.

> This is so not only because nation-states are gradually becoming increasingly permeable but also because knowledge as power is becoming more diffuse, more shared, and less constrained by national boundaries. Economic power is also likely to become more dispersed. In the years to come, no single power is likely to reach the level of 30 percent or so of the world's GDP that America sustained throughout much of this century, not to speak of the 50 percent at which it crested in 1945.[1112]

[1109] Brzezinski, Zbigniew. The Grand Chessboard: American Primacy And Its Geostrategic Imperatives. Basic Books. 1997. Pp. 40-41

[1110] Brzezinski, Zbigniew. The Grand Chessboard: American Primacy And Its Geostrategic Imperatives. Basic Books. 1997.

[1111] Brzezinski, Zbigniew. The Grand Chessboard: American Primacy And Its Geostrategic Imperatives. Basic Books. 1997. P. 211.

[1112] Brzezinski, Zbigniew. The Grand Chessboard: American Primacy And Its Geostrategic Imperatives. Basic Books. 1997. P. 209-210.

Keep in mind that the permeable nature of nation states that Brzezinski refers to is a result of the process of globalization of economies and the harmonization of laws worldwide as well as the globalization of culture.

Also notice that Brzezinski states that the "concentration of hegemonic power" will not be concentrated in the hands of a single state - not that concentrated hegemonic power will cease to exist. Indeed, such world power will simply move from the hands of a perceived national entity to those of an international and global institution.[1113]

Describing "American primacy" as having only a "relatively brief" window of historical opportunity, Brzezinski states that the fall of the American empire will be due to both internal and external reasons – namely, pessimism and addiction to entertainment at home and overextension abroad.[1114]

As quoted above, Brzezinski begins his argument by discussing the lack of will to go to war held by the average American absent the existence of the perception of some serious threat to their safety or the security of the country. He writes,

> Moreover, as America becomes an increasingly multicultural society, it may find it more difficult to fashion a consensus on foreign policy issues, except in the circumstances of a truly massive and widely perceived direct external threat. Such a consensus generally existed throughout World War II and even during the Cold War. It was rooted, however, not only in deeply shared democratic values, which the public sensed were being threatened, but also in a cultural and ethnic affinity for the predominantly European victims of hostile totalitarianisms.

> In the absence of a comparable external challenge, American society may find it much more difficult to reach agreement regarding foreign policies that cannot be directly related to central beliefs and widely shared cultural-ethnic sympathies and that still require an enduring and sometimes costly imperial engagement. If anything, two extremely varying views on the implications of America's historic victory in the Cold War are likely to be politically more appealing: on the one hand, the view that the end of the Cold War justifies a significant reduction in America's global engagement, irrespective of the consequences for America's global standing; and on the other, the perception that the time has come for genuine international multilateralism, to which American should even yield some of its sovereignty.[1115]

Brzezinski thus describes a society that loses its taste for war with other cultures as a result of increased diversity in the makeup of the American public and a lack of cohesion of what has been American culture since the beginning of the country. The fact that America has itself earned the label of the "hostile totalitarianism" that was once foisted onto a number of other countries and governments has finally become too overwhelmingly obvious to hide for many Americans.[1116]

[1113] Brzezinski, Zbigniew. The Grand Chessboard: American Primacy And Its Geostrategic Imperatives. Basic Books. 1997.

[1114] Brzezinski, Zbigniew. The Grand Chessboard: American Primacy And Its Geostrategic Imperatives. Basic Books. 1997.

[1115] Brzezinski, Zbigniew. The Grand Chessboard: American Primacy And Its Geostrategic Imperatives. Basic Books. 1997. P. 211.

[1116] Brzezinski, Zbigniew. The Grand Chessboard: American Primacy And Its Geostrategic

Brzezinski also identifies the fall of the Soviet Union and the end of the Cold War as a potential hindrance to the drive to fight and conquer across the globe. In other words, the lack of the perceived "direct external threat" results in the lack of desire for empire in the minds of the general public. After all, the average person does not desire war or the glory of empire but merely the ability to provide for themselves and live in some level of comfort.[1117] Empire is the goal of psychopaths.

Still, Brzezinski sees the lack of the presence of the Cold War as a potential excuse for the sacrifice of sovereignty under the guise of "genuine international multilateralism" and, of course, globalism and globalization. One can clearly see from reading the Grand Chessboard that this concept only alarms Brzezinski in terms of the possibility that the lack of will to expand the empire might come before America has been exhausted in the pursuit of it.

Unfortunately for those who will be the cannon fodder for any overseas adventure, that perceived direct external threat was provided to them in the form of radical Muslim fundamentalist terrorism in 2001 and, in 2014, the reemergence of the Cold War propaganda between the United States, Russia, and to a lesser degree, China.[1118]

In this regard, Brzezinski appears to avert the question of direct confrontation only to present the possibility in apocalyptic terms. He writes,

> With the more-endowed nations constrained by their own higher technological capacity for self-destruction as well as by self-interest, war may have become a luxury that only the poor peoples of the world can afford. In the foreseeable future, the impoverished two-thirds of humanity may not be motivated by the restraint of the privileged.[1119]

Of course, by "restraint of the privileged" one must read restraint against attacking one's military equal. Restraint is by no means a word that could be used when referring to the policies of Western or "developed" nations toward "undeveloped" countries.

Brzezinski continues by stating,

Imperatives. Basic Books. 1997.

[1117] "Why of course the people don't want war. Why should some poor slob on a farm want to risk his life in a war when the best he can get out of it is to come back to his farm in one piece? Naturally the common people don't want war neither in Russia, nor in England, nor for that matter in Germany. That is understood. But, after all, it is the leaders of the country who determine the policy and it is always a simple matter to drag the people along, whether it is a democracy, or a fascist dictatorship, or a parliament, or a communist dictatorship. Voice or no voice, the people can always be brought to the bidding of the leaders. That is easy. All you have to do is tell them they are being attacked, and denounce the peacemakers for lack of patriotism and exposing the country to danger. It works the same in any country." – Hermann Goering. http://quotes.liberty-tree.ca/quote_blog/Hermann.Goering.Quote.65D2 and http://www.snopes.com/quotes/goering.asp

[1118] Brzezinski, Zbigniew. The Grand Chessboard: American Primacy And Its Geostrategic Imperatives. Basic Books. 1997.

[1119] Brzezinski, Zbigniew. The Grand Chessboard: American Primacy And Its Geostrategic Imperatives. Basic Books. 1997. P. 213.

It is also noteworthy that international conflicts and acts of terrorism have so far been remarkably devoid of any use of the weapons of mass destruction. How long that self-restraint may hold is inherently unpredictable, but the increasing availability, not only to states but also to organized groups, of the means to inflict massive casualties – by the use of nuclear or bacteriological weapons – also inevitably increases the probability of their employment.[1120]

Yet, while the prospect of general war and the employment of nuclear weapons clearly exists, another possibly even more dangerous threat to the American empire is the culture it has deliberately created for the benefit of the ruling class. While Brzezinski presents the American cultural crisis as a threat merely because its hedonism and self-absorption precludes a desire to fight foreign wars, his acknowledgement of the existence of this crisis is revealing in terms of how the American culture has been manipulated into that of egocentrism and entertainment addiction and a type that eschews sacrifice, cultural connection, and identity.

Thus, Brzezinski writes,

> More generally, cultural change in America may also be uncongenial to the sustained exercise abroad of genuinely imperial power. That exercise requires a high degree of doctrinal motivation, intellectual commitment, and patriotic gratification. Yet the dominant culture of the country has become increasingly fixated on mass entertainment that has been heavily dominated by personally hedonistic and socially escapist themes. The cumulative effect has made it increasingly difficult to mobilize the needed political consensus on behalf of sustained, and also occasionally costly, American leadership abroad. Mass communications have been playing a particularly important role in that regard, generating a strong revulsion against any selective use of force that entails even low levels of casualties.

> In addition, both America and Western Europe have been finding it difficult to cope with the cultural consequences of social hedonism and the dramatic decline in the centrality of religious-based values in society. . . . . . . The resulting cultural crisis has been compounded by the spread of drugs and, especially in America, by its linkage to the racial issue. Lastly, the rate of economic growth is no longer able to keep up with growing material expectations; with the latter stimulated by a culture that places a premium on consumption. It is no exaggeration to state that a sense of historical anxiety, perhaps even of pessimism, is becoming palpable in the more articulate sectors of Western society.[1121]

After decades of increasingly decadent, demoralizing, and dehumanizing entertainment, the deliberate dumbing down of each generation, and the intentional destruction of cohesive social and cultural structures, average Americans undoubtedly lack the ability to engage in undertakings that require intellectual commitment or group cohesion that reaches across racial, social, gender, or other divisions.

[1120] Brzezinski, Zbigniew. The Grand Chessboard: American Primacy And Its Geostrategic Imperatives. Basic Books. 1997. P. 213.

[1121] Brzezinski, Zbigniew. The Grand Chessboard: American Primacy And Its Geostrategic Imperatives. Basic Books. 1997. P. 211-212.

The growing egocentric nature of American culture renders most people entirely incapable of the empathy needed to interact with others in a positive and productive manner. In addition, this type of culture negates the value of self-sacrifice required for the undertaking of a project for the common good, particularly if that project requires long-term planning and effort with the ultimate effects that may not be witnessed in the worker's lifetime.

While the lack of motivation to fight foreign wars on the behalf of the ruling class is something that should be encouraged and nurtured, the lack of motivation and desire to engage in any activity outside of oneself or the immediate benefits of such activity spells the death of any culture in short order. Such a culture breeds ignorance, apathy, lack of empathy, and cruelty as well as the destruction of the potential for human progress. The latter, however, is of no real consequence to the ruling class.

Brzezinski also points out the pervasiveness of drugs in a culture that is already obsessed with immediate gratification and escapism. Compounded with the absurd "War on Drugs" which violates the rights of all Americans in immeasurable ways, the persistent spread of drug abuse continues to the point of rendering a significant portion of the American populace unemployable and entirely disconnected from the plight of the nation as a whole or simply incapable of taking effective action to change their own miserable situation.

A culture of hedonism coupled with an economic depression and an entrenched police state has undoubtedly produced what Brzezinski deems a "sense of historical anxiety" and "pessimism" is the order of the day, at least among "the more articulate sectors of Western society."[1122]

Brzezinski writes that this pessimism or "lack of confidence" "has been intensified by widespread disappointment with the consequences of the end of the Cold War."[1123]

"Instead of a 'new world order' based on consensus and harmony," he writes, "'things which have seemed to belong to the past' have all of a sudden become the future."[1124]

Brzezinski's "things which have seemed to belong to the past" is a reference to the writings of historian Hans Kohn, who defined those "things which have seemed to belong to the past" as "fanatical faith, infallible leaders, slavery and massacres, the uprooting of whole populations, ruthlessness and barbarism."[1125]

Brzezinski's answer, of course, is to provide fleeting optimism to the American people in order to keep the empirical ship of state temporarily sailing.[1126]

[1122] Brzezinski, Zbigniew. The Grand Chessboard: American Primacy And Its Geostrategic Imperatives. Basic Books. 1997. P. 212.

[1123] Brzezinski, Zbigniew. The Grand Chessboard: American Primacy And Its Geostrategic Imperatives. Basic Books. 1997. P. 213.

[1124] Brzezinski, Zbigniew. The Grand Chessboard: American Primacy And Its Geostrategic Imperatives. Basic Books. 1997. P. 213.

[1125] Brzezinski, Zbigniew. The Grand Chessboard: American Primacy And Its Geostrategic Imperatives. Basic Books. 1997. P. 212.

[1126] Brzezinski, Zbigniew. The Grand Chessboard: American Primacy And Its Geostrategic Imperatives. Basic Books. 1997. P. 213.

Keep in mind, however, that Brzezinski's analysis does not provide for an indefinite American empire. The United States will lose its empire as well as what little internal wealth it has left.

Thus, whatever optimism is provided to the public, rest assured it will be false and temporary.

The Role Of NATO And The EU On Brzezinski's Grand Chessboard

On the first of May, 2014, Tony Cartalucci of Land Destroyer wrote an article entitled "Ukrainian Crisis Was Always About Containing Russia," where he argued that "NATO's continued existence is hegemonic in nature - its meddling in Ukraine an act of war against Russia."[1127]

In addition, Cartalucci also wrote that "what we have witnessed over the past several months is not 'Russian aggression,' but the premeditated destabilization and overthrow of the elected government of Ukraine, and a resulting, and continuously escalating confrontation with Russia as Moscow reacts to the reappearance of Nazis along its borders, backed by NATO and the EU."[1128]

Cartalucci also discussed the importance of the expansion of NATO, particularly in the context of Ukrainian membership into the organization as a method of expanding the Anglo-European Empire to the doorstep of Russia on yet another front.[1129]

As Cartalucci writes,

> So what is NATO doing with Nazi militants in Ukraine? The same thing Adolf Hitler was doing - establishing "breathing room." While the West attempts publicly to portray the crisis in Ukraine as Europe reacting to Russian aggression, behind semi-closed doors they are very open about their agenda in Ukraine and elsewhere along Russia's peripheries - it is and always was about the expansion of Europe and the containment of Russia.
>
> Recently the corporate-funded NATO think tank, the Atlantic Council, celebrated what it called, "anniversaries of crucial importance to the transatlantic community, including the 25th anniversary of the fall of the Berlin Wall, the 15th anniversary of NATO's first post-Cold War enlargement, and the 10th anniversary of the "big bang" enlargements of both the European Union and NATO."[1130] [1131] These "enlargements"

[1127] Cartalucci, Tony. "Ukrainian Crisis Was Always About Containing Russia." Land Destroyer Report. May 1, 2014. http://landdestroyer.blogspot.com/2014/05/ukrainian-crisis-was-always-about.html

[1128] Cartalucci, Tony. "Ukrainian Crisis Was Always About Containing Russia." Land Destroyer Report. May 1, 2014. http://landdestroyer.blogspot.com/2014/05/ukrainian-crisis-was-always-about.html

[1129] Cartalucci, Tony. "Ukrainian Crisis Was Always About Containing Russia." Land Destroyer Report. May 1, 2014. http://landdestroyer.blogspot.com/2014/05/ukrainian-crisis-was-always-about.html

[1130] "Honor Roll Of Contributors." Atlantic Council. http://www.atlanticcouncil.org/support/supporters

all took place after the fall of the Cold War - in other words, after NATO's mandate for existing expired. Yet the alliance continued to grow, and not only did it grow, in tandem with the European Union, it did so directly toward Moscow's doorstep with every intention of eventually absorbing Russia as well.[1132]

Of course, Cartalucci was correct in pointing out these aspects of the U.S.-Russian conflict surrounding the Ukrainian crisis. On one level, the United States was responsible for the orchestration of a color revolution inside Ukraine as an attempt to scuttle the warming relations between Ukraine and Russia, thus forcing Russia to respond.

On another level, the Anglo-European establishment is attempting to further weaken the geopolitical position of Russia and expand NATO for purposes of containing and eventually dictating policy and demands to the Russian state.

On another level still, the conflict taking place between the Anglo-European NATO alliance is the acting out of a script that has been carefully crafted many years ago with end goal of eliminating the very existence of national sovereignty from across the globe and the ultimate creation of a one-world system with a small but dominant minority reigning at the top of that structure.

One of the architects of the strategy which is currently being implemented by the United States in regards to foreign policy, Zbigniew Brzezinski, is thus a logical source of information when one is attempting to understand the geopolitical movements made by the Anglo-Europeans, Russians, or Chinese.

It should be remembered that it was Brzezinski who, in his book *The Grand Chessboard: American Primacy and Its Geostrategic Imperatives*, uttered the famous statement that "America is too democratic at home to be autocratic abroad. This limits the use of America's power, especially its capacity for military intimidation. Never before has a populist democracy attained international supremacy. But the pursuit of power is not a goal that commands popular passion, except in conditions of a sudden threat or challenge to the public's sense of domestic well-being."[1133]

The book, written in 1997, seemed to lament the fact that the public would not support such blatant imperialism unless they truly viewed the crusade to be in their own immediate self-interest. Only four year later, the public would receive such a "sudden threat or challenge" to their "sense of domestic well-being" in the form of the 9/11 attacks.

However, the *Grand Chessboard* discusses much more than the lack of desire to wage war by the general public absent a perceived external threat. The book discusses in detail

[1131] "Webcast: Toward A Europe Whole And Free." Atlantic Council. http://www.atlanticcouncil.org/events/webcasts/webcast-toward-a-europe-whole-and-free
[1132] Cartalucci, Tony. "Ukrainian Crisis Was Always About Containing Russia." Land Destroyer Report. May 1, 2014. http://landdestroyer.blogspot.com/2014/05/ukrainian-crisis-was-always-about.html
[1133] Brzezinski, Zbigniew. The Grand Chessboard: American Primacy And Its Geostrategic Imperatives. Basic Books. 1997. Pp. 40-41

the various major players in the geopolitical game and the methods they may use to achieve their goals of hegemony.

When one considers the possibility that the events taking place in Eastern Europe are much more than the after effects of seemingly unrelated policy or even those of a series of short-term foreign policy decisions made by one or two world powers, it becomes vitally important to seek out the words of the individuals who would have played a role (and still do play a role) in writing and developing the script the world is now following.

For instance, in the words of Brzezinski,

> As in chess, American global planners must think several moves ahead, anticipating possible countermoves. A sustainable geostrategy must therefore distinguish between the short-run perspective (the next five or so years), the middle term (up to twenty or so years), and the long run (beyond twenty years). Moreover, these phases must be viewed not as watertight compartments but as part of a continuum. The first phase must gradually and consistently lead into the second – indeed, be deliberately pointed toward it – and the second must then lead subsequently into the third.[1134]

Thus, when Brzezinski speaks of the necessity to not only enlarge NATO but to eventually assimilate Russia into the confines of greater Europe, it would be wise to pay attention. Here, in *The Grand Chessboard*, Brzezinski argues that the expansion of NATO and the European Union will serve to reinvigorate greater Europe as well as act as the proverbial carrot by which the more Central and Eastern European countries will be encouraged to facilitate and implement the will of the Anglo-Europeans. The failure to do so, however, runs the risk of awakening a historical Russian imperialism that could challenge Anglo-European hegemony, according to Brzezinski. He writes,

> It follows that a wider Europe and an enlarged NATO will serve well both the short-term and the longer-term goals of U.S. policy. A larger Europe will expand the range of American influence – and, through the admission of new Central European members, also increase in the European councils the number of states with a pro-American proclivity – without simultaneously create a Europe politically so integrated that it could soon challenge the United States on geopolitical matters of high importance to America elsewhere, particularly in the Middle East. A politically defined Europe is also essential to the progressive assimilation of Russia into a system of global cooperation.

> Admittedly, America cannot on its own generate a more united Europe – that is up to the Europeans, especially the French and the Germans – but America can obstruct the emergence of a more united Europe. And that could prove calamitous for stability in Eurasia and thus also for America's own interests. Indeed, unless Europe becomes more united, it is likely to become more disunited again. Accordingly, as stated earlier, it is vital that America work closely with both France and Germany and seeking a Europe that is politically viable, a Europe that remains linked to the United States, and a Europe that widens the scope of the cooperative democratic international system.[1135]

[1134] Brzezinski, Zbigniew. The Grand Chessboard: American Primacy And Its Geostrategic Imperatives. Basic Books. 1997. P.198.
[1135] Brzezinski, Zbigniew. The Grand Chessboard: American Primacy And Its Geostrategic

[...]

The enlargement of NATO and the EU would serve to reinvigorate Europe's own waning sense of a larger vocation, while consolidating, to the benefit of both America and Europe, the democratic gains won through the successful termination of the Cold War. At stake in this effort is nothing less than America's long-range relationship with Europe itself. A new Europe is still taking shape, and if that new Europe is to remain geopolitically a part of the "Euro-Atlantic" space, the expansion of NATO is essential. By the same token, a failure to widen NATO, now that the commitment has been made, would shatter the concept of an expanding Europe and demoralize the Central Europeans. It could even reignite currently dormant or dying Russian geopolitical aspirations in Central Europe.

Indeed, the failure of the American-led effort to expand NATO could reawaken even more ambitious Russian desires. It is not yet evident – and the historical record is strongly to the contrary – that the Russian political elite shares Europe's desire for a strong and enduring American political and military presence. Therefore, while the fostering of an increasingly cooperative relationship with Russia is clearly desirable, it is important for America to send a clear message about its global priorities. If a choice has to be made between a larger Euro-Atlantic system and a better relationship with Russia, the former has to rank incomparably higher to America.[1136]

Brzezinski goes on to describe the framework of an arrangement between the West and Russia that would have very little – if any – benefits to Russia. His requirements are essentially that Russia be neutered with respect to its ability to make effective and influential regional decisions, that it strategically weaken itself militarily, and even reorganize its governmental structure to the form of a confederacy with three co-equal parts. He writes,

For that reason, any accommodation with Russia on the issue of NATO enlargement should not entail an outcome that has the effect of making Russia a defacto decision-making member of the alliance, thereby diluting NATO's special Euro-Atlantic character while simultaneously relegating its newly admitted members to second-class status. That would create opportunities for Russia to resume not only the effort to regain a sphere of influence in Central Europe but to use its presence within NATO to play on any American-European disagreements in order to reduce the American role in European affairs.

It also crucial that, as Central Europe enters NATO, any new security assurances to Russia regarding the region be truly reciprocal and thus mutually reassuring. Restrictions on the deployment of NATO troops and nuclear weapons on the soil of new members can be an important factor in allaying legitimate Russian concerns, but these should be matched by symmetrical Russian assurances regarding the demilitarization of the potentially strategically menacing salient of Kaliningrad and by limits on major troop deployments near the borders of the prospective new members of NATO and the EU. While all of Russia's newly independent western neighbors are anxious to have a stable and cooperative relationship with Russia, the

Imperatives. Basic Books. 1997. P. 199.

[1136] Brzezinski, Zbigniew. The Grand Chessboard: American Primacy And Its Geostrategic Imperatives. Basic Books. 1997. Pp. 200-201.

fact is that they continue to fear it for historically understandable reasons. Hence, the emergence of an equitable NATO/EU accommodation with Russia would be welcomed by all Europeans as a signal that Russia is finally making the much-desired postimperial choice in favor of Europe.[1137]

Russia's longer-term role in Eurasia will depend largely on the historic choice that Russia has to make, perhaps still in the course of this decade, regarding its own self-definition. Even with Europe and China increasing the radius of their respective regional influence, Russia will remain in charge of the world's largest single piece of real estate. It spans ten time zones and is territorially twice as large as either the United States or China, dwarfing in that regard even an enlarged Europe. Hence, territorial deprivation is not Russia's central problem. Rather, the huge Russia has to face squarely and draw the proper implications from the fact that both Europe and China are already economically more powerful and that China is also threatening to outpace Russia on the road to social modernization.

In these circumstances, it should become more evident to the Russian political elite that Russia's first priority is to modernize itself rather than to engage in a futile effort to regain its former status as a global power. Given the enormous size and diversity of the country, a decentralized political system, based on the free market, would be more likely to unleash the creative potential of both the Russian people and the country's vast natural resources. In turn, such a more decentralized Russia would be less susceptible to imperial mobilization. A loosely confederated Russia – composed of a European Russia, a Siberian Republic, and a Far Eastern Republic – would find it easier to cultivate closer economic regulations with Europe, with the new states of Central Asia, and with the Orient, which would thereby accelerate Russia's own development. Each of the three confederated entities would also be more able to tap local creative potential, stifled for centuries by Moscow's heavy bureaucratic hand.[1138]

It is important to note that, when Brzezinski states that a "decentralized political system, based on the free market," is desired for Russia, he means a system that is built on privatization, unfettered Capitalism, and the ability of private corporations to loot and exploit "the country's vast natural resources" as well as its people.

Furthermore, Brzezinski argues that another requirement that West should impose upon Russia is the acceptance of the increase of the sense of nationalism among the countries located in its generally accepted sphere of influence and its national borders. While these countries clearly have a right to their own self-determination and nationalistic identities, Brzezinski is referring more to the radicalization and exploitation of these tendencies than the acceptance of a peoples' right to rule themselves free from outside interference. Brzezinski's requirement would thus only be accepted by Russia to its own detriment. In this regard, he states,

A clear choice by Russia in favor of the European option over the imperial one will be more likely if America successfully pursues the second imperative strand of its strategy toward Russia: namely, reinforcing the prevailing geopolitical pluralism in

---

[1137] Brzezinski, Zbigniew. *The Grand Chessboard: American Primacy And Its Geostrategic Imperatives*. Basic Books. 1997. P. 201.

[1138] Brzezinski, Zbigniew. *The Grand Chessboard: American Primacy And Its Geostrategic Imperatives*. Basic Books. 1997. P. 202.

the post-Soviet space. Such reinforcement will serve to discourage any imperial temptations. A postimperial and Europe-oriented Russia should actually view American efforts to that end as helpful in consolidating regional stability and in reducing the possibility of conflicts along its new, potentially unstable southern frontiers. But the policy of consolidating geopolitical pluralism should not be conditioned on the existence of a good relationship with Russia. Rather, it is also important insurance in case such a good relationship fails to truly develop, as it creates impediments to the reemergence of any truly threatening Russian imperial policy.[1139]

Brzezinski also points to the importance of Ukraine to his anti-Russian policy. He writes,

It follows that political and economic support for the key newly independent states is an integral part of a broader strategy for Eurasia. The consolidation of a sovereign Ukraine, which in the meantime redefines itself as a Central European state and engages in closer integration with Central Europe, is a critically important component of such a policy, as is the fostering of a closer relationship with such strategically pivotal states as Azerbaijan and Uzbekistan, in addition to the more generalized effort to open up Central Asia (in spite of Russian impediments) to the global economy.

Large-scale international investment in an increasingly accessible Caspian – Central Asian region would not only help to consolidate the independence of its new countries but in the long run would also benefit a postimperial and democratic Russia. The tapping of the region's energy and mineral resources would generate prosperity, prompting a greater sense of stability and security in the area, while perhaps also reducing the risks of Balkan-type con-external investment, would also radiate to the adjoining Russian provinces, which tend to be economically underdeveloped. Moreover, once the region's new ruling elites come to realize that Russia acquiesces in the region's integration into the global economy, they will become less fearful of the political consequences of close economic relations with Russia. In time, a nonimperial Russia could thus gain acceptance as the region's preeminent economic partner, even though no longer its imperial ruler.[1140]

It must be remembered that Brzezinski, when discussing the "choices" available to Russia in terms of its place in the world, stated that Russia would "either [choose]to be a part of Europe as well or [choose]to become a Eurasian outcast, neither truly of Europe nor Asia and mired in its 'near abroad' conflicts."[1141]

Notice that, in this statement, the choices provided to Russia by Brzezinski's philosophy are between total fealty to the European Soviet and total irrelevance. No self-respecting nation would choose either of these two options for its future and this is a fact that Brzezinski is undoubtedly aware of. Thus, it is clear that the Russians are being

---

[1139] Brzezinski, Zbigniew. *The Grand Chessboard: American Primacy And Its Geostrategic Imperatives.* Basic Books. 1997. P. 202-203.
[1140] Brzezinski, Zbigniew. *The Grand Chessboard: American Primacy And Its Geostrategic Imperatives.* Basic Books. 1997. P. 203.
[1141] Brzezinski, Zbigniew. *The Grand Chessboard: American Primacy And Its Geostrategic Imperatives.* Basic Books. 1997. P.122

faced with the non-choice that is the Brzezinski doctrine, a philosophy that, when put into practice, makes conflict virtually inevitable.

Russia is thus faced with the choice of willing subservience or a growing NATO and Europe that will inevitably come knocking on its door for "access" to its vast oil and mineral wealth and demand that whatever political clout it may have in the world be erased.

These types of requirements and conditions cannot help but initiate a direct confrontation.

Obama Goes To Vietnam – Says Big Nations Should Not Bully Small Ones

Ever since World War II, the United States has prided itself on being number 1. This classification of superiority has generally been reserved for things at least perceived as being positive attributes, e.g. the biggest economy, the most upward mobility, the most effective military, etc.

However, if the United States were trying to achieve the number 1 position in hypocrisy, then President Barack Obama has made a two week jaunt the crossing of the finish line for a country racing to be labeled as the most hypocritical nation on the face of the earth.

Step 1 was his appearance and speech in Hanoi, Vietnam on May 24. In the course of delivering a speech calling for the peaceful resolution of maritime disputes, particularly in the South China Sea, Obama uttered perhaps one of the most glaringly hypocritical statements to come from the mouth of a U.S. President. Indeed, his statement was even more hypocritical than the general "America represents freedom and democracy" claptrap. "Big nations should not bully smaller ones. Disputes should be resolved peacefully," Obama said.[1142]

Of course, it must be noted that Obama made his statement in small country that was bullied by a big one decades earlier for over ten years with devastating results for the Vietnamese people and a nasty culture war back at home in the United States. The irony of traveling to Vietnam and telling the world that big countries shouldn't bully small ones may have been lost on Americans but, to many people across the world, history was not so easily forgotten.

Indeed, it may be irony for an American President to stand in Hanoi and criticize "bullying" small countries but it is absolute hypocrisy for him to do so at a time when the United States is known the world over for being the biggest bully on the planet. As Libya continues to burn in absolute chaos, Syria fights valiantly against proxy imperialism, Iraq continues to have its legs cut out from underneath it at every turn, and a trail of war and destruction is left all across the world, the fruit of the United States has been borne for all to see.

[1142] Ghosh, Nirmal. "Obama: Resolve Sea Rows Peacefully, Big States Shouldn't Bully Others." The Strait Times. May 25, 2016. http://www.straitstimes.com/asia/se-asia/obama-resolve-sea-rows-peacefully-big-states-shouldnt-bully-others

If the world operated according to reason and rationality, it would not be the United States lecturing other countries on the dangers of bullying; it would be Vietnam, Iraq, Yemen, Syria, Pakistan, Libya, Nicaragua, and much of the Third World lecturing the United States. Unfortunately for Americans, however, empire does always tend to come home eventually. When it does, an apathetic public will no doubt regret their lack of opposition to the war machine.[1143]

U.S. War Policy Has Created The Multi-polar World

As the United States squanders the enormous good will and respect it once had by marching forward on the tired legs of a dying empire, the U.S.' enemies-of-its-own-making are beginning to forge new alliances that might not have been a reality had the U.S. at the very least pursued a strategy of positive reinforcement and cooperation as opposed to a policy of tension, pillage, and war.

The first major crack in the iron curtain of the Anglo-American world hegemon started becoming apparent with the emergence of the U.S. destabilization and proxy war against Syria. While the NATO/American proxy war has left hundreds of thousands of Syrians dead, hundreds of thousands more displaced, and destroyed much of the Syrian infrastructure as well as crippled the Syrian economy, another result of American policy in Syria is that it has strengthened and even created alliances that otherwise may not have existed not only between Middle Eastern countries but European, Asian, and African nations as well.

Unfortunately for the United States, these new alliances of its targets were created out of a political, economic, and military necessity by which to survive the Western onslaught of destabilization, sanctions, and war aimed at these respective nations. Thus, if the West wanted to break resistance to its hegemonic system, it has managed instead to encourage the opposite.

While already an axis of mutual interest, the crisis in Syria has resulted in the strengthening of ties between Syria, Iran, and Hezbollah. Not only a strategic alliance, this arc of resistance has solidified ties that are slowly pulling Iraq away from the influence of the United States. Indeed, the Iraqis are still tethered to the United States due largely to bribery, deception, economic threats, and the decreasing dependency on the United States for military assistance to combat ISIS.

Syria itself is spreading its wings as it mops up America's terrorists. Reaching out to not only the nations of the resistance axis and Russia, it is reaching out and solidifying relationships with Russia and China as well as with other European and African nations like the Czech Republic and Egypt.

Likewise, if the ties between Iran and the Houthis were not strong enough before the U.S.-backed, Saudi-led coalition, they certainly are now. Despite no credible evidence

---

[1143] Turbeville, Brandon. "America's Legacy Will Be Its Downfall: Empire Always Comes Home." Activist Post. May 6, 2016. http://www.activistpost.com/2016/05/americas-legacy-will-be-its-downfall-empire-always-come-home.html

that Iran is providing weapons to the Houthis, there is little doubt that the Iranians are providing whatever support they can in whatever form that can take and that they will do so in the future.

Russia, of course, factors in as the biggest and most important player in the strategic realignment with its insistence (which has come as a result of the U.S. aggression across the planet) in the emergence of a "multi-polar" world. Russia's reunification with Crimea, support of the Ukrainian rebels, as well as its support of Syria is only the tip of the iceberg. A growing cooperation with China and with a host of other nations throughout the world - by virtue of the carrot as opposed to the stick - is rapidly drawing more and more nations into the Russian fold.

Iran, too, having not expressed a desire for empire nonetheless is now beginning to express interest in stretching its muscles and expanding its own influence. How much of this newly expressed desire is innate and how much is simply a necessary act of self-defense against and encroaching war machine that sees Iran as next in line for destruction is unclear. The fact that it is happening, however, is not in doubt.

These new alliances may not have ever taken shape and solidified had the United States not insisted on acting as the battering ram for the Anglo-American system across the world and squandered all the respect and good will that existed for it in so many nations. The U.S. could easily have won many nations over by using positive reinforcement and enticement such as development, higher living standards, and peace. Instead, it has bombed, burned, bribed, and destabilized itself across the globe to the point that it has become the number one threat to world peace, a reality that is being acknowledged by more and more countries by the day.

What could have been the greatest force for peace, stability, democracy, and high living standards has been utterly squandered into being the greatest force for the opposite. If the United States continues down this path of imperialism, it will soon find itself not only hated the world over, but collapsed, weak, and bitter while the nations it has targeted in the final days of its war push have united against it. We can only hope that they have more restraint, good will, and compassion than what the U.S. has shown to them.

Bouthania Shaaban, Assad Advisor, Says We Are Living In A Time That Will Determine The Fate Of The World

As the war in Syria continues to rage on, it is becoming more and more obvious that the battle taking place is about much more than Syria as a country. In this place, the cradle of civilization, there are now two warring ideologies. One that demands total fealty and the absence of all dissent and one that believes a nation's people should decide for themselves the direction of their country. One ideology wants to force its hegemonic world system upon all other nations and the other contends that nations should choose their own direction.

This is not to argue perfection on the part of Syria or Russia by any means. But it is a reality nonetheless.

Even in the United States itself, a battle is raging that will determine whether or not the country will continue to march forward in totalitarianism and decline or whether individual choice and high living standards will rule the day. The elections have been, of course, merely a manifestation of the most vile elements of American society and the battle continues on despite the result.

Those vile elements are exactly those which Syrian President Bashar al-Assad's political and media advisor addressed when she recently took to social media to condemn Western policy in Syria. But it was not only the foreign policy of proxy wars that Shaaban condemned, it was what she described as an attitude of "racism" and "supremacism" that accompanies those policies.

Shaaban wrote,

> In a world where lies and rumors replace facts, and become central to the corporate media narrative; in such a world you only feel absolute comfort when you sit down with friends, allies, and partners who share your principles, values, and ethical standards, and do not dispute the fundamentals of your principles and objectives.

> As you go smoothly through the meeting's agenda, simply because everyone means what he says and does what he promises, you start thinking about the difficulties you face with the other side, and you remember that the reasons behind the pointless discussion with their officials are lack of honesty and the contradictions between their true motives and what they express in public. Right there, you sense what is wrong with our world today, and what is the main source for the troubles we face, ranging from wasting time in pointless discussion all the way to the loss of innocent lives, the destruction of countries, and denying entire generations the right to education and a free and dignified life.

> The foreign ministers of the Russian Federation, the Syrian Arab Republic, and the Islamic Republic of Iran met in Moscow, and it was clear that all of them are departing from a deep belief in the sovereignty of states, a rejection of foreign intervention, the right of people to decide their fate away from foreign dictates, a rejection of land grab by force, and absolute solidarity with peoples suffering injustice and the loss of their rights. And when the discussion is based on such principles, and on the unity of ideas, values, and ethics, it is not too difficult for such a discussion to reach important strategic conclusion, which would shape the future.

> In such a meeting, hegemonic, colonial, and superior attitudes are completely absent; and you start to remember how hateful the racist approach present in meetings with Westerners, which demands you to prove your innocence at every juncture, thus robbing you of your humanity and your right to be treated equal, which should have been a nonissue in the first place.

> In the Moscow meeting, I saw the coming world in which our children and grandchildren would live, a world devoid of racism; a world in which politicians, the media, and all people are honest and respectful of all human beings regardless of race, gender or creed. A world, all the inhabitants of which, wherever they may be, feel a sense of belonging and share a stake in its preservation and progress. A world in which everyone accepts and cherishes the different cultures and languages, and sees them as a gift from God rather than a pretext for national and racial supremacist claims. For despite all what Westerners and their media claim, the truth is that

Western treatment of all other countries is a racist and supremacist treatment that seeks to advance the interests of the West at the expense of the rest of the world.

Looking at this coming world, I feel that the sacrifices of our martyrs and wounded were not only for us, but also for all mankind, for a better world and a better future. Looking at this future world, I am certain that we are living in a difficult phase of history resulting from the difference between what the West says and what it does, because it is fighting to preserve its colonial ways and its preferred methods of humiliating, destroying, and looting other peoples for its own benefit.

Looking at the future of our children and grandchildren, I feel that the battle we are fighting today was inevitable, and that it is for the greater good and for a better future for the coming generations. In this rich and constructive meeting in Moscow, I felt that the entire world is uniting to reject once and for all the concept of hegemony, and to reconstruct international relations on the basis parity, of respect, and shared interests.

Wherever I go, and whenever I write, I never forget to pay homage to the souls of our martyrs, and wish a speedy recovery to our wounded brave soldiers, because their blood and suffering are the torch that lights the path to freedom and dignity. I also do not forget to salute everyone who believed in the inevitability of victory, despite all the difficulties, and worked hard to achieve this victory, offering his life, money, effort, and prayers. As for the traitors, culprits, war profiteers, and those who call on the enemy to invade their country, they will be forgotten and they will never appear in the pages of history ever again.[1144]

Shaaban seems to be picking up on what many people are also starting to surmise, i.e. that we have entered a time that will determine the direction of the world and the planet on which our children and our children's children will live. We will be the ones who determine their future. Many activists have had this feeling for some time and many people who are only tangentially aware of the political sphere are feeling it too.

Shaaban is speaking not only of her country but of the world and the people of the world would do well to recognize that what is happening in Syria will, in one way or the other, affect us all. The battle for Syria is not a Syrian fight alone; it is a fight for the future of the world.

The Results Of Empire At Home – America Is A Police State

Over the years in my own articles, I have used the terms "creeping fascism," "growing police state," and "descent into totalitarianism" among others to describe the domestic situation in which we find ourselves. I have often written that, if Americans do not stand up to the myriad of laws being passed by Federal, State, and local governments we will soon wake up to find ourselves in an Orwellian police state nightmare.

Now, however, I cringe whenever I read those words in contemporary articles. This is because such warnings are so far past their time they are utterly useless. In fact, they

---

[1144] Shaaban, Bouthania. Official Bouthania Shaaban Facebook page. November 5, 2016. https://www.facebook.com/Bouthaina.Shaaban.Official/posts/948675891901959

may do more to hurt any potential for change in American society than they do to promote it.

 These warnings work on the supposition that the U.S. is not a police state yet but, if things do not change, it will become one in the future. Thus, the readers are left with the impression that, while their freedoms are being taken away, the police state is somewhere down the road -in the future - and they have plenty of time to entertain themselves until it comes knocking on their door with a uniform and a bright flashing neon sign that says "ATTENTION!!! POLICE STATE!!!."

But the police state is not coming – it is here.

The United States is a police state.

 Americans may not be able to admit it to themselves but the military soldiers parading on the streets as police officers, police-operated tanks, and horrifying number of imprisoned citizens have spoken for them. The number of Americans brutalized physically and mentally by those who are sworn to "serve and protect" are speaking clearly enough.

 The relatively recent concept of "pain compliance," "rough interrogation," and "rough rides" coupled with the long held tradition but fast increasing commonality of direct beatings, shootings, murders, and "on-site executions" by police in America have had the final say. Since 2003, police have killed more American citizens than were killed by "insurgents" in Iraq, a country whom the US invaded illegally and subsequently imposed a reign of terror upon.

 The United States is now a country where millions of people are locked away in inhuman conditions of confinement, the overwhelming majority of them for crimes in which there was no victim.

 From the Federal, State, and local levels, behavior previously considered normal and innocuous is now mandated and regulated by a tangled web of government agencies. Of course, any disagreement or defiance of those mandates will result in a clash from the militarized police forces mentioned above and an eventual confinement to a cage where the offender is treated like an animal at best.

 In the United States of 2016, children are regularly removed from parents by the State simply because of the parents' economic status, political beliefs, or methods of upbringing. Surely no country that imprisons as many people as America, "enforces" oppressive law with military-style troops, and snatches children away from loving homes simply because those homes are not the ideal model of what the state desires can be called a free country.

 With the recent increase of PC fascism enveloping the nation, even free speech and expression, no matter how ineffectual, is becoming regularly silenced by the long arm of the law.

 Children are being routinely arrested for acting out in elementary school while citizens learn that their first "duty" in America is to "obey" police authority lest they be subject to brutal takedowns, torture, and possibly death.

This is the America many warned about years ago when they protested the militarization of police but were met with responses citing "officer safety" and "growing crime rates." It is the America they warned about when they opposed the drug war but were met with programmed responses of a "drug-addicted youth" and "drug-related crimes." It is the America many could see coming a mile away when the state-sponsored threat of terrorism was used to justify any and all means of "keeping us safe" and providing "security" to the frightened citizens of the world empire.

Those warnings were ignored and now we have the result.

It is now time to call the United States what it is – a police state.

U.S. Takes A Stab At A No Fly Zone In Two Places - Syria And Standing Rock

As the United States marches forward with its war of terror abroad it is, as predicted by researchers and informed observers many years ago, clamping down on the domestic population at home. Indeed, it is virtually inevitable that the great eating machine of the empire returns home to be turned on the people who ignored it while it was grinding up so many innocent lives overseas.[1145] [1146]

So as the war drums beat louder and as America ekes closer toward the impending Clinton coronation and the possibility of the declaration of yet another "no fly zone," this time over Syria, becomes more and more likely, it is poetic justice that a no-fly zone is being declared inside the United States.[1147]

While Russia stands in the way of America's march to create Libya 2.0 in Syria, there is no one willing and virtually no one able to stand in the way of America's declaration of war on itself, personified by the vicious police state brutality being visited upon the protestors at Standing Rock – indigenous and otherwise – and the crackdown on virtually every amendment to the Constitution including the arrest of demonstrators and journalists, some of whom are facing incredibly ridiculous amounts of time in jail.

Indeed, the United States even declared a no-fly zone over the protest area, preventing media coverage of the ensuing bravery of the protestors and brutality of the "Serve and

---

[1145] Watt, Alan. "Blackwater, That Mean Slaughtering Machine, Will Be Coming Home To You." Cutting Through The Matrix. June 4, 2008. Transcription of radio program, Cutting Through the Matrix. http://cuttingthroughthematrix.com/transcripts/Alan_Watt_CTTM_LIVEonRBN_123_Blackwater__that_Mean_Slaughtering_Machine__will_be_Coming_Home_to_You_June042008.html
[1146] Watt, Alan. "Maurice Strong, The U.N.'s King Kong." Cutting Through The Matrix. May 19, 2009. http://cuttingthroughthematrix.com/transcripts/Alan_Watt_CTTM_LIVEonRBN_323_Maurice_Strong__the_UNs_King_Kong_May192009.html
[1147] Turbeville, Brandon. "Turkey Calls For 'Buffer Zone' In Syria As Military Seizes Territory Called For By Brookings, MSM." Activist Post. September 7, 2016. http://www.activistpost.com/2016/09/turkey-calls-for-buffer-zone-in-syria-as-military-seizes-territory-called-for-by-brookings-msm.html

protect" crew who are willing to bash every skull and crush every human right in the quest to "just do their jobs."

One need only take a look at the photos of the protestors vs the heavily armed and militarized police (can we still call them police?) forces amassed around the location to see the crumbling of America into the police state foreseen for Western countries as the rug gets pulled out from under them economically, socially, and culturally despite their use as tools of imperialism abroad. The blunt hammer of Anglo-American hegemony that is the United States is falling apart even as it continues to strike at Syria, Iran, and Russia.[1148]

While police can murder with impunity and Black Lives Matter activists can destroy cities at will, Standing Rock protestors are charged with high crimes for spray painting bulldozers and journalists who dare to even cover the protests are arrested and charged with trespassing, inciting riots, and conspiracy. Even left gate keepers like Amy Goodman have been charged with such crimes. But, while Goodman's charges were eventually dropped, other journalists such as Deia Schlosberg are facing 45 years in prison simply for filming a protest that involved the disruption of the pipeline's operations.[1149]

In regards to the current events taking place at Standing Rock, Jay Syrmopoulos writes,

> This latest flashpoint in the ongoing conflict is north of the larger and more permanent encampments, which have been constructed on federally owned land where over 200 Native American tribes have gathered to oppose the pipeline's construction.
>
> On Wednesday, a heavily militarized law enforcement presence began mobilizing heavy equipment, including Humvees, armored personnel carriers, and buses and demanded the protesters leave the occupied area.
>
> In an ominous sign, the Federal Aviation Administration (FAA) has restricted flights, and banned the use of drones within a radius of about 4 ½ miles of Cannon Ball.[1150] The FAA declared that only aircraft affiliated with the North Dakota Tactical Operation Center are allowed within the restricted airspace. The flight restriction went into effect Wednesday and will last until November 5.

Indian Country Today reports:

> What began with prayers and a single tipi alongside Highway 1806 quickly grew to more than a dozen tipis surrounded by

---

[1148] Watt, Alan. "Fall of the Republic with Alan Watt, Part 1." Youtube. Posted by Cutting Through The Matrix. Posted on December 20, 2000. https://www.youtube.com/watch?v=g-jF4OWjK5E Interview with Alan Watt conducted by Alex Jones for his documentary, "Fall Of The Republic."

[1149] Light, John. "North Dakota Judge Throws Out Charges Against Journalist Amy Goodman." Moyers And Company (Moyers.com). October 17, 2016.
http://billmoyers.com/story/journalists-arrested-north-dakota-pipeline/

[1150] "The Latest: Protester Accused Of Firing 3 Shots At Police." The Bismarck Tribune. October 27, 2016. http://bismarcktribune.com/news/state-and-regional/the-latest-faa-restricts-flights-in-pipeline-protest-area/article_e6360854-ca13-51f2-a8a3-0537cd5d18a9.html

tents, buses, cars and hundreds of water protectors. Some are calling it the "1851 Treaty Camp" to acknowledge their Treaty rights.

Across the road is the encroaching pipeline and a heavily militarized police force with armored vehicles, helicopters, planes, ATVs and busloads of officers. Tensions are growing as unarmed citizens worry that police will use unnecessarily harsh tactics.

In recent weeks, nearly 300 unarmed water protectors who were arrested have been subjected to pepper spray, strip-searches, delayed bail, exaggerated charges and physical violence, according to interviews with several who were taken into custody. The ACLU and National Lawyers Guild recently sent attorneys to Standing Rock to help the Red Owl Collective, a team of volunteer lawyers headed by attorney Bruce Ellison, who are representing many of those arrested.

The massive law enforcement contingent, consisting of sheriff's deputies and officers from numerous other states and counties, as well as National Guard, began staging near the encampment — with scores of Armored Personnel Carriers, buses and Humvees poised at the ready.

"At some point the rule of law has to be enforced," Cass County Sheriff Paul Laney said Wednesday. "We could go down there at any time. We're trying not to."

Dakota Access LLC, the pipeline developer released a statement encouraging trespassers to "vacate the land immediately" or be "removed from the land."[1151]

"Alternatively and in coordination with local law enforcement and county/state officials, all trespassers will be prosecuted to the fullest extent of the law and removed from the land," the company said. "Lawless behavior will not be tolerated."

Just days ago, sheriff's officials had said earlier they didn't have the resources to immediately remove activists from the private land, about 50 miles south of Bismarck. Subsequently, law enforcement officials put out a call for reinforcements, with hundreds of officers from out of state responding.[1152] [1153] [1154]

[1151] "Dakota Access Says Trespassers Will Be 'Removed From The Land' As Law Officers Mobilize." The Bismarck Tribune. October 25, 2016. http://m.bismarcktribune.com/news/state-and-regional/dakota-access-says-trespassers-will-be-removed-from-the-land/article_de20b44d-4a72-5fb0-8a9f-7b44f855b353.html

[1152] Burns, Jack. "As Natives Declare Treaty Rights, Police Admit Defeat – Cite Lack of 'Manpower' To Remove DAPL Protesters." The Free Thought Project. October 25, 2016. http://thefreethoughtproject.com/dapl-morton-county-police-wont-remove-protesters/

[1153] "Obama Holds Private Meeting As Cops Mass Near DAPL Front Lines." Indian Country Today Media Network. October 26, 2016. http://indiancountrytodaymedianetwork.com/2016/10/26/police-presence-grows-civil-rights-leaders-join-water-protectors-166226

[1154] Syrmopolous, Jay. "No-Fly Zone Declared As Militarized Police Prep For Assault on 'Front Line Camp' At Standing Rock." The Free Thought Project. October 27, 2016.

So there is (at the time of the writing of this book) an official "no fly zone" over the Standing Rock protest (which can be seen here at the FAA website) and, on the ground, we have an army of storm troopers no doubt eager to bust heads and fire off some rounds into a group of people who only want clean water, property rights, and the honoring of the legal agreements they signed.[1155]

Across the ocean, however, we await another fly zone.

Of course, the establishment of a "No-Fly Zone" is tantamount to a declaration of war.[1156] [1157] Such has even been admitted by top U.S. Generals when explaining exactly what a No Fly Zone would entail. As General Carter Ham stated,

> We should make no bones about it. It first entails killing a lot of people and destroying the Syrian air defenses and those people who are manning those systems. And then it entails destroying the Syrian air force, preferably on the ground, in the air if necessary. This is a violent combat action that results in lots of casualties and increased risk to our own personnel.[1158]

General Philip Breedlove also echoed this description when he said,

> I know it sounds stark, but what I always tell people when they talk to me about a no-fly zone is . . . it's basically to start a war with that country because you are going to have to go in and kinetically take out their air defense capability.[1159]

When Senator Roger Wicker asked Gen. Joe Dunford what it would take to impose a no fly zone upon Syria, the General responded, "Right now... for us to control all of the airspace in Syria would require us to go to war against Syria and Russia."[1160]

Thus, the entire Western "sphere of influence" is slowly descending down to become a place of no fly zones, riot police, and a boot slowly stamping on the human face. At home, those individuals who resist the "new normal" will be steadily dealt with either by

---

http://thefreethoughtproject.com/militarized-police-mobilize-assault-standing-rock/

[1155] FAA. Gov. Announcement of flight bans over the Standing Rock area. Found previously at this link. http://tfr.faa.gov/save_pages/detail_6_6648.html

[1156] Turbeville, Brandon. "As Russia Bombs Terrorists In Syria, NATO Members Repeat Calls For 'No-Fly Zone' And War." Activist Post. February 18, 2016. http://www.activistpost.com/2016/02/as-russia-bombs-terrorists-in-syria-nato-members-repeat-calls-for-no-fly-zone-and-war.html

[1157] Turbeville, Brandon. "Turkey Calls For 'Buffer Zone' In Syria As Military Seizes Territory Called For By Brookings, MSM." Activist Post. September 7, 2016. http://www.activistpost.com/2016/09/turkey-calls-for-buffer-zone-in-syria-as-military-seizes-territory-called-for-by-brookings-msm.html

[1158] "Face The Nation Transcripts September 28, 2014: Blinken, Kaine, Flournoy." CBS News. September 28, 2014. http://www.cbsnews.com/news/face-the-nation-transcripts-september-28-2014-blinken-kaine-flournoy/

[1159] Vandiver, John. "Breedlove: No-Fly Zone Over Syria Would Constitute An 'Act of War.'" Stars And Stripes. May 31, 2013. http://www.stripes.com/news/breedlove-no-fly-zone-over-syria-would-constitute-act-of-war-1.223788

[1160] Whitney, Mike. "Obama Stepped Back From Brink, Will Hillary?" CounterPunch. October 12, 2016. http://www.counterpunch.org/2016/10/12/obama-stepped-back-from-brink-will-hillary/

economic hardship or a rude reminder that dissenters will be silence, imprisoned, or killed.

Elsewhere, however, the Anglo-American system has begun to encounter nations who are not only willing to fight back but who are able to do so. A dying empire caught in its death throes, trying to remain alive by creating the "absence of dissent" might well launch a third world war with a nuclear power as a last stab at hegemony.

On the other hand, Rome could just burn slowly.

Rest assured, however, the skies above the city will be empty.

America's Legacy Will Be Its Downfall – Empire Always Comes Home

Remember, it's supposed to come right back here because that which the U.S. has created and maybe, perhaps, even the very reason for being that America was set up to do, is almost accomplished. Once it's accomplished, they'll be doing the same thing back home. You'll SUBMERGE into the world system you helped create. -

Alan Watt, CuttingThroughTheMatrix.com

As Western media outlets and the U.S. State Department attempt to gin up public sentiment surrounding alleged bombings of alleged hospitals that may or may not have even existed and that, even if they did, were nothing more than field hospitals for terrorists, the Syrian people are suffering under unimaginable conditions. These true victims, of course, are completely ignored by the same outlets that cry and pine over the deaths and setbacks of jihadists, rapists, torturers, and murderers.

Amidst the constant propaganda and dehumanizing method of reporting "news" in the West, both the humanity and the wishes of the Syrian people are lost completely.

In a video posted by the ANNA News Agency, one is able to see footage of Aleppo where Western-backed terrorists are lobbing missiles and bombs against civilian targets, film that would never be played on Western televisions under the guise of protecting a violence-ridden and violence-obsessed public from the "graphic images" of the results of their own intellectual laziness and lack of moral conviction. Graphic images are no problem when it is movie time, of course, but when violent images come home to roost, trigger warnings are required and censorship is always invoked. That is, unless the necessity of stirring up public support for foreign wars is dire enough to warrant its presentation.

Indeed, scenes from Aleppo will only be shown when media outlets are able to twist the footage into a report on the "crimes of Assad" instead of the natural progression of acts of destabilization set into motion by the United States and its coalition. Indeed, these conditions are entirely the fault of the United States, Britain, France, the GCC, Israel and the NATO powers.

In the ANNA news report, one can view footage that depicts a way of life – only five years old contrary to Western brainwashing – that is unimaginable to any sane person and, five years ago, would have been unimaginable to any Syrian. In the video report, the first scene is shortly after a terrorist bombing in West Aleppo where a young man can be heard speaking to his mother and saying "Hello? Hello? Mama I'll talk to you later. Another bomb fell. Bye, Bye."

Amidst the screaming of women and children, the silence of the dead, and the blaring sirens trying to respond to the fires and carry away the injured, viewers can hear the shouts of men, some in anger and some in frenzied attempts to rescue those buried under rubble or critically injured by the bombs.

In one clip, a woman can be seen shouting at a Syrian soldier, not in anger at the SAA or Assad for "bombing civilians," but for not doing enough to stop America's freedom fighters and moderate terrorists paraded before the Western public as the only hope for Syria. "I'm begging you. I'm begging you," she says. "Aren't you in the army? Save us! Save us please young man!" It should strike American audiences, if they are ever able to view this footage, as odd that a Syrian woman would be shouting for help from the Syrian military to protect her from the "rebels" America is supporting if Assad and the Syrian government are so incredibly cruel.

Another woman is seen shouting similar sentiment. "Aleppo is steadfast, but this is enough!" A man shouts to the cameras, "Where is mercy? Where is God? The US is sending rockets to kill the Syrian people! We don't want this! We want military aid for the Syrian army who are our sons! Our sons! Our sons who are defending us!" Needless to say, we do not expect this footage to be aired on FOX, CNN, or any other major corporate outlet in the United States.

As they are presented by the U.S. media, the Syrian people, like most other people across the world are completely dehumanized. In American media, Syrians are not human. They are numbers. 100 died today. 86 died the day before. Syrians are not mothers or sons. They are not fathers or little children, grandparents. They are blips on a screen and data in a spreadsheet. At least, this is how they are presented to an increasingly hardened American public, a nation that is becoming more and more desensitized to death, destruction, and degradation both at home and abroad.

Each one of the numbers Americans go about their day scarcely aware of had a mother and father. Many had children, girlfriends, husbands, careers, pets, hopes for the future. Each one had a history and a life story. For them, all of that is gone now and, presumably, its absence has left a massive hole in the life of someone else.

In what amounts to three minutes of intense footage, the ANNA News report manages to sum up in minutes what will be the legacy of the United States. In Syria, even if the government is successful in returning the country to some sense of normalcy, a gaping hole in the collective consciousness of the people will remain along with the notable silence of hundreds of thousands of voices who would have been part of the cities, towns, and family dinners had the United States never put the country in its sites. In Libya, America's legacy is thousands dead and a civilized country returned to barbarism and violence. In Iraq, unbelievable destruction and death continue while years of use of depleted uranium will leave a lasting reminder of the presence of America as generations will be born disfigured, deformed, and drastically ill. Even decades on, Vietnam bears the scars of America.

All across the world, America has left a trail of destruction and death, both on massive scales. Only within its own borders does anyone think that the United States represents freedom and democracy. The additional tragedy is that a nation that could have become the greatest force for good in the world has been one of the greatest forces for evil the world has ever known.

As the American people suffer daily under the same Anglo-American control system, it is imperative they understand that their own apathy is the silent acquiescence to the destruction abroad and the inevitable destruction at home. What has been set loose upon foreign peoples overseas cannot help but one day come home. Today it is Syrians who are burying their friends and their children but the meat grinder of empire always eventually comes back to turn on its own inhabitants what it unleashed in foreign lands. If Americans cannot speak out against the destruction of Syria by virtue of their own moral compass and their own humanity, they had better do so out of a sense of self-preservation.

Chapter XII: Upon Returning From the Middle East

To the vast majority of Americans, the Syrian crisis (as well as the state of affairs in Iraq, Libya, Yemen, etc.) is merely a distant blip on a cluttered radar screen. Competing with issues affecting an individual's daily life like wages, taxes, and free trade, that small portion of the American population who hasn't completely zoned out of the political and current-events sphere is increasingly overtaken with the necessities of survival. Those who are able to devote enough time to the Syrian crisis are confronted with an unprecedented onslaught of propaganda demonizing the Syrian government and the Syrian president as "killing his own people," "brutal," and "genocidal." The Syrian people are also victims of the propaganda war as being obsessed with religion, divided, and opposed to their government.

As they are presented by the U.S. media, the Syrian people, like most other people across the world are completely dehumanized. In American media, Syrians are not human. They are numbers. 100 died today. 86 died the day before. Syrians are not mothers or sons. They are not fathers or little children, grandparents. They are blips on a screen and data in a spreadsheet. At least, this is how they are presented to an increasingly hardened American public, a nation that is becoming more and more desensitized to death, destruction, and degradation both at home and abroad.

Having recently concluded a trip to the Middle East, I can safely say that the claims made by Western media are the opposite of the truth.

While my visit centered in Lebanon, we had frequent opportunities to talk with ordinary Syrian citizens either visiting Lebanon or fleeing the ravages of the war in their home country. Indeed, Syrians and Syrian refugees were plentiful in Beirut and many would openly speak about the horrors visited upon them by the West's proxy war and their trials outside Syria.

What is so important about the fact that these Syrians were being interviewed in Lebanon is the unique benefit of talking with someone not living in their home country because one knows with relative certainty that the person speaking has nothing to lose or gain by giving a false perception of the government. After all, one of the frequent accusations leveled by the Western media is that, whenever one speaks to a Syrian actually living in Syria is that they are handicapped by that person's fear of retribution from the Syrian government. According to this train of thought, if a man criticized Assad in Syria, he might be subject to arrest and then, of course, torture, execution, and "barrel bombs."

But that is not the case in Lebanon. In Lebanon, even the most vocal anti-Assad Syrian can speak his mind and be safely out of Assad's reach. Indeed, even out of ear shot by the Syrian government. A Syrian in Lebanon can speak his piece and do so safely in the knowledge that the alleged "brutal dictator" cannot reach him.

That being said, out of all the Syrians I met and spoke to – refugees and visitors, Muslim and Christian, male and female – not one of them supported the "rebels" and all of them – 100% – fully supported their government and Bashar al-Assad. These individuals had nothing but hate for the terrorists and nothing but love for Assad and the Syrian government.

This point needs to be stressed. These individuals were not under threat of a tyrant ready to arrest them if they spoke out against him. They were free of Assad. They could spit on his portrait if they wanted and there is nothing the Syrian government can do to them. Instead, they expressed an incredible amount of pride in their country, their government, and their President.

So, with that in mind, if Assad and the Syrian government are "barrel bombing" their own citizens, committing genocide against the Syrian people, and killing civilians indiscriminately, and if Syrians are free to speak their mind about Assad in Lebanon, why couldn't I find one Syrian who wanted Assad to "step down" or for terrorists to bring them the "freedom and democracy" the West keeps yapping on about? Perhaps I was looking in the wrong places or perhaps the information coming from Western governments and their media mouthpieces are simply propaganda. Personally, I'll put my money on the latter.

One striking aspect of Beirut in the context of the Syrian crisis is that one does not necessarily have to seek out the Syrians in order to speak to them. If one only wears a necklace, t-shirt, or bracelet with the Syrian flag, they will come to you. Any indication of solidarity with their country, especially exhibited by a Westerner (even better, an American) and a man who speaks only one word of English will stop whatever he is doing so that he can have a conversation with the foreigner, even if that conversation is done by body language, hand gestures, broken English, interpreters, or Google Translate alone.

Others more skilled in the English language are willing to have long discussions about their experiences, their support for the government, and their hatred for the terrorists infecting their country. They would tell tales of watching people they knew killed in front of them and having lost family or very close friends at the hands of America's "moderates." Indeed, in Syria, as well as in the diaspora of the last 5 years, it seems impossible to speak with a single Syrian who has not lost someone close to them.

The sheer magnitude of the crisis is unimaginable in scale, much in the way that the horrors inflicted upon the Syrian people by America's democracy loving cannibals are beyond the comprehension of most Western audiences. But despite all the bloodshed, loss, and terror perpetrated on Syria by the United States, the Syrian spirit remains and the Syrian people remain some of the kindest, friendliest, and most hospitable people on the face of the earth.

In addition, Syrians remain a seemingly highly informed audience despite the fact that their country has been crippled by warfare for the past five years and that they themselves have been turned into refugees. Knowledge not only of their own situation, but about the players behind it and the developments taking place in Europe and America is common and, while American audiences watch the 24 hours news cycle in utter befuddlement as to the events taking place in Syria, Syrians are profoundly aware of just who is responsible for the crisis their country is facing.

While Americans chalk the crisis up to the "they have been fighting for thousands of years" line or accept the propaganda that Syria is facing a civil war, Syrians know that what they are facing is a proxy war against their government, against their very way of life, and against Russia. Syrians are fully aware of the fact that the terrorists beheading their way across the country are funded by Saudi Arabia, facilitated by Turkey and Israel, and trained by the United States. They are fully aware that there are no "moderates" fighting against the Syrian government and that the United States is responsible for creating the ISIS terror organization it is claiming to fight.

All of this may come as a surprise to Americans but, in Syria, it is well known.

With that in mind, it is an extraordinary thing that Syrians can welcome foreigners visiting their country with such patience and forgiveness. It is truly amazing that Syrian refugees struggling to survive in a foreign country is willing to sit with a citizen of the very country that destroyed his home and killed his family members, smoke hookah with him, and discuss his homeland. It is an unbelievable act of understanding and forgiveness for a man not to judge an American as the enemy and to separate the American people from their government. I was personally struck by the genuine kindness shown to me by people who have been given every legitimate reason to do otherwise.

What the United States is doing to Syria is truly shameful and immoral but, despite the horrors the U.S. and NATO countries have visited upon Syria, the people have refused to give in.

As Mark Twain said,

> *Damascus has seen all that has ever occurred on earth, and still she lives. She has looked upon the dry bones of a thousand empires, and will see the tombs of a thousand more before she dies.*

Judging by the people I met, I am inclined to agree with him.

About The Author

Brandon Turbeville is a writer out of Florence, South Carolina. He is the author of seven books, *The Road To Damascus- The Anglo-American Assault on Syria, Codex Alimentarius- The End of Health Freedom, Seven Real Conspiracies, Five Sense Solutions, The Difference It Makes: 36 Reasons Hillary Clinton Should Never Be President,* and *Dispatches From A Dissident Vol. 1 and 2.* He is a staff writer for Activist Post and has published over 950 hundred articles dealing with a wide variety of subjects including health, economics, war, government corruption, and civil liberties with a particular focus on the Syrian crisis. He has been a guest on numerous alternative media broadcasts as well as mainstream outlets. Turbeville is also an occasional contributor to other media outlets such as Natural Blaze, The Anti Media, Progressive Gazette, Era of Wisdom, and Off Rail Alliance. His books can be found in the bookstore at BrandonTurbeville.com and Amazon.com.

Turbeville is also the host of Truth on the Tracks, a weekly news round up that serves as a hub for activists, information, and solutions. Truth on the Tracks airs every Monday and Friday night at 9pm EST on UCY.TV/TT.

Pictures From Syria

Readers who wish to see pictures from inside Syria are encouraged to visit BrandonTurbeville.com and access the link "Pictures From Syria." All pictures are used with permission and are available for free.

Made in the USA
Middletown, DE
27 November 2017